EARLIER PUBLICATIONS IN THIS S

THE SUPPLEMENT TO THE THIRTEENTH MENTAL MEASUREMENTS YEARBOOK

THE SUPPLEMENT TO THE THIRTEENTH MENTAL MEASUREMENTS YEARBOOK

BARBARA S. PLAKE and JAMES C. IMPARA

Editors

LINDA L. MURPHY

Managing Editor

The Buros Institute of Mental Measurements
The University of Nebraska-Lincoln
Lincoln, Nebraska

1999
Distributed by The University of Nebraska Press

LC 39-3422
ISBN 910674-46-9

Manufactured in the United States of America.

The paper used in this publication meets the minimum requirements of American National Standard for Information Sciences—Permanence of Paper for Printed Library Materials, ANSI Z39.48-1984.

Note to Users

TABLE OF CONTENTS

INTRODUCTION

This volume, *The Supplement to the Thirteenth Mental Measurements Yearbook (13MMY-S)*, is the fifth in our *Supplement* series. The *Supplements* continue to be well received and feedback indicates they are accomplishing their intended purpose of making evaluative information on key psychological and educational tests available in a timely manner.

The *13MMY-S* contains reviews of tests newly revised since the 1998 publication of the *Thirteenth Mental Measurements Yearbook (13MMY)*. These same reviews will also comprise over a fourth of the *Fourteenth MMY* (projected publication in late 2000). The *13MMY-S* is a bridge between the *Thirteenth* and *Fourteenth Yearbooks* and is useful to professionals whose work and scholarship demand rapid access to critical test reviews written by distinguished measurement experts. The increased numbers of new and revised tests being published makes essential our efforts to publish descriptions and reviews more frequently.

The Buros Institute of Mental Measurements serves the psychological, business, and educational measurement communities. Our frequent publication schedule is consistent with the proud tradition of our founder, Oscar K. Buros, continuing innovative attempts to improve the quality of testing products made available to consumers. These reviews and additional reviews as they are completed are also available electronically through SilverPlatter™ (available in many academic libraries) and via our fax service (information available on our web page www.unl.edu/buros).

THE SUPPLEMENT TO THE THIRTEENTH MENTAL MEASUREMENTS YEARBOOK

The *13MMY-S* contains reviews of tests that are new or significantly revised since the publication of the *Thirteenth MMY* in 1998. We have included reviews of tests that were available before our production deadline of June 15, 1999. These reviews plus reviews of additional new or revised tests received since 1998 will appear in the *Fourteenth MMY*. Reviews, descriptions, and references associated with older tests can be located in other Buros publications such as previous *MMY*s and *Tests in Print V*.

Because of the proliferation of commercially available tests we have adopted a new policy of reviewing in *The Mental Measurements Yearbook* only those tests with at least a minimum of technical and/or developmental information available for review. This new policy is effective with tests reviewed in the *14th MMY*, and therefore, because all reviews in the *Supplement* will be integrated into the *14th MMY*, implementation of the policy begins with this *Supplement*. Under this plan, test reviews will be available sooner but not all commercially available tests will be described and reviewed in the *MMY*. A listing will be included in the *14th MMY* of new and revised tests that did not meet our review criteria. We also continue to include descriptive information for *all* known in-print commercially available tests in *Tests in Print (TIP)*. With our more frequent publication of the *MMY* and because some tests will no longer be reviewed in the *MMY*, it is necessary to provide *TIP* on a more frequent basis. Beginning with *Tests in Print V* (published in August 1999), we have embarked on a plan to publish *TIP* every 5 years.

The contents of the *13MMY-S* include: (a) a bibliography of 101 commercially available tests, new or revised, published as separates for use with English-speaking individuals; (b) 202 critical test reviews by well-qualified professional people who were selected by the editors on the basis of their expertise in measurement and, often, the content of the test being reviewed; (c) a test title index with appropriate cross references; (d) a classified subject index; (e) a publishers directory and index, including contact information and test listings by publisher; (f) a name index including the names of all authors of tests, reviews, or references; (g) an index of acronyms for easy reference when a test acronym, not the full title, is known; and (h) a score index to refer readers to tests featuring particular kinds of scores that are of interest to them.

A list of the names and affiliations of all reviewers contributing to the *13MMY-S* is also included. Typically the *Yearbooks* and *Supplements* also include bibliographies of references for specific tests related to the construction, validity, or use of these tests in various settings. These references are not included in this *Supplement* because all were included in the recently published *Tests in Print V*. Reviewer's references are included in the *13MMY-S* as well as cross references to previous reviews and reference lists.

The volume is organized like an encyclopedia, with tests being ordered alphabetically by title. If the title of a test is known, the reader can locate the test immediately without having to consult the Index of Titles.

The page headings reflect the encyclopedic organization. The page heading of the left-hand page cites the number and title of the first test listed on that page, and the page heading of the right-hand page cites the number and title of the last test listed on that page. All numbers presented in the various indexes are test numbers, not page numbers. Page numbers are important only for the Table of Contents and are indicated at the bottom of each page.

INDEXES

As mentioned earlier, the *13MMY-S* includes six indexes invaluable as aids to effective use: (a) Index of Titles, (b) Index of Acronyms, (c) Classified Subject Index, (d) Publishers Director and index, (e) Index of Names, and (f) Score Index. Additional comment on these indexes is presented below.

Index of Titles. Because the organization of the *13MMY-S* is encyclopedic in nature, with the tests ordered alphabetically by title throughout the volume, the test title index does not have to be consulted to find a test for which the title is known. However, the title index has some features that make it useful beyond its function as a complete title listing. It includes cross-reference information useful for tests with superseded or alternative titles or tests commonly (and sometimes inaccurately) known by multiple titles. It is important to keep in mind that the numbers in this index, like those for all *TIP* and *MMY* indexes, are test numbers and not page numbers.

Index of Acronyms. Some tests seem to be better known by their acronyms than by their full titles. The Index of Acronyms can help in these instances; it refers the reader to the full title of the test and to the relevant descriptive information and reviews.

Classified Subject Index. The Classified Subject Index classifies all tests listed in the *13MMY-S* into 15 major categories: Achievement, Behavior Assessment, Developmental, Education, English and Language, Intelligence and General Aptitude, Mathematics, Miscellaneous, Neuropsychological, Personality, Reading, Science, Sensory-Motor, Speech and Hearing, and Vocations. The additional categories of Fine Arts, Foreign Languages, and Social Studies have no representative tests in this volume but will be represented in the *14th MMY*. Each test entry includes test title, population for which the test is intended, and test number. The Classified Subject Index is of great help to readers who seek a listing of tests in given subject areas. Descriptive definitions of all 18 possible Classifications are provided at the beginning of this index. The Classified Subject Index represents a starting point for readers who know their area of interest but do not know how to further focus that interest in order to identify the best test(s) for their particular purposes.

Publishers Directory and Index. The publishers Directory and Index includes the names and addresses of the publishers of all tests included in the *13MMY-S* plus a listing of test numbers for each individual publisher. Beginning with *TIPV*, this index now also includes telephone and FAX numbers and addresses for electronic access (email and web pages). Publishers were given an opportunity to provide this information if they wanted it listed. For those not providing contact information, only a mailing address is included. This index can be particularly useful in obtaining addresses for specimen sets or catalogs after the test reviews have been read and evaluated. It can also be useful when a reader knows the publisher of a certain test but is uncertain about the test title, or when a reader is interested in the range of tests published by a given publisher.

Index of Names. The Index of Names provides a comprehensive list of names, indicating authorship of a test, test review, or reference.

Score Index. The Score Index is an index to all scores generated by the tests in the *13MMY-S*. Test titles are sometimes misleading or ambiguous, and test content may be difficult to define with precision. But test scores represent operational definitions of the variables the test author is trying to measure, and as such they often define test purpose and content more adequately than other descriptive information. A search for a particular test is more often a search for a test that measures some specific variables. Test scores and their associated labels can often be the best definitions of the variables of interest. It is, in fact, a detailed subject index based on the most critical operational features of any test—the scores and their associated labels.

HOW TO USE THIS SUPPLEMENT

A reference work like the *13MMY-S* can be of far greater benefit to a reader if a little time is taken to become familiar with what it has to offer and how one might use it most effectively to obtain the information wanted. The first step in this process is to read the Introduction to the *13MMY-S* in its entirety. The second step is to become familiar with the six indexes and particularly with the instructions preceding each index listing. The third step is to make actual use of the book by looking up needed information. This

third step is simple if one keeps in mind the following possibilities:

1. If you know the title of the test, use the alphabetical page headings to go directly to the test entry.

2. If you do not know, cannot find, or are unsure of the title of a test, consult the Index of Titles for possible variants of the title or consult the appropriate subject area of the Classified Subject Index for other possible leads or for similar or related tests in the same area. (Other uses for both of these indexes were described earlier.)

3. If you know the author of a test but not the title or publisher, consult the Index of Names and look up the author's titles until you find the test you want.

4. If you know the test publisher but not the title or author, consult the Publishers Directory and Index and look up the publisher's titles until you find the test you want.

5. If you are looking for a test that yields a particular kind of score, but have no knowledge of which test that might be, look up the score in the Score Index and locate the test or tests that include the score variable of interest.

6. Once you have found the test or tests you are looking for, read the descriptive entries for these tests carefully so that you can take advantage of the information provided. A description of the information provided in these test entries will be presented later in this section.

7. Read the test reviews carefully and analytically, as described earlier in this Introduction. The information and evaluation contained in these reviews are meant to assist test consumers in making well-informed decisions about the choice and applications of tests.

8. Once you have read the descriptive information, you may want to order a specimen set for a particular test so that you can examine it first-hand. The Publishers Directory and Index has the address information needed to obtain specimen sets or catalogs.

Keep in mind that the indexes for the *13MMY-S* include information for only the 101 tests reviewed in this publication. If you do not find the information you want in these indexes, you may wish to consult the indexes in *Tests in Print V* and recent volumes of *The Mental Measurements Yearbook*.

Making Effective use of the Test Entries. The test entries include extensive information. For each test, descriptive information is presented in the following order:

a) TITLE. Test titles are printed in boldface type. Secondary or series titles are set off from main titles by a colon.

b) PURPOSE. For each test we have included a brief, clear statement describing the purpose of the test. Often these statements are quotations from the test manual.

c) POPULATION. This is a description of the groups for which the test is intended. The grade, chronological age, semester range, or employment category is usually given. "Grades 1.5–2.5, 2–3, 4–12, 13–17" means that there are four test booklets: a booklet for the middle of first grade through the middle of the second grade, a booklet for the beginning of the second grade through the end of third grade, a booklet for grades 4 through 12 inclusive, and a booklet for undergraduate and graduate students in colleges and universities.

d) PUBLICATION DATE. The inclusive range of publication dates for the various forms, accessories, and editions of a test is reported.

e) ACRONYM. When a test is often referred to by an acronym, the acronym is given in the test entry immediately following the publication date.

f) SCORES. The number of part scores is presented along with their titles or descriptions of what they are intended to represent or measure.

g) ADMINISTRATION. Individual or group administration is indicated. A test is considered a group test unless it may be administered *only* individually.

h) FORMS, PARTS, AND LEVELS. All available forms, parts, and levels are listed.

i) MANUAL. Notation is made if no manual is available. All other manual information is included under Price Data.

j) RESTRICTED DISTRIBUTION. This is noted only for tests that are put on a special market by the publisher. Educational and psychological restrictions are not noted (unless a special training course is required for use).

k) PRICE DATA. Price information is reported for test packages (usually 20 to 35 tests), answer sheets, all other accessories, and specimen sets. The statement "$17.50 per 35 tests" means that all accessories are included unless otherwise indicated by the reporting of separate prices for

accessories. The statement also means 35 tests of one level, one edition, or one part unless stated otherwise. Because test prices can change very quickly, the year that the listed test prices were obtained is also given. Foreign currency is assigned the appropriate symbol. When prices are given in foreign dollars, a qualifying symbol is added (e.g., A$16.50 refers to 16 dollars and 50 cents in Australian currency). Along with cost, the publication date and number of pages on which print occurs is reported for manuals and technical reports (e.g., '98, 102 pages). All types of machine-scorable answer sheets available for use with a specific test are also reported in the descriptive entry. Scoring and reporting services provided by publishers are reported along with information on costs. In a few cases, special computerized scoring and interpretation services are given in separate entries immediately following the test.

l) FOREIGN LANGUAGE, AND OTHER SPECIAL EDITIONS. This section concerns foreign language editions published by the same publisher who sells the English edition. It also indicates special editions (e.g., Braille, large type) available from the same or a different publisher.

m) TIME. The number of minutes of actual working time allowed examinees and the approximate length of time needed for administering a test are reported whenever obtainable. The latter figure is always enclosed in parentheses. Thus, "50(60) minutes" indicates that the examinees are allowed 50 minutes of working time and that a total of 60 minutes is needed to administer the test. A time of "40–50 minutes" indicates an untimed test that takes approximately 45 minutes to administer, or—in a few instances—a test so timed that working time and administration time are very difficult to disentangle. When the time necessary to administer a test is not reported or suggested in the test materials but has been obtained through correspondence with the test publisher or author, the time is enclosed in brackets.

n) COMMENTS. Some entries contain special notations, such as: "for research use only"; "revision of the ABC Test"; "tests administered monthly at centers through the United States"; "subtests available as separates"; and "verbal creativity." A statement such as "verbal creativity" is intended to further describe what the test claims to measure. Some of the test entries include factual statements that imply criticism of the test, such as "1990 test identical with test copyrighted 1980."

o) AUTHOR. For most tests, all authors are reported. In the case of tests that appear in a new form each year, only authors of the most recent forms are listed. Names are reported exactly as printed on test booklets. Names of editors generally are not reported.

p) PUBLISHER. The name of the publisher or distributor is reported for each test. Foreign publishers are identified by listing the country in brackets immediately following the name of the publisher. The Publishers Directory and Index must be consulted for a publisher's address.

q) FOREIGN ADAPTATIONS. Revisions and adaptations of tests for foreign use are listed in a separate paragraph following the original edition.

r) SUBLISTINGS. Levels, editions, subtests, or parts of a test available in separate booklets are sometimes presented as sublistings with titles set in small capitals. Sub-sublistings are indented and titles are set in italic type.

s) CROSS REFERENCES. For tests that have been listed previously in a Buros Institute publication, a test entry includes—if relevant—a final paragraph containing a cross reference to the reviews, excerpts, and references for that test in those volumes. Cross reference "T5:467" refer to test 467 in *Tests in Print V*, "9:1023" refers to test 1023 in *The Ninth Mental Measurements Yearbook*, "T3:144" refers to test 144 in *Tests in Print III*, "7:637" refers to test 637 in *The Seventh Mental Measurements Yearbook*, "P:262" refers to test 262 in *Personality Tests and Reviews I*, "2:1427" refers to test 1427 in *The 1940 Yearbook*, and "1:1110" refers to test 1110 in *The 1938 Yearbook*. Test numbers not preceded by a colon refer to tests in this *Supplement*, for example, "See 45" refers to test 45 in this volume. In the case of batteries and programs, the paragraph also includes cross references—from the battery to the separately listed subtests and vice versa—to entries in this volume and to entries and reviews in earlier editions of *TIP* and *MMY*.

ACKNOWLEDGEMENTS

The publication of any book is a group effort. Among the group who are responsible for this book and who deserve special attention are Linda Murphy, Gary Anderson, Janice Nelsen, Rosemary Sieck, René Tapasak, a long list of reviewers, a dedicated group of graduate students, and our various advisory committees. Our special appreciation is given to Linda Murphy, our Managing Editor whose dedication to the Institute and its publications makes our efforts seem smooth and easy. She accomplishes this in spite of our extensive travel schedule and other distractions.

Gary Anderson, editorial assistant, keeps track of so many things, including our web site, that his continued good humor is both surprising and refreshing. Janice Nelsen's wonderful attitude and willingness to pitch in to help on almost any task is part of the glue that holds the entire Institute together. Similarly, Rosemary Sieck, our data entry specialist continues to perform beyond expectations to ensure accurately typed reviews. René Tapasak's screening and evaluation of tests to assure they met our criteria for review helped to reduce the time between receiving a test and seeking reviewers.

These people in particular, our colleagues, along with those who are recognized below, work very hard at making the *Yearbooks* and the *Supplements* look good. Although our names are listed as the editors, the success of the Institute is really because of their efforts.

In addition to our colleagues in the Institute, we would be remiss if we did not extend our thanks to the many reviewers who have prepared reviews for this book. They take time from their busy schedules to share their expertise by providing thoughtful and insightful test reviews. This way of "giving something back to the profession" deserves not only our thanks, but also the thanks of all those who find the reviews useful. Without them, the *Yearbooks* and the *Supplements* would not be possible.

The Buros Institute of Mental Measurements is one of two Institutes in the Oscar and Luella Buros Center for Testing that is part of the Department of Educational Psychology of the University of Nebraska - Lincoln. Many of the students in the department and from other departments in the university have contributed to the publication of this volume. We express our appreciation to these graduate research assistants who helped with the publication of the *13th MMY-S*: René Ayers, Ouyang Bo, Marta Coleman, Christine Gibbon, Jorge Gonzalez, Jessica Jonson, Gary

Loya, Heidi Paa, Robert Spies, and Elisabeth Sundermeier.

We also rely on the advice and suggestions from our National and Departmental Advisory Committees. These individuals give of their time and expertise on many issues that influence the way we operate. The current members of the National Advisory Committee are: Gary Melton, Anthony Nitko, Charles Peterson, Lawrence Rudner, and Paul Sackett. Our Departmental Advisory Committee members (in addition to Buros Staff) are: John Creswell, Terry Gutkin, Harold Keller, and Gregg Schraw.

SUMMARY

The *MMY* series is a valuable resource for people interested in studying or using testing. Once the process of using the series is understood, a reader can gain rapid access to a wealth of information. Our hope is that with the publication of the *13MMY-S*, test authors and publishers will consider carefully the comments made by the reviewers and continue to refine and perfect their assessment products.

Barbara S. Plake
James C. Impara
November 1999

Tests and Reviews

[1]
Adult Rating of Oral English.

Purpose: "Designed to assess the oral English language skills of secondary and adult students" who speak English as a second language.

Population: Adult and secondary students in vocational education and employment training programs.

Publication Date: 1995.

Acronym: AROE.

Scores, 15: Pronunciation, Grammar, General Vocabulary, Vocational Vocabulary, Building Blocks Subscore; Listener and Speaker scores for Conversation, Instructions, Explanations, Clarification/Verification; Discourse Subscore; Mean Proficiency Score; Total Score.

Administration: Individual.

Price Data, 1997: $75 per training kit including 5 user's handbooks (43 pages) and 25 matrix scoring sheets; $20 per set of 25 matrix scoring sheets; $15 per user's handbook; $10 per technical manual (16 pages); $15 per supplementary video explaining use and purpose.

Time: Untimed.

Comments: A rating scale completed by teachers about individual students' skills; supplementary video explaining use and purpose is available.

Authors: Annette M. Zehler and Patricia A. DiCerbo.

Publisher: Development Associates, Inc.

Review of the Adult Rating of Oral English by ROGER A. RICHARDS, Consultant, Office of Certification and Credentialing, Massachusetts Department of Education, Malden, MA; and Adjunct Professor of Communication, Bunker Hill Community College, Boston, MA:

The Adult Rating of Oral English (AROE) is a scoring matrix for recording teachers' assessments of the English-language skills of adults "within vocational education and employment training programs" (User's Handbook, p. 7). By guiding the teacher through the elements of oral language, it provides a uniform approach to evaluating different individuals by insuring that consistent criteria are applied to all and by eliminating the risk that one or more factors may receive disproportionate weighting in the total assessment.

The rater is required to judge 11 elements of a subject's linguistic proficiency and to assign a score of 0 to 5 to each according to which descriptor is most applicable. The proficiency levels for pronunciation are typical:

Level 0. No ability.

Level 1. Speech is very difficult to understand; repetition is always needed.

Level 2. Speech is difficult to understand; repetition is often needed.

Level 3. Speech is sometimes difficult to understand; repetition is sometimes needed.

Level 4. Speech is seldom difficult to understand; repetition is only occasionally needed.

Level 5. Speech is close to (or the same as) that of a native speaker.

The sum of the ratings for Pronunciation, Grammar, General Vocabulary, and Vocational Vocabulary yields a Building Blocks Score; similarly, rating for Conversation as a Listener, Conversation as a Speaker, Instructions as a Listener, Instructions as a Speaker, Explanations as a Listener, Explanations as a Speaker, and Clarification/Verification are summed to obtain a Discourse score. The total score equals the Building Blocks plus the Discourse score.

The method of administration is described as follows:

> No testing sessions with the students are necessary in using the AROE. The AROE essentially asks teachers to do what you are already doing, that is, to observe your students' skills in English and to make judgments about those skills .... The AROE ratings are based on the teacher's observations of the student's use of English across the variety of situations and topics encountered in the classroom. (User's Handbook, pp. 8–9)

Despite some external trappings that may confuse the uninitiated, the AROE is neither standardized nor a test. (Neither is it an "Adult Rating," whatever that might be; rather, it is a rating of adults' oral English.) There is no uniform content to which all test takers are required to respond, there is no uniform method of administration, there are no objective criteria for determining scores, and there are no norms or other guides to the interpretation of results.

Making the fine distinctions called for would be possible only in a situation in which the teacher knows the students extremely well and has had extensive opportunity to observe their English in a variety of contexts. Even then, differentiating among instructions, explanations, and clarification/verification, for example, must be very difficult. The authors claim that "teachers report feeling comfortable in rating after about 15–30 hours of working with their students" (User's Handbook, p. 9).

A claim of face validity is based on reactions of teachers and other vocational program staff who have reportedly found the instrument useful. As evidence of concurrent/criterion-related validity, the authors offer correlations in the range of .65 to .70 between the AROE and the Basic English Skills Test (BEST) Short Form ($n = 22$) and between the AROE and the Bilingual Vocational Oral Proficiency Test (BVOPT) ($n = 69$). The rationale for such comparison is not clear because the BEST and BVOPT are vehicles for determining language proficiency whereas the AROE is merely a form for recording subjectively assigned judgments of proficiency.

The discussion of reliability provides measures of internal consistency and comparisons of independent ratings assigned by pairs of raters. Concerning the former, the authors state, "Since the AROE components are designed to measure oral language proficiency, items should positively correlate with each other" (Technical Manual, p. 9). The measures of internal consistency all fall within the range of .89 to .99. That being the case, we have to ask, what is the point of determining component scores if they match each other so closely? If each of the scores measures a discrete aspect of oral language, should we not expect lower intercorrelations?

The interrater reliability of the AROE is not impressive. For the 11 component scores, correlation coefficients range from -.12 to .95 for samples of between 9 and 63 students. For the total of nine samples ($N = 197$ for Building Blocks and $N = 284$ for Discourse), the intercorrelations are all in the .70s. These relatively low correlations are hardly surprising. The authors sum up a major flaw of the AROE in acknowledging that:

> The level of agreement between raters varied across sites and teachers but was generally moderately high to high. Variation could be partially accounted for by rater differences in terms of educational background and instructional time with student. (Technical Manual, p. 9)

The AROE does not yield new information about its subjects' performance. It simply provides a format for recording teacher evaluations of performance. It may be helpful in assisting teachers to make more systematic assessments of their students, but a locally developed rating scale could probably prove just as useful and less costly.

Review of the Adult Rating of Oral English by GERALD TINDAL, Professor, Behavioral Research and Teaching, University of Oregon, Eugene, OR:

The Adult Rating of Oral English (AROE) provides qualitative information on the oral proficiency of adult learners of English as a second language. "The focus is on those oral English language skills that are particularly important within on-the-job situations" (p. 7). The ratings are based on teacher observations in classroom situations and topics, with various matrices provided for ensuring the reflections are pertinent to work settings. Both the matrix and video training package were developed with funds from the U.S. Department of Education, Office of Vocational and Adult Education. The instrument is composed of two parts, a Building Blocks matrix and a Discourse matrix, to help define areas of strength and weakness, track progress, and guide placement decisions. The entire instrument is packaged with a User's Handbook, a scoring sheet, a summary information sheet, a training plan, and a technical manual.

The teacher rates the student on each proficiency by selecting one of six levels of proficiency (generally, in all the scales, 0 reflects no ability and 5 reflects the ability of a native English speaker). Three steps are provided for actually rating a student, with the teachers first directed to think back over the past 2–3 weeks in which they have observed the student using English, second to review the rating descriptions, and third to "select the description that best matches the student's most consistent level of performance over the past 2–3 weeks" (p. 9). The authors recommend using the instrument whenever the teacher is comfortable making such decisions (usually after 15–30 hours of working with students).

The manual is divided into sections that organize the two matrices. In the Building Blocks matrix, four basic components of oral proficiency are considered: Pronunciation, Grammar, General Vocabulary, and Vocational Vocabulary. In the Discourse matrix, seven components are included to determine how well the examinee is able to use the Building Blocks in actual communication: Conversation as a Listener, Conversation as a Speaker, Instructions as a Listener, Instructions as a Speaker, Explanations as a Listener, Explanations as a Speaker, and Clarification/Verification. These two matrices provide, therefore, a total of 11 constructs on which to rate proficiency, each of them organized into two opposing pages. In each of these ratings, the examiner is directed to think about "why is it important?" and "what should I look for when rating the construct?" A final section is provided for each construct that raises "issues in rating" (p. 15).

Within each rating level, general descriptions, not specific skills, are listed to help the rater make a selection. For example, in the Building Blocks matrix of Grammar, the examiner is provided one scale that moves from a 0 (No ability) to a 1 ("uses only very few basic forms and structures; errors make all speech very difficult to understand") to a 3 ("uses a range of forms and structures; errors make some speech difficult to under-

stand") to a 5 ("uses forms and structures at a level close to [or the same as] that of a native speaker") (p. 14). And, as an example in the Dicourse matrix for Conversation, the examiner is directed to use the 0–5 scale for making judgments of the student on two related scales: as a listener and as a speaker. The scale guides the examiner with descriptions of understanding and speaking from the low to the high end: with isolated words and phrases, then in the context of everyday topics, next within a context of less familiar topics [with some difficulty or easily], and finally in the context of a native speaker.

In the manual, the examiner is provided guidelines for rating and steps to follow, and then directions for scoring the AROE to determine the student's Total Score and Mean proficiency Level. The Total Score is the sum of all ratings in the Building Blocks and Discourse matrices whereas the Mean Proficiency is simply the average for all components that have been rated. A final section provides several ways the AROE can be used and guides the examiner in how to handle difficult situations (working with shy individuals, students who repeat classes, students with no literacy, etc.). The manual is extremely well organized, designed, and easy to use.

TECHNICAL ADEQUACY OF THE AROE. The AROE was developed by reviewing the vocational curricula and related research, assessing vocational program needs, constructing a pilot instrument, and field-testing it. The two matrices arose from the review of the literature, which then was expanded into a needs assessment of 35 individuals working in 22 vocational education and employment programs serving adult English language learners. Again, the two matrices were further articulated. With its construction and pilot testing, the following procedures have been described in a technical manual. First, discussion sessions were held to define the context for administration (teacher observation within authentic classroom situations using a reflective judgment that requires little time). Second, 12 sites were identified through the National Center for Research in Vocational Education (NCRVE). In this pilot testing, three workshops were held and then a video-training session was conducted.

Summary of technical data includes the following:

1. Ninety four percent of the respondents agreed or strongly agreed that the AROE was a useful measure of language proficiency and that it included the essential indicators of oral proficiency in vocational education and employment training programs.

2. On two other measures of language ability, it correlated about .70 with the Basic English Skills Test (BEST) and .66 with the Bilingual Vocational Oral Proficiency Test.

3. Reliability was investigated by measuring both internal consistency (which ranged from .89 to .99) and rater agreement (median of approximately .80).

4. Item statistics were displayed for all 11 components with four different sites, generally reflecting similar results in three of the four sites.

SUMMARY. This instrument has been very carefully developed and organized. It provides a very useful tool for vocational educators to use with students for whom English is a second language. The essential elements of oral language are well differentiated, easily obtained, and highly useful in the classroom context. As the authors indicate, the instrument can help teachers make many useful decisions about diagnostics, progress, and placement. The manuals and materials are very well organized and professionally published. The technical data are clear and support the use of this instrument in the context described by the authors. In future editions of the test, it might be useful to include factor analysis for documenting the dependence or independence of the traits and student change scores to document the sensitivity of the scale for tracking progress.

[2]
Alcohol Use Disorders Identification Test.

Purpose: A screening procedure "to identify persons whose alcohol consumption has become hazardous or harmful to their health."
Population: Adults.
Publication Date: 1992.
Acronym: AUDIT.
Scores, 2: Core, Clinical.
Administration: Individual or group.
Price Data, 1996: Test and manual (33 pages) are free; $75 per training module.
Time: [2] minutes.
Comments: Developed by World Health Organization and validated on primary care patients in six

countries; available in English, Japanese, Spanish, Norwegian, and Romanian.
Authors: Thomas F. Babor, Juan Ramon de la Fuente, John Saunders, and Marcus Grant.
Publisher: World Health Organization [Switzerland]; also available from Thomas F. Babor.
Cross References: See T5:135 (6 references).

Review of the Alcohol Use Disorders Identification Test by PHILIP ASH, Director, Ash, Blackstone and Cates, Blacksburg, VA:

The Alcohol Use Disorders Identification Test (AUDIT) (Allen & Columbus, 1995, pp. 260-261) was developed in a six-country (Australia, Bulgaria, Kenya, Mexico, Norway, USA) World Health Organization collaborative project to design a screening instrument to identify people whose alcohol consumption has become hazardous and harmful to their health. It should be noted that this is the first instrument of its kind to be derived on the basis of a cross-national study (Babor, de la Fuente, Saunders, & Grant, 1992).

Screening with the AUDIT provides data useful in deciding about treatment alternatives such as brief intervention with heavy drinkers or specialized treatment for more seriously ill patients. The AUDIT package includes the AUDIT Core and an optional Clinical Screening Procedure. This procedure includes two questions about traumatic injury (e.g., "Have you injured your head since your eighteenth birthday?"), five on clinical evaluation (e.g., presence of hand tremor), and a blood test (Serum GGT). Although the Clinical Screening Procedure does not refer directly to problems with alcohol, it may elicit relevant information where patients are defensive toward alcohol-specific questions.

To develop the AUDIT Core, a 150-item assessment schedule was administered to subjects ($N = 1888$) attending representative primary health care facilities in the participating countries. A 10-item self-report questionnaire (the AUDIT) was selected to cover the domains of alcohol consumption, drinking behavior, and alcohol-related problems. It may be paper-and-pencil self-administered or administered in an interview in 2 minutes. Questions 1–3 measure quantitative alcohol consumption, 4–6 drinking behavior, 7–8 adverse reactions, and 9–10 alcohol-related problems. Responses to each question are scored from 0 to 4, for a maximum possible AUDIT score of 40. Among those diagnosed as having hazardous or harmful alcohol use, 92% had an AUDIT score of 8 or more, and 94% of those with nonhazardous consumption had a score of less than 8 (Saunders, Aasland, Babor, de la Fuente, & Grant, 1993).

According to the authors' research report (Saunders et al., 1993, p. 799), the differences between the AUDIT and most other existing questionnaires include the following: (a) it tries to identify problem drinkers at the "less severe end of the spectrum" rather than those with established dependence or alcoholism; (b) it emphasizes hazardous consumption and frequency of intoxication rather than drinking behavior itself and its consequences; and (c) it refers to alcohol experiences in the past year as well as over the patient's lifetime, improving relevance to current drinking status, and it does not require the test-taker to identify himself or herself as a problem drinker. Two questions (9–10) have 3 responses (scored 0, 2, 4). The remaining questions (1–8) have 4-choice responses based upon frequency (from, e.g., "never," "1 or 2" to, e.g., "daily or almost daily," "10 or more"). They yield item scores from 0 (lowest frequency choice) to 4 (highest frequency choice). The authors anticipated that using specific frequency continua will reduce underreporting of adverse effects.

The manual (Babor et al., 1992) is a 28-page document that introduces the AUDIT by discussing the advantages of screening for alcohol problems, the developmental history of the AUDIT, applications of the AUDIT to the early identification of alcohol-related problems, and the scoring and interpretation of the AUDIT. The authors point out that although alcohol screening tests have most often been used to identify who *may probably* be alcohol abusers (case finding), the AUDIT is directed at screening known drinkers to deal with their problems and treatment approaches. The AUDIT is claimed to be the first screening test specifically for use in primary care cases. The seven text chapters of the manual are followed by a list of references and six appendices covering research guidelines, validity evidence in the AUDIT, etc., including a copy of the AUDIT.

Extensive research has been undertaken on the reliability, validity, and other psychometric characteristics of the AUDIT. Both test-retest and internal consistency measures (Fleming, Barry, & MacDonald, 1991) have shown satisfactory reliability. High intrascale reliabilities (alpha coefficient mean values of .93 and .81) were found among the drinking patients' drinking behavior and adverse psychological reactions domains (Saunders et al., 1993, pp. 794–795).

Concurrent, construct, and discriminant validities of the AUDIT were assessed by Bohn, Babor, and Kranzler (1995, p. 425ff). Significant concurrent validities were found against other alcoholism measures such as the MAST (Michigan Alcohol Screening Test: T5:1661) and the MacAndrews scales ($r = .31$ to $r = .887$). Coefficients for the AUDIT Core were consistently higher than for the AUDIT Clinical. Construct validities for five risk factors, four drinking consequences, and three drinking attitudes showed significant correlations ($r = .27$ to $r = .88$) for 11 of the 12 measures for AUDIT Core for male subjects ($n = 107$), but fewer significant correlations for AUDIT Core for female subjects ($n = 91$), or for either sex for AUDIT Clinical scores. An analysis of discriminant validity found a significant difference between nondrinkers and harmful drinkers, but no significant gender or gender x drinker group difference. Similar validity evidence was reported by Babor et al. (1992, p. 21).

SUMMARY. Overall, the AUDIT is a useful device for discriminating between alcoholics and medical patients and in the early detection of hazardous or harmful drinking, and is more successful than the Michigan Alcohol Screening Test (MAST) in discriminating hazardous drinkers from nonhazardous drinkers. A well-written manual and substantial published supporting research commend the instrument for serious consideration in the assessment of people with difficult alcohol problems. Its multinational origins and translations also commend it as a device for conducting cross-cultural alcoholism studies.

REVIEWER'S REFERENCES

Fleming, M. F., Barry, K. L., & MacDonald, R. (1991). The Alcohol Use Disorders Identification Test (AUDIT) in a college sample. *International Journal of the Addictions, 26*, 1173–1185.

Babor, T. F., de la Fuente, J. R., Saunders, J., & Grant, M. (1992). *Programme on Substance Abuse: AUDIT—The Alcohol Use Disorders Test: Guidelines for Use in Primary Health Care* (an update of WHO Document No. WHO/MNH/DAT/89.4 under the same title) [Switzerland]: World Health Organization.

Saunders, J. B., Aasland, O. G., Babor, T. F., de la Fuente, J. R., & Grant, M. (1993). Development of the Alcohol Use Disorders Identification Test (AUDIT): WHO collaborative project on early detection of persons with harmful alcohol consumption—II. *Addiction, 88*, 791–804.

Allen, J. P., & Columbus, M. (Eds.) (1995). *Assessing alcohol problems: A guide for clinicians and researchers.* Washington, DC: National Institute on Alcohol Abuse and Alcoholism.

Bohn, M. J., Babor, T. F., & Kranzler, H. R. (1995). The Alcohol Use Disorders Identification Test (AUDIT): Validation of a screening instrument for use in medical settings. *Journal of Studies on Alcohol, 58*(4), 423–432.

Review of the Alcohol Use Disorders Identification Test by HERBERT BISCHOFF, Licensed Psychologist, Psychology Resources, Anchorage, AK:

The Alcohol Use Disorders Identification Test (AUDIT) is a screening procedure produced by a multicultural collaboration of six nations under the sponsorship of the World Health Organization (WHO). The AUDIT is intended to be used primarily by health care providers to detect harmful or hazardous drinking habits. The AUDIT is not a diagnostic tool, and the authors are clear about its limitations and intended uses. The AUDIT is made up of two components. The first part is a core 10-item questionnaire that addresses drinking patterns including indications of "hazardous alcohol consumption, evidence of dependence symptoms, and harmful alcohol consumption." The second part, which is administered only in cases of a "positive" on the first part, is a clinical screening instrument of eight items covering trauma history, clinical examination, and a blood test.

The intended use of the AUDIT is to detect, or more appropriately screen, persons who may be engaging in dangerous drinking habits, referred to as either harmful, hazardous, or evident of dependence. Referring to the ICD-10 the authors define harmful drinking as, "a pattern of use which is already causing damage to health." Hazardous drinking refers to "an established pattern of use carrying with it a high risk of future damage to health, physical or mental, but which has not yet resulted in significant medical or psychiatric ill effects." Evidence of dependence is defined by symptoms, patterns of behaviors, and debilitating social and occupational consequences of long-term alcohol dependence, as described in the DSM-IV and ICD-10.

The AUDIT has also been found to have high levels of concurrent and construct validity. There have been numerous studies on the efficacy of using the AUDIT screening instrument, and it has been established as providing reliable and valid scores of harmful and hazardous drinking patterns with high levels of accuracy in detecting dependence in multinational and widely varied populations (Bohn, Babor, & Kranzler 1995; MacKenzie, Langa & Brown, 1996; Saunders, Aasland, Babor, de la Fuente, & Grant, 1993). Scores from the AUDIT have been found to be highly reliable in identifying persons who currently demonstrate the above patterns of behavior.

The AUDIT appears to be a highly useable, quickly administered, and cost efficient tool for health care providers to use in the course of various types of clinical interviews. During the short time the AUDIT has been available, it has proven itself when compared to more traditional methods, such as the Michigan Alcohol Screening Test (MAST), TWEAK, and the MMPI's (Minnesota Multiphasic Personality Inventory) MacAndrew Alcoholism scale. Overall, the AUDIT may be an even more reliable indicator of problem drinking patterns with certain populations, such as ethnic minorities and the long-term unemployed (Cherpitel & Clark, 1995; Claussen & Aasland, 1993; Luckie, White, Miller, & Icenogle, 1995).

There are, however, some limitations with the AUDIT and its manual. These include information on how the cutoff point was determined, how results vary from population to population, and how the 10 items were chosen. The information is covered in supplemental material provided by the test authors in the forms of varying research projects that have demonstrated the AUDIT to provide highly reliable and valid scores and to be a useful instrument. Another concern with the test manual is the lack of normative data; nor is there an explanation of how various cultures view harmful or hazardous drinking. This may leave the test administrator confused about the validity of scores from the AUDIT when there are no apparent considerations devoted to the importance of context, other than suggested ideal situations when administering the test. For instance, it is assumed a drink containing 10g of alcohol is the typical quantity per drink cross-culturally. Yet, there is no consideration given to how drinking is viewed culturally, or to the effects of perceived social desirability on the respondents' level of self-reporting. Moreover, there is no discussion on how possibly to control for these potential effects.

SUMMARY. In summation, the AUDIT appears to be an easily administered screening tool that provides reliable scores for health care providers to ascertain if an individual is engaging in potentially damaging drinking patterns. The AUDIT's limitations include limited diagnostic utility and problems with the testing manual. It appears to be a useful tool for health care providers to facilitate treatment or interventions for persons already suffering the effects of alcohol misuse or those soon to be suffering the damaging effects of long-term harmful alcohol consumption.

REVIEWER'S REFERENCES

Claussen, B., & Aasland, O. G. (1993). The Alcohol Use Disorders Identification Test (AUDIT) in a routine health examination of long-term unemployed. *Addiction, 88*(3), 363–368.

Saunders, J. B., Aasland, O. G., Babor, T. F., de la Fuente, J. R., & Grant, M. (1993). Development of the Alcohol Use Disorders Identification Test (AUDIT): WHO collaborative project on early detection of persons with harmful alcohol consumption—II. *Addiction, 88*, 791–804.

Bohn, M. J., Babor, T. F., & Kranzler, H. R. (1995). The Alcohol Use Disorders Identification Test (AUDIT): Validation of a screening instrument for use in medical settings. *Journal of Studies on Alcohol, 56*(4), 423–432.

Cherpitel, C. J., & Clark, W. B. (1995). Ethnic differences in performance of screening instruments for identifying harmful drinking and alcohol dependence in the emergency room. *Alcoholism Clinical and Experimental Research, 19*(3), 628–634.

Luckie, L. F., White, R. E., Miller, W. R., & Icenogle, M. V. (1995). Prevalence of estimates of alcohol problems in a Veterans Administration outpatient population: AUDIT vs. MAST. *Journal of Clinical Psychology, 51*(3), 422–425.

MacKenzie, D. M., Langa, A., & Brown, T. M. (1996). Identifying hazardous or harmful alcohol use in medical admissions: A comparison of AUDIT, CAGE, and Brief MAST. *Alcohol and Alcoholism, 31*(6), 591–599.

[3]
Attention-Deficit Scales for Adults.

Purpose: Designed as an objective measure of attention deficit in adults.
Population: Adults.
Publication Date: 1996.
Acronym: ADSA.
Scores, 11: Attention-Focus/Concentration, Interpersonal, Behavior-Disorganized Activity, Coordination, Academic Theme, Emotive, Consistency/Long Term, Childhood, Negative-Social, Internal Consistency, Total.
Administration: Individual.
Price Data, 1997: $55 per complete kit including manual (30 pages), and 25 instrument/scoring/profile sets; $25 per 25 additional sets; $30 per manual.
Time: Untimed.
Comments: A 54-item, Likert-scale questionnaire to be administered in a clinical setting; self-report.
Authors: Santo James Triolo and Kevin Richard Murphy.
Publisher: Brunner/Mazel, Inc.

Review of the Attention-Deficit Scales for Adults by JOSEPH G. LAW, JR., Associate Professor of Behavioral Science and Educational Technology, University of South Alabama, Mobile, AL:

The Attention-Deficit Scales for Adults (ADSA) is a 54-item self-report designed to assess symptoms of attention-deficit/hyperactivity disorder (ADHD) in adults. Each respondent describes his or her behavior on each item as "Never," "Seldom," "Sometimes," "Often," and "Always." The responses are easily scored by tearing off the cover sheet and filling in boxes for the nine subscales and the total column. Raw scores are then plotted on a separate profile sheet

and transformed into standard scores with a mean of 50 and a standard deviation of 10. The profile sheet also displays scores as percentile ranks. The subscales include an internal consistency measure and total scores as well as nine clinical subscales labeled as: Attention-Focus/Concentration, Interpersonal, Behavior-Disorganized Activity, Coordination, Academic-Theme, Emotive, Consistency/Long-Term, Childhood, and Negative-Social. The names and item content of each subscale were developed to reflect the authors' concern about the multiple effects of ADHD on the lives of adults.

The ADSA was normed on 306 adults, but the authors failed to specify in the manual the age range of their sample. It was indicated that all members of the norm group were 17 years of age or older, had IQs of 80 or higher, no childhood history of attention or hyperactivity problems, no history of alcohol or drug abuse, and no felony convictions. The reported rationale was to duplicate the average population as much as possible. The mean age was reported as 33.95 years ($SD = 11.6$), but no upper age limit or further breakdown by age was evident in the manual. As a test subject diverges in age from 33 years the clinician will have difficulty in determining how appropriate the norms are for that person. This may be an important limitation. This is unfortunate because the manual contains a wealth of useful information on the norm group that should assist the user in applying the test in clinical use.

The 30-page manual reports internal consistency statistics on the ADSA. Cronbach's alpha for the 54 items is .8912 with a split-half correlation of .812. Cronbach's alpha for the nine subscales ranged from .0196 for the Childhood subscale to .8215 for the Emotive subscale. The Academic Theme subscale has an alpha of only -.1124. Although they may provide some useful information, Childhood and Academic Theme only have 2 items per subscale, hence their low reliability. Unfortunately, there were no reported test-retest reliability statistics. Validity information is limited, but promising. In a validation study with 87 subjects diagnosed as having ADHD, the mean total score was 45 points higher than that of the 306-person normative group.

The manual contains the results of a stepwise discriminant analysis predicting group membership of the nine ADSA subscales. Four subscales were identified by the step-wise procedure: Consistency/Long-Term, Attention-Focus/Concentration, Behavior-Disorganized Activity, and Negative-Social. These four subscales had the discriminant power to identify correctly 90.8% of the norm group as non-ADHD and incorrectly classified 9.2% as ADHD. For the 87 clinical subjects reported above, 82% were correctly placed in the ADHD category and 18% were erroneously placed in the normal (non-ADHD) category. Even though these four subscales have the greatest discriminating power, the other subscales may assist the clinician by providing clues into the clients' perceptions of their symptoms. A review of individual item responses on scales such as Emotive, Academic Theme, and Interpersonal may give additional insight. The short length of the ADSA facilitates such a process.

The authors provide six case studies with accompanying profiles to illustrate the use of the ADSA in identifying ADHD in adults. These are well written and helpful in assisting the test user to incorporate the results into a comprehensive diagnostic approach. Unfortunately, on the first two profiles the names of the subscales are not listed, making interpretation difficult for the novice. There are a few small problems with the ADSA manual. For example, as noted earlier, there is no evident report on the upper age limit of the 306-person norm group. A clinical validation study reports 87 subjects in one table and 89 subjects on another page. It is not clear from the manual if these are two different groups or the result of a typographical error. The mean IQ of 111 for the norm group is higher than the national average. The geographical representation of the normative subjects was heavily weighted to the northeastern and southeastern regions of the United States.

SUMMARY. This is a brief and easily administered rating scale with potential use as part of a comprehensive adult evaluation. It draws attention to the need for a broad-based process in assessing adults. The authors stress the importance of using the ADSA as part of a process that includes ruling out physical abnormalities, carrying out clinical and collateral interviews, and other procedures. Future research will be needed on the validity and reliability of scores from the ADSA. Studies of the test-retest reliability of this scale as well as its sensitivity to the effects of various treatment approaches are recommended. Because

of the lack of ADHD-specific scales for adults, the potential utility of this instrument for the study of ADHD in adults far outweighs its limitations. Practicing clinicians are encouraged to include it in their assessment procedures and to begin gathering data for further research on the topic of adult ADHD.

Review of the Attention-Deficit Scales for Adults by JAMES C. REED, Chief Psychologist, St. Luke's Hospital, New Bedford, MA:

The 54 items that comprise the Attention-Deficit Scales for Adults (ADSA) pertain to the syndrome of Attention-Deficit/Hyperactivity Disorder (AD/HD). The respondent is asked to check one of five categories for each item: Never, Seldom, Sometimes, Often, or Always. Most of the items are worded so that marking "Always" indicates a significant AD/HD-related problem. There are, however, 11 items where the scoring is reversed (i.e., "Never" indicates significant problems, and "Always" suggests no AD/HD-related problems). For example, Item 14 reads, "I finish the home projects I start." The marking of "Never" would suggest problems, and marking "Always" suggests no AD/HD problems.

A total score is obtained but nine content subscales can also be scored. The scores can be converted to T scores (mean of 50 and standard deviation of 10) and percentile ranks. The T scores can be plotted on an "MMPI-like" format and a graphic representation of the profile can be made. "The subscales are named and numbered as follows: (I) Attention-Focus/Concentration; (II) Interpersonal; (III) Behavior-Disorganized Activity; (IV) Coordination; (V) Academic Theme; (VI) Emotive; (VII) Consistency/Long Term; (VIII) Childhood; and (IX) Negative-Social" (manual, p. 1). Each scale has items that are unique to it, but it also has items that are shared or overlap with other scales. To illustrate: Subscale I, Attention-Focus/Concentration, has nine items that are unique, one item it shares with Scale VI (Emotive), and two items it shares with Scale VII (Consistency/Long Term). The scale items are based on content validity (e.g., Items 2 and 5 are unique to Scale I, and they are "I tend to daydream" and "I have trouble putting my thoughts down on paper"). Items 10 and 37 appears on both Scale I and VII. They are "Tasks which need persistence frustrate me" and "I need to be reminded of my daily schedule/duties or appointments." The total number of items per scale is variable. Scale V has two items—1 unique and 1 shared with Scale VIII. Scale III has 23 items—11 unique, 3 shared with Scale VI, 7 shared with Scale VII, and 1 with Scale IX. For the Total Scale, a split-half (odd versus even) reliability coefficient was .81, Cronbach alpha was .89. However, as might be anticipated, there was wide variability in the alpha coefficients among the subscales. Four coefficients varied from .71 to .82, three were between .46 and .57, and the remaining two were .02 and .11. The normative sample consisted of 306 persons (139 females and 167 males) who met the following criteria: (a) 17 years or older; (b) No childhood history of problems with attention or hyperactivity; (c) An IQ of 80 or above as estimated by the Shipley Institute of Living Scale (1940); (d) No reported history of drug and/or alcohol abuse; and (e) No reported history of a felony conviction (manual, p. 3). Descriptive characteristics with respect to marital status, ethnicity, Hollingshead Index of Social Position, etc., are given in the manual. The majority of the subjects came from the northeastern and southeastern region of the United States. States included were Georgia, Florida, Massachusetts, Alabama, New York, and New Hampshire (manual, p. 3).

There were 97 clinical subjects previously diagnosed as having AD/HD who participated in an effort to validate the scales. For Total Score, the mean for the clinical group exceeded the norm group's mean by 45 points, a highly significant difference. For each of the scales the mean for the clinical group was higher than the mean for the normative group, but the significance of the differences was not reported. A discriminate analysis showed that 91% of the normative group were accurately classified, and 82% of the clinical group were accurately classified. The authors state "that the ADSA can be a very useful instrument to help identify adults with AD/HD. This is especially so considering that over 88% of cases were classified correctly by the combined scores of only four subscales, without the aid of history, diagnostic interview, collateral findings, and other diagnostic techniques/procedures" (manual, p. 9). ADSA also has a consistency check. There are four pairs of items that ask almost the same question with a variation in wording. Data presented indicate "that intrasubject consistency can be assumed" (manual, p. 6).

GENERAL COMMENTS. There are some limitations that the potential user should consider. First, the usefulness of the ADSA is limited by the geographical restrictions of the normative sample. The subjects were primarily from the northeast and southeast, and whether or not the findings would hold for another geographical area is open to question. Second, although the items on this scale refer to behaviors associated with AD/HD, it is a stretch to assume that nine reliable subscales can be derived from 54 items, particularly when there are so few items on some of the scale (2 on Scale V and 3 on Scale IV). Furthermore, four of the scales have alpha coefficients of .5 or lower, and these are unacceptably low. Third, the reported classification rate for the ADSA is high, but whether this rate would hold with cross validation is another question. It is one problem to distinguish between members of a well-screened normal group and patients in an accurately diagnosed clinical group. There is an additional problem in clinical practice, which is not only to differentiate an AD/HD patient from normal, but also to make the differential diagnosis between AD/HD and, say, conduct disorder, schizophrenia, mental retardation, etc. If one were to administer the ADSA to these last named clinical samples, how many of each would score in the range indicative of AD/HD? The problem is one of test sensitivity as well as test specificity.

SUMMARY. The ASDA scale shows promise. It is in need of further research. The research should be directed toward obtaining a more representative normative sample, a validation of the subscales, and a more definitive evaluation of its sensitivity. In its present form, the ADSA has not been as thoroughly developed as the Adult Attention Deficit Disorders Evaluation Scale (McCarney & Anders, 1996), and the clinician might want to consider this scale as an alternative.

REVIEWER'S REFERENCE

McCarney, S. B., & Anderson, P. D. (1996). Adult Attention Deficit Disorders Evaluation Scale. Columbia, MO: Hawthorne Educational Services, Inc.

[4]

BarOn Emotional Quotient Inventory.

Purpose: Designed to measure emotional intelligence.
Population: Ages 16 and older.
Publication Date: 1997.

Acronym: BarOn EQ-i.

Scores: 21 content scores: Composite Scale scores (Total EQ, Intrapersonal EQ, Interspersonal EQ, Adaptability EQ, Stress Management EQ, General Mood EQ), Intrapersonal subscale scores (Self-Regard, Emotional Self-Awareness, Assertiveness, Independence, Self-Actualization), Interpersonal subscale scores (Empathy, Social Responsibility, Interpersonal Relationship), Adaptability subscale scores (Reality Testing, Flexibility, Problem Solving), Stress Management subscale socres (Stress Tolerance, Impulse Control), General Mood subscale scores (Optimism,Happiness), plus 4 validity indicators (Omission Rate, Inconsistency, Positive Impression, Negative Impression).

Administration: Individual or group.

Price Data, 1999: $10 per summary report; $20 per development report; $36 per group report (volume discounts available); $6 per 3 item booklets (volume discounts available); $42 per mail-in preview package including item booklet, development report, and user's manual; $59.95 per user's set including user's manual, administrator's guide, and facilitator's guide; $24.95 per user's manual; $7.95 per administrator's guide; $39.95 per facilitator's guide; $39.95 per technical manual (234 pages).

Foreign Language Editions: Translations available in Afrikaans, Chinese, Czech, Dutch, French-Canadian, Korean, German, Hebrew, Norwegian, Russian, Spanish (South American), Swedish, Danish, Finnish, French (Euro), Hindi, Indonesian, Italian, Japanese, Portugese, Slovakian, and Slovene.

Time: (30–40) minutes.

Comments: Paper-and-pencil and computer administrations available.

Author: Reuven Bar-On.

Publisher: Multi-Health Systems, Inc.

Review of the BarOn Emotional Quotient Inventory by ANDREW A. COX, Professor of Counseling and Psychology, Troy State University, Phenix City, AL:

The BarOn Emotional Quotient Inventory is designed to assess the construct of emotional intelligence. This concept refers to capabilities, competencies, and skills required to cope with environmental demands and pressures. Emotional intelligence is an aspect of Wechsler's nonintellective factors of intelligence (Wechsler, 1958) and Gardner's (1983) multiple intelligences. Sternberg (1997) and Salovey and Mayer (1990) further elaborate that emotional intelligence involves the ability to monitor and discriminate feelings and emotions of self and others, and use this information to guide thinking and actions (Salovey & Mayer, 1990, p. 189).

The test's author suggests that emotional intelligence is multifactorial in nature. The factorial components of emotional intelligence are measured through the instrument's subscales. There are 15 factorial components described for the construct. Each component is composed of subcomponents.

The inventory consists of 133 items and can be used with test takers 16 years of age or older with at least a sixth grade reading level as estimated with the Flesch formula. Test items were initially drawn from mental health professionals and review of the mental health literature. Final item selection was attained through item analysis procedures. Test takers respond to a 5-point Likert scale as follows: 1—*Very seldom or not true of me*; 2—*Seldom true of me*; 3—*Sometimes true of me*; 4—*Often true of me*; and 5—*Very often true of me or true of me*. Responses are placed on a scannable answer sheet to be returned to the test publisher for scoring. Computer software is available to administer and score the inventory. Though the technical manual and user's manual describe handscorable answer-profile sheets, these materials are not available at this time [February 1999]. The handscorable version will also have fewer items than the currently available measure. Three types of interpretative reports are provided by the publisher. These reports are easy to read and interpret.

Scores are provided for four validity scales, five composite scales, 15 subscales, and a total quotient. Scores are reported as standard scores relative to the test taker's age and gender with a mean of 100 and standard deviation of 15. Interpretative guidelines for scores are adequately described within the technical manual. Higher scores are thought to be more indicative of success in coping with environmental demands whereas low scores represent problematic coping skills.

The test publisher provides several resources useful to test users. These include a technical manual, user's manual, administrator's guide, and facilitator's resource manual. Test manuals and materials are well written and provide detailed information regarding test administration, scoring, and interpretation. Related resources authored by Goleman (1995, 1998) would augment test use.

The instrument has an international normative base with initial normative data from South Africa, Israel, Argentina, Nigeria, India, and Germany. The test was normed on a North American sample of 3,831 individuals, age 15 to over age 60, in the United States and Canada. Characteristics of the North American sample are adequate relative to gender, ethnic origin, age, educational level, and geographic distribution. Age and gender differences within the normative sample resulted in the development of age- and gender-specific norms for use with the instrument.

The instrument's technical characteristics are extensively described within the technical manual. Reported internal consistency and test-retest reliability estimates appear to be adequate. The instrument has an average internal consistency coefficient of .76. Internal consistency reliability estimates were conducted on several international samples as well as the North American sample. Test-retest reliability procedures were provided for South African samples only. Average test-retest coefficients are .85 and .75 for 1- to 4-month time periods.

Test validation included content, factor, construct, criterion-related, and predictive procedures. Validation data are described in both tabular and narrative form within the technical manual. The instrument's validity appears to be generally adequate. However, some of the validation procedures do not include North American samples, which would be a weakness for this instrument. Predictive validation studies are reported for various groups of individuals. Though promising, additional predictive validation for populations representing various categories of psychopathology is necessary. The technical manual indicates that research is currently in progress to develop profiles that include vocational and psychopathology groups. Preliminary profiles are presented with a sample of business leaders, unemployed individuals, financial services employees, and psychologists. This line of research is promising and would assist in further documenting the instrument's predictive validation as well as clinical utility.

As the construct of emotional intelligence is fairly new, construct validation for the instrument was critical. North American samples were included in validation studies using the Sixteen Personality Factor Questionnaire (16PF), Personality Assessment Inventory, Symptom Checklist 90, Zung Self-Rating Scale of Depression, and Short Acculturation Scale. Discriminant, conver-

gent, and divergent construct-related validation studies are cited. These studies suggest adequate construct validation.

Though the manual indicates that the inventory can be used in a variety of business, medical, treatment, or educational settings, the test's author recommends that the instrument be used as part of a comprehensive evaluation. The measure would appear to be of limited value when used in isolation in clinical settings, particularly where individual selection, placement, or prediction of behavior are important clinical decisions. There are few instruments available that measure the construct of emotional intelligence. More research is necessary to delineate the implications of emotional intelligence to human behavior and development. The instrument would serve a useful role in this research activity.

Though only three outcome-based studies are reported for the instrument involving treatment impact, the measure may serve a useful role in outcome assessment within clinical settings. The practitioner should use the inventory in conjunction with more traditional measures of clinical outcome such as depression, anxiety, behavior change, etc. The instrument appears to have limited utility with clinical populations that manifest severe pathology. It would be useful with populations that are reasonably healthy from an emotional perspective but seek clinical services at various life-change transition periods or with adjustment-related disorders. In treatment situations, the instrument would serve a useful role in identifying patient strengths.

SUMMARY. The Emotional Quotient Inventory appears to be an excellent measure of the emotional intelligence concept. Technical characteristics are generally adequate. A representative North American normative sample is provided along with international normative samples that would be useful for cross-cultural clinical activity. Normative, validation, scoring, and interpretation information are well presented in test materials and resources. The addition of hand-scoring procedures currently under development will enhance clinical usage. A weakness of the instrument appears to be relative to the emotional intelligence construct itself. In this era of interest in specific clinical outcomes, the instrument would have limited clinical utility unless used in conjunction with other more specific problem- or adjustment-oriented clinical measures. The test's descriptive materials relate an ambitious research agenda. These studies will further enhance the inventory's clinical use.

REVIEWER'S REFERENCES

Wechsler, D. (1958). *The measurement and appraisal of adult intelligence* (4th ed.). Baltimore: Williams & Wilkins.
Gardner, H. (1983). *Frames of mind: The theory of multiple intelligences.* New York: Basic Books.
Salovey, P., & Mayer, J. D. (1990). Emotional intelligence. *Imagination, Cognition, and Personality, 9,* 185–211.
Goleman, D. (1995). *Emotional intelligence.* New York: Bantam.
Sternberg, R. J. (1997). The concept of intelligence and its role in lifelong learning and success. *American Psychologist, 52,* 1030–1037.
Goleman, D. (1998). *Working with emotional intelligence.* New York: Bantam.

Review of the BarOn Emotional Quotient Inventory by ROBERT M. GUION, Distinguished University Professor Emeritus, Bowling Green State University, Bowling Green, OH:

Psychological well-being requires more than the cognitive abilities called intelligence, and more than passive "adjustment" to events in one's environment; it generally seems to require interpersonal abilities, coping abilities, and others not typically considered a part of intelligence. The Emotional Quotient Inventory (EQ-i) was developed to measure a set of such abilities in work and educational environments, in medical and research settings, and other situations where it can augment ordinary mental ability testing (or perhaps stand alone) to describe or predict effectiveness of functioning for individuals or groups.

The EQ-i developed from Bar-On's professional clinical experience and reading. Generalizations drawn from personal experience do not always hold up well under empirical scrutiny. This inventory is an exception. It was not, despite statements in the manual, developed by raw empiricism, nor is it grounded in systematic theory; indeed, it is described as "theoretically eclectic." Nevertheless, the research data base is extensive and tends to support the initial concepts.

The underlying concept of emotional intelligence differs from but is analogous to conventional ideas of cognitive intelligence. It is "an array of noncognitive capabilities, competencies, and skills that influence one's ability to succeed in coping with environmental demands and pressures" (manual, p. 14). The definition is too broad to be fully satisfying; it could include dexterity, coordination, stamina, and other "noncognitive capabilities" not invoked in developing either the concept or the instrument. Nevertheless, it clearly

sets the concept in the realm of abilities rather than more traditional and more amorphous notions of personality traits. Despite the definition, the author wisely avoids dwelling too much on the inevitably murky boundaries between cognitive and noncognitive abilities. For example, one scale—Problem Solving—is defined in terms of such cognitive processes as problem identification, search for relevant information, generating multiple possible solutions (sometimes called divergent problem solving), and deciding among them. Nevertheless, the items comprising the scale seem to refer to preferences and habitual responses to problem situations—generalizable respondent characteristics that go beyond the ordinary idea of cognition in problem solving. That is as it should be; both cognitive and motivational influences combine to influence the effectiveness of things people do.

The author espouses a hierarchical view of intelligence, whether cognitive or emotional. In both aspects of intelligence, a variety of very specific factors combine to produce more general group factors, and these in turn combine to form a still more general factor. In the present inventory, 15 relatively specific factors combine into 5 group factors, and these in turn combine to form a general factor called an emotional quotient. The term is unfortunate; the abilities and skills it taps are not what people (including psychologists) generally consider emotional, and the danger of reification of an EQ, as has happened with IQ, is very real.

The inventory has 133 items and a 5-point response scale for each, ranging from "Not True of Me" to "True of Me." A Flesch count places the English language version at about a sixth grade reading level. The manual describes inventory development in useful detail, and it helps psychometric evaluation by giving highlights of many studies and thorough data analyses (but more detailed reports are cited). Individual scales are brief—as few as 7 items and not more than 11—so most of them have unimpressive but adequate alpha reliability (estimated in three North American samples and in samples from six other countries). Sample sizes are good, ranging from 168 in a German sample to 3,831 in a nonmilitary North American sample. Scale alpha coefficients across samples ranged from .59 to .90; average alphas (the method of averaging was not described) ranged from .69 to .86. Retest reliabilities were obtained in small South African samples. With a one-month time lapse; these were in the .80s for most scales. With 4 months, they dropped generally to the .70s. Of course, the concept of trait constancy familiar in similar studies of cognitive intelligence is less likely to apply to these abilities.

Validity data are grouped to satisfy any idea of validity readers might hold; nearly any adjective anyone has ever placed before *validity*, from face validity to divergent validity, is covered. Nevertheless, a wealth of data supports the inferences of validity, relatively little of it gives reason for questioning. Exploratory and confirmatory factor analyses, and even a relevant path analysis, provided partial support; however, the exploratory analyses gave a best-fit solution for 13 factors (not 15), and subsequent confirmatory analyses was limited to questions raised by it. Other evidence consisted of appropriate correlations with other measures and the absence of inappropriate ones. Much of the validity discussion could be dropped, especially concerning content and face validity. Face validity means little, and content validity was discussed with no definition of domain boundaries.

Administration of the inventory is not complex. An administrator's manual is available, but the technical manual is probably sufficient to administer the English version. There are also Hebrew, Afrikaans, and other versions, and they may pose problems in administration—but I doubt it.

Scoring is another matter. At present the completed inventories must be sent to the publisher for scoring and for reports. Hand scoring might be possible, but the time requirement to develop a key and do the actual scoring for 15 basic scales, 4 validity scales, and the various composites seems excessive. A special, abridged version of the inventory may be available using the publisher's "QuikScore™" answer sheet. That version deletes about half of the items, so it allows only the overall EQ, the five composite scores, and one of the basic 15. No information is offered about the equivalence of these scores and the corresponding scores based on the full item set.

That omission illustrates my major criticism of the EQ-i and its technical manual: Despite much empirical information, assertions are too often made without supporting data. There is a computer version, and the question of score equiva-

lence is not addressed for it, either. It is asserted that, if more than seven items are skipped (i.e., no response), the overall score should be considered invalid, but no data are offered to support this particular cut point. And so on.

SUMMARY. Nevertheless, my overall evaluation of this inventory is favorable. It has been developed carefully, much research has been done, and the research program is a continuing one. It appears to fill a gap by measuring constructs not often measured or rarely measured well. It is surely worth serious attention as an example of things test developers should address in developing and evaluating their instruments.

[5]
Beck Depression Inventory—II.

Purpose: "Developed for the assessment of symptoms corresponding to criteria for diagnosing depressive disorders listed in the ... DSM IV."
Population: Ages 13 and over.
Publication Dates: 1961–1996.
Acronym: BDI-II.
Scores: Total score only.
Administration: Group or individual.
Price Data, 1999: $57 per complete kit including manual ('96, 38 pages) and 25 recording forms; $27 per manual; $29.50 per 25 recording forms; $112 per 100 recording forms; $29.50 per 25 Spanish recording forms; $112 per 100 Spanish recording forms.
Foreign Language Edition: Available in Spanish.
Time: (5–10) minutes.
Comments: Hand-scored or computer-based administration, scoring, and interpretation available; "revision of BDI based upon new information about depression."
Authors: Aaron T. Beck, Robert A. Steer, and Gregory K. Brown.
Publisher: The Psychological Corporation.
Cross References: See T5:272 (384 references); for reviews by Janet F. Carlson and Niels G. Waller, see 13:31 (1026 references); see also T4:268 (660 references); for reviews by Collie W. Conoley and Norman D. Sundberg of an earlier edition, see 11:31 (286 references).

Review of the Beck Depression Inventory-II by PAUL A. ARBISI, Minneapolis VA Medical Center, Assistant Professor Department of Psychiatry and Assistant Clinical Professor Department of Psychology, University of Minnesota, Minneapolis, MN:

After over 35 years of nearly universal use, the Beck Depression Inventory (BDI) has undergone a major revision. The revised version of the Beck, the BDI-II, represents a significant improvement over the original instrument across all aspects of the instrument including content, psychometric validity, and external validity. The BDI was an effective measure of depressed mood that repeatedly demonstrated utility as evidenced by its widespread use in the clinic as well as by the frequent use of the BDI as a dependent measure in outcome studies of psychotherapy and antidepressant treatment (Piotrowski & Keller, 1989; Piotrowski & Lubin, 1990). The BDI-II should supplant the BDI and readily gain acceptance by surpassing its predecessor in use.

Despite the demonstrated utility of the Beck, times had changed and the diagnostic context within which the instrument was developed had altered considerably over the years (Beck, Ward, Mendelson, Mock, & Erbaugh, 1961). Further, psychometrically, the BDI had some problems with certain items failing to discriminate adequately across the range of depression and other items showing gender bias (Santor, Ramsay, & Zuroff, 1994). Hence the time had come for a conceptual reassessment and psychometrically informed revision of the instrument. Indeed, a mid-course correction had occurred in 1987 as evidenced by the BDI-IA, a version that included rewording of 15 out of the 21 items (Beck & Steer, 1987). This version did not address the limited scope of depressive symptoms of the BDI nor the failure of the BDI to adhere to contemporary diagnostic criteria for depression as codified in the DSM-III. Further, consumers appeared to vote with their feet because, since the publication of the BDI-IA, the original Beck had been cited far more frequently in the literature than the BDI-IA. Therefore, the time had arrived for a major overhaul of the classic BDI and a retooling of the content to reflect diagnostic sensibilities of the 1990s.

In the main, the BDI-II accomplishes these goals and represents a highly successful revamping of a reliable standard. The BDI-II retains the 21-item format with four options under each item, ranging from not present (0) to severe (3). Relative to the BDI-IA, all but three items were altered in some way on the BDI-II. Items dropped from the BDI include body image change, work difficulty, weight loss, and somatic preoccupation. To replace the four lost items, the BDI-II includes

the following new items: agitation, worthlessness, loss of energy, and concentration difficulty. The current item content includes: (a) sadness, (b) pessimism, (c) past failure, (d) loss of pleasure, (e) guilty feelings, (f) punishment feelings, (g) self-dislike, (h) self-criticalness, (i) suicidal thoughts or wishes, (j) crying, (k) agitation, (l) loss of interest, (m) indecisiveness, (n) worthlessness, (o) loss of energy, (p) changes in sleeping pattern, (q) irritability, (r) changes in appetite, (s) concentration difficulty, (t) tiredness or fatigue, and (u) loss of interest in sex. To further reflect DSM-IV diagnostic criteria for depression, both increases and decreases in appetite are assessed in the same item and both hypersomnia and hyposomnia are assessed in another item. And rather than the 1-week time period rated on the BDI, the BDI-II, consistent with DSM-IV, asks for ratings over the past 2 weeks.

The BDI-II retains the advantage of the BDI in its ease of administration (5–10 minutes) and the rather straightforward interpretive guidelines presented in the manual. At the same time, the advantage of a self-report instrument such as the BDI-II may also be a disadvantage. That is, there are no validity indicators contained on the BDI or the BDI-II and the ease of administration of a self-report lends itself to the deliberate tailoring of self-report and distortion of the results. Those of us engaged in clinical practice are often faced with clients who alter their presentation to forward a personal agenda that may not be shared with the clinician. The manual obliquely mentions this problem in an ambivalent and somewhat avoidant fashion. Under the heading, "Memory and Response Sets," the manual blithely discounts the potential problem of a distorted response set by attributing extreme elevation on the BDI-II to "extreme negative thinking" which "may be a central cognitive symptom of severe depression rather than a response set per se because patients with milder depression should show variation in their response ratings" (manual, p. 9). On the other hand, later in the manual, we are told that, "In evaluating BDI-II scores, practitioners should keep in mind that all self-report inventories are subject to response bias" (p. 12). The latter is sound advice and should be highlighted under the heading of response bias.

The manual is well written and provides the reader with significant information regarding norms, factor structure, and notably, nonparametric item-option characteristic curves for each item. Indeed the latter inclusion incorporates the latest in item response theory, which appears to have guided the retention and deletion of items from the BDI (Santor et al., 1994).

Generally the psychometric properties of the BDI-II are quite sound. Coefficient alpha estimates of reliability for the BDI-II with outpatients was .92 and was .93 for the nonclinical sample. Corrected item-total correlation for the outpatient sample ranged from .39 (loss of interest in sex) to .70 (loss of pleasure), for the nonclinical college sample the lowest item-total correlation was .27 (loss of interest in sex) and the highest (.74 (self-dislike). The test-retest reliability coefficient across the period of a week was quite high at .93. The inclusion in the manual of item-option characteristic curves for each BDI-II item is of noted significance. Examination of these curves reveals that, for the most part, the ordinal position of the item options is appropriately assigned for 17 of the 21 items. However, the items addressing punishment feelings, suicidal thought or wishes, agitation, and loss of interest in sex did not display the anticipated rank order indicating ordinal increase in severity of depression across item options. Additionally, although improved over the BDI, Item 10 (crying) Option 3 does not clearly express a more severe level of depression than Option 2 (see Santor et al., 1994). Over all, however, the option choices within each item appear to function as intended across the severity dimension of depression.

The suggested guidelines and cut scores for the interpretation of the BDI-II and placement of individual scores into a range of depression severity are purported to have good sensitivity and moderate specificity, but test parameters such as positive and negative predictive power are not reported (i.e., given score X on the BDI-II, what is the probability that the individual meets criteria for a Major Depressive Disorder, of moderate severity?). According to the manual, the BDI-II was developed as a screening instrument for major depression and, accordingly, cut scores were derived through the use of receiver operating characteristic curves to maximize sensitivity. Of the 127 outpatients used to derive the cut scores, 57 met criteria for either single-episode or recurrent major depression. The relatively high base rate (45%)

for major depression is a bit unrealistic for nonpsychiatric settings and will likely serve to inflate the test parameters. Cross validation of the cut scores on different samples with lower base rates of major depression is warranted due to the fact that a different base rate of major depression may result in a significant change in the proportion of correct decisions based on the suggested cut score (Meehl & Rosen, 1955). Consequently, until the suggested cut scores are cross validated in those populations, caution should be exercised when using the BDI-II as a screen in nonpsychiatric populations where the base rate for major depression may be substantially lower.

Concurrent validity evidence appears solid with the BDI-II demonstrating a moderately high correlation with the Hamilton Psychiatric Rating Scale for Depression—Revised ($r = .71$) in psychiatric outpatients. Of importance to the discriminative validity of the instrument was the relatively moderate correlation between the BDI-II and the Hamilton Rating Scale for Anxiety—Revised ($r = .47$). The manual reports mean BDI-II scores for various groups of psychiatric outpatients by diagnosis. As expected, outpatients had higher scores than college students. Further, individuals with mood disorders had higher scores than those individuals diagnosed with anxiety and adjustment disorders.

The BDI-II is a stronger instrument than the BDI with respect to its factor structure. A two-factor (Somatic-Affective and Cognitive) solution accounted for the majority of the common variance in both an outpatient psychiatric sample and a much smaller nonclinical college sample. Factor Analysis of the BDI-II in a larger nonclinical sample of college students resulted in Cognitive-Affective and Somatic-Vegetative main factors essentially replicating the findings presented in the manual and providing strong evidence for the overall stability of the factor structure across samples (Dozois, Dobson, & Ahnberg, 1998). Unfortunately several of the items such as sadness and crying shifted factor loadings depending upon the type of sample (clinical vs. nonclinical).

SUMMARY. The BDI-II represents a highly successful revision of an acknowledged standard in the measurement of depressed mood. The revision has improved upon the original by updating the items to reflect contemporary diagnostic criteria for depression and utilizing state-of-the-art psychometric techniques to improve the discriminative properties of the instrument. This degree of improvement is no small feat and the BDI-II deserves to replace the BDI as the single most widely used clinically administered instrument for the assessment of depression.

REVIEWER'S REFERENCES

Meehl, P. E., & Rosen, A. (1955). Antecedent probability and the efficiency of psychometric signs, patterns, or cutting scores. *Psychological Bulletin, 52,* 194–216.

Beck, A. T., Ward, C. H., Mendelson, M., Mock, J., & Erbaugh, J. (1961). An inventory for measuring depression. *Archives of General Psychiatry, 4,* 561–571.

Beck, A. T., & Steer, R. A. (1987). *Beck Depression Inventory manual.* San Antonio, TX: The Psychological Corporation.

Piotrowski, C., & Keller, J. W. (1989). Psychological testing in outpatient mental health facilities: A national study. *Professional Psychology: Research and Practice, 20,* 423–425.

Piotrowski, C., & Lubin, B. (1990). Assessment practices of health psychologists; Survey of APA Division 38 clinicians. *Professional Psychology: Research and Practice, 21,* 99–106.

Santor, D. A., Ramsay, J. O., & Zuroff, D. C. (1994). Nonparametric item analyses of the Beck Depression Inventory: Evaluating gender item bias and response option weights. *Psychological Assessment, 6,* 255–270.

Dozois, D. J. A., Dobson, K. S., & Ahnberg, J. L. (1998). A psychometric evaluation of the Beck Depression Inventory-II. *Psychological Assessment, 10,* 83–89.

Review of the Beck Depression Inventory-II by RICHARD F. FARMER, Associate Professor of Psychology, Idaho State University, Pocatello, ID:

The Beck Depression Inventory-II (BDI-II) is the most recent version of a widely used self-report measure of depression severity. Designed for persons 13 years of age and older, the BDI-II represents a significant revision of the original instrument published almost 40 years ago (BDI-I; Beck, Ward, Mendelson, Mock, & Erbaugh, 1961) as well as the subsequent amended version copyrighted in 1978 (BDI-IA; Beck, Rush, Shaw, & Emery, 1979; Beck & Steer, 1987, 1993). Previous editions of the BDI have considerable support for their effectiveness as measures of depression (for reviews, see Beck & Beamesderfer, 1974; Beck, Steer & Garbin, 1988; and Steer, Beck, & Garrison, 1986).

Items found in these earlier versions, many of which were retained in modified form for the BDI-II, were clinically derived and neutral with respect to a particular theory of depression. Like previous versions, the BDI-II contains 21 items, each of which assesses a different symptom or attitude by asking the examinee to consider a group of graded statements that are weighted from 0 to 3 based on intuitively derived levels of severity. If the examinee feels that more than one statement within a group applies, he or she is instructed to circle the highest weighting among the applicable statements. A total score is derived by summing weights corresponding to the statements endorsed over the 21 items. The test

authors provide empirically informed cut scores (derived from receiver operating characteristic [ROC] curve methodology) for indexing the severity of depression based on responses from outpatients with a diagnosed episode of major depression (cutoff scores to index the severity of dysphoria for college samples are suggested by Dozois, Dobson, & Ahnberg, 1998).

The BDI-II can usually be completed within 5 to 10 minutes. In addition to providing guidelines for the oral administration of the test, the manual cautions the user against using the BDI-II as a diagnostic instrument and appropriately recommends that interpretations of test scores should only be undertaken by qualified professionals. Although the manual does not report the reading level associated with the test items, previous research on the BDI-IA suggested that items were written at about the sixth-grade level (Berndt, Schwartz, & Kaiser, 1983).

A number of changes appear in the BDI-II, perhaps the most significant of which is the modification of test directions and item content to be more consistent with the major depressive episode concept as defined in the *Diagnostic and Statistical Manual of Mental Disorders—Fourth Edition* (DSM-IV; American Psychiatric Association, 1994). Whereas the BDI-I and BDI-IA assessed symptoms experienced at the present time and during the past week, respectively, the BDI-II instructs the examinee to respond in terms of how he or she has "been feeling during the *past two weeks, including today*" (manual, p. 8, emphasis in original) so as to be consistent with the DSM-IV time period for the assessment of major depression. Similarly, new items included in the BDI-II address psychomotor agitation, concentration difficulties, sense of worthlessness, and loss of energy so as to make the BDI-II item set more consistent with DSM-IV criteria. Items that appeared in the BDI-I and BDI-IA that were dropped in the second edition were those that assessed weight loss, body image change, somatic preoccupation, and work difficulty. All but three of the items from the BDI-IA retained for inclusion in the BDI-II were reworded in some way. Items that assess changes in sleep patterns and appetite now address both increases and decreases in these areas.

Two samples were retained to evaluate the psychometric characteristics of the BDI-II: (a) a clinical sample (n = 500; 63% female; 91% White) who sought outpatient therapy at one of four outpatient clinics on the U.S. east coast (two of which were located in urban areas, two in suburban areas), and (b) a convenience sample of Canadian college students (n = 120; 56% women; described as "predominantly White"). The average ages of the clinical and student samples were, respectively, 37.2 (SD = 15.91; range = 13–86) and 19.58 (SD = 1.84).

Reliability of the BDI was evaluated with multiple methods. Internal consistency was assessed using corrected item-total correlations (ranges: .39 to .70 for outpatients; .27 to .74 for students) and coefficient alpha (.92 for outpatients; .93 for students). Test-retest reliability was assessed over a 1-week interval among a small subsample of 26 outpatients from one clinic site (r = .93). There was no significant change in scores noted among this outpatient sample between the two testing occasions, a finding that is different from those often obtained with college students who, when tested repeatedly with earlier versions of the BDI, were often observed to have lower scores on subsequent testing occasions (e.g., Hatzenbuehler, Parpal, & Matthews, 1983).

Following the method of Santor, Ramsay, and Zuroff (1994), the test authors also examined the item-option characteristic curves for each of the 21 BDI-II items as endorsed by the 500 outpatients. As noted in a previous review of the BDI (1993 Revised) by Waller (1998), the use of this method to evaluate item performance represents a new standard in test revision. Consistent with findings for depressed outpatients obtained by Santor et al. (1994) on the BDI-IA, most of the BDI-II items performed well as evidenced by the individual item-option curves. All items were reported to display monotonic relationships with the underlying dimension of depression severity. A minority of items were somewhat problematic, however, when the degree of correspondence between estimated and a priori weights associated with item response options was evaluated. For example, on Item 11 (agitation), the response option weighted a value of 1 was more likely to be endorsed than the option weighted 3 across all levels of depression, including depression in the moderate and severe ranges. In general, though, response option weights of the BDI-II items did a good job of discriminating across estimated

levels of depression severity. Unfortunately, the manual does not provide detailed discussion of item-option characteristic curves and their interpretation.

The validity of the BDI-II was evaluated with outpatient subsamples of various sizes. When administered on the same occasion, the correlation between the BDI-II and BDI-IA was quite high (n = 101, r = .93), suggesting that these measures yield similar patterns of scores, even though the BDI-II, on average, produced equated scores that were about 3 points higher. In support of its convergent validity, the BDI-II displayed moderately high correlations with the Beck Hopelessness Scale (n = 158, r = .68) and the Revised Hamilton Psychiatric Rating Scale for Depression (HRSD-R; n = 87, r = .71). The correlation between the BDI-II and the Revised Hamilton Anxiety Rating Scale (n = 87, r = .47) was significantly less than that for the BDI-II and HRSD-R, which was cited as evidence of the BDI-II's discriminant validity. The BDI-II, however, did share a moderately high correlation with the Beck Anxiety Inventory (n = 297; r = .60), a finding consistent with past research on the strong association between self-reported anxiety and depression (e.g., Kendall & Watson, 1989). Additional research published since the manual's release (Steer, Ball, Ranieri, & Beck, 1997) also indicates that the BDI-II shares higher correlations with the SCL-90-R Depression subscale (r = .89) than with the SCL-90-R Anxiety subscale (r = .71), although the latter correlation is still substantial. Other data presented in the test manual indicated that of the 500 outpatients, those diagnosed with mood disorders (n = 264) had higher BDI-II scores than those diagnosed with anxiety (n = 88), adjustment (n = 80), or other (n = 68) disorders. The test authors also cite evidence of validity by separate factor analyses performed on the BDI-II item set for outpatients and students. However, findings from these analyses, which were different in some significant respects, are questionable evidence of the measure's validity as the test was apparently not developed to assess specific dimensions of depression. Factor analytic studies of the BDI have historically produced inconsistent findings (Beck et al., 1988), and preliminary research on the BDI-II suggests some variations in factor structure within both clinical and student samples (Dozois et al., 1998; Steer & Clark, 1997; Steer,

Kumar, Ranieri, & Beck, 1998). Furthermore, one of the authors of the BDI-II (Steer & Clark, 1997) has recently advised that the measure not be scored as separate subscales.

SUMMARY. The BDI-II is presented as a user-friendly self-report measure of depression severity. Strengths of the BDI-II include the very strong empirical foundation on which it was built, namely almost 40 years of research that demonstrates the effectiveness of earlier versions. In the development of the BDI-II, innovative methods were employed to determine optimum cut scores (ROC curves) and evaluate item performance and weighting (item-option curves). The present edition demonstrates very good reliability and impressive test item characteristics. Preliminary evidence of the BDI-II's validity in clinical samples is also encouraging. Despite the many impressive features of this measure, one may wonder why the test developers were not even more thorough in their presentation of the development of the BDI-II and more rigorous in the evaluation of its effectiveness. The test manual is too concise, and often omits important details involving the test development process. The clinical sample used to generate cut scores and evaluate the psychometric properties of the measure seems unrepresentative in many respects (e.g., racial make-up, patient setting, geographic distribution), and other aspects of this sample (e.g., education level, family income) go unmentioned. The student sample is relatively small and, unfortunately, drawn from a single university. Opportunities to address important questions regarding the measure were also missed, such as whether the BDI-II effectively assesses or screens the DSM-IV concept of major depression, and the extent to which it may accomplish this better than earlier versions. This seems to be a particularly important question given that the BDI was originally developed as a measure of the depressive syndrome, not as a screening measure for a nosologic category (Kendall, Hollon, Beck, Hammen, & Ingram, 1987), a distinction that appears to have become somewhat blurred in this most recent edition. Also, not reported in the manual are analyses to examine possible sex biases among the BDI-II item set. Santor et al. (1994) reported that the BDI-IA items were relatively free of sex bias, and given the omission of the most sex-biased item in the BDI-IA (body image change) from the BDI-II, it is possible that this most recent edition may contain even less bias. Similarly absent in the manual is any report on the item-option characteristic curves for nonclinical samples. Santor et al. (1994) reported that for most of the BDI-IA items, response option weights were less discriminating across the range of depression severity among their college sample relative to their clinical sample, an anticipated finding given that students would be less likely to endorse response options hypothesized to be consistent with more severe forms of depression. Also, given that previous editions of the BDI have shown inconsistent associations with social undesirability (e.g., Tanaka-Matsumi & Kameoka, 1986), an opportunity was missed to evaluate the extent to which the BDI-II measures something different than this response set. Despite these relative weaknesses in the development and presentation of the BDI-II, existent evidence suggests that the BDI-II is just as sound if not more so than its earlier versions.

REVIEWER'S REFERENCES

Beck, A. T., Ward, C. H., Mendelson, M., Mock, J., & Erbaugh, J. (1961). An inventory for measuring depression. *Archives of General Psychiatry, 4,* 561–571.

Beck, A. T., & Beamesderfer, A. (1974). Assessment of depression: The Depression Inventory. In P. Pichot & R. Oliver-Martin (Eds.), *Psychological measurements in psychopharmacology: Modern problems in pharmacopsychiatry* (vol. 7, pp. 151–169). Basel: Karger.

Beck, A. T., Rush, A. J., Shaw, B. F., & Emery, G. (1979). *Cognitive therapy of depression.* New York: Guilford.

Berndt, D. J., Schwartz, S., & Kaiser, C. F. (1983). Readability of self-report depression inventories. *Journal of Consulting and Clinical Psychology, 51,* 627–628.

Hatzenbuehler, L. C., Parpal, M., & Matthews, L. (1983). Classifying college students as depressed or nondepressed using the Beck Depression Inventory: An empirical analysis. *Journal of Consulting and Clinical Psychology, 51,* 360–366.

Steer, R. A., Beck, A. T., & Garrison, B. (1986). Applications of the Beck Depression Inventory. In N. Sartorius & T. A. Ban (Eds.), *Assessment of depression* (pp. 123–142). New York: Springer-Verlag.

Tanaka-Matsumi, J., & Kameoka, V. A. (1986). Reliabilities and concurrent validities of popular self-report measures of depression, anxiety, and social desirability. *Journal of Consulting and Clinical Psychology, 54,* 328–333.

Beck, A. T., & Steer, R. A. (1987). *Beck Depression Inventory manual.* San Antonio, TX: The Psychological Corporation.

Kendall, P. C., Hollon, S. D., Beck, A. T., Hammen, C. L., & Ingram, R. E. (1987). Issues and recommendations regarding the use of the Beck Depression Inventory. *Cognitive Therapy and Research, 11,* 289–299.

Beck, A. T., & Steer, R. A., & Garbin, M. G. (1988). Psychometric properties of the Beck Depression Inventory: Twenty-five years of evaluation. *Clinical Psychology Review, 8,* 77–100.

Kendall, P. C., & Watson, D. (Eds.). (1989). *Anxiety and depression: Distinctive and overlapping features.* San Diego, CA: Academic Press.

Beck, A. T., & Steer, R. A. (1993). *Beck Depression Inventory manual.* San Antonio, TX: Psychological Corporation.

American Psychiatric Association. (1994). *Diagnostic and statistical manual of mental disorders* (4th ed.). Washington, DC: Author.

Santor, D. A., Ramsay, J. O., & Zuroff, D. C. (1994). Nonparametric item analyses of the Beck Depression Inventory: Evaluating gender item bias and response option weights. *Psychological Assessment, 6,* 255–270.

Steer, R. A., Ball, R., Ranieri, W. F., & Beck, A. T. (1997). Further evidence for the construct validity of the Beck Depression Inventory—II with psychiatric outpatients. *Psychological Reports, 80,* 443–446.

Steer, R. A., & Clark, D. A. (1997). Psychometric characteristics of the Beck Depression Inventory—II with college students. *Measurement and Evaluation in Counseling and Development, 30,* 128–136.

Dozois, D. J. A., Dobson, K. S., & Ahnberg, J. L. (1998). A psychometric evaluation of the Beck Depression Inventory—II. *Psychological Assessment, 10,* 83–89.

Steer, R. A., Kumar, G., Ranieri, W. F., & Beck, A. T. (1998). Use of the Beck Depression Inventory—II with adolescent psychiatric outpatients. *Journal of Psychopathology and Behavioral Assessment, 20,* 127–137.

Waller, N. G. (1998). [Review of the Beck Depression Inventory—1993 Revised]. In J. C. Impara & B. S. Plake (Eds.), *The thirteenth mental measurements yearbook* (pp. 120–121). Lincoln, NE: The Buros Institute of Mental Measurements.

[6]
Bedside Evaluation of Dysphagia.

Purpose: Designed to assess swallowing abilities and the factors that may influence those abilities.
Population: Adults neurologically impaired.
Publication Date: 1995.
Acronym: BED.
Scores, 13: Behavioral Characteristics, Cognition and Communication Screening (Cognition, Receptive Language, Expressive Language/Speech Production), Oral Motor Examination (Lips, Tongue, Soft Palate, Cheeks, Mandible, Larynx), Oral-Pharyngeal Dysphagia Symptoms Assessment (Oral State, Pharyngeal State, Additional Observations).
Administration: Individual.
Price Data, 1998: $35 per 25 evaluation forms; $45.50 per manual (56 pages) and 25 evaluation forms.
Time: (15–45) minutes.
Author: Edward Hardy.
Publisher: Imaginart International, Inc.

Review of the Bedside Evaluation of Dysphagia by CARLOS INCHAURRALDE, Professor of Linguistics and Psychologist, University of Zaragoza, Zaragoza, Spain:

The Bedside Evaluation of Dysphagia (BED) provides a comprehensive format for the possible diagnosis of dysphagia in a patient by the speech-language pathologist. It has the form of a checklist in which information is collected about behavior, cognition, and communication abilities, and oral-motor capacity. It is claimed to have been developed mainly for use with neurologically impaired adults—the most suitable candidates being patients with right and left CVA, Parkinson's Disease, traumatic brain injury, and dementia.

The manual gives little information about test development: It was developed "following the author's extensive experience with adult patients in a variety of settings" (p. 1), and it used as an initial basis the protocol that appears in Hardy and Robinson (1993). There is no information at all about reliability, validity, or norms, which should be part of any psychometric or clinical instrument of this kind. On the other hand, there are very clear instructions as to how to collect the information in all the sections of the BED. The manual clearly states the procedure and the alternative responses from the patient, with clear specifications as to what may be considered either "within normal limits" or "impaired." At the end of the evaluation form there is a summary report section, in which the observations are summarized and recommendations are made according to the data collected.

The lack of reliability information is a problem with this test. Interscorer reliability would be extremely important here because there are no scores and most of the BED is based on dichotomous judgments, which may be made differently by different evaluators. Proper evaluation of the suitability of the BED would involve knowing whether it can be used reliably by different examiners. Validity is not clearly addressed either. Content validity relies on the protocol that was used as a basis at the development stage, but there are no data available about item analysis, correlations among the different sections, or correlations with other similar instruments.

The main strength of the BED is its detailed assessment of all the factors relevant for the determination of possibly dysphagia. Thus, it is a good checklist for the trained speech-language pathologist to find out about problems in swallowing that may require further exploration. However, there is no scoring that might help to determine the seriousness of the impairment. The recommendations can range from additional examination by other means to compensatory and rehabilitation strategies. This relies on the subjective judgment of the examiner, which may be questionable because the BED's main weakness is its lack of adequate technical information. As has already been mentioned, it has no information about reliability and validity, which makes it unsuitable as the only source of information.

SUMMARY. The BED is a good exploratory checklist for detecting symptoms of dysphagia, and should be useful for the knowledgeable speech-language therapist. It has very detailed instructions, from which interscorer reliability might, in theory, benefit. However, because there are no clear data about development, validity, and reliability, we should be cautious when using this instrument, especially while filling in the recommendations section of the form. The BED is useful for organizing our observations about the patient, but it cannot help us in making judgments other than those suggested by our previous experience.

REVIEWER'S REFERENCE

Hardy, E., & Robinson, N. (1993). *Swallowing Disorders Treatment manual.* Bisbee, AZ: Imaginart.

Review of the Bedside Evaluation of Dysphagia by STEVEN B. LEDER, Professor of Surgery, Yale University School of Medicine, New Haven, CT:

The Bedside Evaluation of Dysphagia (BED) attempts to evaluate basic cognition and communication skills and oral motor functioning prior to beginning a dysphagia evaluation. This information is then used to determine oral feeding status, diet consistency, compensatory strategies, and rehabilitation techniques for the dysphagic patient. An accompanying response form closely parallels the text and allows for recording of data in a clear and concise manner. The specific categories assessed are Cognition and Communication Screening, Oral-Motor Assessment, Oral-Pharyngeal Dysphagia Symptoms Assessment, Summary, and Recommendations. The text also provides a box entitled Clinical Implications for each category in which the author presents clinical insights, caveats, or recommendations for further diagnostic testing or referral to other professionals.

Although a lot of information is collected during a BED, it is unclear how all the information relates to the goal of diagnosing dysphagia. For example, under Clinical Insights in the Cognition and Communication Screening categories the author focuses on their importance in later swallowing intervention strategies. It is unclear how counting 1–10 or saying the days of the week relate to the purpose of the BED (i.e., the diagnosis of dysphagia). How are tasks such as these important during actual oral-pharyngeal dysphagia testing? Many individuals seen for dysphagia testing are demented or disoriented but can be tested reliably and, with proper supervision, can begin an oral diet.

Much time is devoted to direct oral-motor examination of the lips, tongue, soft palate, cheeks, and mandible, with inferred motor functioning of the larynx. The swallow reflex, however, is very robust and although performing non-swallowing-related maneuvers are helpful in assessing motor function with the goal of correlation with swallowing success, no sensitivity or specificity data related to motor assessment are provided to show their predictive value for swallowing success or failure. For example, many individuals with altered oral, pharyngeal, and laryngeal anatomy and physiology due to stroke or head and neck cancer swallow successfully. It is not, therefore, what structures are impaired or removed that is of importance, but rather the functioning of the remaining structures during the act of swallowing that is of primary importance for swallowing success.

Subjectivity is inherent to the scoring of many subsets. For example, the adjectives "Good, Fair, Poor, Diminished, Hypersensitive, Strong, Weak, Mildly, Moderately, and Severely" are used throughout the BED. No correlation statistics for inter- or intraexaminer agreement were reported nor are correlations with outcome variables to determine if these adjectives actually correspond to the degree of physical abnormality they are attempting to describe. Further, it is not known if the various subsets and items within each subset are hierarchical or of equal importance in predicting dysphagia (e.g., does ability to lateralize the jaw impact on swallowing success to a greater degree than tongue sensitivity and, if so, which of the six discrete areas examined on the tongue is most important?).

Although the BED makes good clinical sense and some of the suggestions are correct on face value, a significant drawback is that no corroborating data are provided to substantiate any of the bedside testing methods, feeding recommendations, or rehabilitative strategies suggested. No objective dysphagia testing (e.g., modified barium swallow or fiberoptic endoscopic evaluation of swallowing) was reported in either the same or similar populations of dysphagic individuals to support the efficacy of any of the results or recommendations from the BED.

Finally, another significant drawback is that the final judgment of whether to recommend an objective, instrumental dysphagia assessment is purely subjective. In addition to the rather broad (poor posture/positioning), vague (abnormal voluntary cough, change in vocal quality, and impaired secretion management), incorrect (impaired palatal gag reflex), or impossible to test at bedside (impaired laryngeal evaluation) variables stated as sufficient in and of themselves to make a referral for an instrumental assessment, other even broader variables recommended to generate a referral were any pharyngeal stage abnormalities or documented history of aspiration pneumonia. (Indeed, if the latter was present during history taking there would be no need to proceed further with a BED.)

SUMMARY. In conclusion, the BED incorporates many clinical variables that should be assessed prior to performing an instrumental dysphagia assessment. The response form provides a clear way to record this data. Before the BED can be relied upon, however, to provide adequate sensitivity and specificity in diagnosing oral-pharyngeal dysphagia, making appropriate feeding recommendations and intervention strategies, and referring for objective instrumental dysphagia diagnostics, both more corroborative data based on objective dysphagia testing and appropriate test construct and content validity are needed.

[7]
California Computerized Assessment Package.

Purpose: Designed as a "standardized assessment of reaction time and speed of information processing."
Population: Ages 21–58.
Publication Dates: 1986–1998.
Acronym: CalCAP.
Scores, 7: Simple Reaction Time, Choice Reaction Time for Single Digits, Serial Pattern Matching, Lexical Discrimination, Visual Selective Attention, Response Reversal and Rapid Visual Scanning, Form Discrimination.
Administration: Group.
Forms, 2: Standard, Abbreviated.
Price Data, 1998: $495 per complete kit including manual ('96, 80 pages), standard battery and abbreviated battery; $10 per demonstration program; $15 per manual.
Time: (20–25) minutes.
Foreign Language Editions: Danish, Flemish, French, German, Norwegian, and Spanish editions available.
Comments: IBM AT or compatible, 512K RAM, color display or active color matrix laptop, and MS-DOS 3.1 or greater required.
Author: Eric N. Miller.
Publisher: Norland Software.

Review of the California Computerized Assessment Package by HOWARD A. LLOYD, Neuropsychologist, Hawaii State Hospital, Kaneohe, HI:

The California Computerized Assessment Package (CalCAP) is a computerized assessment tool modeled after the Continuous Performance Task (CPT). There are multiple versions of the Continuous Performance Task, all of which measure sustained attention and reaction time. The CalCAP improves on most standard versions of the CPT by including reaction time tasks that require lexical discrimination, selective visual at-

tention, visual scanning, and form discrimination. The manual provides adequate descriptions of each of the seven tasks that comprise the standard, full-length administration of this test. An abbreviated form of the CalCAP can also be administered. Unlike many psychological tests, the CalCAP is available in multiple languages, for which the author and publishers should be praised.

The CalCAP manual provides a good description of the test and administration procedures. The reference card facilitates ease of administration by eliminating the need to refer to the manual for basic information on starting and running the program. A considerable amount of information regarding how the computer files are organized and how this data can be stored and managed is also included. This is at times technical material and may be of limited interest or usefulness for many users of this test. The manual also provides basic interpretive guidelines that are consistent with the implied intended use of the CalCAP as a screening tool for identification of neuropsychological impairment. Unfortunately, the author does not clearly specify the intended use of this test, and it is left to the examiner to determine how the test should be used. This is of concern particularly because in the introduction section of the manual the author indicates that the CalCAP was designed to "assess a number of cognitive domains, including speed of processing (reaction time), language skills, visual scanning, form discrimination, recognition memory, and divided attention" (p. 1), whereas later in the manual the author indicates that the "cognitive functions assessed by the CalCAP program are best described as timed psychomotor skills requiring focused and sustained attention" (p. 17). Such lack of clarity regarding the intended use of the CalCAP makes it vulnerable to misuse as a more complete neuropsychological instrument than the author seems to have intended. The CalCAP appears to be best used as a screening tool to identify patients in need of further evaluation using traditional neuropsychological tests, and as a measure of focused, sustained, and divided attention.

The CalCAP was normed on a group of 641 men ranging in ages from 21 to 58 years, with a mean education of 16 years. These normative data are reported for the entire sample and for age- and education-stratified groups. The vast majority of the normative subjects were Caucasian (93%), and minority subjects were underrepresented. This raises some concerns about the usefulness of the CalCAP with non-Caucasian individuals. It is also unfortunate that a sample of women was not included. The author does present normative data from an independent group of researchers indicating that there is no difference between the performance of men and women on the CalCAP, though the sample size for this study was relatively small. Supplemental norms gathered by other independent researchers for third, fourth, fifth, and sixth grade children are also reported in the manual. It is also unfortunate that normative data are not available for native speakers of the various languages in which the CalCAP is available.

The psychometric properties of the CalCAP are well within acceptable ranges. The internal consistency reliability coefficients for simple and choice reaction time were high (.77–.95) supporting the consistency with which the CalCAP measures reaction time. The 6-month test-retest coefficients for the CalCAP are more variable (.20–.68), reflecting the impact of state-dependent factors on this reaction time measure (e.g., fatigue). However, it should be noted that the lowest test-retest coefficients were for the Simple Reaction Time measures (.20–.29), and that the Choice Reaction Time test-retest reliability coefficients were more respectable (.43–.68). It is notable that the 6-month test-retest reliability for the CalCAP Choice Reaction Time measures was consistent with the 6-month test-retest reliability of several conventional neuropsychological tests (.47–.77).

The validity evidence for scores from the CalCAP was gathered by correlating performance on the CalCAP with performance on several conventional and commonly used neuropsychological tests (Digit Span, Symbol Digit Substitution, Rey Auditory Verbal Learning Test, Verbal Fluency, Trails A&B, and Grooved Pegboard). These correlations were, however, rather low (.02–.37). It is unfortunate that the author did not attempt a similar comparison between the CalCAP and other computer-administered reaction time measures (e.g., VIGIL, TOVA, Connors CPT). Such a comparison would have been a more appropriate means of assessing construct validity.

SUMMARY. In summary, as stated in the manual, "the skills measured by the CalCAP are best described as timed psychomotor skills requiring focused and sustained attention" (p. 17). This task is a good screening measure for neuropsychological dysfunction, with the emphasis on screening. Major limitations are associated with limited normative information on minorities, women, older adults, and children. As noted above, it is also unfortunate that the CalCAP has not been compared with other computerized measures of reaction time and focused and sustained attention. The strengths of the CalCAP include its relative ease of administration and interpretation, availability of versions in multiple languages, and its usefulness for repeated testing as might be necessary in research or rehabilitation settings.

Review of the California Computerized Assessment Package by GORAN WESTERGREN, Chief Psychologist, and INGELA WESTERGREN, Neuropsychologist and Licensed Psychologist, Department of Clinical Psychology, State Hospital, Halmstad, Sweden:

The California Computerized Assessment Package (CalCAP) is, as the name suggests, a computer-based test developed in the tradition of experimental cognitive laboratories and is modeled on the Continuous Performance Task, a measure of sustained attention and reaction time. Because of this, the test can be administered by technical level personnel and the computer controls the presentation of complex stimuli to the subject. These features reduce variability in test administration.

In its standard design (10 Simple and Choice reaction time measurements), CalCAP gives a broad assessment of a number of the patient's cognitive functions. The functions assessed by the CalCAP program are chiefly described as timed psychomotor skills requiring focused or sustained attention.

Scores from the CalCAP also demonstrate high levels of construct validity compared to traditional neuropsychological tests that measure motor speed and attention (Trail-Making, Grooved Pegboard), verbal memory (Rey Auditory Verbal Learning Task), memory span (Wechsler Adult Intelligence Scale—Revised Digit Span), and verbal fluency.

The computer automatically records subject performance and produces a report in seconds, using age- and education-specific norms derived from 641 men ranging in ages from 21–58 years (with a mean education of 16 years). The final scores are available immediately in tabular and graphical formats. The response measurements are presented as mean and median reaction times as well as total numbers of true and false positive responses. In addition, by using Signal detection theory, the CalCAP offers measurements of the subject's ability to discriminate between the true signal and character items and the degree to which the subject deviates from the optimal likelihood ratio.

In the manual there is also access to normative data for third to sixth grade children, although in limited populations. There are also some normative data for comparison of scores for men and women. There are no statistically significant differences between men and women after adjusting for differences in age and education.

There are no norm data for the foreign language editions (Danish, Flemish, French, German, Norwegian, and Spanish) but there is really no reason to believe that the data from English-speaking environments should not be directly applicable.

From the reliability point of view it is naturally a strength in the CalCAP that the stimulus material is presented under strictly controlled forms and that the responses are measured with the same precision. The constructor of the test believes that the measurements can be used to assess slowed cognition, focused and divided attention, sustained attention, and rapid visual scanning and that this is ideal for longitudinal assessment of cognitive changes due to disease, medications, and cognitive rehabilitation. The test battery is said to have relevance for studies of clinical groups such as multiple sclerosis, hyperbaric nitrogen narcosis, HIV infection, dementia, drug abuse, and traumatic brain injury. This applies to the qualified clinical and research level. However, at a more "everyday" clinic level, a lot of work is required to translate these measurements into terms and functions that are more directly understood by nonpsychologists.

The graphical interface seems a little aged with its DOS environment and ought to be converted to Windows immediately. With this conversion the whole test would be clearer and the administration would be significantly easier. With the fast developments in the IT field there is naturally a problem with computer-based tests

because the graphical construction must continually be updated in order for the test not to appear out-of-date. The test's outward appearance could affect the patient negatively. Due to the current graphical design of the CalCAP, however well thought, the assessment appears to be out-of-date or still at a prototype stage.

SUMMARY. The CalCAP is a broad, cognitive based, reaction time test of most interest for research work and for the advanced clinic. The CalCAP would need to be adapted for the Windows environment to satisfy the normal clinician.

[8]
Campbell-Hallam Team Development Survey.

Purpose: "Designed to give teams standardized feedback on their strengths and weaknesses."
Population: Members of intact working teams.
Publication Date: 1994.
Acronym: TDS.
Scores, 19: Resources (Time and Staffing, Information, Material Resources, Organizational Support, Skills, Commitment), Efficiency (Mission Clarity, Team Coordination, Team Unity, Individual Goals, Empowerment), Improvement (Team Assessment, Innovation, Feedback, Rewards, Leadership), Success (Satisfaction, Performance, Overall Index).
Administration: Group.
Forms, 2: Observer, Member.
Price Data, 1999: $180 per preview package including 10 individual survey booklets, team report, individual report for each team member, manual (216 pages), administrator's guide (15 pages), and facilitator's guide (16 pages); $15 per individual survey and report; $10 per 10 observer survey forms; $60 per team report including scoring of one team report, narrative summary profile, miniature profile, and item response summary; $35 plus $10 per item per supplemental items summary reports; $30 per manual; $10 per administrator's guide; $20 per facilitator's guide; $50 per set of manual, administrator's guide, and facilitator's guide.
Time: (20–25) minutes.
Authors: Glenn Hallam and David Campbell.
Publisher: NCS (Minnetonka).
Cross References: See T5:379 (1 reference).

Review of the Campbell-Hallam Team Development Survey by FREDERICK T. L. LEONG, Associate Professor of Psychology, The Ohio State University at Columbus, Columbus, OH:

The factors that influence work groups and how they can function more effectively has been a longstanding interest in the field of Industrial/ Organizational Psychology (see Dunnette, 1976). However, during the last decade, increased attention has been paid to the importance of teams and team work in organizations from both organizational scientists and practicing managers (e.g., Parker, 1990; Katzenbach & Smith, 1993). The Team Development Survey (TDS) is a recently developed measure of team performance and functioning that fits with this trend. The Team Development Survey purports to measure the strengths and weaknesses of a team as perceived by members of that team. There are 18 scales with the Team Development Survey with measured dimensions such as organization support, mission clarity, team unity, and satisfaction.

The Team Development Survey (TDS) was developed using a combined rational and empirical strategy. The TDS was initially developed based on conceptual and theoretical grounds to measure the various dimensions that are relevant to assessing team performance and functioning. Next, the Team Development Survey was revised empirically through an evaluation of the items and the various psychometric properties to refine and improve the scale until it more closely captured the underlying theoretical conceptual scheme. In combining the rational and empirical approaches to instrument development, the TDS is able to take advantage of the strengths of both approaches.

In general, the TDS has acceptable psychometric properties. For example, the internal consistency is quite adequate with a median Cronbach's alpha of .69 (ranges from .61 to .95). Test/retest stability (17-day interval on average) was also quite good with a median correlation of .80 (ranges from .69–.90). Empirical evidence for the construct validity of the TDS, although not extensive, is adequate. The authors have sought to evaluate the construct validity of the Team Development Survey by comparing the perceptions of the team members with the results of their own individual perceptions. The assumption is that if the TDS is measuring team performance and functioning accurately, then most of the individual team members will perceive the TDS results as consistent with their own perceptions. In other words, it should be found that when asked individually the team members are agreeing that the Team Development Survey results are consistent with their own individual perceptions of how the team is performing. The authors did this by calculating the correlations between the average team scores and the average observer's scores, and they also calculated correlations between the average team scale scores and the performance assessed by observer's team leader and the members as a way of assessing criterion-related validity. Therefore, there seems to be some evidence of the construct and criterion-related validity of scores from the Team Development Survey.

The advantage of the Team Development Survey is that it is a standardized form of assessing team performance that provides feedback to team members and team leaders as to the various dimensions of team functioning and relative strengths and weaknesses. The Team Development Survey also has the advantage of allowing individual members to find out discrepancies between their own individual perceptions and the overall team perceptions of the various dimensions. In addition, the Team Development Survey has normative scores for use in establishing a comparative standing with regards to each team's functioning.

Whereas the TDS is a rigorously developed measure of team performance and functioning, there are a couple of problems with the current version. First, authors of the TDS provided only a partial assessment of the criterion-related validity of the measure. Although the established relationships between the TDS scores and observer scores is one aspect of criterion-related validity, also needed are direct links to outcomes. For example, a more important type of criterion-related validity study would be to demonstrate that TDS scores are actually significantly related to organizational outcomes such as productivity. Theoretically, those teams that have more resources and higher levels of efficiencies (e.g., mission clarity, team unity, and empowerment) should be more productive than those teams with less resources and lower levels of efficiencies as measured by the TDS. In other words, team performance should be meaningfully related to various aspects of work performance. This type of criterion-related validity is still lacking for the TDS and should be collected in future studies.

Second, there are problems with the measurement of a high level phenomenon like team performance. In general, most psychological tests measure phenomena at the individual level of analysis such as a person's level of self-esteem, self-efficacy, or various temperamental characteristics. Whenever psychologists attempt to measure higher level phenomena such as organizational climate and so on, the complexity and challenges are therefore multiplied. This is the same with any attempts to measure team performance and functioning. As indicated by James and Jones (1974) in research with organizational climate there is a potential methodological problem in trying to assess higher level phenomena such as organizational climate by simply summing the responses of all the members of an organization. The same problem pertains here with regards to assessing team performance by summing individual team members' perceptions. This problem has to do with the validity of interpretations of group level phenomena by simply assessing individual perceptions. This remains a thorny methodological issue and is a limitation of the Team Development Survey that was not addressed adequately by the authors and needs to be taken into account in future assessments.

SUMMARY. In conclusion, although there are concerns about the methodological issues of assessing higher order phenomena such as team performance by using individual team members' perceptions and the partial assessment of criterion-related validity, the Team Development Survey is rigorously developed and shows psychometrically sound measurement of team performance that has few parallels or competitors. For example, I refer to the Teamness Index, which was reviewed in *The Eleventh Mental Measurements Yearbook* (11:417) as a comparison and that particular scale has no psychometric validation whatsoever. The TDS is a conceptually developed scale that measures all the major dimensions of team performance and effectiveness quite adequately. The Team Development Survey can be recommended for group organizational interventions and assessment notwithstanding the methodological issues discussed earlier.

REVIEWER'S REFERENCES

James, L. R., & Jones, A. P. (1974). Organizational climate: A review of theory and research. *Psychological Bulletin, 81,* 1096–1112.

Dunnette, M. D. (Ed.). (1976). *Handbook of industrial and organizational psychology.* Chicago: Rand McNally.

Parker, G. M. (1990). *Team players and team work: The new competitive business strategy.* San Francisco: Jossey-Bass.

Katzenbach, J. R., & Smith, D. K. (1993). *The wisdom of teams: Creating the high-performance organization.* Boston: Harvard Business School.

Review of the Campbell–Hallam Team Development Survey by MARY A. LEWIS, Director, Human Resources, Chlor–Alkali and Derivatives, PPG Industries, Inc., Pittsburgh, PA:

The Campbell-Hallam Team Development Survey (TDS) consists of two forms: a 72-item Member Survey for team members (with the option of adding up to 15 supplemental questions) and a 22-item Observer Survey for customers, managers, consultants, or others who work with the team. Minimum team member size is three, and the number of observers can range from 4 to 10. The administrator's guide is well organized and easy to follow, and the survey questionnaires are also well prepared and intuitively easy to complete.

Scores are provided on 18 scales organized around four categories and an overall score based on all items. Each scale is based on from three to six items, and the scale score is reported as a T score, standardized with a mean of 50 and a standard deviation of 10 (note: the Satisfaction scale was designed with a mean of 51). Five items are considered team performance items. The norms were developed from a sample of 1,881 individuals representing 194 teams covering a wide variety of levels and functions. Reliability was estimated for both internal consistency (median Cronbach's alpha = .69) and test-retest (median correlation .80 over a 27-day span).

Two types of reports are provided: a team report, to be used by the facilitator, and a member report. Each member report includes the team profile and team item responses as well as the individual member's personal responses. A narrative summary is also provided, which includes suggested strengths, areas for improvement, and suggested actions for improvement. The team report is similar, without the individual information, and also includes suggested steps for discussing the results. A team facilitator's guide provides detailed and more elaborate recommendations on a process to review and use the results.

The TDS was developed based on an extensive review of theory and research, as well as the practical experience of the authors. This review, which is well documented in the manual provided, led to the development of the Team Success Model. This model, on which the survey is based, proposes that teams build resources, find ways to use them, attend to process that will help them improve, and then measure success based on team performance and team member satisfaction. A

166-item version of the survey was developed and, after several iterations of data collection and refinement, reduced to the 72-item member survey. The data were then rescored using all samples to develop the norms referred to earlier. During the item development and refinement process, an observer booklet was created to get an outside perspective on the team. Observer items were written for each of the 18 scales and five performance items in the Member Booklet.

The TDS manual provides a great deal of data on scale intercorrelations (they are moderate to high) and item intercorrelations by scale (they, too, are moderate to high). Although the scales are conceptually independent, they do not appear to be statistically independent. The validity evidence includes a cursory discussion of face validity and an interesting philosophical treatise on construct validity that raises the issue of the relevance of the concept of "true score" for perception of a team function. Statistical support for construct validity is nontheless provided through member/observer scale/item correlations. Concurrent validity was calculated using the average of the five performance items for team members, for team leaders, and for observers as criterion measures. These three criteria were correlated with the 18 scale scores and the overall score. Median correlations were .37 for average leaders performance items, .5 for average observer, and .6 for average team member. These correlations are moderate to high, and are slightly higher than the intercorrelations of the scales.

It is conceivable that the 18 scales of the TDS are actually some much smaller number of empirical scales, and that the reporting process could be simplified into much fewer dimensions. However, the primary purpose of this tool is to develop teams. The conceptual scales this instrument represents are easily understood by team members, observers, leaders, and facilitators. The instrument is designed to be used with little external support, other than scoring of results, by organization members who have had little technical training. For that reason, the use of these scales makes a great deal of sense. Scale independence is not necessarily an accurate representation of the real world, and in fact is an artifact imposed by statistical models. In this case, scale understanding seems to be a legitimate test construction goal.

Scale scores were examined by a number of demographic characteristics, including gender, age, and race, by dividing teams up into categorical groupings such as all male, all female, and mixed teams to describe the composition of the sample. In addition, scale scores were correlated with such variables as proportion of females on the team, or average leader age. In general, these demographic variables appeared to have little relationship to scale scores, although leader age seemed to be positively related to scale score ($r = .21$) and number of meetings per week was negatively related to scale score ($r = -.16$). It would appear that the scales work equally well across a wide range of teams, both in terms of demographics and job function.

The manual also provides supplemental material on content, importance, and action items for each of the scales. This material, coupled with the facilitator's guide, should provide enough support to allow effective team development sessions.

SUMMARY. The TDS is a well designed, easy-to-administer tool that can provide feedback to drive a team building/team development process. The materials and scales are easily understood, rest on sound theory, were developed using appropriate techniques, and should provide a solid basis for team building. The administrator's guide is self-explanatory, the facilitators' guide is well thought out, and the manual provided enough background information to thoroughly understand the scales and their meaning. I would recommend the TDS as a team building tool, but would strongly recommend that the facilitator selected be someone from outside the team, with presentation and facilitator training.

[9]
Career Decision-Making Self-Efficacy Scale.

Purpose: "Measures an individual's degree of belief that he/she can successfully complete tasks necessary to making career decisions."

Population: College students.

Publication Date: 1983–1994.

Acronym: CDMSE.

Scores, 6: Self-Appraisal, Occupational Information, Goal Selection, Planning, Problem Solving, Total.

Administration: Group.

Price Data: Available from publisher.

Time: Administration time not reported.

Comments: A 25-item short form is also available.

Authors: Nancy E. Betz and Karen M. Taylor.

Publisher: Nancy E. Betz (the author).
Cross References: See T5:403 (1 reference).

Review of the Career Decision-Making Self-Efficacy Scale by JAMES K. BENISH, School Psychologist, Helena Public Schools, Adjunct Professor of Special Education, Carroll College, Helena, MT:

The Career Decision-Making Self-Efficacy Scale (CDMSE) is a tool for measuring "an individual's degree of belief that he/she can successfully complete tasks necessary to making career decisions" (manual, p. 8). The scale was developed for group administration to college students, and has as its foundation Bandura's sources of information regarding the concept of self-efficacy expectations. Previous studies conducted by the authors apply the theories of self-efficacy to vocational psychology and counseling through the application of "Crites' (1978) model of career maturity and assessed in the Career Maturity Inventory" (manual, p. 8). There has been much research in the area of career decision making, and this scale is based on that research.

The CDMSE was developed to provide information regarding "Self-Appraisal, Occupational Information, Goal Selection, Planning, and Problems-Solving" (manual, p. 10). The 50-item scale is intended to be administered in a group setting utilizing generic answer sheets provided by the user. A short version (25-item scale) is also available and retains the same five-factor structure as the complete CDMSE. User qualifications necessitate knowledge of career development and the theories from which this test was based. The CDMSE is a research tool that can be used for career counseling within a classroom setting. Although graduate level training is not specified, it would appear that familiarity with psychometric principles should be adhered to in administering either form. No time limit is given for administration of either form; however, completion time would depend on number of subjects and whether answers are scored electronically or manually. The individual subscales each contain 10 items that, according to the authors, have a "perceived difficulty of career decision-making tasks" (manual, Table 1). Test subjects must respond to each 10-point scale ranging from "Complete Confidence [9] to No Confidence [0]" (manual, p. 9), with each response based on the subject's preconceived ability to accomplish each task.

STANDARDIZATION AND NORMS. The CDMSE was initially administered to 346 midwest college students attending either a private liberal arts college or a large public university. This 1983 validation of the test was used to establish scoring and administration criteria. Of the 346, there were 128 males and 218 females, and data gathered were used to support reliability and validity of the scores including factor analysis. Since then, there have been numerous studies reported in an extensive reference section of the manual. An accompanying journal article underscores the authors' (and others) continuing research of the CDMSE (Betz, & Luzzo, 1996). Clear, concise tables were listed in the manual for item analysis, mean and standard deviation of scores, and gender comparisons for the combined subject group. However, statistical analysis for other normative data, including reliability and validity evidence, was contained within the text of the manual rather than being arranged in a more readable table form.

RELIABILITY. Internal consistency reliability was estimated with coefficient alpha on the five subscales of the CDMSE. These values for Self-Appraisal, Occupational Information, Goal Selection, Planning, and Problem-Solving were .88, .89, .87, .89, and .86 respectively. Total reliability for scores from the 50-item test was .97, and the accompanying journal article reported the 25-item alpha value of .94. These very respectable reliability findings were replicated in more recent follow-up studies provided by the authors and others involved in comparing the CDMSE with other questionnaires. Another unpublished study "reported a coefficient alpha of .93 and test-retest reliability of .83 over a one and one-half month interval" (manual, p. 10).

VALIDITY. A rather expansive narrative within the administration manual highlights various studies and conclusions regarding the authors' discussions of the evidence of content, concurrent, and construct validity of the CDMSE, and how it compares with other tests and research tools. The authors also presented evidence for predictive and discriminant validity based on a plethora of research found throughout the narrative portion of the test manual. Although the test findings support most validity factors, there remains evidence of the need for further study and interpretation of data gathered from the above mentioned research. The CDMSE scores were found to have statistically significant nonzero correlation with scores from Holland, Daiger, and Powers' (1980) My Vocational Situation, with values ranging from .28 to .40. Another interesting finding involving construct validity came from a 1990 study that "reported that the CDMSE significantly differentiated three groups of students categorized on the basis of college major status: Declared Majors (M = 335), Tentative Major Choice (M = 3.8) and Undecided (M = 283)" (manual, p. 15). Finally, although the predictive validity for the CDMSE appears strong, much of the research presented within the manual contains disjointed references of questionable importance for the practitioner.

SUMMARY. The usefulness of the application of the CDMSE for use in vocational psychology and career counseling is strong, especially for students who lack the self-efficacy and career decision making needed for setting goals or achieving success in college. Providing students with the information obtained from their responses might facilitate decision-making skills and reduce frustration with future career planning. As a guidance tool for college age students, the CDMSE is a practical tool that should be given strong consideration. As a research instrument, the CDMSE has proved useful as a forum for ongoing follow-up and scrutiny. It would appear that it has become a standard with which to compare other instruments. Also, it would appear that it has been used to develop new hypotheses for research studies. It appears to be continually evolving as a test instrument to study, and based on the presentation on validity evidence in the manual, for example, this may not be useful for the practitioner searching for a validity table, and finding only a lengthy narrative. Perhaps publishing the CDMSE into a finalized, bound copy would further its practicality and application for those choosing to use it as an assessment tool.

REVIEWER'S REFERENCE

Betz, N. E., & Luzzo, D. A. (1996). Career assessment and the Career Decision-Making Self-Efficacy Scale. *Journal of Career Assessment, 4*, 413–428.

Review of the Career Decision-Making Self-Efficacy Scale by RICHARD W. JOHNSON, Adjunct Professor of Counseling Psychology and Associate Director Emeritus of Counseling & Consultation Services, University Health Services, University of Wisconsin—Madison, Madison, WI:

According to Albert Bandura's theory of self-efficacy, a person's belief in his or her ability to perform a particular behavior significantly affects that person's choices, performance, and persistence. Karen Taylor and Nancy Betz developed the Career Decision-Making Self-Efficacy Scale (CDMSE) as a means of assessing the relevance of this theory to career choice and development.

SCALE COMPOSITION. The CDMSE consists of 50 items that represent critical skills involved in career planning. The authors prepared 10 items to measure each of five career-planning competencies (accurate self-appraisal, gathering occupational information, goal selection, making plans for the future, and problem solving) identified by John Crites (1978) in his model of career maturity. For each item, respondents indicate on a 10-point scale their degree of self-confidence in performing the task mentioned in that item.

NORMATIVE DATA. The CDMSE manual provides means and standard deviations for the Total score, 5 subscales, and 50 items for 346 college students who participated in validation studies. The test authors found little or no significant differences in the mean test scores for men and women or for students enrolled in different types of colleges. Most of the students (79%) in the normative sample were first-year students.

The CDMSE has been designed to be used with college students; however, it can be readily adapted for use with other populations. Relatively little information regarding the influence of cultural background on test scores is available. One study cited in the manual reported that African-American students scored higher than did students from other racial or ethnic groups. Somewhat inconsistent results have been reported in regard to the influence of age, sex, and academic achievement on CDMSE scores.

The average student marked "much confidence" (between 6 and 7 on a scale that runs from 0 to 9) for most of the items. For this reason, the CDMSE may not discriminate as well among students as it would if it had a higher ceiling.

RELIABILITY. Alpha coefficients of consistency are relatively high for all of the subscales (alphas ranged from .86 to .89 for the normative sample described above). The alphas coefficient for the Total score was .97, which indicates that the item content is highly consistent across all 50 items. A test-retest reliability of .83 has been reported for the Total score over a 6-week period.

VALIDITY. Factor analyses do not support the use of the five categories obtained from Crites' theory. The authors suggest that the CDMSE be viewed as "a generalized career self-efficacy measure covering a multifaceted domain of career decision-making behaviors" (p. 11). Despite the results of the factor analyses, the authors recommend retaining the five subscales as a "useful framework" to orient clients to the process of career counseling and career education.

Scores on the CDMSE are highly correlated with scores on other measures of self-confidence, such as self-esteem and occupational self-efficacy scales; however, they also tap unique aspects of self-confidence associated with career planning. In several multiple regression studies, the CDMSE explained more of the variance in career decidedness than all other variables, including measures of self-esteem, occupational self-efficacy, career salience, locus of control, anxiety, verbal ability, and math ability.

As expected, a number of research studies have found high correlation coefficients between scores on the CDMSE and measures of career indecision such as the Career Decision Scale, My Vocational Situation, Career Maturity Inventory, and Fear of Commitment Scale (Betz & Luzzo, 1996). CDMSE scores also have differentiated among students with declared majors, tentative majors, and no majors in the expected manner. All of these studies support the convergent validity of the CDMSE.

To serve as a relatively pure measure of self-confidence in career planning, scores on the CDMSE scores should be independent of ability and social desirability measures. Research studies show low correlations between CDMSE scores and career decision-making skills (as opposed to attitudes), SAT scores, or ACT scores. These data support the discriminant validity of the instrument. No studies of the relationship between CDMSE scores and scores on a measure of social desirability have been reported.

Most of the validity studies conducted with the CDMSE have been based on the relationship between scores on the CDMSE and other measures obtained at the same time or within a short time interval. Longitudinal research studies are needed to determine if CDMSE scores can effectively predict behavioral criteria such as career decidedness, engagement in career planning tasks, and career persistence over longer time periods.

RECENT DEVELOPMENTS. The authors have recently prepared a short, 25-item form of the inventory consisting of the best five items from each subscale (Betz, Klein, & Taylor, 1996). Research conducted thus far with the short form indicates that it may produce higher validity coefficients than the full-scale form. The alpha reliability coefficient for the total scale remains high (alpha = .94). In addition, the authors have recently proposed that the 10-point response continuum be reduced to 5 points to further simplify the form (N. E. Betz, personal communication, March 15, 1998).

SUMMARY AND CONCLUSIONS. The CDMSE has been shown to provide reliable and valid measures of self-confidence in making career decisions in a number of different situations. As such, it can serve a valuable purpose in both research and counseling. In research, it can be used to study factors associated with the causes and consequences of self-confidence in career decision making. In counseling, it can be used to assess the client's need for treatment on this issue and his or her responsiveness to different interventions designed to improve self-confidence in career decision making. Because of its brevity, the short form can be particularly valuable in situations where the instrument is administered more than once. Additional research on the instrument itself is needed in regard to the relationship between the long and short forms, its use in different cultures or with different populations, and its validity in predicting behavioral criteria.

REVIEWER'S REFERENCES
Crites, J. O. (1978). *Career Maturity Inventory.* Monterey, CA: CTB/McGraw-Hill.
Betz, N. E., Klein, K. L., & Taylor, K. M. (1996). Evaluation of a short form of the Career Decision-Making Self-Efficacy Scale. *Journal of Career Assessment, 4,* 47–57.
Betz, N. E., & Luzzo, D. A. (1996). Career assessment and the Career Decision-Making Self-Efficacy Scale. *Journal of Career Assessment, 4,* 413–428.

[10]
Caregiver-Teacher Report Form.

Purpose: Designed "to assess behavioral/emotional problems and identify syndromes of problems that tend to occur together."

Population: Ages 2–5.

Publication Date: 1997.

Acronym: C-TRF.

Scores, 10: Anxious/Obsessive, Depressed/Withdrawn, Fears, Somatic Problems, Immature, Attention

Problems, Aggressive Behavior, Internalizing, Externalizing, Total.

Administration: Group.

Price Data, 1997: $10 per 25 test booklets; $10 per 25 profiles for hand scoring; $10 per guide (67 pages); $7 per templates for hand scoring; $135 per computer scoring program.

Time: Administration time not reported.

Comments: Ratings by daycare providers and preschool teachers.

Author: Thomas M. Achenbach.

Publisher: Child Behavior Checklist.

Review of the Caregiver-Teacher Report Form by KAREN T. CAREY, Professor of Psychology, California State University, Fresno, CA:

The Caregiver-Teacher Report Form (C-TRF) is designed to be completed by daycare providers and preschool teachers who respond to 99 problem area items and several open-ended items. Items are grouped into three categories labeled Internalizing, Neither Internalizing or Externalizing, and Externalizing. These are further broken down into syndromes. The Internalizing grouping is composed of Anxious/Obsessive, Depressed/Withdrawn, and Fears syndromes; the Neither Internalizing or Externalizing grouping is composed of Somatic Problems and Immature syndromes, and the Externalizing grouping is composed of Aggressive Behavior and Attention Problems syndromes. A total scale score is also obtained. The manual provides specific information related to the procedures used for constructing the scale.

Each item is scored 0 for *not true*, 1 for *somewhat or sometimes true*, and 2 for *very true or often true*. Item number 100 provides space for the caregiver/teacher to write in any additional problems the child has that were not addressed by other items of the scale. Three additional open-ended items can be completed that include whether the child has any illness or disability, what concerns the caregiver most about the child, and what the child does best. A profile consisting of each of the seven syndromes can be generated using the protocol and plotting results using *T*-scores or percentiles.

The norm group consisted of 1,076 children between the ages of 2 and 5 with 536 boys and 539 girls from 12 states and Holland. Demographic characteristics include socioeconomic status (upper, middle, and lower), ethnicity (NonLatino White, African-American, Latino, Mixed or Other), region

of U.S.A. (Northeast, North Central, South, West), and respondent (Caregiver and Teacher). Children from upper socioeconomic status, described as NonLatino White, and residing in the Northeast region appear to be overrepresented and caregiver respondents (78) seem to overrepresented as compared to teachers (23) in the sample.

T-scores are obtained from each syndrome and are assigned on the basis of percentiles. Different numbers of items compose each of the syndromes. Normalized *T*-scores were assigned to raw scores on the basis of the percentile represented by raw scores in the norm sample. The *T*-scores were also truncated to low scores so that a child who obtained 0 on two scales did not appear to have more problems in one area than in another. A *T*-score of 50 was assigned to all raw scores that fell at midpoint percentiles up to the 50th percentile. At the high end of the scale *T*-scores were assigned from 71 to 100 in increments because most children obtained scores below the maximum number possible on each syndrome scale. Normal, borderline, and clinical ranges are identified for all scale scores.

In the manual the author states that further reliability and validity studies are needed as this is the first edition of this instrument. However, the initial studies appear to provide adequate technical data. Test-retest reliability of .84 was obtained over intervals averaging 8.7 days. Mean interrater reliability of .66 was obtained. Correlations of the C-TRF with the Child Behavior Checklists/2-3 and 4/18 scales ranged from .14 to .64.

Content validity evidence was based on examination of the items by professionals in the field, parents' feedback, and by findings that respondents' ratings significantly discriminated between referred and nonreferred children. Criterion-related validity was examined based on the ability of each item to discriminate between children who had been referred for behavioral/emotional problems and children from the norm group. Results indicated that the referred sample did differ significantly from the norm sample on most items and scales.

SUMMARY. The C-TRF appears to be a useful instrument to identify behavioral and emotional problems in young children and technical evidence is adequate. Although further studies are needed to confirm technical adequacy, it appears that this instrument will gain the same widespread use as the Child Behavior Checklist (T5:451).

Review of the Caregiver-Teacher Report Form by MICHAEL FURLONG, Professor, and RENEE PAVELSKI, Doctoral Candidate, Counseling, Clinical, School Psychology Program, University of California, Santa Barbara, Graduate School of Education, Santa Barbara, CA:

The Caregiver-Teacher Report Form (C-TRF/2–5), a general measure of child behavioral and emotional problems, is designed to be completed by daycare providers and preschool teachers who have known the child in a school or daycare setting. The C-TRF/2–5, appropriate for 2- to 5-year-olds attending prekindergarten programs or day care, is part of a family of assessment tools including: (a) the Child Behavior Checklist (CBCL/2–3), (b) the CBCL/4–18, (c) the Teacher's Report Form (TRF/5–18), (d) the Youth Self-Report (YSR), (e) the Young Adult Self-Report (YASR), (f) the Young Adult Behavior Checklist (YABCL), (g) the Direct Observation Form (DOF), and (h) the Semistructured Clinical Interview for Children (SCIC). The C-TRF can be thought of as a downward extension of the TRF and as a teacher version of the CBCL. The validity of these tools has been documented in empirical research. Therefore, Achenbach advises that they be used as an integrative unit where appropriate for the age of the individual.

The format of the C-TRF/2–5 is similar to that of the CBCL/2–3. Both contain 99 questions and open-ended items used for describing illnesses, disabilities, concerns the respondent has most about the child, and the best things about the child. Specifically, 82 questions have counterparts on the CBCL/2–3, 56 questions have counterparts on the CBCL/4–18, and 65 questions have counterparts on the TRF.

ADMINISTRATION. The instructions for the C-TRF/2–5 state that staff members who have the most experience with the child over the longest period of time (for a minimum of 2 months) are the best respondents. Responses should be based on the child's behavior within the past 2 months. The same 2-month period used in the Teacher Rating Form (ages 6–17) was selected as sufficient for children's behavior to stabilize in new settings and for respondents to become well acquainted with the children (C-TRF/2–5 manual, p. 49).

The administration of the C-TRF requires no special training and can be completed by assistant and trainee providers and teachers, as well as by more experienced personnel. As different staff members see the child in unique settings, it is best to have as many personnel as possible complete separate C-TRFs on the child based on their individual views. To clarify the role of the respondent, the C-TRF asks about their training and the experience of the child in their care. The type and size of the facility are described, as well as how many hours per week the child attends. If a child has a disability or is in a special class, respondents should base their answers on expectations for typical peers of the child's age. If the respondents lack the information to answer certain questions, one should write in "No chance to observe" or mark 0 to indicate "Not True (as far as you know)."

RESPONSE SCALE. The checklist uses a three-option response scale (from 0 to 2) for each problem item: 0 = *not true (as far as you know) of the child;* 1 = *somewhat or sometimes true;* and 2 = *very true or often true.* It is important to think about these responses in context as each item is weighed equally in subscale scores. The three-option scale, although convenient and economical, assumes that these responses are equally meaningful for all items. It is important for clinicians to get a sense of the caregivers' understanding of these categories in terms of their implied frequency and tolerance/intolerance of specific behaviors.

CONTENT AND SCORING. The scoring profile of the C-TRF/2–5 includes: (a) seven syndrome scales (Anxious/Obsessive, Depressed/Withdrawn, Fears, Somatic Problems, Immature Behavior, Attention Problems, and Aggressive Behavior); (b) a composite Internalizing problem scale score; (c) a composite Externalizing problem scale score; and (d) a Total Problem scale score. Raw scores and their corresponding T-scores for each subscale may be hand tallied and graphed on a profile using templates, or computer-scoring programs can be purchased that will score the profiles based on key entered or machine-read forms.

A number of the items, such as #27 ("Doesn't seem to feel guilty after misbehaving") and #90 ("Unhappy, sad or depressed") involve subjective judgements. The manual emphasizes the importance of obtaining multiple informants to minimize the subjectivity and identify agreements and disagreements between their judgments. Question #100 asks the informant to write in any problems the child has that were not listed above. Proper use requires a thorough review of all item responses prior to any hand or computer scoring.

NORMS. Normative data for the C-TRF/2–5 were drawn from a sample of 1,075 children (536 boys and 539 girls) from a variety of settings at 15 sites in 12 states and Holland. The National Institute of Child Health and Development (NICHD) Study of early Child Care provided data for 753 of these children. This sample is composed of approximately 71% Caucasian, 18% African American, 5% Latino, and 5% mixed or other, and a high representation from upper class SES (47%). The settings included daycare centers, Headstart programs, and preschools. One of the confusing matters of creating a preschool caretaker/teacher report form is that not all preschool youth attend a formal program. Thus, defining what the "norm" sample should be in problematic. The C-TRF/2–5 should not be misunderstood to be an assessment of all preschool children. Eventually it will be necessary to establish norms that describe meaningful subgroupings of children in formal and informal preschool caretaker settings. Another matter is that no data were given in the manual regarding the education level, age, or gender of respondents. This is problematic in outlining norms as this data could confound the interpretation of the results. Greater description of caregiver and teacher demographics would aid in gaining a fuller understanding of these norms. In the future, information about the number of child ratings provided by each caregiver should be provided.

The fact that the C-TRF, like all the other Achenbach scales, focuses exclusively on pathology means that the distribution of subscale scores is highly skewed. Thus, it was necessary to rescale the scores using what is referred to as a "normalized T-score." Of what use are these normalized T-scores for the researcher and the clinician wishing to interpret a child's behavior emotional profile? This is very unclear. The normalized T-score are supposed to provide a more "bell-shaped curve" to the distribution of scores. The user of the C-TRF should recognize that the subscale normalized T-scores are not normally distributed over a full range of behaviors. Because the C-TRF focuses exclusively on problematic behaviors it is only tapping the upper range of the behavioral/emotional continuum. In addition, some of the subscales do a better job of this than others, particularly Depression/Withdrawn, Immaturity, Attention Problems, and Aggressive Behavior. These subscales have a sufficient number of items and these behaviors occur frequently enough among preschool children to obtain a smooth spread of scores across a wider distribution. This means that higher and lower scores on these subscales, in particular, may have clinical meaning. In summary, at the syndrome subscale level, given the various distribution problems, it would be best to use percentile ranking to interpret profiles and to explain them to parents and other consumers.

RELIABILITY. Agreement between different daycare and preschool staff members rating the same child was indicated by a mean $r = .66$. The test/retest reliability of C-TRF scale scores was supported by a mean $r = .84$ over intervals averaging 8.7 days (ranging from .64 to .91). These results should be read with caution, as the sample size was small. However, the cross-informant reliability index for somatic problems was inadequate (.33). This result is surprising, as the questions tend to be less subjective. Curiously, the majority of the test-retest data were derived from ratings provided by Dutch teachers. Given that the C-TRF was developed in English this hardly seems adequate to examine its score stability. The Achenbach series has a long tradition of being translated into other languages, but given that this manual describes its original development and validation, one would have hoped that its psychometric properties would have been firmly established with the English version prior to extending its use to another language and culture. Despite the need for collecting additional reliability data for various sociocultural groups in whichever country the C-TRF is used, the data that are presented show that scores decreased some over about an 8-day interval. The changes were small, but this downward trend is consistent with other research showing that other Achenbach scales produce lower scores on readministration. This is undesirable when used as an outcome measure in program evaluations. This pattern should be kept in mind by clinicians and researchers when evaluating program effectiveness.

VALIDITY. Several kinds of support are presented for validity of scores from the C-TRF. Feedback was received from professionals, parents, teachers, and caregivers. Most of the items and scales scored from the C-TRF ratings discriminated significantly between the referred and normative samples of children. Age, ethnic, and SES differences had little effect on the C-TRF scores. Because the C-TRF/2-5 draws upon the extensive tradition of the Achenbach scales, it has a solid foundation in empirical research about children's mental health.

When considering the validity of scores from the scale, users should recognize that the C-TRF/2-5 has greater power to detect and evaluate externalizing problems. In regression analyses, the syndrome and composite scores were significant predictors of referral status (few differences were found for socioeconomic status, age, or Non-Latino White versus other ethnicities). However, the strongest predictors of referral status were Attention Problems, Aggressive Behavior, and the Externalizing composite. This also may reflect the fact that caregivers identify children in need by observing troubling behaviors as opposed to emotional/internal problems. Preschool children may also be more likely to exhibit their internal turmoil through their behavior. Additional discriminant analyses showed that only the Externalizing composite was a significant predictor of referral status for both boys and girls.

SUMMARY. The C-TRF/2-5 is an interesting component of a complex, evolving, and continually improving assessment package that has become a collection of landmark instruments. Over 1,700 studies have utilized one or more of these instruments and the assessment package has gained international recognition. As a result, the measurements are endorsed and validated by a diverse group of researchers and have been translated into 50 different languages. As a research tool, the C-TRF/2-5 is well established, easy to use, and affordable. Although the long-term utility of the C-TRF/2-5 awaits empirical validation and clinical research, current users of the Achenbach battery of instruments will certainly want to add this instrument to their assessment libraries.

[11]
Child Development Review.

Purpose: A brief screening inventory "designed to help identify children with developmental, behavioral, or health problems."
Population: 18 months to age 5.
Publication Date: 1994.

Acronym: CDR.
Scores, 5: Development (Social, Self-Help, Gross Motor, Fine Motor, Language), Possible Problems, Child Description, Parents' Questions/Concerns, Parents' Functioning.
Administration: Individual.
Price Data, 1998: $10 per 25 parent questionnaire/child development charts; $10 per manual (22 pages).
Time: Administration time not reported.
Comments: Parent-completed questionnaire; scores reflect parents' report of child's present functioning-development.
Author: Harold Ireton.
Publisher: Behavior Science Systems, Inc.

Review of the Child Development Review by TERRY OVERTON, President, Learning and Behavioral Therapies, Inc., Farmville, VA:

DESCRIPTION AND PURPOSE. The Child Development Review manual includes information about the Child Development Review System. This system is composed of the Child Development Review, the Child Development Chart—First Five Years, the Infant Development Inventory, and the Child Development Chart—First 21 Months. This system was designed to serve as a format for reviewing a child's development with the child's parents and to screen for children who may be having developmental problems. The five areas of development assessed are Social, Self-Help, Gross Motor, Fine Motor, and Language. The Child Development Review consists of six open-ended questions for parents concerning the child's strengths, weaknesses, and concerns. A 26-item checklist, containing developmental and behavioral items completes this questionnaire. The parent, the examiner, or both, complete the Child Development Chart—First Five Years, which lists developmental milestones in the five areas. The chart assists with structuring observations or in asking parents for additional information. The final piece of the system is the problems list questions. This is composed of 25 possible problems experienced by children ages birth through 5 years. The Infant Development Inventory and the Child Development Chart are similar instruments to the Child Development Review. These two instruments, for earlier ages, provide a more detailed month-by-month guide of development within the first 21 months of life. The author states that possible developmental problem areas may be further assessed by using a clinical interview format. The author provides examples of using the instrument to structure clinical interview questions.

ADMINISTRATION AND SCORING. The Child Development Review system is administered as an informal criterion-referenced assessment instrument. The parent is given the appropriate interview form for the child's age. This paper-pencil format is easy to administer. The examiner reviews the parents' responses and asks probes about specific problem areas. The examiner and the parent complete the appropriate developmental chart. Instructions for scoring the developmental chart are provided in the manual. The Child Development Chart is scored to determine children whose development is advanced, which is indicated by behavior that is 30% above the level expected for his or her age, around the age expected (behavior is within 30% of the actual age), questionable behavior (behavior that is immature or 30% below the level expected for age), and developmentally delayed (more than 50% below the level expected for age). Suggestions are provided for the examiner to use the results to discuss areas of concern with the parents.

TECHNICAL INFORMATION. The Child Development Review Parent Questionnaire was researched in conjunction with the Preschool Development Questionnaire and the Child Development Review. The manual includes research on all three of these instruments. The sample sizes included in the research ranged from 46 to 2,225 in the four studies. The author reports conclusions from these studies on age and sex differences, common problem areas according to parents, most common problem items, more common problems of early childhood/special education children, and problem items predictive of poor kindergarten performance. The manual does not include specific information on instrument design, item selection, standardization efforts, criterion-related validity data, or detailed descriptive information regarding the samples. The percentages of parents endorsing specific items as problems for their children are included on a table based on a sample of 411 parents. A normative table for ages of 12 months through 5 years is provided for the 30% below and 30% above behaviors for the Child Development Chart—First Five Years. Information about the sample for this table is not included in the table.

Several references are provided that list the studies of the various instruments of the system.

EVALUATION. The Child Development Review System's most appealing attribute is its ease of use for parents, attractiveness, and face validity. The instrument seems to be in line with expected developmental milestones; however, the author fails to explain specific details and provide important research explaining the development of the instrument. This information is imperative for potential consumers in various professions in early childhood. The manual does not include sufficient information about validity and reliability. The construct validity would be greatly enhanced by research on developmental progress using longitudinal research. The manual's format and presentation of specific information is confusing and seems to have little continuity from page to page. The system includes several pieces and each part of the system should receive its own section in the manual rather than requiring the consumer to attempt to sort out research or instructions on one piece from another. Because of the ease of administration and minimum time and effort required for scoring, research on the various pieces of this system in a variety of settings, with both average and clinical samples, would be easily conducted. The individual components of the instrument are affordable.

In summary, this system seems to have great appeal because of its ease of use and understanding by parents, short administration and scoring time, and attractiveness. In order for this instrument to have greater appeal for test consumers, the author should include additional research information and redesign the test manual.

Review of the Child Development Review by GARY J. STAINBACK, Senior Psychologist I, Developmental Evaluation Clinic, East Carolina University School of Medicine, Department of Pediatrics, Greenville, NC:

The Child Development Review (CDR) is a 99-item parent report form that spans the developmental ages from birth to 5 years of age. Areas of Social Development, Self-Help, Gross Motor, Fine-Motor, and Language are addressed. In addition to the 99 developmental items, there are 25 items of possible problems addressing the child's health, growth, habits, vision and hearing, language, motor, and behavioral problems. Developmental behaviors are included within an age interval whereby 75% of normally developing children have developed the behavior by that age.

Parents are directed to examine the chart and check those items that describe what their child is doing regularly, or moderately well. Items are marked with a "B" if their child is only just beginning to do them or does them only sometimes. Items not marked mean the child is not yet doing that developmental task. Parents are further instructed to stop marking in a column representing an area of development (e.g., Social, Self-Help) when three NOs (blanks) in a row have been encountered. For infants under the age of 18 months, it is recommended by the author that a more detailed chart of infant development be used: the Infant Development Inventory (IDI, Ireton, 1994), a copy of which is provided in the Appendix of the CDR.

The CDR is intended to help professionals review the development of young children with the child's parents. It is intended to be a screening instrument for children who may have a developmental problem. It is also intended to be a means for parents to use when talking about their child's development with a professional or child specialist. The CDR has reportedly been used in preschool settings for screening of development, pediatric practices as part of Well Child exams, and as a parent education tool. Items are based on child development research that has included the Minnesota Child Development Inventory (Ireton & Thwing, 1972), Infant Development Inventory (Ireton, 1994), Early Child Development Inventory (Ireton, 1988), and Preschool Development Inventory (Ireton, 1988). Reportedly, this research has included normally developing children, children at risk, and those with developmental disabilities.

Perhaps the most useful purpose of the CDR would be as part of a developmental interview, where direct yes/no questions are avoided. The suggested starting point for a child is one age level below the child's actual age. The suggested stopping point is when all items within a given age interval are answered "NO" or when three items in a row are answered "NO," or when it "makes sense to stop."

Scale interpretation requires using both the problems items and the developmental items. The author points out that 60% of parents of 3- and 4-

year-olds check one or more of the problem items, and gives guidance related to the likelihood of various items accounted for by parents. Scoring the developmental items is accomplished by drawing a line on the chart representing the child's actual age, then two more horizontal lines representing a Below Age Line and Above Age Line. The Below Age Line is drawn at 70% of the child's actual age, and the Above Age Line at 130%. For each area of development, the child's level of development is rated either: *A = Advanced, AA = Around Age, ?D = Questionable Development,* or *DD = Delayed Development.* Advanced is for behavior over 30% above age level, AA for behavior with 30% of the actual age, ?D for behavior that is 30% younger, and DD for behavior that is 50% or more delayed. A chart is provided in the manual starting at 12 months and ascending in 1-month increments up to 5 years, and provides the 30% age levels above and below the given age.

CDR research is addressed through the earlier instruments from which its items have been drawn. These instruments include the Preschool Development Inventory and the Child Development Inventory. Research on the CDR has also been done in a statewide Early Childhood program that screened 3-year-olds, and in a pediatric well-child care program. Each piece of research spoke to the CDR's usefulness for addressing issues pertaining to the child's development and allowing for further discussion, referral for further evaluation, or the provisions for early childhood education services.

No information is provided regarding norms or standardization, nor for reliability or validity of the instrument. The author has been very active in the development of child development inventories, and comparison of the CDR with a separate measure, different from one of his own, would certainly help to provide evidence with regard to validity. Multi-observer ratings may also help to estimate reliability.

In summary, the CDR is a brief parent report measure of the developmental functioning of young children between birth and 5 years of age. It has been used in medical well-child assessments and in settings to help determine eligibility of preschool children for early intervention. It is also useful as a tool to gather parent observations pertaining to their child's development, and direct attention to their developmental concerns. Unfortunately, the CDR does not provide norms or standardization data, nor are issues of reliability or validity addressed. Reported in the manual are some testimonials of the utility of the instrument. More useful, however, would be data relating to criterion-related validity. The CDR appears to be useful as an aid in the medical-parent interview pertaining to the developmental status of the child, but should not be used alone in this process. It should also be used cautiously as a measure of a child's development and for determining eligibility of Early Intervention services.

REVIEWER'S REFERENCES
Ireton, H. R., & Thwing, E. (1972). *Manual for the Minnesota Child Development Inventory.* Minneapolis: Behavior Science Systems.
Ireton, H. (1988). *Early Child Development Inventory manual.* Minneapolis: Behavior Science Systems.
Ireton, H. (1988). *Preschool Development Inventory manual.* Minneapolis: Behavior Science Systems.
Ireton, H. (1992). *Manual for the Child Development Inventory.* Minneapolis: Behavior Science Systems.
Ireton, H. (1994). The Infant Development Inventory. Minneapolis: Behavior Science Systems.

[12]
Children's Depression Rating Scale, Revised.

Purpose: Constructed as a "screening instrument, diagnostic tool, and severity measure of depression in children."
Population: Ages 6–12.
Publication Date: 1996.
Acronym: CDRS—R.
Scores: Total score only.
Administration: Group.
Price Data, 1999: $62.50 per complete kit including manual (91 pages), and 25 administration booklets; $18.50 per 25 administration booklets; $48 per manual.
Time: (15—20) minutes.
Comments: Ratings by health care professionals.
Authors: Elva O. Poznanski and Hartmut B. Mokros.
Publisher: Western Psychological Services.
Cross References: See T5:473 (8 references).

Review of the Children's Depression Rating Scale, Revised by E. THOMAS DOWD, Professor of Psychology, Kent State University, Kent, OH:

The Children's Depression Rating Scale, Revised (CDRS-R) is a clinician-rated scale for assessing childhood depression that is modeled after the Hamilton Rating Scale for Depression, an adult measure. It was designed to be used with children between the ages of 6 and 12. It is an interview-based instrument by which a sensitive clinician elicits information that is used to assess depression in 17 symptom areas. It takes about 20–30 minutes to complete. In addition, the same interview-based scale can be used to obtain information about the child's level of depression from parents and other significant others such as teachers. Thus, it is possible to obtain a comprehensive assessment of the level of childhood depression, a phenomenon that the authors say has been and is considerably underreported. The authors state that this instrument should be used as a preliminary finding to support a follow-up with more exhaustive assessment of childhood depression.

The CDRS-R comes with a manual and an administration booklet. The manual includes an introduction and subsequent chapters on administration and scoring, interpretation and case examples, an excellent review of the literature on depressive disorders in childhood, development and standardization of the instrument, and psychometric properties. There are also two appendices, an interview guide and sample responses for child interviews, and a corresponding guide for parents (and by implication other significant figures in the child's life).

One administration booklet is required for each administration. It consists of a 5- or 7-point rating scale for each of the 17 domains, along with descriptors of each rating and space for comments by the interviewer. The front page contains a "depression thermometer" which includes a total raw score (the Summary Score) as well as a conversion to *t*-scores and percentiles. The *t*-scores are then given an interpretation. There is also a comparison of symptom ratings from all sources (i.e., child, parent, other, as well as a combination Best Descriptor of Child). Apparently, the interpretation is based on previously collected normative data although that is not entirely clear.

The instrument, according to the manual, is administered according to a semistructured interview. This means that, although the interview follows a standard format in conducting the assessment interview, the authors also encourage flexibility in jumping ahead and exploring topics that arise spontaneously even though they may be out off place sequentially. This should be done, according to the manual, to avoid reinforcing any existing sense of alienation and isolation on the part of the child and combine rigor with empathy. Indeed, the consistent demonstration of sensitivity to children in collecting the data is one of the strengths of this instrument and its approach. The appendices provide suggested topics and prompts and sample responses. There are also four case examples to provide guidance in conducting these interviews and scoring the results although, given the flexible approach required, more than four might have been helpful. The flexibility of approach is also demonstrated in the overall Best Description of the Child, which is not simply a rigid and standardized combination of the three separate assessments (child, parent, other). Rather, depending on the circumstances, the child's data may be given precedence or the parent's or teacher's data might. With such a flexible approach, I wondered if extensive training might be necessary to fully utilize the CDRS-R (actually, I still do). However, interrater reliability estimates for the original unrevised instrument between interviewers familiar with the instrument and those unfamiliar with it resulted in similar scores, although there is no definition of "familiarity." Interrater reliability was .74 for interviewers familiar with it and .75 for those unfamiliar with it. Item-total correlations for interviewers familiar with the CDRS had a median of .62 whereas item-total correlations for interviewers unfamiliar with it had a median of .61. Nevertheless, my assessment of the instrument is that training would be required before it could be used well. The very flexibility that allows for empathy and sensitivity may also reduce the standardization and reliability unless the interviewer has had supervised practice.

The original instrument was first published in 1979. Its interrater reliability estimates at that time were good, ranging between .92 and .96. Internal consistency reliability estimates, conducted by correlating each item with a Global Rating of Depression and the Summary Score, resulted in a median correlation of .70. I should note that these reliabilities appear to be based on child assessments only, not parents or others. The CDRS was later revised by adding two symptom areas (Excessive Guilt and Depressed Feelings), renaming some of the symptom areas, and revising the rating anchors. Interrater reliability for the revised scale was estimated as .92 and test-retest (2-week interval) reliability was estimated as .80. Internal consistency reliability (estimated using coefficient alpha) was reported as .85. Validity was demonstrated by a correlation of .87 between the CDRS-R Summary Score and an independently assigned Global Rating of Depression, by a correlation of .48 between the CDRS-R and a modified version of the Hamilton Rating Scale for Depression, and by the ability of the CDRS-R to predict psychiatrically referred children diagnosed with depressive disorders. Scores on the CDRS-R were also found to be associated with independent assessments of suicidal ideation and behavior as well as other depressive symptoms.

SUMMARY. This appears to be a well-designed and researched instrument with years of development, reliability, and validity studies behind it. Its strengths include the semistructured interview-based approach, which is helpful in assessing children who may be more reticent than adults in describing and admitting symptoms. In addition, the authors quite appropriately describe the use of this instrument as a first step in a more comprehensive assessment. Strengths also include the provision for multiple sources of data from parents and others and the flexible combination of these data into a Best Description of the Child.

This very flexibility, however, can lead to loss of both reliability and validity if a standardized format is not followed to some extent. Therefore, I would suggest, perhaps more than the authors do, supervised training and experience in using the CDRS-R. The manual is dense and packed with considerable information, leading to some difficulties in understanding clearly what the authors are saying. This is especially noticeable in Chapter 5, Development and Standardization, and Chapter 6, Psychometric Properties, where reliability and validity data are presented in confusing ways. It would be helpful, for example, to have all the reliability information in one place followed by the validity information. As it is reliability information is provided in both chapters and validity information in Chapter 6 only, leading me to wonder if no validity studies were conducted on the original instrument at all. Some of the terms (e.g., Global Rating of Depression) are not well-defined so that the reader must search throughout the manual to determine what they mean. The interrater reliabilities especially are presented in confusing ways and it was not easy to determine what was being compared to what.

In summary, this appears to be a good instrument for an initial assessment of childhood depression. It should be used by a trained rater, however, and cannot be administered as easily as paper-and-pencil measures.

Review of the Children's Depression Rating Scale, Revised by DONALD LEE STOVALL, Assistant Professor of Counseling & School Psychology, University of Wisconsin—River Falls, River Falls, WI:

The Children's Depression Rating Scale, Revised (CDRS-R) is designed to help psychologists and mental health clinicians assess the level of depression in children from ages 6 through 12. The authors assert the instrument has been used as a screening instrument, diagnostic tool, or as a measure of severity of a child's depression. In clinical settings, the instrument can be used to confirm or document a diagnosis of depression. In nonclinical settings, such as a school psychologist's or physician's office, the CDRS-R can be used to screen for depression in children. A clinical psychologist, clinical social worker, or psychiatrist could refer children in nonclinical settings who obtain an elevated rating on the CDRS-R for a more extensive assessment. As stated by the authors, the CDRS-R is a "first step" in a clinical assessment of a child referred for evaluation. In addition to its use as a diagnostic tool in clinical settings, or as a screening tool in school settings, the CDRS-R also has applications as a research tool involving studies of depression in children. It can be used as a pre- or posttest measure regarding the effectiveness of interventions applied to children.

The CDRS-R assesses 17 symptoms of depression, including those found in the *Diagnostic and Statistical Manual of Mental Disorders* (DSM-IV; American Psychiatric Association, 1994). The symptoms assessed by the instrument include social withdrawal, sleep disturbance, excessive fatigue, and suicidal ideation, among others. The CDRS-R is completed as a semistructured interview with the child, or with the child's parent. The examiner evaluates the child on 14 symptoms, and three other ratings of the child are based upon observations of the child's nonverbal behavior during the interview.

Each symptom covered by the CDRS-R is presented on a continuum and rated on a scale from 1 to 5, or 1 to 7. The lowest score (1) is reserved for "no difficulties." The highest score (5 on 5-point scale, 6/7 on 7-point scale) is reserved for "severe clinically significant difficulties." The scale for Suicidal ideation, for example, begins with a rating of 1 indicating that the child has an understanding of the word suicide, but he or she does not apply that term to himself or herself. The scale for Suicidal Ideation ends with a rating of 7 if the child had made a suicide attempt within the last month, or is considered actively suicidal. Although the rating scale for each item may range from 1 to 5 or 1 to 7, not each scale point has an associated descriptor. The authors present "anchor points," which give the rater specific standards to score. The examiner may use points in between the "anchor points" if he or she is uncertain of the degree to which to rate a child's symptom.

In the manual for the CDRS-R, the authors provide a useful interview guide for conducting an interview with the child, or in conducting the interview with the parent of the child. These guides are contained in the Appendix and they include sample responses and information about how those sample responses would be rated. The protocol is structured to allow results from an interview with the child to be compared with those of the parent, or other person familiar with the child. Additionally, if multiple ratings have been obtained, the clinician can combine information from multiple ratings to develop a summary of the "Best Description of the Child."

The child's raw score on the CDRS-R is converted to a T-score. Interpretation is based upon the T-score range that contains the child's score. If a child obtains a T-score in the 65–74 range, the interpretation is that a depressive disorder "is likely to be confirmed" by a comprehensive diagnostic evaluation. A T-score range of 75–84 indicates that a depressive disorder diagnosis is "very likely" to be confirmed. A T-score of 85 or higher indicates that a depressive disorder diagnosis is "almost certain" to be confirmed. At a T-score level of 85 or higher, the recommendation is made to intervene and evaluate the needs of the child immediately. It is clear from the manual and from the descriptive statements associated with the T-scores that no diagnosis of depression or dysthymic disorder should ever be made based solely on the results of the CDRS-R. The CDRS-R would be one element in a comprehensive assessment of a child, particularly in cases where there are concerns about depression.

The CDRS-R offers a comprehensive set of descriptions of behaviors associated with a clinical diagnosis of depression. The authors present detailed definitions of symptoms of depression that increase the likelihood that users of the measure understand the items, and how symptoms should be rated. The use of "anchor points" provides a good foundation for those rating a child. Both the specificity of the definitions of the symptoms provided by the authors in the manual and the use of the "anchor points" are important elements with regards to the reliability of scores from the instrument, and the usefulness of the instrument as a research tool.

STANDARDIZATION. The CDRS-R norms were developed from a clinical and school sample. The standardization sample, however, is not nationally representative. The sample used is also not culturally diverse. These issues do present some cautions about the use of the instrument. The clinical sample, which involved 78 children, was drawn from children who were involved with the Youth Affective Disorders Clinic at the University of Illinois Medical Center, and the Rush-Presbyterian-St. Luke's Medical Center. These centers were located in Chicago, Illinois. The children in the clinical sample initially met the DSM-III criteria for a depressive disorder, and were followed at 6-week, 6-month, and one-year intervals. The authors reported that 77% of the clinical sample met the criteria for a Depressive Disorder Diagnosis and that 23% met the criteria for some other psychiatric diagnosis. The school sample involved a one-time assessment of 223 children from a magnet school in the Chicago public school system. These children were randomly selected for participation in the study. In addition to the children who were interviewed, 109 parent interviews were also conducted.

The authors do not provide a breakdown of the clinical sample based upon age. This information is provided for the school sample. The authors did not report an attempt to match the sample to a specific census based upon several commonly used demographic or racial factors. They report that both the clinical sample and the school sample fell into the categories of white, black, or mostly Hispanic. Children from Asian or Native-American heritage did not appear to be represented in the sample. Examiners who might work with a significant number of children whose heritage is Asian or Native American would need to be cautious about using the instrument. Certainly, use with more diverse populations is an area

of research with the CDRS-R. The age range of the CDRS-R spans children from age 6 through age 12. This also creates some caution about the standardization. Given the size of the clinical sample, and lack of a specific breakdown based upon age, certain age ranges may have small numbers of children who were involved in the standardization. Again, further research with specific age groups is suggested.

The authors reported various forms of reliability data. Based upon 25 interviews of children within the clinical sample, conducted by pairs of child psychiatrists, a product moment correlation of .92 was reported. Test-retest reliability estimate, based upon a 2-week post intake assessment, was reported at .80. Based upon these assessments of reliability, the CDRS-R appears to produce reliable scores. Reliability when assessing depression can be influenced by many factors, as depression can be a variable state. Some fluctuation in assessments of depression in children can be expected.

The authors reported various forms of validity data. Convergent validity evidence involved the comparison of the CDRS-R with other measures of depression. The authors report a comparison of the CDRS-R results with a Global Rating of Depression score. The Global Rating of Depression score represented clinical judgement assigned by clinicians regarding the severity of depression. The results of the CDRS-R were compared to this score, and a correlation of .87 was found. The summary score from the CDRS-R was also compared to the summary score from the Hamilton Rating Scale for Depression. This comparison yielded a correlation of .46, with $p<.01$. The authors also provide information in the manual indicating that the results from the CDRS-R were able to discriminate children diagnosed with depression from those with some other diagnosis or from children without a diagnosis.

SUMMARY. The CDRS-R is presented as a tool to assist in the diagnosis of depression in children ages 6–12. In nonclinical settings, it can be used as a tool to help professionals screen children for depression. In clinical settings, it can be used as a component in an overall assessment of a child's needs. It can be used as a baseline measure for depression, with the ability to compare data from multiple perspectives. The authors present a detailed manual that provides clear definitions of symptoms associated with depression, and samples of how items might be scored. The use of anchor points provides structure to ratings given by examiners. Information is included in the manual regarding the development and standardization of the instrument. The usefulness of the CDRS-R as a screening device for depression, or as a research tool, is supported. The weakness of the CDRS-R relates to a lack of a national standardization, and failure to include Asian or Native-American children in the clinical or norm sample.

REVIEWER'S REFERENCE

American Psychiatric Association. (1994). *Diagnostic and statistical manual of mental disorders* (4th ed.). Washington, DC: Author.

[13]
Children's Memory Scale.

Purpose: "Designed to evaluate learning and memory functioning" in children and adolescents.
Population: Ages 5–16.
Publication Dates: 1997–1998.
Acronym: CMS.
Scores, 27: 14 Core Battery Subtest Scores: Dot Locations (Learning, Total Score, Long Delay); Stories (Immediate, Delayed, Delayed Recognition); Faces (Immediate, Delayed); Word Pairs (Learning, Total Score, Long Delay, Delayed Recognition); Numbers (Total Score); Sequences (Total Score); 6 supplemental scores from Core subtests: Dot Locations (Short Delay), Stories (Immediate thematic, Delayed Thematic) Word Pairs (Immediate), Numbers (Forward, Backward); 6 supplemental scores from Supplemental subtests: Word Lists (Learning, Delayed, Delayed Recognition), Picture Locations (Total Score), Family Pictures (Immediate, Delayed); 8 Indexes: Visual Immediate, Visual Delayed, Verbal Immediate, Verbal Delayed, General Memory, Attention/Concentration, Learning, Delayed Recognition.
Administration: Individual.
Levels, 2: 5–8, 9–16.
Price Data, 1999: $345.50 per complete kit including manual ('97, 288 pages), 25 record forms for both age levels, 2 stimulus booklets, response grid, 8 chips in a pouch, and 5 family picture cards; $33.50 per record forms (specify level); $84 per manual ('97, 288 pages); $83 per computer Scoring Assistant (available for Windows or Macintosh).
Time: (20–50) minutes.
Author: Morris J. Cohen.
Publisher: The Psychological Corporation.

Review of the Children's Memory Scale by SCOTT A. NAPOLITANO, Adjunct Assistant Professor, Department of Educational Psychology, University of Nebraska-Lincoln, Lincoln, NE, and Pediatric Neuropsychologist, Lincoln Pediatric Group, Lincoln, NE:

The Children's Memory Scale (CMS) is an individually administered instrument developed to evaluate learning and memory in individuals ranging in age from 5 to 16. The complete CMS consists of nine subtests that assess functioning in three domains: (a) auditory/verbal, (b) visual/nonverbal, and (c) attention/concentration. Each domain includes two core subtests and one supplemental subtest. Each subtest in the auditory/verbal domain and the visual/nonverbal domain contains both an immediate memory component and a delayed memory component, with a delay of approximately 30 minutes between the two components. Different combinations of subtests are combined to yield eight index scores: Verbal Immediate, Verbal Delayed, Delayed Recognition, Learning, Visual Immediate, Visual Delayed, Attention/Concentration, and General Memory.

The CMS manual is well written and the test instructions are clearly explained and easy to understand. Comprehensive and easy-to-follow test instructions are also printed directly in the stimulus booklets, facilitating ease of administration. The core battery may be administered in approximately 30–35 minutes of actual test time, and the supplementary battery adds an additional 10–15 minutes of testing time. Each subtest in the auditory/verbal as well as the visual/nonverbal domains also includes a delay task that requires a 30-minute delay from the completion of the immediate memory tasks. The CMS has an optional scoring assistant that greatly simplifies scoring and includes many different report options from a simple summary of index scores to a complete report including background information, score comparisons, and graphs. One drawback to the current version of the scoring assistant is that case reports may not be saved for later review or printing.

The standardization sample for the CMS was stratified by age, sex, race/ethnicity, geographic region, and parent educational level. Census data (U.S. Bureau of the Census, 1995) was utilized for stratification of race/ethnicity, geographic region, and parent education level. The entire sample consisted of 1,000 children equally divided into 10 age groups: 5, 6, 7, 8, 9, 10, 11, 12, 13–14, and 15–16. The sample consisted of 500 males and 500 females, with 50 males and 50 females included in each age group. In terms of race/ethnicity, categories included were: White, African American, Hispanic, Native American,

Eskimo, Aleut, Asian American, Pacific Islander, and Other. In terms of geographic region, the following regions were specified: Northeast, North Central, South, and West. In terms of parent education, the following five categories were included: 8th grade or less, 9th through 12th grade, high school graduate or equivalent, 1 to 3 years of college or technical school, and 4 or more years of college. Overall, the sample closely matched the Census data; however, some case weighting was used to adjust the race/ethnicity and parent education level proportions to those in the Census data.

A unique feature of the CMS is that a subgroup of examinees, referred to as the "linking sample," was also administered either the Wechsler Intelligence Scale for Children—Third Edition (WISC-III) or the Wechsler Preschool and Primary Scale of Intelligence—Revised (WPPSI-R). The linking sample consisted of 300 children, 273 of whom were administered the WISC-III and 27 of whom were administered the WPPSI-R. This feature allows for exploration of relationships and discrepancies between memory and IQ.

Internal consistency was assessed for the majority of subtests using split-half reliabilities corrected by the Spearman-Brown formula. For six subtests, reliability coefficients were estimated using generalizability coefficients due to uniqueness of these subtests, item presentation formats, and inter-item dependency. Reliability coefficients are reported for all age groups across all subtests. Average reliability coefficients for the index scores ranged from .76 to .91. Again averaged across age groups, coefficients for the core battery of subtests ranged from .71 to .91, with an average value of .78. Likewise, average coefficients for the supplementary subtests ranged from .54 to .86, with an overall average value of .72.

Test-retest reliability coefficients were more variable. The mean test-retest interval was 59.6 days. Across all ages, test-retest reliability coefficients ranged from .26 to .88, with a mean value of .71. When these values were corrected for the variability of CMS scores on the first testing, the reliabilities ranged from .29 to .89, with a mean value of .71. Given the low test-retest reliabilities, stability of test scores was further examined by examining the consistency with which a subject was classified into one of the following categories: impaired, borderline to low average, and average to above average. For the index scores, decision

consistency coefficients range from .61 to .93 with a mean value of .78. A practice effect of up to one standard deviation for most scores was revealed, and the CMS manual warns that retesting an examinee within 6 to 8 weeks may result in large practice effects. Interrater reliability was assessed for a subsample of 112 subjects randomly chosen from the standardization sample. Using intraclass correlations, coefficients were obtained that range from .88 to 1.00, with a mean value of .99.

The CMS manual presents information regarding the content, construct, and criterion-related validity of the instrument. Evidence of content validity consists of a description of the test construction procedures. Evidence of construct validity includes subtest and index intercorrelations and results from confirmatory factor analysis. Results from the factor analysis appear to support a three-factor model consisting of Auditory/Verbal memory, Visual/Nonverbal Memory, and Attention/Concentration. To address criterion-related validity, the manual presents data from a series of studies comparing performance on the CMS to performance on measures of general cognitive ability, achievement and academic performance, executive functioning, language skills, and other measures of memory. Additionally, data concerning the CMS performance of children with neurological and neurodevelopmental disorders are also presented. Overall, adequate evidence for the validity of the CMS is presented, thus providing initial support for the use of the instrument. Given the newness of the instrument, further research regarding the validity of the CMS is needed.

SUMMARY. The CMS is an individually administered instrument that was developed to assess memory and learning in children ranging in age from 5 to 16. The CMS is well-designed and standardized, comprehensive, and very user friendly. Furthermore the tasks are engaging and child friendly. The psychometric properties of the CMS are generally quite acceptable, yet users should note that there tends to be a decrease in reliability coefficients for the individual subtests as compared to the index scores, and that the low test-retest reliabilities indicate that the CMS should not be given twice within a 6- to 8-week time frame. There is good evidence for the construct validity of the CMS as well as initial support for the convergent/divergent and discriminant validity of the test. Given these factors, the CMS is not only a welcomed addition to currently available memory assessment tools for children, it is poised to become the instrument of choice for assessing memory and learning in children.

Review of the Children's Memory Scale by MARGOT B. STEIN, Clinical Assistant Professor of Psychiatry, UNC School of Medicine, Director of Training, Center for the Study of Development and Learning, University of North Carolina at Chapel Hill, Chapel Hill, NC:

The Children's Memory Scale (CMS) "was developed to provide school psychologists, child neuropsychologists, and clinical psychologists with a standardized instrument that evaluates the important processes involved in learning and memory" (manual, p. 1). It was designed to help professionals not only to evaluate memory functions of children with neurodevelopmental disabilities such as attention deficit/hyperactivity disorder, speech/language impairment, and learning disabilities, or various neurological disorders such as epilepsy, traumatic brain injury, and brain tumors, but also to formulate treatment recommendations for them.

The battery consists of nine subtests that assess functioning in each of three domains: (a) auditory/verbal learning and memory (verbal), (b) visual/nonverbal learning and memory (visual), and (c) attention/concentration. Each domain is assessed through two core subtests and one supplemental subtest. Core subtests include: Stories, Word Pairs, Dot Locations, Faces, Numbers, and Sequences. Supplemental subtests consist of Word Lists, Family Pictures, and Picture Locations. The core subtest battery can be administered in about 30–35 minutes, according to the manual; the supplemental battery takes an additional 10–15 minutes to administer. There is approximately a 30-minute delay between the immediate memory and the delayed memory portion of each subtest. For each subtest, normative scores are provided for evaluating specific abilities. The index scores associated with each domain reflect various aspects of learning and memory functioning such as short-term memory, delayed memory, learning, and attention/concentration. The General Memory Index represents global memory functioning.

The CMS is intended to be consistent with current theoretical models of memory and learning and with research findings from the neuropsy-

chological assessment of patients with disorders of memory and learning. It also is intended to account for the developmental changes that are expected to occur between ages 5 through 16 and to evaluate the relationship between memory and intelligence. Finally, it is intended to be able to evaluate questions regarding a child's learning style and ability to remember as well as to be "child friendly" (e.g., interesting and motivating) within the constraints of a typical standardized testing situation. As such, the CMS has both clinical and research applications.

In terms of administration and materials, the complete CMS kit includes the administration and scoring manual, test materials, and scoring protocols. There are two different protocols for children of ages 5 to 8 and children of ages 9 to 16. The administration and scoring procedures are clear and easy to follow, but a period of practice contributes significantly to efficiency in both areas. A carrying case is provided and is necessary to carry the test materials conveniently. These materials are well designed, colorful, and sensitive to current issues of gender and culture, holding the interest of the examinees.

The CMS manual contains a great deal of detail about the representativeness of the normal sample. The CMS was normed and standardized based on a sample of 1,000 "normal" children in 10 age groups ranging from age 5 to age 16. These age groups were 5, 6, 7, 8, 9, 10, 11, 12, 13–14, and 15–16, and each age group consisted of 100 children. The sample included 500 females and 500 males from both private and public school settings, with an equal number of both sexes in each of the 10 age groups. In terms of race/ethnicity, the proportion of Whites, African-Americans, Hispanics, and other race/ethnic groups was based on the race/ethnic group proportions of U.S. children ages 5 through 16, based on the 1995 Census. In terms of geographical distribution, children were chosen for the standardized sample in accordance with the proportion of children living in each of four regions of the United States (e.g., Northeast, North Central, South, and West). Specific exclusion criteria for the normal sample included reading below grade level, having repeated a grade, a previous diagnosis of a neurological disorder, referral or receipt of any type of special education or Chapter I remedial services, or previous injury placing one at risk for memory impairment. In addition, in order to assess the clinical sensitivity/utility of CMS data, the CMS was administered to various clinical groups with different neurodevelopmental and neurological disabilities and to a normal control group matched for age, race, sex, and parent education level.

The administration manual also contains an impressive amount of detail on the psychometric properties of the CMS. Reliability coefficients (split-half corrected using Spearman-Brown) are provided for each of the nine subtests for each age, and range from .70 to .94. Scores generally remain relatively stable as children grow older, with the exception of the Long Delay task for Word Pairs and the Verbal Delayed Index score. Indeed, reliability coefficients of the Index scores are greater than the individual subtests making up the index. Test-retest stability coefficients (59.6 mean interval) for CMS Index scores are generally adequate for each of three age bands (5–8, 9–12, 13–16), with the notable exception of Visual Immediate and Visual Delayed Indexes. Information also is included concerning the standard error of measurement for each subtest and index score for each age group.

The manual also includes correlations between scores on the CMS and other standardized measures of general cognitive ability, such as the Wechsler Intelligence Scale for Children—Third Edition (WISC-III), Wechsler Preschool and Primary Scale of Intelligence—Revised (WPPSI-R), Differential Abilities Scale (DAS), and the Otis-Lennon School Ability Test, Sixth Edition (OLSAT-6). These data suggest that the CMS General Memory Index shows a consistent, moderate, positive correlation with general, verbal, and nonverbal intellectual abilities regardless of the instrument used to measure IQ. The Attention/Concentration Index correlates highly with other measures of complex attention, and moderately with most measures of cognitive ability. Correlations of the CMS with measures of academic achievement such as the Wechsler Individual Achievement Test (WIAT), again show a moderate, positive relationship between most CMS measure and measures of academic achievement. The strongest relationship was displayed between the Attention/Concentration Index and total academic achievement. In addition, the manual also presents correlations between the CMS and measures of executive functioning such as the Wisconsin Card Sorting Test (1993) and the Children's

Category Test (1993), with measures of language functioning such as the Clinical Evaluation of Language Fundamentals—Third Edition (1995), and with other measures of memory functioning such as the Wechsler Memory Scale—Third Edition (1997), the Wide Range Assessment of Memory and Learning (1990), and the California Verbal Learning Test—Children's Version (1994).

The CMS joins two other well-established memory scales: the Wechsler Memory Scale—III (WMS-III; T5:2863); and the Wide Range Assessment of Memory and Learning (WRAML; T5:2880). Though the WMS-III is primarily used with adults, like the WRAML, it has norms for adolescents age 16–17. Correlations between the WRAML and CMS indexes are low to high, with the highest correlation between indexes measuring the same subdomain. The WRAML does not have an attention index, although there is a high correlation between the CMS Attention/Concentration Index and three out of four WRAML indexes, which suggests that attention plays an important role in children's performance on that test as well.

To assess the clinical utility of the CMS, data were collected on small clinical groups with various neurological and neurodevelopmental disabilities including children with Temporal Lobe Epilepsy and Traumatic Brain injury, and children with brain tumors, learning disabilities, Attention Deficit/Hyperactivity Disorder, and specific language impairment. Clinical sensitivity of the CMS in detecting mild to moderate memory problems in children with neurodevelopmental disabilities was noted. However, the CMS should have greater sensitivity to learning and memory dysfunction in children with neurological disorders.

SUMMARY. The CMS represents a very valuable contribution to the assessment of children's memory and learning. It is conceptually well grounded in current research, elegantly laid out, and relatively easy to administer and score. To be sure, it has some limitations. In the reviewer's experience, the CMS takes 15 to 30 minutes longer to administer than does the WRAML. Delayed recall procedures on both tests occur no more than 30 minutes after the initial presentation, limiting the assessment of long-term memory accordingly. In addition, it should be noted that a CMS administration with elementary-age children with psychiatric and/or more severe neuropsychological problems can take considerably longer than the estimated administration time. This may compromise the proper administration of delayed tasks. The CMS also makes no attempt to formally evaluate procedural memory. However, its strengths are notable in terms of its conceptual integration of Baddeley and Hitch's "working memory" models (1986, 1994) and other research on the neuroanatomy of memory, its comprehensive approach to memory assessment, and its potential for increasing our understanding and remediation of children's learning problems.

REVIEWER'S REFERENCES

Baddeley, A. (1986). *Working memory*. Oxford, England: Clarendon Press.
Baddeley, A. D., & Hitch, G. J. (1994). Development in the concept of working memory. *Neuropsychology, 8*, 485–493.

[14]

Clinical Observations of Motor and Postural Skills.

Purpose: Designed to assist occupational therapists in performing assessments of children with suspected developmental and coordination disorders.
Population: Ages 5–9.
Publication Date: 1994.
Acronym: COMPS.
Scores: 6 items: Slow Movements, Finger-Nose Touching, Rapid Forearm Rotation, Prone Extension Posture, Asymmetrical Tonic Neck Reflex, Supine Flexion Posture.
Administration: Individual.
Price Data: Not available.
Time: (15–20) minutes.
Comments: Ratings by therapist.
Authors: Brenda N. Wilson, Nancy Pollock, Bonnie J. Kaplan, and Mary Law.
Publisher: The Psychological Corporation.
[Note: The publisher advised in December 1998 that this test is now out of print.]

Review of the Clinical Observations of Motor and Postural Skills by GLEN P. AYLWARD, Professor of Pediatrics, Psychiatry and Behavioral and Social Sciences, Southern Illinois University School of Medicine, Springfield, IL:

The Clinical Observations of Motor and Postural Skills (COMPS) is a screening tool designed to identify subtle, developmental motor coordination problems or "dyspraxias" (manual, p. 2) in children. The test is reported to take 15 to 20 minutes to administer, and is recommended as a general screening tool in situations such as kindergarten motor screening. The COMPS is geared for use by occupational therapists and is not recommended to be given to children with significant motor or cognitive impairments. The COMPS is a descriptive, versus evaluative, tool and basically is a revision and elaboration of clinical observation protocols from Ayres (1976) and others. Therefore, no diagnosis, per se, is derived. The authors of the COMPS have essentially standardized administration and made scoring procedures more objective than was the case with previous clinical observations. Because most of the indicators are "mature" by age 7 to 8 years, the COMPS is applicable for children in the 5- to 9-year age range. The test can be given to older children, and in such applications a positive finding would be of clinical utility (indicating dysfunction); however, a negative finding would not be as clinically meaningful.

The COMPS consists of six indicators. These are: (a) Slow Movements measuring the child's ability to move the upper extremities slowly and symmetrically. This indicator is considered to measure cerebellar function over a 6-second time span, with symmetry, quality of performance, and speed each being scored on a 3-point scale. (b) Rapid Forearm Rotation assessing the number of forearm rotations accurately completed within 10-seconds. Diadochokinesis (cerebellar-vestibular integrity), assessed in this manner, matures at age 7–8 years. (c) Finger-Nose Touching requires the child to touch the nose and then the finger of the other hand that is extended as far as possible from the face. The task is performed both with eyes open and closed. This maneuver is thought to reflect cerebellar coordination and also matures by age 7 years. (d) Prone Extension Posture measures the child's ability to assume and maintain an arched-back position against gravity with arms and legs extended in a sort of "superman" or "supergirl" flying posture. It involves vestibular-proprioceptive function. (e) Asymmetrical Tonic Neck Reflex (ATNR) measures the presence of the asymmetrical tonic neck reflex in the quadruped position. This item requires the attachment of a plastic measuring tool to the child's arms in order to measure elbow flexion. (f) Supine Flexion Posture assesses the child's ability to assume and maintain a flexed posture in the supine position, with the child bringing knees to the chest and crunching up in a "ball." Duration and measurement of six flexion components is involved.

COMPS materials include a manual, four-page scoring forms, two plastic measuring devices with velcro fasteners (with lines to facilitate measuring elbow angles), and a carrying case. A stopwatch, mat, and two chairs are necessary, and this reviewer suggests use of a calculator as well. The authors recommend that the sequence of item presentation remain as outlined, this being underscored for the last three items in particular because of the facilitation effects of stretch and flexor activities.

The authors emphasize that one of the strengths of the COMPS lies in its objective scoring. However, the scoring is somewhat complex and time-consuming for a screening test. Scores are summed and then compared to one of three weighted score tables that are based on age (5 years 0 months to 5 years 11 months, 6 years 0 months to 7 years 11 months, and 8 years 0 months to 9 years 11 months). Converted scores range from -2.16 to 7.92, depending on task and age of the child. The six weighted scores are then totaled, an "adjustment" is subtracted (7.61, 8.54, or 9.80, depending on age), and a weighted total score is derived. A weighted total score less than zero is considered indicative of problems in postural and motor skills, and scores greater than zero are indicative of normal functioning. Interpretation of a score of exactly zero is not specified.

The normative sample consisted of 123 children, 67 who displayed developmental coordination disorders (DCD), and 56 children with no known motor problems. Diagnostic criteria warranting the diagnosis of DCD, ages of the children, gender, and other demographic information are not contained in the manual. Instead, the prospective test user is referred to an article by Wilson, Pollock, Kaplan, Law, and Farris (1992) for more detailed information on test development. It would seem that this information should be provided in the manual, as a substantial number of test users might not necessarily attempt to seek out the reference. Moreover, the high base rate of purported coordination/motor problems would affect statistical descriptors such as sensitivity.

Test-retest reliability over a 2-week time span in the total sample (r = 48) was estimated to be .93; it was .87 in the DCD group (n = 20) and .76 in the non-DCD group (n = 28). Interrater reliability was measured using four individuals: two with experience in pediatrics, one with no experience in pediatrics, and one occupational

therapy student. Sample sizes used for comparisons ranged from 30 to 72, and reported intraclass correlation coefficients ranged from .57 to .90. The highest correlations were found between the two "pediatrics experienced" examiners. In general, test-retest reliability needs to be more rigorously examined.

Internal consistency reliability, using Cronbach's alpha coefficient, was estimated to be .77 for the total test. Correlations between the individual items and total test score ranged from .33 (ATNR) to .53 (finger-nose touching).

Construct validity was measured via use of MANOVAs, with age as a covariate (MANCOVA). DCD and non-DCD children (n = 64) were compared on total COMPS scores (not weighted total scores) and were found to differ significantly. Additional comparisons, not covarying for age, revealed significant between-group differences as well (ns = 22, 22, and 20, for each of the three age groups). Discriminant analyses (DCD and non-DCD group membership as grouping variable) produced a reported 73% correct classification rate. Weights derived from this procedure were employed in the aforementioned three age-specific weighted score conversion tables in the manual, which are used in the computation of the final weighted total score. The previously mentioned adjustment score is an intercept that is subtracted to denote the cutoff score of zero, which is the same for all ages.

The authors also report sensitivity and specificity values for a sample of 64 children (ages not specified). Reported sensitivity ranged from 82% to 100%; specificity from 63% to 90%. However, given the vagueness of the reference diagnosis, the high base rate of "dysfunction," and the lack of specific numbers in the comparisons, these terms may not be appropriate. Co-positivity and co-negativity may be more applicable.

Concurrent validity involving score comparisons between the COMPS weighted total score and the Test of Visual Motor Integration, Standing Balance-Eyes Open and Closed tests, the Motor Accuracy Test—Revised, and the Bruininks-Oseretsky Test of Motor Proficiency produced correlations ranging from .18 to .48 (ns ranging from 27 to 64). Correlations between the six COMPS subtest scores and these concurrent measures ranged from .07 to .65. The authors also describe at length a comparison between eight children with motor and sensory integration problems who also had been given the COMPS and the Sensory Integration and Praxis Tests (SIPT; Ayres, 1989). Given the small sample size, this discussion is of limited utility and is rather speculative.

SUMMARY. In summary, the main strength of the COMPS is found in the emphasis on refinement of administration and scoring of clinical observations of motor coordination items, frequently used to assess neurologic "soft signs." Administration directions are well presented and clear. Moreover, in addition to occupational therapists, the test can be useful for other professionals such as early developmental neuropsychologists (Aylward, 1997). That being said, drawbacks include a small sample size (with inadequate description in the manual), a high base rate for motor problems in the original sample, a relatively lengthy administration time and labor-intensive scoring (if the test is to be used as a screen), and the need for additional research as to the "diagnostic utility" of the COMPS.

REVIEWER'S REFERENCES

Ayres, A. J. (1976). *Interpreting the Southern California sensory integration tests.* Los Angeles: Western Psychological Services.
Ayres, A. J. (1989). *Sensory integration and praxis tests.* Los Angeles: Western Psychological Services.
Wilson, B., Pollack, N., Kaplan, B. J., Law, M., & Faris, P. (1992). Reliability and construct validity of the Clinical Observations of Motor and Postural Skills. *The American Journal of Occupational Therapy, 9,* 775–783.
Aylward, G. P. (1997). *Infant and early childhood neuropsychology.* New York: Plenum.

Review of the Clinical Observations of Motor and Postural Skills by WILLIAM R. MERZ, SR., Professor-School Psychology Training Program, California State University, Sacramento, CA:

The Clinical Observation of Motor and Postural Skills (COMPS) is designed to assist occupational therapists in performing valid and reliable assessments of suspected developmental coordination disorders in children ages 5 to 9. It is a revision of and elaboration on clinical observations used by pediatric occupational therapists. Standardizing tasks and developing objective scoring criteria were the primary goals for developing the COMPS. The COMPS is a screening tool rather than an evaluative instrument for assessing change over time. Although screening for the presence or absence of motor problems that have a postural component is the instrument's primary function, it also accurately identifies from 73% to 95% of children in the norm group with motor problems that have a postural component. The

COMPS is made up of six tasks: Slow Movements: the ability to move slowly and symmetrically—a reflection of cerebellar function; Rapid Forearm Rotation: the number of forearm rotations accurately completed within 10 seconds—a test of cerebellar-vestibular integrity; Finger-Nose Touching: the ability to touch index finger to nose and then touch finger to the extended index finger of the other hand—a measure of cerebellar coordination; Prone Extension Posture: the ability to assume and maintain an arched back position against gravity—a task related to vestibular-proprioceptive processing dysfunction; Asymmetrical Tonic Neck Reflex: the degree of inhibition of the Asymmetrical Tonic Neck Reflex—a measure of postural stability; and Supine Flexion Posture: the ability to assume and maintain a flexed posture in the supine position over time—a task associated with somato-dyspraxia.

It takes 15 to 20 minutes to administer the COMPS as a general screening device for motor problems in children 5 to 9 years old. The authors warn against using it with children younger than 5 years. They urge cautious use with children older than 9 years when a child has motor difficulties but, then, only as an indication that the child has motor difficulties. They also recommend against using it with children who have known neurological or neuromotor problems or with children who manifest general intellectual delays. As a screening tool it gives a global picture of a child's functional performance. The authors do not presently recommend it as a measure of change over time. Occupational therapists and physical therapists with some experience in assessing children can use this set of observations. Although students and therapists without pediatric experience can use the COMPS, the authors suggest that examiners have at least 1 to 2 years of experience in testing children.

This set of observations uses a 3- or 4-point scale based on qualitative descriptions of behaviors to derive scores; the values are presumed to be on an equal interval scale. The order of administration proceeds from easier, briefer tasks and progresses to more complex tasks. Raw scores are converted weighted scores for each of three age groups (5-0 to 5-11, 6-0 to 7-11, and 8-0 to 9-11). These weighted scores are summed across tasks and an adjustment number is subtracted to yield a weighted total score. Scores less than zero indicate problems in Postural and Motor Skills; scores greater than zero indicate normal function. The authors suggest in the section of the manual on interpretation that the assessor examine each of the subtest results to look for tasks that may be more difficult for the child. They also state that performance may be used to aid in treatment planning with children who already have identified problems. They maintain that the six tasks tap different areas of neuromotor function but caution that they are not totally discrete. Therefore, they suggest that the COMPS be interpreted primarily as a cluster of skills in light of presenting functional problems.

The test was developed, standardized, and normed in Canada on a small sample of children in the Province of Alberta. Although the authors do not report the actual sample size of the norm group, the numbers in the reliability and validity studies range from 20 to 119; that number gives an idea of how small the norm group may be. The authors report estimates of test-retest (within a 2-week period) reliabilities of .76 for their nondisabled sample, .87 for their disabled sample, and .93 for the entire sample. Interrater reliabilities are wider ranging and a good deal lower for the disabled group: .57 to .76; they are .81 to .90 in the nondisabled group. Internal consistency reliabilities computed as correlations between item and total test score range from .33 to .53 and from .46 to .54 when computed as Cronbach's alpha with the item score deleted. These coefficients urge caution in generalizing behavior based on these observations to typical behaviors.

Construct evidence of validity is presented by analyzing scores of 64 children with MANOVA and Discriminant Function Analysis. Using age as a covariate, mean differences on total test scores between the disabled and nondisabled were statistically significant. Means between the disabled and nondisabled children for the different age groups without covariation were statistically significant for all age groups. Discriminant functions were statistically significant for each of the six tasks and indicated that the scores detect dysfunction correctly 73% of the time across age groups. The authors report concurrent evidence of validity by correlating COMPS nonweighted scores with measures collected during the same period. Correlations for nonweighted item scores with the other tasks range from .07 to .65; correlations for weighted total scores with the other measures range from .18 to .48. One can infer content evidence of validity from the authors' drawing tasks reported in the current literature on motor skills and tasks commonly used by pediatric therapists.

SUMMARY. The COMPS is a test with a narrow purpose designed for professionally trained pediatric occupational and physical therapists to use for screening 5- to 9-year-olds for motor problems. Trials with small samples demonstrate that the COMPS discriminates fairly well between children who have motor problems and those who do not. The evidence about reliability and validity needs further exploration because, at first glance, the magnitudes of correlations do not seem impressive. Examples are the magnitude of the reliability coefficients among tasks taken by the disabled group and item correlations with criterion measures used to present evidence of validity. Because the disabled group is smaller, has a more restricted range of scores, and more than likely has less variability than the nondisabled group, the magnitudes of correlation coefficients are attenuated. With item-total score correlations, restriction in range would attenuate correlation magnitudes. Discussion of these issues would better describe how the instrument functions in achieving its screening purpose.

There is great need for instruments that assess motor skills in the 5- to 9-year-old population. Psychologists use fairly gross measures; more specialized measures used by people trained specifically in the motor function of children would help identify children who need accommodation. It would help delineate the nature and specifics of that accommodation. In that regard, the COMPS has much to recommend. It does, however, need more work with larger sample sizes taken from a more geographically diverse population. Working with the COMPS in American public schools would provide valuable information on an extremely diverse population of children. Assessment of motor skills in the United States would benefit from standardized, norm-referenced instruments that identify children with need and evaluate progress with training. Instruments that allow assessment of progress during training would be very helpful, as well. Standardized, norm-referenced assessment tools for children age 10 or older would be extremely helpful.

The COMPS must be used cautiously by trained professionals who recognize that generalization is restricted by the norm group and standardization sample. It is a valuable step in the right direction.

[15]

The Clock Test.

Purpose: "Developed as a screening tool for the assessment of dementia in the elderly."
Population: Ages 65 and older.
Publication Date: 1995.
Scores, 3: Clock Reading, Clock Drawing, Clock Setting.
Administration: Individual.
Price Data, 1999: $160 per test kit including 25 QuikScore™ forms, 25 profile sheets, administration test, and manual (85 pages); $60 per 25 QuikScore™ forms; $10 per 25 profile sheets; $60 per administration tent; $40 per manual.
Time: [15–30] minutes.
Authors: H. Tuokko, T. Hadjistavropoulos, J. A. Miller, A. Horton, and B. L. Beattie.
Publisher: Multi-Health Systems, Inc.

Review of The Clock Test by HOWARD A. LLOYD, Neuropsychologist, Hawaii State Hospital, Kaneohe, HI:

The Clock Test was designed as a screening tool for assessment of cognitive impairment in the elderly. The authors have attempted to standardize the administration and scoring of traditional clock drawing tasks while adding components to measure clock setting and clock reading abilities. The manual provides a thorough and detailed explanation of the uses of the Clock Drawing Test, as well as a historical review of similar techniques. This serves to educate the user of this test about the conceptual foundations upon which The Clock Test is based. To their credit, the authors clearly state the limitations of this measure and caution against the use of The Clock Test as the sole diagnostic measure of cognitive impairment. User qualifications are also clearly delineated in the manual.

The Clock Test comprises three separate tasks. Clock Drawing requires subjects to place numbers on a predrawn clock face and set the hands of the clock to a specified time (10 after 11). Clock Setting requires the subject to set the hands on five predrawn clocks with the number omitted, to five different times (1 o'clock, 10 after 11, 3 o'clock, 9:15, and 7:30). Clock reading requires subjects to read the time set on five predrawn clocks (numbers omitted) with the hands set at the same times used in the clock setting task. Scoring of the Clock Drawing and Clock Setting conditions is facilitated by a standard scoring form on which the stimuli are printed. Carbon paper is used to transfer the subject's drawings onto this form. The one flaw to this system is that the carbon paper must be placed properly for the form to work as it was designed. There is no instruction in the manual about this and the forms received by this reviewer for review required that the carbon paper be reversed in order to work. This is a minor flaw but one that may result in some initial administration errors due to failure to have the subject's drawings transferred to the scoring form. Otherwise, the scoring form serves its purpose of facilitating ease of scoring this test in a standardized manner. The manual provides detailed scoring instructions and examples.

The Clock Test was normed on a sample of 1,753 normal elderly subjects ranging in age from 65 to 100. A clinical sample of 269 subjects over the age of 65 who had been diagnosed with dementia was also included. An additional sample of 64 community dwelling older adults aged 50 and above was used for cross-validation purposes. This normative sample appears appropriate to the purpose of this test and is of sufficient size to allow for reasonable standardization. The psychometric properties of The Clock Test are well within acceptable ranges.

Interrater reliability for the scoring procedures ranged from .90 to .99, which is quite high. This high interrater reliability is particularly important given the nature of The Clock Test as a screening tool for cognitive impairment. Test-retest reliability (time interval specified as "within days") was assessed for the Clock Drawing Test using a subsample of the clinical group. Retesting resulted in a test-retest reliability coefficient of .70. This is actually rather low, particularly for such a short retest interval. Although the test-retest reliability of such a measure may be less important than interrater reliability, it is also unfortunate that the authors did not conduct a similar examination of the stability of scores on The Clock Test for a subsample of their normal group. This would have been a more appropriate measure of the test-retest reliability of The Clock Test.

The validity of The Clock Test was investigated using multiple approaches including measures of sensitivity and specificity, and convergent and discriminant validity. The authors clearly put considerable effort into analyzing the validity of scores from The Clock Test. Detailed information is provided in the manual that strongly supports the validity of scores from this test. Sensitivity indices ranged from 80% to 93% and specificity indices ranged from 82% to 94%. The Clock Test correlates well with a variety of traditional neuropsychological measures. The authors have done a good job establishing strong evidence of the validity of scores from The Clock Test using a variety of appropriate approaches to validity estimation.

SUMMARY. In summary, The Clock Test has been well designed and has strong normative and psychometric properties. One minor design flaw was noted in an otherwise admirable attempt to facilitate standard scoring of The Clock Test. This measure is likely to be useful to generalist psychologists as well as specialists in neuropsychology. The authors should be commended for standardizing a frequently used, but heretofore often qualitatively interpreted, screening task.

Review of The Clock Test by ANTHONY M. PAOLO, Coordinator of Assessment and Evaluation, University of Kansas Medical Center, Kansas City, KS:

The Clock Test was designed as a brief screening test for dementia in the elderly. It measures visuo-spatial construction, visual perception, and abstract conceptualization. The test consists of three subtests: Clock Drawing, Clock Setting, and Clock Reading. The interrelation for normal persons among the three subtests ranges from -.26 for Clock Drawing and Reading to .38 for Clock Reading and Setting. These relatively small relationships are to be expected because the tasks are different, but all of them tap some component of cognitive functioning. The correlations increase in magnitude for persons with dementia ranging from -.51 to .71. The higher correlations likely reflect increased variability of performance in persons with brain dysfunction.

To obtain a total score, the user counts different types of errors that the patient makes. There are seven error types and at least three subcategories under each error type. Interrater reliability for raters scoring the clock test was very good and ranged from .73–1.00 for Clock Drawing, .95 to .98 for Clock Setting, and .99 for Clock

Reading. Test-retest stability over a 4-day period for 32 persons with suspected dementia was .70 for Clock Drawing. Although the magnitude of this coefficient is adequate, the 4-day test-retest interval is not one typically used in clinical settings. The stability of the Clock Setting and Clock Reading subtests is not provided. In addition, standard errors should be provided to allow users to be able to compute when changes in Clock Drawing scores reflect real change, rather than measurement error.

The Clock Test demonstrates adequate convergent and divergent validity evidenced by moderate correlations of -.27 to .77 with other measures of cognitive abilities (i.e., selected subtests from the Wechsler Adult Intelligence Scale—Revised, verbal fluency, and Buschke Selective Reminding Test) and lower correlations (.05 to -.19) with measures of mood (i.e., selected subtests from the Multifocal Assessment Scale). Additional evidence of validity comes from The Clock Test's ability to distinguish normal elderly persons from those with suspected dementia. In general, the sensitivity and specificity estimates are good and range from 80% to 94%. The manual notes that distinguishing between normal and demented elderly is better for the young-old group (i.e., ages 65 to 70) rather than the older groups (i.e., persons older than 70 years). This suggests that The Clock Test may be best suited as a screening tool for the young-old rather than the old-old.

Age-dependent cutoff scores are provided for a large ($N = 1,753$) healthy elderly sample. This sample was 58% female and ranged in age from 65 to 100 years (Median = 75 years). The median education level was 11 years. No information is provided concerning how representative this sample is of elderly persons. If the sample is not representative, but merely a sample of convenience, then the results presented in the manual may not generalize well to other elderly persons. The manual does refer users to an article published in the *Canadian Medical Association Journal* that may provide users with a more detailed description of the standardization sample. It is this reviewer's opinion that test authors and publishers should provide all relevant information in the test manual. Finally, the normative information provided is only for total scores. No information on the prevalence of the different error types among normal or demented elderly is provided. This is unfortunate because the presence of certain clock errors (i.e., stimulus boundness) have a long clinical heritage. Providing hard numbers to such a clinical heritage would be extremely helpful for clinicians.

The use of clock drawing as a screening device for cognitive impairment has a long history. This version of The Clock Test provides a large norm sample and good standardized administration and scoring procedures. The reported reliability and validity values for scores from The Clock Test are adequate for a screening device. Providing sensitivity and specificity information is essential for a screening device and the authors are commended for presenting this data. The lack of a clinically relevant retest interval and standard errors makes any change in scores on retesting difficult to interpret. Knowing how representative the standardization sample is would also be helpful. Overall, The Clock Test is a good choice for persons needing a well-standardized version of a screening device that has a long and rich history in neurology and neuropsychology.

[16]
Closed Head Injury Screener.

Purpose: "Designed to help medical doctors and psychologists assess whether patient symptoms are suggestive of closed-head injuries."
Population: English-speaking adults.
Publication Date: 1994.
Acronym: CHIS.
Scores: 3 ratings: Medical Facts, Presenting Complaints, Response Validity.
Administration: Individual.
Price Data, 1998: $25 per sampler set including manual (20 pages), questionnaire/answer sheet, and scoring directions; $100 per permission set including sampler set plus permission to reproduce up to 200 copies of the instrument.
Time: Approximately 30 minutes.
Comments: To be used as a supplement to a full face-to-face patient interview; partial paper and pencil/partial oral interview; results interpreted by administrator; not to be used with patients with cognitive deficits that are explainable by a previous diagnosis.
Author: Michael Ivan Friedman.
Publisher: Mind Garden, Inc.

Review of the Closed Head Injury Screener by THOMAS J. CULLEN, JR., Clinical Psychologist, Cullen Psychological Services, P.C., Fairless Hills, PA:

The author makes a clear statement regarding the appropriate uses of the Closed Head Injury Screener. He notes that clinicians are often faced with situations where they must make decisions regarding the necessity of referring patients for neuropsychological evaluation. He also notes that in many cases symptoms may be biased as a function of situations involving legal actions. Therefore, the test is designed to aid the clinician in screening for the consequences of a closed-head injury while at the same time helping the clinician to be alert to the possibility of bias in a patient's responding.

He cites the case that the conceptual status of post-concussion syndrome as a diagnostic entity has been controversial and has changed over the years. He presents a definition of the syndrome as encompassing a variety of emotional symptoms and motivational and cognitive deficits that make their appearance shortly after the patient has been involved in a concussive event of some sort. He goes on to note that the cognitive deficits typically involve the areas of attention, memory, and reasoning. The motivational deficits are noted to include sleep disruption and poor general vitality as well as disinterest in appetitive, recreational, and social behavior. The emotional symptoms include both dysphoria and irritability. He states that the most commonly encountered concussive event is the motor vehicle accident with additional significant contributions from both assault and sports.

He goes on to present studies by a number of authors showing the effects of concussive events including those involving no contact with the head and only very brief unconsciousness. The studies found disruptive effects in skill and a characteristic distribution of microscopic lesions. From these studies, it has been concluded that concussions are acceleration-deceleration injuries. As such, the author notes that there is a high incidence of events that may produce such acceleration-deceleration injuries. Indeed, today's clinician may be faced with any number of situations where neuropsychological examination appears appropriate. It is noted that neurobehavioral consequences of closed-head injuries, especially in milder forms, are often quite subtle and are often ascribed to an emotional response to physical trauma. At the same time, the clinician must be aware of the possibility of biased responding by individuals simply seeking compensations for damages. The Closed Head Injury Screener therefore provides a structure for an interview that elicits symptoms of post-concussion syndrome and provides guidelines for the interpretations of the obtained results. It also enables the clinician to be aware of biased responding before proceeding with a lengthy testing process.

The author notes that for the most part the Screener is administered in a question-and-answer format over a period of about one-half hour. (There is also a Questionnaire Format that is intended as an adjunct to the full interview and that may allow a considerable saving of time in the case of patients who are capable of responding "to" and responding "in" written form.) There are four sections to the full interview instrument. The first elicits medical facts associated with the events of the trauma. The second prompts the report of any neurobehavioral symptoms that appear to be consequentially related to the initial trauma. The last two sections provide an indication of the validity of the patient's responses to the interview.

The manual is clear and presents the administration procedures in a straightforward manner. The instrument reporting procedures are also elucidated. It is noted that certain evidence documenting compromised cortical functions, the existence of a concussive event, and a certain score on the Learning and Recall sections must be present before suggesting there is evidence of a closed-head injury. Nevertheless, the author makes it clear that because the instrument is a screener, it cannot provide the basis for a diagnosis of a closed-head injury. Its stated purpose is to assist the clinician in judging whether a full neuropsychological evaluation is appropriate in a particular case. It is important to note that no reliability data are presented. And no predictive validity data are presented. The content validity is such that the Screener closely mimics the areas of impairment noted in the stated definition of post-concussion syndrome. The instrument is not biased with regard to any demographic characteristics except for English-language proficiency.

SUMMARY. Overall, the Closed Head Injury Screener provides a useful tool in the battery of tests available to psychologists working with possible closed-head injury patients. It taps a number of areas typically measured by a variety of other tests. In this sense it provides a relatively quick measure of possible neuropsychological impairment. It also provides an important measure of a patient's motivational integrity. However, it should be noted that it does not measure every possible area and misses some of the major cognitive functional areas tapped by other specialized tests. A variety of functional areas have been identified as being important in a neuropsychological screening instrument. These areas include lateral dominance; motor functioning; auditory, tactile, and visual sensation; spatial-perceptual organization; language skills; general information; and memory processes. The Closed Head Injury screener does not measure lateral dominance, motor functioning, tactile sensation, spatial-perceptual organization, language skills, general information, or specific memory processes beyond self-reported global memory difficulties. It does, however, detail the elements of post-concussion syndrome quite well.

Review of the Closed Head Injury Screener by SCOTT A. NAPOLITANO, Adjunct Assistant Professor, Department of Educational Psychology, University of Nebraska–Lincoln, Lincoln, NE, and Pediatric Neuropsychologist, Lincoln Pediatric Group, Lincoln, NE:

The Closed Head Injury Screener (CHIS) is a semi-structured interview designed "to assess whether or not the presentation of a given case suggests a closed-head injury" (manual, p. 18), and "to assist the clinician in judging whether or not a full neuro-psychological evaluation is appropriate in any particular case" (manual, p. 17). The CHIS consists of four sections: (a) Medical Facts, (b) Presenting Complaints, (c) Learning, and (d) Recall. The Medical Facts section of the interview elicits information from the patient regarding the medical facts of the injury such as loss of consciousness, confusion, and post-traumatic amnesia. The Presenting Complaints section of the interview elicits information from the patient regarding neurobehavioral changes following an injury such as changes in memory, attention, and sensory abilities. The Learning and Recall sections are included as a validity index of the patient's truthfulness in responding. The patient is first presented with a list of 20 words and instructed to learn them and be able to remember them. Then the patient is shown a list of 20 word pairs. In each pair there is one familiar word and one new word, and the patient must indicate which word is the familiar word. In addition to the four sections described above, the CHIS includes an optional Questionnaire Format, which can serve as an adjunct to the complete interview. When the Questionnaire Format is utilized, the patient first completes the questionnaire, which is in yes/no format and which parallels the full interview, and then the examiner reviews the questionnaire with the patient eliciting further detail.

The CHIS manual is quite brief and is lacking much information that seems necessary to use the instrument in clinical practice or to make a decision as to whether or not to proceed with further neuropsychological testing, which is one of the stated purposes of the test. To begin with, no information regarding for what ages the CHIS is appropriate has been provided. It seems as though many of the questions would be difficult for children to answer. The author does state that the Questionnaire Format is not appropriate for children, but does not provide specific ages or reading levels at which it becomes appropriate. No objective rating, scoring, or decision-making system is explained, with the exception of the validity index, on which the author states that at least 16 correct recognitions should be achieved to be sure of the patient's motivational integrity. Furthermore, even though this criterion is provided, no specific empirical rationale for using 16 as a cutoff is provided. Again, related to the age issue, it is unclear whether the author is advocating the use of this cutoff for all ages (i.e., is 16 the cutoff for both a 5-year-old and a 35-year old?). As far as the other scales are concerned, the manual is very vague regarding making decisions about whether a closed-head injury is present or not. For example, for the Presenting Complaints section the manual states "as the number of complaints increases, so does the probability of a positive screening decision" (p. 18). However, no specific numbers or cutoffs are described to aid in the decision-making process.

No information regarding the CHIS's psychometric properties is presented in the CHIS manual. Additionally, no research studies are presented to support the CHIS's usefulness for the purposes for which it was designed. Specifically, no examination of interrater reliability, test-retest reliability, construct validity, or the criterion-related validity of the CHIS is presented. Although the CHIS would appear to be somewhat useful in

obtaining a thorough clinical history, the absence of this information makes it unacceptable for its intended purpose of making significant decisions regarding whether or not to identify as having a closed-head injury, or whether or not to complete a neuropsychological assessment following a head injury.

SUMMARY. Given the serious limitations of the CHIS described above including the lack of sufficient decision criteria and the complete absence of research investigating reliability and validity, it is not possible to recommend this instrument for clinical use. The author has the obligation to provide sufficient information regarding the basic psychometric properties of an instrument, including whether it measures what it is supposed to measure.

[17]
Cognitive Symptom Checklists.

Purpose: "Developed to assist in the identification and treatment of problems in five basic cognitive areas."
Population: Ages 16 and older.
Publication Date: 1993.
Acronym: CSC.
Scores: 5 checklists: Attention/Concentration, Memory, Visual Processes, Language, Executive Functions.
Administration: Group.
Price Data: Price data available from publisher for complete kit including manual (26 pages), and 10 each of Attention/Concentration, Memory, Visual Processes, Language, and Executive Functions checklists.
Time: (10) minutes per checklist.
Comments: Checklists can be used separately or in any combination.
Authors: Christine O'Hara, Minnie Harrell, Eileen Bellingrath, and Katherine Lisicia.
Publisher: Psychological Assessment Resources, Inc.

Review of the Cognitive Symptom Checklists by THOMAS J. CULLEN, JR., Clinical Psychologist, Cullen Psychological Services, P.C., Fairless Hills, PA:

The Cognitive Symptom Checklists (CSC) are actually a set of five checklists that were designed to elicit information about difficulties in daily living that a client may be experiencing as a result of impaired cognitive functioning. The authors state that the CSC may be used with individuals 16 years of age and older who have neurological disorders or developmental disorders. The appropriate settings for the use of the test, according to the authors, includes residential settings, outpatient facilities, school settings, and clinician's offices. The instrument was reportedly developed for use within a treatment model that focuses on identifying cognitive problems, teaching strategies, and generalizing strategies and skills to real-life situations. The authors further state that the CSC was developed as "a clinical tool to assist clients in determining missing links and to target real-life, functional areas in treatment" (clinician's guide, p. 21).

The administration of the CSC is accomplished in four phases. These are the Checklist Selection, Administration, Inquiry, and Interpretation. The authors note that the Administration may be carried out by individuals with no formal training in psychology so long as that individual is familiar with self-report instruments and that individual has access to a supervising clinician for consultation. The Selection, Inquiry, and Interpretation phases must be carried out by a clinician familiar with brain/behavior relationships and with therapeutic approaches to rehabilitation of cognition. The authors also state that the instrument may be self-administered. It is also stated that the five checklists may be used either individually or in various combinations depending on the needs of the client or the clinician. As examples, the authors cite the difference in needs of a client with diffuse brain injury as compared to the needs of a client with a learning disability.

The five checklists correspond to "five core cognitive areas in which clients often experience problems" (p. 1). The five areas, as well as the individual items, were apparently chosen by the authors as "representing critical problems observed in their clinical work and reported by survivors of brain injury and other neurological disorders" (p. 21). They note that the CSC was "developed to provide information that is typically not obtained through the use of traditional standardized tests" (p. 21). Indeed, this last statement seems to be eminently clear. Although formal neuropsychological evaluation often yields invaluable information, the day-to-day or real-life consequences of neurological dysfunction often go unspoken. It is in this area that the CSC excels. It provides a vehicle for conveying the much needed objective descriptions of some of the problems encountered by the client with neurological dysfunction. By reporting on specific identified behaviors, the clinician is able to tie the abstract conceptualizations presented in a neuropsychological evaluation to the more concrete and real problems experienced by the individual client.

Despite the need for behavioral checklists in the area of neuropsychological dysfunction, it should be noted that the psychometric value of the instrument is questioned. In line with this, the authors appropriately cite several clinical caveats for use of the CSC. They point out that, "As with all self-report instruments, the CSC may not accurately reflect all of a client's symptoms" (p. 7). It is also noted that there may be an under- or overreporting of information by the client due to a number of factors. It is noted that the CSC is a clinical tool and not a standardized test. This is of utmost importance and must be firmly stressed. It is appropriately stated that the checklists were not designed for formal scoring beyond an examination of specific items and clusters of symptoms. The CSC is designed to supplement and complement other clinical tools.

SUMMARY. The sample population is not clearly identified or defined. The authors state that "validation of sections occurred through consensus of four clinicians, representing psychology, speech, and counseling disciplines, who independently identified, grouped, and categorized items" (p. 21). Nevertheless, despite face validity for certain clinical populations, there are no data presented to quantify the validity or reliability of scores from the instrument. Therefore, although the authors suggest that the instrument might be used to measure treatment progress or to establish a baseline for cognitive problem areas, it must be used with much caution in this respect. There are no quantified reliability measures making the instrument of questionable utility as a psychometric instrument.

Review of the Cognitive Symptom Checklists by MICHAEL LEE RUSSELL, Commander, 47th Combat Support Hospital, Fort Lewis, WA:

The Cognitive Symptom Checklists (CSC) is a useful set of structured inventories that can assist in the identification of neurological problem areas. The CSC will allow the clinician to refine which symptoms of cognitive difficulty may require more formal neuropsychological testing. The format of these questionnaires is actually five separate four-page booklets, each of which is color coded and targeted to a different cognitive function. They can be given in any combination, depending on the patient's presenting problem, and average approximately 70 questions per inventory. These checklists, when combined with a brief screening instrument such as the COGNISTAT (Northern California Neurobehavioral Group, 1995) can make a fairly comprehensive 50-minute neuro-screening interview.

The questions asked in the inventory are fairly standard neurological and neuropsychological screening questions used by most clinicians. The great advantage of this instrument is that its standardized format would insure that important areas are not omitted in an interview, and to allow administration by a technician for later review by the clinician. The manual suggests self-administration as another option, but I would only recommend this for a very high functioning neurological population: The questions asked are sometimes complex, and there are a large number of them (389 plus 7 redundant demographic questions if all 5 questionnaires are given). It asks the individual to rate difficulties in several subtests of cognitive function, then to go back and circle those areas of most concern. The manual suggests that a clinician remain present until the questionnaires are completed to provide structure and answer questions, which is certainly prudent.

The fundamental flaw of the questionnaire approach in assessing cognitive dysfunction is that it presupposes accurate self-appraisal: The individual must be cognitively intact enough to realize their own limitations in order to accurately report them. In essence, they must manifest intact executive ability for the data collected to be meaningful. Even though this is often the case in stroke and attention-deficit disorders, it is unlikely for most cases of cortical dementia. As the manual cautions, it is clearly a problem in the Executive and Memory questionnaires, and these should not be seen as a substitute for an objective memory test or a set of objective mental problems, which may be of more value in observing dysfunction in these areas.

The manual is well written, and addresses well the theoretical basis and limitations of the questionnaires. The administration instructions are clear and well written, including a procedure for inquiry. There are no formal scoring criteria.

SUMMARY. The development and validation of the CSC was as a "clinical tool," rather than a psychological test: The items were selected by clinical judgment of the authors, sampling items they felt to be critical in assessing a patient's cognitive ability, and guided by their own Rehabilitation Model. They refined the tool with the input of other clinicians and patients, although no formal reliability or validity data are reported. As their clinical judgment of what constitutes important questions to ask closely aligns with my own, it appears as a fairly useful clinical tool, as long as it is used in conjunction with formal testing and objective assessment methods.

REVIEWER'S REFERENCE

The Northern California Neurobehavioral Group. (1995). *Manual for COGNISTAT (The Neurobehavioral Cognitive Status Examination)*. Fairfax, CA: Author.

[18]
Communication Profile: A Functional Skills Survey.

Purpose: Designed to assess the importance of 26 everyday communication skills to elderly clients from diverse educational, cultural, and socioeconomic backgrounds.
Population: Elderly adults.
Publication Date: 1994.
Scores: Item scores only.
Administration: Individual.
Price Data: Not available.
Time: Administration time not reported.
Comments: Orally administered; survey used for elderly clients with health problems that have impaired or potentially could impair the ability to communicate; administrator scored.
Author: Joan C. Payne.
Publisher: The Psychological Corporation.
[Note: The publisher advised in March 1999 that this test is now out of print.]

Review of the Communication Profile: A Functional Skills Survey by ELAINE CLARK, Professor of Educational Psychology, University of Utah, Salt Lake City, UT:

The Communication Profile: A Functional Skills Survey assesses the importance of a broad range of communication skills in the daily lives of older adults (e.g., verbal expression and comprehension, reading comprehension, writing, and math). It is intended to be used in treatment planning for elderly people who are experiencing functional communication problems. The 26 items in the survey were chosen for their "broad applicability to the lives of older adults, regardless of their heterogeneity in education, living circumstances, financial resources, gender, ethnic background, or job experiences" (manual, p. 1). According to the author, there are similar measures of communication problems (e.g., Sarno's Functional Communication Profile and Lomas' Communication Effectiveness Index); however, the Communication Profile is unique in its assessment of what examinees perceive to be important communication skills. For example, the Profile asks adults to rate how important it is for them to be able to read an appointment card, talk on the phone with family and friends, or write checks to pay bills. It does not, however, assess a person's competence to perform these tasks. The title may be somewhat misleading to potential users who do not read carefully that this is a survey, not a functional skills analysis. The Profile is intended to be used alone or in conjunction with other measures; however, from this reviewer's perspective, there would be little advantage to give only the Communication Profile. For one, there would be no way to verify if a communication problem exists. Secondly, it would be ineffective, not to mention inefficient, to target only perceived problems for rehabilitation.

ADMINISTRATION AND SCORING. According to the manual, the Communication Profile is to be administered by a clinician. It is not entirely clear, however, to whom the term clinician refers. One might assume that this refers to someone who has experience with an aging population, or those for whom the instrument was intended. The fact the author felt compelled to include in the manual suggestions to insure examinees can see the materials and hear the questions (e.g., wearing their glasses and hearing aids), however, suggests that more novice examiners are expected to administer the survey. There are no indications that any training is needed to administer the scale, or that there are any requirements other than the ability to read the 26 items in a face-to-face situation. Administration instructions are clearly written and, for the most part, the scoring is self-explanatory.

All survey items are answered using either a 1-to-5 or 1-to-3 Likert-type rating scale. Although the 1-to-5 scale is the standard format, a shorter 3-point rating scale can be used by those who are unable to use a 5-point scale. It is unclear who should use the shorter rating system, as no suggestions were made in the manual. If examiners elect to use the short form rating scale, however, they need to be cautious in scoring the items. The examiner's scoring form only has the 5-point ratings, and the numbers assigned to the 3-point rating system (i.e., 1 = *not important at all*, 2 = *somewhat important*, and 3 = *important*) are not the same as the 5-point system (1 = *not important at all*, 2 = *not too important*, 3 = *somewhat important*, 4 = *important*, and 5 = *very important*). This may make it somewhat confusing to examiners and could lead to scoring errors. For example, if an examinee taking the test uses the 3-point scale and responds to an item with a rating of 2, the examiner is apt to record the answer as "not too important," whereas the correct answer would be "somewhat important." This is a rather minor problem, and is certainly not insurmountable; however, some mention of this in the manual (or an additional scoring sheet with the 3-point scale) may be helpful. The author did include two separate rating scale sheets for examinees to refer to while rating the survey questions. One is to be used for the 5-point scale, and the other for the 3-point scale. The two rating sheets are reproducible and have large block letters to assist those with reduced vision.

A Personal Profile form is also included and is to be used in conjunction with the 26-item survey. The form asks demographic questions but is extremely limited (e.g., asks questions about the examinee's age, gender, ethnic background, level of education, type of job and employment status, annual income, and living situation). It is surprising that the form does not ask questions about the examinee's health history, especially given the author's statement on page 2 of the manual that the Communication Profile is intended to be used with aging adults whose health has compromised their ability to communicate. Because it is assumed that this includes adults with stroke histories and dementing illnesses, some place on the form needs to be provided to obtain this information. Targeting high-risk aging adults (e.g., adults at risk for aphasic disorders secondary to cerebral vascular accidents) may extend the usefulness of the Communication Profile. As the Personal Profile form stands, there is no place to write any additional comments that may be relevant to assessment and treatment of communication problems.

SCALE DEVELOPMENT, RELIABILITY, AND VALIDITY. Survey items were developed by a work group that consisted of the author and three individuals who had experience with the "normal elderly" and elderly individuals in rehabilitation settings (e.g., a gerontologist, geriatric social worker, and speech and language pathologist). The work group who constructed the items also had experience with elderly people from culturally diverse backgrounds. In addition to these individuals, four speech and language pathologists were asked to evaluate a preliminary survey to determine if the items met the following criteria: independence of each item, appropriateness for the elderly, appropriateness for elderly from culturally diverse backgrounds, and items representing functional communication. The interjudge agreement among the four evaluators was .97.

Following pilot testing and reviews, the final 26-item Communication Profile was administered to 257 elderly adults (100 males and 157 females; 143 Africa-American and 114 Caucasian) for field testing. The sample was "selected" (it is not clear how) from 300 elderly adults in churches, nursing homes, and senior centers in the midwest and northeastern region of the United States. Staff at the various sites apparently referred potential subjects for testing if they felt they met criteria (i.e., no history of neurological damage, significant unaided hearing problems, or dementia). The subjects were between the ages of 65 and 94 (139 were 65 to 74, and 118 were between the ages of 75 and 94), and lived in community or institutional settings. The number of individuals with annual incomes over or below $30,000 was approximately equal; however, there was an overrepresentation of individuals with post-high school education and white collar jobs.

Results of the field testing showed that there were no significant group differences for gender, ethnicity, or education. There were, however, significant differences for community-living status (i.e., living alone or with others), living arrangements (community or nursing home), personal income, and type of job. Summary profile information across the eight demographic variables is provided to assist users in understanding what skills the field-test group found particularly important; that is, what they consistently rated as skills having high priority for them. For example, subjects living in the community who have a high

school education or less rated "telling the doctor what bothers you" as being a more important skill than did the other groups. Individuals 75 or older and living in nursing homes rated being able to read prescription labels as being highly important, and more so than the other groups.

Internal consistency reliability data are provided. The Cronbach alpha for the 26-item survey was .82. The number of subjects used to calculate the alpha for the 26-item survey was 257. The Guttman split-half technique and the Spearman-Brown formula were also calculated for the reliability of the 26-item survey (the Guttman produced a coefficient of .74 and the Spearman-Brown, a reliability coefficient of .77). No test-retest reliability data were provided, which is unfortunate given the potential for variable responding by elderly adults who have dementing illnesses and other neurologic problems compromising their communication. The only analyses reported in the manual for adults with disabilities were those pertaining to 100 aging adults with mental retardation, and 100 aging adults with hearing impairments. The reported data, however, were limited to Cronbach alpha coefficients.

TEST SCORE INTERPRETATION. The survey is intended to provide a "profile" of skills viewed as important for therapy. There is no total score to be derived, and according to the author, "there are no right or wrong answers ... no basal or ceiling scores" (manual, p. 2). The author suggests that examiners look for items that receive a score of 4 (important) or 5 (very important) when planning for treatment. Obviously, this system has to be adapted for examinees who use the 3-point scale (e.g., targeting items that are given a rating of 3, a score that represents an "important" skill).

Although the author states that examiners can use the fielded-test profile data provided in the manual to compare examinees' responses to those of nonneurologically impaired adults with similar demographic features, it is unclear how useful this information would be. The fact that nonneurologically impaired adults 65 to 75 years of age, living in the community, and having an annual income of less than $30,000, rate being able to ask the date as more important than other groups provides little information on which to base an intervention program. In addition, given the way information is presented, it is not even practical to look up this type of data. It also seems impractical to compare an examinee's skill rating with their own demographic data (i.e., data provided on the Personal Profile). Although the author suggests using the Profile data in this manner, interpretive suggestions such as these do not appear helpful, and are difficult to understand.

CONCLUSIONS. The Communication Profile represents a good attempt at providing information about communication skills that older adults view as important in their daily life. Although the Profile does not lend itself to the direct assessment of skill deficits, and provides little in the way of treatment information (i.e., other than information about examinees' perceptions of skill importance), the Communication Profile can be used to help target skills that may need further evaluation and intervention. Fortunately, the survey is easy to use and takes very little time to administer and score. Potential users, however, need to be aware of the limited information that is derived from the Profile, and the limited population with which the instrument was field tested. No older adults with neurologic impairments such as strokes and dementias were included in the field tests. In fact, the only groups tested besides normals (i.e., nonneurologically impaired older adults) were aging adults with mental retardation and hearing impairments. As a result, it is difficult to determine who would actually benefit from being given the Profile. Although the 26 items appear appropriate for demented adults and those with strokes, these data are missing. It is hoped that data supporting the usefulness of the instrument will be forthcoming, in particular, the relationship between the survey data and intervention strategies.

Review of the Communication Profile: A Functional Skills Survey by D. ASHLEY COHEN, Clinical Neuropsychologist, CogniMetrix, San Jose, CA:

Statements at the beginning of the Communication Profile (CP) manual are ones with which almost everyone in the gerontology field would agree: that intact functional language skills aid elders in being able to remain independent and maintain well-being, and that the "systematic study" of these everyday communication skills in older adults has been lacking. Sadly, this instrument will do little to help professionals restore functional communication skills to those who have lost a portion of them, and nothing to help maintain the skills in unimpaired elders.

Despite its title, the CP does not survey or measure in any way the *actual* functional communication skills of examinees. What is rated is the perceived importance of various communication skills to the person being interviewed. Perhaps of most concern is that only a skewed sample of very healthy subjects with little or no communication problems was used in standardization, even though the test is recommended for use with older adults with various speech and language handicaps, along with other cognitive and physical impairments.

NORMATIVE SAMPLE AND INSTRUMENT DEVELOPMENT. Items were generated by a committee of four persons, and informally validated by four others. We are told that "the theoretical framework for the CP was developed from a nontraditional paradigm of a broad range of variables that should be considered for aging clients" (manual, p. 7). However, the theories discussed—relating to racial and sexual differences—bear little relation to the instrument presented.

Diversity and ethnicity are heavily discussed, but the author concludes that Black and White older adults did not differ significantly in their responses. Although she also quotes others that aging is "a gendered process," most of her results show no differences based on gender. Further, because one of the author's stated aims is to develop more ethnically and culturally relevant instruments, it is unfortunate that no older Hispanics or Asians were included.

The final normative sample of 257 was 61% female, 56% Black and 44% White. Demographic data were tabulated in the manual, although only in raw numbers, leaving the reader to calculate percentages. This table would have been more meaningful if the sample data were compared with figures from U.S. citizens age 65 and over. For example, her data reveal that 52% of the sample had some college education up to post-graduate degrees, which is far from representative of the current cohort of older adults.

The normative sample was drawn from the northeastern U.S. and some midwestern sites. This limitation is regrettable as a recent study (Klein, 1998) found that the counties in the U.S. with the highest percentage of seniors are located in Florida, California, Arizona, and Nevada.

Subjects were obtained from senior centers, churches, and nursing homes; potential subjects were suggested by ministers or staff members. Thus, no independent-living subjects were included if they were not affiliated with a social organization of some type. As has often been observed (Birren, Sloane, & Cohen, 1992; Butler, Lewis, & Sunderland, 1991) elders who are not involved in activities such as church or senior centers can be very different from older adults who do belong to these organizations: Some are more isolated, ill or depressed, whereas others are much more independent.

Only very healthy elders were selected for inclusion; even subjects with hearing loss were excluded. Particularly when studying older persons, restricting one's sample to the healthy restricts the range acutely (by as much as 80%), and decreases the variance unacceptably, as well as making generalization to the entire elderly population a questionable proposition (LaRue & Markee, 1995).

The manual concedes that "there is a certain amount of selection bias in how subjects were identified and included in the study" (p. 24). The manual then reassures us: "However, it was felt that the size of the sample would eliminate much of the bias in subject selection" (p. 24). In the opinion of this reviewer, 257 individuals is not that large a sample for development of a new instrument. Second, and most important, it is impossible to make up for a restriction of range in a population sample simply by adding more subjects who are essentially the same; heterogeneity cannot be produced in a homogenous sample, no matter how many similar cases are included.

USES FOR THIS INSTRUMENT. The manual identified the primary purpose of this instrument as being determination of the importance of various practical language skills to older adults who have a language impairment. Other uses suggested were assisting therapists in selecting training goals important to the patient, measuring changes in the patient's priorities following a change in situation, and employing the instrument as a component of a thorough language assessment. Finally, it is said the Communication Profile can provide comparative premorbid and postmorbid data.

Regarding the last suggested use, the author seems to be suggesting using the rankings of her healthy normative sample to gauge the likely past importance of certain language skills to a current patient, prior to the onset of his or her brain disorder, and then compare that hypothesized ranking to the patient's present ranking. No means is conceivable to validate this use based on the test development data described in the manual.

The manual lists four groups with whom the test can be used effectively: (a) diffuse neurological disorders, (b) hearing impairments, (c) mental retardation, and (d) aphasia (mild to moderate) from cerebrovascular accidents and traumatic brain injuries.

Although older mentally retarded adults and older persons with hearing impairments were "field tested" in the development of this instrument, none of the findings from these two groups is presented in the manual, nor are data presented for those with neurological disorders or aphasia. It is troubling that the author suggests using the CP with demented, CVA, and TBI patients, who often have extensive and multifaceted cognitive difficulties, when they have not been examined during test development. For example, persons with language impairments may not understand the test items, or may not be able to rate them accurately.

POSITIVE FEATURES. As the test developer noted, there is a need for instruments targeted to elders, and she has attempted to address this need both in her normative sampling and in the format of her measure. For example, two levels of response complexity are available for more intact or more impaired persons. It is also welcome that individuals can respond by speaking their answers, gesturing, or writing, in an attempt to accommodate those with various physical handicaps.

Administration instructions are clear. The manual discusses common problems that may arise during testing, and suggests strategies for overcoming them. Purchasers are urged to reproduce pages of the manual for their own use. There are "Additional Activities" and situational role playing items suggested for therapy, which may expand the possible use of the instrument.

MINOR PROBLEMS. There is an excessive amount of repetition in the manual. This did not produce an overly long document, however, as the entire text runs to 24 pages, with large type and very generous margins. Unusual or incorrect usage of neuropsychological terms is annoyingly frequent. For example, on page 5 she writes "partial or complete blindness in one eye (hemiopsia) [sic]" and on page 2 she lists "Diffuse neurological disorders (e.g., Alzheimer's and progressive neuropathies)." There are minor inaccuracies in other areas as well (e.g., in Table I, instead of 257 subjects described elsewhere, a total of 272 subjects were reported for Income Data).

In the author's Conclusions section, many of the explanations advanced for the findings appear post hoc. For example, it was found that persons who lived with others put more importance on communication skills than those who lived alone. The author reasons that one would need better ability to communicate when living with someone else, but it could as easily be argued that those who live alone have no one else on whom to depend, and must therefore have reliable functional communication skills.

SUMMARY. Did this need to be a "test" at all? With improved statistical analysis, this work may have made an interesting journal article, and could have been the beginning of a useful instrument, particularly if it had included measurement of actual skills, along with patient ratings of their priorities.

Despite its attention to the needs of older adults, and to the priorities of patients in rehabilitation, the CP's deficiencies—a demographically limited and skewed normative sample, standardization on only very healthy older persons, and faulty and inadequate statistical analysis—seriously limit the usefulness of this measure.

REVIEWER'S REFERENCES

Butler, R. N., Lewis, M., & Sunderland, T. (1991). *Aging and mental health* (4th ed.). New York: Macmillan.
Birren, J. E., Sloane, R. B., & Cohen, G. D. (Eds.). (1992). *Handbook of mental health and aging.* San Diego: Academic Press.
LaRue, A., & Markee, T. (1995). Clinical assessment research with older adults. *Psychological Assessment, 7*(3), 376–386.
Klein, H. E. (1998). Retirement migration in America. *Psychotherapy Finances—Special Report; Statistics and Demographics, 24*(1), 6.

[19]
Communication Skills Profile.

Purpose: "Designed to help people who want to gain a thorough knowledge of the processes of communication and to improve their effectiveness as communicators."

Population: Individuals or teams within organizations.

Publication Date: 1997.

Scores: 6 scales: Slowing My Thought Processes, Making Myself Understood, Testing My Conclusions, Listening Constructively, Getting to the Essence, Exploring Disagreement.

Administration: Group.

Price Data, 1997: $12.95 per test booklet.

Time: Administration time not reported.

Author: Elena Tosca.

Publisher: Jossey-Bass Pfeiffer.

Review of the Communication Skills Profile by ROBERT BROWN, Carl A. Happold Distinguished Professor of Educational Psychology Emeritus, University of Nebraska-Lincoln, and Senior Associate, Aspen Professional Development Associates, Lincoln, NE:

The Communication Skills Profile (CSP) is a self-report instrument that includes eight questions for each of the six subscales, three of which focus on expressing one's own opinions (Slowing Thought Processes, Making Myself Understood, and Testing My Conclusions) and three on Listening and Understanding (Listening Constructively, Getting to the Essence, and Exploring Disagreement). Respondents use a 6-point Likert-like scale (6 = *Nearly always true*, 1 = *Never true*) to respond. After completing the scales, respondents are asked to predict their average score for each of the subscales before calculating their actual average scores.

Next, respondents plot their scores within a circle that has lines representing the six scales radiating from the center with gradations from "1" near the center to "6" near the circumference. The dots representing the scores are then connected to form a polygon. Sample polygons represent profiles with generally low scores, mixed high and low scores, and generally high scores. The author suggests that a "gap analysis" be made between the individual's score and the ideal score of "6." At this juncture, the respondent reads a page-length set of bromides for each of the six scales, which suggest how to improve his or her communication skills. Finally, the respondent is asked to develop an action plan for improvement and obtain feedback from others.

The manual includes no psychometric data regarding norms, reliability, or validity so it is not possible to comment on these characteristics of the instrument from a data-based perspective. The CSP appears to be a tool that would be more useful in a workshop setting than as an instrument to analyze an individual's communication skills for any diagnostic or prescriptive purposes. Nevertheless, the author asserts that the CSP "was designed to help people who want to gain a thorough knowledge of the processes of communication and to improve their effectiveness as communicators" (manual, p. 1); as such, the psychometric properties of the CSP should be available to potential users.

Choosing among alternative instruments will depend on the specific purposes of the users. Even if the user desires only to stimulate discussion within a group, the CSP might not be the best alternative. Many of the questions are abstract and, though understandable, may not provide individuals with enough concrete feedback to enable them to understand, much less improve, their communication skills. And how valid are self-perceptions of one's communication skills? The discrepancies between what an individual thinks he or she has communicated and what the listener understands are too frequent in everyday life for much credibility to be given to a self-report skill profile.

Assessment of communication skills lends itself naturally to a performance-based approach to measurement. Having individuals make presentations or observing individuals in communications settings is just one alternative. Televised vignettes or role-playing situations could be used to provide respondents with a context in which they could comment on the portrayals or even be asked to suggest how they would handle the situation. The creative possibilities are numerous and they could be tailor-made for the specific communication setting.

SUMMARY. Examination of the CSP may provide potential users with useful ideas if they are thinking about a workshop-like situation. Even then, without major adaptations to the specific context, the CSP would not likely be of much benefit. If the user wants a true assessment of communications skills, consideration must be given to a performance-based assessment procedure. I cannot recommend the CSP.

Review of the Communication Skills Profile by THOMAS P. HOGAN, Professor of Psychology and Director of Assessment and Institutional Research, University of Scranton, Scranton, PA:

PURPOSE AND TARGET POPULATION. The Communication Skills Profile (CSP) is a 48-item, self-report questionnaire regarding one's own communication practices. According to the CSP booklet, it is "designed to help people who want to gain a thorough knowledge of the processes of communication and to improve their effectiveness as communicators" (manual, p. 1). Communication, of course, is a very broad topic, encompassing reading, writing, public speaking, the broadcast media, etc. The CSP booklet does not explicitly differentiate among these subdivisions of the field. However, discussion in the booklet makes it clear that the CSP focuses on interpersonal communication of the one-on-one or one-on-small group variety, especially in the oral mode.

The CSP booklet indicates that the questionnaire may be completed individually or in groups. Beyond that, the booklet does not identify a target audience or administration procedures. One infers from the discussions in the CSP booklet that the target audience is adults working in organizational settings. There are no time limits or suggested timing arrangements. It appears that an adult of normal intelligence and motivation could complete the questionnaire in about 15 minutes.

MATERIALS, ITEMS, SCORES. The CSP consists of a 48-page booklet that provides a description of the rationale for the questionnaire, the questionnaire items themselves, pages for profiling scores, and suggestions for follow-up activities. Each person completing the questionnaire gets one of these booklets.

The CSP's 48 items are divided into the following six sections, with 8 items per section: Slowing My Thought Processes, Making Myself Understood, Testing My Conclusions, Listening Constructively, Getting to the Essence, and Exploring Disagreement. The booklet indicates that the first three of these sections comprise Area 1: The Ability to Express One's Own Opinion, and the last three sections comprise Area 2: The Ability to Listen and Understand Others. However, neither the text nor the score profiles suggest obtaining total scores from the section scores for these two broader areas.

Each of the 48 items calls for a self-report on a 6-point Likert-type scale ranging from 6: *nearly always true* to 1: *never true*. Each item is a one-sentence statement, such as "I try to find the cause of a disagreement in order to understand its origins." Numerical responses to the items are summed within each section, then averaged (divided by 8), and profiled. Two types of profiles are provided in the CSP booklet. The first is a bar chart showing the six scores. The second is a Holland-type hexagon with the six scales radiating from the center. Unfortunately, this arrangement easily gives the impression that high points on certain scales form polar opposites. This was probably not intended and the CSP text does not suggest it. Nevertheless, the visual appearance of the axes in the polygon invites such an interpretation.

TECHNICAL CHARACTERISTICS. The CSP has no norms, no reliability data, and no validity data. In fact, none of these terms nor concepts related to them are mentioned in the CSP booklet. The author and publisher are, apparently, oblivious to these concepts or simply consider them irrelevant for the CSP.

In the absence of any normative data, one could conceivably view the average scores on the six scales and their accompanying bar charts or polygon projections as amenable to criterion-referenced interpretation. In fact, that is what the CSP booklet does, without calling it criterion-referenced interpretation. However, there does not seem to be any basis for such interpretation of the scores. No rationale is provided for claiming that the statements in each of the six areas are somehow representative of their respective domains. A low score in one area may be a function of the peculiar wording of a few items in that area rather than a real deficiency in the area. The CSP booklet contains no discussion of how the eight items in each area were constructed or why they are thought to be representative of the area.

The CSP booklet contains no reliability data or any discussion of the concept of stability of scores. One infers that the author just assumes that responses to the items are perfectly reliable. The CSP booklet contains no data on the validity of the measures. At the most elementary level, even lacking any data, one would expect presentation of a rationale for having 6 scales rather than 1, or 10, or 30. No such rationale is provided.

SUMMARY. The CSP should not be considered a test or psychometric measure in any ordinary sense of those terms. It has no standardized administrative procedure, no rationale for interpreting scores (either norm-referenced or criterion-referenced), no systematic method of development, no reliability data, and no validity data. The CSP may be useful for purposes of

generating discussion in professional development seminars. However, it is not useful for measurement purposes. If one needs a measure of interpersonal communication skills or knowledge of such skills, one needs to look elsewhere.

[20]
Conners' Rating Scales—Revised.

Purpose: Constructed to assess psychopathology and problem behaviors.
Population: Ages 3–17; self-report scales can be completed by 12- to 17-year-olds.
Publication Dates: 1989–1997.
Acronym: CRS-R.
Administration: Group.
Price Data, 1999: $425 per complete kit including manual ('97, 226 pages), 25 feedback forms for each of the CPRS-R:L, CPRS-R:S, CTRS-R:L, CTRS-R:S, CASS:L, CASS:S, CADS-Parent, CADS-Teacher, CADS-Self-Report, 25 Global Index-Teacher Forms, 25 Global Index-Parent Forms, 15 CRS-R Treatment Progress Color Plot, and 100 Teacher Information Forms; $26 per 25 Quick Score forms (specify test and version); $22 per feedback forms (specify test and version); $46 per technical manual; $40 per user's manual; $45 per Windows preview version including 3 administrations/interpretive reports, and user's manual; $10 per computer interpretive report; $4 per computer profile report.
Comments: Ratings by parents and teachers and adolescent self-report.
Author: C. Keith Conners.
Publisher: Multi-Health Systems, Inc.
a) CONNERS' PARENT RATING SCALE—REVISED.
Acronym: CPRS.
Scores, 13: Oppositional, Cognitive Problems/Inattention, Hyperactivity, Anxious-Shy, Perfectionism, Social Problems, Psychosomatic, ADHD Index, Conners' Global Index: Restless-Impulsive and Emotional Lability, DSM-IV Inattentive, DSM-IV Hyperactive-Impulsive, DSM-IV Total.
Forms, 2: Long, Short.
Time: (15–20) minutes.
b) CONNERS' TEACHER RATING SCALE—REVISED.
Acronym: CTRS.
Scores: Same as *a* above.
Forms, 2: Long, Short.
Time: (15) minutes.
c) CONNERS-WELLS' ADOLESCENT SELF-REPORT SCALE.
Acronym: CASS.
Scores, 10: Conduct Problems, Cognitive Problems/Inattention, Hyperactivity, ADHD Index,

Family Problems, Anger Control Problems, Emotional Problems, DSM-IV Inattentive, DSM-IV Hyperactive-Impulsive, DSM-IV Total.
Forms, 2: Long, Short.
Time: (15–20) minutes.
d) CONNERS' GLOBAL INDEX.
Acronym: CGI.
Scores, 3: Emotional Lability, Restless-Impulsive, Total.
Forms, 2: Parent, Teacher.
Time: (5) minutes.
e) CONNERS' ADHD/DSM-IV™ SCALES.
Acronym: CADS.
Scores, 4: Conners' ADHD Index, DSM-IV: Inattentive, DSM-IV: Hyperactive/Impulsive, DSM-IV Total.
Forms, 3: Parent, Teacher, Adolescent.
Time: (5–10) minutes.
Cross References: See T5:681 (99 references) and T4:636 (50 references); for reviews by Brian K. Martens and Judy Oehler-Stinnett of the original edition, see 11:87 (83 references).

Review of the Conners' Rating Scales—Revised by ALLEN K. HESS, Distinguished Research Professor and Department Head, Department of Psychology, Auburn University at Montgomery, Montgomery, AL:

"Conners (1990–1991) has produced a family of rating scales that are [sic] useful for identifying hyperactivity and other behavioral problems in children" (Gregory, 1996, p. 327). The fruits of his three decades of work are provided in the Technical Manual for the Conners' Rating Scales (CRS), containing a wealth of information in its 208 pages. The CRS began as a brief set of phrases forming a checklist given free to clinicians to use with parents and teachers. It has grown to include both long- and short-form parent scales and teacher scales by which to rate boys and girls from ages 3 to 17, and a set of self-report adolescent scales for youth from 12 to 17 years of age.

The set of parent and teacher rating scales includes subscales putatively tapping Oppositionalism, Cognitive Problems, Hyperactivity, Anxiety-Shyness, Perfectionism, Social Problems, Psychosomatic Concerns (parent scales only), Global Hyperactivity (including emotional lability and restless-impulsive components), Attention-Deficit/Hyperactivity Disorder (ADHD), and DSM-IV Symptoms (including inattentive and hyperactive-impulsive components). The adolescent scales include subscales for Family Problems and Anger Control problems subscales in addition to the Conduct Problems, Cognitive Problems and DSM-IV Symptoms subscales, and a Hyperactivity ADHD index. The parent-teacher, parent-child, and teacher-child contrasts can yield fascinating information (e.g., if the child and teacher see problems that the parents do not perceive).

PSYCHOMETRIC CHARACTERISTICS. The Conners rating scales are face valid. Teachers respond to items such as "fidgets with hands or feet or squirms in seat," "disturbs other children," and "talks excessively"; parents respond to items such as "easily frustrated in efforts," "argues with adults," and "messy or disorganized at home or school." Children answer questions such as "I feel like crying," "I break rules," and "I am behind in my studies."

RELIABILITY. Standard errors of measurement are presented for observed and predicted scores. They show that the scales provide stable scores to assess both the individual at a given time and the changes that might occur in an individual over time. The items seem to cohere to their assigned scale as seen by the impressive internal reliability coefficients. However, no interjudge reliability estimates are presented. This is a serious omission in observer-based measures. Six- to 8-week test-retest reliability coefficients are as low as .47 for the CTRS-R:L Cognitive-Problems and DSM-IV-Hyperactive-Impulsive scales, and the CPRS-R:L Anxious-Shy scale. However, the other test-retest coefficients average in the .70s with the CTRS-R:L scales averaging .82. In contrast to the norms that have an 11,000 total subject base, the test-retest reliability coefficients for the teacher, parent, and adolescent scales are based on samples of but 50 subjects each.

NORMS. A Canadian- and United States-based sample provides norms in 3-year age groupings for the parent and teacher's forms (from 3–5, 6–8, 9–11, 12–14, and 15–17 years) and for the adolescent self-report form (from 12–14 and 15–17 years). Norms for the parent scales tend to overrepresent white and underrepresent black parents; norms for the teacher scales are racially proportional; the norms for the adolescent scales overrepresent blacks. Native-American norms were collected and reveal elevations on most scales when compared with the norms of other ethnic groups. The problem of whether to use one set of norms for all children, based on the fact that the test subjects will be measured by a societal standard, or whether to use norms as specific to the tested person as possible is a question that is larger than the Conners' Scales or this review can address adequately, but the CRS does provide enough information for the user to sculpt a test report for either perspective.

EMPIRICAL VALIDITY. The CRS have been used in a variety of studies over the years but surprisingly the manual does not refer to any of the studies. There is a serious need for the manual to examine concurrent and predictive validity. With the exception of a study using the Children's Depression Inventory, the research reviewed in the manual is exclusively concerned with the relationships between various forms of the CRS, and these relationships are modest.

The manual cites one study concerning "discriminant validity." Conners idiosyncratically defines discriminant validity as the "instrument's ability to distinguish between relevant subject groups" (manual, p. 133). In fact, discriminant validity is defined by psychometricians as the degree to which measures do not correlate with variables from which they should differ. The manual does not cite any discriminant validity studies that show, for example, elevated hyperactivity scales and nonelevated obsessive-compulsive or anxiety-shyness scales with a hyperactive sample. Conversely, a measure with discriminant validity would show elevations on anxiety-shyness scales but not on hyperactivity scales in a group of anxious children. Such studies would provide discriminant validity [previous *MMY* reviews cite such evidence (Martens, 1992; Oehler-Stinnett, 1992), but this manual is strangely silent on this issue. These two reviews in the *Eleventh MMY* are excellent, are still pertinent in their observations about the CRS, and are essential resources for the reader interested in using the CRS or one of its competitors].

Conners' definition of discriminant validity actually is closer to what is usually termed "classification efficiency," or the degree to which a measure correctly classifies people. Classification efficiency is often determined by linear discriminant function analysis, which may account for the definitional problem. The manual reports a study showing the subscales differ when assessing a "nonclinical," ADHD, and emotional disturbance group. However, the degree to which true positive and true negative (hits) and false positive and false negative (misses) decisions occur is not reported so we do not know how efficient the CPRS-R:L is in helping with classification decisions.

The differences between the groups portrayed on the scales are interesting, statistically significant, and consistent. But because the prevalence of hyperactivity is some 3% in the general population and the study included 91 "nonclinical," 91 ADHD, and 55 emotional problem children, there is no way to determine the utility of the CRS in detecting ADHD from the "nonclinical" and emotional problems group. That is, when the samples are roughly a third ADHD there are statistical differences but will the CRS be useful in detecting ADHD when applied to populations where the prevalence rate is closer to 3%? The Fs were statistically significant but tell us nothing about classification efficiency nor the magnitude of effect or clinical significance of the differences. Sensitivity, the degree to which a measure detects disordered people in a population, and specificity, the degree to which a measure distinguishes between disorders, are yet to be determined for the CRS.

The manual shows male and female matrices to have similar factor solutions. Studies presented in the manual, and published in peer-reviewed journals only after the publication of the manual, appear to support three factor solutions featuring the Oppositionalism, Cognitive Problems, and Hyperactivity scales. Recall that the CRS posit six or more scales in the various forms. But surprisingly, a study supporting the six scales/factors model is not cited. Trites, Blouin, and Laprade (1982) report a six-factor solution for the CPRS-39, with the Hyperactivity factor accounting for 36% of the variance. There is little question that the CRS is tapping something important, that there is strong evidence for a three-factor structure, that the six scales model received only partial support, and that the factorial validity studies are consistent in showing the CRS to be useful in assessing ADHD at the least. But there is an equal certainty that more research by the author and by independent researchers needs to be published in peer-reviewed journals, and that the manual needs to include peer-reviewed validity research.

CONCLUSIONS. The 30-year anniversary is a time for Conners to celebrate the prominence of the CRS in clinical and research activities, particularly those addressing questions of hyperactivity. However, there is a greater urgency to address the paucity of peer-reviewed externally published validity research and the need to determine the classification accuracy of the CRS than there is a need to celebrate. Anyone engaging in educational or child clinical assessment or in research concerning child clinical syndromes generally and hyperactivity specifically, needs to consider using the CRS, weighing the limitations cited above against the flaws and benefits extant in other measures.

REVIEWER'S REFERENCES

Trites, R. L., Blouin, A. G. A., & Laprade, K. (1982). Factor analysis of the Conners' Teacher Rating Scale based on a large normative sample. *Journal of Consulting and Clinical Psychology, 50,* 615–623.

Martens, B. K. (1992). [Review of Conners' Rating Scales.] *The eleventh mental measurements yearbook* (pp. 233–234). Lincoln, NE: Buros Institute of Mental Measurements.

Oehler-Stinnett, J. (1992). [Review of Conners' Rating Scales.] *The eleventh mental measurements yearbook* (pp. 234–241). Lincoln, NE: Buros Institute of Mental Measurements.

Gregory, R. J. (1996). *Psychological testing: History, principles, and applications* (2nd ed.). Boston: Allyn and Bacon.

Review of the Conners' Rating Scales—Revised by HOWARD M. KNOFF, Professor of School Psychology, University of South Florida, Tampa, FL:

Published for the first time in 1989, the Conners' Rating Scales—Revised (CRS-R) has been revised and restandardized with three primary goals in mind: (a) to align the CRS-R with, especially, the Attention-Deficit/Hyperactivity Disorder (ADHD) criteria of the *Diagnostic and Statistical Manual of Mental Disorders* (4th Edition; DSM-IV; APA, 1994); (b) to update the norms using a large, representative normative sample; and (c) to add an adolescent self-report scale such that the CRS-R can now elicit multiple response sets from parents, teachers, and adolescents from ages 12 through 17 (to complement the parent and teacher analyses available from ages 3 to 11). With this restandardization and its main focus on the assessment of ADHD, the CRS-R reinforces its distinction as one of the best instruments in this area relative to development, psychometric integrity, and functional utility. As such, except for the three DSM-IV Symptom subscales on the Adolescent Self-Report Scales (Long and Short), the CRS-R can be used for screening, comprehensive assessment, treatment monitoring, and research.

The CRS-R actually comprises five clusters of scales: the Parent Rating Scales (Long and Short versions), the Teacher Rating Scales (Long and Short versions), the Adolescent Self-Report Scales (Long and Short versions), the Parent and Teacher Global Indexes, and the Parent, Teacher, and Adolescent versions of the ADHD/DSM-IV Scales. Usually given under the direction of a school psychologist or other psychologist, all of these scales can be used for children and youth aged 3 to 17, except the Adolescent Scales, which are used between the ages 12 and 17. Completed within the context of the child or adolescent's behavior during the last month, the Parent and Teacher scales have "reading ease" scores, using the Flesch Reading Ease Formula, at the 9th and 10th grade reading equivalents, and the Adolescent scales score at the 6th grade reading equivalent.

Overall, the CRS-R has short- and long-form versions for parents, teachers, and adolescents (via self-report), respectively. As organized by the items on its protocols, the Long version of the Parent Rating Scale (80 items) consists of seven "clinical" subscales (Oppositional, Cognitive Problems, Hyperactivity, Anxious-Shy, Perfectionism, Social Problems, Psychosomatic), the Global Indexes (Restless-Impulsive, Emotional Lability), the ADHD Index, and the DSM-IV subscale (with its Inattentive and Hyperactive-Impulsive factors). The Parent Rating Scale-Short Form (27 items) consists of three shortened clinical subscales (Oppositional, Cognitive Problems, Hyperactivity—which happen to be the three scales accounting for the most variance on the Long Form), and a shortened ADHD Index. Although there are separate protocols that allow the clinician to combine the Parent Rating Scale—Short Form (with its 27 items) with the Parent Global Index (10 items) and the Parent ADHD/DSM-IV Scales (26 items), it would appear easier and more clinically sound to give a parent *one* 80-item Parent Rating Scale—Long Form rather than *three separate* shorter form protocols totaling 63 items. Even though the Short Form scales have good psychometric properties, the integrated Long Form scale has more items (increasing its clinical reliability) and more explained variance.

Except for the Psychosomatic subscale, the Long Form of the Teacher Rating Scale (59 items) has the same subscales as the Parent Scale—Long Form along with a substantial, but not complete, overlap of individual items. The same is true for the Short Form of the Teacher Scale (28 items), which again consists of the three shortened Oppositional, Cognitive Problems, Hyperactivity subscales, and the shortened ADHD Index. The Long Form of the Adolescent Self-Report Scale (87 items) consists of six clinical subscales (Family, Emotional, Conduct, Cognitive, and Anger Control Problems, respectively, and Hyperactivity), the ADHD Index, and the DSM-IV subscales. The Adolescent Short Form (27 items) consists of the Conduct Problem, Cognitive Problem, Hyperactive-Impulsive, and ADHD Index subscales. Because some of the adapted items overlap across the Adolescent Scale and the Parent and Teacher scales, care needs to be taken when attempting to interpret results across these scales and their similar sounding subscales. This is especially true given the expected low or nonsignificant correlations between the Adolescent and the Parent and Teacher scales, respectively, that are reported in the manual.

DEVELOPMENT, PSYCHOMETRIC PROPERTIES, AND EVALUATION OF THE CRS-R. Relative to the development of the CRS-R, it appears that all of the scales, except for the DSM-IV Symptoms Subscales, were factor analytically derived (the manual reports that the DSM-IV subscales were rationally created). These factors were derived from a pilot study that involved 10 sites from eight states, and responses from (a) the parents of 2,200 students, (b) the teachers of 1,702 students, and (c) 1,749 self-reporting adolescents. Additional information about the pilot samples and the item loadings on the various factor analyses are needed (see evaluation below). The manual also needs to report the empirical research underlying the items chosen for the scales, and which items (of the 131 teacher, 193 parent, and 102 self-report items) were not retained in the scales' final versions. In addition, the author needs to clarify a statement in the manual (p. 86) that suggests the preliminary pool of items was selected to cover seven preselected content areas (i.e., conduct, activity, attention, learning, and social problems, respectively, and emotionality, and perfectionism). Although this a priori organization is not problematic per se, it *is* important to demonstrate that they have an empirical basis relative to ADHD. This preselection takes on additional importance when the final clinical scales, and their factor structures, are considered. Clearly, the close resemblance of the final scales with their original conceptualizations demonstrates the integrity of the item selection process, as well as the construct validity of the CRS-R.

Based on the factor analytic results of the pilot study, the final CRS-R norms were derived from over 8,000 cases from over 45 states and 10 provinces across the U.S. and Canada. The Long Form of the Parent Scale was based on 2,482 cases. The Short Form sample (involving 2,426 cases) overlapped substantially with the Long Form sample with the protocols simply being rescored to generate separate norms. Limited demographic and stratification data were provided (see below). The median annual household income for participating parents was between $40,0001 and $50,000. As this appears to be above the median income for the country as a whole, the possibility exists that the norms may not be representative of "typical" children and adolescents in the U.S. either due to differences in parent perceptions and ratings or to the actual behavior of those in more upper-income homes. Ultimately, this is an empirical question that is offset by some of the convergent and discriminant validity data reported in the manual.

The Teacher and Adolescent Self-Report scales similarly used large samples in their norming processes (approximately 2,000 children and adolescents for the Teacher Scale and 3,400 adolescents for the Self-Report Scale). Their respective Short Form samples also largely overlapped with the Long Form samples through the rescoring of the reorganized protocols. Although the size of the normative samples used is impressive, discrepancies were noted relative to the racial distribution of rated children and adolescents. Specifically, the percentage of Caucasian students rated was approximately 83% for the Parent Scale, 78%–81% for the Teacher Scale, and 62% for the Adolescent Scale (the percentage ranges reflect differences between the Long and Short Forms of a scale). For African-American students rated, the percentages were 4%–5% for the Parent Scale, 7%–10% for the Teacher Scale, and 30% for the Adolescent Scale. The percentage of Hispanic students rated ranges from 3% to 6% of the sample across the three scales, and between 1% to 2% of the samples involved Asian, Native American, or other-racial-background students, respectively.

Although the impact of these discrepancies is unknown, the CRS-R manual did note a number of significant ethnic differences among certain scales across the Long and Short Forms of all three (Parent, Teacher, and Self-Report) CRS-R scales. In the end, clinicians will need to be careful when making comparisons and conclusions for profiles across the Parent, Teacher, and Self-Report scales of the CRS-R, both because of the demographic differences across the normative samples and the fact that correlations between these respondents are typically low.

From a psychometric perspective, the CRS-R manual reports the reliability and validity data expected for this type of tool. Relative to the reliability, internal consistency, reliability estimates appear acceptable, ranging from .72 to .95. Six- to 8-week test-retest reliabilities are similarly acceptable, ranging from .47 to .92. Relative to the validity, factorial validity was reported for the Long and Short Forms, respectively, of the Parent, Teacher, and Self-Report Scales looking at both the intercorrelations between the subscales and the factorial structures for males and females. Once again, based on the data provided in the manual, both the intercorrelations among the subtests for the Long and Short Forms of the three scales and the confirmatory factor analyses reported for the Short Forms of the scales appear acceptable.

Finally, the manual addresses construct validity by reporting the CRS-R's convergent validity (primarily through interrespondent correlations) and its discriminant validity (primarily through investigating three different clinical or nonclinical groups of adolescents). As expected, there was considerable variability in the intersubscale correlations between the parent and teacher ratings; low or nonsignificant correlations between parent and adolescent self-report ratings and teacher and adolescent self-report ratings also were reported. Although the samples and data collection methods used were not well-described, the discriminant validity findings across an ADHD, "emotional problem," and randomly selected CRS-R normative group did reveal significant differences in most of the predicted directions across all of the subscales for the Parent, Teacher, and Self-Report Scales, respectively.

CRITICAL OMISSIONS. Even though the CRS-R is well organized and is very detailed throughout, there are a number of omissions that made specific aspects of the CRS-R difficult to evaluate. Some of the notable omissions include the lack of information regarding: (a) how the sites and participants in the pilot and norming processes were chosen (e.g., randomly, by convenience, or in a different manner); (b) how reflective the 10 pilot sites were of the demographics of the country and (later) of the norming sample; (c) the specific item correlations from the pilot study's factor analytic results that largely determined which items were included in the final CRS-R; (d) the demographic stratification of the parent participants *and the students who were rated* in the norming process across the country (especially by gender, age, race, and SES), and how these demographics compared with the U.S. Census; (e) the teachers and adolescents who participated in the norming and their descriptive characteristics (e.g., the teachers' degrees, years of experience, gender with race, etc.; the adolescents' age and gender with race, their grade-point averages, etc.); (f) where and how the Canadian participants were fit into the norming process and statistical analyses; (g) how many mothers versus fathers participated in the Parent norming process, and the statistical analyses to demonstrate that the CRS-R's profiles can be used with either parent respondent; (h) the statistical rationale for separating the norms into the five (3–5, 6–8, 9–11, 12–14, 15–17 year) age group clusters, and the factor analytic/construct validity of the CRS-R across these age clusters; (i) the normative and discriminant validity support for the recommendation that children or youth scoring at the 65T level be evaluated further; and (j) how the CRS-R accommodated for the racial differences found and reported in the manual.

In the face of the large standardization sample and the reliability and validity data reported, these omissions are important but they do not undermine the overall strength of the CRS-R. Nonetheless, these issues should be addressed in future revisions of the manual. If done, this would only make the general use of the CRS-R unquestioned.

SUMMARY. Given its revision, restandardization, psychometric integrity, and functional utility, the Conners' Rating Scales—Revised maintains its place as one of the best instruments available relative to assessing ADHD and its concomitant behaviors for children and adolescents aged 3 to 17. The CRS-R now appears to be well aligned with the ADHD criteria of the DSM-IV, it has updated its norms using a large sample of children and adolescents drawn from across the country and Canada, and it has added an adolescent self-report scale (for ages 12 through 17) such that multirespondent data can be collected from parents, teachers, and adolescents.

The CRS-R is now composed of five clusters of scales: the Parent Rating Scales (Long and Short versions), the Teacher Rating Scales (Long and Short versions), the Adolescent Self-Report Scales (Long and Short versions), the Parent and Teacher Global Indexes, and the Parent, Teacher, and Adolescent versions of the ADHD/DSM-IV Scales. Each scale comes with a separate protocol and profile form that provides easy-to-understand directions and scoring approaches that minimize errors. Although the manual needs some added description, especially relative to the samples used to pilot and norm the CRS-R and the factor analyses used to demonstrate the scale's construct validity across the age and gender groups used, it provides an exceptional amount of information that is clear and well organized, and that includes interpretive guidelines and a series of prototypical case studies.

Overall, except for the three DSM-IV Symptom subscales on the Adolescent Self-Report Scales (Long and Short), the CRS-R can continue to be used for its intended screening, comprehensive assessment, treatment monitoring, and research purposes. Although additional research is needed to replicate and validate the work reported in the manual, it is clear that the CRS-R is a well-crafted and important tool in the assessment of ADHD children and adolescents.

[21]
Contextual Memory Test.

Purpose: Designed to assess awareness of memory capacity, strategy use, and recall in adults with memory dysfunction.
Population: Adults.
Publication Date: 1993.
Acronym: CMT.
Scores, 12: Recall Score (Immediate Recall, Delayed Recall, Total Recall), Cued Recall, Recognition, Awareness Score (Prediction, Estimation of Performance Following Recall, Response to General Questioning [Prior to Recall, Following Recall]), Strategy Use (Effect of Context, Order of Recall, Total Strategy Score).
Administration: Individual.
Price Data, 1999: $89 per complete kit including manual (138 pages), 2 test cards, 14 cut-apart sheets of 80 picture cards, 25 score sheets (12 pages), and carrying case; $32 per 25 score sheets.

Time: Administration time not reported.
Author: Joan P. Toglia.
Publisher: Therapy Skill Builders—A Division of The Psychological Corporation.

Review of the Contextual Memory Test by KAREN MACKLER, School Psychologist, Lawrence Public Schools, Lawrence, NY:

The Contextual Memory Test (CMT) examines different aspects of an individual's knowledge of their memory limitations, following such events as head trauma, CVAs, dementia, brain tumor, etc. It also assists in determining how responsive a patient is to using cues to enhance recall. The author states that "this information is directly related to choosing and designing a compensatory or remedial treatment program" (p. 1). It is understood that the instrument is not diagnostic in nature, and the information should be used to supplement more conventional measures of memory and cognition.

The CMT has two equivalent versions. Each consists of a picture card containing 20 drawings of items relating to either a Restaurant or a Morning scene. The test is given in two parts. Part I (noncontext) requires recall without being told the theme. Part II is given only if the patient scores below criterion on Part I, and the theme is told to the patient. If recall does not improve significantly after being given the schema, a task involving cued recall and recognition can be used. These additional tasks were not included in the original research. In addition to the recall tasks, the patient is asked to respond to questions regarding estimation of memory capacity, awareness of actual performance, and strategies used to recall.

The basic test takes approximately 5–10 minutes to administer, with a 15–20-minute time interval before the delayed recall task is given. If the patient demonstrates difficulty, the time is increased to include cued recall and recognition tasks.

The manual is written in a straightforward manner. Directions for administration become clearer upon familiarity with the protocol. Strengths and limitations of the measure are stated explicitly in the manual. Although administration is easy, scoring and interpretation are more difficult. Twelve scores are obtained. Raw scores are compared to norms to determine norm-referenced scores.

A weakness of this measure is its norms. The measure was standardized on 375 adults, ages

17 to 86, from the New York City area. Eighty-three percent of the sample was Caucasian, indicating inadequate ethnic diversity. In addition, 50% of the group held a college degree. Demographic variables such as educational level and age significantly influenced recall scores. The text offers many disclaimers as to the use of the scores. Perhaps more important than comparing scores to normed scores is to examine the pattern of scores relative to one's own performance. Many suggestions for remediation of specific weaknesses are included within the manual. These strategies are helpful and sensible. Several case studies are presented to illustrate different profiles.

The Morning and Restaurant versions of the measure are considered appropriate alternative forms if used with their corresponding standard score conversion tables. The tables are different to account for differences found in difficulty level between the two versions.

A sample population of 112 individuals with brain injury aged 17–88 was tested to assess reliability and validity. This group was similar in sex to the control group, but differed in education (lower), race (more diverse), and mean age (higher). In addition, these individuals covered a wide range of diagnoses. As such, it cannot be said with certainty that the scores obtained are representative for a specific patient experiencing memory impairment. Clinically it has been noted that some patients benefit from the context version of the test, whereas others do not.

Recall scores were analyzed for reliability using parallel form, test-retest, and Rasch analysis. Parallel form reliability compared the Morning and Restaurant versions of the test. These estimates ranged from .73 to .81, with higher reliability estimates for the context versions. A quasi-test-retest reliability estimate was obtained by correlating immediate recall scores with delayed recall scores. Full test administration procedures were not followed for the delayed score, voiding the potential for a true test-retest reliability score. These estimates ranged from .74 to .87 for the control group and .85 to .94 for the subjects with brain injury.

Rasch analysis generates item separation scores and person separation scores. For the full sample (control and patients with brain injury), person separation reliabilities ranged from .75 to .77 with immediate and delayed recall scores taken separately. When the recall scores were combined, reliability improved to .89 to .90. Overall reliability estimates indicate that the measure stands up over time.

Prediction scores were found to be highly reliable, with a correlation score of .90. Strategy scores correlated at .75 between the two versions of the test.

Concurrent validity was assessed by correlating recall scores on this measure with those obtained on the Rivermead Behavioral Memory Test. Results of these correlations were in the upper .70s to mid .80s.

Discriminant function analysis was used to assess the ability of the CMT to discriminate between nondisabled individuals and those with brain injury. An overall hit rate of .873 was obtained with immediate and delayed recall scores. Adding in the total strategy score resulted in a high rate of .911. The addition of the discrepancy score did not improve the hit rate (.907).

Overall, the Contextual Memory Test (CMT) is an easily administered measure that appears to have potential usefulness in the assessment of an individual's knowledge of and use of specific memory strategies. It is questionable how useful the normed scores are. Rather, the instrument provides a structured method for obtaining information regarding current strategies used and gives some useful suggestions for translating test performance into remediation and treatment goals.

Review of the Contextual Memory Test by ALAN J. RAPHAEL, President, International Assessment Systems, Inc., Miami, FL:

Published in 1993 by Therapy Skills Builders, a Division of The Psychological Corporation, the Contextual Memory Test (CMT) is a 40-item measure designed to assess awareness of memory capacity, strategy use, and recall in adults with bonafide memory dysfunction.

According to the test developer, the CMT is not diagnostic in purpose and is intended solely to provide information that can supplement traditional measures of memory and cognition. This distinction is contradictory and confusing, as it is labeled as a test, yet denies the essential diagnostic qualities of a test.

Although the test has a large normative sample of 375, the sample is biased with only about 25% of the subjects possessing a high school education or less. There is also an overemphasis on younger people, yet no material is provided on the interaction between age and education, which is likely to occur in skewed normative samples. The overemphasis on younger subjects is also problematic given that memory dysfunctions are more relevant to middle-aged and older populations. There is information on age and education correlates; however, norms provided present only gross correlations for age and none at all for education despite a higher correlation of education with test indices. Raw scores are transformed into "standard" scores; however, the mean and standard deviation of these scores is not provided (although standard error of the mean scores are presented). There are clear directions for labeling scores normal or abnormal, but the reasoning behind such distinctions is unclear.

The normative data are questionable as well. The CMT has been standardized on subjects without obvious memory dysfunction who are 18 years old and older and has purportedly demonstrated evidence of reliable and valid interpretations for adults who have organic memory dysfunction. According to the author, the test is unique in that it examines different aspects of individuals' self-awareness of their memory limitations.

Testing based on one brain-injured group is presented, but the demographic characteristics of this and the normal groups are quite different. The brain-injured group consists primarily of people with CVAs, tumors, and dementia, and is much older and less educated than the normal group. The author makes no attempt to look at diagnostic differences between the brain-injured group and a matched group of control clients, although general comparisons are made on some score distributions without correcting for demographic information.

The test generates many measures that have unclear scoring. There are no factor analytic or other procedures to indicate how the different scores relate to one another.

Like many self-report measures, this instrument has no method of controlling for test-taking attitude or external influences like work avoidance, depression, malingering, deception, or random responding. This is particularly significant for memory measures that are often involved in rehabilitation matters or personal injury litigation

where secondary gain matters like financial compensation abound.

Reliability data on the measure are generally good, with parallel form reliability estimated along with correlations with the Rivermead Behavioral Memory Test. Reliabilities generally fell in the .70+ range, consistent with other reliable tests of memory function. The authors also report what they call "quasi test-retest reliability" (p. 1) by correlating immediate and delayed memory.

Overall, from an empirical viewpoint, this test has value as a measure of memory function. However, the measure as it currently stands possesses significant limitations as a clinical instrument and should be limited to use as a research instrument until further research clarifies its value, validity, and reliability for use in diverse populations. It should not be used to determine memory function or memory impairment in individuals whose status potentially or definitely supports a claim seeking compensation for injuries or illnesses related to memory impairment.

[22]
Coolidge Axis II Inventory.

Purpose: Designed as a measure of personality disorders.
Population: Ages 15 and older.
Publication Date: 1993.
Acronym: CATI.
Scores, 45: 13 Personality Disorder Scales (Antisocial, Avoidant, Borderline, Dependent, Histrionic, Narcissistic, Obsessive Compulsive, Paranoid, Passive Aggressive, Schizotypal, Schizoid, Sadistic, Self-Defeating); 4 Validity Scales (Random Responding, Tendency to Look Good or Bad, Tendency to Deny Blatant Pathology, Answer Choice Frequency); 7 Axis I Scales (Anxiety, Depression, Post-traumatic Stress Disorder, Schizophrenia, Psychotic Thinking, Social Phobia, Withdrawal); 4 Neuropsychological Dysfunction Scale and Subscales (Neuropsychological Dysfunction, Memory and Concentration, Language Dysfunction, Somatic); 4 Executive Functions Scale and Subscales (Executive Functions, Poor Planning, Decision-Making Problems, Task Incompletion); 3 Hostility Scales (Anger, Dangerousness, Impulsiveness); 4 other clinical scales (Indecisiveness, Emotional Lability, Apathy, Adjustment); Normal Clinical Scale (Introversion-Extraversion); 5 Non-normative scales (Drug and Alcohol, Sexuality, Depersonalization, Frustration Tolerance, Eccentricity).
Administration: Group.
Forms, 2: Self-report, Significant Other.

Price Data, 1996: $10 per evaluation kit including demo disk, manual on disk, 2 test booklets, and limited-use scoring software; $199 per complete kit including computer scoring software (unlimited use), manual ('93, 41 pages), and 25 test booklets; $349 per multi-user kit (same as complete kit, for use by 2 or more clinicians at the same address); $20 per 25 test booklets; $7.50 per manual.

Time: (30–45) minutes.

Comments: Computer scoring program requires DOS version 3.1 or higher and at least 640K RAM.

Author: Frederick L. Coolidge.

Publisher: The CATI Corporation.

Cross References: See T5:690 (3 references).

Review of the Coolidge Axis II Inventory by KEVIN L. MORELAND, *Psychologist, Private Practice, Ft. Walton Beach, FL:*

The Coolidge Axis II Inventory (CATI) was originally developed in the early 1980s to measure the personality disorders defined in the *DSM-III* (American Psychiatric Association, 1980; see Grana, Coolidge, & Merwin, 1989). The inventory was expanded to 200 items during the late 1980s, partly to help measure the two experimental personality disorders added to the *DSM-III-R* (1987), a number of Axis I scales, and three validity scales (Coolidge & Merwin, 1992). The current test booklet has 225 items, but the last 25 are not scored.

The inventory is advertised as *DSM-IV* (American Psychiatric Association, 1994) compatible, though no information is provided on alterations made to effect this change. That may not be as big a problem as it sounds for the Axis II scales. In the *DSM-IV*, Antisocial Personality (ASP) criteria were changed by deleting two items, combining two items, and simplifying the relationship between ASP and Conduct Disorder. One item was added to the Borderline (BDL) criteria. The Passive-Aggressive diagnosis was relegated to an appendix and two *DSM-III-R* experimental disorders, Sadistic and Self-Defeating, were dropped. This review will consider only those personality disorders listed in the *DSM-IV*.

ITEM AND SCALE DEVELOPMENT. The items were developed rationally. They are answered on a 4-point scale from *Strongly False* to *Strongly True*. Most of the scales include roughly half as many items keyed in the false direction as in the true direction to offset symptom claiming. The number of items per scale ranges from 16 for Avoidant Personality (AVD) to 45 for ASP.

Considering two or more Axis II items keyed in the same direction, item overlap among scales ranges from 25% between AVD and the other scales to 64% between ASP and the other scales (cf. Coolidge & Merwin, 1992). It would be helpful to have a table of the empirical intercorrelations among the scales to evaluate its effects.

RELIABILITY. Thirty-nine college students took the CATI twice, one week apart. The mean stability coefficient was .90, with a range from .78 for the Obsessive-Compulsive (OCD) scale to .97 for the Schizoid (SZD) scale. Unfortunately, the individual values were not reported.

The coefficient alpha reliability estimates for all the scales were calculated on the 609 "purportedly normal" individuals who were predominantly young, Caucasian, single, and well educated. These reliabilities ranged from .68 for the OCD scale to .87 for the Dependent (DEP) scale with a median of .79.

STRUCTURAL VALIDITY. A principal factor analysis was conducted with varimax rotation on data from the 609 participants previously described. The three factors extracted accounted for about 65% of the common variance but did not conform to the rational classification used in the *DSM* or factors developed using other instruments. This may have been due to the presence of the three scales dropped from the *DSM-IV*. However, the three factors did match Horney's theory that people move toward others (Histrionic loading = .91), away from others (AVD = .89), or against others (ASP = .89).

CONTENT VALIDITY. In addition, Coolidge and Merwin (1992) asked mainly depressed clients of 11 "licensed clinicians" to complete the CATI and the Millon Clinical Multiaxial Inventory-II (MCMI-II; Millon, 1987), and the clinicians rated their clients on a personality disorder checklist. Using a criterion of 1 *SD* above the mean on the CATI as evidence of a disorder, the CATI and clinician diagnoses agreed 12 out of 24 times, using a Base Rate Score of 75 as a criterion, agreement was 14/24 with the MCMI-II.

The CATI was related to the original version of the NEO Personality Inventory (Costa & McCrae, 1985) for 223 college students (Coolidge, Becker, DiRito, Durham, Kinlaw, & Philbrick, 1994). Zero-order correlations were largely in line with theoretical expectations. Significant correlations between the CATI and NEO neuroticism scale were positive, except for SZD (-.41); the correlations with NEO Extraversion were negative except for Histrionic (HST; .46); the correlations with Agreeableness were negative, and, finally, the correlations with Conscientiousness were all negative.

Fifty-two married participants, mostly white, in their mid 30s, and with at least some college took the CATI and were rated on the Axis II constructs by their spouse and a friend. Participant/spouse correlations ranged from .27 (PAR, n.s.) to .63 (HIS) with a median of .57, and participant/friend correlations ranged from .22 (BDL, NAR, n.s.) to .61 (OCD) with a median of .40 (HIS). This is similar to correlations found in such studies with other instruments.

NORMS. The norm sample described in the 1993 test manual included 937 individuals. Most were female (62%), young (mean age = 29), Caucasian (89%), single (57%), and had at least some college (70%).

SUMMARY. Even though the CATI has been under thoughtful development for nearly 20 years, it has generated only a handful of studies published in the peer-reviewed literature. Moreover, Dr. Coolidge and his colleagues have published all these, most employing college students and other "purported normals" as participants.

Given these factors I cannot recommend the CATI for clinical use absent local trials. Even though scoring is unlimited, given the competition, the $200 (as of early 1999) price of the scoring software may be preventing practitioners and researchers from trying the CATI. Dr. Coolidge and his publisher may wish to rethink their marketing strategy.

REVIEWER'S REFERENCES

American Psychiatric Association. (1980). *Diagnostic and statistical manual of mental disorders* (3rd ed.). Washington, DC: Author.

Costa, P. T., Jr., & McCrae, R. R. (1985). *The NEO Personality Inventory manual.* Odessa, FL: Psychological Assessment Resources.

American Psychiatric Association. (1987). *Diagnostic and statistical manual of mental disorders* (3rd ed. Rev.). Washington, DC: Author.

Millon, T. (1987). *Millon Clinical Multiaxial Inventory-II: Manual for the MCMI-II.* Minneapolis: National Computer Systems.

Grana, A. S., Coolidge, F. L., & Merwin, M. M. (1989). Personality profiles of the morbidly obese. *Journal of Clinical Psychology, 45,* 762–765.

Coolidge, F. L., & Merwin, M. M. (1992). Reliability and validity of the Coolidge Axis II Inventory: A new inventory for the assessment of personality disorders. *Journal of Personality Assessment, 59,* 223–238.

American Psychiatric Association. (1994). *Diagnostic and statistical manual of mental disorders* (4th ed.). Washington, DC: Author.

Coolidge, F. L., Becker, L. A., DiRito, D. C., Durham, R. L., Kinlaw, M. M., & Philbrick, P. B. (1994). On the relationship of the five-factor personality model to personality disorders: Four reservations. *Psychological Reports, 75,* 11–21.

Review of the Coolidge Axis II Inventory by PAUL RETZLAFF, *Professor, Psychology Department, University of Northern Colorado, Greeley, CO:*

The Coolidge Axis II Inventory (CATI) is an odd mix of scales. Although the title implies personality disorder scales, the test also includes a number of Axis I scales, a few neuropsychological scales, some hostility scales, and, finally, a group of "other" scales.

Generally, the manual is dated both in terms of the discipline and the current version of the test. Much has changed since *DSM-III-R* and the MCMI-II. Further, the manual is at best barely adequate.

The test is primarily made up of *DSM-III-R* personality disorder criteria rewritten into psychological test item format. These items are endorsed by patients on a 1 to 4 *Strongly False* to *Strongly True* metric. The manual talks about a 200-item version of the test but the current test is 225 items. It is not readily apparent where the other 25 items came from.

The scales include 13 personality disorder scales (Antisocial, Avoidant, Borderline, Dependent, Histrionic, Narcissistic, Obsessive-Compulsive, Paranoid, Passive-Aggressive, Schizotypal, Schizoid, Sadistic, and Self-Defeating). There are 7 Axis I scales including Anxiety, Depression, Post-traumatic Stress Disorder, Psychotic Thinking, Social Phobia, and Withdrawal. There are 4 neuropsychological function scales, one an overall Neuropsychological Dysfunction scale and three subscales (Memory and Concentration, Language Dysfunction, and Somatic). There are 3 Hostility scales including Anger, Dangerousness, and Impulsiveness. There are 4 "Other Clinical Scales" including Indecisiveness (Executive Functions), Emotional Lability, Apathy, and Adjustment. There is 1 "Normal Clinical Scale," which is Introversion-Extraversion. Finally, there are 5 "Non-normative" scales including Drug and Alcohol, Sexuality, Depersonalization, Frustration Tolerance, and Eccentricity. This amounts to over 30 scales.

The biggest problem with the test is that it started out being a test of personality disorders and then became a test that included many domains. Those additional scales were built using the original personality disorder items. Judging from the item keying, the neuropsychology scales have new items but it is not apparent from the manual that many of the other scales were developed using new items.

The reliability estimates presented in the manual are only for the personality disorder scales and used "normal" subjects. Cronbach alphas are needed for all the scales. In addition, a large sample of patients is far more appropriate to the intent of the test.

Validity for scores from the personality disorder scales is unimpressive. A study with a total of 24 patients including only three males is presented as criterion validity evidence. No scale-specific validity evidence is presented due to the large number of scales per subject. The author has arbitrarily chosen a cutscore of 1 standard deviation above the normative sample's mean as indicative of a personality disorder. Obviously, a data-based decision would have been better. Construct validity evidence for scores from the Axis I scales correlated against MCMI-II and MMPI type scales are all generally in the .60s. An intercorrelation matrix of the CATI scales would have been nice to determine scale specificity.

The validity of scores from the neuropsychological scales hinges on a study of only 17 clinical subjects. Further, it appears that the subscales were developed through a factor analysis of the items using the normal subjects' data. Here, a development procedure that used actual patients would have been stronger. There appears to be no reliability or validity data for the Hostility scales, the "Other Clinical" scale, the "Normal Clinical" scale, or the "Non-normative" scales.

SUMMARY. In sum, the CATI provides an odd mixture of scales. Scores from some are probably reliable and some probably valid. The manual is inadequate and the number of actual clinical subjects is inadequate. Given that the competition is the MCMI-III (T5:1687), there is little reason to use the CATI.

[23]
Coping Inventory for Stressful Situations.

Purpose: Scale for measuring multidimensional aspects of coping with stress.
Population: Adults, Adolescents.
Publication Date: 1990.
Acronym: CISS.
Scores, 5: Task, Emotion, Avoidance, Distraction, Social Diversion.
Administration: Individual or group.
Forms, 2: Adult, Adolescent.

Price Data, 1999: $40 per complete kit including manual (78 pages) and 25 QuikScore™ forms (specify Adult or Adolescent Version); $22 per 25 Adult or Adolescent QuikScore™ forms; $25 per manual; $160 per IBM MS DOS 50-use 3.5-inch disk for administration and scoring.
Foreign Language Editions: French, German, Spanish editions available.
Time: (10) minutes.
Comments: Paper-and-pencil or computer administered.
Authors: Norman S. Endler and James D. A. Parker.
Publisher: Multi-Health Systems, Inc.
Cross References: See T5:696 (2 references).
[Note: The publisher advised in September 1999 that a Second Edition (1999) is now available for this test addressing several concerns raised by reviews of the 1990 edition. The Second Edition will be reviewed in the *15th MMY*.]

Review of the Coping Inventory for Stressful Situations by E. THOMAS DOWD, Professor of Psychology, Kent State University, Kent, OH:

The Coping Inventory for Stressful Situations (CISS) is a 48-item self-report, paper-and-pencil measure of coping along three dimensions consisting of 16 items each: Task-oriented, Emotion-oriented, and Avoidance-oriented coping. The latter scale in turn consists of two subscales, Distraction (8 items) and Social Diversion (5 items). The instrument is based theoretically on an interactional model of anxiety, stress, and coping, in which person variables (e.g., trait anxiety, vulnerability, cognitive style) interact with situation variables (e.g., life events, hassles, crises) to produce perception of threat, leading in turn to increases in state anxiety and subsequent physical and psychological reactions to this state anxiety. The model is presented as an integration of an intraindividual approach to coping (in which an individual's coping is compared across different types of situations) and an interindividual approach to coping (in which coping scores of the same individual are assessed over different occasions representing a stable score). These different approaches have differing implications for reliability estimates; one would expect it to be lower for the intraindividual approach than for the interindividual approach. Functionally, the CISS appears to be more interindividual, however; indeed, the manual states that it was developed to assess preferred coping *styles* or strategies *typically* used. Work on the instrument began in 1986 and it was formerly called the Multidimensional Coping Inventory (MCI). There is both an adult and an adolescent version, the latter constructed by rewording six items in the adult version in more simple words.

The package comes with a manual and a combination answer sheet and scoring grid, which enable the user to plot individual scores against normative data. The manual consists of seven chapters, including a general description of the instrument, computer administration and scoring instructions, interpretation and use, instrument development, description of normative samples, and reliability and validity evidence. There are several case studies indicating how the instrument might be used in clinical situations.

The inventory was created by developing a pool of 120 items representing (in the view of a number of psychologists and graduate students) diverse coping behaviors. This pool was reduced to 70 items by removing redundant and biased items (not stated is how this was done or what "biased" means). The 70-item scale was administered to 559 undergraduates and a factor analysis conducted, resulting in 19 factors. Based on the scree test criteria, the first three factors were rotated. Subsequently, items that did not load about .40 were discarded with a few exceptions. The resulting rotated factors were labeled "task-oriented coping," "emotion-oriented coping," and "avoidance-oriented coping." A later factor analysis identified two subfactors of the Avoidance scale. From the description, however, it is not clear how only three factors were ultimately identified. Were the three factors identified in advance or arrived at strictly empirically?

The authors present both coefficient alpha and test-retest reliability estimates. The former, by each factor and by gender, ranged from .92–.73, with the majority in the .90s and .80s. Test-retest reliabilities ranged from .73–.51. These reliabilities, although decent, are not high, especially the test-retest, indicating perhaps that coping style is not an especially stable construct. Item-remainder correlations (those between each item and the rest of the items) for each factor ranged from .12 to .71. Many of these correlations are quite low and I am surprised that some of the lower correlating items were not eliminated earlier in the test development.

Validity was investigated by factor analyses on subsequent samples, resulting in the same three factors, and by relatively low intercorrelations of the CISS factor scales. These results, the authors say, speak to the multidimensionality of the scale and presumably to validity. Construct validity was demonstrated by theoretically expected correlations between the factor scales of the CISS and the Ways of Coping Scale (WOC), the Basic Personality Inventory (BPI), the Beck Depression Inventory (BDI), the Endler Multidimensional Anxiety Scales (EMAS), the Eysenck Personality Inventory (EPI), and selected scales of the MMPI-2. Although the theoretical logic behind some of the many correlations was apparent, the logic behind others was not. In general, Emotion-focussed coping was related to various measures of psychological distress and Task-focussed coping either was not related to psychological distress or was negatively related. Avoidance-focussed coping was generally not related to psychological distress.

Emotion-focussed coping in this instrument appears to be an unmitigated problem with no redeeming features at all and associated with a wide variety of psychological problems. Aside from the situational differences in coping styles (one might use Task-focussed coping in one situation and Emotion-focussed in another), the stress literature does not present Emotion-focussed coping in such a universally negative light. Even the case examples present it this way; those individuals in distress are high on Emotion-focussed coping and low or moderate on Task-focussed and Avoidance-focussed coping. Indeed, I was left wondering how this instrument would have differential utility over instruments measuring general psychological distress.

SUMMARY. This is a reasonably well-designed instrument for which specific utility is not always clear. What, other than providing another look at general distress, is to be done with the results? Perhaps one implication is its use as an initial assessment instrument prior to training individual to use more Task-focussed and fewer Emotion-focussed coping strategies that are undefined by this instrument. In addition, I would suggest the authors revise the instrument to eliminate some of the very low item-remainder correlations. I suspect they might be reducing the reliability. Finally, I would like to know exactly how the specific factors and subfactors were identified.

Review of the Coping Inventory for Stressful Situations by STEPHANIE STEIN, Professor of Psychology, Central Washington University, Ellensburg, WA:

The Coping Inventory for Stressful Situations (CISS) is a revision of the former Multidimensional Coping Inventory. The CISS is a brief self-report measure of coping styles used by an individual in a "difficult, stressful, or upsetting situation" (manual, p. 5). Each item on the inventory is a single descriptive phrase that is rated by the respondent on a Likert-type scale from 1 (*not at all*) to 5 (*very much*). The 48 items combine to provide *T*-scores in five types of coping styles: Task, Emotion, Avoidance, Avoidance-Distraction, and Avoidance-Social Diversion. The adolescent version of the inventory is apparently identical to the adult version except that some of the vocabulary is simplified. The inventory is quick and easy to administer and score.

The manual that accompanies the inventory is well organized and complete. It provides thorough guidelines on administration and scoring of the CISS. However, the chapter on interpretation of the inventory is a bit vague. The authors describe two methods of profile analysis: eyeballing and pattern analysis. It is surprising to see eyeballing listed as a recommended method of interpretation, especially without additional guidelines, because untrained individuals using that technique tend to underestimate or overestimate differences between the scales or differences over time. In contrast to the informal eyeballing method, the authors also recommend pattern analysis using "*statistically* based decision rules regarding *confidence intervals*" (manual, p. 14). However, they do not explain how to do this, nor do they provide confidence intervals or the standard error of measurement on the different scales. They do include several case studies, which are accompanied by score profiles. Unfortunately, the authors provide only very general interpretations of the case studies for the most part, indicating whether a scale score was high or low but not giving much information about the implications of these scores. Another minor problem with the case studies is that the interpretation of the scores is inconsistent. For example, the guidelines indicate that a *T*-score of 32 or 33 is "much below average" but in some of the case studies a score of 33 is described as "low" and in one case study a score of 32 is considered "somewhat below average." It is questionable whether the average test user would know how to interpret a CISS profile meaningfully after reading this chapter.

A detailed description is given of the development of the CISS including a theoretically based rationale for the inventory and factor analysis of the five scales. Several normative samples are described for the English version of the CISS: 537 adults, 1,242 college undergraduates, 302 psychiatric inpatients, 313 young adolescents between the ages of 13 and 15 years, and 504 older adolescents between the ages of 16 to 18 years. Other than gender, the manual does not provide any further information about the normative populations. Therefore, the test user has no way of knowing whether the normative sample is similar to the test user's subjects in terms of SES, race/ethnicity, geographic region, or any other relevant demographic characteristic. The authors only say that the adult and college samples were English-speaking North Americans, which is likely to mean Canadians because that is where the authors lived.

Reliability data on the CISS are adequate. The authors present internal consistency reliability coefficients ranging from a low of .69 for female psychiatric patients on the Distraction scale to a high of .92 for male early adolescents on the Task scale. Most of the Cronbach alpha coefficients are between .80 and .90. Test-retest reliability information (based on a 6-week interval) is also provided for a small subgroup of college undergraduates. The test-retest correlations range from .68 to .72 on the Task and Emotion scales and are slightly lower for the Avoidance scale and two subscales, ranging from .51 to .60.

In support of the validity of the CISS, the authors present factor analyses data that provide evidence for the multidimensionality of the inventory. In addition, nonsignificant or low intercorrelations were found between the Task, Emotion, and Avoidance scales. The intercorrelations were somewhat higher between the Avoidance scale and the two Avoidance subscales, which is not surprising because they share some of the same items in each scale. Finally, the authors present evidence for the construct validity of scores from their instrument by correlating scores with other instruments such as the Marlowe-Crowne Social Desirability Scales (low or nonsignificant correlations) and the Ways of Coping Questionnaire (moderate correlations). They also correlate the different CISS scales with various measures of psychopathology such as the Basic Personality Inventory, the MMPI-2, the Beck Depression Inventory, the Psychosomatic Symptom Checklist, and others. The authors found that the Emotion scale was highly correlated with a number of measures of "psychological distress, psychopathology, and somatization. Task-oriented coping and avoidance-oriented coping, on the other hand, appear to be unrelated to these negative variables" (manual, p. 63). Actually, the Task scale is negatively correlated with some of the measures of psychopathology, which is consistent with the authors' theory. However, the general lack of correlation between the Avoidance scale and the two subscales of Distraction and Social Diversion with almost anything else leads one to question the inclusion of these scales.

SUMMARY. The CISS appears to be a technically adequate measure of coping styles. More information could and should be provided, though, on the characteristics of the norming samples so that test users can judge the appropriateness of the measure for their subjects. The biggest weakness of this instrument is that the implications of the scores are unclear, especially on the Avoidance scale and subscales. It leaves the test user responding "So what?" after the instrument is administered and scored. Additional guidelines from the authors on interpretation and use of the instrument would be helpful. Despite these problems, the CISS is probably the best measure of its kind because other measures of coping styles have even more problems related to reliability and factor structure.

[24]
Das-Naglieri Cognitive Assessment System.

Purpose: "Developed to evaluate cognitive processes of children … using the PASS theory of intelligence."
Population: Ages 5 to 17-11.
Publication Date: 1997.
Acronym: CAS.
Levels, 2: Ages 5–7, ages 8–17.
Price Data, 1999: $595 per complete kit with carrying case; $520 per complete kit without case; $48 per Administration and Scoring Manual (305 pages); $48 per Interpretive Handbook; $27 per 25 Record Forms (ages 5–17); $16.50 per 25 Response Books (specify ages 5–7 or ages 8–17); $16.50 per 25 Figure

Memory Response Books (ages 5–17); $24 per 30 Multi-Pack of Forms; $64 per Assessment of Cognitive Processes: The PASS Theory of Intelligence (256 pages).
Comments: PASS theory reconceptualizes intelligence as cognitive processes.
Authors: Jack A. Naglieri and J. P. Das.
Publisher: Riverside Publishing.
   a) STANDARD BATTERY.
   Scores: 4 scales with 13 subtests: Planning (Matching Numbers, Planned Codes, Planned Connections), Simultaneous (Nonverbal Matrices, Verbal-Spatial Relations, Figure Memory), Attention (Expressive Attention, Number Detection, Receptive Attention), Successive (Word Series, Sentence Repetition, Speech Rate, Sentence Questions).
   Time: [60] minutes.
   b) BASIC BATTERY.
   Scores: 4 scales with 8 subtests: Planning (Matching Numbers, Planned Codes), Simultaneous (Nonverbal Matrices, Verbal-Spatial Relations), Attention (Expressive Attention, Number Detection), Successive (Word Series, Sentence Repetition).
   Time: [40] minutes.
Cross References: See T5:763 (5 references).

Review of the Das-Naglieri Cognitive Assessment System by JOYCE MEIKAMP, Associate Professor of Special Education, Marshall University Graduate College, South Charleston, WV:

NATURE AND USES. The Das-Naglieri Cognitive Assessment System (CAS) is a clinical instrument for assessing intelligence based on a battery of cognitive tasks. The CAS reflects the authors' more than 20 years of research and development. Utilizing an innovative, nontraditional approach for assessing individual differences in intelligence, both theory and applied psychology are incorporated in this instrument. Based upon Luria's PASS theory, intelligence is reconceptualized as consisting of four cognitive processes. These mental activities include planning, attention, simultaneous, and successive (PASS) processing. The CAS is designed for identifying relative cognitive processing strengths and weaknesses, predicting achievement or classification, determining eligibility, and designing treatment, instructional, or remedial programs.

Operationalizing the PASS theory, the CAS has two forms: a Standard Battery and a Basic Battery. Both forms consist of Planning, Attention, Simultaneous, and Successive Scales. For the Standard Battery, each of the four PASS scales consists of three subtests, whereas the Basic Battery PASS scales utilize two subtests each. Within each PASS scale scores are combined to yield a standard score with a mean of 100 and *SD* of 15. A Full Scale standard score, derived from the sum of the subtest scaled scores, is generated for either the Standard or Basic Batteries.

Each PASS scale subtest was developed to operationalize a particular process for task completion. These subtests incorporate a variety of tasks, representing diversity in content, modality, and complexity. Uniquely, the CAS employs Planning and Attention scales, two constructs not typically incorporated in traditional measures of intelligence. For example, the Planning scale subtests present relatively easy paper-and-pencil tasks requiring the individual to make decisions about solving novel tasks. Not only must a plan of action be created, but also applied, verified, and modified as needed.

Emphasizing cognitive processing strategies, the examiner records not only time and accuracy, but also the strategies the subject both appears to be and reports to be utilizing. Although this feature is unique and holds much promise for understanding an individual's cognitive processing, identification of relative strengths and weaknesses, and designing treatment and instructional programs, caution is in order for exceptional populations. For example, questioning individuals who may be either mentally retarded or learning disabled is problematic because these populations frequently have great difficulty verbalizing strategies utilized to solve problems. Thus, there may be great uncertainty as to whether or not they are even utilizing problem-solving strategies. Moreover, given the examiner accuracy, timing, and observed and reported strategies requirements, and the nature of the demands placed on the examiner, potential for error exists for the Planning subtests.

Attention is felt by the authors to be central to cognitive processing. The Attention Scale requires the child to focus on a task, selectively attend to a specific stimulus, and suppress irrelevant stimuli. A variety of creative tasks with familiar stimuli are in each of the subtests.

Conversely, the Simultaneous scale subtests include a predominance of information coding tasks requiring perception of parts into wholes or a single gestalt. Interrelating parts into a perceptual whole, the subtests require the individual to acquire, store, and retrieve information. According to the CAS authors, simultaneous processing involves both nonverbal spatial as well as verbal-grammatical activities.

The Successive Processing subtests tasks require the processing of information in a linear and sequential manner. For each of the subtests the individual deals with verbally presented information in a specific chain-like order and for which the order drives the meaning. According to the CAS authors, each element is only related to those that precede it, and these stimuli are not interrelated. Unlike the other CAS scales, the Successive scale subtests stimuli are only presented auditorily to the individual and then the individual is asked to respond verbally. Given the diversity of modalities and modes of presentation utilized in the other Pass scales, one has to wonder why the authors uncharacteristically opted to rely so heavily on verbal task demands for this particular scale.

DEVELOPMENT AND STANDARDIZATION. The CAS was standardized on a national sample of 2,200 children (aged 5-0 to 17-11) randomly stratified for age, gender, race, Hispanic origin, geographic region, parental educational attainment, and community setting. Approximately 13% of the sample was drawn from children who were receiving special education services. All scores are expressed as normalized standard scores and as percentile ranks. Although conversions of CAS subtest raw scores to age equivalents are also available, the authors caution about doing so.

RELIABILITY AND VALIDITY. Split-half reliability coefficients ranging from .70 to .96 were reported for Simultaneous and Successive subtests (except Speech Rate). Test-retest reliability coefficients (median delay = 21 days) for the Planning and Attention subtests as well as Speech Rate ranged from .64 to .92. The formula for the reliability of linear combinations was utilized to compute reliability coefficients for the Standard and Basic Battery PASS scales and Full Scale standard scores. Standard Battery PASS scale reliability coefficients were from .84 to .95, and for the Basic Battery they ranged from .81 to .93. Standard Full Scale coefficients were from .95 to .97 and Basic Full Scale coefficients ranged from .85 to .90.

In addition to content validity built into the tests through item and subtest analyses via task analyses and examination, analyses conducted on the standardization sample contributed to evidence of construct validity. Data were provided from factor analyses of subtests, age differences, and internal consistency of subtests and scales, as well as CAS Basic and Standard Batteries. However, factor analyses of subtests indicated some support for a 4-factor PASS solution as well as for a 3-factor solution. Thus, Planning and Attention as separate factors may be debatable.

Criterion-related validity against the Woodcock-Johnson—Revised Tests of Achievement was investigated with a sample of 1,600, with resulting correlations appearing to be promising. Several other investigations, with small groups of exceptional children, also reported promising correlations.

INTERPRETIVE HAZARDS. An important goal of the CAS is to reconceptualize human cognitive processing in order to gain a broader understanding of both interindividual and intraindividual differences. Ultimately this information is to be used to make informed decisions about diagnosis, eligibility, and intervention. However, comparing the PASS scales and subtest scores for intraindividual differences and discrepancies may open the way for misinterpretation. Such ipsative interpretation is highly controversial given these procedures violate the assumptions of typical statistics (Kerlinger, 1973).

Regarding intervention, the authors acknowledge the validity of assessment-intervention linkages is ongoing and an emerging area of research. Although a summary of such research is provided, few intervention studies with exceptional populations are cited. Thus, caution should be exercised in prescribing PASS-based remedial instruction for exceptional students.

SUMMARY. The CAS is an innovative instrument and its development meets high standards of technical adequacy. Despite interpretation cautions with exceptional populations, this instrument creatively bridges the gap between theory and applied psychology.

REVIEWER'S REFERENCE
Kerlinger, F. N. (1973). *Foundations of behavioral research* (2nd ed.). New York: Holt, Rinehart, & Winston.

Review of the Das-Naglieri Cognitive Assessment System by DONALD THOMPSON, Dean and Professor of Counseling and Psychology, Troy State University Montgomery, Montgomery, AL:

The Das-Naglieri Cognitive Assessment System (CAS) is a test of general ability that consists of a battery of subtests designed to assess cognitive processing based on the authors' PASS theory of intellect "which reconceptualizes intelligence as cognitive processes" (Interpretive Handbook, p. 2). The user's manual indicates that the CAS was developed:

> To integrate theoretical and applied areas of psychological knowledge using a theory of cognitive processing and tests designed to measure those processes. More specifically, the CAS was developed to evaluate Planning, Attention, Simultaneous, and Successive (PASS) cognitive processes of individuals between the ages of 5 and 17 years. (p. 1)

The complete CAS kit includes the Administration and Scoring Manual, Interpretive Handbook, and 25 each of the Record Form, Response Book, and Figure Memory Response Books. The test has two forms: The Standard Battery is composed of 13 subtests (only 12 are used in any administration, however), and the Basic Battery is composed for 8 subtests. Although both the Standard and Basic Batteries include Planning, Attention, Simultaneous, and Successive (PASS) scales, in the Basic Battery the scales are composed of two subtests each, whereas on the Standard Battery, the scales have three subtests each. All subtests yield standard scores, and the standard score scale for each subtests has a mean of 10 and standard deviation of 3. The Full Scale score on the test is determined by combining the subtests scaled scores. The Full Scale score is a standard score scale that has a mean of 100 and a standard deviation of 15.

The CAS is an individually administered test that requires 40 minutes for the Basic Battery and 60 minutes for the Standard Battery. The reported reliability data for the Full Scale and PASS subscales indicate the test has high internal consistency and test-retest reliability. The Full Scale reliability coefficients range from .95 to .97 (Spearman corrected split-half estimate), and the average reliabilities for the Standard Battery PASS scales are reported as .88 (Planning), .88 (Attention), .93 (Simultaneous), and .93 (Successive). The Interpretive Handbook also reports data on content, construct, and criterion-related validity. These data provide generally strong support for the construct, and the criterion-related validity studies suggest that the CAS is highly correlated to other well-established measures of ability and achievement such as the Woodcock-Johnson Psycho-Educational Battery—Revised (WJ-R; T5:2901) and the Wechsler Preschool and Primary Scale of Intelligence—Revised (WPPSI-R; T5:2864).

CAS norms are based on a sample of 2,200 children ranging in age from 5 years to 17 years, 11 months. The standardization sample was distributed geographically to be representative of the United States for gender, age, racial and ethnic origin, and socioeconomic factors. The data reported in the Interpretive Handbook suggest that this was a very well-done standardization. The representativeness of the norm data should insure that the individual scores can be accurately interpreted for all individuals for whom the test is intended.

Although the primary purpose of the CAS is to assess cognitive processing (or general intellectual functioning/ability level), the authors suggest that PASS scores can be especially useful in the identification of attention-deficit/hyperactivity disorders, traumatic brain injury, learning disabilities, mental retardation, and giftedness.

The CAS has many strong features that make it a desirable test. It is not difficult to learn to administer the test, and the directions for administration and scoring are clear and straightforward. Also, when compared to other individually administered general ability tests, such as the Stanford-Binet (T5:2485) or the Wechsler scales (98; T5:2862; T5:2863; T5:2864), it take less time to administer. As noted earlier, the CAS definition of cognitive functioning (intelligence) is based on the four components of planning, attention, simultaneous, and successive processing. This is a different view of intelligence, but it also makes sense if you follow the reasoning. Test administrators who used the CAS for this review liked the idea of four specific assessment areas rather than just Verbal or Quantitative scores provided by the Wechsler Scales. It is easy to explain the test scores to parents and teachers because the full scale and subtests scaled scores have means and standard deviations that are the same as the Wechsler Scales. This also makes it easy to interpret and compare to other test scores. In fact, the Record Form contains a very handy

chart for making a direct calculation of ability/achievement discrepancy scores using the WJ-R Achievement Test results. The interpretive handbook is very helpful in making judgments regarding the meaning of test scores and making interpretations for individual test takers; however, the lack of an index made it difficult to find specific material quickly. Having the option of the Basic or Standard Battery adds flexibility and still provides the full scale score and all four cognitive processing scores.

The CAS is a relatively new entry into the field of ability testing. The amount of empirical research supporting the PASS construct is limited, and most of this comes from the authors. Although the test materials were generally judged to be of high quality, the administrators who used the CAS for this review were unimpressed with the scoring templates that are used as overlays on the subject's Response Book answer sheets. The overlays are made of translucent paper, as opposed to a more durable plastic material. The templates are likely to tear, fall apart, or be disfigured in long-term use. Several test subjects expressed dislike for the Sentence Repetition and Sentence Questions subtests. They complained that both the subtests were particularly difficult because the sentences were so silly. The Figure Memory subtest is similar to the Bock Design subtest on Wechsler Scales, but it is both more difficult to administer, and appears to be more difficult for subjects to perform. The ratio conversion scores are rather confusing. The method of scoring is clear, but the meaning of the scores is rather hazy. Although the complete test battery kit costs less than either the Wechsler or Binet Scales, the cost of consumables per administration (about $2.20) does raise the long range cost.

SUMMARY. Overall, the CAS was judged by this reviewer to be a strong entry into the ability testing field for children and adolescents. It would seem particularly useful for testing special populations as noted earlier. The PASS concept makes logical sense, but more empirical research is needed. The test materials are of generally high quality, and ease of use is a strong feature. Generally, I found the CAS to be a better measure than the current version of the Stanford-Binet, but in terms of ease of use and score interpretation, I prefer the Wechsler Scales.

[25]
Davidson Trauma Scale.

Purpose: Developed to assess post traumatic stress disorder (PTSD) symptoms and aid in treatment.
Population: Adults who have been exposed to a serious trauma.
Publication Date: 1996.
Acronym: DTS.
Scores, 4: Intrusion, Avoidance/Numbing, Hyperarousal, Total.
Administration: Individual or group.
Price Data, 1997: $45 per complete kit including manual (42 pages), and 25 QuikScore™ forms; $22 per 25 QuikScore™ forms; $27 per manual.
Foreign Language Edition: French-Canadian QuikScore™ forms available.
Time: (10) minutes.
Author: Jonathan Davidson.
Publisher: Multi-Health Systems, Inc.

Review of the Davidson Trauma Scale by JANET F. CARLSON, Professor of Counseling and Psychological Services, Associate Dean School of Education, Oswego State University, Oswego, NY:

The Davidson Trauma Scale (DTS) is a recently published, paper-and-pencil, self-report inventory that assesses frequency and severity of posttraumatic stress disorder (PTSD) symptoms in adults. The DTS was developed by Jonathan Davidson, Director of the Anxiety and Traumatic Stress Program at Duke University Medical Center. The items of the scale consist of 17 symptoms that mirror closely the diagnostic criteria of PTSD, contained in the fourth edition of the *Diagnostic and Statistical Manual of Mental Disorders* (DSM-IV; American Psychiatric Association, 1994). Using the past week as a frame of reference and a 0 to 4 rating scale, test takers are asked to rate each item for the frequency of its occurrence and the subjective distress accompanying the symptom. The items comprise three symptom clusters associated with the major dimensions of PTSD symptomatology—intrusion into everyday life, acts or experiences that avoid or numb feelings connected with the trauma, and hyperarousal.

APPLICATIONS. The test author recommends the DTS for use in providing feedback to patients undergoing treatment for PTSD and to assess treatment response. Further, it may be used as a screening instrument or for research purposes. Appropriately, the test author advises potential users that the DTS is best regarded as an adjunct or supplement to clinical assessment, rather than as a replacement for same. It is not intended as a diagnostic instrument.

The intended uses of the DTS include the assessment of PTSD symptoms experienced by adults who have been exposed to serious traumata. In this context, trauma is a clinically significant term denoting an event that is "outside of everyday experience and [is] markedly distressing to the great majority" (manual, p. 2). The test author notes that such an event must have "involved actual or threatened death or serious injury, or threat to the physical integrity of self or others, and induced a response of intense fear, helplessness, or horror" (p. 1). Such events include but are not limited to criminal or sexual assault, combat, natural disaster, torture, and bereavement.

ADMINISTRATION, SCORING, AND INTERPRETATION. The DTS may be administered individually or in group format. It also is possible to modify procedures slightly to permit oral administration if, for instance, the test taker were visually impaired. Instructions to the test taker are simple, and the test author indicates that completion of the scale requires only an eighth-grade reading level. General guidelines for test administration are provided in the test manual, including suggestions for prompting respondents if necessary. Total administration time is no more than 10 minutes; scoring takes even less time than administration.

Test takers respond by writing numbers corresponding to their ratings of frequency and severity of the 17 symptoms in boxes on the record form. A carbonized sheet transfers responses to the underlying score sheet, consisting of a set of boxes that are meaningfully grouped to yield a Total Frequency score, Total Severity score, and Total DTS score. In addition, separate cluster scores for Intrusion, Avoidance/Numbing, and Hyperarousal are readily obtained by simple addition.

Interpretation stems from tabled data that present relative frequencies of various Total DTS scores for persons with and without PTSD. The table appears in the manual and is reproduced as part of the DTS QuikScore form. Interpretation is based primarily on the total score, which may range from 0 to 136. The test author suggests that the tabled data provide a measure of diagnostic probability, and offers the score of 20 as "a useful flag that PTSD is a likely probability" (manual, p. 15). However, elsewhere in the manual (p. 23) a cut point of 40 is identified as "perhaps the most clinically accurate." As noted above, cluster scores are obtainable, but data-derived interpretive procedures are not specified in the test manual for scores other than the Total DTS score. The test author suggests that subscale scores, frequency, and severity ratings be examined to assist in treatment planning or assessment of treatment response.

TECHNICAL ASPECTS. The section of the test manual that covers psychometric characteristics presents information from four studies to generate reliability estimates and provide evidence of scale validation. All studies used clinical samples, ranging in size from 53 to 110. The study used to examine test-retest reliability consisted of 102 individuals, who completed the DTS two times, with a one-week interval, and an assessment by a third party that their clinical picture had remained constant. The resulting coefficient was .86. Split-half reliability estimates are reported as .95 and .97 for frequency and severity, respectively, but it is not clear from the manual how these coefficients were determined. Alpha reliability coefficients were based on combined data from these studies (n = 241). The test author describes the coefficients as "high" and indicates that the values exceeded .90 for the total scale and for the frequency and severity scale scores. A separate study of 50 women who survived childhood sexual abuse produced alpha reliability estimates of .93 for the total scale, and .85, .83, and .87 for Intrusion, Avoidance/Numbing, and Hyperarousal cluster scores, respectively. Item-total correlations ranged from .60 to .89, with most falling in the .80s.

Validation evidence for the DTS is provided in the test manual with attention to classification accuracy, convergent validity, divergent validity, group differences, and treatment change. All of these are best viewed as construct validation efforts. The test author discusses classification accuracy in terms of the interdependence of sensitivity and specificity and provides examples of how each factor is clinically relevant, as well as how each is affected by the selection of different cut points. Convergent validity was assessed by comparing the DTS with the Clinician-Administered PTSD Scale (n = 102), the Impact of Events Scale (n = 180), and the Symptom Checklist-90-R (n = 123). Correlation coefficients of Total DTS scores with the corresponding total score for each of these instruments were .78, .64, and .57, respec-

tively. A related study compared the frequency and severity scales of the DTS with the total score from the Trauma Symptom Checklist 40, with resulting coefficients of .31 and .24, respectively. In addressing divergent validity, the Total DTS score was compared with an extraversion measure from the Eysenck Personality Inventory, using 78 subjects. Appropriately, the scores were unrelated (r = .04). The test author reports significant findings concerning the scale's ability to discriminate PTSD from non-PTSD patients, and to distinguish patients who respond to treatment from those who do not. Changes in symptoms and overall clinical condition, as assessed by the treating physicians, paralleled changes in DTS scores.

A factor analysis using a clinical sample (n = 133) was conducted. Some of the findings are presented briefly in the test manual. The test author notes that in this analysis a single very strong factor emerged, with a second much weaker factor present. Other studies found three factors. The number of factors extracted may be due, in part, to the characteristics of the samples used, and the method of extraction employed.

CRITIQUE. Not surprisingly, the information presented in the test manual is favorable and supportive of the DTS as far as its use with the intended population. Still, potential users must be prepared to ferret out some information beyond that presented in the test manual that may affect their choice of instruments. In particular, test users should bear in mind that the DTS is not intended to be a diagnostic instrument, and should not be used as such. Thus, in clinical applications, it is best regarded as a screening instrument for PTSD or as an indicator of the frequency and extent of related symptoms.

The test manual is uneven in its presentation of information. In the discussion of studies bearing on the psychometric properties, for example, sample sizes or procedures employed are only sometimes specified. Other times, rather descriptive labels are used, making it difficult for a potential user to assess relevant features of the scale. Particularly problematic are the guidelines pertaining to interpretation, which appear driven almost exclusively by clinical judgment. Therefore, use of the DTS by persons who lack considerable clinical experience with trauma victims is not recommended. Use of the scale by persons with substantial experience will not add greatly to such persons' understanding of the patient or population with whom they work. However, as a means of documenting symptoms numerically, or assessing treatment response, experienced clinicians may find the DTS somewhat useful.

There are no filler items on the DTS, as all items contribute to the total score. Items clearly are aimed at assessing aspects of PTSD. The response options for each item are presented in order of increasing severity or frequency. The items themselves are grouped by clusters. Although these characteristics make administration, scoring, and interpretation straightforward and probably add to the intrinsic appeal of the instrument, they also make faking extremely easy, because what is being assessed and which responses will garner the greatest clinical "weight" are obvious. In cases where test takers might be motivated to deceive (e.g., competency to stand trial, custody hearings, involuntary commitment procedures, social desirability), the test user is advised to use additional or less transparent means of assessment. Test users are left to their own devices as far as the detection of malingering.

SUMMARY. The DTS is a relatively new instrument, intended to be used and integrated with other available information, in order to document and understand PTSD symptomatology among clinical populations. Likely, it will find applications in related arenas, including research, screening, and assessment of therapeutic outcomes. Working in its favor are the facts that it is a simple measure that is easily and rapidly administered and scored, may be modifiable for use with individuals with disabilities, encompasses the major symptoms of PTSD, and is reasonably priced. Evidence concerning its usefulness is most likely to accumulate from its use in clinical settings and data generated from these applications. In the test manual, the test author expresses interest in receiving such information.

REVIEWER'S REFERENCE

American Psychiatric Association. (1994). *Diagnostic and statistical manual of mental disorders* (4th ed.). Washington, DC: Author.

Review of the Davidson Trauma Scale by WILLIAM E. MARTIN, JR., *Professor of Educational Psychology, Northern Arizona University, Flagstaff, AZ:*

The Davidson Trauma Scale (DTS) was designed for use with adults who have experienced a serious trauma as operationalized by the 1994 *Diagnostic and Statistical Manual of Mental Disorders* (DSM-IV; American Psychiatric Association, 1994). The scale is intended to cover *all* types of trauma including accident, combat, sexual assault, criminal assault, natural disaster, torture, burns, loss of property, near death experiences, and bereavement.

The DTS consists of 17 questions organized into three subscales and three total scales that directly reflect the 17 symptoms of Criteria B, C, and D of the DSM-IV for Posttraumatic Stress Disorder (PTSD). The three subscales are Intrusion (5 questions/symptoms), Avoidance/Numbing (7 questions/symptoms), and Hyperarousal (5 questions/symptoms). Additionally, the three total scales are Total Frequency (17 questions/symptoms), Total Severity (17 questions/symptoms), and DTS Total (17 questions/symptoms).

ADMINISTRATION, SCORING, AND INTERPRETATION. A user of the DTS is asked first to provide an open-ended response that identifies the trauma that is most disturbing him or her. Then, the user responds in two ways to 17 questions reflecting trauma symptoms. First, the respondent is asked to identify the frequency of symptoms for the last week on each questions using a 5-point rating scale (0 = *Not At All*, 1 = *Once Only*, 2 = *2–3 Times*, 3 = *4–6 Times*, and 4 = *Every Day*). Second, the respondent identifies the severity of each symptom using a 5-point scale ranging from 0 = *Not At All Distressing* to 4 = *Extremely Distressing*. The DTS is presented on a carbonized 3-page form that is used for both administering and scoring the instrument. The test-taking process takes less than 10 minutes according to the DTS manual.

Completion of the DTS culminates in three subscale scores (Intrusion, Avoidance/Numbing, Hyperarousal), a Total Frequency score, a Total Severity score, and a DTS Total score. The three subscale scores and the DTS Total score are obtained by combining the frequency and severity ratings for all those questions that are associated with the three subscales and the total scale.

The DTS manual provides guidelines for interpreting the DTS results that focus on examining the DTS Total score, subscale scores, and the frequency and severity of symptoms scores. A table containing ratios of expected number of individuals with PTSD to individuals without

PTSD is provided to assist the examiner in interpreting the DTS Total scores. Accordingly, higher ratios indicate higher probability of having PTSD. Unfortunately, there is a lack of information on how the ratios furnished in the table were obtained. Likewise, it is unclear which scores to use given the information provided in the table. The manual presents interpretations for six case studies representing differing traumas and clinical contexts.

DEVELOPMENT OF THE SCALES. The DTS was constructed to reflect directly the DSM-IV Criteria B, C, and D for Posttraumatic Stress Disorder.

RELIABILITY AND VALIDITY. Estimates of reliability and validity for scores from the DTS were derived primarily from four clinical research studies. The clinical groups in the four studies were female rape victims ($n = 78$), hurricane victims ($n = 53$), male combat veterans ($n = 110$), and individuals in multicenter clinical trials ($n = 102$). The ethnocultural profile of the first three clinical groups was reported as African American (24%), Hispanic (6%), and Caucasian (70%).

A one-week test-retest reliability estimate of $r = .86$ ($n = 21$) was reported. A split-half reliability estimate was $r = .95$ but the sample used was not specified. Coefficient alphas were over .90 for the Frequency, Severity, and DTS Total scales using the first three clinical groups combined. Item-total correlations ($n = 241$) ranged from .60 to .88 for the frequency items and .76–.89 for the severity items.

Classification accuracy values were reported as indicators of validity. For example, a positive predictive value of .92, a negative predictive value of -.79, and a diagnostic accuracy of .83 were given for a Total DTS score of 40. It is unclear, however, how these values were derived. Scores from the DTS were correlated with three other related measures to demonstrate evidence of convergent validity. The measures and associated correlation coefficients of the total scores were: (a) PTSD Scale ($r = .78$, $n = 102$), (b) Impact of Events Scale ($r = .64$, $n = 180$), and (c) Symptom Checklist-90-R ($r = .57$, $n = 123$). Additionally, a divergent validity measure is reported at $r = .04$ ($n = 78$). Further evidence of construct validity was reported based upon studies demonstrating group differences, treatment change, and severity differences. Finally, a small sample size ($n = 131$) principal components analysis was briefly discussed indicating a lack of clarity as to the factor structure of the DTS.

SUMMARY. The DTS provides a clinician with standardized self-report information from a respondent, reflecting perceived symptomatology directly related to the DSM-IV criteria for Posttraumatic Stress Disorder. This information used in conjunction with other data sources, including clinical assessment, would be useful in screening and for supplementing diagnoses to develop intervention plans. However, the DTS should not be used singly for diagnosis of PTSD. Although there is evidence supporting the psychometric properties of the DTS, considerably more data are needed. For example, there is a need for additional studies with larger sample sizes representing more trauma types in varying contexts. Furthermore, it would be valuable to initiate an intentional research agenda to study more fully the effects of sex, ethnocultural background, and socioeconomic status on DTS scores.

The case studies presented in the manual were useful in demonstrating how the DTS can be interpreted in a variety of clinical contexts. However, the table of ratios of expected numbers of individuals with PTSD to individuals without PTSD needs further explanation relative to both its origin and its use in interpreting DTS scores. Moreover, the authors might consider developing specific norm-referenced scores to supplement the interpretation process. Not only would standard scores be useful for interpretation but they could generate valuable data for the next DSM revision.

Although there are empirical strengths to the DSM process used to develop the criteria for PTSD that constitute the DTS, there also are restrictions to using the results. The data gathered in the DSM process focus on providing evidence to support optimal clinical diagnostic decision making, not to discover the traits and factors that comprise the psychological construct of posttraumatic stress. As such, the DTS is most suited for clinicians who want to connect their diagnoses and interventions directly to the DSM process.

REVIEWER'S REFERENCE
American Psychiatric Association. (1994). *Diagnostic and statistical manual of mental disorders* (4th ed.). Washington, DC: Author.

[26]
Dyslexia Screening Instrument.
Purpose: Designed to identify students with dyslexia.
Population: Grades 1–12, ages 6–21.
Publication Date: 1994.

Scores, 4: Passed, Failed, Inconclusive, Cannot Be Scored.
Administration: Individual.
Price Data, 1999: $74.50 per complete kit including teacher rating scale, manual (40 pages), and scoring program software; $13 per 50 rating forms.
Time: (15–20) minutes.
Comments: Rating form is completed by student's teacher; computer scored, DOS 3.0 or higher.
Authors: Kathryn B. Coon, Mary Jo Polk, and Melissa McCoy Waguespack.
Publisher: The Psychological Corporation.

Review of the Dyslexia Screening Instrument by JANET E. SPECTOR, Assistant Professor of Education and Human Development, University of Maine, Orono, ME:

The Dyslexia Screening Instrument (DSI) assesses the degree to which a student displays characteristics associated with Dyslexia. According to the authors, the DSI is useful for screening students in grades 1–12 to identify those at risk for dyslexia. The authors also recommend the DSI as part of a multidisciplinary evaluation to document a student's disability as required by either Section 504 of the Rehabilitation Act of 1973 or the Individuals with Disabilities Education Act (IDEA).

The measure comprises 33 statements, each of which describes a problem (e.g., inadequate spelling for grade level; low self-esteem). A rater, typically the target student's teacher, indicates on a 5-point Likert-type scale the degree to which the student demonstrates each behavior. Administration is easily accomplished, even for novice evaluators. Scoring is slightly less straightforward. Because items are weighted to reflect their contribution in discriminating between students with and without dyslexia, the measure must be scored using software that comes with the scale. The program is available only for PC users, a notable limitation for teachers in schools with Apple or Macintosh computers. For PC users, the computer software is easy to use. According to the authors, rating and scoring takes no more than 15 to 20 minutes per student.

The DSI yields a classification rather than a norm-referenced score such as a standard score of percentile rank: *Passed* (i.e., the student's score is most similar to students in the norm group who did not have dyslexia); *Failed* (i.e., the student's score is most similar to students in the norm group who were identified as dyslexic); *Inconclusive* (i.e., the score is not similar to either of the above groups); and *Cannot Be Scored* (i.e., more than three items were omitted by the rater). For students who fail the screening, the manual recommends completion of additional assessments in accordance with state and district policies for identifying students with special education needs. Follow-up is also recommended for students with an inconclusive rating and for students who pass the screening if they were referred due to academic problems.

The test manual contains brief but well-organized sections on reliability, validity, and standardization procedures. Test reliability was estimated using two approaches, internal consistency and interrater reliability. Although it would be desirable to study interrater reliability in a larger sample and to investigate test-retest reliability, the measure shows sufficient reliability for a screening device (i.e., all coefficients exceeded .85).

The DSI may appeal to school personnel who are searching for a quick way to identify students at risk for dyslexia. Unfortunately, it has several serious shortcomings. First, the authors fail to provide a definition of dyslexia, a construct for which meaning varies widely across researchers, practitioners, and policy makers (e.g., Lyon, 1995). Without a definition, it is impossible to judge construct or content validity. The only definition the authors provide is for learning disabilities, and this serves merely to document that dyslexia is widely regarded as a form of learning disability. The manual includes a brief discussion of content validity that focuses on item selection. Items were generated based on a review of the literature and then validated by teachers and other professionals with prior experience with dyslexia. The final set of items was selected for their ability to distinguish between dyslexic and nondyslexic students in the standardization sample. The authors acknowledge that the behaviors on the scale also describe students with learning disabilities and attentional or behavioral difficulties, but they do not believe that this undermines the use of the measure for differential diagnosis. Their argument would be more compelling if they were able to relate the behaviors to a definition of dyslexia and, better still, to a theory of dyslexia. In addition, the authors do not indicate to prospective users which items contribute most to student scores.

If this information were provided, it might be possible to evaluate retrospectively the match between items and current definitions and theories of dyslexia.

A second weakness of the DSI is the nonrepresentativeness of its norms, a problem that compromises its potential as a screening device. The scale was developed in a single metropolitan school district with a sample of 386 students ranging in age from 5 to 21 years old. In comparison to the U.S. population, DSI race and socioeconomic breakdowns reflect overrepresentation of Africa-American students (36.8% of the sample) and students from lower socioeconomic levels (47.7% of the sample qualified for free or reduced-price lunch). Users in geographic regions or districts with noncomparable demographics should definitely not use the DSI. Similarly, prospective users cannot assume comparability between the DSI's dyslexic/nondyslexic students and the dyslexic/nondyslexic population in their district. Unfortunately, no achievement or cognitive data are provided to enable a comparison.

Finally, although the authors present some promising statistics to support validity, key questions remain unaddressed. Two studies are described that demonstrate potential for differential diagnosis. One study indicated the effectiveness of the instrument in not identifying high-performing students ($n = 74$) as dyslexic (100% accuracy). Another study investigated the DSI's ability to distinguish between ADD and dyslexia. Among students with ADD ($n = 51$), the percentage of students (63%) who received passing (i.e., nondyslexic) scores was consistent with results of previous research on the percentage of students with ADD who do not have reading and spelling problems (i.e., 50%).

With respect to predictive validity, the DSI was about 73% accurate in identifying which second graders ($n = 34$) who had been referred for a dyslexia program would be found to be dyslexic based on more lengthy diagnostic procedures and teacher judgment. Among nine middle and high school students, DSI results and district diagnostic procedures were congruent in all but one case. In a more comprehensive study, the test was used to screen for dyslexia in a population of 762 elementary, middle, and high school students who had never been referred for testing. The demographics of the sample resembled that of the standardization sample (i.e., overrepresentation of African-Americans and students from a lower socioeconomic group). The DSI identified 20% of the students ($n = 152$) as Failing (i.e., dyslexic) or Inconclusive. Unfortunately, the rate of hits and false positives cannot be established because outcomes for failing and inconclusive scores are not separated. However, among these students, only 24% ($n = 36$) were later diagnosed as dyslexic, suggesting a potentially high rate of false positives. False negatives cannot be estimated because no follow-up testing was done for students who passed the screening.

Is the DSI an efficient and effective screening measure? Clearly, additional data are needed to address this question. In particular, it would be helpful to compare the DSI's hit rate to that of other measures. Many school districts use group-administered achievement tests to identify students with problems such as dyslexia. If the DSI is not a better predictor of dyslexia than achievement data, it will be superfluous in districts with group-administered testing programs.

Overall, the DSI is an easily administered rating scale that may be attractive to school personnel who need to identify students who are at risk for dyslexia. However, given the absence of a guiding definition of dyslexia, the nonrepresentativeness of the standardization sample, and the indeterminacy of validity studies, the measure falls short of its promise. Until the authors address these issues, the test is not recommended as a screening measure.

REVIEWER'S REFERENCE

Lyon, G. R. (1995). Toward a definition of dyslexia. *Annals of Dyslexia, 45,* 3–31.

Review of the Dyslexia Screening Instrument by BETSY WATERMAN, Associate Professor, Counseling and Psychological Services Department, State University of New York at Oswego, Oswego, NY:

The Dyslexia Screening Instrument is a recently developed (1994) measure for which the purpose is to help identify children or adolescents who demonstrate those characteristics often associated with dyslexia (i.e., reading, spelling, writing, or language-processing difficulties). It is also suggested that the results of this test may help to provide information required for documentation of eligibility for services under Section 504 of the Rehabilitation Act of 1973 and the Individuals with Disabilities Education Act (IDEA).

The Dyslexia Screening Instrument is a 5-point rating scale that is completed by a teacher who is acquainted with the targeted student's reading, English, or language abilities. The scale consists of 33 declarative phrases (e.g., "easily distracted") to which a teacher may respond with one of five possible numbers: 1-never exhibits; 2-seldom exhibits; 3-sometimes exhibits; 4-often exhibits; and, 5-always exhibits. Scoring is completed using an IBM-format computer program that accompanies the test. Concrete instructions for installing and using the computerized program are included in the manual. There are four possible outcomes or "scores" that may be assigned to the targeted student based on the teacher's responses—Passed (behavioral characteristics not consistent with dyslexia), Failed (behavioral characteristics consistent with dyslexia), Inconclusive (behavioral characteristics that are inconsistent with either group), and Cannot Be Scored (the result of more than three questions unanswered).

In developing this instrument, an initial pool of 70 research-based statements was reviewed by teachers, and later, by other professionals (i.e., psychologists, college teachers, and reading specialists) with 43 statements retained.

A total of 386 students, 172 from elementary grades and 214 from secondary grades, from a large, city school district, made up the development sample. Of these students, 103 were in the dyslexia program. In an effort to determine the "best weighted combination of statement scores" (manual, p. 17), the 43 items were subjected to discriminant analysis. Those items that had low discriminant weights, were highly correlated with each other, or were frequently omitted during testing were ultimately eliminated from the statement pool. The 33 items that remained comprise the current test. The authors also used the posterior probability of group membership, with the probability set at 95% in order to be classified as a member of a given group.

Internal consistency for items on the Dyslexia Screening Instrument was reported at .99 for the elementary students and .98 for the secondary students. Interrater reliability was completed with 27 elementary and 29 secondary at-risk students who had received multiple teacher ratings. A correlation of .86 was reported for elementary students and .91 for secondary students. The authors reported 100% and 97% agreement on classification for elementary and secondary students respectively.

Content, construct, and predictive validity studies were also conducted. The test authors report that the Dyslexia Screening Instrument is based on current research and reviewed by experts in the field. The authors report that discriminant analysis predicted placement with 98.2% at the elementary level and 98.6% at the secondary level and 100% accuracy with high achieving students at both elementary and secondary levels. In a study completed with children classified with Attention Deficit Disorder (ADD), the test authors found that 63% of ADD children were classified as nondyslexic, 25% were classified as dyslexic, and 12% as "Inconclusive," consistent with other research findings on ADD/dyslexia overlap. Predictive validity was investigated in two studies using students who had been referred for dyslexia screening. These students were rated by teachers using the Dyslexia Screening Instrument and also evaluated in the school district's typical manner (i.e., cognitive assessment, discrepancies in achievement performances). The authors report that 73% to 100% of students who "Failed" the Dyslexia Screening Instrument were classified as dyslexic and over 73% of those who "Passed" the Dyslexia Screening Instrument were not classified as dyslexic. A final screening study was completed on 474 elementary, 189 middle school, and 99 high school students who had never been referred for testing. White (322), African-American (416), and other (24) racial groups were represented. Students who "Failed" or were classified as "Inconclusive" were further assessed for cognitive and achievement abilities. Of those, 54% of elementary students, 70% of middle school students, and 100% of high school students were ultimately diagnosed as dyslexic.

SUMMARY. The Dyslexia Screening Instrument appears to be a quick measure that is useful in identifying students who have behavioral characteristics that are consistent with other students diagnosed with dyslexia and that shows reasonable evidence for score validity and reliability. Statements on the rating scale appear consistent with current literature in the field and are written in generally concrete, observable, "non-child-blaming" terms. From a psychometric standpoint, the instrument appears adequate although samples are small and from one geographic area.

The greatest concern related to the current measure is the absence of any discussion related to the definition of dyslexia. Because this term is not universally used in state definitions of disabilities and it is used in many different ways by both lay people and professionals, the lack of a clear definition may result in confusion as this test is applied and interpreted. Finally, although the computer scoring program is generally easy to use, the instructions need to be updated to include the latest versions of Windows currently in use (i.e., Windows 3.X, and Window 95 and 98). Also, the program generates a report so brief that it offers little specific useful information.

Overall, this screening instrument appears appropriate for the purpose for which it is intended and may offer preliminary information that would be helpful in further assessment and in the development of interventions.

[27]

Firestone Assessment of Self-Destructive Thoughts.

Purpose: Constructed "for the clinical assessment of a patient's suicidal potential."
Population: Ages 16–80.
Publication Date: 1996.
Acronym: FAST.
Scores: No scores.
Administration: Group.
Price Data, 1998: $120.50 per complete kit including manual (176 pages) and 25 ReadyScore® response booklets; $51.50 per 25 response booklets, $73.50 per manual.
Time: (20) minutes.
Comments: Includes 11 levels of progressively self-destructive thoughts on a continuum ranging from Social Isolation, Eating Disorders, Substance Abuse, Self-Mutilation, and Suicide.
Authors: Robert W. Firestone and Lisa A. Firestone.
Publisher: The Psychological Corporation.

Review of the Firestone Assessment of Self-Destructive Thoughts by WILLIAM E. MARTIN, JR., Professor of Educational Psychology, Northern Arizona University, Flagstaff, AZ:

The Firestone Assessment of Self-Destructive Thoughts (FAST) is designed to measure the "Continuum of Negative Thought Patterns" as they relate to a client's level of self-destructive potential or suicidality. The authors recommend the FAST to be used for screening, diagnosis, treatment progress, treatment outcome, research,

and therapy. The FAST is theoretically grounded in what the authors refer to as the "concept of the voice," which refers to negative thoughts and attitudes that are said to be at the core of maladaptive behavior.

The FAST consists of 84 items that provide self-report information from a respondent on how frequently he or she is experiencing various negative thoughts directed toward himself or herself. Four "composites" and 11 linked "continuum levels" comprise the FAST. One composite is named Self-Defeating and has five continuum levels (Self-Depreciation, Self-Denial, Cynical Attitudes, Isolation, and Self-Contempt). Addictions is another composite with addictions listed as its continuum level. A third composite is Self-Annihilating with four continuum levels (Hopelessness, Giving Up, Self-Harm, Suicide Plans, and Suicide Injunctions). The last composite is Suicide Intent and no continuum levels are identified.

ADMINISTRATION, SCORING, AND INTERPRETATION. The FAST instrument is a seven-page perforated, self-carbon form used for responding to items, scoring responses, and graphing the results. T scores are derived for the 11 continuum levels, four composites, and for the total score. Percentiles and 90% confidence interval bands also are available for use. The T scores are plotted on the T-Score profile graph, which has shaded partitions that indicate if the T scores fall within a *nonclinical range, equivocal range,* or clinical ranges that include *elevated* and *extremely elevated.*

The normative sample for the FAST was a clinical sample of outpatient clients undergoing psychotherapy. A T score of 50 on any scale represents the average performance of an individual who was in outpatient treatment with no suicide ideation from the normative sample. The nonclinical range is a T score between 20 and 41 whereas the equivocal range is 42–48. The two clinical ranges are elevated (42–59) and extremely elevated (60+). Any score that falls above the equivocal range is treated with concern and anyone scoring in the extremely elevated range on levels 7–11, the Self-Annihilating Composite, the Suicide Intent Composite, or the Total score should be immediately assessed for suicide potential.

DEVELOPMENT OF THE SCALES. The items for the FAST were derived from actual statements of 21 clinical outpatients who were receiving "voice therapy" in groups. Nine of the outpatients had a previous history of serious suicide attempts and the others exhibited less severe self-defeating behaviors including self-denial, isolation, substance abuse, and eating disorders. The list of items was further refined from a study conducted to select those factors that significantly discriminated between suicide attempters and nonattempters. Then items were retained or deleted based upon their psychometric relationship to hypothesized constructs, resulting in the current 84-item version of the FAST.

RELIABILITY AND VALIDITY. Cronbach's alpha reliability coefficients ranging from .76 to .91 (Mdn = .84) are reported for the 11 level scores. Standard errors of measurement and 90% confidence intervals also are provided. However, sample sizes and descriptions are not provided for these measures. Test-retest reliability coefficients (1–266 days) ranged from .63–.94 (M = .82) using a sample (N = 131) of nonclinical, psychotherapy outpatients, and psychiatric inpatients.

Content validity of the FAST was investigated using a Guttman Scalogram Analysis resulting in a coefficient of reproducibility of .91 and a coefficient of scalability of .66. FAST Total Scores were correlated with the Suicide Ideation subscale of the Suicide Probability Scale (r = .72) as indicators of convergent validity. An exploratory factor analysis was conducted using 579 outpatients resulting in a 3-factor solution (Self-Annihilating, Self-Defeating, and Addictions), which provided support for construct validity. Evidence for criterion-related validity was demonstrated from studies showing how FAST scores were able to discriminate inpatient and outpatient ideators from nonideators and to identify individuals who made prior suicide attempts.

SUMMARY. The authors have put forth empirical evidence that supports the psychometric properties of the FAST. However, continuing studies are needed, especially related to the effectiveness of the FAST in diagnosing and predicting chemical addictive behavior. Furthermore, the construct validity of scores from the FAST needs further consideration. First, the items for the FAST were generated from a small (N = 21) somewhat restricted focus group of persons receiving "voice therapy." Second, the FAST is closely anchored to a theoretical orientation known as "concept of the voice" in which additional studies are needed to validate.

Overall, the FAST is a measure worth considering for professionals working with individuals who have exhibited self-destructive potential or suicidality. However, I encourage professionals to study the theoretical orientation underlying the FAST and determine if it is congruent with their own expectations for clinical outcomes prior to extensive use of the instrument.

Review of the Firestone Assessment of Self-Destructive Thoughts by ROBERT C. REINEHR, Professor of Psychology, Southwestern University, Georgetown, TX:

The Firestone Assessment of Self-Destructive Thoughts (FAST) is a self-report questionnaire intended to provide clinicians with a tool for the assessment of a patient's suicide potential. Respondents are asked to endorse how frequently they are experiencing various negative thoughts directed toward themselves. The items were derived from the actual statements of clinical outpatients who were members of therapy groups in which the techniques of Voice Therapy were used.

Voice Therapy is a technique developed by the senior test author as a means of giving language to the negative thought processes that influence self-limiting, self-destructive behaviors and lifestyles. The FAST includes items intended to assess each of 11 levels of a Continuum of Negative Thought Patterns. Items were assigned to levels based on the judgments of advanced graduate students and psychologists with training in Voice Therapy.

In the standardization process, the FAST was administered to a sample of 478 clients who were currently receiving outpatient psychotherapy and who did not have any current (within the last month) suicide ideation, suicide threats, or suicide attempts. Standard scores were calculated for the Total Score, for four composite scores derived by factor analysis and other statistical procedures, and for each of the 11 levels of negative thought patterns.

Estimates of internal consistency are based on a single sample, the size of which is not reported in the manual. They range from .76 to .97, with the majority falling between .81 and .88. Test-retest reliability estimates are reported for three samples with intervals from 28–266 days in one study and 1–31 days in another: psychiatric inpatients (n = 28), psychotherapy outpatients (n = 68), and nonclinical college students (n = 35). Reliabilities for the various levels of the negative-thought continuum range from .63 to .94, with the higher coefficients generally being found among the nonclinical respondents. Test-retest reliability estimates for the various composite scores and for the total score are somewhat higher, ranging from .79 to .94.

As an indication of construct validity, FAST scores were compared to scores on the Beck Depression Inventory (BDI), the Beck Suicide Inventory (BSI), and the Suicide Probability Scale (SPS). The FAST Total score had its highest correlations with the BDI (.73), the BSI (.72), and the Suicide Ideations subscale of the SPS (.76). The composite scores and the various level scores had lower correlations with the subscales of the Beck instruments or the SPS.

The FAST was administered to groups of inpatients and outpatients with various diagnoses including Adjustment Disorder, Anxiety Disorder, Bipolar Disorder, Depression, Personality Disorder, Schizophrenia, and Substance Abuse, and to a nonclinical sample of 172 college students. Each of the clinical groups was further subdivided into suicide Ideators and Nonideators. Ideators had higher average FAST Total scores than did Nonideators and clinical groups had higher average FAST Total scores than did the nonclinical group. Information is provided in the manual with respect to the relationships between the various FAST subscales and the diagnostic groups and subgroups.

SUMMARY. In general, it would appear that the FAST is similar in many ways to other depression and suicide inventories. Total Scores tend to be higher for respondents in diagnostic groups than for nonclinical respondents, and within diagnostic groups, Suicide Ideators score more highly than do Nonideators.

Within the limits of these findings, the FAST may be useful to clinicians as an indication of how a given respondent's answers compare to those of various diagnostic groups. It might also be possible to use the scale as a clinical tool for the evaluation of change during therapy, although use as a psychometric instrument is not justified on the basis of the evidence presented in the manual.

[28]
General Ability Measure for Adults.

Purpose: "Designed to evaluate intellectual ability using abstract designs."

Population: Ages 18–96.
Publication Date: 1997.
Acronym: GAMA.
Scores, 5: Matching, Analogies, Sequences, Construction, GAMA IQ Score.
Administration: Individual and/or group.
Price Data: Available from publisher.
Time: (25) minutes.
Comments: May be self-administered.
Authors: Jack A. Naglieri and Achilles N. Bardos.
Publisher: NCS (Minnetonka).

Review of the General Ability Measure for Adults by ROBERT FITZPATRICK, Consulting Psychologist, Cranberry Township, PA:

The authors designed the General Ability Measure for Adults (GAMA) to measure general cognitive ability, or intelligence, in an efficient manner. It is nonverbal except for the instructions and requires no motor skill beyond filling in an answer sheet. It is normed for adults only. Readily administered to groups of examinees, it can even be self-administered. A Spanish language version is available.

For the most part, the GAMA appears to have been developed with care and with technical sophistication. Particular attention was paid to avoiding differential item functioning and other manifestations of bias. Whether justified or not, claims of bias against those who are culturally or otherwise out of the mainstream continue to plague tests of cognitive ability. Hence, any effort to achieve both the appearance and the reality of fairness is to be welcomed.

All items call for reasoning or problem solving based on abstract figures in two or more colors. Each of four subtests is intended to measure the same construct of general intelligence. Yet, the manual suggests comparing subtest scores for a given examinee. "Although variation among subtest scores is not considered to reflect different abilities (because the GAMA is a general ability test), varying scores could reflect performance differences related to the demands and structure of the individual subtests" (manual, p. 25). Suggested interpretations of subtest variations seem sensible enough, but are unsupported by evidence. It would be helpful to have data on the relationships of the subtests to a variety of spatial tests. Lacking such data, users are advised to be cautious in interpreting subtest scores.

The GAMA has 66 items, with a time limit of 25 minutes. The manual does not indicate what proportion of examinees can be expected to answer all the items, but it seems likely from inspection that such an event would be rare. The informed use of guessing, skipping item types the examinee finds especially difficult, and other coachable strategies might well be effective with the GAMA. Hence, the GAMA might be contraindicated for users potentially vulnerable to outside coaching.

Subtest scaled scores are based on norms from a United States standardization sample of more than 2,000, stratified by geographic region, age, gender, education, and race or ethnic group. Raw scores are converted to scaled scores and then to a deviation IQ score, based on norms for 11 age groups, ranging from 18–19 to 80+. (Sample sizes in the age groups range from 91 to 310.) Users should be aware that, with this type of scoring, the expected decrement of cognitive ability with age is taken into account, so that scores should be interpreted only in relation to those of others of similar age.

The test booklet and the manual are handsomely printed, partly in "colors that have been shown to be the least problematic for those with color-impaired vision" (p. 2). The test instructions are written at about a third-grade level of difficulty. The manual is generally well written, although the description of the self-scored answer sheet is hard to follow.

The results of internal consistency (average split-half correlations across the 11 age groups ranged from a low of .65 to a high of .81 for the subtests and equaled .90 for total GAMA IQ score; test-retest correlation was .67 for GAMA IQ score) and test-retest reliability studies are generally favorable though less so at the higher age levels. However, the test-retest (2–6-week interval) results are based on a single study with sample size of only 86, and should not be relied upon greatly.

The manual reports fairly high correlations of GAMA scores with those of other tests of cognitive ability, albeit more so for relatively nonverbal tests than for tests with high verbal content. Also reported are four studies using the GAMA to study special populations. In one of these studies, the GAMA was administered, with apparent success, to deaf adults using American Sign Language. The publisher has indicated that further studies are under way.

SUMMARY. A final verdict on the GAMA awaits those further studies and experience in application. Nevertheless, the evidence reported in the manual, along with the careful procedures in test development, support the authors' contention that the GAMA IQ score is an effective measure of cognitive ability for U.S. residents. It is not necessarily limited to special populations, but rather might be useful in a variety of situations where the user needs a short test that seems as fair to a variety of examinees as current test technology permits.

Review of the General Ability Measure for Adults by BERT A. GOLDMAN, Professor of Education, Curriculum and Instruction, School of Education, University of North Carolina at Greensboro, Greensboro, NC:

Naglieri and Bardos indicate that their "GAMA test evaluates an individual's overall general ability with items that require the application of reasoning and logic to solve problems that exclusively use abstract designs and shapes" (manual, p. 1). The test, consisting of four sample items followed by 66 items to be answered in 25 minutes, was normed on 2,360 people who ranged in age from 18 to 96.

The GAMA includes four subtests containing nonverbal items: Matching, Analogies, Sequences, and Construction. By using one of 11 age group conversion tables, the raw score earned on each subtest is converted to a scaled score with a mean of 10 and a standard deviation of 3. These four converted scores are summed and the total is converted to a GAMA IQ score that has a mean of 100 and a standard deviation of 15.

In addition to the test book and test manual, there are two kinds of answer sheets: a self-scoring answer sheet and a computer scannable one along with software scoring and reporting. All materials are attractively printed and the directions for administering, scoring, and interpreting scores are clearly presented and easily followed.

Detailed information concerning the GAMA standardization sample is presented and includes numbers and percentages of the various age groups, education levels, gender, geographic regions, and race or ethnic groups comprising the sample. The percentages of these groups are similar to the percentages obtained from the U.S. Department of Commerce, thus supporting the GAMA authors' claim that the test "was standardized using a carefully designed stratified random sampling plan" (manual, p. 31).

Reliability was estimated by the split-half method with the Spearman-Brown correction for each of the 11 age groups and for the total standardization sample. The average of these corrected reliabilities for two of the four subtests was low (i.e., .65 and .66). The other two were higher at .79 and .81. However, a linear composite of these reliabilities produced a coefficient of .90, which suggests a reliable total GAMA score.

Estimates of test-retest reliability within an interval of 2 to 6 weeks were determined from a sample of 86 people comprising both sexes, several ethnic or racial backgrounds, and varying education levels. The test means for each of the four subtests and for the total score are similar to those of the retest, suggesting that the scores remain stable over time. However, the test-retest reliability coefficient for each subtest and for the total score are low, ranging from .38 to .74, suggesting that over time the scores are not very stable.

The idea of providing a 25-minute nonverbal test of intellectual ability has merit. However, the authors provide little specific explanation for their selection of the four types of items comprising the GAMA. They indicate that "the GAMA test evaluates an individual's overall general ability; that it is designed to evaluate intellectual ability using abstract designs" (manual, p. 1). Although four types of items employing abstract designs are contained in the test format, this reviewer has difficulty accepting the notion that so limited an array of item types can adequately measure "overall general ability." The Full Scale WAIS-R, in this reviewer's opinion, may be considered more a test of an individual's overall general ability than the GAMA. A sample of 194 people provided a correlation of only .75 between the Full Scale WAIS-R and the GAMA. When the GAMA was compared to the Performance (nonverbal) half of the WAIS-R, a correlation of only .74 was produced. Although these correlations are statistically significant at $p < .001$, they do not reveal, to a very high degree, that the GAMA measures "overall general ability."

Evidence is presented suggesting that the GAMA may be used with a variety of special populations including adults with learning disabilities, deaf adults, elderly nursing home residents, adults with traumatic brain injury, and adults with mental retardation. Again, to say that the GAMA is measuring the "overall general ability" of these groups may be misleading.

In summary, the GAMA appears to measure the ability to apply reasoning and logic to solve problems involving abstract designs and shapes. This reflects an aspect of intelligence rather than being a measure of overall general ability. The standardization sample was carefully selected to represent the U.S. population for ages 18 to 96. Internal consistency data for the total test are excellent, but test-retest reliability data suggest poor to fair stability of scores over time. Validity evidence for use of test scores as measures of overall general ability has not been shown. However, one might cautiously use the GAMA as a relatively quick screening device for measuring a limited aspect of intelligence.

[29]

Gibson Spiral Maze, Second Edition.

Purpose: Measures "the speed, accuracy, and general style of people's muscular reactions in response to carefully controlled stimuli."
Population: Children and adults.
Publication Dates: 1961–1965.
Scores, 2: Time score, Error score.
Administration: Individual.
Price Data, 1999: £10 per test 20 copies; manual and specimen set are now out of print.
Time: (2) minutes.
Comments: Forms part of the Clifton Assessment Procedures for the Elderly (T5:537).
Author: H. B. Gibson.
Publisher: Hodder and Stoughton Educational [England].
Cross References: See T4:1037 (3 references), T3:955 (1 reference), T2:1191 (3 references), 7:82 (3 references), and P:90 (2 references).

Review of the Gibson Spiral Maze, Second Edition by WILLIAM K. WILKINSON, Consulting Psychologist, Boleybeg, Barna, Co. Galway, Ireland:

The Gibson Spiral Maze (GSM) purports to measure psychomotor skill. It was first published in England in 1965 and the technical manual was updated in 1977. Why the instrument is under review 21 years later is a mystery. The potential user is immediately warned that the technical references are now outdated.

The GSM consists of a single Spiral figure made of continuously flowing concentric circles. Because the figure is not square and does not contain blind alleys, it is not a traditional maze, like the Mazes subtest of the Wechsler Intelligence Scale for Children, Third Edition (WISC-III). In fact, it may be more accurate to refer to it as the Gibson Spiral Figure, because reference to "Maze" may mislead potential users.

The Figure consists of small circles placed at different spacings within each spiral. The object is to trace an exit from the middle of the figure without touching the small circles or the path lines. The two scores available are Time (T) and Errors (E)—the latter score the sum total of the number of times the individual touched the inner circles or path walls.

Atypical in this test are the directions to test administrators to focus the test-taker on the time element. Specifically, at 15-second intervals the administrator is to sharply and authoritatively comment, "go as quickly as you can!" and to further stress speed by reiterating these comments at 15-second intervals. The author notes that the usefulness of the test depends on the administrator's skill in creating time-stress. I did not find a compelling rationale for emphasizing speed. One would think that the use of a stopwatch and the nature of the task would insure that examinees will work as quickly as they can. A serious difficulty with this procedure, as the author notes, is the creation of test administrator error (e.g., variations in voice tone, language, rapport with test-taker, etc.).

A positive feature of the GSM is that it is quick to administer and easy to score. The scores have demonstrated interrater reliability ($r = .98$). The manual provides limited test-retest reliability. It seems that in children ages 8 to 10, T decreases but E does not.

The author has developed a peculiar position with respect to norms. Because the test depends on the administrator's skill in stressing speed, the author urges GSM users to develop local norms. In addition, test scores will depend entirely on an individual sample's T and E score distribution. Therefore, the author suggests that GSM users obtain a sample's raw score distributions to form a scatterplot, with T and E regressed on each other. It is unclear how a test user interprets an individual's score before a sample distribution is obtained. Further, it is doubtful that test users will believe it part of their responsibility to collect a GSM database and perform somewhat sophisticated statistical analyses on this data (unless they use the GSM purely for research purposes).

Based on regression analyses, the author developed four interpretive quadrants, "quick and accurate," "slow and accurate," "quick and careless," and "slow and careless." A person's score will fall into one of these four divisions after the local database is collected and analyzed.

At this point, the use of the GSM moves beyond its initial scope—as a measure of psychomotor speed. Using the four quadrants as a guide, it becomes a measure of "maladjustment," "neurotic styles," and purportedly discriminates between various clinical samples. For example, "naughty" boys are more likely to be quick and careless whereas "good" boys are more likely to be "quick and accurate." The lure for potential users is to consider the "styles" as indicative of personality disturbance. If anything, these are cognitive styles, because the test is purportedly a cognitive one. That is, psychomotor speed is a cognitive, neuropsychological variable first and foremost. If a test user wants to measure "personality" aberrations there are a number of "personality" tests specifically for this purpose.

An essential question is, "how well does the GSM measure psychomotor speed?" Although the GSM appears face valid as a measure of psychomotor speed, there is little construct validation evidence for this claim. There is a weak, albeit statistically significant, correlation of .33 with its precursor, the Porteus Mazes (Q-score). Unfortunately, greater effort is made to prove the usefulness of the GSM in distinguishing maladjusted children from their adjusted peers.

It is odd that the GSM was not correlated with other tests purporting to measure psychomotor speed. For example, the Coding and Symbol Search subtests of the Wechsler Intelligence Scale for Children—III (WISC-III, T5:2862) would seem parallel measures of paper-and-pencil speed. Oddly, the author compares the GSM to the WISC-III Block Design subtest, although it seems more similar to Coding and Symbol Search. Again, part of the problem is that the technical manual is outdated, so it is unknown how well the GSM correlates with more recently developed measures of psychomotor speed. For example, it would be interesting to see the correlation of the GSM on a reaction time measure, such as the processing Speed Index of the Continuous Performance Test (T5:679). Convergent/Divergent validity studies such as these would seem a useful, indeed, essential, line of inquiry.

SUMMARY. Overall, the GSM may have a place in research, particularly neuropsychological research. However, the test is too limited and out of date to be considered a viable clinical instrument. If one wants to measure psychomotor speed the new Processing Speed Index of the WISC-III appears far more valid than the GSM. Again, one should not use this instrument as a measure of "personality" style or "deviation."

Review of the Gibson Spiral Maze, Second Edition by JAMES YSSELDYKE, Birkmaier Professor of Educational Leadership, University of Minnesota, Minneapolis, MN:

The Gibson Spiral Maze (GSM) test is a psychomotor test designed to measure the speed, accuracy, and style of people's muscular reactions in response to carefully designed stimuli. The authors claim that the test can be used in assessment of intelligence and "special skills," and in personality research. The conceptual/theoretical basis for the test is extremely dated, and there have been major developments in the assessment of psychomotor skills since the publication of the Gibson in 1965.

The GSM is a one-prompt test. Individuals are asked to trace a path through a spiral design printed on a large card. Small circles are in the spiral, and these are defined as "obstacles," which the examinee is to avoid. The test takes less than 2 minutes to administer. The administrator is instructed to tell the examinee in firm, sharp, repeated commands to go as quickly as he or she can. These injunctions to hurry are to be repeated every 15 seconds, and not more frequently. Thus, the test is described as a "time-stress" test.

The test is scored for time and number of errors. Errors are counted each time the subject touches an obstacle (1-point error), penetrates an obstacle or line (2-point error), or touches a line (1-point error if less than one inch, 2-point error if it touches for more than one inch). There are two ways to interpret the scores obtained. Users

are told to construct their own norms by creating a graph in which time is plotted along the abscissa and errors plotted along the ordinate. Regression lines of Time on Error and Error on Time are plotted. The examiner uses the self-generated chart to assign one of four ratings to the subject: quick and careless, slow and careless, quick and accurate, and slow and accurate. An alternate way of reporting performance is to use norms printed in the test manual. These norms are based on data from 392 boys in primary schools. Other than knowing that the norms are for boys, the norm group is not described. The author also reports quartile and median scores for the following referent groups: office girls, factory girls, "approved school girls," secondary schoolboys, junior boys in a "remand" home, boys in a senior approved school, maladjusted schoolboys, and depressive patients (median age 55) before and after treatment (manual, p. 9).

Data on interscorer reliability are reported for secondary studies. Reliability estimates exceed .90. Data on test-retest reliability are also from secondary studies using samples, which are not described. Test-retest (over a period of one year) reliability estimates are consistently below .80. Data on validity are dated, limited, and highly questionable. For example, the author reports criterion group data on "good boys, average boys, and naughty boys" (manual, p. 11).

SUMMARY. In my opinion there is no specific reason why examiners would want to know how individuals perform on this test. If one did know, it is uncertain how the data would, could, or should be used. Very many superior devices are readily available for use in assessing psychomotor skills.

[30]
High/Scope Child Observation Record for Ages 2 1/2–6.

Purpose: Designed to assess children's development, learning, and interests.
Population: Ages 2 1/2–6 years.
Publication Date: 1992.
Acronym: COR.
Scores, 6: Initiative, Social Relations, Creative Representation, Music and Movement, Language and Literacy, Logic and Mathematics.
Administration: Group.
Price Data: Available from publisher.
Time: Administration time not reported.

Comments: Ratings by teachers.
Author: High/Scope Educational Research Foundation.
Publisher: High/Scope Educational Research Foundation.

Review of the High/Scope Child Observation Record for Ages 2 1/2–6 by GLEN P. AYLWARD, Professor of Pediatrics, Psychiatry and Behavioral and Social Sciences, Southern Illinois University School of Medicine, Springfield, IL:

The High/Scope Child Observation Record (COR) is an observational instrument designed to allow staff members of early childhood educational programs, preschools, and similar child-care facilities to record behaviors in children ages 2 years, 6 months to 6 years. Observations are made in normal program activities and are grouped into six developmental categories: (a) Initiative (expressing choices, solving problems, engaging in complex play, cooperating in program routines); (b) Social Relations (relating to adults, relating to other children, making friends with other children, engaging in problem solving, understanding and expressing feelings); (c) Creative Representation (making and building, drawing and painting, pretending), (d) Music and Movement (exhibiting body coordination, exhibiting manual coordination, imitating movements to a steady beat, following music and movement directions); (e) Language and Literacy (understanding speech, speaking, showing interest in reading activities, demonstrating knowledge about books, beginning reading, beginning writing), and (f) Logic and Mathematics (sorting, using the words *not, some, all,* arranging materials in graduated order, using comparison words, comparing numbers of objects, counting objects, describing spatial relations, describing sequence and time). The COR therefore contains a total of 30 items, each scored on a 5-point scale. Essentially, the observer chooses a statement that best represents the presumed highest level of behavior characteristic of the child under observation. For example, in the Initiative category, the *solving problems* subscale includes options ranging from "child does not yet identify problems" (score of 1) to "child tries alternative methods to solve a problem and is highly involved and persistent" (score of 5). Most items are initiated by the child, versus being elicited by the examiner.

The complete High/Scope COR kit includes a 52-page manual, assessment booklets (each can be used three times for the same child), anecdotal notecards, parent report forms, and a COR poster. The instrument can be used to evaluate individual children or groups, curricula (or parts of a curriculum), or specific characteristics of particular groups being served such as bilingual children or those with special needs. The COR can be used to provide feedback to parents, staff, administrators, program evaluators, or researchers.

The COR is the result of previous efforts to assess outcomes of the High/Scope Preschool Curriculum. Originally, items had three to seven scoring options, but in the present version, all have five possible scores; several items were added and others deleted from the original version to produce the current 30-item version. The end result is an instrument that could be applied to a variety of curricula.

A total of 64 teams, each consisting of a Head Start teacher and an assistant teacher collected data on 484 children who were attending preschool programs in southeastern Michigan. Of these, 51% were African American, 26% were white, 14% middle Eastern, 7% Hispanic, 2% Asian, and 1% Native American. A major drawback is that the specific ages of the children were not stated. Teams underwent 3 days of initial training and were supported and monitored throughout data collection. The authors emphasize the need for periodic refresher sessions to enhance reliability in routine COR usage.

Alpha coefficients for teachers ranged from .80 to .93; for assistants, values ranged from .72 to .91 (based on a sample of 50 teachers, 50 assistants, and 484 children). Pearson correlations between teacher and assistant scores ranged from .61 to .72.

"Factor loadings" for subscales and the six developmental categories, based on the responses of 51 teachers and 484 children, are reported to range from .57 to .82, with most being above .75. Correlations between the six factors (developmental scales) were .69 to .84 ($M = .75$), based on a sample of 484 children and 50 teachers. The authors report relationships between teacher-rated COR items from Fall to Spring, with ratings increasing by .9 points over this period, from 2.6 to 3.4; correlations between ratings ranged from .29 to .60. The samples were not described in detail, and they appeared to be of a mixed nature (i.e., cross-sectional and longitudinal, with ns of 484 and 415, respectively).

Validity evidence included correlations between COR ratings and the McCarthy Scales of Children's Abilities (MSC) (n = 98); these ranged from .27 to .66. The COR language and Literacy scale had the highest correlations with the MSCA (.53–.66), whereas Music and Movement had the lowest (.27–.46). In regard to demographic variables, correlations between COR ratings and age were .51–.61 (n = 385), gender .00–.07 (n = 376), and socioeconomic variables .14–.28 (parent schooling and employment). The socioeconomic variables are not well described and their influence may have been underestimated, due to the homogeneity (i.e., generally low SES) of the sample.

The COR Assessment Booklet contains a summary page where the examiner transfers subscale scores from preceding pages and produces an average score for each of the six developmental categories. Unfortunately, there are no directions as to what to do with these scores, or how best to interpret them. This issue underscores the problem of not specifying ages of the sample children. It would enhance interpretation if mean scores and standard deviations for each age were presented. Along these lines, item statistics (Table 1 in the manual) are rendered meaningless because the user has no idea as to the ages of the children involved. As it now stands, it is assumed that each subscale scoring option represents an increment in the child's developmental level, although it was not indicated how this assumed developmental sequence was validated.

The intent of the COR is in line with the new models or "visions" of developmental assessment of infants and young children, namely moving away from norm-referenced testing to criterion-referenced, curriculum-based, or performance assessments (particularly the latter). Given that the movement espouses assessment that involves multiple sources of information and multiple components, avoidance of unfamiliar surroundings, use of a familiar assessor, and decreased reliance on formal tests and tools, the COR has potential. However, the authors have indicated that individuals not familiar with a child would have a difficult time completing the COR, requiring at least three contacts before completing the instrument reliably. Moreover, time taken to complete

the instrument is not specified. These factors may make the instrument rather time-consuming. Conversely, the COR does tap the child's level and pattern of organizing experience and functional capacities, with integration of cognitive, social, and emotional abilities. Moreover, it bridges the gap between assessment and intervention and allows for cultural and ethnic differences, particularly with the use of the option of additional descriptors. Unfortunately, it may do so at the cost of psychometric rigor.

Review of the High/Scope Child Observation Record for Ages 2 1/2–6 by MARY MATHAI CHITTOORAN, UC Foundation Assistant Professor of School Psychology, The University of Tennessee at Chattanooga, Chattanooga, TN:

The High/Scope Child Observation Record (COR) is described by the authors as a developmentally appropriate assessment instrument for use in early childhood settings. It is designed to allow teachers to assess young children's developmental progress by gathering semistructured observations of their behaviors over a period of several months. The COR offers a nonintrusive alternative to "artificial and limited testing situations" (manual, p. 3) and allows teachers to observe children as they engage in daily instructional activities. Observations may be made on six subscales: Initiative, which assesses the ability to begin and follow through on tasks; Social Relations, which assesses social interactions with peers and adults; Creative Representation, which measures the ability to represent objects and experiences through symbolic means such as imagination, language, and art; Music and Movement, which assesses musical abilities as well as fine and gross motor skills; Language and Literacy, which evaluates listening, speaking, reading, and writing; and finally, Logic and Mathematics, which assesses logical thinking and mathematical reasoning.

The COR has 30 items grouped under the major subscales. Each item includes five descriptive statements that represent a range of functioning, from very poor (rated 1) to very superior (rated 5). The rater selects the statement that best describes the functioning level of the child and adds relevant notes about the child's behaviors. Although behaviors are preferably self-initiated, the COR does allow observers to structure situations or ask questions to prompt a desired behavior. Ratings are transferred to the Summary of Scores sheet. Subscale scores, which represent the average rating for all items on a subscale during a single observation period, may be computed.

The COR was developed and validated over a 2-year period beginning in 1989. Sixty-four teaching teams and nine home-based teachers representing eight Head Start programs in Southeastern Michigan were recruited, trained, and paid for their involvement. Teaching teams were responsible for approximately 2,500 children a year who were ethnically representative of Head Start programs across the nation.

Teachers' COR ratings showed an average increase of .9 between fall and spring ratings for the 1990–1991 school year. Pearson product-moment correlations between the two sets of teacher ratings ranged from .29 to .60 and factor loadings of items completed for the six COR categories ranged from .57 to .82, with only four items loading below .70. Factor correlations between scales ranged from .69 to .84. With regard to reliability, the manual reports intraobserver alpha coefficients ranging from .80 to .93 for teachers and .72 to .91 for assistant teachers. Interobserver Pearson product-moment correlations for ratings completed by 50 teaching teams (n = 484) were found to range between .61 and .72.

Concurrent validity evidence was collected from a sample of 98 children who were evaluated with both the COR and the McCarthy Scales of Children's Abilities. The manual reports correlations ranging from a high of .66 between the COR's Language and Literacy subscale and the McCarthy's Perceptual-Performance scale and a low of .27 between the COR's Music and Movement subscale and the McCarthy's Verbal subscale. The manual also reports correlations ranging from a low of .37 to a high of .53 on four pairs of similar scales. COR ratings showed moderate correlations with children's age and low to negligible correlations with variables such as child's gender and parental schooling and employment. A related study demonstrated the feasibility of training teaching staff to use the COR; 10 research assistants were provided with 3 days of training and practice and achieved a 92.8% agreement rate.

CRITIQUE. The High/Scope Child Observation Record provides a systematic way of gathering information about young children that obviates the difficulties associated with traditional methods of assessment. COR materials are attractive and aid in ease of administration. Anecdotal notecards allow teachers to document children's behaviors over the course of several months and the Assessment Booklet, which can be used three times, provides a convenient summary of developmental progress. The items and their associated descriptors are particularly helpful. For example, on the item, "Child distinguishes between *some* and *all* and uses these terms in categorizing" the descriptor is, "When watering plants, Diana says, 'these are all plants; some of them are cactus plants.'" The Parent Report, also available in Spanish, affords teachers an easy way to communicate assessment information to parents. Behavioral indicators in each domain simplify the development of short-term instructional objectives and may be particularly useful for teachers of children with special needs.

One rather obvious omission in the manual is a clear discussion of how to interpret and use COR subscale scores. Such information would be invaluable for teachers who want to use assessment results for instructional planning. Factor correlations are rather high, indicating not only that children's behavior remains consistent across domains of functioning and that observers tend to rate individuals consistently, as the authors suggest, but that the six subscales may be related to one another, at least in this preschool population. A child's functioning in one domain may not be independent of his or her functioning in another domain.

The COR's technical features are its weakest area. The authors offer very little information about the actual development of the COR, stating only that it was developed in several versions over the course of a decade. With the exception of ethnic composition, there is little information provided about the validation sample or about the teaching teams who participated in the study. Such information would appear to be critically important. The issue of content validity is only tangentially addressed. Although the COR is based on the High/Scope Preschool Curriculum, there is no indication that efforts were made to judge the degree of agreement between the two, or between the COR and other preschool curricula. A panel of experts might have been profitably used to address content validity and to comment on item content and format. The manual does not provide evidence of construct validity although the COR purports to measure several important constructs in early childhood development. Concurrent validity correlations with scores on the McCarthy are low. The McCarthy differs from the COR in intent and format, so correlations could hardly be expected to be high. More information on criterion-related validity would be useful; for example, do documented delays at this stage necessarily mean that children will experience deficits later? Does superior performance on the COR suggest fewer problems in the elementary years? Given the purpose of Head Start and preschool programs like it, the answers to such questions may very well be important.

Internal consistency reliability estimates appear to be adequate; however, interobserver reliability is not as impressive. There are too few items, both on the total scale and on the subscales; for example, both the Initiative and the Music and Movement subscales only have four items. The feasibility study was conducted using research assistants, not regular teachers or teaching assistants, and as such, offers limited generalizability.

Technical issues must be addressed before the COR can be recommended without reservation. However, given its limitations, the COR may still be profitably used as part of a comprehensive assessment battery if results are interpreted with caution.

[31]
Holden Psychological Screening Inventory.

Purpose: "To provide a very brief measure of psychiatric symptomatology, social symptomatology, and depression."

Population: Ages 14 and older.

Publication Date: 1996.

Acronym: HPSI.

Scores, 4: Psychiatric Symptomatology, Social Symptomatology, Depression, Total.

Administration: Individual or group.

Price Data, 1999: $48 per complete kit including manual (50 pages) and 25 QuikScore™ forms; $25 per 25 QuikScore™ forms (English or French-Canadian); $30 per manual; $33 per specimen set including manual and 3 QuikScore™ forms.

Comments: Windows™ version computer administration and scoring available on CD or 3.5-inch disk.

Foreign Language Editions: French-Canadian QuikScore™ forms available.

Time: [5–7] minutes.

Author: Ronald R. Holden.

Publisher: Multi-Health Systems, Inc.

Cross References: See T5:1213 (1 reference).

Review of the Holden Psychological Screening Inventory by STEPHEN N. AXFORD, Psychologist, Pueblo School District No. Sixty, Pueblo, CO, and University of Phoenix, Colorado Springs, CO:

The Holden psychological Screening Inventory (HPSI) is a self-report, paper-and-pencil format, individual- or group-administered clinical screening instrument, normed for use with adolescent and adult ("people over 14 years old," manual, p. 3) nonclinical, psychiatric, and forensic populations. As noted by the publisher, the HPSI can be used efficiently and quickly for determining potential need for more comprehensive assessment. The author states that although the HPSI "is not intended to offer a complete psychological assessment," it is designed to serve as a "component" of comprehensive diagnostic evaluation, to include "extensive interviewing, examining, and testing" (manual, p. 3). As stated by the author:

> The HPSI was developed to fulfill a need for a short, reliable, and valid questionnaire that focuses generally on the broad domain of psychopathology and, in particular, on the underlying dimensions associated with the MMPI. (manual, p. 3)

The HPSI purportedly can also be utilized for program evaluation and as a method for monitoring treatment efficacy. Truly a brief measure, the HPSI consists of 36 five-point Likert-type scale items and requires 5 to 7 minutes to complete. The author states that individuals with reading difficulties, psychiatric problems, or whose first language is not English may require "slightly" more administration time. The HPSI may not be appropriate for psychotic and certain physically disabled subjects, according to the author.

Comprising three scales, the HPSI is based on a three-factor model involving specific components of psychopathology: Psychiatric Symptomatology (aspects of hypochondriasis, persecutory ideas, anxiety, thinking disorders, and deviation), Social Symptomatology (aspects of interpersonal problems, alienation, persecutory ideas, impulse expression, and deviation), and Depression (aspects of depression, social introversion, and self-depreciation). The factors were identified through multivariate latent analysis of the Minnesota Multiphasic Personality Inventory (MMPI), Differential Personality Inventory, and Basic Personality Inventory.

A well-organized manual provides in-depth discussions on the HPSI's item development and psychometric properties. A detailed schematic illustration outlines steps in HPSI scale construction, including factor analysis, item selection, validation, and norming. The final version of the HPSI was normed on several samples: A general adult sample ranging in age from 18 years to above 70 years (main normative group, N = 564), high school students (N = 139), university students (N = 326), adult psychiatric patients (N = 64), and adult male psychiatric offenders (N = 277). The main normative group comprised respondents randomly selected from a community-based Canadian consumer mailing list. Although the norming samples represent a good start, the HPSI would benefit from additional norming employing larger sample sizes and broader demographic representation. As a point of reference for comparison, the Personality Assessment Screener (PAS; Morey, 1997)—a 22-item clinical screening instrument having similar purposes as the HPSI but derived from the Personality Assessment Inventory (PAI; T5:1959) instead of the MMPI (T5:1697)—is normed on a sample of 2,631 individuals in community and clinical settings, utilizing 1995 U.S. Census-based quotas.

As noted by the author, a major demographic concern regarding the norming samples is limited representation of racial/ethnic minorities. The HPSI adult normative sample yielded the following race/ethnicity composition percentages: White = 85.1, Asian = 7.5, African Canadian = 1.1, Hispanic = .7, First Nations = .4, and other = 5.3. As the author correctly points out, this places severe restrictions on generalizing normative results to non-Caucasian populations. Until additional norming is conducted with larger sample sizes, the HPSI should not be used with non-Caucasian subjects. In a section of the manual entitled "Directions for Future Research," the author acknowledges the HPSI was normed on primarily English-speaking North American (Canadian) Caucasian samples and that studies sampling other populations are needed. As noted by the author, this would address the issues of: (a) whether separate norms may be needed for differ-

ent ethnic/racial groups, and (b) "establishment of psychometric properties for the HPSI in non-white populations" (manual, p. 37).

As the HPSI may well receive attention in the United States, given the size of the U.S. market and the appeal of the HPSI as an efficient and economical screening instrument, it would be encouraging to see additional norming and validation research targeting Black, Hispanic, Native American, and Asian American populations. Indeed, as the HPSI manual identifies both U.S. and Canadian customer service centers, there seems to be intention to market in both nations.

Regarding internal consistency reliability, six studies are cited by the author, with median coefficient alpha values across samples (N ranging from 61 to 564) of .73 for Social Symptomatology, .74 for Psychiatric Symptomatology, .84 for Depression, and .83 for Total Psychopathology. As noted by the author, higher coefficient alpha values were observed for the clinical samples, as would be expected "where more measurement variance would be anticipated" (manual, p. 31). Regarding test-retest reliability, a single study is cited by the author, involving 108 undergraduates, with a 4-week retesting interval, yielding the following coefficients: Psychiatric Symptomatology = .83, Social Symptomatology = .84, Depression = .86, and Total Psychopathology = .88. Particularly for a screening instrument, these are adequate correlation coefficients, indicating internal consistency and stability. However, additional research in this area sampling a greater diversity of populations is needed.

A detailed section addressing validation is provided in the manual. HPSI scale validity coefficients ranging from .28 to .75 for two studies involving self-report and observer ratings for undergraduate and clinical populations are reported. Generally, coefficients were observed to be higher for the clinical population. Coefficients reported for the student population, involving roommate observations, are somewhat low, although in the direction predicted.

In an effort to address criterion validity, the author compares mean HPSI scores for clinical versus nonclinical populations, further differentiated by gender. For each gender, means differ significantly (.01 level) for all HPSI scales. In that the HPSI successfully differentiates clinical from nonclinical populations, this lends credence to the HPSI's criterion validity. It thus appears that the

HPSI meets its main criterion as a clinical screening instrument.

Regarding convergent validity, the author reports correlations between the HPSI and theoretically connected self-report scales, specifically: the MMPI-2, Basic Personality Inventory (BPI), Carlson Psychological Survey (CPS), and Jackson Personality Inventory (JPI). In general, the coefficients are of sufficient magnitude and in the directions predicted, supporting the validity of the HPSI as this relates to measuring constructs it purports to measure.

The author also reports research investigating the HPSI's utility in detecting clinical change, thus addressing the claim that the instrument may appropriately be used in monitoring treatment and program effectiveness. In general, the research supports that the HPSI is a sensitive measure for detecting clinical change. Review of the HPSI answer sheet reveals clinically relevant and carefully constructed items, generally written in the present tense. From a face validity perspective, the HPSI presents as a useful instrument for monitoring intervention efficacy.

The HPSI manual's sections on test administration, scoring, interpretation, and use are concise and clear, with examples of scoring and sample case studies. Although the scoring materials are user friendly, requiring no templates or additional tables other than provided in the protocol, two options for computer administration and scoring are available utilizing IBM-compatible hardware and software: on-line administration (on-screen presentation of items) and a personal computer data entry and scoring program (QuikScore). Both options yield a computer-generated interpretive report. Network accessibility is available. HPSI computer services are retailed on a per use basis (i.e., the programs include an invisible counter).

The HPSI yields a composite T-score (Total psychopathology and T-scores for the three factors (Psychiatric Symptomatology Scale, Social Symptomatology Scale, and Depression Scale). Representing the only validity index for the HPSI, the Total Psychopathology raw score is used as a measure of excessive impression management (i.e., "faking good/faking bad"). The HPSI manual provides a table of cutoff scores for determining invalidity. According to the author, the HPSI validity index was empirically derived utilizing the fact that heavily biased responding results in sub-

stantially correlated scales; in contrast, a sincere pattern of responding should result in relatively independent scales. The author notes that "norms for general adult and general psychiatric patient populations" (p. 11) were also considered in the development of cutoff scores. To the author's credit, the test user is cautioned to utilize social ecological factors when interpreting validity index data. A high validity index score may accurately be indicative of severe maladjustment.

The author is to be commended for including a section in the HPSI manual on "Directions for Future Research" (p. 37) addressing limitations of the instrument and empirical issues requiring further investigation. Specifically, the HPSI is in need of additional norming utilizing larger and demographically representative samples, and specific HPSI scales require further investigation (e.g., how does the HPSI validity index compare to validity indicators for other measures? Does the Social Symptomatology Scale predict workplace adjustment?).

In summary, although considerable theoretically well-grounded work has been invested in item development/selection, the HPSI appears to be in its formative stages of development with regard to norming and research aiding interpretation of test results. The author has established a good foundation for future investigation of what appears to be a promising clinical screening instrument. The major limitation of the instrument, as the author acknowledges, is a limited norming sample. At the present time, the HPSI should be restricted to use with Caucasian subjects. Users of the HPSI should find the materials (manual, protocol, scoring forms) to be of professional quality and very convenient. The HPSI meets its primary goal as an efficient method for clinical screening. The prospect of the HPSI generating research that could potentially result in health services benefits related to efficient triage and treatment/program efficacy evaluation is encouraging.

REVIEWER'S REFERENCE

Morey, L. C. (1997). *Personality Assessment Screener professional manual.* Odessa, FL: Psychological Assessment Resources.

Review of the Holden Psychological Screening Inventory by JANET F. CARLSON, Professor of Counseling and Psychological Services, Associate Dean School of Education, Oswego State University, Oswego, NY:

The Holden Psychological Screening Inventory (HPSI) is a recently published, brief, paper-and-pencil, self-report inventory that assesses three major dimensions of psychopathology in persons over the age of 14. The HPSI was developed with an eye toward psychometric soundness and practicality. The test author notes that the inventory is predicated on the scale structure of traditional but much lengthier personality inventories. The inventory consists of 36 five-point Likert-type items, with 12 items representing each of the major dimensions tapped—psychiatric symptoms, social symptoms, and depression. A total score is also obtained. Test takers are asked to rate some items according to the frequency with which the statements listed apply (e.g., "I behave recklessly"), and other items on the basis of the extent to which respondents agree or disagree with the statements posed (e.g., "Trying something new is scary").

APPLICATIONS. The test author recommends the HPSI for use with clinical and nonclinical populations, as a component of comprehensive assessment. The inventory may be used to assess treatment response, to screen for psychopathology or to identify areas where further testing is warranted, and for research purposes. Appropriately, the test author advises potential users that the HPSI is best regarded as an adjunct or supplement to clinical assessment, rather than as a replacement for same. It is not intended as a diagnostic instrument.

ADMINISTRATION, SCORING, AND INTERPRETATION. The HPSI may be administered individually or in group format. It may be possible to modify procedures slightly to permit oral administration if, for instance, the test taker were visually impaired. However, the test author warns that the inventory may not be appropriate for use with individuals with disabilities, generally. Its appropriateness would need to be considered in light of the nature of the disability. Instructions to the test taker are easy to understand and follow. General guidelines for test administration are provided in the test manual. Typically, administration time is between 5 and 7 minutes; scoring takes about the same amount of time as administration.

Test takers respond by circling letters corresponding to their ratings of frequency (Items 1–19) or agreement (Items 20–36) for each of the 36 statements on the record form. A carbonized sheet transfers responses to the underlying score sheet, consisting of a grid with differential shading that expedites scoring. Responses are associated with numerical ratings, shown on the score sheet that is beneath the carbonized sheet. To score the inventory, one simply transposes the numbers to one of three appropriately shaded columns, each of which corresponds to a scale. The values within each column are then summed to produce scale scores for Psychiatric Symptomatology, Social Symptomatology, and Depression. Raw scores for each scale may range from 0 to 48. Scale scores are summed to yield a Total Psychopathology score. The total raw score may range from 0 to 144. Raw scores are converted to T-scores by plotting the scores on a profile form, which is part of the QuikScore response sheet.

Interpretation begins with an assessment of profile validity, which is largely a function of the Total psychopathology score. In general, extreme scores (greater than 80 or less than 20) on the total scale are indicative of an invalid profile that typically is associated with dishonest responding. Less extreme scores (greater than 70 or less than 30) are suggestive of the possibility that the profile is not valid. The validity index is intended to detect faking or attempts to present oneself in an overly positive or overly negative way. Cutoff scores that assist in the assessment of deception were derived empirically. The test author is careful to note that working hypotheses other than faking—such as severe disturbance—should be considered, even when scores are extreme.

Narrative interpretive guidelines associated with T-score ranges are presented in the test manual, and are used to interpret the three scale scores once the profile has been deemed valid. As well, percentiles associated with raw score values are presented by sex, for each scale and the total score. The test author suggests that individual responses may be queried, in an effort to identify isolated areas of difficulty that may benefit from intervention. Further, the test author suggests that HPSI findings be integrated with other available assessment information. Computer software is available from the publisher. The HPSI Computer Program runs on IBM-compatible personal computers with Microsoft Windows installed, and is launched from PsychManger. The program scores and interprets the HPSI, as well as several other instruments developed by the same publisher.

TECHNICAL ASPECTS. Several types of samples were used to establish norms. The main normative group consisted of a community-based sample of 304 women and 259 men from Canada, sampled during 1994. Although demographic descriptions are provided in the test manual, comparison figures (e.g., from the U.S. Bureau of the Census) are not given, so it is not easy to establish the degree to which the sample mirrors any specific population. Still, with less than 15% of the normative group being nonwhite, it is apparent that the normative group overrepresents whites and underrepresents nonwhites, for North American populations. The test author acknowledges that "the current adult HPSI norms cannot be recommended for nonwhites" (manual, p. 30). It also appears that individuals whose marital status is separated or divorced were underrepresented, whereas individuals with at least a college education were overrepresented.

Additional data in the form of means and standard deviations for several groups with special characteristics are provided in tables in the test manual. For example, the manual contains normative data for high school students, university students, psychiatric patients, and psychiatric offenders. The test author specifies that the data for high school students should be used in place of the data on the profile forms when the respondent is between the ages of 14 and 17. Similar instructions are not provided for the other samples for whom normative data are provided.

The section of the test manual that covers psychometric characteristics presents information about reliability estimates and provides evidence of scale validation. Internal consistency reliability estimates were examined using eight studies, ranging in size from 61 to 564 respondents, and varying in composition from students, to male, females, offenders, and adults. Overall, the coefficients are high, generally running in the mid-.60s to .90 range. Test-retest reliability was examined in a single study, using a 4-week interval and 108 undergraduate students. The reliability coefficients for Psychiatric Symptomatology, Social Symptomatology, Depression, and Total Psychopathology were .83, .84, .86, and .88, respectively.

Validation evidence for the HPSI is provided in the test manual, including consideration of criterion validity, classification accuracy, convergent validity, and treatment change. Two sets of validity coefficients were determined using a nonclinical sample of 150 students and a clinical sample of 64 adult psychiatric patients. In both studies, respondents completed the HPSI, as did a second party who was well acquainted with the respondent but unaware of the HPSI results. Validity coefficients were at least in the moderate range, varying from .28 to .75.

Classification accuracy was assessed using an experimental faking study. The HPSI correctly classified 67% of respondents using the more conservative T-score cutoff of <30, and 77% when the less conservative T-score of <20 was used as the cutoff score. Further, mean scores for the three scales and the total score differed at the .01 level of probability, between clinical and nonclinical samples, indicating that individuals with and without psychiatric disorders can be discriminated on the basis of their HPSI profiles.

Convergent validity was assessed using a sample of 84 patients, and comparing HPSI Psychiatric Symptomatology scale scores with related MMPI-2 (Butcher, Dahlstrom, Graham, Tellegen, & Kaemmer, 1989) scales and Jackson's Basic Personality Inventory (Jackson, 1976). Resulting correlation coefficients averaged .56 and .58, respectively. Similar comparisons using the Social Symptomatology scale scores produced average coefficients of .37 and .51, respectively, and the Depression scale score yielded average coefficients of .57 and .60, respectively. Findings reported by other researchers, and presented in the HPSI test manual as well, were largely consistent with these results.

Two small scale studies are reported in the test manual in support of the HPSI's ability to detect clinical changes. Both studies were conducted using a pretest/posttest paradigm. In general, changes in scale scores and total score were in the predicted directions. The test author also presents the results of five factor analyses, employing anywhere from 64 to 564 participants, and confirmatory principal components analyses. On balance, the HPSI's factor structure supports the scoring key.

CRITIQUE. In favor of the HPSI is the fact that it is a straightforward measure that is easily and rapidly administered, and easily and rapidly scored and interpreted. Its theoretical base was borrowed from tried and true measures with lengthy histories of development and related research. For a rather recently published instrument, the HPSI has been well-researched, can be scored and interpreted via computer software, and is reasonably priced compared to other screening or research tools that require individual administration. Data accumulated to date concerning its psychometric properties are encouraging, in that they support the inventory's reliability and validity. The presence of a validity index, in the form of the Total Psychopathology score, is unusual but welcome in a brief instrument such as this one.

Test users should be mindful of the fact that the HPSI is not intended to be a diagnostic instrument, and should not be used as such. Thus, in clinical applications, it is best regarded as a screening instrument that assesses three traditional dimensions of psychopathology. As suggested earlier, it may function as an indicator of clinical change in paradigms examining treatment response or outcome, in clinical or empirical applications.

As noted by the test author, use of the HPSI with nonwhite individuals is not recommended, given the relative lack of nonwhite participants in the main normative group. Other questions about the representativeness of the normative group are present as well, as suggested earlier. In addition, the interpretation of scores for youth between the ages of 14 and 17 is considerably more complex, given that the manual instructs the test user to use the norms in the manual rather than those contained—and presented conveniently in graph form—on the QuikScore form. Procedures for using the data in the manual to interpret scores for adolescents are vague, leaving the test user somewhat to his or her own devices. A table of T-score conversions for this age group could be included in the test manual, which would spare this confusion.

SUMMARY. The HPSI is a relatively new instrument, although it has been in development for several years. The number of studies that support its psychometric soundness is larger than for most tests first published in 1996. It is intended to be used and integrated with other available information, as part of a more comprehensive psychological assessment aimed at illuminating major dimensions of psychopathology. Likely, the HPSI will find additional applications in related arenas, including research and assessment of therapeutic outcomes. It is a simple measure that is easily understood and rapidly administered, scored, and interpreted, and may be modifiable for use with some individuals with disabilities. Group administration is possible, and computer software for scoring is available. Additional evidence concerning the HPSI's usefulness is likely to accumulate from its use in clinical settings and data generated from these applications.

REVIEWER'S REFERENCES
Jackson, D. N. (1976). Basic Personality Inventory. Port Huron, MI: Sigma Assessment Systems.
Butcher, J. N., Dahlstrom, W. G., Graham, J. R., Tellegen, A., & Kaemmer, B. (1989). *Minnesota Multiphasic Personality Inventory-2: Manual for administration and scoring.* Minneapolis: University of Minnesota Press.

[32]
Independent Living Scales.

Purpose: Designed to assess adults' competence in instrumental activities of daily living.
Population: Adults with cognitive impairments.
Publication Date: 1996.
Acronym: ILS.
Scores, 6: Memory/Orientation, Managing Money, Managing Home and Transportation, Health and Safety, Social Adjustment, Total.
Administration: Individual.
Price Data, 1999: $209.50 per complete kit including manual (119 pages), 25 record forms, stimulus booklet, and a pouch containing a facsimile of a driver's license, credit card, and key; $31 per 25 record forms.
Time: (45) minutes.
Comments: Four screening items are used to determine whether the examinee has a vision, speech, or hearing impairment; the stimulus booklet is designed for adults who can hear and those with a hearing impairment.
Author: Patricia Anderten Loeb.
Publisher: The Psychological Corporation.

Review of the Independent Living Scales by LIBBY G. COHEN, Professor of Special Education, University of Southern Maine, Gorham, ME:

The Independent Living Scales (ILS) is an individually administered test that ostensibly assesses selected independent living skills of adults. However, the specific purpose of the instrument is unclear because several different descriptions are used throughout the manual to indicate what the test assesses. These include: "instrumental activities of daily living" (manual, p. 1), "functional competence" (manual, p. 68), living arrangements, competency in managing personal property and affairs, guardianship decisions, needs for support services, adaptations, or instruction.

The ILS kit includes a manual, stimulus book, record forms, and a plastic case containing a key, a poor imitation of a credit card, and a driver's license. The examiner must provide the remaining materials needed for administration including a stopwatch, money (both coins and bills), a telephone book, and a telephone. The test consists of seven screening items and five subscales: Memory/Orientation (8 items), Managing Money (17 items), Managing Home and Transportation (15 items), Health and Safety (20 items), and Social Adjustment (10 items).

The subscales can be administered in any order. Several items are ambiguous or poorly worded. One example of a poorly worded item on the Managing Home and Transportation subscale is "What are two routine tasks that you do at home, but less often than every day?" One item asks the respondent to read the time on an analog clock rather than a digital clock. The stimulus book is used throughout the test administration.

Items are scored 2, 1, or 0. Although the manual provides suggested guidelines for scoring items, a great deal of interpretation is left to individual test administrators.

The development and administration of the ILS does not take into consideration the diversity of the U.S. population. The test assumes that respondents are able to read, write, hear, and speak English. There is no consideration for testing accommodations for adults who may have physical disabilities and many potential respondents of this test may have physical disabilities. The test scores of respondents who have one or more sensory disabilities may be penalized because of the way the items are administered and scored.

Several samples were used in the development of the ILS. A clinical sample composed of 248 adults, ages 17 years and older, had diverse clinical diagnoses including mental retardation, traumatic brain injury, psychiatric problems, or dementia. A nonclinical sample consisting of 590 adults, ages 65 years and older, was divided into three groups according to living status: Independent, Semi-independent, and Dependent. The ILS standard scores are only based on the Independent group. There is a great deal of disparity when the characteristics of the Independent group are compared to the U.S. population, ages 65 and older, according to the 1993 Census with regard to educational level, race/ethnicity, and geographical region.

Raw scores are converted to standard scores (standard T scores with a mean of 50 and a standard deviation of 10) for the subscales and both factors. The Full Scale is a sum of the five standard subscale scores (deviation IQ scores with a mean of 100 and a standard deviation of 15). All of the standard scores were derived from nonnormalized distributions because the distribution of the underlying raw scores was based on the minimal requirements for competence.

Reliability was determined only for the nonclinical sample and was not based on a sample of adults for whom this test is intended. Internal consistency reliability was based on the 590 respondents from the nonclinical sample. Coefficients for the subscales ranged from .72 (Social Adjustment) to .87 (Managing Money). As expected when the items were arranged into the two factors, the internal consistency reliability increased (Problem Solving .86, Performance/Information .92). Full Scale internal consistency was .88. Test-retest reliability (7–24-day interval) was based on 80 adults from the nonclinical sample. The coefficients for the subscales, factors, and Full Scale ranged from .81 (Social Adjustment) to .92 (Managing Money). Interrater reliabilities were all in the high .90s.

According to the manual, content validity was examined through the use of a Q sort. The test items were sorted into the subscales by areas of competence. For example, items relating to managing the home, transportation, mobility, communication, and use of the telephone were placed in the Managing Home and Transportation subscale. Although the ILS contains five subscales, the only two factors that were identified are problem solving and performance/information. Five of the 8 items on the Memory/Orientation subscale and 6 of the 10 items on the Social Adjustment subscale did not align with either of these factors.

The purpose of the cut scores is to aid in predicting the functional competence of the respondents to live independently. Criterion-referenced cut scores, according to living status, were developed for the subscale, factor, and Full Scale scores. Percentages of adults in the nonclinical Dependent and nonclinical Independent groups were classified as having dependent, semi-independent, or independent living status. There are several problems with the development of these cut scores. First, the samples from which the cut scores were derived are small and not representative of older adults according to the U.S. Census. Secondly, no studies are reported in the manual that confirm that these scores do, in fact, accurately predict functional competence. Finally, there is some support in the manual that demonstrates that, upon retesting, decision making is very inconsistent and unstable.

Several studies were conducted that investigated concurrent validity of the ILS. The Wechsler Adult Intelligence Scale—Revised (WAIS-R) was administered to 90 adults from the nonclinical sample. The results of this study demonstrated that the ILS and the WAIS-R assess different constructs. The MicroCog and the ILS were administered to 47 adults in the nonclinical sample. The MicroCog is a computer-administered and scored test of neurocognitive functioning. The results showed that the MicroCog and the ILS test similar constructs. The Activities of Daily Living Domain (ADL) and the ILS were administered to 90 adults from the nonclinical sample. The results demonstrated that the ADL and the ILS assess somewhat similar constructs.

The ILS was administered to small samples of individuals who were diagnosed with some type of cognitive impairments such as mental retardation, traumatic brain injury, dementia, or psychiatric disturbance. These studies showed that the ILS is not a precise instrument and that the results are open to interpretation.

SUMMARY. The ILS is an instrument that should be used cautiously. Because of the emphasis on respondents being able to read, write, hear, and speak English, this instrument may not be useful with all individuals for whom it was intended. The standardization sample is not representative of the U.S. population. Although reliability is satisfactory, validity is inadequate. Caution should be exercised when interpreting the results of this instrument.

Review of the Independent Living Scales by JACK A. CUMMINGS, Professor and Chair, Department of Counseling and Educational Psychology, Indiana University, Bloomington, IN:

The Independent Living Scales (ILS) was designed to assess "adults' competence in instrumental activities of daily living" (manual, p. 1). The purpose of the ILS is to evaluate an individual's skills associated with various levels of independent living. In contrast to current measures, the ILS requires the individual to demonstrate various adaptive skills. The ILS does not rely on third party informants or self-report. Loeb's (the test author's) intent was to create a "direct, more objective assessment of functioning in daily life" (manual, p. 1).

STANDARDIZATION. A sample of 590 individuals, ages 65 and above, served as the standardization sample. The sample was stratified into five age groups at intervals of 5 years starting at age 65. Within the sample, individuals were in one of three living arrangements: Independent (*n* = 400), Semi-independent (*n* = 100), and Dependent (*n* = 90). Those classified as Independent typically lived in a private home and were capable of all self-care skills. Semi-independent individuals often lived in a retirement home and needed some assistance with a limited number of daily living activities. Those in the Dependent category needed full-time supervision and help with most daily living skills. Adults in the three categories of living arrangement were evenly distributed across the age levels. Men and women were proportionally represented.

In the section of the manual on standardization, Loeb reports that two samples were collected. She refers to the group of 590 adults as the "nonclinical" sample. The clinical sample was not actually a standardization sample, but rather separate validation samples including individuals with mental retardation, dementia, traumatic brain injury, and chronic psychiatric disturbances. No norms are provided for individuals representing the aforementioned groups. Despite the age stratification in the nonclinical sample, the norms are collapsed for all individuals. This means that regardless of the adult's age, there is a single norm table that is used to generate subscale and factor scores. As developmental cognitive and psychomotor changes have been documented with adults in the age range from 65 to 85+, there should have been some discussion in the manual of the relationship between age and performance on the ILS. Beyond the issue of age, the decision to aggregate the scores of individuals across independent, semi-independent, and dependent living situations also merits discussion by the author. As the standardization sample is composed, approximately two thirds are living independently, one sixth semi-independently, and one sixth dependently. What is the rationale for allocating those proportions in the sample? An alternative approach to the use of a single table would have been to have separate norms for those in the three levels of living with each category stratified by age. This would be similar to the use of separate norm tables with the AAMR Adaptive Behavior Scale—School, Second Edition (Lambert, Nihira, & Leland, 1993; T5:2).

RELIABILITY. Coefficient alphas were calculated to estimate the internal consistency of the Full Scale score, two factor scores, and five subscale scores. The coefficients for the Full Scale and factor scores exceeded .85. Scores from the subscales of Managing Money, Managing Home and Transportation, and Health and Safety were reported to have coefficients in the mid-80s. The reliability of scores from the Social Adjustment and Memory/Orientation subscales was slightly lower at .72 and .77, respectively. Loeb notes in the manual that the lower internal consistency estimates of the latter two subscales are a function of relatively fewer items as compared to the other subscales. Overall, the coefficient alphas provide support for the author's contention that scores from the ILS have adequate internal consistency.

Stability was assessed by readministering the scale to 80 nonclinical adults. The average interval between testings was 2 weeks (range 7 to 24 days). The coefficients were impressive: .91 for the Full Scale, .90 and above for both factor scores, and .81 to .92 for the subscales. These coefficients indicate adequate stability.

Loeb also reports decision consistency based on the test-retest data. The question was whether an individual's classification as high, moderate, or low functioning would be comparable across testing sessions. For those initially scoring in the high classification, 92.6% scored high in the second administration. Likewise, there was consistency for those initially classified as functioning in the low range: 81.3% were in the same classification after the second testing. However, the stability of the classification for those labeled moderate was considerably less consistent. Only 47.6% were classified as moderate on the second testing. More than half of those in the moderate category on the first testing scored in the high range on the second administration. This is likely a function of a practice effect or, as Loeb suggests, partially explained by elderly individuals feeling more comfortable with the testing format on the second sitting.

VALIDITY. The description of the initial item development is vague. An unspecified number of "professionals knowledgeable about competency issues … [and] older adults" identified items and subscales that were important in regard to competent functioning (manual, p. 60). Once the items were developed, four experts in the psychology of aging sorted items into categories. The content validity phase of scale development could have been improved by having experts judge how effectively the various items represent a given domain, as well as judging the adequacy of the item format. Despite this caveat, the present reviewer does not see gaps in item coverage or problems with format.

Criterion-related validity was established with concurrent validity studies where scores from the ILS was correlated with scores from the Wechsler Adult Intelligence Scale—Revised (Wechsler, 1981), MicroCog (Powell, Kaplan, Whitla, Weintraub, & Funkenstein, 1993), and an unpublished activities of daily living self-report measure. Although the resultant coefficients were in the moderate range, none of the concurrent measures would have been expected to serve as an ideal anchor for the ILS. Another form of criterion-related validity was demonstrated by considering the performance of individuals in the three different living circumstances.

CONCLUSIONS AND SUMMARY. The value of the ILS lies in the selection of items; it provides a useful guide for a practitioner to reflect on the various roles associated with independent living. The ILS provides a format to observe an individual's response to common situations wherein adults have to perform actions to maintain an independent life style. This allows the examiner to gain another perspective on the individual's abilities, a perspective that can supplement data form third party informants. It is not a scale that should be interpreted rigidly. For instance, an individual may be performing at the top of the distribution in the areas of Memory/Orientation, Managing Money, Health and Safety, and Social Adjustment. A high Full Scale may place the individual in the independent category, but there could be a mobility issue that would require assistance. Loeb points to another issue: An individual may score poorly in a given area because a spouse or someone else takes responsibility for the function. As with other assessments, scores from the ILS must be interpreted in light of background information, observations, interviews, and other data.

REVIEWER'S REFERENCES

Wechsler, D. (1981). Wechsler Adult Intelligence Scale—Revised. San Antonio, TX: Psychological Corporation.

Lambert, N., Nihira, K., & Leland, H. (1993). AAMR Adaptive Behavior Scale—School, Second Edition. Austin, TX: PRO-ED.

Powell, D. H., Kaplan, E. F., Whitla, D., Weintraub, S., & Funkenstein, H. H. (1993). MicroCog: Assessment of Cognitive Functioning. San Antonio, TX: Psychological Corporation.

[33]
Infant Development Inventory.

Purpose: Designed "for screening the development of infants in the first eighteen months."
Population: Birth to 18 months.
Publication Dates: 1980–1995.
Acronym: IDI.
Scores, 5: Social, Self-Help, Gross Motor, Fine Motor, Language.
Administration: Individual.
Manual: Brief Instructions only.
Price Data, 1995: $10 per 25 parent questionnaires.
Time: Administration time not reported.
Comments: New version of the Minnesota Infant Development Inventory (T4:1642); observations by mother.
Author: Harold Ireton.
Publisher: Behavior Science Systems.
Cross References: See T5:1259 (2 references); for information on the earlier edition, see T4:1642 (1 reference); for a review by Bonnie W. Camp of the earlier edition, see 9:714.

Review of the Infant Development Inventory by ALAN S. KAUFMAN, Clinical Professor of Psychology, Yale University School of Medicine, and NADEEN L. KAUFMAN, Lecturer, Clinical Faculty, Yale University School of Medicine, New Haven, CT:

The Infant Development Inventory (IDI), for ages 1–18 months, is a revision of the Minnesota Infant Development Inventory (MIDI; Ireton & Thwing, 1980), which, in turn, evolved from Ireton's prior work with the Minnesota Child Development Inventory (MCDI; Ireton & Thwing, 1974). The IDI is intended to offer "a convenient way of obtaining and summarizing the mother's observations of her baby's development" (Ireton, 1995). The author sees the IDI as a time-saving device: "The professional may save time assessing the infant's development by reviewing the mother's IDI report before examining the

baby, and then confirming a few age-relevant items by observation or testing" (IDI instructions, p. 1).

Mothers are shown a Child Development Chart that lists five columns of behaviors (Social, Self-Help, Gross Motor, Fine Motor, Language), which are sequenced developmentally from birth to 21 months. The Chart is constructed as a grid such that each column is composed of 17 boxes, the first 15 depicting one-month intervals (i.e., Birth–1 mo., 1–2 mos., and so forth, to 1–15 mos.), and the last two boxes denoting 3-month intervals (15–18 mos. and 18–21 mos.). Age-appropriate behaviors are printed in the pertinent box within each column. Mothers are supposed to check off the "behaviors that describe the things that your baby is doing regularly or pretty well" and to "mark with a B those things that your baby is only just beginning to do or only does sometimes." Mothers are to go down each column until they come to three "NOs" in a row; then they go on to the next column. There are a total of 89 behaviors listed, ranging from 13 in the Self-Help column to 22 in the Language column. Most boxes include a single behavior, although some boxes are empty (four in Self-Help) and several list two behaviors (six in Language and three in Gross Motor). In addition to filling out the Chart, mothers are asked to write, within two small boxes, a description of their baby and a response to "How are you doing as a parent?"

To use and interpret the IDI Chart, test users are provided with an 8.5 x 11-inch pink card. The front of the card tells about the uses of the IDI and instructs professionals, in three brief paragraphs, to integrate the parent's report with their professional observations and knowledge. The back of the card instructs test users how to graph the results of the mother's responses to the Chart, and provides a table for determining which age levels of behavior correspond to Delayed development (30% below the infant's chronological age) or Advanced development (30% above the infant's chronological age). When computing the infant's age, the days of prematurity are subtracted before the age is rounded down to the nearest half-month (below age 12 months) or month (age 12 months and above). Half-months can be gleaned from the Chart because each box is subdivided; some behaviors are printed in the top half of the box and others are printed in the bottom half. Advanced and Delayed development are determined for each of the five areas separately. When evaluating the infant's developmental level, test users are told to consider only the checked behaviors; those behaviors marked with a "B" are treated as secondary information.

The lack of a manual makes it difficult to evaluate the IDI. The author provided only the pink card, the copy of the Chart, a one-page Appendix that devoted the left column to the IDI, and an article that related the Bayley Scales of Infant Development (Bayley, 1969) Mental Scale to the earlier version of the IDI, the 1980 MIDI (Creighton & Sauve, 1988). The Appendix indicates that the IDI items were drawn from prior research with the MCDI and that "Developmental age norms have been established for these items." There is no mention of how these age norms were established or whether any attempt was made to obtain standardization data or otherwise update what are most likely outdated norms. No reliability or validity data are reported for the IDI.

The Creighton and Sauve (1988) investigation suggests that the MIDI shows promise as a predictor of Bayley Mental age performance for 86 high risk 7–10-month-olds (mean = 8 months). However, the Bayley's 30-year-old norms are long outdated—the most well-respected test of infant development has been replaced by a second edition (Bayley, 1993)—and the MIDI has been supplanted by the IDI. Ireton does not indicate how closely the IDI resembles its predecessor, whether items were moved from one age level to another based on new data, or what steps were undertaken to modify the MIDI. The fact that the IDI Chart lists some age levels with two items and others with none indicates that the IDI represents at least a slight modification of the MIDI. In her review of the MIDI in the *Ninth Mental Measurements Yearbook* (*MMY*), Camp (1985) noted, "There is one item for each month of age in each of five areas" (p. 995). Also, the "stop" rule was changed from 5 to 3 "NOs," and the directions to the mother are more precise in the IDI than for its predecessor; for the MIDI, mothers were asked "to read each statement and decide if it describes 'what your baby is doing'" (Camp, 1985, p. 995). Furthermore, the age range of birth to 18 months differs for the IDI from the birth-to-15-months range indicated for the MIDI in the *9th MMY*.

However, the major criticisms made by Camp (1985) of the MIDI still apply to the IDI: (a) the standardization of the MCDI did not include infants below age 6 months, so the criterion for placement of items below that level is unclear; (b) no validity or reliability data were provided either for Ireton's instrument or for the MCDI within the age range of the MIDI; (c) it is not possible to know exactly how parents will interpret the wording of the behavioral statements; (d) there is no justification for the 30% criterion for determining Delayed or Advanced development; and (e) it is unclear how to interpret Delayed development in a single area of behavior—what it denotes and what to do about it.

The wording of the IDI items is a concern because some of the behavioral statements are vague. For example, a 2-month Gross Motor item on the IDI is "Holds head steady when held sitting." On the Bayley Scales of Infant Development—Second Edition (Bayley-II; Bayley, 1993), holding one's head steady for 3 seconds is achieved at the age of one month whereas holding one's head steady for 15 seconds is 2-month behavior. Another illustration of wording that might confuse mothers is the distinction between the Fine Motor items "Marks with pencil or crayon" (listed on the Chart between 14 and 15 months) and "Scribbles with pencil or crayon" (between 15 and 18 months).

Of greater concern is the placement of items on the IDI Chart by Ireton in view of the questionable data base for making such decisions. An appropriate criterion for evaluating the "correctness" of the IDI developmental ages is the Bayley-II, for which norms are both representative and recent. A comparison of similar items on the IDI and Bayley-II reveals some notable differences. For example, "Kicks a ball forward" is an IDI Gross Motor item listed as occurring at about 18 to 19 months; on the Bayley-II, the item, "Swings leg to kick ball" has a developmental age of 26 months. "Imitates sounds that you make" is an IDI Language item listed as occurring at about 9 months; on the Bayley-II, "Imitates vocalization" has a developmental age of only 5 months. "Transfers objects from one hand to the other" is an IDI Fine Motor item listed as occurring at about 6 to 6.5 months; on the Bayley-II, the item, "Transfers object from hand to hand" is a 5-month item. Although a number of IDI items are placed correctly, based on the Bayley-II criterion, the discrepancies are numerous and occasionally extreme. The validity of the developmental ages yielded by the IDI in each of the five areas is, therefore, open to challenge. Whereas the burden of validating a test ordinarily falls on the author, this burden was not dealt with in any way by Ireton.

SUMMARY. The IDI is intended to provide a measure of an infant's development, Advanced and Delayed, in five areas of behavior, as observed by the mother. It lacks data-based support for its placement of behaviors at specific developmental levels, reliability or stability of the infant's obtained age levels, and validity of the mother's classifications of her infant as Advanced, Delayed, or "normal." The wording of some behaviors is imprecise and the developmental levels assigned to some behaviors differ substantially from the empirically derived levels reported for the Bayley-II (Bayley, 1993). Professionals who are seeking an instrument for obtaining an infant's developmental level based on the mother's (or, more appropriately, the primary caregiver's) observations are not advised to use the IDI. A much better choice is the Kent Infant Development (KID) Scale (3rd ed.) (Reuter & Wozniak, 1996; 38) for ages 1–15 months. The KID Scale is administered to the infant's primary caregiver. It includes a much wider array of behaviors than the IDI, and these behaviors were selected as a result of considerable test research and development efforts. Psychometric properties were addressed by the KID Scale authors, and its applications cross-culturally have been documented by empirical research.

REVIEWERS' REFERENCES

Bayley, N. (1969). *Bayley Scales of Infant Development manual.* San Antonio, TX: The Psychological Corporation.

Ireton, H., & Thwing, E. (1974). Minnesota Child Development Inventory. Minneapolis, MN: Behavior Science Systems.

Ireton, H., & Thwing, E. (1980). Minnesota Infant Development Inventory. Minneapolis, MN: Behavior Science Systems.

Camp, B. W. (1985) [Review of Minnesota Infant Development Inventory.] In J. V. Mitchell, Jr. (Ed.), *The ninth mental measurements yearbook* (pp. 995–996). Lincoln, NE: Buros Institute of Mental Measurements.

Creighton, D. E., & Sauve, R. S. (1988). The Minnesota Infant Development Inventory in the developmental screening of high-risk infants at eight months. *Canadian Journal of Behavioral Science, 20,* 424–433.

Bayley, N. (1993). *Bayley Scales of infant Development: Manual (2nd ed.).* San Antonio, TX: The Psychological Corporation.

Reuter, J. M., & Wozniak, J. R. (1996). *Kent Infant Development (KID) Scale (3rd ed.): User's guide & technical manual.* Kent, OH: Kent Developmental Metrics.

Review of the Infant Development Inventory by JOHN J. VACCA, Certified School Psychologist, Assistant Professor of Special Education, Advisor, Graduate Program in Early Intervention, Loyola College, Baltimore, MD:

TEST COVERAGE AND USE. The purpose of the Infant Development Inventory (IDI; adapted version of the Minnesota Infant Development Inventory, 1980) is to provide a means for professionals and mothers to screen the developmental status of infants in the first 18 months of life. Though a manual for the scale is not provided, a page of instructions for administration and interpretation is included for the professional, and a limited set of instructions is included for the mother. The format of the IDI is intended to assist mothers in summarizing their own observations of their infants' development. The author makes reference to the infant's mother only without indicating that another caregiver could complete the scale. In light of the changing makeup of today's family, the fact that the author only makes reference to the "mother" is a drawback of the scale. The child would be better assessed if the IDI could be completed by any caregiver directly familiar with the child, including the parents (if available) to allow multiple perspectives on the child's functioning capabilities. In combination, multiple perspectives are not only a legal requirement for early childhood assessment, but also help to provide a link between the results gained from formal and informal evaluation techniques.

Eighty-nine pass/fail items on the IDI are categorized according to the areas of Social, Self-Help, Gross Motor, Fine Motor, and Language. Additionally, a limited amount of space is provided for the mother to address the following open-ended questions: "Please describe your baby; What questions or concerns do you have about your baby's health: Development? Behavior? Other?; How are you doing as a parent?" Through review of these observations and answers to such questions, professionals are presumed to be able to determine whether the infant is developing in a normal pattern or has delays. Further, the author states that "the professional may save time assessing the infant's development by reviewing the mother's IDI report before examining the baby, and then confirming a few age-relevant items by observation or testing" (instructions, p. 1). Although the inclusion of parent/caregiver report is crucial in the appropriate evaluation of an infant or young child, this information should not be used to gauge time needed for an evaluation or to determine the amount of items from a normative measure to be administered to the child. Instead, the professional should comply with principles of best practice for assessment by employing a complete battery of evaluative measures with the child, and by using the data from observations to assist in the interpretation of the normative data. For instance, many infants may not respond to items the way the test author expected them to respond for a variety of reasons, including novelty of the testing situation (room, materials, clinician), motivation, sleep/awake cycles, illness, or fatigue. In these situations, observations about the child received from someone who sees the child on a daily basis may assist the professional to determine the representativeness of the child's responses on the items on the normative measure.

TEST ADMINISTRATION. With respect to procedures for test administration, the author does not provide suggestions for the professional regarding how and when to introduce the IDI to the infant's mother. Based on a review of the IDI material, it appears that the mother is given the IDI to complete first. This assumes that she is able to read and comprehend the statements. The author mentions that the IDI can be used as a guide in a parent interview when it is suspected that the mother is unable to complete the scale independently. Although this can be beneficial to the mother, such use of different forms of administration of the IDI can greatly affect the reliability of the results. For example, when the IDI is used in the context of a parent interview, verbal exchange occurs between the professional and the mother. This may facilitate a higher level of clarification regarding test items than that of a mother who completes the IDI independently and may make her own judgments on an item's meaning. Therefore, it would be critical for a professional using the IDI to always verify with the mother who completes the scale independently that she completely understands both the content of the items and the criteria for responding to the items.

According to the brief set of instructions provided for the mother, the first thing she is required to do is to answer the series of open-ended questions about her baby. Second, she is instructed to proceed to the back of the sheet and review the items that "tell us what [her] child is doing in each area of development." The mother places a check beside those things her baby is "doing regularly or pretty well," and a "B for those

things that [the baby] is only just beginning to do or only does sometimes."

In terms of scoring, the directions for the professional are brief. They enable the professional to determine whether the child is considered by the mother to be functioning in a normal manner or to have delays. A score that falls 30% below the child's chronological age is used as the benchmark for determining developmental delay.

APPROPRIATE SAMPLES FOR TEST VALIDATION AND NORMING. No information relating to test validation and norming issues is included on the IDI instruction sheet. The instruction sheet simply indicates that the scale addresses development from birth to 21 months. The author states that the items on the IDI were drawn from earlier research with the Minnesota Child Development Inventory (1980), and that the developmental age norms have been established. Documentation supporting these statements is not included in the current IDI material. Therefore, it is not clear whether or with what population the IDI was field tested. It is also unclear how the items on the IDI were developed and subsequently selected. All of this information should be provided to allow the professional to determine if the scale would be appropriate for use with a given child and family.

RELIABILITY. In terms of reliability, the author did not include information on the revised IDI forms. An area that needs to be discussed in particular is internal consistency. Due to the fact that no information was available to address item selection, the degree to which the items are consistent with one another cannot be determined.

PREDICTIVE VALIDITY. In a study completed by Creighton and Sauve (1988), the Minnesota Infant Development Inventory (MIDI) was compared with the Bayley Scales of Infant Development (BSID) in the screening of capabilities of high-risk infants, 8 months of age ($n = 86$). Based on correlation results, the authors reported that the scores from the MIDI and BSID were significantly consistent ($p < .001$). Creighton and Sauve prefaced their discussion of results, however, by identifying that "the study sample was an abnormal sample … and hence showed a higher frequency of developmental problems on the BSID than one would anticipate in an unselected population of infants" (p. 430). Therefore, because the children in the sample had a significant postnatal history for developmental problems, the similarities in the responses received for both the MIDI and BSID need to be treated cautiously. In looking at the results, the correlations for both raw scores and index scores ranged from .46 to .58. Although these reflect a moderate degree of relationship (although statistically significant), the authors indicated that the data "[did] not indicate whether the MIDI has predictive utility for later infancy and childhood development" (p. 431).

SUMMARY. A major strength of the IDI is that it was designed with the intent of capturing the opinions of mothers concerning their babies in a formal manner. Too often, the input of caregivers is heard but not formally appreciated in a given evaluation. The IDI provides a vehicle for parent input to be considered in tandem with other normative measures. It is this type of input that is vital to the appropriate assessment of an infant or young child. In some cases, parent input helps in the translation of scaled scores. Even though the intent of the IDI is to incorporate parent report into the eligibility equation, professionals are cautioned to ascertain fully whether the mother understands the items and completion requirements of the IDI. Parent report is often the vehicle by which children are referred for screening. It should not be, however, the only vehicle by which children are identified for services. If the concepts of sensitivity and specificity are to be upheld, parent report should be augmented by norm-referenced screening tools such as the Developmental Indicators for the Assessment of Learning—Revised (DIAL-R; T5:809), AGS Early Screening Profiles (T5:124), Screening Profile for the Battelle Developmental Inventory (T5:266), or the Early Screening Inventory (T5:889). Throughout this review, issues regarding the utility of the IDI have been identified. Due to the fact that issues of sampling, item selection, validity, and reliability with the IDI have not been reconciled, professionals are urged to treat results from administration cautiously.

REVIEWER'S REFERENCE

Creighton, D. E., & Sauve, R. S. (1988). The Minnesota Infant Development Inventory in the developmental screening of high-risk infants at eight months. *Canadian Journal of Behavioral Science, 20,* 424–433.

[34]

Infant Developmental Screening Scale.

Purpose: Designed as a clinical instrument to be used to assess the current developmental status of the newborn.

Population: Newborns.
Publication Date: 1995.
Acronym: IDSS.
Scores, 24: Habituation, Attention/Interaction (Visual Orientation, Auditory Orientation, Alertness, Irritability), Motor Responses (General Tone, Movements, Activity Level, Symmetry), Physiological System (Respiratory/Circulation, Other Stress Signals), Abnormal Posture or Movements, Reflexes (Root, Suck, Hand Grasp, Toe Grasp, Babinski, Ankle Clonus, Positive Support, Walk, Placing, Crawl, Asymmetric Tonic Neck Reflex, Moro).
Administration: Individual.
Price Data: Not available.
Time: (10–20) minutes.
Author: W. June Proctor.
Publisher: The Psychological Corporation.
[Note: The publisher advised in March 1999 that this test is now out of print.]

Review of the Infant Developmental Screening Scale by JEFFREY A. ATLAS, Associate Clinical Professor (Psychiatry), Bronx Children's Psychiatric Center, Albert Einstein College of Medicine, Bronx, NY:

The Infant Development Screening Scale (IDSS) is described by the publisher as a "clinical instrument to be used to assess the current developmental status of the newborn" (manual, p. 1). In the 26-page manual, the IDSS is noted to be a "clinical tool in the experimental phase of construction" (p. 24), one for which the author invites feedback from users for further refinement of the scale. Although this invitation is a valuable one to the infant health community in the research and practical development of the field, it is important to consider the differences between a clinical instrument and an experimental scale carefully in determining the usefulness of the IDSS in particular applied settings.

The IDSS comprises scales for Habituation, Attention/Interaction, Motor Responses, Physiological Systems, Abnormal Movements, and Reflexes. The scales vary in construction from Reflex check-offs (e.g., Babinski absent or exaggerated) to observations combining physiological impressions and counts of stress signals, to multidimensional assessments combining stimulation of responses and general observation (Attention/Interaction). The ordinal scaling of these measures appears sensible, and their presumed treatment as equal-interval scales for purposes of later correlational analysis and predictive validity is not in serious contrast to psychometric principles. However, the variations in anchor points and summary stores (e.g., ranging from 1–3 for Habituation to 4 to 20 for Attention/Interaction and Motor Responses) is contrary to our expectations of more congruent scaling with such measures as the Brazelton Neonatal Assessment Scale (T4:321) from which the IDSS draws heavily. The Brazelton, in addition, contains some more refined individual measures, such as Defensive movements (to cloth on face), which this reviewer has found valuable in testing infants for viability of neurobehavioral integration. The more global assessments of the IDSS and its fledgling research status bring up the question of the need for an additional scale at this juncture.

One advantage of the IDSS is that, in part, due to its relative simplicity, extensive training is not required in contrast to the Brazelton. As such, it may find a current niche as a screening device in settings used to suggest the need for further evaluation or early intervention. It may also furnish a set of individual findings that may be psychoeducational for parents, sensitizing them to their baby's needs and possible problems. The manual presents some impressive follow-through studies showing significant predictive value of IDSS scores and infants' Bayley developmental quotient scores at 4-, 9-, and 15-month intervals. A number of qualifiers to these good results should be noted: the small (n = 106) and demographically restricted nature of the sample (the sample comprising a preponderance of inhabitants from Guam, and 1% ethnic Caucasions); interrater agreement estimates relying on global "percentage" of agreement versus proximity of agreement (e.g., such as used in alpha ratings); and a high number of false positives (50 of 81 children predicted by the IDSS to be at risk had normal Bayley scores).

In summary, the IDSS is to be recommended as a "work in progress" screening device for infants at risk (premature, exposed in-utero to toxic substances), which does not require an intense training regimen and which may provide useful information to parents in concert with pediatric health workers. Infant health professionals, researchers, and students desiring a more tested clinical instrument might do well to consider the revised Brazelton book as an established, and to this point preferred, alternative.

Review of the Infant Developmental Screening Scale by CYNTHIA A. ROHRBECK, Associate Professor of Psychology, The George Washington University, Washington, DC:

The Infant Developmental Screening Scale, or IDSS, was developed to provide an assessment of potential developmental delays in newborns from 38–42 weeks gestational age and to teach parents more about their babies' behavior. The IDSS manual also provides recommendations for using the IDSS to assess premature infants. IDSS items were developed from, and are similar to, items from other neonatal scales such as the Neonatal Behavioral Assessment Scale (Brazelton, 1984; T4:321).

In contrast to some of these other measures, the IDSS was designed to be administered and scored quickly and easily. According to the manual, it takes about 10–20 minutes to administer and 5–10 minutes to score. This aspect appears to be the only rationale for developing a new infant screener; other evidence for the IDSS' strengths compared to other infant screeners is not provided.

The IDSS includes 12 behavioral items (covering Habituation, Attention/Interaction, Motor Responses, Physiological System, and Abnormal Posture or Movements). Items are scored from "1" (the best score) to "5" (the least desirable) except for Habituation items, which are scored on a 1–3 scale. Summary scores for each behavioral area are recorded on a profile sheet, divided into "Normal," "Questionable," and "High Risk." Twelve reflex items are scored as "absent," "present/weak," "present/normal," or "exaggerated." A summary score is recorded on the profile sheet. The test comes with a bright toy and a rattle that are used as manipulatives.

It should be noted (and it is stated several times in the manual) that the IDSS should *not* be used as an isolated measure to predict future infant development or to make intervention decisions. In addition, results may vary depending on the infant's state when the test is administered. It is also suggested that the IDSS could be used as an intervention tool (e.g., demonstrating techniques of arousal and soothing to new parents) although there is no evidence of the measure's reliability or validity when used for that purpose.

In fact, there is limited reliability evidence for the IDSS in general. Interrater reliability estimates (ranging from .83 to .96) are based on percent agreement of only four examiners' scoring of eight infants. Internal consistency and test-retest reliability and norms are not available. Furthermore, it should be noted that this sample was from one hospital in Guam; further evidence of the measure's generalizability is needed.

The manual also provides only preliminary validity evidence for the IDSS. Content validity is suggested by basing the items on items from other neonatal scales. One sample of 106 at-risk (i.e., low birth weight, low Apgar score) infants at the University of Guam was used to provide preliminary evidence of construct validity. In this sample, the mean gestational age was 35, the sample was roughly equal boys and girls, and the predominant ethnic groups were Chamorro and Filipino. At follow-up visits, 4 months (n = 83), 9 months (n = 65), and 15 months (n = 60), the Bayley Scales were administered. At each follow-up, IDSS scores were significantly related to Bayley scores and predicted more of the variance in Bayley mental and psychomotor scores than other important variables such as birth weight, mother's education, or severity of neonatal complications (number of days hospitalized after birth). This study provides preliminary evidence for using the IDSS to identify infants eligible for intervention services.

SUMMARY. Future research is needed to provide additional evidence of test score validity. Studies need to sample from different populations to provide support for generalizability. As noted by the test developer, scores on newborn tests have not shown strong relationships with later development. Future research is needed to see whether or not the IDSS will predict future behavior better than other infant measures.

REVIEWER'S REFERENCES

Brazelton, T. B. (1984). Neonatal Behavioral Assessment Scale (2nd ed.). *Clinics in Developmental Medicine, No. 88.* Philadelphia: Lippincott.

[35]

Integrated Writing Test.

Purpose: "Designed to evaluate major components of good writing in students' writing samples."
Population: Grades 2–12.
Publication Date: 1993.
Acronym: IWT.
Scores, 7: Productivity, Clarity, Vocabulary, Spelling, Punctuation, Legibility, Total Test Language Quotient.
Administration: Group.

Levels, 5: Grades 2/3, Grade 4, Grades 5/6, Grades 7 to 9, Grades 10 to 12.
Price Data, 1997: $132.95 per kit including manual (66 pages) and 35 booklets for each grade level; $22.95 per package of 35 booklets; $22.95 per manual.
Time: 15(20) minutes.
Comments: Academic extension of the Developmental Test of Visual-Motor Integration (T5:815); also based upon the National Assessment of Educational Progress Writing Test.
Authors: Keith E. Beery with assistance from the Integrated Teaching Team.
Publisher: Golden Educational Center.

Review of the Integrated Writing Test by C. DALE CARPENTER, Professor of Special Education, Western Carolina University, Cullowhee, NC:

DESCRIPTION. The Integrated Writing Test (IWT) is a short, simple assessment tool designed to evaluate "good writing" by having students write for 15 minutes to a teacher-chosen prompt. Percentile ranks and standard scores are calculated for six subtests and the total test. Productivity is the number of words written. This is a standard method of assessing writing fluency. However, students are not allowed time to reflect on the topic nor are they allowed any other prewriting time to engage in brainstorming, webbing, outlining, discussing, or other activities that might lead to good writing and that are often suggested by written expression experts.

Clarity is a content score that refers to clarity of presentation. Students are told that they should write as if they were reporters for a newspaper. How well they address the following reportorial questions is evaluated: Who? When? Where? What? How? Why? Each of these questions receives a score of 0 for "Unclear" to 3 for "Detailed." This is the most subjective subtest and is at least partially dependent on the teacher-selected topic. Some topics such as "Discovery of America" might be more amenable to this kind of writing than others such as "Photosynthesis." Examiners are told to decide on a topic that will elicit the required questions and is interrelated with a topic being taught in a content area.

Vocabulary is scored by counting the number of words with seven or more letters and comparing this to the total number of words written yielding a ratio of long words to total words written. This is a standard, objective, and reliable method of scoring vocabulary. Spelling is also a ratio, counting number of words misspelled to total number of words. Unlike Vocabulary, which only counts the same long word once, misspelled words are counted whenever they occur even if they are consistently misspelled.

Punctuation is another ratio measure calculated the same way as Spelling except that punctuation errors are counted. Scorers are instructed to circle all punctuation errors including omissions. Examiners are directed to sections of dictionaries for punctuation rules. Although this subtest appears to be objective, all sources do not agree on punctuation rules, particularly on comma use, and examiners must have a basic knowledge to know where to question punctuation.

Legibility is a measure of number of words to total words with adequate legibility. A word with poor legibility includes such things as poor spacing, letter distortions, or any word that makes the reader pause to decipher.

The Total Test score is a composite of three or more subtests and is available as a quotient or percentile.

The Integrated Writing Test is based on the National Assessment of Educational Progress (NAEP) in Writing and is compared throughout the manual to the NAEP. Unlike the NAEP, the IWT allows examiners to score the entire writing sample or to score only five lines of the writing sample for all but the Clarity subtest. This approach reduces the time required to score each test and is reported in the manual to correlate at very high levels with full sample scoring.

A separate response form is required for each student to use and is also used to record. Five versions of the response form are available based on the grade level of the student and differ only in the line space provided. Besides a writing instrument, a watch, and the record form, the test requires no other materials to administer the test. A manual is required to score as well as is, presumably, a standard guide to punctuation rules.

NORM SAMPLE. The IWT was normed on approximately 1,000 students at 11 age levels with appropriate proportions of ethnic groups and balanced for gender. No information is provided about the inclusion of students with disabilities.

RELIABILITY. Because of the subjective nature of some of the scoring, interrater reliability is critical. On a sample of 20 protocols of fifth grade students, two scorers achieved interscorer reliabilities above .90 for all subtests except Legibility (.85) using the sample and full scoring methods. Internal consistency coefficients averaged .73 (Vocabulary) to .99 (Productivity). Test-retest reliability was estimated using two fourth grade classes writing within 2-days of each other. Coefficients using the sample method of scoring ranged from .23 (Punctuation) to .81 (Productivity) and using the full scoring method ranged from .49 (Punctuation) to .84 (Spelling).

VALIDITY. The authors present content validity information by stating reasons for each of the subtests and the method of scoring chosen. The topic selection for the writing sample is the most controversial aspect of the IWT and in this case, the manual states narratively, without presenting data, that no significant difference was found between action-oriented topics but significant differences were obtained between action-oriented topics and passive topics. Criterion-related validity is shown by comparing selected subtests of the IWT with the developmental curves of the NAEP Writing and comparing total test scores for the IWT with the Test of Written Language-2 and the California Test of Basic Skills. Construct validity evidence is presented in four ways. IWT subtest intercorrelations show low to moderate coefficients indicating that subtests do not assess the same thing. Developmental curves affirm that the constructs measured are indeed developmental. Third, the manual presents scores for 22 students identified as learning disabled showing their average scaled scores in an attempt to indicate group differentiation. Yet, the scores presented are not significantly different from nondisabled students in the standardization sample. Finally, the manual presents data from a study of two fourth grade classes using the test and showing gains after approximately 7 months of instruction.

SUMMARY. The Integrated Writing Test is promising and deserves to be used by researchers and practitioners. It offers a quick and authentic way to measure important aspects of writing. The manual provides reasonably clear directions for administering and scoring. However, the option of two scoring methods, a sample method and a full scoring method, may appear confusing to some users. The choice of a topic to which students are to write is the most problematic feature of the instrument. Although the authors address how to choose a topic, the information about variations in scores based on topic is not adequate.

Technical data regarding standardization sample, reliability, and validity are not overwhelming, but are adequate to merit further use of the instrument. Reliability and validity studies use small samples and focus on the intermediate grades rather than including the entire age range of the norm sample. Therefore, the IWT appears better suited to these grades than to second grade students and secondary aged students. The instrument would benefit, as would most, from more study. Nonetheless, the IWT currently offers an acceptable alternative to other popular writing tests.

Review of the Integrated Writing Test by RI-CHARD M. WOLF, Professor of Psychology and Education, Teachers College, Columbia University, New York, NY:

The Integrated Writing Test (IWT) is a test of reportorial writing ability intended for use by classroom teachers in grades 2–12. Students are given 15 minutes to write a passage on an assigned topic, pretending that he or she is a reporter "who is writing the story for a newspaper" (test booklet, p. 1). The test booklet, outside of a cover sheet for recording name and other information, consists simply of three pages of ruled lines on which to write the story. Unfortunately, teachers are furnished virtually no guidance about a topic on which students are to write. The manual simply says, "Decide upon [a] topic which will elicit the *Who?, When?, Where?, What?, How?, and Why?* questions of reportorial writing. The topic should also interrelate with a topic currently being taught in another subject such as Language, Science, or Social Studies" (manual, p. 5). Unfortunately, no examples of topics are furnished.

Scores are obtained on the following six dimensions: Productivity (the number of words in a five-line sample—usually lines 10 through 14 of the story), Vocabulary (the number of words of seven letters or more in a five-line sample), Spelling (number of misspelled words in a five-line sample), Punctuation (the number of punctuation errors in a five-line sample), Legibility (the number of words judged "poor legibility" in a five-line sample), and Clarity (a rating of 1 to 6 for judged clarity of the entire story). Except for Clarity, the scoring can be done on either the full story or a five-line sample from the story. Norms are provided for each of the dimensions. Scaled scores and percentile ranks are provided for each of the six dimensions whereas scaled scores, percentile ranks, "quotients," T scores, and NCEs (normal curve equivalents) are provided for total scores. The norms are based on samples ranging from 78 to 110 students at each grade level, drawn from different sections of the United States. The use of "quotients" is highly questionable for two reasons. First, they are not quotients at all, but rather standard scores with a mean of 100 and a standard deviation of 15. Second, they resemble Wechsler Intelligence Scale scores and thus may lead some users to regard them as immutable. This seems dangerous.

Validity evidence on the IWT inheres primarily in the selection of the dimensions on which the stories are scored. It appears to parallel the scoring dimensions of the National Assessment of Educational Progress (NAEP), Grill and Kerwin's (1989) Written Language Assessment (WLA; T4:3005), and Hammill and Larsen's (1988) Test of Written Language (TOWL-2; T4:2804). However, the authors acknowledge that some of the scores may be less important than others, namely Clarity, Spelling, and Punctuation. Evidence of construct validity is furnished by showing that the developmental curves for many of the scores parallel those of other tests of writing proficiency. Raw score correlations with grade levels range from .36 for Punctuation and Legibility to .67 for Productivity. Correlations between IWT scores and other measures are fairly high (i.e., .6 to .7), although the samples sizes on which they are based are often quite small.

The author presents the results of a number of investigations undertaken to establish the reliabilities of the various scales. Although the results show generally high reliability estimates with values in the .7 to .9 range, these studies suffer from two defects. First, the sample sizes are generally quite small (as low as 10 students in an analysis). Second, analyses were conducted combining age/grade groups. This inflates the variability considerably and results in high correlations. It would have been better to conduct analyses separately at each age/grade level.

One issue of particular interest to test users, particularly teachers, is the amount of time required to score the IWT. The author provides two procedures. The first involves scoring the full story and the second requires only a scoring of five lines of the story (lines 10–14 are recommended). To determine whether the five-line scoring was sufficient, the author and a graduate student in English each scored 20 protocols from an average fifth grade class on both the five-line sample as well as the full scoring. As expected, the correlations for the full scoring were higher (.87 to .97) than for the five-line sample scoring (.85 to .97). The median correlation for the full story scoring was .965 whereas the median correlation for the sample scoring was .925. It appears that the five-line sample scoring is adequate although if there is a question about an individual's performance, full story scoring should probably be done.

In summary, the IWT appears to be a carefully developed measure of reportorial writing ability for students in grades 2–12. It yields scores on six dimensions. If these dimensions are ones that a teacher feels are important, then its use should be given consideration. If other types of writing are to be assessed (e.g., narrative writing), a user will need to look elsewhere or devise a different measure. Validity and reliability information are based on relatively small samples and may be somewhat inflated by combining results across age/grade levels. Unfortunately, users are given little guidance with regard to the selection of topics on which students should write.

REVIEWER'S REFERENCES

Hammill, D. D., & Larsen, S. C. (1988). *Test of Written Language* (TOWL-2). Austin, TX: PRO-ED.
Grill, J. J., & Kirwin, M. M. (1989). *Written Language Assessment Manual.* Novato, CA: Academic Therapy Publications.

[36]
Interpersonal Adjective Scales.

Purpose: "A self-report instrument designed to measure two important dimensions of interpersonal transactions: Dominance and Nurturance."
Population: Ages 18 and up.
Publication Date: 1995.
Acronym: IAS.
Scores, 10: Assured-Dominant, Arrogant-Calculating, Cold-hearted, Aloof-Introverted, Unassured-Submissive, Unassuming-Ingenious, Warm-Agreeable, Gregarious-Extraverted, Dominance, Nurturance.
Administration: Individual or group.
Price Data: Price information available from publisher for introductory kit including manual (143 pages), 25 test booklets, 25 scoring booklets, and 25 glossaries.
Time: (15–20) minutes.

Comments: Separate norms are available for college students and adults; glossary is included to be used by subjects during testing.
Author: Jerry S. Wiggins.
Publisher: Psychological Assessment Resources, Inc.
Cross References: See T5:1288 (2 references).

Review of the Interpersonal Adjective Scales by STEVEN J. LINDNER, Executive Director, Industrial/Organizational Psychologist, The WorkPlace Group, Inc., Morristown, NJ:

The Interpersonal Adjective Scales (IAS) describe the behaviors individuals are likely to manifest when interacting with others. Individuals use an 8-point Likert scale to rate the extent to which 64 adjectives accurately describe them as a person. Based on these ratings, a profile of an individual's interpersonal behaviors is generated. Profiles show individuals' standings on eight different interpersonal scales arranged on a circle having two primary axes: Dominance and Nurturance. The shape of an individual's profile defines his or her general interpersonal style or type, the intensity with which behaviors associated with that type are likely to be manifested, and the likelihood of behaviors associated with each of the remaining interpersonal scales.

The IAS is appropriately used to assess the interpersonal styles of college students and adults. Normative data are provided for both college and adult men and women with separate norms available for each group. Separate norms for both college and adult men and women allow individuals' interpersonal profiles to be interpreted with respect to the most meaningful referent group.

The IAS requires a 10th grade reading level when administered with its accompanying glossary, which defines the 64 adjectives that appear in it. Because of its high reading level, the IAS may not be appropriate for individuals whose primary language is not English. However, the IAS has been translated into Chinese, Dutch, German, Spanish, and Swedish (manual, p. 59). Although no formal training is required for administering and scoring the IAS, professional training in psychology is required for interpreting the IAS. Only general information regarding interpersonal types and the behaviors associated with types are provided in the test's manual. A detailed interpretation of an individual's profile requires professional understanding of interpersonal behaviors, personality, psychopathology, clinical assessment, and for work place applications, "knowledge of laws governing the use of tests for that purpose, along with psychometric concepts such as job relevance" (manual, pp. 7–8).

In clinical settings, IAS profiles should not serve as the only diagnostic measure of psychopathology. Interpretation of an individual's IAS profile should be supported by information obtained from additional assessment instruments, such as personality measures, and family, social, and work histories.

In other settings, such as research or the workplace, the purpose and use of IAS scores may justify its appropriateness as a stand-alone test.

Each of the eight scales of the IAS has strong internal consistency, providing a reliability index that suggests items making up each of these scales are cohesive in measuring the underlying characteristics they have been assigned to measure. Although the scores from the IAS have strong reliability with respect to internal consistency, the test manual provides no information regarding the consistency with which individuals assess themselves over multiple occasions (test-retest reliability) or the extent to which ratings of individuals by independent others agree (interrater reliability).

With respect to validity, the structural arrangement of the IAS interpersonal scales along the dimensions of dominance and nurturance has substantial theoretical and conceptual support. This theoretical and conceptual evidence comes from research conducted by others examining concepts and constructs related to the IAS. In limited cases, the test manual refers directly to studies using the IAS.

Studies directly using the IAS have shown that peer ratings of dominance and nurturance correlate with corresponding facets of the NEO Personality Inventory (Costa & McCrae, 1992). In addition, IAS scales have been found to correspond with self-reported behaviors (Buss & Craik, 1983; Buss, 1984; Buss, Gomes, Higgins, & Lauterbach, 1987) and observed nonverbal behaviors (Gifford & O'Connor, 1987). Convergence between two different measures of similar characteristics suggests that the IAS is measuring the underlying interpersonal constructs it purports to measure. Correspondence between IAS ratings and behaviors also supports the notion that inferences made from individuals' standings on the IAS are descriptive of their actual behaviors.

SUMMARY. The IAS is a useful measure for assessing the interpersonal styles of adults and college students along two important dimensions of interpersonal behavior: dominance and nurturance. Those using the IAS to make clinical assessments need to supplement IAS results with information from other instruments and sources. Those using the IAS for making workplace-related decisions (e.g., employee selection) need to establish the job relatedness of the IAS for the jobs in question. The strong theoretical and conceptual foundation of the IAS, along with its substantial empirical evidence supporting the appropriateness of its structure, makes it a good instrument for describing the behaviors individuals are likely to manifest when interacting with others.

REVIEWER'S REFERENCES

Buss, D. M., & Craik, K. H. (1983). The act frequency approach to personality. *Psychological Review, 90,* 105–126.
Buss, D. M. (1984). Toward a psychology of person-environment (PE) correlation: The role of spouse selection. *Journal of Personality and Social Psychology, 47,* 361–377.
Buss, D. M., Gomes, M., Higgins, D. S., & Lauterbach, K. (1987). Tactics of manipulation. *Journal of Personality and Social Psychology, 52,* 1219–1229.
Gifford, R., & O'Connor, B. (1987). The interpersonal circumplex as a behavioral map. *Journal of Personality and Social Psychology, 52,* 1019–1026.
Costa, P. T., & McCrae, R. R. (1992, June). *Comparability of alternative measures of the five factor model.* Paper presented at the annual meeting of the American Psychological Society, San Diego, CA.

Review of the Interpersonal Adjective Scales by GERALD R. SCHNECK, *Professor of Rehabilitation Counseling, Mankato State University, Mankato, MN:*

The Interpersonal Adjective Scales (IAS) is a "self-report instrument that is designed to measure two important dimensions of interpersonal transactions: Dominance (DOM) and Nurturance (LOV)" (manual, p. 1). The IAS test booklet contains 64 items that consist of adjectives, which are descriptive of interpersonal interactions. The test respondent rates each of the items on an 8-point Likert scale, according to how accurately each adjective describes them as an individual. The accuracy of self-description is rated on the Likert scale, which ranges from 1 (Extremely Inaccurate) to 8 (Extremely Accurate). Scores on the instrument are "ordered around an interpersonal circumplex with Dominance and Nurturance as the primary axes" (manual, p. 1). The IAS also measure the respondents' interpersonal type and the intensity of type.

The majority of the content of the professional manual for the IAS centers its focus on the psychological and clinical assessment of individuals. It also includes a relatively thorough explanation of the development of the instrument, procedures for administration and scoring, normative group descriptions, and scoring tables, as well as developmental and psychometric properties of the instrument.

The author indicates that the IAS is appropriate for use with college students and adults, with separate norms being provided for each. A reading level analysis of the IAS test items and the IAS glossary sheet adjective definitions indicated that a 10th-grade reading ability is necessary to complete the test. It is recommended the test user use care in the administration of the IAS to persons whose native or first language is not English, and who do not have the physical and emotional capabilities for meeting "the normal demands of testing with self-report instrument" (manual, p. 7). Additional care is emphasized if the user will be testing persons with "psychological disorder(s), or who display confusion, psychomotor retardation, distractibility, or extreme emotional distress" (manual, p. 7).

Administration and scoring of the IAS "can be performed by individuals with no formal training in psychology or related fields." However, "(T)raining in the administration and scoring of the IAS should be provided by a qualified psychologist. In a psychiatric setting, for example, an appropriately trained ward staff member can administer the IAS" (manual, p. 7). The test manual does emphasize that "interpretation of the IAS requires professional training in clinical or counseling psychology," and that "interpretation should not be attempted without a firm understanding of theories of personality and psychopathology and a knowledge of the appropriate uses and limitations of self-report inventories" (manual, p. 7). Other professional qualifications may be essential, beyond these basic requirements, depending on the setting and the purpose(s) for which the IAS is utilized. In administering the IAS, the professional manual, a four-page IAS test booklet, a one-page glossary (printed definitions are included on both sides of the page), and a four-page scoring booklet are used. The respondent uses the glossary sheet whenever they are unsure of the meaning of one of the descriptive word items.

The manual states that most respondents will complete the instrument in approximately 10–15 minutes. The test administrator should encourage the respondent to complete all unanswered items, prior to completing scoring of the instrument. The scoring booklet is then used to complete the lengthy and involved manner of scoring the completed instrument. Raw octant scores, average raw octant scores, and T-scores are determined for each of eight personality type categories. T-score values for each of the personality type categories are then combined in order to calculate the Dominance (DOM) and Nurturance (LOV) scores. Angular location, vector length, and vector length T-score are then calculated prior to being plotted on the circumplex, which provides a graphic profile on the instrument for the respondent. A relatively extensive discussion and several case studies are offered and are meant to aid the qualified test user in interpreting the resulting respondent profile that is represented on the circumplex.

Normative samples for the IAS were drawn from several sources, including: (a) participants in the Baltimore Longitudinal Study of Aging (McCrae & Costa, 1989) ($N = 344$); (b) a volunteer sample that was recruited through churches and civic organizations ($N = 377$); (c) a sample of volunteer undergraduate college students from the University of British Columbia (Wiggins & Broughton, 1991) ($N = 2,988$); and (d) an employment sample of applicants for fire fighter positions in a large southwestern city ($N = 362$). Descriptive information regarding the composition of each normative group was provided and differences among sample groups were analyzed and resulting data were presented.

A very thorough discussion of the theoretical basis for inclusion of self-descriptive adjectives within the instrument, study of items to include and exclude for the final scales, reliability, structural and convergent validity, varying applications to which the instrument might be applied, and the evolution of the IAS circumplex as a behavioral map were presented within the manual. Internal consistency reliability of IAS scales was estimated using Cronbach's alpha; results for the IAS scales ranged from .755 to .865 for the Adult sample and from .733 to .865 for the College student sample. Factor analysis was performed as part of the structural validity analysis of the circumplex model. Correlational analysis of the IAS scales was performed as part of the convergent validity analysis of the instrument. A relatively extensive presentation of data and discussion of its implications was presented for both the structural and convergent validity analyses of the IAS.

The IAS appears to be a well-developed assessment tool based upon a substantial amount of theoretical foundation and research evidence. The professional manual and instrumentation provide a well-organized and thoughtfully written presentation of the information that would be most useful to a professional who wishes to identify and utilize an instrument such as this, within mental health or other therapeutic settings. The IAS presents itself as an important supportive tool within a therapeutic milieu and as a welcome adjunct to other measures of psychopathology or psychological type. In the hands of a well-qualified professional, significant information can be drawn from respondent results on this instrument, to aid in the exploration of those dimensions and issues that have brought the individual to seek out therapeutic assistance.

REVIEWER'S REFERENCES

McCrae, R. R., & Costa, P. T., Jr. (1989). The structure of interpersonal traits: Wiggins' circumplex and the five-factor model. *Journal of Personality and Social Psychology, 56,* 586–595.
Wiggins, J. S., & Broughton, R. (1991). A geometric taxonomy of personality scales. *European Journal of Personality, 5,* 343–365.

[37]
The Jesness Inventory.

Purpose: Designed to measure "several relevant personality dimensions."
Population: Ages 8 and older.
Publication Dates: 1962–1996.
Acronym: JI.
Scores, 22: Conventional Scales (Social Maladjustment, Value Orientation, Immaturity, Autism, Alienation, Manifest Aggression, Withdrawal-Depression, Social Anxiety, Repression, Denial, Asocial Index), Validity Scales (Lie, Random Response), Subtype Classification (Undersocialized—Active, Undersocialized—Passive, Immature Conformist/Conformist, Cultural Conformist/Group-Oriented, Manipulator/Pragmatist, Neurotic—Acting-out/Autonomy-Oriented, Neurotic—Anxious/Introspective, Situational/Inhibited, Cultural Identifier/Adaptive).
Administration: Individual or group.
Price Data, 1999: $70 per complete kit including manual, 10 test booklets, and 25 QuikScore™ forms; $13 per 10 reusable test booklets (specify English, Spanish or French-Canadian); $27 per 25 QuikScore™ forms (specify English or Spanish); $40 per manual; $42 per specimen set including manual, 1 test booklet, and 3 QuikScore™ forms; $75 per set of scoring templates and computer program for Windows.

Foreign Language Edition: Spanish and French-Canadian forms available.
Time: Administration time not reported.
Comments: Self-report; "Originally developed for use in the assessment and classification of male delinquent youths."
Author: Carl F. Jesness.
Publisher: Multi-Health Systems, Inc.
Cross References: See T5:1341 (3 references) and T3:1209 (9 references); for a review by Dorcas Susan Butt of an earlier edition, see 8:595 (14 references); see also T2:1249 (5 references); for a review by Sheldon A. Weintraub of the Youth Edition of the earlier edition, see 7:94 (10 references); see also P:133 (3 references).

Review of The Jesness Inventory by ROBERT M. GUION, Distinguished University Professor Emeritus, Bowling Green State University, Bowling Green, OH:

This 155-item inventory was initially developed for the assessment of "youth at risk," whether delinquents or those with psychological or behavioral problems; it is also suggested for adults. It was developed in recognition of the extensive individual differences among a less-than-homogeneous group known as delinquent. For respondents with at least a fourth grade reading level, it provides both a taxonomy of personality variables and a classification scheme, offering scores on 11 personality scales and 9 classification scales. It is an aid, not a substitute, for judgment; although administering and scoring the inventory is rather simple, interpretation of the scores requires advanced education and relevant experience. The emphasis in this review is on the basic personality scales.

The personality scales stem from an initial 250-item pool. Three of them (Social Maladjustment, Value Orientation, and Immaturity) were developed by item analyses comparing a priori groups. Seven scales resulted from cluster analysis. The 11th scale (Asocial Index) is a weighted composite of the other scales based on discriminant function analysis, distinguishing between offenders and nonoffenders. According to the manual, no item appears on more than one scale unless scored in opposite directions, but that assertion needs qualifying: An item scored for one of the seven cluster analytic scales is not scored in the same direction on any of the other six cluster scales. Several items are scored for a cluster scale and for two of the first three scales. Overlapping items produces some redundancy. For example, the 65-item Social Maladjustment scale and the 26-item Alienation scale have 14 items in common, and the correlation between them is .66. Correction for attenuation using the reported alpha coefficients raises the correlation estimate to .81—not quite totally redundant. Using the less friendly test-retest reliabilities, however, gives a corrected coefficient of .99. The median intercorrelation was lower, .38, but alpha coefficients were lower than one would wish (especially for the Immaturity scale, where alpha = .43) with several in the .60s. Coefficients reported for retesting after a year were lower still, although the likelihood that attitudes of delinquents would fluctuate suggested that moderate retest reliabilities simply reflect scale sensitivity. All things considered, several scales appear to be redundant, some do not. It seems likely that all useful variance could be expressed in not more than three factors—one very large factor, a secondary one combining Immaturity and Repression, and perhaps a third one defined mainly by the Social Anxiety scale. Is this a serious problem? Perhaps not. The manual emphasizes frequently that the inventory is to be an aid in assessment, not the sole basis. Such a caveat suggests that scores on individual scales are not considered definitive but can guide the search for other relevant information about individual respondents. For such screening, the reliabilities are probably adequate for most of the 11 scales, and there may be enough unique meaning in the scores to be useful in practice. The scales should not, however, be considered a scientifically useful taxonomy of personality variables.

The normative data samples, totaling more than 3,000 cases, included both male and female delinquents and nondelinquents. Ages ranged from 8 to 19, although there were no female delinquents under age 12. Scores of nondelinquents were converted to "T-scores" for the various age and sex groupings in the nondelinquent samples, and these are the reported norms. (The manual does not say whether these are normalized T-scores or linear transformations.) Data from these samples were collected in 1961 and 1962. Have there been enough social changes in the more than three decades since then to change the norms? Many modal attitudes have changed, including attitudes toward many kinds of behavior. Are girls under 12 still less likely than boys to be committed as delinquent? Is behavior once considered a form

of delinquency now considered ordinary? Does it now require more serious social transgressions to be classed as delinquent? Do item responses mean now the same things they meant nearly 40 years ago? It seems to me that renorming is needed, and to whatever extent the reliability estimates come from these same data, they should be brought up to date as well.

Validity evidence, primarily construct validity, includes more recent studies. Many of these studies involve correlations with other measures. I would have liked to have seen more argument presented about why certain correlations are deemed to support the interpretations intended for scores from the various scales—not because of doubts but because the nature of the author's arguments would help clarify the sometimes murky nature of the intended constructs. It is nice to have sections of a test manual giving information in support of construct validity, but they are not very meaningful if the nature of the construct has not been well defined. For some of these scales, the nature of constructs is discernible but not wholly clear. For example, "Value Orientation" is (or "reflects") a "tendency to share attitudes characteristic of individuals of low socioeconomic status" (manual, p. 5). A statement of why a negative correlation with the CPI Tolerance scale, or a positive correlation with the MMPI Pt scale, supports such an inference would clarify the construct as the author has intended it. Other validity information seems more pragmatic. Data are presented showing that scores can distinguish delinquents from nondelinquents or first time from repeat offenders. However, prediction of delinquency is not very successful (because of low base rates, according to the manual).

SUMMARY. The Jesness Inventory was developed with a lot of thought and care. I do not doubt its usefulness in the practical setting of screening young people (or even adults) who may have violated laws—when such screening is done by well-trained people with access to supplementary information. I am concerned, however, about its age. Like far too many other personality measures, there is a tendency to assume that an instrument developed in one zeitgeist will retain all of its desirable characteristics as the zeitgeist changes—and maybe even discard any undesirable characteristics over time. Such assumptions need to be challenged, and developers of the instruments need to maintain a chronological history of various kinds of item statistics and evidences of scale validities. In the case of the Jesness Inventory, item revisions in 1972 were to make the inventory useful for adults and females. Further revision of one key scale (Social Maladjustment) was done in 1986. The reader is not told what effect these changes had on norms, reliabilities, or validities. Ten years after the most recent item changes the current manual was published—but it reflects little new information in its list of references. There may have been little or no psychometric reason to revise anything said about the inventory since 1972, but I see no sign that such an assumption has been investigated. This concern, of course, applies equally well to nearly all personality measures developed during the flurry of test development of the 1950s and 1960s.

Review of the Jesness Inventory by SUSANA URBINA, Professor of Psychology, University of North Florida, Jacksonville, FL:

BACKGROUND INFORMATION. The Jesness Inventory (JI) was developed, in the early 1960s, as part of a long-term project aimed at evaluating the effectiveness of a treatment program for young male delinquents. Its author, Carl F. Jesness, wanted a multidimensional instrument that could be used with subjects as young as 8 years of age and that would be helpful in predicting delinquency and assessing change. At the time the JI was developed, there were no other self-report inventories specifically designed for adolescents, let alone deviant adolescents. Thus, the JI was rightly seen by an earlier reviewer as "a useful addition to measurement in the study and treatment of young offenders" (Butt, 1978, p. 876).

Since its introduction, the JI has undergone minor revisions that purportedly make it appropriate for use with adults and with females, and there has been some refinement of two of its scales, but it has otherwise remained essentially unchanged. The inventory is being reviewed now because its manual has been revised to consolidate information spread over several publications and to incorporate more recent research. Therefore, this review will simply describe the basic components of the JI and outline its strengths and weaknesses from a contemporary perspective. Prospective users are urged to consult earlier *Mental Measure-* *ments Yearbooks* and Mooney's comprehensive review (1984) for additional details on the JI.

It is worth noting that since the 1960s, several instruments that could be used for the same population and purposes for which the JI was intended have been published. Among these are: the Basic Personality Inventory (BPI; T5:256), the Millon Adolescent Clinical Inventory (MACI; T5:1685), the Minnesota Multiphasic Personality Inventory—Adolescent (MMPI-A; T5:1698), and the Personality Inventory for Youth (PIY; T5:1963), all of which attempt to assess maladaptive tendencies in adolescents. An instrument for adult male offenders, the Carlson Psychological Survey (CPS; T5:427), has also been published. Thus, test users in the field can now choose the most suitable instrument(s) for their purposes from among several.

GENERAL DESCRIPTION. The JI comprises 155 true/false items that require approximately 30 minutes to complete and at least a fourth-grade reading level. Scoring can be done directly from the Quikscore™ answer form or by computer. The inventory can also be administered by computer and a computer-generated narrative report is available as well.

Normative samples for the JI consisted of 970 delinquent and 1,075 nondelinquent males between the ages of 8 and 18 as well as 450 delinquent females, aged 12 to 19, and 811 nondelinquent females between the ages of 8 and 18. Data were collected in California in 1961 and 1962. The nondelinquent samples, mostly lower class, came from 10 public schools and, according to Jesness, contained at least some delinquents.

Two distinct sets of results can be gathered from the JI. One set consists of 11 "conventional" personality scales and the other of nine "I-level" scales used to classify respondents. The personality scales aim to differentiate delinquents from nondelinquents and to describe respondents. *T*-score norm comparisons on these scales are based on the nondelinquent samples, separated by sex and age level. Three of the personality scales—Social Maladjustment (SM), Value Orientation (VO), and Immaturity (Imm)—have items that were selected based on whether they differentiated, respectively, (a) delinquents from nondelinquents, (b) youths from different social class groups, and (c) youths from different age groups. Seven other personality scales, developed through cluster analyses, assess maladaptive traits, such as Alienation, Manifest Aggression, and Withdrawal-Depression. The remaining personality scale score, an "Asocial Index" (AI) derived through discriminant function analysis, combines information from eight of the other personality scales and is regarded as the best JI measure of one's generalized tendency to transgress social rules.

Comprising the second set of JI results are nine "I-level" scales that classify respondents into types such as "Unsocialized Aggressive" or "Immature Conformist." Although the "I" in "I-level" is never spelled out in the manual, it apparently refers to interpersonal maturity level as postulated in M.Q. Warren's theory (cited in the manual, pp. 33-35), which was the basis for the JI typology. The I-level scales were constructed from the responses of 206 delinquents classified as "ideal" representatives of their types. Norms for each scale were then derived from a different sample of 2,000 delinquent males. The rules for classifying test takers into types were empirically determined based on combinations of scores on the nine scales. The goal of these scales is to help in differential treatment planning for those already identified as delinquents.

An evaluation of response sets that might invalidate results is particularly relevant for the population targeted by the JI. Yet, the inventory provides only two validity scales—of five items each—designed to assess random responding and tendency to "fake good." These scales, described as "experimental," are offered only with the JI scoring software and need empirical validation. Pinsoneault (1998), however, has recently developed two promising response inconsistency scales to detect random and acquiescent response sets on the JI.

EVALUATION OF STRENGTHS AND WEAKNESSES. It is easy to understand why, according to Pinkerman, Haynes, and Keiser (as cited by Pinsoneault, 1998), the JI is the second most widely used personality inventory in juvenile court clinics in the U.S. The inventory grew out of the author's extensive experience with delinquent youths and of his knowledge of the theoretical and empirical literature in the field. The JI has gathered a solid research base spanning thee decades and several countries (75 PsycINFO entries from 1967 to 1998). Its brevity, low reading level

requirement, and normative base of (male) delinquents as young as 8 years make it uniquely suitable for juvenile forensic settings. In addition, validity data on the Asocial Index show that the JI can certainly contribute to identifying or predicting delinquency in young males. The remaining scales and subtype classification system provide a good source of hypotheses for individual assessment and research. Descriptions of typical attitudes, behavior, background variables, and treatment recommendations provided in the manual for each JI type should prove helpful to counselors and of heuristic value.

In spite of its potential usefulness, there are several areas in which the JI could be improved. First, and most important, is the issue of its applicability to groups other than adolescent male delinquents, which is questionable in light of the way the JI was developed. Adult norms are altogether lacking and norms for delinquent females are only available for ages 12 to 19. In addition, the JI norms now date back almost 40 years. Another matter, important in view of the goals of the inventory, is the generally low stability (ranging from coefficients of .40 to .79) of the personality scales over an 8-month interval, and the relatively low rate of subtype classification agreement (52%) over the same period. Furthermore, the manual has a number of errors that could easily be corrected. Among the more significant of these are the sketchy fashion in which validity data are provided, the allusion to an important table (4.2) that is not presented (manual, p. 27), and discrepancies between the text and the tables.

SUMMARY. The JI may prove clinically useful in the assessment of young delinquent males, especially if used in conjunction with other tools. For young female delinquents, clinical use is not as well supported and for adult offenders, it is not supported at all. Updating and extension of the JI norms, as well as further investigation of its stability and of its validity for females and adults, would be highly desirable.

REVIEWER'S REFERENCES

Butt, D. S. (1978). [Review of the Jesness Inventory.] In O. K. Buros (Ed.), *The eighth mental measurements yearbook* (pp. 876–878). Highland Park, NJ: The Gryphon Press.

Mooney, K. C. (1984). [Review of the Jesness Inventory.] In D. J. Keyser & R. C. Sweetland (Eds.), *Test critiques* (vol. I, pp. 380–392). Kansas City: Test Corporation of America.

Pinsoneault, T. B. (1998). A Variable Response Inconsistency scale and a True Response Inconsistency scale for the Jesness Inventory. *Psychological Assessment, 10,* 21–32.

[38]

Kent Inventory of Developmental Skills [1996 Standardization].

Purpose: Designed to assess the developmental status and progress of healthy infants, infants at risk, and young children with developmental disabilities.

Population: Infants up to 15 months of age and young children whose developmental age is less than 15 months.

Publication Dates: 1978–1999.

Acronym: KIDS.

Scores, 12: Developmental Ages and Standard Scores for: Cognitive, Motor, Language, Self-Help, Social Domains, Full Scale.

Administration: Individual.

Price Data: Price information available from publisher for complete kit including 25 profile sheets, 25 answer sheets, reusable administration and scoring booklet, 5 scoring templates, set of developmental timetables, manual, and 2-use disk for on-site computer scoring and interpretation.

Time: (45) minutes.

Comments: Relies on caregiver report; also yields individualized developmental timetables; includes hand-scoring materials and an expanded computer report, including a list of developmentally appropriate activities selected to match each child's specific competencies; earlier editions entitled The Kent Infant Development Scale.

Authors: Jeanette Reuter with Lewis Katoff and Jeffrey Wozniak (3rd edition of the test manual and user's guide) and James Whiteman (computer-scoring disk).

Publisher: Western Psychological Services.

Cross References: See T5:1391 (2 references); for reviews by Candice Feiring and Edward S. Shapiro of an earlier edition, see 10:163 (2 references); for a review by Candice Feiring of an earlier version, see 9:567; see also T3:1246 (1 reference).

[Note: The publisher advised in September 1999 that this test has been changed but that the following reviews, based on materials for The Kent Infant Development Scale, Third Edition [1990 Standardization], are still appropriate for the new edition. Major changes are ones of packaging and usage. Hand scoring is now available as well as an expanded computer report.]

Review of The Kent Infant Development Scale, Third Edition [1990 Standardization] by DIANE J. SAWYER, Murfree Professor of Dyslexic Studies, Middle Tennessee State University, Murfreesboro, TN:

DESCRIPTION. The Kent Infant Development Scale, Third Edition, consists of 252 items sampling five domains of development: Cognitive, Motor, Language, Self-Help, and Social. These items are ordered in a hierarchical progression that the authors indicate are consistent with the developmental progression observed in normal children. The scale was designed to be used by any caretaker with at least a 4th grade level of reading ability. However, the authors indicate that the scale items may be read to caretakers who do not have reading skills consistent with the demands of the test. For each item, the caretaker indicates the child's current status—yes, the child can perform the task; yes, the child used to perform the task but outgrew it; no, the child cannot do this task yet. On the accompanying answer sheet, the caretaker fills in the #1 if the child can do the task, the #2 if the child has outgrown the task, or the #3 if the child cannot yet do the task.

Raw scores in each domain are calculated by counting the numbers of ones and twos that have been circled. Templates are provided to distinguish the items that fall into each domain. Raw scores are then converted into a Developmental Age, in months, using a profile sheet provided by the authors. The developmental age for each domain and for the full scale may be obtained. Finally, the developmental status may be determined by consulting the Delay Chart provided by the authors. This chart permits a comparison of the child's chronological age with the full scale developmental age obtained. Determination of status—no delay, at risk, or developmentally delayed—is based upon standard deviations from the mean of the norming sample. A classification of developmentally delayed would be associated with the difference between the developmental age and the chronological age of more than two full standard deviations. A computer scoring procedure is also available. Conversion of raw scores to standard scores (mean of 100, *S.D.* of 15) is possible for children ages 2–14 months using conversion tables provided. The authors state that the full scale standard score provides the best guide for determining developmental status (manual, p. 9).

To interpret developmental status, in each of the domains, into a plan for intervention, developmental timetables are provided. In these timetables, a given item number is associated with the age norm at which that item is expected to be accomplished. It is suggested that intervention begin at the point at which the caretaker identifies three consecutive items in the domain as #3 (child cannot do it yet). Intervention is interpreted as special attention from the caregivers. Professional consultation is suggested to assist the caregiver in interpreting the scale results, in planning intervention, or in determining if referral to early intervention programs or particular specialists should be made. A clinical case study is provided to assist test users in interpreting test results to determine the developmental status and to assess strengths and weaknesses.

DEVELOPMENT OF THE SCALE. The Kent Infant Development Scale has evolved through three separate normative studies. Profiles obtained on more than 1,500 children have contributed to item selection, and the development of all normative data provided. These children were described as normal, healthy babies and young children representing at least two different socioeconomic groups.

RELIABILITY. Reliability is reported with respect to internal consistency, test/retest reliability, and interjudge reliability. Internal consistency is high; Cronbach alpha coefficients of .93 to .99 are reported for the five domains and the Full Scale. Test/retest reliability coefficients (administration interval ranges from 2 weeks to 2 months) from four different studies are reported. Generally, these are high and consistent, ranging from .91 to .99 for the domain and full scale scores. One study, however, involving 331 children, yielded much lower coefficients. In this instance, coefficients ranged from .77 to .86. This particular study was part of the Hungarian language form of the scale. Interrater reliability is reported for six studies. These studies include those associated with the development of the scales in other languages. Overall, the reliability coefficients ranged from .68 to .99. In all studies, mothers' and fathers' ratings were compared. However, a number of nonparental caregivers were also included in some of the computations. The two lowest coefficients attained across all studies involved samples of severely or profoundly mentally retarded children and children with diagnosed brain damage. Within both samples, the lowest coefficients were obtained for the Language domain.

VALIDITY. Validity of the scales was examined with respect to construct validity, concurrent validity, and predictive validity. With respect to construct validity, the authors note correlation coefficients of .88 to .93 for scores obtained on the scale with the ages represented in the samples of healthy infants.

Concurrent validity has been examined through a comparison of the scale with the Bayley Scales of Infant Development. Degrees of agreement in the assessment of "delayed or not delayed" across the two measures, over five studies, are reported to be between .44 and .91. Decision agreement based upon the Full Scale score only, ranged from .59 to .97.

The authors report three studies that explored the predictive validity of the scales. Two studies examined child behavior on the scales over periods of 4 months, 6 months, and 7 months. One study shows a high degree of predictive validity (.90 to .97) for a sample of 71 children tested at a 6-month interval. Much lower predictive values were obtained in another study which examined prediction over a 4-month span (a sample of 256 children) and a 7-month span (a sample of 96 children). Values of .70 to .77 were obtained for a 4-month interval and values of .41 to .54 were obtained for a 7-month interval. In a third study, the ability of the scales to predict outcome measures on the Bayley Scales and the Stanford-Binet was examined. This latter study yielded the lowest prediction values (.46 at 1 year of age), .33 at 2 years of age, and .20 at 3 years of age based upon an assessment at age 6 months).

SUMMARY. The Kent Infant Development Scale, Third Edition, is a relatively brief and easy-to-use instrument. It addresses development in five critical domains and is perhaps best suited as a screen for the possible identification of children with developmental delays. Reported test/retest reliability is reasonably strong but interrater reliability is relatively weaker. This may be due, of course, to the familiarity of the rater with the child's behavior on a day-to-day basis. Among mother/father pairs of raters, it is likely that one parent will have many more clock hours of contact with the child each day than may be possible for the other parent. The range of interrater reliability coefficients reported appears to underscore the importance of ratings obtained from the primary caregiver.

Estimates of concurrent validity vary greatly (.44 for the Self-Help to .91 for the Social and Motor domains) when compared to the Bayley Scales of Infant Development. When compared to the Vineland Adaptive Behavior Scales, the validity index ranges from .85 for the Self-Help scale to .97 for the Full Scale. These data, however, were derived from a sample of only 25 children. Again, the estimates of concurrent validity raises the question of rater familiarity with the child as well as the question of objectivity of the rater in the use of any of the scales for the evaluation of development.

The power of the Kent Scales to predict performance on these scales or other scales at a future time is extremely variable. Prediction to a second administration of the scales at 4 months was .77, at 6 months was .97, and at 7 months was .54 based upon the Full-Scale score, across three studies. Such wide variability may simply underscore individual variability in development among individuals previously diagnosed as developmentally delayed or disabled. The ability of the Kent Scales to predict performance on the Bayley Scales 6 months and 18 months later is quite low (.46 and .33 respectively).

The data presented by the authors suggests that the primary utility of the Kent Scales may be to identify developmental status at the time of assessment, but not to predict future behavior among individuals with developmental handicaps. As a screen, the Kent Scales may be facilitative in identifying areas of slower than expected development and in assisting with decisions regarding referral for further assessment or for supportive stimulation.

Review of The Kent Infant Development Scale, Third Edition [1990 Standardization] by GARY J. STAINBACK, Senior Psychologist I, Developmental Evaluation Clinic, East Carolina University School of Medicine, Department of Pediatrics, Greenville, NC:

The Kent Infant Development Scale, Third Edition (KID Scale) is a 252-item parent assessment of their child's development up to the age of 15 months. It precedes two earlier editions and normative studies from 1978, 1982, and 1990. The KID Scale is reported to be appropriate for the assessment of normally developing, at risk, and developmentally delayed children, even those whose level of developmental functioning falls below a 15-month level. The Full Scale score is recommended for determining the developmental status of an infant; however scales are also provided for Cognitive, Motor, Language, Self-Help, and So-

cial domains. Developmental Age (DA) and Standard Scores are provided for the Full Scale score total, as well as for each domain scale. Several foreign language versions are available as well as a computer-scoring program, which offers a slightly greater analysis than would traditionally be available through hand scoring and analysis.

Parents or primary caregivers are asked to rate each of the 252 items, either 1 (Yes, can do it), 2 (Yes, used to do it but outgrew it), or 3 (No, cannot do it yet). The standardization sample of the third edition of the KID Scale consisted of 706 infants between .3 and 15.8 months of age, who by parent report were full term and without any significant medical complications or serious illnesses. An equivalent number of male and female infants were involved in the standardization. Developmental Ages were smoothed so Full Scale raw scores offer a DA in tenths of a month, ranging from .1 to 15.5. Standard scores have a mean of 100 and standard deviation of 15. In addition to standard scores and developmental ages, the manual offers item age norms and a Consistency Scale. Item age norms reflect the approximate age an item may be observed in the development of a child. The Consistency Scale can be used as a validity check on the scoring responses of the caregiver. In the KID Scale are 53 pairs of items that describe similar behaviors. If responses for essentially the same behavior are inconsistent, the caregiver may have responded carelessly and the resulting scores may not be valid. The Consistency Scale is equal to the number of item pairs that were found to be answered in an inconsistent manner. It is only available, however, when the KID Scale is scored by computer.

The KID Scale manual presents an impressive array of psychometric data, illustrating its sound evidence of reliability and validity. Internal consistency measures, test-retest, interjudge reliability, and generalizability indices are provided for reliability measures. Concurrent, predictive, and construct validity measures are also available and very acceptable. Normative studies have also been undertaken in the Netherlands (1990), Spain (1996), Hungary (1996), Germany (1992), the Czech Republic (1996), and South Vietnam (1989). The overall order of behavioral acquisition across all cultures was found to be very similar, with rank order correlations of .80 and above. However, some cultural variations were noted; therefore, cultural factors would need to be accounted for in assessing the developmental timetables for some cases.

Perhaps one of the more impressive features of the KID Scale came from research comparing scores from the KID Scale with those from the Bayley Scales of Infant Development (BSID), the Motor Scale and Mental Scale. Strong validity measures were obtained even for a clinical sample of developmentally disabled children, as well as with children at risk.

Scoring of the KID Scale may be accomplished through the use of templates or the computer-scoring program, that may be loaded on a personal computer or by mailing the results to the publisher. The computer program requires an IBM or compatible computer running Microsoft's Disk Operating System (MS-DOS) and having at least 350K of RAM and a floppy disk drive. From the computer program three report formats are available: short report (only scores and DAs, no narrative text), professional report (scores, DAs, list of items and their responses, and no narrative text), or the full report, which has all of the above plus a narrative text that explains the domains and scores. It is anticipated that about 6 to 12 minutes would be involved in keying in the client information and responses to the 252 items, and about 4 to 10 minutes to print the report. Template scoring is accomplished by counting the number of 1s and 2s on the answer sheet (without the template). Templates are used for determining the score for each domain. Tables are provided for converting Full Scale and Domain Raw Scores to DAs and Standard Scores. A graphic display is then plotted on the Profile Sheet, where approximate Domain and Full Scale Raw Scores can be read along the right and left hand margins. From this profile, strengths and areas of weakness may be identified.

If more than five items were left unanswered by the caregiver, the scale should be considered invalid. An invalid scale should also be considered if the Consistency Scale Score is greater than 4. Care should also be undertaken for computing the correct age of the child, as well as adjusting for chronological age when necessary, in order to obtain valid estimates of the child's developmental status. A Delay Chart is provided and provides a developmental status for the child's chronological age to the nearest .5 of a month, and a rating for the amount of delay. Delays are rated as No Delay, At Risk, or Developmentally Delayed, depending on the difference between the obtained score and the chronological age or corrected gestational age. Essentially, ratings of Developmentally Delayed represent standard scores <71 whereas At Risk represents standard scores between 70 and <86.

Analysis of results may also involve an analysis of the developmental timetables, where emergent behaviors may be identified. This may be particularly useful for programming purposes in Early Intervention programs, as well as an aid for programming for the clinically delayed. Emergent behaviors can then be identified for each domain area and activities provided to help the child in acquiring these behaviors within the next month (assuming a normal course of development).

SUMMARY. In review, the KID Scale follows a sound evolution of the scale from the doctoral dissertation of L. Katoff. Earlier editions were psychometrically sound (see ninth and tenth editions of the Buros *Mental Measurements Yearbooks* for reviews), and the current edition remains so. A computer-scoring program is also available, which makes possible an added level of analysis to the results, namely the Consistency Scale, which can serve as a validity check for scoring purposes. The KID Scale is recommended in the developmental assessment of children up to 15 months, or of those developmentally delayed and whose level of functioning falls within this range. It may even prove more useful in the developmental assessment of culturally different children, especially those whose family cultures follow very close to those of their heritage.

[39]
Learning and Memory Battery.

Purpose: Used for assessing both specificity and sensitivity to diverse memory problems.
Population: Ages 20 to 80.
Publication Date: 1995.
Acronym: LAMB.
Scores: 7 subtests: Paragraph Learning, Word List, Word Pairs, Digit Span, Supraspan Digit, Simple Figure, Complex Figure.
Administration: Individual.
Price Data, 1999: $295 per complete kit including 25 recording forms, 25 profile/summary sheets, 100 Simple and Complex Figure drawing forms, adminis-

tration tents, standard score conversion booklet, and manual (171 pages); $55 per manual; $65 per 25 recording forms; $12 per Standard Score Conversion Booklet; $10 per 100 Simple and Complex Figure Drawing Forms; $180 per administration tents (set of 2); $295 per LAMB Score Windows™ CD or 3.5-inch disk (unlimited use); price information available from publisher for Administration Windows™ 3.5-inch (per usage).

Time: (45–60) minutes.
Authors: James P. Schmidt and Tom N. Tombaugh.
Publisher: Multi-Health Systems, Inc.

Review of the Learning and Memory Battery by CHARLES J. LONG, Professor of Psychology, and MICHELE L. RIES, Research Assistant, Psychology Department, The University of Memphis, Memphis, TN:

The Learning and Memory Battery (LAMB) was designed to serve as a relatively comprehensive measure of learning and memory abilities. This instrument was developed to overcome the limited scope, weak theoretical foundations, and psychometric deficits found in many of the other memory tests that are presently available. The selection of memory constructs assessed by the LAMB was based on research literature on those memory types that have been found to be anatomically and functionally distinct as well as clinically useful. The content of several of the subtests was largely derived from already established memory tests, and therefore should be familiar to clinicians and researchers who evaluate memory functions. Subtests of this battery were selected to assess various types of memory (e.g., verbal vs. nonverbal) and various phases of memory (e.g., short-term vs. long-term). Repeated presentation of materials within each subtest provides information on the rate and pattern of learning over multiple exposures. Immediate free recall, cued recall, recognition, and delayed recall measures are utilized to distinguish among problems in consolidation, storage, retrieval, etc.

The instrument consists of seven subtests. Three subtests are verbal (Paragraph Learning, Word List, and Word Pairs); two are numerical (Digit Span and Supraspan Digit); and two are visual (Simple and Complex Figure). The test is relatively easy to administer and score, but this process is rather time intensive. About 60 to 90 minutes should be allotted for the full administration; about 30 to 60 minutes should be allotted for

scoring. Meaningful information can be derived by administering individual subtests (without completing the full battery of tests) because each subtest is independent in content and has its own normative data. The test materials include two administration tents, Simple and Complex Figure drawing sheets, recording forms, trial-by-trial summary sheets, and profile sheets. A computerized scoring program called LAMB Score is also available for purchase. Directions for the administration and scoring of the LAMB are available in the manual and on the side of the administration tents viewed by the examiner. Overall, the materials are user-friendly and instructions are clear and easy for the examiner and test taker to understand.

Raw scores are obtained for each trial within each subtest by tallying the correct answers obtained during that trial. Cumulative percentile scores for each trial can be found in the manual. Total raw scores for each subtest are obtained by summing raw scores of the learning trials. The raw scores for trial 1, total, and retention are entered onto the summary table on the front page of the recording form. Standard scores are available in the Standard Scores Conversions Tables booklet (these scores are broken down by age groups); the standard error of measurement for total learning scores is reported in the manual. Because the authors stress the independence of the memory functions evaluated by this instrument, and thus the independence of the subtest scores, no composite memory score is calculated.

The normative sample for this instrument included 480 individuals age 20 to 79 who had no history of neurological disease or depression. The gender, education level, and intelligence of the normative group paralleled that of the normal population. The effect of age on memory test performance was controlled for by establishing separate norms for 10-year age groups from ages 20 to 60 and 5-year age groups from ages 60 to 80. Seventy individuals were included in each of the first four groups; 50 individuals were included in each of the last four groups.

The authors of this instrument employed coefficient alpha and split-half reliability measures as indices of internal consistency. Subtest reliabilities obtained by calculating coefficient alphas range from .62 to .95. Lower reliabilities found for verbal tests were explained in several ways (e.g., recency and primacy effects in list memorization act to mitigate against the equal chance of items to be answered in a certain direction). Subtest reliabilities obtained by computing split-half reliability coefficients ranged from .76 to .96. Simple Figure was the only subtest that displayed low reliability estimates for both measures of internal consistency (.74 and .76 respectively). The authors state that this low reliability level reflects the ease of this task that leads to a rapid ceiling effect in most test takers. Interrater reliability was evaluated for the scoring of the Simple and Complex Figure subtests. High interrater reliability (.99) was demonstrated for both subtests. Test-retest reliability was evaluated using a sample of 20 neuropsychologically impaired individuals (the specific impairments were not described). The mean time lapse between administrations of the LAMB was 15.4 months (range 4 to 46 months). The authors report reliability coefficients ranging from -.03 to .86 (median = .73). The use of a neuropsychologically impaired sample in assessing test-retest reliability makes it difficult to interpret these coefficients (especially because the specific impairments of those within the sample are not described). Individuals in this clinical population may exhibit variability in performance due to progression of their neurological condition. It is thus difficult to ascertain how much fluctuation in test scores is due to instability of the test itself and how much reflects an actual change in performance of the individuals due to progression of neurological impairment. The effort to determine the test-retest reliability of any memory test encounters problems because practice effects and long-term retention of material render two administrations of the test nonindependent. The only logical way to attempt to overcome this difficulty would be to administer the battery to a sample of normal individuals with a lengthy time lapse between the administrations.

The LAMB is presented as a comprehensive measure of memory, yet it obviously does not tap every empirically validated form of memory. In the test manual, the authors provide a thorough overview of the domains of memory assessed by the LAMB and a rationale for this choice of targeted memory domains. To assess concurrent validity of the LAMB, the verbal and visual subtests were compared to other established tests of verbal and visual memory (e.g., Wechsler Memory Scale—Revised [WMS-R], Benton Visual Retention Test,

Rey Auditory Verbal Learning Test). The LAMB subtests correlated significantly with these memory tests, yet these correlations were only of moderate size (ranging from .17 to .59). The authors attributed the moderate correlation sizes to low reliability of the established memory measures. The LAMB demonstrated sufficient ability to discriminate between individuals with neurological deficits (i.e., individuals with traumatic brain injury, epilepsy, and Alzheimer's disease) and normal individuals. Sensitivity and specificity of the LAMB for detection of neurological deficits was not reported.

The LAMB serves as a useful instrument for the assessment of memory. It is comparable to the WMS-R in its psychometric properties. The use of multiple learning trials on all subtests and the availability of trial-by-trial performance norms for the evaluation of learning curves are unique features of the LAMB. Other unique features include a comprehensive manual outlining the theoretical rationale for the subtests, comprehensive age-based norms, individual subtest scoring, an easy-to-interpret profile of subtest performance, and a number of representative clinical cases. In conclusion, although the clinical information obtained through the use of the LAMB may be redundant with that which is assessed by other memory tests, it does serve as another source of valid and reliable information about a number of clinically relevant memory types.

REVIEWER'S REFERENCE
Tombaugh, T. N., & Schmidt, J. P. (1992). The Learning and Memory Battery (LAMB): Development and standardization. *Psychological Assessment, 4,* 193–206.

Review of the Learning and Memory Battery by WILFRED G. VAN GORP, Associate Professor of Psychology in Psychiatry, Director, Neuropsychology, New York Hospital—Cornell Medical Center Mental Health System, New York, NY:

The test authors assert that the Learning and Memory Battery (LAMB) was developed based upon an information-processing framework in response to significant failings of prior memory measures. The authors note that historically, memory tests have been limited because multiple aspects of memory processes have not been adequately assessed.

In response to this perceived need, the authors developed a new memory battery that assesses a range of processes including delayed recall of paragraph information as well as recognition of this information. The battery also assesses learning, as well as free and cued recall, of a word list in addition to word pairs, emphasizing the "difficult" word pairs. Nonverbal memory is assessed through recall of simple and complex figures. Primary memory is assessed by both digit span and supraspan learning tasks. The authors have collected normative data from a final sample of 480 subjects, recruited largely from Ottawa, Canada (potential subjects were excluded who scored greater than 12 on the Geriatric Depression Scale or less than 25 on the Mini-Mental State Examination).

From a psychometric perspective, the scores from the LAMB appear to be adequately reliable. Internal consistency estimates (Cronbach's alpha) for the various subtests of the LAMB range from .62 for Digit Span backwards to .95 for the Complex Figure subtest (Table 7–9, p. 87, manual). Subsequent factor analytic studies reported in the manual have demonstrated three factors underlying the LAMB: a verbal factor, a visual factor, as well as a general intelligence factor (Table 7–14, p. 91, manual). The authors further provide useful data on the validity of scores from the battery by comparing performance on the seven subtests for four different clinical populations.

The authors are to be commended for working hard to develop an improved aggregate memory battery relative to what existed when they began their work. Ten years ago, when the LAMB was first developed, there was a critical need to improve upon existing memory measures in neuropsychology; the original Wechsler Memory Scale, which was in widespread use, did not include measures of delayed recall. Additionally, there was an emphasis in the original Wechsler Memory Scale upon an aggregate "memory quotient," which implied that memory was a unitary phenomenon and largely ignored its component parts. The LAMB was developed in order to improve upon these and other limitations of existing instruments.

Things have changed greatly in the past 10 years, and the authors' publication of the LAMB may be just a bit too late to make it a widely used and popular memory test. Around the time of the development of the LAMB, others noted the same need for improved memory measures, and this resulted in such developments as the Wechsler Memory Scale—Revised (WMS-R: T4:2940),

which included index scores of attention and concentration, verbal memory, nonverbal memory, general memory, and delayed memory. There is now a third edition of the Wechsler Memory Scale (Wechsler Memory Scale—III, WMS-III; T5:2863), which contains further improvements upon the WMS-R with a number of new subscales and indices. Perhaps the greatest strength of the WMS-III is that the norms are based upon a large and nationwide sample of demographically heterogeneous adults.

This strength of the WMS-III also represents the greatest limitation of the LAMB. The normative data for the LAMB are based upon a Canadian sample, largely from one location, of 480 subjects that appears to be a "sample of convenience" in that individuals were recruited by word of mouth, from shopping malls, personal contacts, etc. Information on the ethnicity of the sample is not given, though in the absence of information to the contrary, it is assumed to be a relatively homogeneous sample. It is not clear the degree to which the norms from the LAMB may be appropriately applied to other North American or English-speaking groups, or to individuals of various ethnicities. This factor alone is sufficient for the WMS-III to be considered a superior tool to the LAMB in order to assess a range of memory functions for most adults in North America.

The test stimuli for the LAMB are quite appropriate and are a strength of the battery. The stimuli are presented in booklet format in very large print and are shown to the patient or subject. They are easily read (particularly important for older adults who may have vision difficulties) and appear to be easily administered. The manual is very readable and contains complete information on administration, scoring, and interpretation.

In sum, the greatest limitation of the LAMB is that it has now been replaced by a new generation of memory measures that contain even more sophisticated methods of assessment of memory processes, generate a broader range of test scores, and contain a more appropriate, demographically heterogeneous standardization sample than is true for the LAMB. As such, despite admirable efforts, it may be that some of the same criticisms that have been leveled at older measures of memory by the authors of the LAMB may now be leveled, unfortunately, at this test.

[40]

Leiter International Performance Scale—Revised.

Purpose: Constructed as a "nonverbal cognitive assessment."

Population: Ages 2.0–20.11, adults.

Publication Dates: 1936–1998.

Acronym: Leiter-R.

Scores, 31: Visualization and Reasoning (Figure Ground, Design Analogies, Form Completion, Matching, Sequential Order, Repeated Patterns, Picture Context, Classification, Paper Folding, Figure Rotation), VR Composite (Fluid Reasoning, Brief IQ, Fundamental Visualization, Spatial Visualization, Full IQ), Attention and Memory Associated Pairs, Immediate Recognition, Forward Memory, Attention Sustained, Reverse Memory, Visual Coding, Spatial Memory, Delayed Pairs, Delayed Recognition, Attention Divided), AM Composite (Memory Screen, Associative Memory, Memory Span, Attention, Memory Process, Recognition Memory).

Administration: Individual.

Price Data, 2000: $850 per complete kit (in cloth carrying case) including manual ('97, 378 pages), 3 easel books, VR response cards, AM response cards, manipulatives, 20 each VR and AM record forms, Attention Sustained booklets A, B, and C, and the Growth Profile Booklet and the rating scales; $25 per 20 record forms (specify battery); $15 per 20 Attention Sustained booklets (specify form); $10 per 20 rating scale record forms (specify form); $25 per 20 Growth Profile booklets, $75 per manual.

Time: (90) minutes.

Comments: May calculate growth scores (criterion-referenced scores) to assess improvement in cognitive skills; computer scoring software available requiring Windows 3.1, Windows 95, or Windows 98 operating systems.

Authors: Gale H. Roid and Lucy J. Miller.

Publisher: Stoelting Co.

Cross References: See T5:1485 (64 references), T4:1446 (33 references), T3:1319 (16 references), and T2:505 (18 references); for a review of the original version by Emmy E. Werner, see 6:526 (10 references); see also 5:408 (17 references); for a review by Gwen F. Arnold and an excerpted review by Laurance F. Shaffer, see 4:349 (25 references).

Review of the Leiter International Performance Scale—Revised by GARY L. MARCO, Consultant, Chapin, SC:

The Leiter International Performance Scale has recently been updated and standardized on over 2,000 children and adolescents. Its primary purpose continues to be assessing in a nonverbal way the cognitive development of special populations of individuals aged 2 years up to 21 years for whom the usual tests of cognitive abilities are inappropriate. Examples of these populations include those who are deaf, mentally handicapped, speech and language impaired, learning disabled, brain injured, and ESL populations. It is also intended for use in evaluating speech and language disorders, including attention deficit disorders. The revision, based on modern psychometric and cognitive theory, is substantial; most of the subtests and materials used for the test have been revised and new subtests have been added. The revision and its supporting documentation are impressive, and in this reviewer's judgment makes the instrument an outstanding example of nonverbal cognitive assessment. Because of the instrument's complexity, this review does not cover some aspects (e.g., cut-scores) of instrument development.

TEST DESCRIPTION. The Leiter International Performance Scale—Revised (Leiter-R) consists of 20 subtests in four domains. The first 10 subtests form the Visualization and Reasoning (VR) Battery; the second 10, the Attention and Memory (AM) Battery. The AM Battery was added to this edition to make the scale more useful for individuals with learning disabilities. The VR and AM batteries take about 40 minutes each to administer and may be administered separately, depending on the needs of the individual to be assessed. Optional rating scales (Examiner, Parent, Self, and Teacher) may be used to collect additional, observational information about an individual. Brief versions of the VR Battery ("IQ screener") and AM Battery ("Memory Process screener") are available to make tentative decisions about intellectual development or to distinguish individuals with attention deficit disorders from those with learning disabilities.

Carroll's (1993) work and Gustafsson's (1984) hierarchical model of cognitive abilities guided the revision. This development is impressive in that it represents a major rework of the item content of the battery. Although the primary domains (Reasoning, Visualization, Attention, Memory, and Memory Span) are represented at each of the age levels tested by the battery, the subdomains change somewhat and increase in complexity with age.

TEST KIT. The test kit consists of an impressive set of materials that are geared towards making the test materials lighter and easier to use than those in the previous version. Foremost among these materials are the three plastic easel books that provide the 20 subtest items and directions for administration and scoring. The three item types represented on the Leiter-R are those that require the examinee to (a) place response cards in the easel tray, (b) arrange manipulative response shapes, and (c) point to stimulus material. Besides the easel booklets, the kit includes three Attention Sustained booklets for ages 2–3, 4–5, and 6–21 and a packet containing scoring keys, laminated grids, and picture plates for three of the AM subtests.

Other testing materials for the examinee include response cards and manipulative response shapes. Materials for the examiner include record forms for the VR and AM batteries and record forms for growth scores and rating scales. Also included in the kit are the rating scales for examiner (provided at the end of the record forms), teacher, parent, and self. A timer and a colored marker complete the kit.

TEST ADMINISTRATION. The Leiter-R is administered individually using response easels and stimulus cards. Test materials consist of three easels of stimulus material, picture cards, physical objects (manipulatives), and printed material. The examinee is asked to place the cards and manipulatives into slots on a frame. Not all subtests are appropriate for each age level. The Examiners Manual lists the recommended subtests for a given age level and the order of administration (p. 20).

The directions for administering and scoring the subtest tasks are conveniently given on the back side of the easel sheet on which the task is presented. They are also shown in the Examiners Manual. The directions are clear but may still pose some difficulty in administration until the examiner is well acquainted with the subtests. The method of communicating directions to the examinees is through pantomime. The examiner is, however, permitted considerable freedom in pantomiming the instructions—this could possibly lead to individual differences that depend on examiner variation. The directions provided in the Examiners Manual and the easel charts are very thorough and thus, except for the pantomiming requirement, go a long way toward providing the necessary standardization.

Examiners are well advised to practice giving the battery before actually using it in an operational setting. In this reviewer's opinion, to ensure smooth standardized administrations, supplemental practice and instruction in giving the instrument are necessary. Special training in administering the battery is available through the test publisher as well as college and university courses.

SCORING. The scoring directions for each subtest are provided in the Examiners Manual and on the back of the appropriate easel card. The directions are very clear, and forms are provided for recording the test results.

The test publisher also makes available a Computer Scoring Software System and User's Guide that prepares a score report for an examinee once scores are entered into templates. The system works with Windows 95 and Windows 98 operating systems. Chapters in the User's Manual tell how to install the system, how to use the basic system, how to input data, how to prepare reports, and how to interpret scores (selected portions from the Leiter-R Examiners Manual). Although the scoring software and guide are very clear, the printed reports generated are very ordinary in appearance. In this modern era of personal computers, scoring software is a welcome addition to the testing battery.

SCALED SCORES. The normative scales for the VR Battery are based on a nationally representative sample of 1,719 individuals; those for the AM Battery, on 763 individuals. Subtest scores are expressed on a normative scale with a mean of 10 and a standard deviation of 3 for each age group (55 age brackets, ranging from 2 years, 0 months to 20 years, 11 months). For general intellectual ability a deviation IQ (mean of 100 and standard deviation of 15) is used based on the subtest scaled scores. Growth increments are expressed on a scale developed using the Rasch item response theory model (see Embretson, 1996; Hambleton, Swaminathan, & Rogers, 1991; Wright & Stone, 1979). Extensive documentation of the scaling and tables for converting raw scores to scaled scores is provided in the Examiners Manual.

SCORE USE. The Examiners Manual appropriately recommends that the test results not be used apart from nontest information (e.g., academic and family background). It also suggests caution in using the battery with individuals from cultures that may not be familiar with testing.

The Examiners Manual suggests that score interpretation proceed from general IQ scores, to composite scores on two or more subtests, to specific subtest scores, and finally to detailed, diagnostic level information. In addition, it shows how to use growth scores, based on item response theory, and provides for measuring growth between two testings. Interpretive information provided with growth scores includes item difficulty values that are on the same scale as the test scores and growth norms. In the chapter on score interpretation, the Examiners Manual provides a number of useful examples of various types of score uses, including clinical interpretation, and describes what the subtests measure. This chapter should be very helpful to score users.

TRYOUT AND STANDARDIZATION ADMINISTRATIONS. Tryout testing occurred in 1994, and standardization testing in 1995. The total sample for the pilot administration consisted of 550 children and adults, including 225 children without disabilities. For the separate age groups, the sample sizes for these analyses were small, numbering no more than 50 at each of five age brackets for the pilot testing.

Two samples were used for the standardization administration, one for the VR Battery and one for the AM Battery. The VR sample consisted of 1,719 typical children and the AM sample, 763 typical children—a subset of the VR sample—administered both batteries on two occasions. The AM sample provide at least 42 examinees for each of 18 age brackets. Such sample sizes within age brackets may seem small compared to those in norming samples for nationally normed individually administered intelligence tests, but compare favorably with those used for other memory and neuropsychological instruments such as the Wechsler Memory Scale (T5:2863). In addition, the standardization edition was administered to 701 atypical children with such disabilities as severe speech or language impairment, severe hearing impairment, and significant cognitive delay, and with ESL, LD, and ADD/ADHD groups.

Representation in terms of geographic region, community size, socioeconomic status, gender, race, and ethnicity for both the tryout and standardization administrations was slightly distorted in some cases, but certainly adequate for purposes of the item analyses, scaling, and other statistical analyses that were carried out.

ITEM AND SUBTEST SELECTION. Twenty-three subtests and 704 items were included in the tryout edition of the test. Based on the item analyses, 20 subtests and 691 items were included in the standardization edition, and 20 subtests and 549 items were chosen for the final edition. For both the tryout and standardization administrations, items were selected by examining a number of variables (e.g., item difficulties, item-total correlations, Rasch fit statistics, internal consistency of items within subtests, correlations with criterion variables, differential item function indices, and ratings by examiners). The extensiveness of the item selection for the Leiter-R is impressive and led to an appropriately refined final edition.

NORMS. Norms for different population segments are not provided in the Examiners Manual. However, the scores themselves are normative in that they have set means and standard deviations (e.g., 10 and 3 for subtests) and as such may be referred to the normal curve to obtain percentile ranks. The Examiners Manual does provide mean scores for 11 special criterion groups (severe speech or language impairment, severe hearing impairment, etc.), and percentile ranks and Normal Curve Equivalents for the rating composite standardized scores. Additional normative data by gender and racial/ethnic group would help with score interpretation.

RELIABILITY INFORMATION AND SCORE DIFFERENCES. Consistent with modern psychometric developments, classical and item response theory approaches to reliability were used. Reliability information reported in the Examiners Manual consisted of internal consistency reliabilities (alpha coefficients), test-retest reliabilities, standard errors of measurement, and test information curves. The average coefficients (alphas) across the various age brackets range from .75 to .90 for the VR subtests. The average coefficients (alphas and retest reliabilities—for times subtests) range from .69 to .87 for the AM subtests. Reliability coefficients and standard errors of measurement are also reported for the AM Battery Special Diagnostic Scales and for rating subscales for the examiner, parent, teacher, and self-rating scales. In addition, reliabilities of IQ and composite scores are reported for three age brackets. Moreover, test-retest reliability coefficients are reported based on samples of 163 children and adolescents for the VR Battery and 45 children for the AM Battery. (The time between occasions is not reported in the Examiners Manual but was presumably only a few days.) The sizes of the test-retest reliability coefficients vary considerably because of the small sample sizes but still are reasonably similar to the alpha coefficients. Several of the subtests and composite scores showed practice effects. Also, scores on the AM Battery subtests and composite scores were less stable than scores on the VR Battery.

Decision consistency reliability is reported for the Brief IQ Screener and the Full Scale IQ for identifying children with cognitive delay (those below the cutoff scores). In addition, test information curves are reported for these scales. This kind of reliability information is more relevant than coefficient alphas and retest reliabilities for such decisions.

These reliability analyses, although based on small sample sizes, are clearly presented and comprehensive. The test publisher's use of modern psychometric theory for developing reliability information is to be commended. The reliability information reported in the manual should provide users with what they need to evaluate score consistency.

A caveat here is that the reliability analyses and some of the analyses to be reported under validity were apparently derived from test scores generated by dropping items from tests given in the 1995 standardization administration. Others were apparently based on the actual tests given at the tryout and standardization administrations. The Examiners Manual does not necessarily make clear which scores were actually used in many of the analyses. Reliability and validity results would best be based on scores from a real administration of the final edition of the Leiter-R and not from administrations of the tryout and standardization editions. Presumably studies reporting reliabilities and validities based on giving the final edition of the Leiter-R will be forthcoming in the research literature.

VALIDITY. The validity perspective taken with respect to the Leiter-R is one that stresses the importance of multiple validities for the various interpretations of test scores. This view is consistent with current testing standards. Obviously, studying validity is an ongoing process; thus, one

can only expect the publisher's documentation to provide evidence for the most important validity considerations.

CONTENT VALIDITY. Content validity evidence for the test comes from ratings provided by 60 examiners involved in the tryout phase and 114 examiners involved in the standardization phase of data collection. Carroll's (1993) delineation of cognitive factors was used to categorize both the original Leiter items and the items that were added later. Only those subtests that received high ratings were retained in the final version of the test. Content validity evidence also comes from the careful procedures used to select the items for the subtests (see the section on item and subtest selection).

CRITERION-RELATED VALIDITY. Criterion-related validity evidence consisted of percentages of correctly classified examinees, correlations among the Leiter-R scores and scores on other intellectual ability tests, and differences between typical and atypical examinees. The Examiners manual provided information on classification accuracy in identifying cognitive delay or giftedness and attention deficit disorders or learning disabilities. The classification results are very promising, but the Examiners Manual wisely cautions score users not to use the Leiter-R scores in isolation for clinical diagnosis. The classification accuracy is especially good for identifying cognitive delay. A difficulty with these cut-score analyses, however, is that separate samples were not used to first develop the cut-scores and then to assess classification accuracy. Because the analyses probably overstate the value of the scales for classification, the test publisher is encouraged to perform additional studies of classification accuracy.

Criterion-related information was also represented in the form of correlations with other instruments that measure similar abilities. Included in the manual are correlations of the Brief IQ, Full IQ, and certain other scores on the Leiter-R with scores on the original Leiter, the Wechsler Intelligence Scale for Children (WISC-III), selected subtests on the Stanford-Binet Intelligence Scale—Fourth Edition, the Wide Range Assessment of Learning and Memory, and the Test of memory and Learning. These data also suffer from small sample sizes (ranging from 18 to slightly over 100). Correlations with the original Leiter were quite high (.85 to .93). The other correlations tended to be lower but still high enough to suggest that similar abilities are being measured.

Other criterion-related validity information consisted of correlations with group-administered achievement tests (from the California Achievement Test, Comprehensive Test of Basic Skills, and Stanford Achievement Test batteries). All of these correlations were in the low to moderate range.

CONSTRUCT VALIDITY. A number of analyses relevant to construct validity were completed on the tryout and standardization editions of the Leiter-R. Mean scores on the Growth Scale (based on four Brief IQ subtests) increased monotonically with age, starting to level off at about 10 years of age and plateauing at about 15 years of age. In addition, factor analytic studies (both exploratory and confirmatory) provided evidence for the multidimensionality of the Leiter-R and for the existence of reasoning, visualization, attention, and memory factors (Bos, 1995, and Bos, Gridley, and Roid, 1996). One confirmatory analysis supported four- or five-factor hierarchical models for the Leiter-R for three different age brackets. Moreover, the ideal patterns of common variance greater than specific variance and specific variance greater than error variance were generally supported, although four of the subtests had very low specific variances. A cross-battery analysis demonstrated the convergence of nonverbal factors on the WISC-III and the Leiter-R.

A final piece of construct validity evidence relates to fairness across ethnic groups. Studies of bias at the subtest level yielded few significant differences between Caucasian and Hispanic samples and between Navajo and normative samples (see, for example, Flemmer & Roid, 1996). Clearly, however, more fairness studies are needed.

For a test that is new the validity evidence presented in the Examiners Manual is reasonably comprehensive and supports the factorial nature of the Leiter-R. Other validity evidence will accumulate as researchers undertake special studies and present their results. This reviewer encourages the test publisher to study particularly the validity of the test for discriminating among different types of special groups.

SUMMARY. The Leiter-R is a carefully developed battery that is based on a well-specific cognitive model. Excellent test materials, along with a comprehensive Examiners Manual that also serves as a technical manual, go a long way toward making the Leiter-R a solid measurement instrument. Although more study is needed, the evidence so far suggests that the Leiter-R is an effective instrument for identifying and evaluating those with speech and language disorders and for estimating the cognitive ability of such individuals.

REVIEWER'S REFERENCES

Wright, B. D., & Stone, M. H. (1979). *Best test design.* Chicago: MESA Press.
Gustafsson, J. E. (1984). A unifying model for the structure of intellectual abilities. *Intelligence, 8,* 179–203.
Hambleton, R. K., Swaminathan, H., & Rogers, H. J. (1991). *Fundamentals of item response theory.* Newbury Park, CA: Sage.
Carroll, J. B. (1993). *Human cognitive abilities: A survey of factor-analytic studies.* New York: Cambridge University Press.
Bos, J. (1995). *Factor structure of the field edition of the Leiter International Performance Scale—Revised.* Unpublished doctoral dissertation, George Fox University, Newberg, OR.
Bos, J., Gridley, B. E., & Roid, G. H. (1996, August). *Factor structure of nonverbal cognitive abilities: Construct validity of Leiter-R.* Paper presented at the annual meeting of the American Psychological Association, Toronto, Canada.
Embretson, S. E. (1996). The new rules of measurement. *Psychological Assessment, 8,* 341-349.
Flemmer, D., & Roid, G. H. (1996, August). *Nonverbal cognitive performance of Hispanic and speech-impaired adolescents.* Paper presented at the annual meeting of the American Psychological Association, Toronto, Canada.

Review of the Leiter International Performance Scale—Revised by TERRY A. STINNETT, Associate Professor, School Psychology Programs, Oklahoma State University, Stillwater, OK:

The Leiter International Performance Scale—Revised (Leiter-R) represents a significant modernization and upgrade of an historic icon. The instrument measures nonverbal intellectual ability, memory, and attention and is appropriate for use with children and youth aged 2 years through 20 years, 11 months. It may be particularly useful for children with communication disorders, cognitive delays, English as a second language, hearing impairments, motor impairments, traumatic brain injury, and attention and/or learning difficulties.

The Leiter-R contains 20 subtests that comprise two batteries, Visualization and Reasoning (VR) and Attention and Memory (AM). They have separate record forms. There are four optional rating scales including separate forms for the Examiner, Parent, Self, and Teacher. The subtests given for the VR and AM batteries vary for different age groups and not all subtests are administered at a given age. There is a recommended order of administration for the four distinct age groupings of 2–3, 4–5, 6–10, and 11–20 years. The items to be presented to a child are based on specific age-based starting points and all subtests begin with teaching trials. Items are presented through pointing, gesture, facial expression, and pantomime. There are three types of response formats; the child might place response cards in a particular order, or arrange manipulative shapes, or point to the correct response on the easel. There are standard rules for restarting if the start-point items are too difficult for the child and standard discontinue rules based on cumulative rather than consecutive errors. All subtest demands, materials, teaching items, and scoring guides are printed on the back of easel pages before the first item of each subtest. The record forms also include start points, stop rules, time limits, and some cues for item content to facilitate administration.

There are 10 VR subtests: Figure Ground (FG), Design Analogies (DA), Form Completion (FC), Matching (M), Sequential Order (SO), Repeated Patterns (RP), Picture Context (PC), Classification (C), Paper Folding (PF), and Figure Rotation (FR). There are 10 AM subtests: Associated Pairs (AP), Immediate Recognition (IR), Forward Memory (FM), Attention Sustained (AS), Reverse Memory (RM), Visual Coding (VC), Spatial Memory (SM), Delayed Pairs (DP), Delayed Recognition (DR), and Attention Divided (AD).

LEITER-R RATING SCALES. The optional rating scales are to assess social-emotional functioning and all four yield composite scores for Cognitive/Social and Emotions/Regulation. The Examiner Rating Scale includes the subscales of Attention, Organization/Impulse Control, Activity Level, Sociability, Energy and Feelings, Mood and Regulation, Anxiety, and Sensory Reactivity. The Parent Rating Scale subscales include Attention, Activity Level, Impulsivity, Social Abilities, Adaptation, Moods and Confidence, Energy and Feelings, and Sensitivity and Regulation. The Self Rating Scale (used only for children aged 9–20 years) has four subscales: Organization/Responsibility, Activity Level and Mood, Feelings and Reactions, and Self Esteem. The Teacher Rating Scale subscales are Attention, Organization/Impulsivity, Activity Level, Social Abilities, Mood and Regulation, Temperament, Reactivity, and Adaptation. The Examiner and Teacher Scales both have excellent internal consistency reliability (Cronbach's alphas) across the ages (mid .80s to upper .90s). The Parent Scale generally has very

good internal consistency (alphas generally in the mid .80s). The estimates for the Self Rating Scale were lower (range from .69 to .83). The temporal stability of the Examiner Rating Scale was also examined, but the length of the interval between ratings was not specified. The test-retest stability was best at the 2–5-year level with all estimates falling in the upper .80s and .90s. Estimates were lower at the other two age groups. The Cognitive/Social composite reliabilities were acceptable across the three age groups (2–5 years = .90; 6–10 = .87; and 11–20 = .80). The Emotions/Regulation composite followed a similar pattern but was not very stable at the 11–20-year age group (2–5, .94; 6–10, .87; and 11–20, .76).

A series of factor analyses of the rating scales suggested two fairly distinct factors, Cognitive/Social (CS) and Emotions/Regulation (ER). Although the scales appear structurally sound, the authors indicate additional validity work is needed. The Leiter-R manual is not too specific about how to use the rating scale information. It suggests the rating scale data can be combined with the battery data to develop hypotheses. The authors did report studies that used cutoff scores for the Examiner C/S composite to examine classification accuracy in samples of children with ADHD, but the results were not promising. I would recommend that systems like the Behavior Assessment System for Children (Reynolds & Kamphaus, 1992; T5:280) or the Child Behavior Checklist (Achenbach, 1991; T5:451) be used for assessment of behavioral and emotional adjustment until further support for the Leiter-R scales is accumulated.

LEITER-R SCORES. Raw scores for each of the VR and AM subtests can be converted to age-based scaled scores ($M = 10$, $SD = 3$) that range from 1 to 19. Percentile rank scores for the subtests are not available in the manual but can be derived through the Leiter-R computer scoring software (described later in this review). [Editor's Note: The publisher advises the percentile ranks for the subtests may be found in Appendix K.] Combinations of VR battery subtests scaled scores yield estimates of nonverbal general ability ($M = 100$, $SD = 15$). There is a Full Scale IQ for ages 2–5 and 6–20 and a Brief IQ Screener for all ages. The authors state the IQ score reflects nonverbal "g." The VR battery subtests can also provide composite scores for Fluid Reasoning, Fundamental Visualization, and Spatial Visualization, but the test's authors recommend calculating only those composites that are needed to answer questions specific to the child being assessed. There are six AM composite scores that reflect aspects of attention or memory: Memory Screener (for ages 2–20), Associative Memory (6–20), Memory Span (6–20), Attention (6–20), Memory Process (6–20), and Recognition Memory (4–10).

The IQ and composite score norms are collapsed into a single table for all ages rather than being separated by age groups. Percentile rank scores for the IQ derivatives and VR and AM composite scores are available. The standard errors of measurement for all Leiter-R scores are also presented in the manual. Confidence intervals at the .95, .90, and .68 levels can also be calculated and the values needed to construct the intervals are presented in the manual for three age groups (2–5, 6–10, and 11–20). Examiners should note that the confidence intervals are based on obtained score rather than the predicted true score method that is most appropriate for describing the examinee's current functioning on a given test at that point in time they were tested (Glutting, McDermott, & Stanley, 1987). The Leiter-R also provides Growth Scores for all subtests, composites, and IQs for interpreting a child's performance in a criterion-referenced fashion. Because the child's overall ability and task performance ability are placed on the same continuum, these scores can be considered in conjunction to allow for estimation of the difficulty that items may have for the child, which can then be used to target skills at the appropriate level for intervention.

LEITER-R COMPUTER SCORING SOFTWARE. The manual recommends a hierarchical interpretive model to describe the child's cognitive strengths and weaknesses. For the convenience of their users, a computer scoring software system and user guide (Roid & Madsen, 1998) can be purchased separately. Those familiar with the score-difference method will recognize the Leiter-R interpretive model as similar (e.g., see Kaufman, 1979, 1994; Wechsler, 1991; Sattler, 1992). There is disagreement in the literature among experts about the value of subtest-level interpretation (Glutting, McDermott, Watkins, Kush, & Konold, 1997; Kaufman, 1994; Sattler, 1992). However, the authors do stress that not all levels of the interpretive model must be used. They also emphasize that the statistical significance of score differences as well as the frequency of differences in the normative population (base rate) should be evaluated. To be maximally clinically useful, a score difference needs to be statistically significant and rare in the normal population.

Raw score data are entered by the examiner and automatically converted to scaled scores and IQs. There are six data entry forms: Identification, VR Battery, AM Battery, AM Diagnostic Scales, Examiner and Parent (EP) Rating Scales, and Teacher and Student (TS) Rating Scales. Two report versions can be printed: a five-page summary of tables of the results and a nine-page report containing tables and profiles. The system does not provide interpretive narratives and does not generate hypotheses for the user, which should prohibit those without sufficient background with the test's theory and concepts from using the program to write reports. As would be expected, the system allows its summaries to be saved to a file so that a user can access and edit them with other software such as a word processing program. Most would likely use this feature to reduce the standard output before cutting, copying, and pasting Leiter-R results into a more individualized, comprehensive interpretive psychological or psycho-educational assessment report. The program calculates 90% confidence intervals for all score points and there is no way to specify otherwise. The authors include a brief section in the guide related to ethics and computer-assisted interpretation.

DEVELOPMENT AND CONTENT VALIDITY. The Leiter-R was developed with careful attention to theoretical and psychometric excellence. A literature review and input from subject matter experts and Leiter users were used to compile a variety of items into 23 subtests that reflected the content that logically would be expected for a nonverbal IQ test. Examiners at both the tryout and standardization phase provided content and procedural ratings for each subtest. Only subtests that received high ratings were retained without revision. Items were also categorized according to Carroll's (1993) groupings of cognitive factors. This was an impressive effort to make the Leiter-R a solid theoretically based test. A comparison of the proposed structure of the test to the theory shows that it was designed to reflect nonverbal components of a multifactor, hierarchical "g" model like the three-stratum theory of cognitive abilities (see Carroll, 1993; Carroll, 1997; Gustafson, 1984). Item-level analyses included calculation of item difficulties for five age groups, estimation of item-total correlations, assessment of item stability (test-retest), differential item functioning between gender and ethnic subgroups, qualitative analysis of items by examiners and examinees, and item-response theory scaling.

CONSTRUCT VALIDITY. After the item analyses, subtest-level analyses were completed. Exploratory and confirmatory factor analyses generated a series of models to describe the Leiter-R's internal structure (Bos, 1995; Bos, Gridley, & Roid, 1996 as cited in the 1997 Leiter-R Examiners Manual.). In sum, the Leiter-R tryout edition fit the underlying theoretical model fairly well with adolescents showing more differentiated cognitive abilities than younger children did and an invariant, unidimensional, and robust "g" factor composed of the FG, FC, RP, and SO subtests was demonstrated at all ages. The Leiter-R final edition was also subjected to a series of exploratory and confirmatory factor analyses. The exploratory analyses (principal axes) employed four age groups (2–3, 4–5, 6–10, and 11–20 years) to reflect the different starting ages of the subtests. Reasoning, visualization, attention, and memory factors emerged across all age groups although there was some variation in the way the subtests loaded across the ages. Confirmation models were again examined following the exploratory analyses and justified four factors at ages 4–5 and five-factor models at ages 6–10 and 11–20 as the best fitting. All are hierarchical models with "g" at the highest level, with subordinate second-level broad abilities, followed by even more specific and narrow third level abilities. For the 4–5-year age group Fluid Reasoning, Broad Visualization, Attention, and Recognition Memory were confirmed; at ages 6–10 Nonverbal Reasoning, Visuospatial Reasoning, Attention, Recognition Memory, and Associative Memory Span were confirmed; and at ages 11–20 Nonverbal Reasoning, Visuospatial Reasoning, Attention, Associative Memory, and Span Working Memory were confirmed.

At the 2–5-year-old age group most of the individual subtests were fair estimates of "g" with C, FC, M, and AS (loadings ranged from .60 to .66) providing the strongest measures of the construct. The best measures of "g" at the 6–10-year

group were only fair: FG, FC, DR, SO (.55 to .65), DA and DP (both at .53), and IR (.49). For the 11–20-year group SO (.70) and PF (.70) were strongly associated with "g" whereas DA, FC, RP, FR, AP, VC, and SM were good measures of "g" (.54 to .62).

STANDARDIZATION. The test has a superb standardization sample that is nationally representative. A stratified random sampling design was used based on the population survey of the 1993 U.S. Census. The VR Battery was standardized on 1,719 children and the AM Battery on a subset ($N = 763$) of that group. There is an impressive match between the sample demographics and the census data on gender, ethnicity (including Caucasian, African-American, Hispanic, Asian, and Native American), parental education level, and geographic region. The sample is specified into 18 age groupings; for the VR Battery there are approximately 100 children in each half-year grouping for ages 2–5 and about 100 children and youth in each of the remaining 10 age groups. For the AM Battery sample there are a minimum of 42 children at each of 18 age levels. The standardization sample is presented in cross-tabulated form for a variety of variables and users can evaluate the relevance of the sample for their uses in great detail.

LEITER-R RELIABILITY. Stability over time was estimated for Leiter-R VR subtests and composite scores for three age groups (2–5, 6–10, 11–20) but there is no indication of the length of the interval between testing. The AM battery data are also presented but were derived from a single 6–17-year-old group. The VR subtests were more reliable at the 11–20-year age group than at the other age groups with most test-retest coefficients falling in the .80s. The estimates for these subtests at the younger ages were lower. The reliabilities for the composite scores and IQs for the VR battery were acceptable (upper .80s or .90s) except for Fluid Reasoning at the 2–5- and 6–10-year levels (both were .83). The AM battery subtests generally were too low to be considered stable over time. They ranged from .55 to .85 with a median estimate of .62. The AM composite score reliabilities were somewhat better ranging from .61 to .85. However, only the Attention composite (.85) was sufficiently stable to be used for diagnostic purposes. None of the other test-retest estimates broke .80.

Internal consistency reliabilities are reported for the VR battery subtests, the AM battery subtests, and the special diagnostic scales of the AM battery. Most of the estimates are Cronbach's alpha coefficients, except for the timed AS and AD tests, which are test-retest estimates. For the VR battery the average alpha reliabilities ranged from .75 to .90 with a median alpha value of .82. For the AM battery the average reliabilities ranged from .67 to .87 with a median alpha value of .83. The alphas for the AM special diagnostic scales ranged from .74 to .87.

SUBTEST SPECIFICITY ESTIMATES. Common, specific, and error variance associated with the Leiter-R subtests are presented in the manual and were derived using the communalities from the principal axes analyses of the three age groupings and the reliability estimates just presented. For the most part, the Leiter-R subtests follow the Common > Unique > Error variance pattern. To their credit the authors caution users about subtests at different ages, which have excess error variance.

ADDITIONAL VALIDITY STUDIES. Classification accuracy statistics are reported for the Leiter-R for a variety of groups (e.g., children with mental retardation, children who are gifted, children with learning disabilities including verbal and nonverbal subgroups, and children with ADHD including hyperactive and inattentive without hyperactivity subgroups). Using a cutoff IQ score of 70 resulted in good specificity and sensitivity with low rates of false positives and false negatives for the children with mental retardation. The Leiter-R was not very effective in reclassifying students who had previously been identified as gifted. The Leiter-R fared even worse for classifying children with attention problems and children with learning disabilities. Various cutpoints were examined using the Memory Process Composite (MPC), the Examiner rating scale Cognitive/Social Composite, and the two combined for classification of these groups. The best classification compromise was a combination of the MPC cutoff score of 90 and C/S composite score of 85, which produced moderate sensitivity (.50 to .60) and an acceptable false positive rate (5.4 to 6.3). Classification of the LD groups was also problematic with a similar pattern of low sensitivity (.40 to .67) using the MPC and unacceptable false positive rates (.20 to .24).

A variety of criterion groups were also contrasted by comparison of group means. For "typical" children the median IQ was 101, whereas children with mental retardation had a median IQ of 58, and children who had been identified as gifted-talented had a median IQ of 115. The hearing-impaired and English-as-Second Language groups were only approximately a third of a standard deviation below the normative sample mean. Also the Growth Scale scores show an increase across age, which suggests the scores are age-sensitive and performing as expected.

The Leiter-R Brief and Full IQs are also correlated with the WISC-III Full Scale and Performance IQs (.85 to .86). The Leiter-R AM Memory Process Composite was related to the WISC-III Freedom from Distractibility Index (.78) and the AM Attention composite was related to the WISC-III Processing Speed Index (.83). These data indicate the Leiter-R has convergent validity with established independent measures of intelligence but is also capable of providing some additional description of a child's intellectual abilities that would not be evident with the Wechsler.

The Leiter-R IQs are also moderately related to certain subtests of the Stanford-Binet Intelligence Scale—Fourth Edition (SB-IV, Thorndike, Hagen, & Sattler, 1986), and to subtests of the Wide Range Assessment of Learning and Memory (WRAML, Adams & Sheslow, 1990), and to subtests of the Test of Memory and Learning (TOMAL, Reynolds & Bigler, 1994). Taken as a whole these data support that the Leiter-R has overlapping variance between independent measures of reasoning, visualization, and memory.

The Leiter-R IQs are also related to tests of academic achievement including the Wechsler Individual Achievement Test (WIAT; Psychological Corporation, 1992) Reading and Math (.69 to .83), the Woodcock-Johnson Psycho-Educational Battery—Revised (WJ-R; Woodcock & Johnson, 1989) Broad Reading and Mathematics (.79 to .82), and the Wide Range Achievement Test—3 (WRAT-3; Wilkinson, 1993) Word Recognition and Arithmetic subtests (.62 to .73). The Leiter-R IQs are also related to several group-administered achievement tests (e.g., California Achievement Test [CAT], Comprehensive Test of Basic Skills [CTBS], and Stanford Achievement Test [SAT]). The SAT Math and Reading and the CAT Math were moderately related to the Leiter-R scores (.48 to .70). The Leiter-R was not highly related to the CAT Reading, CTBS Math, and CTBS Reading scores (.24 to .31).

SUMMARY. The Leiter-R is recommended as an excellent contemporary test of nonverbal intellectual ability. This is a theoretically derived instrument and careful attention has been paid to all aspects of its development and psychometric qualities. Does the Leiter-R have some problems? Yes, but the test's strong points far outweigh its negatives and to their credit, the test authors have presented the test's strengths and weaknesses in an honest and straightforward manner. They have left no stone unturned. It will be exciting to observe the further validation of the Leiter-R by independent researchers in the years to come. No doubt this revision has ensured the Leiter-R will continue to be used by modern psychologists rather than becoming a historical artifact.

REVIEWER'S REFERENCES

Kaufman, A. S. (1979). *Intelligent testing with the WISC-R.* New York: John Wiley & Sons, Inc.

Gustafsson, J. E. (1984). A unifying model for the structure of intellectual abilities. *Intelligence, 8,* 179–203.

Thorndike, R. L., Hagen, E. P., & Sattler, J. M. *Assessment of children* (3rd Ed. Rev. and updated). San Diego: The author.

Glutting, J. J., McDermott, P. A., & Stanley, J. C. (1987). Resolving differences among methods of establishing confidence limits for test scores. *Educational and Psychological Measurement, 45,* 607–614.

Woodcock, R. W., & Johnson, M. B. (1989). Woodcock-Johnson Psycho-Educational Battery—Revised. Itasca, IL: Riverside.

Adams, W., & Sheslow, D. (1990). Wide Range Assessment of Memory and Learning (WRAML). Wilmington, DE: Wide Range, Inc.

Achenbach, T. M. (1991). *Manual for the Child Behavior Checklist/4–18 and 1991 Profile.* Burlington: University of Vermont, Department of Psychiatry.

Wechsler, D. (1991). *Manual for the Wechsler Intelligence Scale for Children* (3rd Ed.). San Antonio: The Psychological Corporation.

Psychological Corporation. (1992). Wechsler Individual Achievement Test. San Antonio, TX: The author.

Reynolds, C. R., & Kamphaus, R. W. (1992). Behavior Assessment System for Children. Circle Pines, MN: American Guidance Service.

Sattler, J. M. (1992). *Assessment of children* (3rd Ed. Rev. and updated). San Diego: The author.

Carroll, J. B. (1993). *Human cognitive abilities: A survey of factor-analytic studies.* New York: Cambridge University Press.

Wilkinson, G. S. (1993). Wide Range Achievement Test-3. Wilmington, DE: Jastak Associates/Wide Range, Inc.

Kaufman, A. S. (1994). *Intelligent testing with the WISC-III.* New York: John Wiley & Sons, Inc.

Reynolds, C. R., & Bigler, E. D. (1994). Test of Memory and Learning (TOMAL). Austin, TX: PRO-ED.

Carroll, J. B. (1997). The three-stratum theory of cognitive abilities. In D. P. Flanagan, J. L. Genshaft, & P. L. Harrison (Eds.), *Contemporary intellectual assessment: Theories, tests, and issues* (pp. 122–130). New York: The Guilford Press.

Glutting, J. J., McDermott, P. A., Watkins, M. M., Kush, J. C., & Konold, T. R. (1997). The base rate problem and its consequences for interpreting children's ability profiles. *School Psychology Review, 26,* 176–188.

Roid, G. H., & Madsen, D. H. (1998). *Leiter-R computer scoring software system user's guide.* Wood Dale, IL: Stoelting Company.

[41]
Management & Leadership Systems.

Purpose: Designed to assess management and leadership skills and team effectiveness.
Population: Management personnel.
Publication Dates: 1992–1996.

Acronym: MLS
Administration: Group.
Price Data, 1996: $295 per facilitator's kit including manual ('96, 207 pages), Guide to Management & Leadership, Project Management Workbook, 6 Management Leadership Profiles, 6 Team Effectiveness Profiles, and transparency masters; $35 per Guide to Management & Leadership; $40 per Project Management Workbook; $95 per scoring software including software disks (specify 3.5-inch or 5.25-inch), Code Lock, Operating manual.
Foreign Language Editions: Available in English, Spanish, and French.
Time: Administration time not reported.
Comments: Microcomputer software requirements are DOS version 3.0 or newer, 1 MB RAM, 1 Mg free in hard drive; the option to have ASI generate the MLP and TEP is available, thus eliminating purchase of the scoring software.
Author: Curtiss S. Peck.
Publisher: Assessment Systems International, Inc.

a) MANAGEMENT & LEADERSHIP PROFILE.
Purpose: Designed to measure "both present behavior and desired behavior based on the needs and expectations of the people who are evaluating the manager."
Acronym: MLS.
Scores, 15: Clarity of Purpose (Goals, Communication), Planning and problem Avoidance (Planning, Involvement, Decision Making), Task Accomplishment (Competence, Motivation, Work Facilitation), Providing Feedback (Feedback), Exercising Control (Managing Performance, Accountability, Delegation), Individual & Team Relationships (Relationships, Linking, Teamwork).

b) TEAM EFFECTIVENESS PROFILE.
Purpose: "Provides a way of measuring and giving feedback to teams on how they manage their processes and projects."
Acronym: TEP.
Scores, 15: Clarity of Purpose (Goals, Communication), Planning and Problem Avoidance (Planning, Involvement, Innovation/Risk, Decision Making), Task Accomplishment (Values, Competence, Motivation, Quality/Continuous Improvement), Providing Feedback (Feedback), Exercising Control (Control, Delegation), Individual & Team Relationships (Linking, Teamwork).

Review of the Management & Leadership Systems by STEPHEN F. DAVIS, Professor of Psychology, Emporia State University, Emporia, KS:

The core of the Management & Leadership Systems (MLS) consists of the Management & Leadership Profile (MLP) and the Team Effectiveness Profile (TEP). (Other components not available for review include the *Guide to Management & Leadership, Project Management Workbook, High-Performing Teams Workbook,* and scoring software.) The MLS User's Manual indicates that the goals of the MLS are to "develop and/or strengthen the management and leadership skills of people who will be instrumental in inspiring commitment to the positive changes needed for companies to be competitive and successful" (p. 1) and to evaluate and provide guidance and evaluation to teams within an organization. It is felt that "teams can be incredibly successful when they have guidance and regularly evaluate and discuss their work processes, rather than just focusing on their outputs" (p. 1).

According to Curtiss S. Peck, the developer of these materials, a two-fold impetus prompted the development of the MLS: A large number of managers have never read any material on management and leadership skills, whereas other managers have received academic training that does not transfer to the work environment. These two situations pointed to the need to provide assistance for managers and leaders in business. In turn, Peck developed the Work Flow Process Model, which is well-suited for facilitating collaborative relationships and "empowering people at all levels to do the right things at the right times" (p. 11). All components of this theoretical model revolve around customers and mission. "Satisfying the needs of the customers and the mission of the organization, function, and/or team" (p. 12) interfaces with the next layer of the model: the six phases that guide action. In order these phases are Clarity of Purpose, Planning and Problem Avoidance, Task Accomplishment, Feedback, Exercising Control, and Individual and Team Relationships. The final (outermost) layer of the model involves the process of continuous improvement and utilizes such steps as Plan/Replan, Activity, Performance Measurement, and Analysis. Because the MLP and TEP are driven by the Work Flow Process Model, it is important to understand the model. The User's Manual clearly describes the basic model and how it supports these two instruments. (The User's Manual is a definite plus for the MLS package. In addition to providing information on the theoretical background of the system, this extensive manual presents detailed, yet readable, chapters on the MLP and TEP, feedback, project administration, and statistical analysis.)

The 15 dimensions or categories measured by the MLP are embedded within the six phases that guide action. For example, Managing Performance, Accountability, and Delegation are the dimensions measured within the Exercising Control phase. The MLP consists of 119 questions that are answered on a Likert-type scale ranging from 1 (*never*) to 5 (*always*). The respondent provides two answers for each question. One answer indicates the current frequency of occurrence (*Is*), whereas the second answer indicates how often the described behavior *Should* occur.

The TEP also evaluates 15 dimensions or categories that are embedded within the six phases that guide action. For example, Values, Competence, Motivation, and Quality/Continuous Improvement are the dimensions measured within the Task Accomplishment phase. The TEP consists of 87 questions that are answered on the same scale and in the same manner as are the questions on the MLP. The questions that comprise the MLP and TEP are easily understood; moreover, the physical layout of each answer sheet facilitates responding.

Although provisions and instructions are included for the involvement of both an internal coordinator and an external consultant, the responsibilities of these two positions are sufficiently similar that the project can be handled by one of these individuals. In any event, the designated individual will be in charge of coordinating the entire test administration program, arranging for the scoring of the profiles, providing feedback once the scored profiles are returned, and conducting reassessment to ascertain program effectiveness.

Once the MLP and TEP profiles are completed, the user can opt to have them scored by Assessment Systems International, Inc. (ASI) or the forms can be scored in house using software purchased from ASI. Although the latter alternative is appealing, there appear to be several potential drawbacks. First, because the ASI software is now quite dated (e.g., it was designed for 3.0 DOS and is available on 3.5-inch and 5.25-inch disks), some users may not choose this option because of system limitations. Second, an individual must undergo ASI certification training in order to be able to use the software. Third, in-house scoring appears to be reasonably expensive. Finally, the fact that the employment of an external consultant (likely an ASI employee) is highly recommended makes processing of profiles by ASI easier and more appealing.

The scored materials for the MLP and TEP are presented in graphical form that depicts both the "Is" and "Should" scores for the major categories and on a question-by-question basis. For the MLP these Is and Should scores are depicted for specific individuals, as well as the individual's boss and staff.

Likewise, the TEP depicts the value of the differential between "Is" and "Should" for the 15 major categories and for each individual question. These responses are presented for the team leader, the team members, and customers.

This approach to scoring makes it easy to determine strengths (small or no gaps between "Is" and "Should") and improvement areas (large gaps between "Is" and "Should") as perceived by the various constituencies. Plotting the "Is" and "Should" differential also lends itself quite well to evaluating the effects of change via a subsequent reassessment(s).

SUMMARY. The ease of coordination, administration, and interpretation suggest that the MLP and TEP have the potential to be effective instruments in an organization's evaluation of its effectiveness. The option to readminister these scales in order to determine the effectiveness of a program or modification that has been implemented is an appealing bonus. Strong support services from ASI also are desirable aspects of the overall evaluation program. However, before deciding to use the MLP or TEP, the costs involved should be considered; they may be substantial. However, the benefits to be derived may clearly outweigh the costs.

Review of the Management & Leadership Systems by WILLIAM J. WALDRON, Administrator, Employee Testing & Assessment, TECO Energy, Inc., Tampa, FL:

INTRODUCTION. The Management & Leadership Systems (MLS) is a package of multirater feedback instruments and support materials designed to assess management and leadership skills (the *Management & Leadership Profile; MLP*) and team effectiveness (the *Team Effectiveness Profile; TEP*). A detailed manual/facilitators' guide accompanies the instruments, and optional workbooks and other associated developmental materials are available. Scoring of the instruments and report generation are typically performed by the publisher, but DOS/Windows software is available for on-site scoring as well. The publisher conducts training workshops for organizations that want to conduct the entire feedback process in-house.

Both the MLP and TEP instruments are based upon the publisher's own theory of effectiveness, referred to as either the "Work Flow Process" or "Management Task Cycle" model in various parts of the manual/guide. This model describes management and team effectiveness in terms of 15 dimensions grouped into six broad areas. The MLP contains 119 behavioral statements, each of which is rated on two 5-point frequency scales: How often *does* this occur, and how often *should* this occur. The TEP contains 90 statements, each of which is rated using the same two scales.

Both instruments are designed to be used by multiple raters: For a manager using the MLP, ratings would typically be performed by self, boss, direct reports, and peers; for the TEP, the team rates itself, as does the team leader and perhaps customers. The reports graphically present the "is" and "should" dimension ratings by each source, as well as normative percentiles on the "is" scales. A summary of top-rated strengths and development areas is provided, as is a detailed section containing individual item results.

CRITIQUE. The quality of the guide/manual accompanying the instruments is variable. The quality of the sections describing administration procedures is very high, with attention paid to the proper use and potential misuses of the instruments. Many other sections, however, are written in rather rambling and unclear prose; the manual is much longer than it needs to be to convey the information it contains. Even given its length (143 pages plus appendices), there is a clear lack of information describing the development of the theory/model underlying the instruments.

The feedback reports provided by the publisher are nicely done, presenting the results in a clear fashion. The reports would be further improved by expanding the introductory section about the reports' contents and how to use them; in particular, information about the source of the normative data (percentiles) presented in the reports is needed but missing.

SUMMARY. Multirater or "360-degree" feedback is currently extremely popular in organizations today. As an organizational development intervention, the effectiveness of these programs is a function of many factors, among them (a) the quality of the instrument (including the fit between the dimensions measured and the organization's particular needs), (b) the clarity and ease-of-use of reports and supporting materials, and (c) the skills of the external and/or internal staff implementing them. I cannot evaluate the Management & Leadership Systems on the third factor; on the first two, perhaps all that can be said is that these instruments should be among those reviewed by organizations desiring to implement a multirater feedback program. Others are of course available, many with a more fully described theoretical foundation and better quality statistical data available (Clark & Clark, 1990). The publisher would do well to rewrite key sections of the manual to improve their clarity and incorporate more and better information about the statistical characteristics of the instruments.

REVIEWER'S REFERENCE

Clark, K. E., & Clark, M. B. (Eds.). (1990). *Measures of leadership*. West Orange, NJ: Leadership Library of America.

[42]
Matching Person and Technology.

Purpose: Designed for "selecting and evaluating technologies used in rehabilitation, education, the workplace and other settings."
Population: Clients, students, or employees.
Publication Dates: 1991–1994.
Acronym: MPT.
Administration: Group.
Forms, 2: Consumer, Professional.
Price Data: Available from publisher.
Time: (15) minutes per test.
Author: Marcia J. Scherer.
Publisher: The Institute for Matching Person & Technology, Inc.
a) SURVEY OF TECHNOLOGY USE.
Purpose: Constructed to measure "the consumer's present experiences and feelings toward technological devices."
Acronym: SOTU.
Scores: 4 categories: Experience with Current Technologies, Perspectives on Technologies, Typical Activities, Personal/Social Characteristics.
b) ASSISTIVE TECHNOLOGY DEVICE PREDISPOSITION ASSESSMENT.
Purpose: Designed to "help individuals select appropriate assistive technologies."

Acronym: ATD PA.
Scores: 5 categories: Disability, Environment, Temperament, Device, Degree of Match.
c) EDUCATIONAL TECHNOLOGY PREDISPOSITION ASSESSMENT.
Purpose: Designed "for teachers who are helping students use technology to reach educational goals."
Acronym: ET PA.
Scores: 4 categories: Educational Goal, The Student, Educational Technology, Educational Environment.
d) WORKPLACE TECHNOLOGY PREDISPOSITION ASSESSMENT.
Purpose: "Designed to assist employers in identifying factors that might inhibit the acceptance or use of a new technology in the workplace."
Acronym: WT PA.
Scores: 4 categories: The Technology, The Employee Being Trained to Use the Technology, The Workplace Environment, Match Between Person and Technology.
e) HEALTH CARE TECHNOLOGY PREDISPOSITION ASSESSMENT.
Purpose: "Developed to assist health care professionals in identifying factors that might inhibit the acceptance or appropriate use of health care technologies."
Acronym: HCT PA.
Scores: 5 categories: Health Problem, Consequences of HCT Use, Characteristics of the Health Care Technology, Personal Issues, Attitudes of Others.

Review of Matching Person and Technology by PATRICIA A. BACHELOR, *Professor of Psychology, California State University at Long Beach, Long Beach, CA:*

Matching Person and Technology (MPT) is designed to be a series of assessment instruments to facilitate the selection and evaluation of technologies used in education, rehabilitation, and workplace settings. The five assessment instruments are the Survey of Technology Use (SOTU), the Assistive Technology Device Predisposition Assessment (ATD PA), the Educational Technology Predisposition Assessment (ET PA), the Workplace Technology Predisposition Assessment (WT PA), and the Health Care Technology Predisposition Assessment (HCT PA). The SOTU elicits present experiences and feelings about technological devices. Issues of self-esteem and well-being surrounding the use of technology are assessed using a 3-point semantic differential. The

ATD PA is used by rehabilitation specialists to aid individuals in selecting assistive technologies. The checklist taps satisfaction with current progress and prioritizes aspects of recovery. The user's view about an assistive device or devices is captured on a 5-point or 7-point scale. The ET PA uses a checklist to identify educational goals/targets as well as student, teacher, and psychosocial environmental characteristics. The WT PA is designed to identify factors that may inhibit the use or acceptance of technology in the workplace. Employers can thereby plan training to assist employees in skill enhancement. The HCT PA was designed to assist health care professionals to identify factors that may facilitate or inhibit the acceptance of appropriate use of health care devices. Except for the HCT PA, each instrument has a version designed for the provider of technologies (therapist, rehabilitator, teacher, trainer, etc.) and a version designed for the user of technology (client, student, employee, etc.).

The MPT assessment process enables the individual to enter into a collaborative decision-making environment designed to assist technology users and providers in making choices based upon the needs of the user, the environment, and the personality of the user. Users' expectations and preferences, personal and social factors, economic and situational characteristics, as well as the training requirements will add to the blend of qualities and traits needed for an effective/successful pairing of person and technology. The successful pairing of each user to the appropriate technological device should save the frustration and economic losses of a mismatch.

No specific scoring system is used. However, the patterns of positive and negative responses are expected to reveal to the users and providers sufficient insight to select a technological device with the best chance of success.

The targeted population includes individuals with physical or sensory disabilities. No specific age limits are recommended; however, the ability to read is required.

RELIABILITY. The interrater agreement of the SOTU was reported to be 80% or higher on more than two-thirds of the items. Eighty-six to 91% was the consistency reported across ET PA raters. Overall, the agreement is higher among technology items than on user psychosocial characteristics. These findings provide a preliminary

step in the process of demonstrating the consistency of the MPT scales. In order to conform with the *Standards for Educational and Psychological Testing* (AERA, APA, & NCME, 1985), estimates of internal consistency need to be assessed prior to an enthusiastic acceptance of the psychometric merit of the MPT scales. Without evidence of internal consistency, the dependability of assessments made with the instrument is dubious. Consequently, the application and use of the MPT scales should be restricted to research applications.

VALIDITY. Content validity was suggested by using items reflective of a person's actual experiences with technology. Discussions with professionals and ongoing literature reviews were offered as evidence for content validity of the scales. A few contrasted group studies were used to support claims of criterion-related validity. The SOTU and ET PA were used in a study designed to identify the characteristics of 120 students from eight schools in Maine who would be successful in a distance learning course in American Sign Language. Results indicated that selected items from the SOTU and ET PA were modest predictors of grades and satisfaction/proficiency with course technologies. The ET PA was used in a study with 59 middle-school students to assess successful performance in multimedia instruction. Results based on descriptive outcome measures were suggestive of a relationship between the ET PA and performance. These predominantly descriptive studies are not compelling evidence of the predictive and/or criterion-related validity of scores from the MPT. Further research studies are needed to show convincing support for claims of predictive and/or criterion-related validity of all of the MPT scales. The careful appraisal of such validity will enable users to use and interpret the scales with confidence about the accuracy of the test results. The dissemination of evidence based upon validity studies is warranted prior to use of the MPT scales beyond research settings.

NORMATIVE GROUPS. Limited information was provided on the standardization sample or normative groups. The purpose of the MPT does not readily lend itself to such comparisons. This is primarily a personalized assessment strategy.

SUMMARY. The MPT system is an innovative approach to the difficult issue of pairing persons with sensory or physical disabilities with assistive technology. The needs, abilities, environment, personality, and social characteristics of the individual are used to facilitate a match. These aspects blend to create technology matches that one hopes will avoid frustration and mismatches leading to nonuse and economic losses. These types of assessments are particularly important now that technology is available in many forms for disabled and sensory impaired persons. Support for the psychometric qualities of the MPT subscales has been, to date, preliminary and basically descriptive. Appropriate evaluations of the internal consistency and criterion-related validity are expected to be conducted prior to an enthusiastic endorsement of the psychometric merit of the scales of the MPT.

REVIEWER'S REFERENCE

American Educational Research Association, American Psychological Association, & National Council on Measurement in Education. (1985). *Standards for educational and psychological testing.* Washington, DC: American Psychological Association, Inc.

Review of Matching Person and Technology by LAURA L. B. BARNES, Associate Professor of Educational Research and Evaluation, School of Education Studies, and CARRIE L. WINTEROWD, Assistant Professor of Counseling Psychology, College of Education, Oklahoma State University, Stillwater, OK:

Matching Person and Technology (MPT) is a collection of five individual assessments designed for use by technology providers (educators, rehabilitation professionals, health care professionals, or employers) to help identify obstacles to the successful use of technology for each individual consumer. These assessments help professionals consider whether or not a technology is a good match for individual consumers given personal and environmental factors. The individual assessments target somewhat different populations of technology users and providers. Except for the Assistive Technology Device Predisposition Assessment (ATD PA), there appear to be no restrictions placed on the types of technology under consideration. For example, the Educational Technology Predisposition Assessment (ET PA) may be appropriate for studying the outcomes of distance learning with general undergraduate students, or it may be used to evaluate the feasibility of using special computer enhancements for a student with a physical disability.

The MPT is described as being grounded in a theoretical model in which the degree of successful technology use depends on characteristics of the technology user in interaction with characteristics of the technology and the environment in which the technology is being used. Thus, each of the MPT assessments contains items developed to measure each of these three areas. Each of the assessment instruments (except for the Health Care Technology Predisposition Assessment; HCT PA) is a pair of instruments—one to be completed by the technology user and a similar one for use by the technology provider to help the user and provider work together to make choices about technologies and training strategies.

There are no norms reported for any of the MPT assessments. Scores on the individual instruments are to be interpreted subjectively and used to supplement clinical judgement. For some of the instruments, discrepancies between the technology user's self-report ratings and the technology provider's ratings of the same or similar items can provide useful insight into differing perspectives on the barriers that influence technology use. The amount of interpretive guidance given in the manual varies across the instruments, from a great deal for the ADT PA to very little for the WT PA.

In general, there is very little psychometric information contained in the brief (48-page) manual. The shortage of information on the reliability and validity of MPT scores pertains to all five of the instruments. Neither does the manual describe how the instruments were developed, though test development is often cited in the manual as the basis for validity. For example, the author claims content validity for the Survey of Technology Use (SOTU) because "the SOTU was created from the experiences of people who used or did not use a technology provided to them" (manual, p. 10) but provides no supportive information about the instrument's development. Likewise, the manual provides no information to support the statement that the Assistive Technology Device Predisposition Assessment (ATD PA) was developed from research that examined differences between users and nonusers of assistive technology. Purchasers of the MPT assessments are promised reliability and validity updates as they become available.

Following are brief reviews of each of the instruments in the MPT collection.

SURVEY OF TECHNOLOGY USE (SOTU). The Survey of Technology Use is a two-part survey. The first part purports to measure attitudes toward technology experiences; the second part seeks to measure aspects of general affect, mood, and typical activities. The SOTU could help professionals evaluate the effectiveness of technology interventions, particularly with consumers who are initially reluctant to use technology, and to identify those who may be at risk of abandoning technology.

With respect to reliability, interrater agreement of 80% on most of the SOTU items was reported for a group of undergraduate students (no sample size given) who were shown a videotape of a "student considering using a computer" (manual, p. 9). A semester-long test-retest study involving self-ratings by the same students was reported, according to the author, to show reasonable stability although no coefficients or other statistics were presented. No validity evidence is presented in the manual. One study not included in the manual (Keefe, Scherer, & McKee, 1996) showed SOTU items and ET PA items were predictive of course grades and teacher ratings in two distance learning courses in which American Sign Language was taught. The same study reported a fairly strong correlation (.64) between nonspecified items from the SOTU and ET PA with the Tennessee Self-Concept scale.

EDUCATIONAL TECHNOLOGY PREDISPOSITION ASSESSMENT (ET PA). The Educational Technology Predisposition Assessment was developed to identify characteristics of (a) the educational goals, (b) the technology, (c) the learner, and (d) the learning environment that would influence the successful use of the technology. Both the teacher and student forms provide a checklist of learner characteristics (e.g., impatience, physical dexterity, preference for group or individual work, likes computers). Questions about the technology and the educational environment must be responded to separately for each different type of technology being considered.

Scoring of the ET PA can be extremely complex and requires a great deal of time, effort, and subjective judgment on the part of the teacher/professional. For each of the 32 learner characteristic items on both the teacher and student forms, the teacher must decide whether that characteristic will facilitate or discourage the use of the particular technology under consideration. Once each item has been marked as an incentive or disincentive, the teacher must then assign to each

item a strength rating from 1 (strong disincentive) to 5 (strong incentive). Items not selected as representing this particular learner's characteristics must be scored in reverse (e.g., a score of 1 would be assigned to a strong incentive item that was not selected). A similar process is required on the Educational Environment section of the student form. The whole scoring process for this assessment instrument is so cumbersome and time-consuming that it seems improbable it would facilitate decision making more than once. On the other hand, the ET PA might be a reasonably useful tool if only a single technology were used repeatedly so that the strength ratings could be pre-assigned. Further, it may be informative to have the students themselves evaluate whether or not their own responses (regarding personal and learning characteristics and educational environment issues) would facilitate or hinder their use of educational technology.

In a study published subsequent to the publication of the MPT, Albaugh and Fayne (1996) reported an average interrater agreement of 87% for nine incentive items and 91% for nine disincentive items when CD-ROM technology was the target. Some evidence for validity comes from studies reported in the manual and two other studies (Albaugh & Fayne, 1996; Keefe, Scherer, & McKee, 1996) that showed some items from the ET PA were useful in predicting student satisfaction and grade outcomes for courses delivered electronically (computer conferencing, HyperCard, satellite video, CD-ROM).

The ET PA has some very practical applications for educators who work with students needing educational technology services. The Educational Goal section of the Student Form may be useful in promoting successful use of educational technology devices by helping educators better understand student perceptions of the goal and their levels of motivation in achieving such a goal. The manual also provides examples of educational goals and a useful discussion on matching educational goals with instructional strategies.

ASSISTIVE TECHNOLOGY DEVICE PREDISPOSITION ASSESSMENT (ATD PA). The Assistive Technology Device Predisposition Assessment is designed to promote collaboration between professionals and consumers in selecting assistive devices. The consumer form primarily assesses the influences of disability, environment, consumer personality, and device characteristics on ATD use. The professional form helps assess consumer and environmental characteristics that may affect ATD use and evaluate device requirements compared to consumer resources. The ATD PA has scoring requirements similar to the ET PA. Once again, scoring of either form is a daunting task (there are 6 pages of scoring instructions) and represents a major drawback to use.

Predictive validity of the instrument would appear to be critical; however, the only information given in the manual is that the ATD PA was more sensitive than another instrument in distinguishing between users and nonusers of listening devices in two groups of hearing-impaired adults. The only reference to reliability for the ATD PA was a report of "good inter-rater reliability, particularly for items regarding the AT and disability" (manual, p. 23) among a group of psychology students and four groups of rehabilitation professionals.

Although the author does not specify when the ATD PA should be administered, it is assumed that it could be administered prior to discharge from a rehabilitation hospital by a rehabilitation professional who has a good working relationship with the client. In addition, the ATD PA could be administered in an outpatient vocational rehabilitation setting after the rehabilitation counselor has developed a good working relationship with the client. The ATD PA would not be appropriate to administer until the professional has a good understanding of the client's attitudes, feelings, personality style, and level of environmental support.

In general, the forms hold a great deal of promise for rehabilitation professionals and their clients. The professional form may help rehabilitation professionals organize their conceptualizations about the client-technology match.

WORKPLACE TECHNOLOGY PREDISPOSITION ASSESSMENT (WT PA). The Workplace Technology Predisposition Assessment is designed to supply employers with "individual information on your employees' perspectives of new technologies" (manual, p. 37) to facilitate decisions about training, orientations, "even to the point of accommodating differing learning styles" (p. 37). The employer and employee forms ask for ratings to be given to aspects of the technology (e.g., length of time for training), the person using

the technology (e.g., previous success with new technology), and the workplace (e.g., is mastery of technology rewarded?). The items appear highly relevant to issues that influence the successful implementation of a new technology in the workplace. Both forms provide space for respondents to identify any discrepancies between the employee's and employer's perceptions of work technology use by the employee or any potential negative influences on such use. In addition, space is provided to document necessary accommodations, interventions, and/or training plans to increase workplace technology use. The WT PA has the potential to be very useful in helping employers or workplace consultants identify employees' concerns about technology implementation and could be an important planning tool. For example, it may provide information that would be useful in establishing an implementation and training schedule in a company that is adopting a complex new database system, or it may help employers and employees work together to comply with the Americans with Disabilities Act by adding or modifying technology. Unfortunately, no reliability nor validity data were available in the manual or made available for this review.

HEALTH CARE TECHNOLOGIES PREDISPOSITION ASSESSMENT (HCT PA). The Health Care Technologies Predisposition Assessment is a checklist to be completed by the healthcare provider. The HCT PA contains 43 items that address characteristics of the health problem, consequences of health care technology use, characteristics of the health care technology, personal issues, and attitudes of others. The categories represented in the instrument are said to be "areas of influence that impact most on a patient's use or non-use of a technology" (manual, p. 40). The HCT PA has no scoring criteria and may be used as an interview guide and "visual aid to help you organize your impressions about your patient" (p. 41). Again, no reliability nor validity data were presented. It would be important to know how the items were developed and the degree to which responses to these items do, in fact, point to barriers to successful technology use.

The advantage of the HCT PA is its short, checklist format for screening potential barriers to health care technology use. However, the fact that there is no scoring system may make it difficult to scan the items quickly for meaning or to identify major themes. A factor analysis of this instrument may help to identify specific constructs related to health care technology use.

GENERAL COMMENTS ON THE MPT. The only way in which the organization of the MPT suggests its use as a "battery" is through two worksheets and flowchart. One worksheet is used to record the technology user's specific limitations, goals, and desired interventions in 11 potential areas. Examples are provided of technologies and environmental accommodations for each of these areas to help professionals develop goals and/or interventions with the consumer. The other worksheet helps professionals identify: (a) the person's limitation(s); (b) technologies that the person is currently using (includes months used, percent of daily use, and level of satisfaction with technology); (c) technologies used previously (includes months used, percent of daily use, satisfaction with technology, and reasons for not using this technology now); and (d) technologies needed for that person. These two worksheets provide professionals with a well-organized format to document client/consumer information pertinent to technology use. Depending on the type of interventions planned, the technology provider is directed by the flowchart to one or more of the MPT assessment instruments. Unfortunately, the manual's interpretive guides for scores are strictly "within instrument." There are no discussions aimed at examining profiles across tests for consistency or discrepancies. Further, several of the instruments measure the same basic characteristics—for example, both the AT PA and the ET PA measure family support, self-concept, coping skills, etc., which must be evaluated as an incentive or disincentive to using each specific technology being considered. If multiple assessments are to be used, the instrument should be organized to minimize redundancy. In the current format, several of the assessments are far too long for reasonable use in combination.

Although these assessment instruments were developed to supplement professional opinions, one major limitation of these assessments is the lack of specific scoring keys to interpret item responses or subscale scores. For the SOTU, the ATD PA, and the ET PA, professionals simply look at subscale scores or tallies and determine which subscale has the lowest score or tally. The lowest subscale score is then identified as an "area of concern" to discuss further with the consumer. For the HCT PA and the WT PA, professionals have to extrapolate major themes on their own by exploring individual item responses. It is unclear how this current scoring system provides meaning to the items, except to identify areas for further assessment.

SUMMARY. Our general impression of the MPT is that the author has tried to do too much with it and has succeeded in doing only some of it well. If the MPT is thought of as a conventional test, it fails in many respects—many of the instruments are too long, the scoring is cumbersome and time-consuming, there is no formal mechanism for interpreting the scores so laboriously obtained, and data are sorely lacking on the reliability and validity of the scores. Very little information is presented on the validity of the instruments for counseling and rehabilitation—almost nothing, in fact. Though some information is provided to support their use as outcomes measures, it is still inadequate. This is unfortunate because there appears to be a great need for outcome measures, particularly in the area of assistive technology. However, if the process of completing and scoring the MPT can be viewed as part of a helping process—as a vehicle for fostering collaborative decision making and goal setting, and for promoting self-understanding, then these shortcomings become less serious. This would suggest that the consumer/client become more involved in the scoring process of these instruments than the manual suggests—for example, by deciding to what extent personal and environmental characteristics are incentives or disincentives to technology use. If the MPT is to be used as a guide to organizing therapeutic approaches to technology decision making, or as a learning activity, it may be highly effective. However, we cannot recommend that scores derived from the MPT be used for ranking, sorting, classifying, categorizing, describing, predicting, or for any other purpose that assumes the scores have meaning. There is simply too little evidence to support such traditional use. The strength of the MPT is the theoretical model upon which it is based and its wide applicability.

REVIEWERS' REFERENCES

Albaugh, P. R., & Fayne, H. (1996). The ETPA for predicting technology success with learning disabled students: Lessons from a multimedia study. *Technology and Disability, 5,* 313–318.

Keefe, B., Scherer, M. J., & McKee, B. G. (1996). Mainepoint: Outcomes of teaching American sign language via distance learning. *Technology and Disability, 5,* 319–326.

Mathematics Competency Test.

Purpose: Constructed to assess "mathematics achievement."

Population: Ages 11 to adult.

Publication Dates: 1995–1996.

Scores: Total score only.

Administration: Group.

Price Data: Available from publisher.

Time: (40) minutes.

Authors: P. E. Vernon, K. M. Miller, and J. F. Izard.

Publisher: Australian Council for Educational Research [Australia] and Hodder & Stoughton Educational [England].

Review of the Mathematics Competency Test by JOSEPH C. CIECHALSKI, Professor of Counselor and Adult Education, East Carolina University, Greenville, NC:

The Mathematics Competency Test (MCT) is the descendant of the Graded Arithmetic Test (GAT) published in 1949 and later revised in 1971 and 1976. Published in 1995–96, the MCT retained 18 items from the 1976 GAT and added 28 new items for a total of 46 items.

All of the items are open-ended and were constructed to assess math skills in four areas. These areas include: Using and Applying Mathematics (12 items), Number and Algebra (20 items), Shape and Space (8 items), and Handling Data (6 items). Items are arranged in order of difficulty. The MCT may be used in schools, colleges, and employment settings.

ADMINISTRATION AND SCORING. The administration section in the manual is divided into three parts: preparation, instructions for administration, and using the test with poor readers. This section of the manual was well written and informative.

Scoring the test is easy. The authors point out that, unlike scoring multiple-choice items, more skill is needed to score open-ended questions. Scorers of the MCT must be able to recognize alternate correct answers. Therefore, the scoring key contains acceptable alternate answers as well as information on responses that are not acceptable. The scoring key, included in the manual, was designed to correspond with the responses made by the examinee in the test booklet. Directions for scoring the test also included suggestions for avoiding errors in determining the total score and the scores for each of the subscales.

Scores are reported in raw score, percentiles, stanines, percentile ranges, and MCT scaled scores using the conversion Table (Table 2). Error scores are also reported in Table 2. In addition, percentile ranks by age group are provided in Table 3.

NORMS. The norming group was developed by sampling students and employment applicants from the United Kingdom ($n = 575$) and Australia ($n = 264$). It was noted by the authors that, because of the voluntary nature of the sample, the norms may not be a representative sample. The norming data for both sample groups were combined because a statistical analysis indicated that the level of difficulty for individual items was consistent between the two groups. Unfortunately, the difficulty indices for individual items were not included in the manual. Table 4 also includes the means, standard deviations, internal consistencies estimates, and standard errors of measurement of the norming group ($n = 839$) for the full test and subscales.

RELIABILITY. Evidence for reliability was reported by calculating the internal consistency estimates for the total test and the four subscales. The reliability coefficients ranged from .65 for the Handling Data subscale to a high of .94 for the total test. However, the manual does not describe which internal consistency method was used in calculating these coefficients. Standard errors were reported for the MCT and ranged from .95 for Handling Data to 2.55 for the total test.

No evidence of test-retest reliability is reported in the manual. Although the scoring key contains alternative correct answers that may be supplied by the examinee, scorers still must be able to recognize other correct responses. Therefore, evidence of scorer reliability is needed.

VALIDITY. Evidence of content validity was reported in the table of specifications (Table 1). This table contains information on the four content areas, the specific items included in each area, and the total number of items in each area.

Concurrent validity coefficient was reported as .80 by correlating the MCT with the ACER Test of Employment Entry Mathematics (TEEM). The tests were administered so that half of the group took the TEEM first and the other half took it second.

Test validation by means of interscale correlations was reported. The four subscales were correlated with each other and with the total test. Coefficients among the subscales ranged from .66 to .82 and from .84 to .96 between each subscale and the total test.

INTERPRETATION. A profile is provided on the back page of the test booklet to aid in the interpretation of test scores. Using the profile, information about an individual's total score and subscale scores can be easily obtained. The directions for interpreting the results are clearly written and the examples are straightforward.

The total score can be interpreted easily by completing the graph on the right side of the profile. When completed, this graph provides a shaded region representing a banded score based on the standard error of measurement for the total test. Using this banded score, one may compare the results of several individuals or the results of an individual who was retested. When the graphs are aligned, one can readily determine whether the shaded regions overlap or not. If they overlap, then one may assume that the level of mathematics skills is likely the same. Likewise, if they do not overlap, then the level of mathematics skills is most likely not the same. In addition, spaces are provided at the bottom of the profile for recording stanine, percentile rank, and percentile range scores for the total test.

To interpret the results of the four subscales, graphs representing each subscale are included on the profile. These graphs contain a list of the item numbers for each subscale arranged in order of difficulty. To complete these graphs, one needs to find the items missed on the test and mark them on the corresponding graph. Using these results, one may determine which mathematics skills need additional work.

SUMMARY. The MCT is designed to assess mathematics skills. Directions for administering, scoring, and interpreting the test are clearly presented in the manual and illustrated with easy-to-follow examples. The profiles provide useful information that can be used to determine math achievement as well as areas needing improvement. Although evidence of validity and reliability are reported, evidence of test-retest and scorer reliability are not. The MCT is a power test; however, no information is provided in the manual on the difficulty index of individual items. These concerns need to be considered before selecting this instrument.

Review of the Mathematics Competency Test by G. MICHAEL POTEAT, Associate Professor of Psychology, East Carolina University, Greenville, NC:

The Mathematics Competency Test (MCT) is a brief (46-item), group-administered, timed (30 minutes) instrument designed to measure the math skills of individuals from 11 years of age to adulthood. The test is designed as a measure that will allow: (a) the identification of individuals with ability or weakness in mathematical skills, (b) the identification of group strengths and weaknesses, (c) information to use in instructional planning, and (d) the development of a profile of individual math skills. The questions on the MCT are intended to measure four areas of mathematical skill: (a) Using and Applying Mathematics (12 items), (b) Number and Algebra Skills (20 items), (c) the Use of Shape and Space (8 items), and (d) the Ability to Handle Data (6 items). The MCT is recommended by the test developers for use in employment, school, and college settings.

An 8-page test booklet consists of a cover page, 6 pages of items, and a profile sheet. Simple instructions for administering the test are included in the 31-page user's manual. The 46 items are hand scored and a scoring key is included. A number of the items require responses that would not be amenable to the use of a multiple-choice format and the development of machine scoring would not appear to be practical. The MCT was developed and published in the United Kingdom and Australia, and several of the items would need modification to be used in the U.S. (e.g., the substitution of dollars for pounds). Inspection of the content of the items suggests the MCT covers material no more difficult than what would be taught in a typical high school general mathematics course in the U.S. Examples of two of the more difficult items are to compute the square of a decimal fraction and determine the hypotenuse of a right triangle—which requires computing the square root of a perfect square.

The profile sheet is used to plot raw scores for the total score and the four subscales. The number correct on each subscale corresponds to different heights on the profile bars because of the variation in the number of items between the subscales. The total test raw score can be converted to percentile ranks, stanines, and MCT scaled scores (which range from -5.2 to 4.97). Percentile ranks are also provided for the total score by 6-month intervals starting at 11 years, 6 months to 15 years, 11 months. MCT scaled scores are provided for the four subscales, but Shape and Space and Handling Data consist of so few items that the interpretation of the subscales is problematic.

Technically the MCT can be characterized as underdeveloped. Norms are based on samples of 575 subjects from the United Kingdom and 264 subjects from Australia. The reference group is otherwise not described and is not claimed to be representative. The manual addresses this weakness by making an argument for the use of the MCT as a measure of skill (i.e., as a criterion-referenced test). A measure of internal consistency reliability is provided for the total test (.94) and for each of the subscales. Handling Data, which consists of only six items, has a reported internal consistency value of .65 and a standard error of measurement of .95. The other three subscales have internal consistency coefficients of .78 (Using and Applying Mathematics), .89 (Number and Algebra), and .73 (Shape and Space). Content validity is addressed by stating that the items on the MCT are similar to items in other mathematics tests. Criterion-related validity is addressed by reporting a correlation of .80 between a short form of the ACER Test of Employment Entry Mathematics and the MCT. The administration of the two instruments was counterbalanced, but the number of subjects involved was not specified.

The MCT contains some interesting items and can be administered quickly by individuals with little training in testing. The scoring of responses and converting of raw score to percentile ranks should present no problem to anyone who has even minimal training in statistics or testing. However, the use of the MCT cannot be recommended. The norms are totally inadequate and the evidence for both content and criterion-related validity is extremely limited. The internal consistency reliability estimates for the total test and "number and algebra" subscale are adequate, but the other three subscales should only be interpreted with extreme caution. The use of the MCT scaled score is confusing, and the basis for its calculation is not clear. If the number of items on the MCT was increased and adequate norms developed, it might potentially provide useful information especially in the employment applica-

tions. In its present form it is inadequately developed and there are a number of other measures of mathematical ability that provide more reliable information. As a measure of mathematical competence, the MCT does provide some criterion-related information, but similar and more complete data could be obtained by developing a mathematics test based on any of a number of standard curricula.

[44]
Mathematics Self-Efficacy Scale.

Purpose: Intended to measure beliefs regarding ability to perform various math-related tasks and behaviors.
Population: College freshmen.
Publication Date: 1993.
Acronym: MSES.
Scores, 3: Mathematics Task Self-Efficacy, Math-Related School Subjects Self-Efficacy, Total Mathematics Self-Efficacy Score.
Administration: Group.
Forms, 2: A, B.
Price Data, 1998: $25 per sampler set including manual (22 pages); $100 per one-year permission to reproduce up to 200 administrations of the test.
Time: (15) minutes.
Authors: Nancy E. Betz and Gail Hackett.
Publisher: Mind Garden, Inc.
Cross References: See T5:1602 (1 reference).

Review of the Mathematics Self-Efficacy Scale by JOSEPH C. CIECHALSKI, Professor of Counselor and Adult Education, East Carolina University, Greenville, NC:

The Mathematics Self-Efficacy Scale (MSES) is designed to assess one's beliefs that he or she is capable of performing math-related tasks and behaviors. Although the manual indicates otherwise, there is only one form of the test. The MSES contains 34 items divided into two parts: Everyday Math Tasks (18 items) and Math-Related Courses (16 items).

In Part 1, examinees rate each item based on how much confidence they have in themselves to solve everyday math problems. Part 2 contains a list of 16 math-related courses that require examinees to rate the amount of confidence they have in completing the courses with a grade of "A" or "B."

Development of the MSES is extensive. The original instrument contained 75 items divided into three parts: math problems (18 items), math tasks (30 items), and a list of math-related college courses (27 items). An analysis of these items resulted in the development of the 1983 version. This version contained 52 items divided into three parts: Math Tasks (18 items), Math Problems (18 items), and Math-Related Courses (16 items). According to the manual, the 1993 version of the MSES retained only the Math Tasks and Math Problems subscales. However, in reviewing the test booklet, the two subscales that were actually retained were the Math Tasks and Math Courses.

ADMINISTRATION. The directions for administering the MSES are clearly written. A practice example is provided in Part 1 to ensure that the examinees understand how they are to respond to each item on the test. The test is not timed but should take no more than 15 minutes to administer. According to the manual, the MSES is designed to be used with an answer sheet; however, no answer sheet was included in the package. In reviewing the example in the test booklet, it appears that examinees are expected to respond to each item by circling their response in the test booklet.

Examinees rate each item based on a 10-point scale ranging from 0 to 9: *No Confidence at All* (0); *Very Little Confidence* (1–3); *Some Confidence* (4–5); *Much Confidence* (6–7); and *Complete Confidence* (8–9). Some examinees may have a problem in using this 10-point scale. For example, examinees who believe that they have "very little confidence" with a given math task may have difficulty deciding whether to rate their response a 1, 2, or 3. A 5-point scale may be sufficient.

SCORING. Scoring the MSES is easy. The MSES yields three subscale scores ranging from 0 to 162 (Math Tasks); 0 to 144 (College Courses); and 0 to 306 (Total score). Directions for obtaining average scores for each part and a total average score are described in detail. The total average score may be converted to percentiles using the conversion table (Table 2). According to the manual, the most useful score is the total average score.

NORMS. Table 1 includes the norming data developed from a 1983 sample population of undergraduates from the Ohio State University (n = 262). Norming data developed from a 1989 sample population of undergraduates from the University of Utah (n = 148) are also included in Table 1. No norming data are reported for the 1993 version of the MSES.

RELIABILITY. The authors report internal consistency reliability coefficients of .96 for the Total scale, and .92, .96, and .92 for the Math Tasks,

Problems (no longer a part of the MSES), and Courses subscales respectively. In addition, coefficient alpha (.92) and test-retest reliability (2-week interval) (.94) are reported. However, all of the reliability estimates reported are for the 1983 version. No reliability coefficients are reported for the 1993 version.

VALIDITY. Evidence of content, concurrent, and construct validity coefficients are reported in the studies cited, but all are based on the 1983 version of the MSES. No validity coefficients are reported for the 1993 version.

INTERPRETATION. To interpret an individual's score, a table (Table 2) of percentile equivalents is used. Using this table, one can convert a person's total average score into percentile equivalents based on gender. The authors are careful to point out that these scores should not be overinterpreted due to significant gender differences regarding math self-efficacy. Again, the information contained in this table is based on the 1983 norming group. therefore, users of the 1993 version need to be extremely cautious when interpreting the results.

SUMMARY. It is evident that extensive research and effort went into the development of the MSES. Like the 1983 version, the 1993 MSES is theory based and easy to administer and score. Unfortunately, what is troublesome for this reviewer is that there are problems with some of the information contained in the manual. Almost all of the information contained in it refers to the 1983 version. For example, the manual indicates that there are two forms of the MSES (FORMS A & B) but only one form is available. The norms included in the manual are old and need to be revised for the 1993 version of the MSES. Validity and reliability coefficients are reported in the manual but are all based on the 1983 version. In addition, some information contained in the manual needs to be rewritten or corrected. Until these problems and concerns are corrected in the manual, the 1993 version of the MSES cannot be recommended for use.

Review of the Mathematics Self-Efficacy Scale by EVERETT V. SMITH JR., Assistant Professor of Educational Psychology, University of Illinois, Chicago, IL:

The Mathematics Self-Efficacy Scale (MSES) is intended to measure a person's beliefs in their ability to accomplish math tasks and related behaviors. The MSES consists of 34 self-report items answered on a 0 to 9 confidence scale with labels of *No Confidence at all* (0 on the response scale), *Very Little Confidence* (1, 2, or 3), *Some Confidence* (4 or 5), *Much Confidence* (6 or 7), and *Complete Confidence* (8 or 9). Modification of this 10-point response scale may be desirable as the current scale does not evenly distribute the rating points among the anchors. For example, there are 3 rating points to choose from for *Very Little Confidence*, 1 point for *No Confidence at all*, and 2 points for *Complete Confidence*. This distribution loads the response scale in favor of *Very Little Confidence*. In addition, if one can have more than one level of *Complete Confidence*, why not more than one level of *No Confidence at all?*

The first 18 items of the MSES are intended to measure Mathematics Task Self-Efficacy. Instructions ask participants to respond to the question "Please indicate how much confidence you have that you could *successfully* [emphasis added] accomplish each of these tasks by circling the number according to the following 10-point confidence scale." Examples of math tasks include "Determining the amount of sales tax on a clothing purchase" and "Calculating recipe quantities for a dinner for 3 when the original recipe is for 12 people." The remaining 16 items are intended to measure Math-Related School Subjects Self-Efficacy. Instructions ask participants to "Please rate the following college courses according to how much *confidence* [emphasis added] you have that you could complete the course with a *final grade* [emphasis added] of 'A' or 'B.' Circle your answer according to the 10-point scale below." Examples of math-related school subjects include Economics, Calculus, Accounting, and Biochemistry.

The MSES is easily administered to individuals or groups of participants. Completion time is estimated to take no longer than 15 minutes. Scoring for each dimension (Math Tasks and Math-Related School Subjects) follows the traditional summated rating scale technique in which the responses to the items corresponding to each dimension are summed and then divided by the number of items representing each dimension. The authors also suggest calculating an average score by summing the responses to all 34 items and dividing by 34. The justification provided in the manual for creating an average total score is that "The most useful score is the Total Mathematics Self-Efficacy Scale score ... because it includes both types of item content" (manual, p. 11). Implicit in the creation of this average total score is the notion that both scales measure the same construct. However, no empirical evidence (a simple correlation would suffice) is provided to justify combining the two scales to form a single scale. In addition, no evidence is provided to support the statement that the average total score is the most useful of the three scores. Until such evidence is accumulated, it is recommended that the two scale scores be used as two indicators of mathematics self-efficacy. With respect to missing data, the authors suggest that if less than four responses are omitted, then simply sum the responses to the items that were completed and divide by the number of items completed to arrive at a scale score. If four or more responses are omitted, the authors claim the scores can no longer be considered valid.

Evidence for the reliability of the scores consists of estimates of internal consistency and test-retest coefficients. Across studies the internal consistency estimates were all above .90 for the original three scales (discussed below) and the total scale. A modified version of the Math-Related School Subjects scale had a 2-week test-retest coefficient of .94. A Japanese version had test-retest coefficients (4-week interval) of .68, .72, and .75 for the Math Tasks, Math Problems, and Math-Related School Subjects scales, respectively. A significant omission is information regarding the standard error of measurement, which would be essential for interpreting individual scores.

Validity evidence is reported in the traditional content, concurrent, and construct validity paradigm. The content of the original MSES was based on a review of existing measures of mathematics anxiety and confidence. From this review three domains were identified: solving math problems, math behaviors in everyday life, and college math-related courses. Seventy-five items were generated for these three domains by adapting items from existing measures, using examples of math tasks generated by students, and using courses perceived by college students as requiring a math background and knowledge. Using data from 115 undergraduates, the authors used traditional item discrimination and internal consistency indices as well as item difficulty ratings provided by the students and an examination of item content to reduce the total item pool to 52. The manual elaborates only on the Math Tasks and Math-Related School Subjects scales. The Math Problems scale was dropped from this version for "ease of administration and simplicity of instructions" (manual, p. 9). Evidence for concurrent validity is supported using correlations with other measures of attitude toward mathematics. Specifically, the MSES Total score was found to be correlated with math anxiety ($r = .56$; because this correlation is positive, it is assumed that higher scores on the math anxiety measure indicate lower levels of anxiety as self-efficacy and anxiety are hypothesized to be inversely related), confidence in doing math ($r = .66$), perceived usefulness of math ($r = .47$), and effectance motivation in math ($r = .46$) (Betz & Hackett, 1983). Studies have also found that math self-efficacy contributes to the selection of science-based college majors, perceived math- and nonmath-related career options, and to the prediction of mathematics performance. Construct validity evidence is supported using the "known" groups technique. The authors hypothesized that because math has traditionally been a male domain, females would report lower levels of math self-efficacy. These hypothesized relationships have been demonstrated in a number of studies (Betz & Hackett, 1983; Lapan, Boggs, & Morrill, 1989) for all three of the original scales as well as the total scale score. It is noted that these differences may exist as the result of females having fewer mathematics courses.

Normative data were obtained on samples of undergraduates (predominantly freshman) from two research universities. A series of studies conducted comparing males and females at each university on the Math Tasks, Math-Related School Subjects, and average Total scores indicated statistically significant differences on all three scores, with males demonstrating higher levels of self-efficacy. Score interpretation is facilitated by a table of approximate percentile equivalents based on the average Total scores. These percentiles are provided for each gender and are derived from an averaging of the average total scores and standard deviations from the two samples. With the samples being drawn from two large research universities and the intended population being college freshman, the representativeness of the normative

sample may not be adequate. Potential users of the MSES may wish to develop local norms.

The manual recommends that the MSES be used to help investigate problems associated with low math self-efficacy and the related math avoidance and approach behaviors with respect to the pursuit of careers in science and engineering by women and minorities. The manual also suggests that the MSES may be used to help identify students in need of an "efficacy" intervention with treatment focusing on the four influences on self-efficacy (i.e., performance accomplishments, vicarious learning, verbal persuasion, and emotional arousal).

The manual itself contains several typographical errors and oversights, making for difficult and frustrating reading. For example, the cover of the manual, the Table of Contents, the test booklet, and the scoring guide indicate that two forms of the MSES exist. However, this reviewer found no evidence of a second version. Other minor typographical errors or oversights include incorrect page numbering in the Table of Contents, incorrectly stating the number of items per scale at various points in the manual, stating that the Math Problems scale was retained for this version when in fact the Math-Related School Subjects scale was retained, an incorrect spelling of an author's name, the failure to create separate headings for the evidence of concurrent and construct validity (the manual lists the evidence of content, concurrent, and construct validity all under the heading of Content Validity), and the unusual practice of citing Table 2 prior to citing Table 1. For those wishing to pursue the topic of mathematics self-efficacy further, the list of references may also prove problematic. More than 10 citations in the manual had no corresponding entry in the Reference section.

In conclusion, the MSES has made an important contribution toward the measurement of mathematics self-efficacy. It is a simple and short assessment that may be used for research, assessment, and intervention purposes. It is recommended that future versions of the MSES include a more representative norming sample, additional psychometric studies investigating the dimensionality of the responses, and attention to the other recommendations mentioned in this review.

REVIEWER'S REFERENCES

Betz, N. E., & Hackett, G. (1983). The relationship of mathematics self-efficacy expectations to the selection of science-based college majors. *Journal of Vocational Behavior, 23,* 329–345.

Lapan, R. T., Boggs, K. R., & Morrill, W. H. (1989). Self-efficacy as a mediator of Investigative and Realistic General Occupational Themes on the Strong Interest Inventory. *Journal of Counseling Psychology, 36*, 176–182.

[45]

The MbM Questionnaire: Managing by Motivation, Third Edition.

Purpose: Designed for "helping managers understand their own needs" … and "to identify the needs of their employees."
Population: Managers and supervisors.
Publication Dates: 1986–1996.
Acronym: The MbM Questionnaire.
Scores: 4 scales: Safety/Security, Social/Belonging, Self-Esteem, Self-Actualization.
Administration: Group.
Price Data: Available from publisher.
Time: (10) minutes.
Author: Marshall Sashkin.
Publisher: Human Resource Development Press.

Review of The MbM Questionnaire: Managing by Motivation, Third Edition by JOHN W. FLEENOR, Director of Knowledge Management, Center for Creative Leadership, Greensboro, NC:

Based on Maslow's (1943) classic theory of motivation, the MbM Questionnaire: Managing by Motivation (MbM) is designed to increase the effectiveness of managers by improving their motivational skills. The MbM provides scores on four scales representing Maslow's hierarchy of needs—Security, Social, Self-Esteem, and Self-Actualization. Security includes safety and survival needs, Social includes the need for belonging, Self-Esteem includes the need for interpersonal relationships, and Self-Actualization includes the need for self-development. The instrument is intended to help managers understand their own motivations, as well as their employees' motivations, related to job performance. According to the author, the MbM encourages managers to focus on the intrinsic motivators of their employees, rather than on external motivators that are less relevant.

The first edition of the MbM was developed for training purposes in 1985; the second edition was published in 1990. The third edition of the MbM which includes revised scoring and interpretive material, was published in 1996. A form was included in the third edition on which respondents can plot and visually compare their scale scores. Additionally, the discussion of the underlying theories of motivation was expanded in the third edition.

The MbM is a 20-item questionnaire that can be completed and self-scored in 10–15 minutes. Directions for scoring and brief interpretive materials are included in the test booklet. On the instrument, respondents indicate the extent to which they agree or disagree with each item (e.g., "Chasing after dreams is a waste of time"). According to the author, the MbM is primarily a tool for increasing self-understanding; therefore, there are no right or wrong answers.

MANUAL. A 24-page trainer's guide includes a summary of theories of motivation, suggestions for workshop design, norms, technical information, and references.

ADMINISTRATION AND SCORING. The instrument is self-scored. Directions instruct test-takers on how to convert their responses to numerical scores. One score is calculated for each of the four needs (Security, Social, Self-Esteem, and Self-Actualization). There are five items on each scale; possible scores range from 5 to 25.

NORMS. Norms are available for the scores on each need. Normative data are presented for five samples: Managers (*n* = 46), team leaders (*n* = 30), retail store managers (*n* = 54), MBA students (*n* = 13), and sales clerks (*n = 188*).

RELIABILITY. According to the manual, interitem correlations were calculated using a large dataset during the second revision of the MbM. Items that did not correlate highly with others on the same scales were revised. Although scale reliabilities are alluded to in the manual, no reliability data are reported for the instrument.

VALIDITY. The manual indicates that construct validity of the scale scores was investigated using factor analyses. Eight factors were identified which were combined to form the four dimensions of Maslow's (1943) model; however, no further description of the factor structure is presented. The manual states that the result of this analysis "does not mean that The MbM Questionnaire accurately measures an individual's motivational state or that the questionnaire accurately predicts individuals' behaviors" (p. 5). The primary purpose of the instrument, therefore, is to acquaint managers with the basic concepts of work motivation, rather than attempting to measure the levels of motivation present in the respondents.

SUMMARY. The MbM is a fairly engaging presentation of Maslow's (1943) hierarchy which can be used to provide managers with a hands-on technique for understanding work motivation. It shows some promise as a training tool to increase managers' self-insights in areas related to motivation. The author clearly states that the MbM has not been validated as a measure of work motivation, and he presents no reliability or validity data for the instrument. Additionally, the norms for the MbM are based on small samples and are probably not representative of the population of test-takers. The norms, therefore, should be used with caution. In summary, the instrument was not developed, nor is it recommended, for use as a measure of individual differences in levels of motivation.

REVIEWER'S REFERENCE

Maslow, A. (1943). A theory of human motivation. *Psychological Review, 50,* 370–396.

Review of The MbM Questionnaire: Managing by motivation, Third Edition by ROBERT K. GABLE, Professor of Educational Psychology, and Associate Director, Bureau of Educational Research and Service, University of Connecticut, Storrs, CT:

The Managing by Motivation (MbM) self-report questionnaire is based on Maslow's Need Hierarchy and Herzberg's Motivator-Hygiene theories. The 20-item questionnaire purports to assess four dimensions, each with five items. An atypical 5-point Likert scale is employed and contains four gradations of agree and one disagree option (*Agree Completely, Agree Mostly, Agree Partly, Agree Slightly, Do Not Agree*). Although the four "agree" labels appear to represent a continuum, no empirical evidence or discussion is offered to support the use of the rating format. It may be that previous pilots of traditionally balanced "disagree-agree" formats resulted in extremely skewed distributions favoring the "agree" option. Item response theory assessment of the accuracy of these multistep response options is necessary before this format can be supported.

ADMINISTRATION. The author's suggestion that The MbM Questionnaire can be group administered in 10 minutes is appropriate.

VALIDITY. Although not labeled as such, the content validity of The MbM Questionnaire is well supported through discussions of the Maslow and Herzberg theories. In addition to brief literature reviews, the Trainer Guide provides a content analysis/rationale for each item-dimension assignment. Unfortunately, the Technical Considerations section contains no empirical evidence of construct validity. The statement "The technical development of this instrument has demonstrated … the validity of the constructs, the basic ideas of the dimensions (as shown by the factor analyses)" (p. 5) does not meet the *Standards for Educational and Psychological Testing* (APA, AERA, NCME, 1985). Readers need access to exploratory or confirmatory factor analytic studies that support this statement. The author's statement that "The purpose of this instrument is to teach people, especially managers, some basic concepts of human work motivation" (p. 5) does not preclude the inclusion of empirical support for the constructs underlying meaningful score interpretations.

Five of the 20 items are negative statements (e.g., "Job security is not especially important to me"). Given the confirmatory factor analysis (Pilotte & Gable, 1990) and item response theory (Wright & Masters, 1982) research on the use of positive/negative item stems, the inclusion of some "reversed scored" items is an empirically unsupported approach to instrument development. It could be that the positive and negative items access different aspects of the targeted affective constructs.

RELIABILITY. The earlier reference to technical development demonstrating "a degree of scale reliability (as shown by intercorrelations)" (p. 5) is not adequate. Item analysis and scale level alpha internal consistency and possibly stability reliabilities are necessary before users can be confident that The MbM Questionnaire provides accurate assessments. Following the statement regarding reliability and validity (p. 5) the author states: "This does not mean that the MbM accurately measures an individual's motivational state or that the questionnaire accurately predicts individual's behaviors" (p. 5). Again, we note that stating that "the purpose of the instrument is to teach people … basic concepts of human work motivation" (p. 5) does not excuse the author from following the *Standards* by providing users with empirical evidence of reliability and validity to allow accurate and meaningful score interpretations.

SCORING AND SCORE INTERPRETATION. The MbM Questionnaire booklet contains an easily used scoring grid to facilitate hand scoring. The scores can then be plotted on a chart for comparison with some small norm groups (e.g., MBA students, $N = 46$; retail store managers, $N =$

54; female retail sales personnel—national cosmetics firm, N = 188). The Trainer's Guide presents scale-level means and standard deviations for five such groups. The Guide also contains a form for respondents to indicate expected and actual scores. A well-done interpretive guide section is also included based on Maslow's and Herzberg's theories.

SUMMARY. The MbM Questionnaire is clearly designed to introduce basic concepts of motivation during leadership training seminars. Although the questionnaire is based on well-documented theories of motivation, the materials available lack any empirical evidence of construct validity and reliability. Without the empirical information required by the *Standards for Educational and Psychological Testing* (AERA, APA, & NCME, 1985), it is unclear if the data obtained provide valid interpretations. Unfortunately, several users will ignore the lack of validity and reliability data and assume their score interpretations are meaningful and accurate, but the jury is still out.

REVIEWER'S REFERENCES

Wright, B. D., & Masters, G. N. (1982). *Rating scale analysis.* Chicago: Mesa Press.

American Educational Research Association, American Psychological Association, & National Council on Measurement in Education. (1985). *Standards for educational and psychological testing.* Washington, DC: American Psychological Association, Inc.

Pilotte, W. J., & Gable, R. K. (1990). The impact of positive and negative item stems on the validity of a computer anxiety scale. *Educational and Psychological Measurement, 50,* 603–610.

[46]

The MIDAS: Multiple Intelligence Developmental Assessment Scales.

Purpose: "Designed to provide an objective measure of the multiple intelligences."

Population: Age 14 to adult.

Publication Dates: 1994–1996.

Acronym: MIDAS.

Scores: 10 scales with 27 subscales: Musical (Appreciation, Instrument, Vocal, Composer), Kinesthetic (Athletic, Dexterity), Logical-Mathematical (School Math, Science, Logic Games, Everyday Math, Everyday Problem-Solving), Spatial (Spatial Awareness, Art Design, Working with Objects), Linguistic (Expressive, Rhetorical, Written/Reading), Interpersonal (Persuasion, Sensitivity, Working with People), Intrapersonal (Personal Knowledge, Calculations, Spatial Problem-Solving, Effectiveness), Leadership (Communication, Management, Social), General Logic, Innovative.

Administration: Group.

Price Data, 1996: $25 (plus shipping and handling) per manual ('96, 128 pages).

Time: (30) minutes.

Comments: May be group administered via self-completion or individually as a structured interview; based on Howard Gardner's theory of Multiple Intelligences.

Author: C. Branton Shearer.

Publisher: Multiple Intelligences Research and Consulting, Inc.

Review of the MIDAS: Multiple Intelligence Developmental Assessment Scales by ABBOT PACKARD, Instructor, Educational Psychology and Foundations, University of Northern Iowa, Cedar Falls, IA:

This test is intended as a screening instrument to determine the characteristics of an individual's multiple-intelligence disposition. The Multiple Intelligence Developmental Assessment Scales (MIDAS) are proposed to provide an objective measure of the multiple intelligences as reported by the person or by a knowledgeable informant. The test was created to provide information about the individual's intellectual development and/or to aid curriculum design and enhance the counseling process. The MIDAS is based on Howard Gardner's theory of multiple intelligence providing information in four broad categories. First, it gives an estimate of the person's intellectual abilities in each of the seven constructs (Linguistic, Logical-Mathematical, Spatial, Musical, Kinesthetic, Interpersonal, and Intrapersonal). Second, it give 25 types of skills that are associated with each type of intelligence (e.g., navigator and advertising for Spatial). Third, three additional scales assess the person's inclination for Innovation, General Logic, and Leadership. Fourth, qualitative information is provided to deepen information gained through the measure's questions.

This test is intended for use with individuals from 14 years of age through adulthood. It can be a self-completion test or it can be administered via a structured interview. Individuals who are unable to read at a sixth grade level should have the test administered via a structured interview. Other individuals who should have the test administered by structured interview are those who are either unable or unwilling to cooperate in responding in an honest manner. Respondents with a very limited education or conceptual ability should answer the questions with the aid of a knowledgeable friend or family member. The publisher suggests that the users of the MIDAS instrument should have "an understanding of basic assessment principles and the limitations of psychometric interpretation" (manual, p. 11). Anyone interpreting results of the test should be trained in the use of this instrument with a minimum of a master's degree in psychology, education, or a related field to insure proper use and interpretation.

Psychometric properties were assessed against standards used to evaluate objective tests. An exploratory study using 349 participants addressed the question of whether the MIDAS was able to determine the seven distinct scales or constructs as described by Gardner's theory of multiple intelligences. The results indicated that seven hypothetical constructs could be determined. Discriminant and convergent validity were investigated yielding evidence that the MIDAS had the ability to discriminate each construct. The information provided the reviewer stated "while these results are not perfect they provide evidence that the questionnaire obtain a 'reasonable estimate' of a person's multiple intelligence profile" (manual, p. 67). Four studies were conducted over a 6-year period using more than 700 individuals. Construct validity was examined using 349 participants to determine if the MIDAS was able to assess specific intellectual abilities (constructs) suggested by H. Gardner. During this stage it was determined that the questionnaire was able to distinguish the hypothetical constructs. Concurrent validity was examined using 56 participants to determine that the MIDAS's subscales and appropriate cognitive tests showed correlational values ranging from .35 to .65 (most values above .48). Predictive validity evidence was gathered using 224 university students. These college students' self-reports were compared with "expert ratings" provided by their instructors; an 86% agreement was found for one category.

Four studies examined the internal consistency of the items in each scale. The mean alpha coefficients for the seven scales ranges from .76 for Kinesthetic to .87 for three other scales giving a grand mean of .85 for all seven scales. Temporal stability examination was conducted using two studies to determine if respondents changed their rating during the retest of the questionnaire. Twenty subjects in phase one completed the retest with a week delay yielding an 89% agreement. A later study using 32 participants with an 8–10-week delay indicated an average .81 agreement. An interrater reliability study was conducted to estimate the reliability of an informant's responses as well as to obtain information regarding construct validity. The rate of pairwise agreement for individual items ranged from 75% to 85% using a total of 212 people. Cultural bias was investigated using 119 college students with the results suggesting that the MIDAS is not prone to cultural bias.

Complete instructions are given with forms for both self-assessment and assessment by a knowledgeable informant. The steps in administration are simple and direct, providing guidance for each step and condition. The test is scored by two methods: DOS-based computerized scoring program or a mail-in computerized scoring service. The results are reported with a multipage profile of the individual.

The profile includes several items to help with the interpretation of the MIDAS results: (a) an introduction to the assessment with its limitations and definitions of terms, (b) seven main scale scores, (c) 25 subscale scores, and (d) a listing of high and low key items (available in the extended report option). An interpretative packet is available for educational, career, and counseling uses. Included are the following items: (a) Cover letter introducing the nature of profile, (b) brief learning and skill summary describing areas of both strength and limitations, (c) brief descriptions of the main and subscales, (d) strategies for each intelligence, (e) college majors selection help, and (f) activities and occupations associated with the multiple intelligences. Also included are steps to understanding, interpretation, and action planning.

SUMMARY. Further studies are needed to support the value of the initial assessments. With more support, the strength of estimating a person's intellectual skills in H. Gardner's seven constructs would increase the test's desirability. This information could aid in developing a curriculum design or adding information to the counseling proceeding of an individual.

Review of the MIDAS: Multiple Intelligence Developmental Assessment Scales by MICHAEL S. TREVISAN, Assistant Professor, Department of Educational Leadership and Counseling Psychology, Washington State University, Pullman, WA:

Gardner (1993) has offered a multiple-intelligence model that includes the following dimensions: linguistic, logical-mathematical, spatial, kinesthetic, musical, interpersonal, and intrapersonal. These intelligences are flexible and dynamic and can be enhanced or improved through education and/or life experiences.

Ideas of multiple intelligences, particularly Gardner's model, resonate well with many educators. A school district in Washington state, for example, has instituted a curriculum designed specifically to foster Gardner's multiple intelligences at the elementary school years. Recently, a school district in the midwest posted a position announcement with the job responsibility of developing, implementing, and evaluating a curriculum focused on Gardner's multiple intelligences.

Given the movement in some school districts toward embracing Gardner's multiple-intelligence model, the development of the Multiple Intelligence Development Assessment Scales (MIDAS) seems a timely and welcome addition to the current curricular and instructional strategies designed to enhance Gardner's multiple intelligences. In fact, this reviewer is not aware of any other existing psychometric assessment designed to assess Gardner's multiple intelligences.

The MIDAS was developed in 1996 and is designed to be administered to individuals from age 14 to adulthood. The questionnaire consists of 106 five-point Likert scales with scale anchors specific to the content of the item. The reading level of the questionnaire is approximately sixth grade. Items ask the respondents about their (a) level of skill, (b) amount of participation, or (c) amount of enthusiasm, relative to the activities of personal preferences reflected in the item.

In addition to the aforementioned seven constructs from Gardner (1993), the items provide information on 25 subskills associated with each intelligence. Three "research scales" are also provided, which assess an individual's tendency for Innovation, General Logic, and Leadership.

The MIDAS can be individually or group administered and takes approximately 25–35 minutes. The MIDAS can also be administered with a structured interview, which takes approximately an hour. Clear, readable directions for administration are provided in the documentation accompanying the MIDAS, although there are some misspelled words in the administration manual that should be located and corrected in future documentation. The manual includes directions for both self-completion and when conducting administration with an interview.

Two options exist for scoring. One, a DOS scoring system, can be obtained from the publisher and used in-house. Two, a computerized scoring service, is available from the publisher. The second approach requires the use of a computer-scannable answer sheet. Directions for preparation of the scannable forms are included with the MIDAS documentation.

Two key sets of documents form the basis for score interpretation and consultation with the respondent. The first is referred to as the MIDAS Profile. The profile provides percent scores for the seven Gardner (1993) constructs, 25 subscales, and three research scales. A brief description of the assessment and limitations is also provided with the profile.

The Interpretative Packet is the second set of documents provided for consultation with clients. Included in the packet are a description of the scale and ways of interpreting the results, study strategies for each intelligence, strategies for selecting a college major, and activities and occupations associated with each intelligence.

Several reliability studies were conducted to estimate the consistency of scores obtained from the MIDAS. The first study estimated the extent to which the items within a scale go together or are internally consistent. Reliability estimates ranged from a low of .76 to a high of .87, providing evidence that items within a scale are measuring the same dimensions. Second, test-retest reliability estimates (based on a one-week interval) were computed to determine whether respondents change their ratings during a second administration of the questionnaire. Reliability estimates ranged from a low of .69 to a high of .86, suggesting that scores obtained from the MIDAS are relatively stable over time. Third, two studies were conducted to determine level of rater agreement, particularly when an informant conducts a structured interview with a test taker. However, the presentation of this section of the reliability studies is somewhat confusing. The author states, for example, that items not meeting agreement expectations were slated for removal or reconsidered but does not specifically state what actually happened to the items (although in a previous chapter the author specifically states that items were, in fact, eliminated). The author also defines anything below 65% agreement as unacceptable but no rationale was given for this arbitrary cutoff. Given the importance of accurately documenting test taker responses in a structured interview, this reviewer recommends rethinking the reliability evidence for rater agreement and its presentation. Assuming high agreement is desired, the author is encouraged to consider two central facets of high rater agreement when further refining the MIDAS: (a) clear criteria, and (b) training of raters (Herman, Aschbacher, & Winters, 1992).

Attempts to develop a scale that will produce valid scores is apparent in the documentation. Specifically, in the initial stages of development, items were written that were thought to tap into the various intelligences. After statistical analysis and expert review (including Howard Gardner as a reviewer) a finished set of items was retained that showed evidence for the seven scales inherent in Gardner's (1993) multiple intelligence theory. Further study showed moderate correlations with similar measures of intelligence, providing evidence of concurrent validity. In yet another validity study, a sample of college students' MIDAS scores showed some agreement with their college instructors' assessment of their multiple intelligences. Also, little evidence of cultural bias was shown in an investigation of its existence in the MIDAS.

These validity studies, however, appear to be unconnected. When the MIDAS is revised, the author is urged to develop a validity framework (Shepard, 1993) rather than an unconnected collection of validity studies. Given the high goal of assessing Gardner's (1993) multiple intelligences, this practice should markedly improve the assessment.

The MIDAS is a self-report measure. The author is clear about this limitation and offers guidelines for assessing whether an individual is capable of this type of reflection. Nevertheless, caution is warranted, particularly when using this measure for classification or diagnostic purposes in the context of a local program. Moreover, because this is a self-report measure of what one thinks their ability and cognitive styles might be rather than an actual measure of cognitive ability, in its current form the MIDAS is not equivalent to conventional intelligence and ability tests such as the Stanford-Binet or Wechsler Scales. Thus, even though the term "intelligence" appears in the title, this measure does not currently provide the kind of information needed for classification and diagnosis in the context of federal programs such as special education.

SUMMARY. Despite limitations previously mentioned, this measure appears to be a fine addition to the field. Some district officials made complementary statements about the MIDAS in the accompanying documentation and applaud its use. The author has made a professional attempt to build a quality psychometric assessment and further refinement will ensure its continued use in the future.

REVIEWER'S REFERENCES

Herman, J. L., Aschbacher, P. R., & Winters, L. (1992). *A practical guide to alternative assessment.* Alexandria, VA: Association for Supervision and Curriculum Development.
Gardner, H. (1993). *Frames of mind* (rev. ed.). New York, NY: Basic Books.
Shepard, L. A. (1993). Evaluating test validity. In L. Darling-Hammond (Ed.), *Review of research in education* (vol. 19, pp. 405–450). Washington, DC: American Educational Research Association.

[47]
Minnesota Clerical Assessment Battery.

Purpose: "Designed to assess knowledge and skills required for a number of clerical jobs."

Population: Secretaries and other clerical workers.

Publication Dates: 1988–1995.

Acronym: MCAB.

Scores: 3 composite scores: Secretaries, Clerk-Typists, Generalists.

Administration: Group.

Price Data, 1995: $260 per complete system, limited-use license administration units; $1,495 per single machine, unlimited-use license; $5,995 per single building site license; additional license and volume discount information available from publisher.

Comments: Composite scores are derived from two or more subtests; requires MS-DOS or PC-DOS computer to administer.

Author: Assessment Systems Corporation.

Publisher: Assessment Systems Corporation.

a) TYPING/KEYBOARDING.

Scores, 3: Gross Speed, Accuracy, Net Speed.

Time: (2–4) minutes.

b) PROOFREADING.

Scores, 3: Initially Incorrect, Initially Correct, Total.

Time: (45) minutes.

c) FILING.

Scores, 3: Alphabetical, Numerical, Total.

Time: (50) minutes.

d) BUSINESS VOCABULARY.

Scores: Total score only.

Time: (25) minutes.

e) BUSINESS MATH.

Scores: Total score only.

Time: (60) minutes.

f) CLERICAL KNOWLEDGE.
Scores: Total score only.
Time: (25) minutes.

Review of the Minnesota Clerical Assessment Battery by ROBERT FITZPATRICK, Consulting Psychologist, Cranberry Township, PA:

The Minnesota Clerical Assessment Battery (MCAB), not to be confused with the Minnesota Clerical Test (T5:1693), is administered and scored by personal computer using a DOS operating system. The tests can be administered separately or in batteries. The using organization may use predesigned batteries or may specify its own.

The tests were developed by a content strategy; that is, a job analysis presumably dictated the choice and development of the tests. According to the user's manual, "a test is valid for the job if it consists of a sample of the types of things that a person could be expected to do on that job" (p. 5-1). Hence, it is said, there is no need for other evidence of validity. No criterion-related evidence, to show that test scores are related to clerical job performance, is presented. A weak claim for construct validity is based on data showing that test scores tended to be higher for norm group members who had relatively more reported experience with matters related to test content. The manual asserts that the user must "determine whether the tests are valid for a particular purpose and intended use" (p. 5-1). Most users, however, are limited in the resources they can devote to validation, and expect at least initial evidence and guidance from the publisher.

Even for the limited purpose of describing a content strategy, the manual is inadequate. The job analysis, insofar as it relates to the content of the tests, is described in quite general terms: Two previous job analysis studies (dated 1975 and 1981) and three secretarial handbooks were reviewed, and somehow the tests and their contents were derived. Further job analysis efforts were devoted to (a) establishing three norm groups representing different types of clerical workers and (b) aiding in the assignment of weights to test scores when tests are used in battery to produce an overall score. These efforts seem only marginally useful.

Except for the Typing/Keyboarding test, ample time is allowed, so that almost all examinees can finish each test. In some ways, this is a desirable feature because the psychometric characteristics of speeded tests are difficult to interpret.

On the other hand, some clerical tasks call for quick *and* accurate work, so that pure accuracy is not necessarily what is wanted. Time to administer all six tests, judging from the experience of the norm groups, would average about 2 hours, and it could take as long as 4 hours.

The norm groups are limited in size and representativeness. The groups are made up of incumbent clerical workers, for most purposes divided into secretaries, typists, and "generalists" on the basis of time and importance of clerical activities in which the workers engage.

Reliabilities were estimated from internal consistency statistics for most of the tests. For the Typing/Keyboarding and Proofreading tests, the two parts were treated as alternate forms for the purpose of estimating reliability. The reliability numbers are high enough to be encouraging, but the lack of other reliability evidence is unfortunate. Test-retest correlations ought to have been obtained.

No information is provided about the intercorrelations of the tests, or of any of the tests with other measures. The tests appear to be similar to a number of other tests of clerical aptitude or ability. However, in the absence of data showing similarity in use, it would be risky to assume that scores from these tests are as valid for selecting successful clerks as others have been shown to be.

TYPING/KEYBOARDING. This is a straight copy test using two short passages that appear to be reasonably similar to material often encountered in a typical office. The text is shown in the top half of a split computer screen, and the examinee's production appears in the bottom half. The examinee is told that errors may be corrected only before the next word is completed. However, it is not clear whether it is good strategy for the examinee to correct errors. Scoring is automatic and complicated; it is doubtful that the scores are comparable to those that would be obtained in the usual typing test from separate printed copy.

PROOFREADING. This test is not a proofreading test in the traditional sense of detecting deviations from error-free copy. Rather, it presents 3 brief passages with a number of errors in spelling, grammar, capitalization, and punctuation. The examinee is to detect the errors and use the computer keyboard to correct them. Problems can arise if an examinee chooses to change the passage in ways not recognized by the program, or if an error is made in attempting a recognized correction.

FILING. This is a test of ability to place items in alphabetical or numerical order. Requiring up to an hour to administer, it seems inordinately long. Other similar tests can be completed in 10 minutes or so, with little if any loss in reliability.

BUSINESS VOCABULARY. The stem words for this test are said by the manual to have been "drawn from indices and glossaries of three secretarial handbooks" (p. 10-1), selecting words "that appeared both difficult and significant enough to include in a test" (p. 10-1). The sampling method is vaguely described and seems inadequate. Some of the keyed answers are difficult to justify, even after reference to a dictionary. (The tests are not accompanied by keys to correct responses, so that the user is apparently expected to trust the publisher to have keyed correctly.) It seems likely that this test is highly similar in function to a typical test of word knowledge or to a test of general cognitive ability.

BUSINESS MATH. This test deals with discounts and other percentage problems, fractions, and decimals. Items were partly based on the contents of three business math textbooks. Calculators are not allowed, but it is suggested that paper and pencil be made available. Surely, most clerks these days do not make calculations in this way.

CLERICAL KNOWLEDGE. The content of this test was based on the same three secretarial handbooks used for the Business Vocabulary Test, along with input from seven "business teachers from vocational-technical schools" (p. 12-1). Internal consistency reliability estimates for these items are relatively low (alpha = .80); it is not clear just what this test is measuring. It seems likely that it is substantially correlated with Business Vocabulary and general cognitive ability.

SUMMARY. These tests might be useful to an organization for which the content can be shown to be job-relevant and in which testing time is not an important consideration. For others, the doubtful job analysis and content relevance, the high testing time, the dearth of validity and other data, the limited reliability information, and the absence of justification for adding to the already bulging store of clerical tests

make the MCAB a poor investment. An efficient alternative for most of the tests can be found, for example, in the Short Tests of Clerical Ability (T5:2408) or the Office Skills Tests (T5:1836), both of which come with ample validity and other evidence and which can be computer administered.

Review of the Minnesota Clerical Assessment Battery by BIKKAR S. RANDHAWA, Professor of Educational Psychology, University of Saskatchewan, Saskatoon, Canada:

The Minnesota Clerical Assessment Battery (MCAB), Edition 1.5, was published in 1995. It was intended for use in assessing the knowledge and skills of prospective employees for secretarial, clerical, and general clerical and secretarial positions, labeled here as "generalists." The previous version of this battery (Edition 1.0) was released in 1988 and reviewed by Stutzman and Veres III (1990). From the current manual it is not clear if any changes were made to the content of the tests in the battery, norms, results, and the manual itself.

The battery consists of six separate tests: Typing, Proofreading, Filing, Business Vocabulary, Business Math, and Clerical Knowledge. An interesting and a novel feature of this battery is that it is administered and scored on an IBM-compatible personal computer. As a result, it requires that the test administrator be reasonably computer literate and have the ability to cope with frustrations due to unexpected computer- or software-related glitches. The supplied diskettes do not allow making a backup copy of the MCAB Key Diskette to be used in case of a computer emergency. I can appreciate the need to control for the unauthorized use of the battery. However, the user's inability to have a working backup diskette handy in case of emergency is a serious problem. The planned testing cannot proceed unless a replacement is released by the publisher, which might take days. I personally ran into difficulties in accessing the tests for review. I either had to wait for days to get a replacement from the supplier after they had received the defective diskette back or receive a replacement from the Buros Institute personnel immediately after I informed them of my dilemma via e-mail. There ought to be another alternative for the developers to consider what is more convenient for the administrators of the battery in case something goes wrong with the original diskette.

The test development was preceded by an analysis of the jobs performed by clerical personnel in public service and the insurance industry. From this initial analysis the basic content of the six MCAB tests was determined. Also, a 25-task questionnaire, partitioned into seven content areas, was developed.

The job analysis questionnaire and the initial battery of six tests were administered to 414 employees from six organizations. The range of the number of examinees in the so-called "norming sample" from these organizations was 3 to 189. However, 46 of these examinees were excluded from the norming study because these respondents did not meet the criterion for inclusion, that is, spending at least half of their time doing tasks directly related to the tasks appropriate for the MCAB. These excluded examinees from the norming study were "combined with another sample of nonclerical individuals for use in refining the psychometric quality of the tests" (manual, p. 6-4). No further details of this group and how they were used for the above purpose are given in the manual. The remaining sample of 368 examinees were divided based on an iterative cluster analysis procedure into three subgroups, secretarial (187), clerk-typist (98), and general office clerk (83), for establishing separate norms. It is not evident how the cluster analysis categories represent actual reported job classifications of the individuals. Therefore, how one would relate to the norms results from MCAB for recruitment for a specific job is problematic.

The total sample consisted of 17 males and 346 females. The manual also reports the ethnic distribution of the total norming sample and concludes that "minority representation in the sample was slightly higher than that in the United States population at the time of the norming study" (manual, p. 6-4). Furthermore, norming samples clearly were convenience samples only and their representativeness or not to the U.S. population is incidental.

The Typing/Keyboarding Test was purportedly designed to measure the six tasks included in the job analysis questionnaire for this cluster. This is a direct typing test displayed on a split-monitor screen such that the stimulus text appears in the top window of the screen and the text that an examinee types appears in the bottom window. The examinee is given instructions on the computer screen on how to take the test and a practice passage is presented. Timing for typing the passage begins with the examinee's first keystroke. In terms of keystroke intensity and syllabic intensity as measures of difficulty, it is claimed that the first passage is typical of most general office correspondence and that the second passage is representative of professional or technical writing. Although three scores (gross speed, accuracy, and net) are obtained for each passage, standard error of measurement (*SEM*) is provided only for the gross speed for each passage and for the average gross speed.

The Proofreading Test consists of three passages, each about 100 words in length and contains 20 typographical errors, about two per line of text. It assesses, therefore, the examinee's ability to find and correct typographical errors on the computer screen. The developers admit that the proofreading passages are not authentic because it is rare to find a document in a business environment that would contain, on the average, two errors per line of text (manual, p. 8-1). The lack of authenticity is further exacerbated because there are 39 spelling errors in total, which would be rare to find given that most modern offices are equipped with the automated spelling checker. The exaggeration of errors was necessitated, it is argued, in order to make the test of reasonable length.

The primary score for the Proofreading Test is the net correctness, errors corrected minus the number of errors introduced, over the three passages. The minimum score may be less than zero. This results when an examinee introduces more errors than are corrected. The authors claim that several intermediate results are also provided for this test for diagnostic purposes (manual, p. 8-2). Interpretative guidance is provided for the use of these diagnostic scores through descriptive data in separate tables. However, norms are available by subgroup for the net correctness score. The internal consistency reported as alpha reliability coefficient, .92, for this score is reasonable.

The Filing Test is designed to assess the basic ability to file and retrieve items alphabetically and numerically. It is claimed to be a power test because 99% of the sample tested finished the test within the 25-minute limit imposed separately for the numerical and alphabetical portions of the test. Each portion of the test consists of two kinds of items. The first requires the examinee to indicate which of the nine labeled drawers will be selected for filing or retrieving a given document. The other requires the examinee to identify which in a list of nine has a pair of names or numbers out of sequence. The test consists of a total of 100 items, 50 alphabetical and 50 numerical.

Three raw scores and their corresponding standard scores are produced from the Filing Test, alphabetical, numerical, and total. For this test, norms are provided for the total group because the means for the three subgroups were not statistically different. However, the number of examinees used for establishing the norms for this test was considerably smaller (254) than the total eligible group of 353. There is no explanation for this discrepancy in the number of examinees. From the examination of the mean scores for the alphabetical (45), numerical (46), and total (91), it is obvious that this test was too easy and nondiscriminating. The test suffers from the ceiling effect and the placement of examinees into different skill levels with a difference between raw scores of one point for two successive levels in the top six levels of alphabetical and numerical components is not advisable. For these components, the authors report the alpha reliabilities of .90 and .91, respectively.

The Business Vocabulary Test, consisting of 60 items, assesses familiarity with words required for business communication. The items are four option multiple choice. The examinee is instructed to choose the word most similar to the stem word. There is no other text that accompanies each item. The stem words were chosen from indices and glossaries of three secretarial handbooks published between 1981 and 1984. As a result, some of the contemporary words in the business environment of computer applications are not represented in these items. Although a time limit of 25 minutes is set for this test, 99% of the examinees completed it within this time frame. A single raw score, representing the items answered correctly, is computed for this test. Norms for the total sample used are provided because it is claimed the subgroups were not significantly different on this test. However, no statistical data for the subgroups are provided in the manual.

The mean and standard deviation of the total score was 46 and 9, respectively with an alpha reliability coefficient of .91. The test was again quite easy for the norming group because the average score was 77% correct and it is reported that "some examinees were able to answer all of the items correctly" (manual, p. 10-2). The minimum score on the test was 13, which is slightly below the chance score of 15. In spite of these problems, the reliability estimate was reasonable.

The Business Math Test consists of 25 four-option multiple-choice items. The items test examinees' problem-solving ability, presented as word problems involving decimals, percentages or proportions, and fractions. Examinees in the norming group were not allowed to use calculators. Thus, the manual recommends that future "examinees be allowed to use only paper and pencil. This will control for differential familiarity with calculators, result in more standardization across examinees, and match the conditions under which norming data were collected" (manual, pp. 11-2, 11-3). This is sound advice to the test users. The maximum time allowed for the test was 60 minutes and about 98% of the examinees in the norming sample completed all the test items.

Norms for the total group are provide because there were no significant differences in the means of the various subgroups.

The Clerical Knowledge Test initially administered to the norming group consisted of 110 items but reduced after administration to 60 items. A serious problem arises from changing the length and context of the items in the original in order to assemble the final version of the test without readministering it. Fatigue would be a critical factor in such a drastic reduction from 110 items to 60 items. Also, other psychological processes such as proactive and retroactive facilitation and inhibition are ignored in making these changes to the content of the test.

A single raw score was obtained and was linked to the corresponding T-score. It is stated that the means of the subgroups on this test were significantly different. Therefore, norms for each subgroup are provided.

Users are encouraged to create their weighting system for creating composite scores for assessing secretaries, clerk-typists, and generalists. For the user-created weighting system for tests to be included, the MCAB provides skill-level norms in terms of T-scores. There is much emphasis put on the job analysis questionnaire originally used with the standardization of the MCAB. However, users are advised to assess the time spent on taks and the importance of those in a test to approximate the weights to be used. The composite score norms in the manual suffer from the lack of separation among the top six skill levels as has been the case with the individual tests in this battery. If group-specific composites are justified, I do not see the need to include the norms for the total group in the norming sample. A serious limitation in these composites is the absence of descriptive statistics necessary for interpreting the results.

Validity evidence for the tests rests on the job analysis and the content contained in the early 1980s handbooks for secretarial courses. Much has changed since in terms of technology and office practices. Content validity of the six tests in the battery in terms of tasks and their importance on the job is important but it is not the only requirement for tests that might be used for selection and promotion in various organizations. Other aspects of validity evidence are also necessary (see Messick, 1989; American Educational Research Association, American Psychological Association, & National Council on Measurement in Education, 1985). The only reliability evidence provided for the various tests in the MCAB is the internal consistency estimate. Can we interpret the test results properly if examinees are retested? How stable are the test scores? What are the actual and potential consequences of misplacements of examinees in skill levels? The impression given in the tables of norms is that the skill level of an examinee is the absolute placement without any regard to the measurement problems, notably the *SEM*. Suitable cautions in the interpretation of scores that suffer from drastic misclassifications are essential. Not much evidence of this is given in the manual. Also, users should be cautioned of the consequences of alterations to the content of tests in terms of the measured constructs. Altering the content of an instrument in a small way might seriously compromise the initial conception intended in the design and validation of the test. This battery encourages users to alter the content of the tests. How could they still use the norms provided for the tests? It is possible to simulate the norms for composites based on different weightings by the users but it would not be possible to provide suitable interpretative aids if tests are altered.

The norming group was a convenience sample of experienced employees in related occupations. Unless research evidence is available that shows that new recruits perform as well as the norming group(s) on the tests in the MCAB, the use of this battery should be made with extreme caution. Also, extreme caution is necessary if tests are altered by the user organization. Regardless, local norms or criterion scores should be established before altered tests are used for selection purposes.

SUMMARY. The MCAB is an interesting computer-administered instrument for assessing clerical and secretarial skills. Prospective and current employees can be classified into skill categories. However, caution is recommended because separations between successive skill levels are not sufficiently large to permit such decisions with confidence.

REVIEWER'S REFERENCES
American Educational Research Association, American Psychological Association, & National Council on Measurement in Education. (1985). *Standards for educational and psychological testing.* Washington, DC: American Psychological Association, Inc.
Messick, S. (1989). Validity. In R. L. Linn (Ed.), *Educational measurement* (pp. 13–103). New York: Macmillan Publishing Company.
Stutzman, T. M., & Veres, J. G., III. (1990). Review of the Minnesota Clerical Assessment Battery. In J. Hogan & R. Hogan (Eds.), *Business and industry testing: Current practices and test reviews* (pp. 493–507). Austin, TX: PRO-ED.

[48]
Motor-Free Visual Perception Test—Revised.

Purpose: Designed as a test of visual perception that avoids any motor involvement.
Population: Ages 4–11, adults.
Publication Dates: 1972–1996.
Acronym: MVPT-R.
Scores, 2: Perceptual Quotient, Perceptual Age.
Administration: Individual.
Price Data, 2000: $85 per test kit including manual ('96, 40 pages), test plates, and 50 recording forms in vinyl folder; $27 per manual; $40 per test plates; $15 per 50 recording forms; $9 per pad of 50 remedial checklists (optional); $27 per specimen set including manual and sample form.
Time: (10) minutes.
Authors: Ronald P. Colarusso and Donald D. Hammill.
Publisher: Academic Therapy Publications, Inc.
Cross References: See T5:1725 (8 references) and T4:1677 (6 references); for a review by Carl L. Rosen of an earlier edition and an excerpted review by Alan Krichev, see 8:883 (9 references).

Review of the Motor-Free Visual Perception Test—Revised by NANCY B. BOLOGNA, Clinical Assistant Professor of Psychiatry, Louisiana State

University Medical Center, Program Director, Touro Senior Day Center, New Orleans, LA:

The Motor-Free Visual Perception Test—Revised (MVPT-R) is an updated edition of the Motor Free Visual Perception Test first introduced in 1972. The revised edition offers norms from a new standardization sample, and an expanded age range (4 through 11 years vs. the original 4 through 8 years). The original MVPT was developed to provide a general measure of visual perceptual processing ability that is uncontaminated by motor performance. Although the new edition offers norms for ages 4 through 11 years, the maturity of the human visual perceptual system by age 10 to 11 years suggests that the age 11 norms would be appropriate for adult use. In fact, a review of the raw score means for each age in the standardization sample reveals a negatively accelerating curve, reaching a plateau at about age 9 years, further supporting the use of age 11 norms as "adult." The MVPT-R has been used with both children and adults in a wide range of clinical populations, including mentally retarded children and adults, schizophrenics, cerebral palsied individuals, and brain-damaged adults. Because the test does not rely on graphemic responses, unlike many other visual perceptual measures, it may be particularly useful with populations who are motorically impaired.

The standardization sample consisted of 912 children residing in northern California and Georgia. The numbers of children in each age group ranged from a low of 100 (age 9) to a high of 135 (age 11). Fifty percent of the children in the total population were male and 50% female, with the gender ratio within each age nearly 50/50. The racial characteristics of the population were close to those reported by the U.S. Bureau of the Census, 1988. Sixty three percent of the sample population was white (compared to 70% of the U.S. population), 10% black, 16% Hispanic and 11% "other" (as compared to 15%, 11%, and 4%, respectively, from the census data). Children included in the standardization sample were described as "not identified as having motor, sensory or learning disabilities" (manual, p. 13), but no details were provided of any screening techniques used to eliminate such individuals. Although the test manual mentions studies in clinical populations, no norms are presented for comparison with similarly impaired individuals.

The selection of individual test items for the revised edition was determined by point biserial correlation of each potential item with the total score. Those yielding coefficients between .30 and .80 were considered acceptable for inclusion. Test-retest, split half, and Kuder-Richardson reliabilities were determined for the original Motor-Free Visual Perception Test within each age range (4 years through 8 years). All reliability coefficients were noted to fall between .71 and .84. Reliability measures were not calculated for the revised edition and are not available for the expanded age range. Similarly, the validity coefficients offered reflect studies with the original MVPT. In fairness, strong correlations between the original MVPT and the MVPT-R support the carryover of both reliability and validity measures from the original edition.

There are five aspects of visual perception that are sampled by the MVPT-R: spatial relationships, visual discrimination (of form, color, and position), figure-ground discrimination, visual closure, and visual memory. Although the test provides items in each of these areas, only a single composite score is generated, reflecting a general perceptual ability. The authors clearly warn against attempting to use item cluster scores as measures of subareas of visual perception, citing significant interrelatedness among these abilities. Even through skills, such as visual closure, may in theory exist separately from other aspects of visual perception, studies as far back as Thurstone (1944) have consistently reported strong intercorrelations among the various constructs that form visual perception.

The MVPT-R is an individually administered, multiple-choice test. Instructions are simple and straightforward. The 40 multiple-choice test items are presented in a spiral-bound book that includes on each page clear, easy-to-read instructions to the examiner. Test items seem engaging, and are well presented with little chance for confusion about instructions or other nonperceptual factors. Although the test is not timed, completion should take less than 10 minutes. Scoring the MVPT-R consists of simply summing the number of correct responses, then comparing that raw score to the correct column in a normative table to derive a perceptual quotient and a perceptual age. A perceptual quotient of 85 or less (1 standard deviation below the mean) is considered indicative of visual perceptual inadequacy. Perceptual age is reported as a range (based on the mean and standard error of measurement), generally used as an easily interpreted value for lay persons.

SUMMARY. The MVPT-R is a quick, easily administered measure of general visual perceptual ability. Reliability and validity evidence have been presented for an earlier version of the instrument, which correlates well with the revised edition. The instrument will be useful within its limited scope. Independent research articles may provide suggestions for using this instrument in clinical populations; however, no norms currently exist for that purpose.

REVIEWER'S REFERENCE

Thurstone, L. L. (1944). *A factorial study of perception.* Chicago, IL: The University of Chicago Press.

Review of the Motor-Free Visual Perception Test—Revised by THERESA VOLPE-JOHNSTONE, Clinical and School Psychologist, Pleasanton, CA:

The Motor-Free Visual Perception Test—Revised (MVPT-R) is a revision of the original test developed by Ronald P. Colarusso and Donald D. Hammill in 1972. It is an untimed, individually administered test "designed for screening, diagnostic, and research purposes … of overall visual perceptual processing ability in children and adults" (manual, p. 7). The items themselves do not require knowledge, skill, or ability outside the visual perceptual realm. The MVPT-R requires no graphomotor output. Therefore, visual perception can be isolated from populations with a visual motor or motor skill deficit. Primary changes to the original include updated norms, an expanded age range (through age 11 years), and the addition of four new test plates bringing the item total to 40. Administration directions are easy to follow and accompany each plate. Plates consist of a target stimulus with horizontally placed response choices. Subjects may respond by pointing or may use another gestural system. The one-page scoring sheet is simple, objective, and inexpensive, with correct responses in boldface type. Each category has an example for which the correct answer may be given with an explanation should the examinee incorrectly respond.

The original MVPT had norm data for children without any specific disability. The authors suggest that the revised test can be used for a variety of purposes with different populations but did not perform any analyses to confirm group differences. The MVPT-R seemed relatively pure for item bias. The use of Delta values yielded high correlations (.78 to .92) for all racial groups with no significant differences upon comparison.

Interpretation of test results is explained in the introduction section. The two scores that may be obtained are perceptual quotients and perceptual ages. This reviewer recommends perceptual quotients because perceptual ages may be misleading, particularly below age 5 or above age 10. The manual specifically indicates that no attempt should be made to generate subtests scores for the five separate visual perceptual skills or to identify specific strengths or weaknesses in the subareas. This suggestion is a good one because there are too few items in some groupings to make definitive statements. Further, the authors do not establish that these five areas are mutually exclusive (Compton, 1990), nor do they adequately define the areas.

In terms of test construction, the test is divided into five areas by category for ease of administration. These areas are visual discrimination, visual closure, visual memory, spatial relationships, and figure-ground. Based on the revised test item analysis distribution, it seemed that most of one's visual perceptual development is complete by about age 8-0, supported by item difficulty greater than .75 for approximately 70% of total items by this age. Unless there was compelling rationale for administering the first three categories past age 8, there was not enough variation in scores to be useful once the skill is fully developed. Barring neurological injury to visual processing or perceptual areas, the MVPT-R would permit stable estimates of performance above the test age range without re-administration of the test. The test is objectively scored and although coefficients for interrater reliability were not indicated, the scoring format would likely yield high correlations.

Reliability and validity were not established for scores from the revised MVPT. The data from the original sample were referenced because the authors concluded that the extremely high correlation between the original and the revised edition ($r = .85$) would allow it. Because the visual perceptual construct is dependent upon neurophysiological maturation, this would make sense. However, when considering using this test, one should keep in mind that the original studies used an *N* of 881 for ages 4 through 8 (racial composition not reported), with uneven distribution through the age range. Reliability and validity coefficients for age 4 was based on a small *N* and there are no data for groups over age 8 years. Interpretation for these age groups should be cautious. Current demographics have an *N* = 912 with over 100 at each age group between 4 and 11 years. Its racial composition is weighted slightly more heavily toward minorities. It seems, therefore, that using the MVPT-R as a screening tool would be appropriate up to age 8, but should be interpreted very cautiously for ages 4, 9, and above.

If accepting data from the MVPT regarding reliability and validity, the reliability coefficients would suggest that scores from the test do have a high degree of stability. This is presumed more from split-half and Kuder-Richardson reliability coefficients because test-retest data may have been confounded by time-sampling (standardization population was tested 20 days after pretesting). Mean coefficients were .86 (KR-20) and .88 (split half), yielding a split-half coefficient stronger than that for all other motor-free tests referenced in the manual.

Validity was reported to be discussed in three ways: content, construct, and criterion-related. Content validity was investigated by the degree that there is high correlation with other tests that purport to measure the same domain. Construct validity was reportedly demonstrated based on low discriminant validity coefficients and high convergent validity coefficients. A criticism is that these test coefficients were based on infrequently used tests, tests that have since been renormed and/or revised in some important way, or tests that were not highly reliable themselves. Internal consistency was considered using the point biserial correlation technique with Plates 1–36 evidencing statistical significance at least once for the age range 5 through 7 years. The MVPT-R did not give information showing that the test accurately distinguishes between people who are known to have different levels of the construct due to poor neurophysiological growth but did report age differentiation based on the original MVPT sample population. Criterion-related validity was not discussed but it seemed likely that performance on the MVPT-R would be used to estimate current status and not be used in a predictive way.

SUMMARY. Primary benefits of the MVPT-R include easy administration and scoring, clear and simple instructions in the manual, and total testing time of about 10 minutes. Additionally, no verbal responses are required, the test can be used for individuals with limited language ability, receptive language requirements are minimal, and it can easily be interpreted to other languages. Further, additional instructions are permitted on trial items, slow response time is not penalized, and the authors are planning a vertical position plate booklet for individuals with hemispatial visual neglect. Limitations include the reliability and validity data being based on the 1972 sample and no research cited to support the suggestion that the visual perceptual system was completely developed by age 10 years 11 months (except the high pass rate in the item analysis summary). There was no evidence that the four additional plates substantially discriminated at half-year intervals from year 9-0 through 11-6, which could then be extrapolated to adult populations based on item difficulty levels. Further, based on reviewer administration of 17-year-old females, new information was not attained because of the additional plates. Correlation data between the MVPT and other tests of visual perception did not describe the children in the comparison. Content validity was not adequately established and the resources referenced for instructional materials and ideas were from 1964–1971.

REVIEWER'S REFERENCE

Compton, C. (1990). "Motor-Free Visual Perception Test" in *A guide to 85 tests for special education*. Fearon, Janus, Quercas: Belmont, CA.

[49]

Movement Assessment Battery for Children.

Purpose: Designed to assess motor skills and motor development difficulties.
Population: Ages 4–12 years.
Publication Dates: 1972–1992.
Acronym: Movement ABC.
Administration: Individual or group.
Price Data, 1999: $463.50 per complete kit including checklist, manual ('92, 250 pages), record forms, and all necessary manipulatives in an attaché case; $14 per 50 checklists; $40 per 25 record forms (specify level).
Authors: Sheila E. Henderson and David A. Sugden.
Publisher: The Psychological Corporation Limited [United Kingdom]; distributed by The Psychological Corporation.
a) MOVEMENT ABC.
  Scores, 3: Manual Dexterity, Ball Skills, Static and Dynamic Balance.
  Administration: Individual.

Levels, 4: Age Band 1 (Ages 4–6); Age Band 2 (Ages 7–8); Age Band 3 (Ages 9–10); Age Band 4 (Ages 11–12).
Time: (20–30) minutes.
Comments: Developed from the Test of Motor Impairment (9:1265).
b) MOVEMENT ABC CHECKLIST.
Scores, 5: Child Stationary/Environment Stable, Child Moving/Environment Stable, Child Stationary/Environment Changing, Child Moving/Environment Changing, Behavioral Problems Related to Motor Difficulties.
Administration: Individual or group.
Time: Administration time not reported.
Comments: Behavior checklist used by teachers, parents, and other professionals.
Cross References: See T5:1725 (8 references); for a review by Jerome D. Pauker of an earlier edition, see 8:881 (2 references); see also T2:1904 (4 references).

Review of the Movement Assessment Battery for Children by LARRY M. BOLEN, Professor and School Psychology Trainer, East Carolina University, Greenville, NC:

The Movement Assessment Battery for Children is the product of 20 years of research and provides a comprehensive and systematic assessment system for screening, identifying, planning intervention, and program evaluation for children with motor problems. The test battery is composed of three basic parts: The Movement ABC Test, designed by S. E. Henderson, D. H. Stott, and F. A. Moyes; The Movement ABC Checklist, developed by D. A. Sugden and L. Sugden; and The Movement ABC Manual, which includes a thorough presentation of a Cognitive-Motor theoretical approach to intervention, compiled by Henderson and Sugden.

The Movement ABC Test is based in large part on the Test of Motor Impairment (TOMI; Stott, D. H., Moyes, F. A., & Henderson, S. E., 1972). Specifically, the Movement ABC Test follows from the 1984 revision of the TOMI by Henderson (Stott, D. H., Moyes, F. A., & Henderson, S. E., 1984). The 1972 TOMI had 45 items, 5 at each of nine age levels, reflecting the format of the Oseretsky Test of Motor Proficiency (Oseretsky, 1923, 1948). The Henderson revision of the TOMI (1984) involved substantial modifications. The 1984 TOMI was reorganized into three sections covering Manual Dexterity, Ball Skills, and Static and Dynamic Balance. Additionally, a decision was made to increase sensitiv-

ity at the lower end of the scale. Thus, test items were organized into four sets of eight, with each set corresponding to one of four age bands ranging from age 4 to 12.

The Movement ABC is the direct descendant of the TOMI and includes all features of the 1984 Henderson revision of the TOMI. Two additions, however, make the clinical usefulness of the Movement ABC superior to the TOMI: First, the authors utilize a strong underlying theoretical (Cognitive-Motor) framework in interpreting and developing practical interventions for children with motor problems. Second, the refinement of Stott's (1972) Checklist and inclusion as part of the current test battery extends the scope for classroom-based assessment and screening as well as for home-based assessment and screening.

Standardization and item representation remain basically unchanged from the Henderson revision of the 1984 TOMI. Modifications involved clarifying test instructions, providing pictorials to help standardize test item presentation, improving the scoring system (from a 3-point scale to a 6-point scale) to sensitize measurement for small improvements in motor performance, and expanding the record form. A major modification involved the addition of norms for children 4 years of age, recognizing the need for preschool assessment and screening.

The United States standardization of the Movement ABC included 1,234 children divided into four geographic samples: Northeast, North Central, South, and West. Both urban and rural areas were represented with 24 testing centers across the U.S. The case quotas spanned four age bands from 4 through 12 years: Age Band 1: 4 to 6 years of age (*n* = 493); Age Band 2: 7 to 8 (*n* = 264); Age Band 3: 9 to 10 (*n* = 257); and Age Band 4: 11 and over (*n* = 220).

The South sample was underrepresented (U.S. population percentage 34.6, test sample 12.6%) and the West sample was overrepresented (U.S. 18.9%, test sample 34.6%). Ethnicity was very adequately represented across the four age bands proportionally to U.S. population percentages. Although standardization was also stratified based on parents' educational background, the test norms do not adequately represent the less educated parent. Children with motor problems with parents having 12 years or less of education are significantly underrepresented and the better educated parents are slightly overrepresented. The authors state that the effect on the norms is considered slight. Followup analysis of "socioeconomic status," represented as mother's education level, and Movement ABC test scores supports this notion. Analysis of a group of children aged 4 to 6 years and of children aged 7 to 12 found no significant relationship of Total impairment scores and mother's educational level.

Item reliability data were provided for samples of children for Age Bands 1, 2, and 3 over a 2-week period. Percentage agreement for each of the eight items comprising each age band ranged from 62% to 100%. The median agreement for Age Band 1 was 90%; Age Band 2 = 84%; and Age Band 3 = 80%. These percentage agreements are quite high considering they represent individual items rather than total score. The stability of the Total impairment scores were: 97% for Age Band 1, 91% for Age Band 2, and 73% for Age Band 3. Percentage agreement data for Age Band 4 was not reported and should be presumed as low.

Validity evidence was assessed in a number of ways. Concurrent validity was considered by comparing performance on the Movement ABC with the Bruininks-Oseretsky ($n = 63$). Construct validity was investigated by comparing assessment outcome with various experts (e.g., teachers, therapists, pediatricians, various clinics, etc., where children with known impairment received services). In all cases, the Movement ABC differentiated motor-impaired children from matched samples of normal functioning children. Moreover, the test was also able to discriminate subtle changes in motor movement following intervention efforts.

The Movement ABC Checklist, designed to be used by teachers, parents, and other professionals, provides a qualitative aspect to the standardized assessment. Originally developed in 1972 by Sugden, the content of the Checklist was modified as well as reorganized following a behavior-environment interactional model. This allows for examining children's motor behavior (passive/moving) in different settings as well as contrasting environmental demand differences (stable/changing). As with the Movement ABC Test, the Checklist is thoroughly explained and detailed in the manual.

Although user qualifications are discussed, the authors maintain no special training is required. Keeping in mind that only experienced professionals, including special service teachers, would be expected to use the test, it seems quite clear that the usefulness of the test will directly reflect the background and training of the professional using it. It is my opinion that not only training in standardized procedures is necessary but that adequate background knowledge with regard to motor development is essential for proper and effective utilization of this test.

The test equipment is first rate. The design and motor behavior measured have high face validity. The manual is clear and detailed. The manual is also a monograph outlining in considerable depth the theory, structure, and evolution of the Movement ABC (i.e., providing detailed background knowledge in motor movement). The authors utilize a persuasive Cognitive-Motor theoretical framework for understanding test performance (degree and kind of motor impairment) and effect on the learning process. For therapist and teachers, the manual presents chapters on intervention, linking assessment to behavior management, and the teaching of individual skills.

In sum, the Movement ABC appears to be an excellent instrument for the measurement of motor difficulties for young children. Caution is advised in the use of the test for Age Band 4 (ages 11–12) until data are provided showing reliability and validity of measurement at this level.

Review of the Movement Assessment Battery for Children by CAROL E. KESSLER, Assistant Professor of Education, Chestnut Hill College, Philadelphia, PA, and Adjunct Professor of Special Education, West Chester University, West Chester, PA:

This Battery, appropriate for children 4–12 years of age, originated from the works of Stott (who developed the Test of Motor Impairment [TOMI]) and Keogh (who produced the original Checklist). Thirty years of work have produced this new package. The main test (TOMI) was first published in 1972, revised by Henderson in 1984, and newly formatted as The Movement ABC in 1992 by Henderson and Sugden. This hybrid is a direct descendent of these previous editions, but additionally emphasizes practical application and intervention, creating fresh opportunities for classroom-based screening and assessment. Stott was concerned with investigating the relationship between possible perinatal trauma and later developmental disorders, specifically "clumsiness" in childhood; whereas Keogh, working with another strand of inquiry, was interested in alerting teachers to movement difficulties and their subsequent educational significance in children.

The Movement Assessment Battery for Children (Movement ABC) incorporates both of these perspectives into an assessment battery that contains two component parts. The "performance Test" requires individual administration and entails a series of motor tasks that the child must complete in a standardized fashion. It contains 32 items organized in four age bands of eight tasks. The first age band is for ages 4–6; the next is for children 7–8 years; the third band is for 9–10 year-old-children; and finally, the last band is for youngsters between the ages of 11 and 12 years. The requirements are identical for each of the eight tasks within the four bands. The eight test items or tasks are grouped under three dimensions: Manual Dexterity (3), Ball Skills (2), and Static (1)/Dynamic Behavior (2). The total score is a composite of these eight estimates of movement competence and is translated in terms of age-related norms. Additionally, a section where qualitative observations are to be noted accompanies each task. Further, upon conclusion of the test administration, the examiner is to comment on the influences on performance and summarize the qualitative observations. This portion should take 20–40 minutes, thereby easily maintaining the interest of the child. The Total Impairment Score on the Test portion indicates the extent to which a child demonstrates movement difficulties when compared to her/his same-age peers. Any score below the 5th percentile indicates a definite motor delay requiring immediate intervention. Similarly, a score between the 5th and 15th percentile suggests borderline motoric functioning.

The Checklist, ideal for screening purposes, is the second component of the Battery. This section is to be completed by an adult who is very familiar with the child's everyday movement capabilities. The 48 items are divided into four sections, each of which entails evaluating and rating the child in progressively more complex situations (Child Stationary/Environment Stable, Child Moving/Environment Stable, Child Stationary/Environment Changing, Child Moving/Environment Changing). Section 5 of the Checklist provides a qualitative assessment regarding the child's feelings and attitudes that may affect movement functioning. The Checklist, according to the manual, will probably identify more children as having deficits than will the Movement ABC Test, but will most likely yield similar scores for youngsters who are competent. This combination of quantitative and qualitative information is a definite strength of this assessment device.

The format of this well-constructed test is easy to follow. The instrument is designed to measure a child's motoric competence, not the ability to remember or understand directions. Therefore, numerous demonstrations can be given; instructions can be simplified, modified, and/or repeated; and testing may be done over the course of more than one session. A 0 item score indicates success whereas the measure of motor impairments is tabulated using a 1–5 score range.

In general, the manual is comprehensible and each item description has a matching picture of a child performing the task, which is extremely helpful. The instructions and scoring criteria are very clear, as well. Thus, the Test is easy to administer and score and is appropriate for the age range tested. Also, the instrument does not seem to pose any risk of physical injury, would be equally relevant to various cultural backgrounds, and includes tasks that are equally familiar to both sexes. Further, all of the materials supplied (my kit was missing the pegboard with 16 green pegs as well as the plastic target disk) were of very high quality. In addition, all of the necessary items fit neatly into the attaché case provided. One limitation inherent in the test pertains to the specifications regarding the room requirements, which are: a space that is at least 18 by 12 feet, a floor that is uncarpeted, and a blank wall that is smooth (I suppose the school gymnasium would satisfactorily meet these stipulations). The manual indicates that the instructions have been clarified, the scoring system has been improved, and norms for 4-year-olds have been added in the 1992 Battery—very critical improvements when compared to the previous editions. Also, the addition of the Checklist and the explanation of the cognitive-motor approach to educational intervention (which appears in the manual) are very helpful.

The age norms for the Test, which are provided for children 4–12 years of age, are based on a representative sample of 1,234 youngsters. For the Test, the geographic spread included the

Northeast, North Central, South, and West regions (the standardization of the Test was completed in the United States whereas the Checklist was based in the United Kingdom). Both rural and urban areas were represented. Further, in terms of gender, parental education, and ethnic origin, the sample seems to satisfactorily represent the general population of children in the U.S.

In preparing the impairment score scale and the test items for the newest edition, there was a deliberate focus on the low end of the distribution of motor proficiency. Because there was a statistically significant difference in variability among the 4–5-year-old band and the older children on the Total Impairment scores, two sets of total score norms were prepared.

When examining the reliability data for the Test, there seems to be stability over time when the items and Total Impairment scores are statistically analyzed. However, additional reliability data are necessary because the sample size was small. In investigating the construct validity for the Test, comparisons between groups of children known to have difficulties were made. In various studies, children with learning disabilities, as well as children with low birth weight and/or prematurity were compared with the standardization sample. These high-risk children consistently demonstrated motor difficulties (obtained elevated scores) in comparison to normal children. Additionally, the Movement ABC Test was examined in relationship to the Bruininks-Oseretsky Test. Although these tests are similar in some respects, they also differ radically. The ABC Test focuses primarily on the identification of impairment and the Bruininks Test is intended to indicate ability across the entire spectrum. A coefficient of -0.53 resulted (the true direction of the relationship is positive because the composite scores of these tests are scaled in the opposite direction). Because these two tests are only moderately comparable (a very high correlation should not be expected to occur), it is suggested that additional test comparisons be conducted to gain a more comprehensive validity examination of scores from the Test.

When examining the statistical adequacy of the Checklist, only children between the ages of 6–10 years were examined. The authors make a commitment to collect data in the future that include children who have just begun school and those who are entering puberty.

It can be hoped that with more extensive study these limitations regarding the technical characteristics of this instrument will be addressed adequately. In summation, I recommend this Battery for examiners who are interested in assessing a child's movement capabilities and in increasing their knowledge pertaining to the management and remediation of motor impairments.

[50]
Mullen Scales of Early Learning: AGS Edition.

Purpose: A comprehensive measure of cognitive functioning for infants and preschool children.
Population: Birth to 68 months.
Publication Dates: 1984–1995.
Scores, 6: Gross Motor Scale, Cognitive Scales (Visual Reception, Fine Motor, Receptive Language, Expressive Language), Early Learning Composite.
Administration: Individual.
Price Data, 1999: $599 per complete kit; $25.95 per 25 record forms; $149.95 per Mullen ASSIST (specify for IBM, Macintosh, or Windows).
Time: (15–60) minutes.
Comments: Previous editions entitled Infant Mullen Scales of Early Learning and Preschool Mullen Scales of Early Learning.
Author: Eileen M. Mullen.
Publisher: American Guidance Service, Inc.
Cross References: See T5:1728 (2 references); for a review by Verna Hart of the earlier edition, see 11:177.

Review of the Mullen Scales of Early Learning: AGS Edition by MARY MATHAI CHITTOORAN, UC Foundation Assistant Professor of School Psychology, The University of Tennessee at Chattanooga, Chattanooga, TN:

The Mullen Scales of Early Learning: AGS Edition is a revised version of the original Mullen Scales of Early Learning (MSEL) and combines the Infant MSEL with the Preschool MSEL. It is an individually administered, standardized measure of cognitive functioning in infants and preschoolers from birth through 68 months. The Mullen is theory-based and consists of a Gross Motor Scale, which is administered to children from birth through 33 months, and four Cognitive Scales (Visual Reception, Fine Motor, Receptive Language, and Expressive Language), which can be used with children from birth through 68 months. Performance on individual scales is reported as *T*-scores (X = 50; *SD* = 10) and the optional Early Learning Composite (X = 100; *SD* = 15) is a derivation from the *T*-scores of the four Cognitive Scales, and serves as an overall estimate of cognitive functioning. Also available are percentile ranks and age equivalents. Because scales on the Mullen correspond with federal mandates for infant and preschool assessment, results of the test may be used for eligibility decisions, as well as for program planning and early intervention services.

The test kit includes a number of bright and attractive test materials. Although they are generally durable and safe for use with young children, there were some notable exceptions; cards for some items are flimsy and unlikely to stand up to continued use, the table leg arrived broken, and the formboard, which appears to be made of painted particle board, is poorly sanded and was covered with paint flakes. Examiners are also expected to supply supplemental materials such as paper and coins; however, the author does provide a comprehensive list of necessary materials. The Item Administration Book includes directions for administration and scoring and is nicely done; however, there are only a few items in each area, and in some cases only two at certain age levels. The Stimulus Booklet may have been more useful with an easel back. Further, its small size, and the fact that there are often many items crowded onto a page, may be problematic for young children. The single-sheet fold-out Record Form could have been better designed; the print is miniscule, giving it a rather "busy" appearance, and the flap that contains stimuli for items on the Receptive and Expressive Language Scales is oddly placed.

Training requirements are minimal and administration should be simple for those with early childhood experience. The examiner may choose to give all or some of the subscales without sacrificing accuracy and is allowed to vary the order of administration to maintain examinee interest. Although most items involve observing the child actually performing a task, there are some that may be scored by interviewing the parent, and others that allow the parent to assist in elicitation of a response. Scoring and interpretation are enhanced by the inclusion of clearly organized tables, case studies, and ASSIST software.

Seventy-one clinicians participated in the standardization of the Mullen over a period of 8 years. The normative sample included 1,849 children between the ages of 2 days and 69 months grouped into 16 age groups ranging from 2-month age intervals at the youngest age level to 5-month age intervals at the upper age level. Children in the normative sample were 51.3% male and 48.7% female and included Caucasian, African American, Hispanic, and Native American individuals in proportion to the U.S. Census of 1990. Females are underrepresented at some age levels (e.g., 5–6 months) and males are underrepresented at others (e.g., 27–32 months). Other stratification variables included socioeconomic status, geographic region, and community size. Results of the Mullen may be affected by the fact that the standardization sample did not include children with a primary language other than English or children with known exceptionalities; separate norms for children with special needs might have been useful. Also potentially problematic is the fact that the sample only included children whose parents gave permission for participation.

Item analyses using the Rasch one-parameter IRT model were conducted to determine the final item set for all five scales of the Mullen as well as to establish basal and ceiling rules. Developmental progression of raw scores and intercorrelations between scales are offered as evidence of construct validity and principal-factor loadings (ranging from .55 to .90) lend support for the Early Learning Composite as a measure of general cognitive ability.

Concurrent validity with the Bayley Scales of Infant Development was studied in a sample of 103 "normal" children ages 6 to 15 months. Moderately high correlations were obtained between the Bayley's Mental Development Index and both the Early Learning Composite (.70) and the four cognitive scales (.53 to .59). The Gross Motor Scale correlated with the Bayley's Psychomotor Development Index at .76. Divergent validity was illustrated by relatively low correlations with scales measuring unrelated abilities. High convergent and divergent validity were also established by examining correlations between measures of receptive and expressive abilities on the Mullen and the Preschool Language Assessment (*N* = 65; ages 15–59 months). The Mullen had high to moderate correlations with the Motor subtest of the Brigance, the Peabody Fine Motor Scale, and the Metropolitan Readiness Test. According to the author, the Mullen is able to discriminate between children with developmental delays and those without. Content validity is not directly mentioned; however, evidence of criterion-related and construct validity can also be used to establish content validity.

Modified split-half internal consistency coefficients for the scales had median values ranging from .75 to .83 and the composite had a median value of .91. Four coefficients were not used in the calculation of median values because of ceiling effects on the Visual Reception Scale and floor and ceiling effects on the Receptive Language Scale. The standard error of measurement had median values ranging from 4.1 to 5.0 for the Cognitive Scales and 4.5 for the Early Learning Composite. Test-retest reliability was measured for two age groups (1–24 months and 25–56 months) with a mean retest interval of 11 days. Among the younger age group, stability coefficients ranged from a low of .82 for the Fine Motor Scale (N = 50) to a high of .96 for the Gross Motor Scale (N = 38); among the older age group, coefficients ranged from a low of .71 for the Expressive Language Scale (N = 47) to a high of .79 for the Fine Motor Scale (N = 47). Interscorer reliability for four age groups of children between 1 and 44 months (N = 81) ranged from .91 to .99. Although validity and reliability evidence appears to be adequate, it must be mentioned that results reported are based on studies completed with previous versions of the Mullen and samples that are either rather small or that have inadequate representation of older children.

SUMMARY. The concerns noted with regard to standardization, reliability, and validity warrant a cautious interpretation of the test, particularly for older children or children with exceptionalities. Despite these deficiencies, the Mullen appears to be a satisfactory alternative to other measures of functioning for early childhood populations, particularly if it is used as part of a comprehensive assessment battery.

Review of the Mullen Scales of Early Learning: AGS Edition by CAROL E. KESSLER, Assistant Professor of Education, Chestnut Hill College, Philadelphia, PA, and Adjunct Professor of Special Education, West Chester University, West Chester, PA:

There is an increased need to assess young children, particularly those from birth to 68 months, because of the passage of P.L. 999-457. The

Mullen Scales enables early childhood specialists to design developmentally appropriate individualized educational plans based on the child's profile of cognitive abilities and weaknesses, which underlies her/his learning style. These Scales assist the examiner in facilitating eligibility decisions regarding the need for special services but, as the author notes, should be used in conjunction with measures of social-emotional development and adaptive skills to provide a comprehensive assessment.

Dr. Eileen M. Mullen, a developmental psychologist, has extensive experience in diagnosing children with developmental disabilities. This interactive test model, which includes both intrasensory and intersensory components, views intelligence as "a network of interrelated but functionally distinct cognitive skills" (manual, p. 1). This assessment device consists of a Gross Motor Scale and four Cognitive Scales (Visual Reception, Fine Motor, Receptive Language, Expressive Language). Also, an Early Learning Composite score is included, which represents general intelligence.

In her theoretical framework, Mullen asserts that visual and auditory conceptual development has as its foundation gross motor learning. Each score provides a T score, percentile rank, descriptive category (which is very helpful for the practitioner), and an age equivalent. T scores are to be used for program eligibility. If a child receives a T score of 30 or less on any Scale (2 standard deviations or more below the mean), this would indicate a significant delay and would certainly warrant early intervention services. Further, T scores of 31–35 (1.5 standard deviations below the mean) are indicative of a child at risk for delay and should also be considered for special services.

The manual provides outstanding explanations regarding all the important features of the Scales and includes examples of profile interpretations within case study reports. The test kit contains an ASSIST computer software program, which is available in Macintosh, DOS, and Windows versions. The program calculates derived scores and give interpretive information for the five Scales and the Early Learning Composite. Also, it includes activities for intervention for birth through 36 months. It is suggested that these intervention tasks be extended upward to include children 45+ months. Further, the manipulatives included are of high interest to young children and are of very sturdy quality. An exception would be the child's safety scissors. These should be of a higher quality if children are expected to cut accurately and comfortably for Item 24 of the Fine Motor Scale. Also, white chalk and/or a 10-foot colored tape should be included (specified in the manual to be supplied by the examiner). Inclusion of these items would make preparation a great deal easier for the examiner.

The Scales are presented in nontechnical terms and are easy to administer and score. Also, the directions have numerous diagrams to aid comprehension and are of very superior quality. The administration time, 15–60 minutes, is certainly within an acceptable range and thus allows the interest of the child to be maintained easily. All five scores can stand alone for scoring and administrative purposes. Separate scores are available for both receptive and expressive responses, which should be considered a definite strength of this test.

Standardization data are provided on 1,849 children ranging in age from 2 days to 69 months. More than 100 sites, in four geographic regions of the U.S. (Northeast, South, West, Central), were used. The standardization testing began in the Northeast region and continued over a period of 8 years. Stratified variables included sex, race/ethnicity, father's occupation, and urban/rural residence. The description of the sample indicates that it is a very close representation of the U.S. population. The examiner should be cognizant of the fact that only children with parental consent were included in the sample. An item analysis and normative scores (these recomputed norms are different from the ones provided in previous versions) are provided.

The psychometric properties appear technically adequate. Internal consistency was estimated using a split-half procedure. Very satisfactory median internal consistency values for the five Scales were obtained (.75 to .83). However, some ceiling effect is present for the Perceptive Language Scale and the Visual Perception Scale. Also, a floor effect is evident for the Receptive Language Scale, which reflects reduced score variance and concomitantly reduces reliability estimates. Negligible practice effects were demonstrated (test-retest reliability), which indicates a high degree of score stability over time. The interscorer reliability ranges from .91 to .99 and thus the Scales appear to be interpreted similarly by multiple examiners. Further, the construct and concurrent validity appears to be technically sound. The author uses developmental progression of scores, intercorrelations of the Scales, and principal-axis factor analysis in support of the construct validity of this assessment instrument. Also, concurrent validity was substantiated using the Bayley Scales of Infant Development, the Preschool Language Assessment, and the Peabody Fine Motor Scale with different age ranges. Again, correlations between the Mullen Measures and the Bayley Measures support convergent and divergent validity of the scores. The results, when compared to the PLA Measures, yield similarly good evidence. Finally, when investigating and comparing the fine motor scales, again the Mullen Scale shows substantial correlations supporting the concurrent validity of this instrument.

Some of the earlier psychometric concerns regarding the Infant Mullen Scales of Early Learning have been addressed adequately and thus the examiner can be more confident when using these Scales to assess learning patterns and capacities of children. In summary, I highly recommend this assessment tool when the examiner is interested in measuring a young child's cognitive abilities and gross motor base for learning.

[51]
The Multidimensional Addictions and Personality Profile.

Purpose: Designed as "an objective measure of substance abuse and personal adjustment problems."

Population: Adolescents and adults experiencing substance abuse and mental health disorders.

Publication Dates: 1988–1996.

Acronym: MAPP.

Scores, 15: Substance Abuse Subscales (Psychological Dependence, Abusive/Secretive/Irresponsible Use, Interference, Signs of Withdrawal, Total), Personal Adjustment Subscales (Frustration Problems, Interpersonal Problems, Self-Image Problems, Total), Defensiveness and Inconsistency Scores (Defensiveness, Inconsistency, Total); Minimizing Response Pattern Scales (Substance Abuse, Personal Adjustment, Total).

Administration: Group or individual.

Price Data, 1995: $65 per 50 answer booklets; $30 per manual ('96, 110 pages); $22 per French and Spanish translation package including written and audiotaped instructions and questions; $170 per Advanced Computer scoring package including 50 tests and a research module.

Foreign Language Edition: French and Spanish translation package available (including printed questions with audio tape).

Time: (20-25) minutes.

Comments: Previous edition entitled The COMPASS; IBM or compatible with 2 disk drives and at least 640K RAM, monitor, and printer required for computer scoring option.

Authors: John R. Craig and Phyllis Craig.

Publisher: Diagnostic Counseling Services, Inc.

Review of The Multidimensional Addictions and Personality Profile by CARL ISENHART, Coordinator, Addictive Disorders Section, VA Medical Center, Minneapolis, MN:

The Multidimensional Addictions and Personality Profile (MAPP; a revision of "The COMPASS") is a 98-item self-report questionnaire that assesses an individual's (adolescent or adult) substance abuse and personal adjustment. It can be administered in 20–25 minutes either individually or in a group. The manual states that "no minimum reading skill or educational level is required" (manual, p. 19) because an illiterate person could have the items read to him or her.

The Substance Abuse section consists of four, 14-item subscales and one total scale that assess Psychological Dependence; Abusive, Secretive, and Irresponsible Use; Interference; and Signs of Withdrawal. The Personal Adjustment scales consists of three, 14-item subscales (actually, seven, 2-item pairs with opposite content) and one total scale that assess Frustration, Interpersonal Problems, and Self-Image Problems. An Inconsistency and Defensiveness scale are derived from the Personal Adjustment items. The Inconsistency scale assesses the test-taker's response consistency and contains the 21, 2-item Personal Adjustment scale items. The Defensiveness scale assesses the person's willingness to admit to problems. The response options for all the items consist of five options: *always, usually, occasionally, seldom,* and *never.* Each text term is associated with a number; for example, *always* = 4 and *never* = 0.

ADMINISTRATION AND SCORING. The MAPP items are administered orally or in writing, and the examinee's responses are transferred via a carbonless sheet to a scoring sheet that is used by the examiner to tally the raw scores. The scale scores are obtained by tallying the examinee's responses to each item then converting the raw scores to percentiles. The Defensiveness score is obtained by counting the number of *never* responses on the three Personal Adjustment subscales. The Inconsistency score is obtained by summing the absolute differences between the 21 pairs of items that make up the Personal Adjustment subscales. The manual provides guidelines (but no rationale) for when to question or reject protocols based on the Defensiveness and Inconsistency scales.

NORMS. There are major problems with the standardization description. The standardization sample consisted of "inpatients" and the "general population"; a table provides details of each sample's sex, race, and age. There is no description of the inpatient sample in terms of background or substance use dimensions, and there was no discussion of how these individuals were selected for inclusion. There was a large age difference between the inpatient and general population sample (31% of the inpatient and 71% of the general population was under 21, respectively), but there was no analysis of the statistical significance of that and other possible differences between the two groups. The authors do not provide the means and standard deviations of the standardization sample's scores from the MAPP. The only means and standard deviations that are provided are from a sample of 131 people used in the test-retest reliability sample. With this limited sample, the standard deviations show a high level of variation. There is no information about the distribution of the samples. There was no evaluation of any demographic differences on any of the MAPP scales.

SCALE DEVELOPMENT AND CONTENT. The substance abuse scale items "were selected primarily from rational-theoretical considerations rather than by factor-analytical or empirical techniques ... to meet the definition of substance abuse as set forth in this manual and in DSM-III-R" (manual, p. 9). These items were "provided to substance abuse evaluation specialists" (manual, p. 9) for further refinement. The Personal Adjustment scale items were "limited to those areas which dealt with the most commonly occurring problems of daily living" (manual, p. 9). There is no discussion of the refinement of items and justification for the types and number of items in each scale. For example, there was no empirical evaluation of whether the subscales assess truly unique and independent dimensions: The reported Substance Abuse subscale correlations ranged from .57 to .85. There was also no justification for needing 21 pairs of items for the Inconsistency scale; it is likely fewer items would serve the same purpose. Also, there is no empirical support that the Inconsistency scale item pairs do represent opposite content.

RELIABILITY. The quality of the reliability data is poor. Test-retest reliability was reported for 131 people with an interval of 7 days between administrations; no other intervals were reported. The correlations ranged from .50 to .91. Each scale's standard error of measurement (*SEM*) was reported; however, the large *SEM*s seem to actually call into question the test's reliability. For example, the *SEM* is approximately 11 for the Total Substance Abuse score. Given a score of 23 (which is at the 50th percentile), 68% of the time the true score will fall between a range of 12 and 34; this represents percentiles of 30 and 65, respectively. This is a large range and questions the repeatability and consistency of the scores. Of course, this problem is further exacerbated if two *SEM*s were to be used (which is typical). In addition, the authors reported "internal consistency measures" to support reliability. However, instead of examining the consistency of item responses within the subscales and total scales and calculating coefficient alphas, they correlated the subscales with the total scale. This does not represent item consistency but rather shared variance across the scales (which is different). Because they reported substance abuse subscales and the total score correlations between .83 to almost .86, this further questions the independence and uniqueness of these scales.

VALIDITY. The validity data presented in the manual are weak. *T*-test analysis showed that the MAPP scales significantly differentiated between "chemically dependent" patients and the general population and between a new sample of inpatients (again, there is no demographic or background information provided) and patients with a first and prior arrests and those with and without prior DUIs. However, *t*-tests do not control for making multiple comparisons and do not control for the high correlations between the subscales. These results do little to support the validity of the instrument. In addition, because of the high correlations between the substance abuse and distress scales, the differences that do occur between the inpatients and the general population may be attributable to the distress and not substance use per se. Demographic differences, which were not examined, could also explain the differences. There are no comparisons of the MAPP scores with external criteria, such as other measures of substance abuse, diagnostic criteria, or other indicators of substance-related problems.

SUMMARY. This reviewer cannot support the use of the MAPP. The evaluation of the MAPP vis a vis the standardization sample is inadequate, and there is limited support for the reliability and validity of the instrument.

Review of The Multidimensional Addictions and Personality Profile by KEITH F. WIDAMAN, Professor of Psychology, University of California at Davis, Davis, CA:

The Multidimensional Addictions and Personality profile (MAPP) is a measure of substance use problems and accompanying personal adjustment problems. Alcohol and drug use and abuse are pressing problems in the U.S. so reliable and valid measures of substance use problems are valuable tools in psychological evaluation in general and personnel selection in particular. Personal adjustment problems may precipitate substance use problems or may result from such problems. The MAPP takes no stand on the causal relations between substance use and personal adjustment problems, simply opting to assess the types of adjustment problems that appear to represent significant comorbidity with substance abuse.

DESCRIPTION. The MAPP is a 98-item scale that contains items answered on a frequency scale, ranging from 0 = *Never* to 4 = *Always*. The 98 items are divided into seven primary content scales, with 14 items per scale. Four content scales directly assess substance use problems. These four scales are labeled Psychological Dependence (PD), Abusive, Secretive, and Irresponsible Use (ASI), Interference (INT), and Signs of Withdrawal (SOW). These scale scores can be aggregated into an overall Total Substance Abuse Scales score, which is the simple sum of the PD, ASI, INT, and SOW scale scores. All substance use questions are positively worded (i.e., none are negatively worded), so acquiescence response bias might well be confounded in all four substance use problems scales.

The remaining three content scales measure Personal Adjustment problems accompanying substance use problems. These three scales are Frustration Problems (FP), Interpersonal Problems (IP), and Self-Image Problems (SIP). The aggregated Total Personal Adjustment Scales score is the simple sum of the FP, IP, and SIP scale scores. One-half of the items for each personal Adjustment problem scale are positively worded, and one-half are negatively worded, which would control for acquiescence response bias.

There are also two sets of style scales. The first set consists of two scales, Defensiveness (DEF) and Inconsistency (INC), which can be summed into a total score. The second set of style scales consists of "minimizing" response style scales. One may obtain a score for each subject on a Substance Abuse Minimizing Response Pattern Scale, a Personal Adjustment Minimizing Response Pattern Scale, and a Total Minimizing Response Pattern Scale, which is the sum of the previous two scale scores.

ADMINISTRATION. The MAPP may be administered in either group or individual formats. The instructions for the MAPP are simple and straightforward, with the respondent told to describe his or her behavior during the past 6 months when choosing a response on the 0 = *Never* to 4 = *Always* scale for each item. One confusing aspect of the MAPP is the fact that the 98 items are presented under the title of COMPASS Questionnaire. The COMPASS was an earlier name for the questionnaire now identified as the MAPP, and this inconsistency should be rectified.

SCORING. The scoring of the seven content scales is easily completed. As respondents answer each item, a carbon copy of item responses is transferred directly onto a scoring template, and item scores are easily summed into scale scores for the seven content scales.

With regard to style scales, the DEF scale score is obtained by counting the number of 0 (or *never*) responses across the Personal Adjustment problem scales of FP, IP, and SIP. The INC scale scores is the absolute difference between responses on pairs of items from the FP, IP, and SIP scales, after appropriate reversing of the scores on negatively worded items. This rescoring of the items from the Personal Adjustment problems scales may be problematic, leading to contaminated correlations among scale scores due to item overlap.

In addition, the DEF and INC scales are fairly crude attempts to identify defensiveness and inconsistency of responding. The final style scales, identified as "minimizing response pattern" scales, are poorly described, and the method for obtaining scale scores on these items is not included in the MAPP scoring template.

The standardization samples consisted of an inpatient sample of 424 persons and a general population sample of 1,668 persons. In the general population sample, 1,180 persons were under 21 years of age, 460 were 21 years and over, and 28 declined to state their age. These samples were used to generate two conversion tables, one for persons under 21 years of age and the second for those 21 years and older. The conversion tables provide only percentile scores, which have a uniform distribution. The knowledgeable user could use these conversion tables to transform scores into a *T*-score or IQ score metric, but this would require a nonlinear transformation of percentiles into another metric and is not provided in the manual. Also, raw scores on each of the seven content scales have a potential range from 0 to 56. The raw scores on these scales are likely to be positively skewed, so conversion to another metric using percentiles would be recommended when using these variables in statistical models.

RELIABILITY. Test-retest reliability estimates based on a sample of 131 respondents, are reported for all content scales and for the DEF and INC style scales, as well as the total scores derived from the several sections. The test-retest interval was 7 days. The test-retest reliability coefficients for the substance use problems scales were fairly high, ranging from .89 to .91. The reliability estimates for the interpersonal adjustment problems scales were lower, ranging from .78 to .87. Test-retest reliability estimates for the style scales of Defensiveness and Inconsistency were much lower, ranging between .50 and .67. No test-retest reliabilities were provided for the Minimizing response pattern scales.

The accompanying values for the standard error of measurement (*SEM*) for each scale are given for the raw score metric only. The *SEM* values appear reasonably small for most scales, but are difficult to interpret given the differing means and standard deviations for each scale.

VALIDITY. The authors reported correlations among Substance Abuse scales and among

Personal Adjustment problem scales, referring to these as indices of internal consistency reliability. However, these are more correctly seen as indices of validity, particularly discriminant validity. That is, correlations among scales within a given domain should be sufficiently low to support a contention that empirically distinct constructs are assessed. Across the three samples of persons under 21 years, persons 21 years and over, and inpatients, the correlations among the substance abuse scales ranged between .57 and .85. Across these same three samples, the correlations among the Personal Adjustment scales ranged between .50 and .76. If corrected for attenuation (or unreliability), most of these correlations among scales would be over .80, with many above .90. These results suggest that there is little discriminant validity among the four Substance Abuse scales and little discriminant validity among the Personal Adjustment scales. No correlations were provided between Substance Abuse and Personal Adjustment scales, so the discriminant validity between these two domains is unknown. Also, no correlations among style scales were reported in the manual.

The only other type of validity evidence presented is a series of group mean comparisons between the inpatient sample with other contrast groups. The inpatient sample had a mean level of response placing them at or beyond the 99th percentile on most scales, representing a rather extreme contrast group. Not surprisingly, the inpatient sample had significantly different mean scores on all scales when compared to persons under 21 years of age, persons 21 years and older, persons with a first offense for drug use, persons with two or more arrests for drug use, and persons arrested for driving under the influence with or without prior arrests. No comparisons among the latter groups were reported.

No factor analytic results on the MAPP are reported, and no correlations with other similar instruments are reported. As a result, the dimensional structure of the MAPP has yet to be tested.

SUMMARY. The MAPP is an easy-to-administer, direct measure of substance abuse and the personal adjustment problems associated with substance use. Although levels of reliability are adequate, the MAPP has several deficiencies. Among these deficiencies are the potential contamination of acquiescence response bias on the substance use scales and the lack of clear discriminant validity among many of the scales derived from the MAPP. Persons wanting a measure of alcohol use might consider the Alcohol Use Inventory (T5:136), by K. W. Wanberg, J. L. Horn, and F. M. Foster, which has a much wider array of reliability and validity information available. The MAPP appears to be a promising instrument, but additional reliability and validity data are needed to ensure confident interpretation of its scale scores.

[52]
Multiscore Depression Inventory for Children.

Purpose: Designed to assess depression and "features related to depression."
Population: Ages 8–17.
Publication Date: 1996.
Acronym: MDI-C.
Scores, 9: Anxiety, Self-Esteem, Sad Mood, Instrumental Helplessness, Social Introversion, Low Energy, Pessimism, Defiance, Total.
Administration: Group.
Price Data, 1999: $125 per complete kit including manual (54 pages), 25 AutoScore™ test forms, 25 profile forms, 2 prepaid mail-in answer sheets for computer scoring and interpretation, 2-use disk, and 2 PC answer sheets for on-site computer scoring and interpretation; $32.50 per 25 AutoScore™ test forms; $16.50 per mail-in answer sheet; $14.50 per 50 profile forms; $45 per manual; $299 per MDI-C microcomputer disk including 25 uses (IBM or compatible and Microsoft Windows 3.1 or above; 3.5-inch); $15 per 100 microcomputer answer sheets; $12.50 per FAX service scoring.
Time: (10–20) minutes.
Authors: David J. Berndt and Charles F. Kaiser.
Publisher: Western Psychological Services.

Review of the Multiscore Depression Inventory for Children by JILL ANN JENKINS, Psychologist, Mary Sheridan Child Development Centre, London, United Kingdom:

The Multiscore Depression Inventory for Children (MDI-C) is a 79-item self-report depression inventory for children ages 8 to 17. Based on the adult Multiscore Depression Inventory (MDI) (Berndt, 1986; T4:1693), administration time is approximately 20 minutes and the test can be given on a group or individual basis.

The MDI-C was developed to investigate not only whether depression is present, but also what different features of depression are manifested in the children tested. It therefore boasts not only the ability to diagnose depression as do other self-report tools such as the Children's Depression Inventory (CDI) (Kovacs & Beck, 1977) and the Center for Epidemiologic Depression Studies—Depression Scale Modified for Children (CES-DC) (Weissman, Orvaschel, & Padian, 1980), but assists in specific treatment planning on an individual basis. The only other self-report depression inventory for children that also investigates characteristics of depression is the Children's Depression Scale (CDS) (Tisher & Lang, 1983). The CDS scales, however, are fewer and less specific than those found in the MDI-C.

The MDI for adults analyzes 12 constructs of depression. Two of the 10 constructs of the MDI were altered to conform to child-related issues for the MDI-C. The first, "Irritability" was transformed into "Defiance" to measure symptoms related to Oppositional Defiant Disorder and Conduct Disorder. Some of the items from "Cognitive Difficulty" (which relates to indecision, confusion, and bewilderment) were added to an "Anxiety" construct for children.

After an impressive sampling of 1,465 children ages 8 to 17 years from a geographically diverse sample in the USA, two of the initial scales were eliminated (Guilt and Learned Helplessness) due to inadequate reliability, as were two additional constructs that had been added (Somatic Problems and Suicidal Ideation). In the final version, the authors added a single question regarding suicidal ideation, which is to be analyzed separately from the remaining eight constructs (Anxiety, Self-Esteem, Social Introversion, Instrumental Helplessness, Sad Mood, Pessimism, Low Energy, and Defiance). The item questions themselves were written by children to ensure that the language was suited to children.

The sample of 1,465 children described above also provided the means and standard deviations for scoring. The sample was divided into three age groups: 8 through 10, 11 through 13, and 14 through 17.

The internal consistency reliability of the MDI-C total score and scales scores was evaluated for children in the age range of 11 to 13, with all of the alpha coefficients at or above .75. The other two age ranges, although showing very acceptable total score alphas (.92 for ages 8–10 years and .92 for ages 14–17), found six of the eight scales

unable to meet alpha coefficients of .70. The upper and lower age groupings perhaps would have yielded better internal consistency scores if divided into more age ranges. It seems quite plausible, for example, in the upper age range grouping, that a girl of 14.0 years would have different developmental issues related to depression than a girl of 17.11 years.

Showing more optimistic findings, a cross validation sample of 254 junior high school and high school students found all of the scales, except for Pessimism, to be at or above alpha .70. Incidentally, Pessimism was also one of the scales that did not reach alpha of .70 with the normative sample as well.

Test-retest reliability was examined with a sample of 145 junior high and high school aged subjects ranging in age from 11 to 18. Subjects were tested 4 weeks after completing their initial MDI-C. Test-retest reliability estimates were quite high, with a Pearson correlation for the total score of .92, and a range of acceptable scale correlations from .77 to .86. Despite the homogeneity of the sample used (where all of the subjects were from the same demographic area), the results are quite impressive.

In a study of diverse, nonclinical children ages 9 to 17 (N = 163), criterion validity investigations found a correlation of .84 between the popularly used CDI (Kovacs, 1981) and the MDI-C total scores. The correlation of the scales of the MDI-C and the CDI total score were lower (ranging from a correlation of .52 to .76), indicating that although the two scales are testing for the same overall concept of depression, the scales of the MDI-C are tapping different issues (as they were intended to do).

Seventy-one children (age range not provided) with various psychiatric diagnosis were also pooled to evaluate the predictive validity of the MDI-C. Predictive validity with clinician's ratings and the MDI-C of severity of depression was .61 (a substantial difference from that with the currently popular CDI, which was .44). Scores of the MDI-C were also highly predictive of the Piers-Harris Children's Self-Concept Scale (Piers & Harris, 1983) in a study of 147 children in the age range of 11 to 13.

When both the adult MDI and MDI-C were given to adolescents (n = 170) ranging from ages 13 to 18, moderate to high correlations were indicated between the scales, despite the fact that the scales of the MDI were altered to be more developmentally appropriate. The total score of the MDI and MDI-C had a very respectable correlation of .83.

The test was carefully constructed to ensure content validity. Items of the scale were included if a point biserial correlation of the item with its corresponding scale was higher than the item's correlation with any of the other seven scales. Initial and cross validation samples found highly significant total correlations of each item and their corresponding scales (p<.001).

Face validity was also fully analyzed and found to be satisfactory and the readability of the questionnaire acceptable. Construct validity via factor analyses on all of the MDI-C items was thoroughly evaluated with the normative sample (n = 1,114) and a cross-validation sample (N = 250). In both instances it was found to be acceptable.

SUMMARY. Scores from the MDI-C provide valid and reliable evidence of child depression. The inventory has been well researched. It offers the unique characteristic of looking at features of depression, in addition to indicating an overall score for depression, allowing the examiner to use it for not only diagnosis but also treatment planning. The well-established evidence of test-retest reliability may additionally be useful in screening and in research evaluating treatment effectiveness.

Research indicates that scale results are more valid for children in the age range of 11 to 13. The Pessimism scale should be viewed cautiously due to lower validity scores. If the clinician is looking for a tool that offers a wider age range for which to test, they may be better suited with the CDI, which has norms for children ages 6 to 17. In addition, there are other tests available which, unlike the MDI-C, allow for parent, teacher, and sibling evaluations of the child simultaneously to the child's self-report, such as the Children's Depression Scale (Tisher & Lang, 1983), the structured interview Kiddie SADS (Puig-Antich & Ryan, 1986), and the Bellvue Index of Depression (Petti, 1978). This may be critically important due to the current belief that agreement from more than one source is essential for appropriate assessment of childhood depression (Kaslow & Rehm, 1991).

REVIEWER'S REFERENCES

Kovacs, M., & Beck, A. T. (1977). An empirical-clinical approach toward a definition of childhood depression. In J. G. Schulterbrandt & A. Rasking (Eds.), *Depression in childhood: Diagnosis, treatment, and conceptual models* (pp. 1–25). New York: Raven Press.

Petti, T. A. (1978). Depression in hospitalized child psychiatry patients. *Journal of the American Academy of Child Psychiatry, 17,* 49–59.

Weissman, M. M., Orvaschel, H., & Padian, N. (1980). Children's symptom and social functioning self report scales: Comparison of mothers' and children's reports. *Journal of Nervous and Mental Disease, 168,* 736–740.

Kovacs, M. (1981). Rating scales to assess depression in school aged children. *Acta Paedopsychiatrica, 46,* 305–315.

Piers, E. V., & Harris, D. B. (1983). Piers-Harris Children's Self-Concept Scale (PHCSCS). Los Angeles, CA: Western Psychological Services.

Tisher, M., & Lang, M. (1983). The children's depression scale: Review and further developments. In D. P. Cantwell & G. A. Carlson (Eds.), *Affective disorders in childhood and adolescence: An update* (pp. 375–415). New York: Spectrum.

Berndt, D. J. (1986). *Multiscore Depression Inventory (MDI) manual.* Los Angeles, CA: Western Psychological Services.

Puig-Antich, J., & Ryan, N. (1986). *Schedule for affective disorder and schizophrenia for school-age children (6–18 years)—Kiddie SADS (K-SADS).* Unpublished manuscript. Pittsburgh: Western Psychiatric Institute and Clinic.

Kaslow, N. J., & Rehm, L. P. (1991). Childhood depression. In R. R. Kratochwill & R. J. Morris (Eds.), *The practice of child therapy* (2nd ed.) (pp. 43–75). New York: Pergamon.

Review of the Multiscore Depression Inventory for Children by MICHAEL G. KAVAN, Associate Dean for Student Affairs and Associate Professor of Family Practice, Creighton University School of Medicine, Omaha, NE:

The Multiscore Depression Inventory for Children (MDI-C) is a 79-item self-report measure designed to assess "depression and features related to depression" (manual, p. 1) in children between the ages of 8 and 17 years. It is meant to be used both as a screening instrument to "identify high risk children and as an aid in clinical assessment" (manual, p. 1). The MDI-C is adapted from the well-developed and respected adult Multiscore Depression Inventory (MDI; T4:1693). Like its predecessor, the MDI-C provides a total score for depression and subscale scores deemed useful in a broad range of clinical applications.

ADMINISTRATION AND SCORING. The MDI-C may be administered and scored by an "appropriately trained and supervised clerk" (p. 3) to individuals or to groups. For administration of the MDI-C, children are requested to complete the necessary background information on the answer form. They are then asked to read the printed instructions silently as the administrator reads them aloud. Children are to respond by circling "T" (true) or "F" (false) to each item by indicating how they "usually feel." The manual states that the items are readable at a mid first-grade reading level in one section, a second-grade reading level in another section, and a third-grade reading level in yet another section. Despite the authors' lack of clarity on this issue, experience with the MDI-C demonstrates that most MDI-C items are, in fact, clear and easy to understand. However, some younger children may have difficulty with the meaning of "suicide" and thus, the administrator may need to assist them in defining this word. Administration time is predicted to be 20 minutes, but most children should be able to complete the measure within 10 minutes.

The MDI-C may be scored by hand or microcomputer. Scoring may also be done by the test publisher through fax or mail services. For hand scoring, the administrator tears the perforated answer form in order to reveal the scoring page. A total score, which is meant to measure the severity of overall depression, and eight subscale scores (i.e., Anxiety, Self-Esteem, Sad Mood, Instrumental Helplessness, Social Introversion, Low Energy, Pessimism, and Defiance) are tabulated on this page and then transferred to a profile form for plotting. A suicide item is also included and contributes to the total score, but does not appear on any subscale. In addition, the scoring form includes an infrequency score column in order to measure response bias and/or malingering. Total scores can range from 0 to 79, whereas subscale scores can range from 8 to 13. The manual includes information on profile validity, total and subscale definitions, along with several case examples to assist in the interpretation of the MDI-C.

RELIABILITY. Within the manual, information is provided on both internal consistency and test-retest reliability. Coefficient alpha was figured for each MDI-C scale using the 1,465 children within the normative sample. Alpha coefficients for the entire group ranged from .70 (Low Energy) to .94 (Total score). Internal consistency holds up fairly well when examined within the three age ranges. One will, however, want to interpret some subscales within certain age groups with caution because alpha coefficients occasionally dip into the mid .60s. Internal consistencies were also calculated on a separate group of 254 junior high school and high school students (no other information was provided within the manual on this group) with alpha coefficients ranging from .66 (Pessimism) to .94 (Total). Four-week test-retest reliability was examined with 145 junior high and senior high school students (ages 11 to 18 years) from Charleston, South Carolina. Reliability coefficients ranged from .77 (Low Energy) to .92 (Total) indicating that the total score and subscale scores are fairly stable over time. No data, however, were provided on test-retest reliability for younger children. Therefore, caution should be urged when using the MDI-C for measuring treatment efficacy in younger children.

VALIDITY. The authors borrowed test construction techniques from the MDI in developing the MDI-C. Items were generated by the authors to match scales roughly equivalent to the MDI. These were then rewritten with the assistance of children so that a younger audience could more easily understand them. A survey by the authors found that most children viewed the items as age appropriate and a Q-sort demonstrated that children participating were able to sort successfully the majority of items into their respective subscale piles. Other evidence of content validity comes from the MDI-C coverage of the *Diagnostic and Statistical Manual of Mental Disorders—Fourth Edition* (DSM-IV) (APA, 1994) criteria for major depressive episode. With depression in children and adolescents being similar to that in adults, except for some age-specific symptoms, the MDI-C items cover fully or partially eight of nine DSM-IV symptom categories. The MDI-C does not, however, assess the temporal dimensions of the mood problem, nor does it address exclusion criteria as recommended by the DSM-IV. In terms of criterion-related validity, the MDI-C total score has been shown to correlate .84 with the Children's Depression Inventory in a sample of children and adolescents from the Midwest and Southeast. It correlated .83 with the MDI total scores (subscale range from .12 to .82) in a sample of adolescents ages 13 to 18 years. The MDI-C total score was also found to correlate -.83 with the total score from the Piers-Harris Self-Concept Scale (subscale range from -.26 to -.83). The authors failed to assess any children within the normative sample with both the MDI-C and a clinical or structured interview, which is typically thought of as the "gold standard" for diagnostic purposes. They do cite item and scale development procedures along with convergent and discriminant validity for the MDI-C in support of construct validity. Their own factor-analytic studies found that "scales intercorrelated sufficiently to justify use of a single general dimension and were sufficiently different to justify a preliminary view of the scales as separate" (p. 31). Further analyses identified five factors consisting of demoralization, tension and stress, alienation, defiance, and an "uninterpretable" factor.

NORMS. The normative sample for the MDI-C consisted of 1,465 children between the ages of 8 and 17 years within grades 3 to 12 in Florida, Illinois, Michigan, Montana, Nebraska, North Carolina, South Carolina, and Washington. The authors note that a review of participating school demographics indicate that the relative proportion of Blacks and Native Americans to the general population is most likely high, whereas the number of Asians and Hispanics is low. No data, however, were specifically collected on the normative sample regarding this issue. Despite research suggesting that racial differences exist in the expression of depression in children (Politano, Nelson, Evans, Sorenson, & Zeman, 1986), no racial data are provided for the MDI-C within the manual.

SUMMARY. The MDI-C is a well-constructed self-report measure designed to assess depression and related features in children and adolescents. Administration and scoring of the MDI-C to children individually or in groups is quick and easy. Test-retest reliability and internal consistency reliability are solid for the total score and most subscale scores. Validity evidence appears strong in the limited studies that have been completed on the MDI-C to date. Interpretation will be made easier and more accurate as additional research data are generated on the MDI-C. Normative data for minority children and adolescents are sketchy at best, and thus, may limit the use of the MDI-C in these populations. In general, the MDI-C is a promising instrument for the assessment of depression in children and adolescents in both research and clinical settings. As additional validity data accumulates, the MDI-C is likely to develop into one of the best, if not the best, screening instrument available for this purpose. For diagnostic purposes, the MDI-C, as with any self-report measure, should only be used as part of a larger battery that includes a structured clinical interview (Fristad, Emery, & Beck, 1997).

REVIEWER'S REFERENCES

Politano, P. M., Nelson, W. M., Evans, H. E., Sorenson, S. B., & Zeman, D. J. (1986). Factor analytic evaluation of differences between Black and Caucasian emotionally disturbed children on the Children's Depression Inventory. *Journal of Psychopathology and Behavioral Assessment, 8,* 1–7.
American Psychiatric Association. (1994). *Diagnostic and statistical manual of mental disorders* (4th ed., rev.). Washington, DC: Author.
Fristad, M. A., Emery, B. L., & Beck, S. J. (1997). Use and abuse of the Children's Depression Inventory. *Journal of Consulting and Clinical Psychology, 65,* 699–702.

[53]
NEPSY: A Developmental Neuropsychological Assessment.

Purpose: "Designed to assess neuropsychological development.:

Population: Ages 3–12.

Publication Date: 1998.

Acronym: NEPSY.

Scores, 32: Attention/Executive (Tower, Auditory Attention and Response Set, Visual Attention, Statue, Design Fluency, Knock and Tap, Total), Language (Body Part Naming, Phonological Processing, Speeded Naming, Comprehension of Instructions, Repetition of Nonsense Words, Verbal Fluency, Oromotor Sequences, Total), Sensorimotor (Fingertip Tapping, Imitating Hand Positions, Visuomotor Precision, Manual Motor Sequences, Finger Discrimination, Total), Visuospatial (Design Copying, Arrows, Block Construction, Route Finding, Total), Memory and Learning (Memory for Faces, Memory for Names, Narrative Memory, Sentence Repetition, List Learning, Total).

Administration: Individual.

Forms, 2: Ages 3–4, Ages 5–12.

Price Data, 1999: $499 per complete kit including manual (464 pages), 10 record forms for both Ages 3–4 version and Ages 5–12 version, 10 response booklets for both Ages 3–4 version and Ages 5–12 version, scoring templates and manipulables packaged in a bright nylon bag; $21 per 25 Ages 3–4 response booklets; $26.50 per 25 Ages 5–12 response booklets; $23.50 per 25 Ages 3–4 record forms; $29 per 25 Ages 5–12 record forms; $79 per manual; $93.50 per stimulus booklet; $79 per tower (with 3 balls).

Time: (45–60) minutes for preschool-aged children; (65–120) minutes for school-aged children.

Comments: Also includes optional qualitative behavioral observations and supplemental scores.

Authors: Marit Korkman, Ursula Kirk, and Sally Kemp.

Publisher: The Psychological Corporation.

Review of the NEPSY: A Developmental Neuropsychological Assessment by SANDRA D. HAYNES, Assistant Professor, Department of Human Services, The Metropolitan State College of Denver, Denver, CO:

The shortened title, NEPSY, could easily leave one wondering about the purpose of this test instrument. Even knowledge of the acronym's origin, however, provides scanty information regarding the purpose of the test. NEPSY is an acronym taken from the word neuropsychology, with NE representing neuro and PSY representing psychology. After reviewing or using NEPSY, however, the aim of the test is unmistakable.

NEPSY, as the extended title suggests, was designed to assess neuropsychological development in children ages 3–12, with separate forms for children ages 3–4 and 5–12. The development of a measure specifically for children is a distinction among comprehensive neuropsychological tests that have historically been designed to assess neurological function in adults and then modified for use with children (e.g., the Halstead-Reitan Neuropsychological Test Battery, T5:1164).

The NEPSY was developed for four interrelated purposes. The first purpose is to detect subtle deficiencies that might interfere with a child's learning. Secondly, the NEPSY can be used to detect and clarify the degree to which brain damage or dysfunction affects the capacity to process information in a particular area of neuropsychological functioning or functional domain, such as language. In addition, the NEPSY can be used to determine how this impairment may impact or be impacted by the child's operating capacity in other functional domains. The third purpose is to provide for long-term follow-up of a patient to determine how functioning changes over time and with development. Finally, the NEPSY was designed "to create a reliable and valid instrument for the study of normal and atypical neuropsychological development in preschool and school-age children" (manual, p. 3). Two of these purposes are particularly noteworthy. First, the comparison between functional domains is in line with Luria's theory that emphasizes the interrelatedness of brain operations. This feature of the NEPSY allows the clinician to design more complete treatment plans with attention to all areas that may need remediation. Secondly, attention to continued research into normal and abnormal neuropsychological development is an important contribution of the NEPSY.

The NEPSY assesses the development of five neuropsychological domains: Attention/Executive Functions, Language, Sensorimotor Functions, Visuospatial Processing, and Memory and Learning. Thus the NEPSY focuses on assessment of impairment in the major categories of neuropsychological functioning. Further, functioning in each domain is measured using a graduated series of subtests with six in the Attention/Executive Functions domain, seven in the Language domain, five in the Sensorimotor Functions domain, four in the Visuospatial Processing do-

main, and five in the Memory and Learning domain for a total of 27 subtests. In addition to a score for each individual subtest, each domain yields a total score for an overall total of 32 scores. Supplemental scores for many subtests can also be calculated in the Attention/Executive Function, Language, Sensorimotor Function, and Memory and Learning domains. Such scores provide additional useful information regarding neuropsychological functioning such as time to completion, response set, immediate and delayed memory, and free versus cued recall. Subtest scores are based on sound neuropsychological theory (especially Luria). Raw scores are converted into scaled scores based on age or, as in the case of some of the Expanded Range subtests, into percentile ranks. The test manual provides information for forming confidence intervals for each score and a place for listing this information is found on the profile sheet. Such flexibility in score representation and attention to reporting confidence intervals is a strength of this test.

Not all subtests are administered in all cases. Tests to be given depend on the child's age, referral question, needs of the child, time constraints, and setting. Subtests within each domain are divided into core subtests and expanded subtests. Core subtests represent a sample of performance from each domain and were chosen based on the psychometric qualities of the test as well as "clinical considerations." Expanded subtests provide additional information regarding functioning within each of the domains. The test authors recommend administering all core subtests for all individuals to obtain a good overview of function in all five domains. When only core subtests are used the assessment is referred to as a Core assessment. The authors identify three other types of assessment: Expanded, Selective, and Full. Expanded assessment involves the administration of all core subtests and administration of expanded subtests only within a domain in which there has been a previously identified problem. Selective assessment involves the administration of expanded subtests in different domains that may help to explain difficulties noted during administration of NEPSY core subtests. The authors recommend that expanded subtests be selected not only from domains in which the child demonstrated difficulty but also from domains that may be related to the apparent impairment. Thus, selection of expanded subtests should be based on theory and research findings. In this way, further information can be gathered regarding what deficiencies underlie the difficulties noted. Again, flexibility is a plus for this test as is use of multiple-domain assessment. Clinicians are able to measure relative strengths and weaknesses of each child within and across different functional domains. Knowledge of the interrelatedness of strengths and weaknesses can be used to develop the best treatment/education plan. Additionally, the profile approach can provide the clinician with invaluable information that can be easily communicated to others involved in the child's treatment. At first glance, the existence of 27 subtests appears time-consuming. In actuality the test requires only 45 minutes to 2 hours to administer, another strength of this test especially given that it is designed for children.

Although having a number of representative subtests is a strength, it is also the primary difficulty with NEPSY. One must be highly familiar with all subtests to do an efficient administration including knowing where to start within the subtest, when to return to the beginning, and when to stop subtest administration. Given 27 subtests, this can be quite a task. Practice is also necessary as appropriate use of props, hand positions, and written materials is required.

The NEPSY was originally developed and used in Finland (1980 & 1988). After proving successful in that country, the authors set to revising the instrument for use in the United States (1998). Revisions take into account the multicultural nature of the United States population; diversity in geographic, socioeconomic, urban, suburban, and rural living situations; and age at which children begin formal education. Normative data for the U.S. version of the NEPSY were developed using an adequate sample with regard to size and heterogeneity of subjects.

Perhaps the greatest strength of the NEPSY is the comprehensive evaluation of reliability and validity that produced consistently laudable results. Internal consistency was measured via split-half or test-retest reliability measures depending on the nature of the subtest. The average length of time between test administration for test-retest measures was 38 days. The results indicate that scores from most of the NEPSY subtests have moderate to high stability. Scores from tests requiring some degree of subjective scoring (e.g., design copying) were evaluated using interrater reliability and found to have a high degree of reliability.

Criterion-related validity was assessed in a number of published clinical studies using subtests from the 1988 Finnish version of the NEPSY. Most of the subtests in the current NEPSY had a high degree of correspondence to the Finnish version. Additionally more validity studies comparing various clinical groups to matched controls (on the current version) are provided in the NEPSY manual. Content validity was assessed via literature searches, and review by a panel of experts that included pediatric neuropsychologists and school psychologist from around the United States. Finally, construct validity was assessed by comparing the NEPSY to several other tests measuring similar content, including the Wechsler Intelligence Scale for Children, Third Edition and its subscales, the Wechsler Preschool and Primary Scale of Intelligence, Bayley Scales of Infant Development, Second Edition, the Wechsler Individual Achievement Test, the Benton Neuropsychological Tests, and several single neuropsychological tests. The results suggest that the NEPSY exhibits evidence for convergent and discriminant validity.

Perhaps a minor flaw but nonetheless a vexatious aspect of the NEPSY is the set-up of the manual and protocol forms. A great deal of complicated information is put into a paperback manual with no index, making access to information laborious and reading instructions during test administration unwieldy. Additionally, both the manual and protocol forms have poor figure-ground configuration. More attention paid to these details would make administration and scoring a much easier task.

SUMMARY. Overall, the NEPSY appears to be a strong developmental neuropsychological instrument based on sound theory and research that should prove a valuable assessment instrument in the field.

Review of the NEPSY: A Developmental Neuropsychological Assessment by DANIEL C. MILLER, Associate Professor of Psychology, Texas Woman's University, Denton, TX:

In the past, neuropsychological assessment with children has been principally restricted to downward extensions of tests initially designed for adults. The NEPSY has shattered that mold in an elegant fashion. The NEPSY is a comprehensive instrument designed to assess neuropsychological development in preschool and school age children. The authors point out that the NEPSY is unique as compared to other neuropsychological tests because: It is specifically designed for children ages 3–12, the subtests were standardized on a single sample of children, and the test was administered concurrently with other validity measures. The NEPSY was developed with four purposes in mind: (a) a psychometrically sound instrument sensitive to subtle neuropsychological deficits; (b) an instrument that helps evaluate "the effects of brain damage in young children"; (c) an instrument that could be used for "long-term follow-up"; and (d) an instrument for "the study of normal and atypical neuropsychological development in preschool and school-age children" (manual, pp. 2–3).

The NEPSY has a strong theoretical foundation in the Lurian perspective that is reflected in the assessment of a child's neuropsychological status across five functional domains, and in both quantitative and qualitative scoring. The five functional domains include: (a) Attention/Executive Functions, (b) Language, (c) Sensorimotor Functions, (d) Visuospatial Processing, and (e) Memory and Learning. The test consists of 27 subtests used in various combinations based upon the needs of the child and the assessment goals of the examiner. There is a suggested set of Core subtests for children ages 3–4 and 5–12, and a suggested set of Expanded subtests for the same age ranges. The administration times vary from 45–120 minutes based on the number of subtests administered and the age of the child.

The NEPSY comes with an administration, scoring, and interpretation manual, a stimulus booklet, and several manipulatives, all within a carrying case. The NEPSY manual is well organized with an easy-to-use guide indicating what materials are to be used with each subtest. The record forms are also easy to use and conceptually well designed, with discontinuation rules and time guidelines clearly printed. The NEPSY manual provides a variety of scores used in the quantification of a child's neuropsychological status, including standard scores, scaled scores, and percentile ranks. Most subtests also include supplemental scores that allow for intrasubtest pattern analysis of performance strengths and weaknesses. Finally, the qualitative behaviors observed during testing may be compared to the frequency of occurrence within the standardization sample.

From a neurocognitive interpretative perspective, the most useful features of the NEPSY are the different levels of scoring and interpretation, particularly the supplemental scores and qualitative analyses. It may be too easy for some users to report only the standard scores for the Core domains and perhaps the scaled scores of the subtests, without interpreting the pattern of the child's strengths and weaknesses and qualitative behaviors. Potential users of the NEPSY should seek out training specific to the test administration and interpretation, and have some graduate-level training in brain-behavior relationships.

Most NEPSY subtests are easy to administer and score; however, a few of the subtests such as Tower and Auditory Attention and Response Set require practice before actual administration. Currently, the NEPSY must be hand-scored; however, it is hoped that user demand will encourage the publisher to release a computer-scoring program in the future. [Editor's Note: The publisher has advised in October 1999 that a computer-scoring program was recently released.] The NEPSY manual that accompanies the test kit is excellent, with chapters on the theoretical foundations and history, development and standardization, testing and scoring considerations, subtest administration, psychometric and statistical properties, and interpretation. The appendices of the manual include several useful forms including a Comprehensive Clinical History form, a Handedness Inventory, and an Orientation (a mini mental status exam) interview form. The Handedness Inventory and the Orientation Form have helpful norm tables that compare to the frequencies of the standardization sample.

The NEPSY standardization sample was derived from an adequate, stratified random group of children based on 1995 U.S. Census data. The Core Domain Scores exhibit moderately high internal consistency scores ranging from .69 to .91 and moderate stability coefficients ranging from .67 to .76 across the five domains for the average 5–12 age groups. The authors reported that there is a practice effect evident on the test-retest administrations of the NEPSY, particularly in subtests that measure memory or learning. Actually, there is a fairly strong practice effect across all domains, which increases with age, thus lowering the stability coefficients as age increases.

The NEPSY manual includes an excellent chapter on the validity evidence for the test. The content validity was reviewed twice for possible item biases and face validity by a panel of experts. The patterns of the correlations among the Domain subtests provide good support for the construct validity of the NEPSY, particularly within the Language Domain. Ample evidence for the convergent and divergent validity of the NEPSY's scores is provided in the manual based on correlational studies with the test compared to general measures of cognitive abilities, tests and indicators of achievement, and specific tests of neuropsychological functions. The Validity chapter of the manual also reports on several studies of the NEPSY used with several clinical groups including Attention-Deficit/Hyperactivity Disorder, ADHD with a Learning Disability, Reading Disabled, Language Disorders, Pervasive Developmental Disorders—Autistic Disorder, Fetal Alcohol Syndrome, Traumatic Brain Injury, and Hearing Impaired. Norms for each clinical group along with matched control sample norms and areas of clinical significance are presented in the manual. Future research needs to better control for clinical group membership and examine potential within-group or subtype differences. For example, the clinical group composed of ADHD with a Learning Disability is too broad given the subtypes of ADHD and LD.

SUMMARY. The NEPSY is a welcome addition to the fields of child clinical neuropsychology and school psychology. The test is rooted in strong theory and prior years of clinical research and is relatively easy to administer and score. Interpretation of scores from the NEPSY will be the challenge to some users. It is recommended that potential users of the test seek out training in the test's administration and score interpretation. Given the good psychometric properties of the NEPSY, the test is ideally suited for research into the neurodevelopmental functioning of school-age children who may have a wide variety of acquired and congenital brain impairments. The clinical validity studies reported in the manual are a good first step in understanding the clinical utility of the test.

Opinions About Deaf People Scale.

Purpose: To measure hearing adults' beliefs about the capabilities of deaf adults.
Population: Adults.
Publication Date: Undated.
Scores: Total score only.
Administration: Group.
Price Data, 1995: $11.50 per development and validation manual (127 pages); $1 per administration guide including reproducible copy of the scale; $5 per disk of both.
Time: Administration time not reported.
Authors: Paul James Berkay, J. Emmett Gardener, and Patricia L. Smith.
Publisher: National Clearinghouse of Rehabilitation Training Materials.

Review of Opinions About Deaf People Scale by JEFFERY P. BRADEN, Professor, School Psychology Program, Department of Educational Psychology, University of Wisconsin-Madison, Madison, WI:

TEST COVERAGE AND USE. The Opinions about Deaf People Scale (ODPS) is a 20-item, Likert-scale instrument intended to measure the opinions people hold regarding persons who are deaf. [Reviewer's Note: In keeping with the authors of the scale, and the customs of the Deaf community in North America, I will use "deaf people" instead of "people who are deaf" throughout the rest of this review.] The suggested uses of the instrument include measuring (and targeting for change) negative attitudes to improve relationships among deaf and hearing employees, and measuring how parental attitudes towards deaf people affects the performance of their deaf children in scholastic tasks.

SCALE DEVELOPMENT. The ODPS was developed in a three-step process: (a) specification of the domain to be sampled, (b) development and trial of a 35-item pilot version on a small ($N = 35$) group of undergraduate students; and (c) a second administration to a larger ($N = 299$) group of students. The authors (Berkay et al.) meticulously describe the decisions made in the domain specification, item generation, item selection, and final scale format and content stages of scale development (see also Berkay, Gardner, & Smith, 1995).

RELIABILITY. The reliability of scores from the ODPS was estimated via internal item consistency. Two versions of the ODPS are described in the manual: a preliminary version of 35 items, and a final version of 20 items. The reliability indices for the preliminary version were good to excellent (a = .90; split-half r = .86). The reliability estimates of the final 20-item version were good (*alpha* = .83; split-half r = .82). No stability (test-retest correlations) are reported, nor are parallel forms or other measures of reliability included in the manual.

VALIDITY. The validity of scores from the ODPS was investigated in two ways. First, Berkay et al. define the domain of attitudes towards deafness using a content/item mapping strategy. That is, they identified the types of attitudes (especially negative stereotypes) that individuals might have about deaf people in a number of domains (e.g., the intelligence of deaf people, their work skills, their academic abilities). They then explained how the ODPS sampled from these domains. This procedure culminated in appropriate item sampling of the identified domains, and reflected the relative weights that Berkay et al. assigned to these domains. Furthermore, items were constructed to be scored positively or negatively to balance response set tendencies across content domains.

The second method for validating scores from the ODPS was to correlate it with the Attitudes to Deafness (AD) Scale (Cowen, Rockway, Bobrove, & Stevenson, 1967). The AD scale also purports to measure attitudes about deafness. Berkay et al. do not explain why a second scale to measure attitudes about deafness is needed, although they refer to the dated content and norms of the AD scale. The correlation between the ODPS and the AD scale was high (r = .75), suggesting convergence between the two scales.

Unfortunately, Berkay et al. did not study the validity of the scores from the ODPS for either of its stated purposes. That is, Berkay et al. do not provide evidence regarding how the ODPS might identify negative attitudes in the workplace, evaluate the efficacy of programs intended to change attitudes, or how the ODPS might be used in research to link attitudes to other psychologically relevant constructs. Although Berkay et al. suggest the ODPS has treatment utility for changing attitudes among employees (that is, the instrument would point to treatments that would alter or improve the attitudes people may hold about deaf people), they do not provide evidence to

support this use. Likewise, they do not demonstrate its use in measuring parental attitudes towards their deaf children, nor the link between those attitudes and the academic achievement of deaf children.

DISCUSSION. The ODPS appears to sample attitudes (hearing) people have toward deaf people. The items appear to have appropriate content validity, and the item/domain mapping employed in the development of the scale is exceptionally clear and rigorous. The instrument also demonstrates good internal consistency. A third virtue of this instrument is its cost—Berkay et al. clearly want to make this instrument available to people without regard to fiscal remuneration. It is inexpensive to order, and is available in the public domain (Berkay, Gardner, & Smith, 1994). I wish other test developers shared Berkay et al.'s scholarly values on this point.

The ODPS has some significant shortcomings. The definition of the domain sampled (that is, which domains one should sample in assessing people's attitudes toward deaf people) is arbitrary. I do not fault Berkay et al.'s choice of domains, but I do not have a clear sense that they chose the best domains to sample. The scoring of some items also appears arbitrary. For example, agreement with the pilot item "Deaf people do not have levels of achievement commensurate with hearing people" was indicative of a negative attitude. However, objective data show that deaf people have high rates of functional illiteracy, and the median reading level for deaf individuals who *graduate* from high school is approximately a fourth grade level. Although this pilot item does not appear on the final version of the ODPS, it illustrates the problem of defining the domain of attitudes towards deaf people, and of separating negative stereotyping from accurate appraisal.

A second shortcoming of this instrument is its insufficient validation. Berkay et al. wisely avoid recommending score classifications (e.g., cutoffs to identify positive, neutral, or negative attitudes) from their college sample data. However, by failing to develop meaningful score standards, they undermine the use of the ODPS for its stated purpose. For example, how would employers know which ODPS scores reflect negative attitudes?

The other purpose of the ODPS (studying the relationship between parental attitudes and their deaf children's achievements) is unusually narrow. I suspect Berkay et al. intend the broader purpose of facilitating research on how opinions of deaf people influence behaviors and outcomes, but this purpose is not stated. Neither the narrow purpose, nor the broader application to research, is directly studied in the manual.

Given the current level of knowledge regarding the ODPS, its most appropriate use would be further research on the instrument itself. Item content suggests that it samples people's attitudes toward deaf adults, the reliability indexes suggest it does so with reasonable accuracy, and it has some construct validity support. There is no evidence in the manual to support the clinical/applied use of the ODPS, although the ODPS offers a promising (and inexpensive) platform for facilitating research.

REVIEWER'S REFERENCES

Cowen, E. L., Rockway, A. M., Bobrove, P. H., & Stevenson, J. (1967). Development and evaluation of an attitudes to deafness scale. *Journal of Personality and Social Psychology, 6*(2), 183–191.

Berkay, P. J., Gardner, J. E., & Smith, P. L. (1994, April). *Administration guide for the Opinion about Deaf People Scale: A Scale to Measure Hearing Adults' Beliefs about the Capabilities of Deaf Adults* (ERIC Document No. ED372122). Paper presented at the Annual Meeting of the American Educational Research Association, New Orleans, LA.

Berkay, P. J., Gardner, J. E., & Smith, P. L. (1995). The development of the Opinions about Deaf People Scale: A Scale to Measure Hearing Adults' Beliefs about the Capabilities of Deaf Adults. *Educational and Psychological Measurement, 55*(1), 105–114.

Review of the Opinions About Deaf People Scale by VINCENT J. SAMAR, Associate Professor, and ILA PARASNIS, Associate Professor, Department of Applied Language and Cognition Research, National Technical Institute for the Deaf, Rochester Institute of Technology, Rochester, NY:

The Opinions About Deaf People Scale (OADP) is a 20-item scale designed to measure the beliefs of hearing adults about the capabilities of deaf adults. The authors' intention in developing this scale was to provide a research tool and was motivated by the "belief that one of the first steps in changing negative attitudes toward deaf people is to measure and determine the attitudes that need to be changed" (Development and Validation manual, p. i). As a contemporary research instrument, however, the scale suffers from construct validity problems as detailed below.

TEST FORMAT AND DESCRIPTION. The OADP scale is supplied with an administration guide and a separate unpublished booklet that exhaustively documents the development and validation efforts for scores from the scale. The final version of the OADP scale contains 20 scale items, each of which requires respondents to indicate their agreement with the item using a 4-point Likert scale. The four anchors are: *strongly disagree, mildly disagree, mildly agree,* and *strongly agree.* The absence of a neutral point was based on the assumption that there is generally no neutral attitude toward deaf people (Development and Validation manual, p. 18) and was intended to prevent respondents from avoiding comment on what might be uncomfortable subjects.

The items on the OADP scale fall into six major categories of attitudes toward deaf people. These categories are intelligence, ability to deal with traffic, job skills, ability to live independently, communication skills, and academic skills. The nature of the categories is based on the perceptions of deaf and hearing professionals and previous literature on the nature of common misconceptions about deaf people. The numbers of items in each category are proportional to the frequency with which deaf and hearing informants and literature sources identified specific misconceptions about deaf people in each category. There are an equal number of negatively and positively phrased items.

TEST COVERAGE AND USE. The OADP scale is intended for use with hearing adults. The scale items are designed to measure beliefs about a specific subset of the deaf population. The subset includes young to middle-aged deaf adults only. The OADP scale was explicitly not intended to measure beliefs about deaf children and senior citizens. The authors believe that there are certain distinct misconceptions held by hearing people regarding these latter groups of deaf people and that attempting to include them in the same scale would produce too general an instrument. Given the authors' explicitly stated belief and their careful consideration of the scope of use of their scale during its development, it is unfortunate that they chose to title the instrument as if it applied to all deaf people, rather than indicating directly in the title that the targeted population was only young and middle-aged deaf adults. Because there is no mention of this restriction in the administration guide itself, there is a real danger that the scale might be indiscriminately used in research and other data gathering settings that apply to deaf children or senior citizens.

A second difficulty with the scope of the OADP scale is the operational definition that the authors assumed of a deaf individual. They define a deaf individual as follows:

> A deaf individual is someone who cannot hear and/or distinguish speech sounds even with amplification. Although the primary mode of communication for most deaf adults in the United States is American Sign Language, many of them take advantage of their residual (remaining) hearing and use speech and lip-reading skills to some extent. There are also deaf oralists who communicate through lip reading and speech and do not use sign language. Deaf individuals should be differentiated from hard-of-hearing individuals who can hear and distinguish speech sounds with amplification and primarily communicate through speech and lipreading. (Development and Validation manual, p. 1)

It is good that the authors recognize that individuals with significant hearing losses comprise diverse language and cultural groups. However, their audiometric definition of the target population for their instrument is both overly restrictive and itself suffers from a serious misconception about deaf people. The deaf community in the United States certainly does not define itself audiometrically, that is, according to whether or not its members "can hear and/or distinguish speech sounds even with amplification." Many members of the deaf community have some degree of residual hearing useful for perceiving speech sounds.

Nor is it reasonable to believe that the intended respondents for this scale, namely hearing individuals as a group, use such a restrictive audiometric criterion to determine whether or not a person is deaf. In fact, the most visible emblem to a hearing person of an individual's deafness is a hearing aid, most likely indicating to the hearing person that some deaf people have usable hearing. Even the authors' definition above suggests this conclusion when they point out that many deaf adults take advantage of their residual hearing.

Finally, the relevance of the ability to "hear and/or distinguish speech sounds" to the classification of individuals as members of the deaf versus hard-of-hearing community is a topic of ongoing debate. Although subgroup membership tends to correlate somewhat with audiometric characteristics, it is not a foregone conclusion that speech perception skill or the total lack of it is a necessary criterion for membership in either of these subgroups. In fact, the total absence of hearing and speech discrimination is even more restrictive than the standard audiometric definition of deaf and hard-of-hearing individuals. In any case, there are no instructions to hearing respondents in the OADP scale administration guide that would direct them to restrict their opinions to an audiometrically deaf as opposed to a hard-of-hearing population as restrictively defined by the authors. Therefore, it is doubtful that the authors' scale selectively targets deaf individuals who "cannot hear and/or distinguish speech sounds even with amplification." In reality, the scope of the OADP scale is more likely to be individuals who are perceived by hearing people to be members of the larger deaf community, including, potentially, at least some audiometrically hard-of-hearing individuals and not including, potentially, some audiometrically deaf individuals. This is a much more diverse group with much more varied communication characteristics than the authors envision their scale to address.

APPROPRIATENESS OF SAMPLES FOR TEST VALIDATION AND NORMING. An initial 35-item version of the OADP scale was piloted on a sample of 38 hearing students from an upper-level teacher education program population. Based on the results of the pilot administration, the final 20-item OADP scale was normed on a sample of 290 undergraduate students whom the authors regard as representative of a typical upper-level undergraduate student population. However, the sampling was not random over the university, but rather was restricted to students in a particular general education course entitled "Sociology of Family." This resulted in a high proportion of students from the college of arts and sciences (53%) and relatively low proportions of students from other colleges (e.g., only 7% of the sample were students from the College of Engineering). Therefore, not only are the norms for the OADP scale based on a highly educated population, they also tend to underrepresent populations from several significant academic and professional sectors.

This sampling bias in the normative data is potentially very important. The authors' intention in developing this scale was to provide a research instrument to assess hearing people's attitudes toward deaf people as a prelude to designing effective methods to change the beliefs of hearing people toward deaf people. And, they explicitly state that they intend this instrument to be used in a variety of settings, including employment settings such as large corporations and with parent groups (Development and Validation manual, p. v). Presumably, future users of this instrument will be motivated to apply it in the settings that are most likely to engender negative attitudes toward deaf people. Undoubtedly, the attitudes of the target populations in these settings will be influenced by factors such as their level of education, the cultural history of their profession, their familiarity with deafness, and the social, communication, and functional demands of the setting. It seems unlikely that the population of students interested in the sociology of family can provide a suitable normative model for the sorts of real world employment settings where negative perspectives on deaf employees are likely to be harbored. Neither does it seem reasonable that this student population is an adequate model for the general population of hearing parents of deaf children, most of whom will be confronted rather suddenly with their child's deafness and its real implications for their child's education and development and for the social dynamics of their family. Therefore, extreme caution must be exercised in applying this scale to populations other than the unlikely one on which it was normed.

RELIABILITY. The documentation reports a coefficient alpha reliability estimate of .91 and a Guttman split-half reliability value of .92. These results suggest generally good internal consistency reliability for the instrument.

CONTENT AND CONSTRUCT VALIDITY. The content of the OADP scale is based on the perspective of a few deaf informants and previous researchers on the misconceptions that typify hearing people's attitudes toward deaf people. A reasonably good correlation ($r = 75$) with the widely used Attitudes to Deafness Scale (Cowen, Rockway, Bobrove, & Stevenson, 1967) suggests that the general construct assessed by the OADP scale is in line with the construct underlying that measure. However, the construct underlying the Attitudes to Deafness Scale was developed 30 years ago, when the general hearing society was not as informed about deafness and deaf people as it is today. Therefore, this correlation is not strong evidence for good construct validity for the OADP scale.

It is difficult to assess the actual construct validity of the OADP scale. Presumably, the intended construct for the OADP scale is the full spectrum of significant misconceptions about deaf people held by hearing people in today's society. However, it is questionable to what extent the OADP scale samples this domain fairly. The process of generating the prototype list of misconceptions for the OADP scale involved interviewing a group of "deaf professionals and deaf people" with a series of open-ended critical-incident questions. (Oddly, the OADP scale documentation refers to these informants as including hearing people working in the field of deafness.) This is a reasonable approach to identifying the universe of significant contemporary misconceptions that comprise the construct. However, there is no information given on the number of people interviewed, on their professional roles and experiences with deaf people, on their demographic characteristics, or on their cultural identities. Therefore, it is impossible to determine to what extent the sampling of misconceptions generated by this group is representative of the educated experiences of professionals working in deafness or of the deaf community itself.

The authors speculate, based on their literature review and informants' responses, that there are two subconstructs measured by the OADP items, namely attitudes toward the intelligence of deaf people and attitudes toward the skills of deaf people. Their factor analysis data intimate but do not clearly show differential factor loading patterns for the intelligence and skill items respectively. However, the scale only included two clear intelligence-related items, so it is difficult to assess the factor structure in this respect.

More importantly, it appears from the factor analyses on both the 35-item pilot version and the 20-item final version that the construct underlying hearing people's attitudes toward deaf people is intricate. These factor structures suggest that additional subconstructs determining hearing people's attitudes may include a dimension of perceived danger stemming from the inability to hear and a consequent concern for the safety of deaf people in specific situations, a dimension of concern regarding the existence of barriers to equal access in educational settings, a dimension of specific knowledge about the relationship between speech and intelligence, a dimension of knowledge about the nature of sign language, a dimension of general knowledge of deafness, and a dimension of conceptions about the roles and responsibilities of interpreters. If so, then further revisions of the OADP scale are in order to refine the item sampling of such constructs. In this sense, the construct validity of the OADP scale at this stage, even for the limited population on which it was normed, is incomplete in its sensitivity to the full range of attitude-relevant subconstructs that appear to influence the scale as it stands.

Furthermore, it is clear that the OADP scale falls short on at least two major dimensions of misconceptions held by hearing people, namely the communication and language abilities of deaf people and the cultural identities of deaf people. There is only one question related to sign language on the OADP scale, and that question only probes for the understanding that sign language is a fully developed human language like spoken languages. There are no items that would assess the respondent's understanding of the relationships among American Sign Language, signed English, and spoken English, the bilingual and bicultural status of deaf individuals in American society, the ability of deaf individuals to read and write and to communicate with hearing individuals in a variety of modes and a variety of settings, the existence of cross-cultural differences between deaf and hearing cultures, the existence of cultural diversity within the deaf population itself, and so on. Clearly, a research instrument intended to help change negative attitudes toward deaf people must expose the crucial underpinnings of those attitudes on the part of hearing people today. Historically, those underpinnings have proven to be misconceptions about language, thought, and culture. The OADP scale is inadequate in this respect. It does not assess attitudes regarding the major contemporary themes that educators and other professionals currently regard as central to the development, acceptance, and success of deaf people in society today.

Finally, it should be noted that attitudes toward deafness and deaf people held by hearing people (DeCaro, Dowaliby, & Maruggi, 1983; Parasnis, DeCaro, & Raman, 1996) and deaf people (Parasnis, Samar, & Mandke, 1996) vary from society to society. Hence, the construct represented by the OADP scale or its possible future revisions based on American respondents may not generalize to other countries.

TEST ADMINISTRATION. The administration of the OADP scale is relatively straightforward and should require about 5–10 minutes to complete. Care must be taken, however, in tallying the scores because both negative and positively stated items occur. This requires the user to reverse the numerical values assigned to half of the scale items. The authors have provided a scoring key to remind the user which items must be assigned which order of numerical values.

There is a troubling issue about the administration guide. The administration guide contains the following statement:

> This scale measures hearing adults' beliefs about the capabilities of deaf adults. It should be apparent that there is a discrepancy between the scale's title and its actual measure. There was some concern that if the intent of the scale was explicitly stated, subjects might respond in a socially desirable manner. That is why the scale's title is somewhat ambiguous. If this scale is used to conduct research, subjects should be debriefed and informed of the scale's true purpose following the collection of data. (p. 1)

We find this statement mysterious and uninterpretable. The nature of the supposed discrepancy between the title and the stated purpose of the scale is, in fact, not apparent. This statement, therefore, is likely to confuse scale administrators and possibly to create a significant source of variation in their instructions to respondents if they try to compensate for whatever they imagine the discrepancy to be. The authors should revise their instructions to eliminate this claim or to include a specific and clear statement of its meaning and implications for administration.

SUMMARY. The OADP scale is a very limited instrument. It was validated on a population that is not representative of the populations to which the scale would most likely be applied and it does not sample the range of attitudes toward deafness that is needed in a useful research instrument today. The contemporary attitudes of hearing people toward deaf people are determined by greater subtleties of misconception than in previous times due to changes in people's world knowledge and their exposure to specific information and misinformation about deafness and deaf people. The OADP scale fails to capture these subtleties. It might be useful, for example, for crude screening in organizational settings. However, it is inadequate for use in serious psychosocial or organizational research.

REVIEWERS' REFERENCES

Cowen, E. L., Bobrove, P. H., Rockway, A. M., & Stevenson, J. (1967). Development and evaluation of an attitudes to deafness scale. *Journal of Personality and Social Psychology, 6*(2), 183–191.

DeCaro, J. J., Dowaliby, F. J., & Maruggi, E. A. (1983). A cross-cultural examination of parents' and teachers' expectations for deaf youth regarding careers. *British Journal of Educational Psychology, 53*, 358–363.

Parasnis, I., DeCaro, J. J., & Raman, M. (1996). Attitudes of teachers and parents in India toward career choices for deaf and hearing people. *American Annals of the Deaf, 141*, 303–308.

Parasnis, I., Samar, V. J., & Mandke, K. (1996). Deaf adults' attitudes toward career choices for deaf and hearing people in India. *American Annals of the Deaf, 141*, 333–339.

[55]
Oral and Written Language Scales: Listening Comprehension and Oral Expression.

Purpose: Designed to assess "receptive and expressive ... language."

Population: Ages 3–21.

Publication Date: 1995.

Acronym: OWLS.

Scores, 3: Listening Comprehension, Oral Expression, Oral Composite.

Administration: Individual.

Price Data, 1999: $169.95 per complete kit including manual (212 pages), Listening Comprehension Easel, Oral Expression Easel, and 25 record forms; $24.95 per 25 record forms; $149.95 per AGS computer ASSIST™ for OWLS LC/OE (IBM or Macintosh).

Time: (15–40) minutes.

Author: Elizabeth Carrow-Woolfolk.

Publisher: American Guidance Service, Inc.

Review of the Oral and Written Language Scales: Listening Comprehension and Oral Expression by STEVE GRAHAM, Professor of Special Education, University of Maryland, College Park, MD:

The Oral and Written Language Scales (OWLS) contains three subtests: Listening Comprehension, Oral Expression, and Written Expression. Although the three subtests were developed and normed as part of the same assessment, the Written Expression subtest was packaged as a separate test (see 56) and is not reviewed here. The decision to package the Written Expression subtest separately was unfortunate, as it complicates comparing students' performance in these three areas.

The Listening Comprehension and Oral Expression subtests of the OWLS are administered individually to children and young adults, aged 3 to 21. Listening Comprehension is measured by asking the examinee to select one of four pictures that best depicts a statement (e.g., "In which picture is she not walking to school") made by the examiner. Oral expression is assessed by asking the examinee to look at one or more line drawings and respond verbally to a statement made by the examiner (e.g., "Tell me what is happening here and how the mother feels"). Contrary to the author's claim, these tasks are not typical of those found in the classroom, and like other language tests of this nature, concerns about the ecological validity of the instrument need to be addressed in the test manual.

An interesting feature of the Oral Expression subtest is that the examiner can conduct a descriptive analysis of correct and incorrect responses. For all but 30 of the 96 items on this subtest, correct responses can be categorized as preferred or acceptable responses, providing additional information on how well the examinee understood the oral expression task. In contrast, incorrect responses can further be classified as a miscue involving grammar or a miscue involving semantic and/or pragmatic aspects of language. Although the manual provides item-by-item scoring rules for making these decisions, no data are provided on the reliability of these scores.

A notable strength of the OWLS is that both the Listening Comprehension and Oral Expression subtests were constructed on the basis of a strong theoretical foundation. Items were constructed to measure important aspects of listening and oral language performance. The author's description of this process is incomplete, however, as no table was provided to indicate what each item supposedly measured nor was the expert review process adequately described.

Both subtests are easy to administer, requiring only about 15 to 40 minutes depending upon the age of the child. The establishment of the basal and ceiling for the Oral Expression subtest involves some uncertainty, as the scoring information provided on the record form may not be adequate for correctly scoring all items. More complete scoring information is provided in the test manual. A solution to this problem is to provide the needed information in the same place that instructions for administering each item are provided.

The authors are to be commended for providing clear and easy-to-follow directions for scoring as well as determining normative scores. More attention, however, should have been directed to establishing the cautions that examiners need to exercise in interpreting these scores. This is especially the case for test-age equivalents that can be derived for each subtest and a composite score for the whole test.

According to the author, the OWLS provides a broad measure of an individual's competence in listening comprehension and oral expression. It is also claimed that the instrument can be used to help in the identification of students with learning disabilities, predict academic success, and monitor progress over time. The support that the author provided for each of these claims was uneven. For example, seven studies demonstrated that students with special needs scored lower on the OWLS than children included in the standardization sample that were matched on age, gender, race/ethnicity, and SES. This included children with learning disabilities in reading, learning disabilities in general academic skills, speech impairments, language delays, language impairments, hearing difficulties, and mental handicaps. The findings from these studies provide strong support for using the OWLS to help in the identification of students with learning disabilities as well as other disabilities involving language and cognitive difficulties.

In contrast, little evidence was available to support the claim that the instrument can be used to monitor progress over time. The only evidence relevant to this claim was the means and standard deviations for the raw scores of each subtest for the standardization sample. The standard deviations for each age level were typically larger than the mean difference between ages, and differences between one age level and the next were relatively small after children reached the age of 9. Notably absent in the test manual were data showing that scores for the OWLS are responsive to the effects of instruction.

The claim that the instrument can be used to predict academic success was only partially substantiated by the information provided by the author. In several studies conducted in conjunction with standardization of the OWLS, children's performance on the instrument was related to their current academic performance and, as noted earlier, students with severe academic difficulties (e.g., learning disabilities) did not perform as well on the test as matched students in the standardization sample. Nevertheless, there was no statistically significant difference in the test scores of students with less severe academic difficulties and a matched sample of students participating in the standardization process. Even more importantly, studies examining the validity of using scores from the OWLS to predict future academic performance were conspicuously absent in the test manual.

Finally, there was relatively strong support for the author's primary claim that the instrument provides a valid measure of general listening and speaking skills. First, scores on the OWLS were moderately to highly correlated with scores on other measures of language development. Second, measures of achievement and cognitive development were also moderately to highly correlated with OWLS scores. Previous research has established that school learning is dependent on language ability and that there is a substantial relationship between the development of cognitive and language skills. Third, mean scores of students in the standardization sample increased from one age to the next. As expected, differentiation was greatest for young children and least for older students and young adults. Fourth, as noted earlier, students with language difficulties, such as a hearing or language impairment, obtained lower scores on the test than matched students in the standardization sample.

With the exception of the Listening Comprehension scale, the reliability of scores from the instrument was adequate. Correlations for test-retest reliability and internal consistency for the Oral Expression scale and the composite score for both scales were almost always above .80. For the Listening Comprehension subtest, however, measures of reliability were below .80 for children aged 6 to 9, suggesting that this particular scales appears to be best suited as a screening device at these ages.

Finally, the OWLS was standardized on 1,795 examinees at 74 sites nationwide. The author is to be commended for the care taken in conducting the standardization, and the resulting sample was reasonably representative of the population of children in the United States in 1991.

In summary, the OWLS provides reliable and valid scores for determining the language competence of individual children. The only exception involves the Listening Comprehension measure, which appears to be best suited as a screening device for children 6 to 9 years of age.

Review of the Oral and Written Language Scales: Listening Comprehension and Oral Expression by KORESSA KUTSICK MALCOLM, School Psychologist, Augusta County School Board, Fishersville, VA:

The development of the Oral and Written Language Scales (OWLS) represents a positive advancement in the realm of language assessment. The OWLS was created to provide a quick and comprehensive evaluation of expressive and receptive language functions. The author indicated that her test can be used to determine "broad levels of language skills as well as specific performance in the areas of listening, speaking, and writing" (p. 1). The OWLS addresses these areas in a fashion that taps into everyday language functioning more so than do other language tests. Because the Listening Comprehension and Oral Expression Scales are packaged separated from the Written Expression Scale, they will be reviewed together. A review of the Written Expression Scale will be presented on its own in this *MMY* (56).

The Listening Comprehension Scale taps the understanding of spoken language. This scale requires examinees to select one of four pictures that depicts the verbal information presented by the examiner. Three levels of language skills are assessed by the Listening Comprehension Scale. These three levels include lexical, syntactic, and supralinguistic skills. Administration time takes 5 to 15 minutes, depending on the age of the examinee.

The Oral Expression scale was developed to measure the understanding and use of spoken language. Examinees must respond to questions, complete a sentence, or generate one or more sentences, based on a presented verbal and pictorial stimuli. This scale takes 10 to 25 minutes to administer.

The items on both the Listening Comprehension and Oral Expression Scales are presented in ascending developmental order. Basal and ceiling rules are clearly presented. The ceiling rule of stopping after failing five out of seven items on the Listening Comprehension Scale and six out of seven on the Oral Expression scale is always cumbersome for examiners. Rationales presented in the manual for this procedure, however, provide

good reasoning for using this process to increase the reliability of the test while decreasing effects of fatigue on test performance.

The manual for the Listening Comprehension and Oral Expression Scales of the OWLS is very clear and informative. Administration and scoring procedures are presented in good detail. Administration of both scales is relatively easy. Scoring may present some challenge until examiners are familiar with necessary criteria. Many examples are provided that will help examiners work through the scoring of these scales.

Several positive administration and scoring procedures are present in the OWLS. Each scale provides ample items to help examinees understand presented directions. Teaching of these items is also possible when examinees do not grasp the direction. Another positive feature of this test is that the OWLS allows for an item analysis for examining the types of errors or patterns of language that the examinee tends to demonstrate. This analysis allows examiners to pinpoint specific functions of an examinee's language that need to be addressed in therapy.

Computer scoring and interpretation are available for both the Listening Comprehension and Oral Expression Scales. IBM and Windows versions of these programs are available. The usual normative scores as well as descriptive reports can be obtained from the use of the programs.

The most positive feature of the OWLS is its base in theoretical constructs related to the development of language processes. The manual highlights the essential theoretic positions utilized to formulate the purposes of the OWLS. A clear relationship was established between these positions and the applications and purposes of the OWLS scales.

Whereas previous tests of language development tend to focus only on the receptive or expressive components of language, and then only at the one-word level in many cases, the OWLS attempts to capture the pragmatic and supralinguistic (higher order thinking) structures of language. The test provides an opportunity to observe an examinee's ability to understand and produce connected language. Students with language processing difficulties often score well on more traditional measures of singular dimension language tests, yet have great difficulty using language to function in school or social settings. These students miss subtle nuances of language that cause communication difficulties in real life settings. The Listening Comprehension and Oral Expression Scales attempt to incorporate processes of language constructions not directly related to lexical or grammatical information. These scales attempt to tap the understanding of idioms, humor, exaggerations, and sarcasm used in conversational speech.

There are several positive test construction features of the Listening Comprehension and Oral Expression Scales of the OWLS. The author stated that items were written and reviewed by many experts in the fields of speech/language pathology, school psychology, and other related disciplines. Correct responses for the Oral Expression scale were not formulated a priori. Rather, responses from the standardization sample were reviewed to determine the language content and structures used by the examinees. Scoring criteria were then developed based on this sample of responses.

The standardization process of the Listening Comprehension and Oral Expression Scales was very appropriate. The sample size consisted of 1,795 subjects who ranged in age from 3 to 21 years. Subjects were grouped by 6-month age intervals for ages 3-0 to 4-11; 1-year intervals for ages 5-0 to 11-0; and then by ages 12–13, 14–15, 16–18, and 19–21. The total sample was representative of the U.S. population for gender, geographical region, race/ethnicity, and socioeconomic status as determined by maternal employment. Norms were established by age level. Mean scaled scores for both the Listening Comprehension and Oral Expression Scales were 100 with a standard deviation of 15. This makes comparisons with scores obtained on most of the major psychological and educational batteries easily done.

The OWLS Listening Comprehension and Oral Expression Scales can be administered to children and young adults ages 3 to 21 years. The upper age levels of this span are very positive features for this test. Many of the language tests only provide norms to the middle teen years. The band to age 21 allows examiners to assess language functions in older students and to trace the development of language competencies throughout their school careers.

The only apparent weakness of this test is its art work. Stimulus materials consist of black-and-white line drawings. Many of these drawings seem vague to the concepts to be tapped by the items. As the items increase in developmental difficulty, they become much more detailed and subtle in their differences. Students who do not attend well to visual detail, or who have short attention spans, may miss the cues and details presented in the materials that are used to prompt them for the appropriate language responses.

Statistical properties of the OWLS are good and reflect the trends in test development to provide this information before a test is marketed. Reliability studies conducted for the scales were not as extensive as the validity reports; however, they were adequate. Test-retest reliability for the short term (median of 8 weeks) by three different age groups was within the .58 to .85 range. One interrater reliability study evidenced good consistency in scoring with trained examiners for the Oral Expression Scale. Reliability coefficients ranged from .90 to .99.

Validity information presented in the manual was very impressive. Several studies were highlighted that compare results of the Listening Comprehension and Oral Expression Scales, by age levels, with commonly used measures of ability (Kaufman Assessment Battery for Children, Wechsler Intelligence Scales for Children—Third Edition, and the Kaufman Brief Intelligence Scale) other measures of language (Test for Auditory Comprehension of Language—Revised, Peabody Picture Vocabulary Test—Revised, and Clinical Evaluation of Language Fundamentals—Revised) and tests of academic achievement (Kaufman Test of Educational Achievement, Comprehensive Form, Peabody Individual Achievement Test—Revised, and Woodcock Reading Mastery Test—Revised). Correlations with other language tests were moderate to high, reflecting similarities between the tests. The use of the OWLS can be justified by the more extensive nature of the test and its age ranges. Correlations with IQ measures indicate strong positive relationships between the Listening Comprehension and Oral Expression Scales and various tests of verbal ability. Moderate correlations were obtained between these scales and the nonverbal sections of the IQ batteries. Moderate correlations were also obtained between the OWLS Scales and various measures of verbal achievement. Low correlations were obtained between these scales and measures of math achievement. The author offered these correlations as evidence of divergent validity, especially in areas where low correlations were obtained between the OWLS and various subtests of math achievement. Validity studies conducted with clinical populations (students with speech impairments, language delays, and language impairments) indicated the more involved the speech or language difficulty, the lower the scores on the OWLS. This would indicate that the test is able to identify students with difficulties in the language functions.

SUMMARY. The OWLS Listening Comprehension and Oral Expression Scales may prove to be one of the more popular and widely used language tests. The scales can be administered by school psychologists, speech pathologists, educational diagnosticians, and other professionals who need to assess language functions in students. Examiners may find that the OWLS provides information on language functions that are not tapped by other language tests they are currently using.

[56]
Oral and Written Language Scales: Written Expression.

Purpose: Constructed as an "assessment of written language."
Population: Ages 5–21.
Publication Date: 1996.
Acronym: OWLS Written Expression.
Scores, 2: Written Expression, Language Composite (when used with OWL Listening Comprehension and Oral Expression Scales).
Administration: Individual or group.
Price Data, 1999: $84.95 per complete kit including manual (255 pages), response booklets, record forms, and administration card; $23.95 per 25 response booklets; $19.95 per 25 record forms; $62.95 per manual; $149.95 per AGS Computer ASSIST™ for OWLS Written Expression (IBM or Macintosh).
Time: (15–25) minutes.
Comments: May be used alone or in combination with OWLS Listening Comprehension and Oral Expression (55).
Author: Elizabeth Carrow-Woolfolk.
Publisher: American Guidance Service, Inc.

Review of the Oral and Written Language Scales: Written Expression by DALE CARPENTER, Professor of Special Education, Western Carolina University, Cullowhee, NC:

DESCRIPTION. The Oral and Written Language Scales: Written Expression (OWLS Written Expression) is intended to assess three aspects of written expression—Conventions, Linguistics, and Content. It may also be used as part of three scales comprising Oral and Written Language Scales, the other two being Listening Comprehension and Oral Expression (55). Although these three scales were conormed, they may be used individually and provide useful independent data.

OWLS Written Expression contains 39 items grouped in four overlapping sets for children ages 5 to 7, 8 to 11, 12 to 14, and youth 15 to 21. There are no basals and ceilings as all the items in a set are administered depending on the child's age. The following tasks are included: (a) Students write dictated sentences; (b) students write questions or notes, or interpret information from a table; (c) students complete stories; (d) students retell stories; (e) students use brief descriptive writing such as interpreting a quote or describing a cartoon character; (f) students use expository writing to convey information. All of the items are relatively short and, with rare exception, students receive a score of 1 or 0 for a point on an item. Some items are scored for only one point such as spelling whereas others are scored for as many as 7 or more points including such domains as meaningful content, details, and supporting ideas.

OWLS Written Expression is designed to be administered individually but may be administered to small groups. Administration requires a response booklet, record form, and a laminated Written Expression Scale administration card. All are well designed for clarity and ease of use. The manual may be used in lieu of the administration card and is necessary for scoring.

Scoring is complex and examiners must carefully read and understand the overall scoring scheme as well as follow instructions for each item. The manual provides clear, detailed instructions and examples of correct and incorrect answers for each item. Age- and grade-based standard scores are available as well as percentiles, normal curve equivalents (NCEs), stanines, and age and grade equivalents. OWLS comes with software for Macintosh and Windows formats to assist with finding and reporting derived scores. If the Listening Comprehension and Oral Expression scales are used, a Language Composite standard score is also available. In addition, the manual provides a reproducible Descriptive Analysis Worksheet for each of the four sets of items. This allows the examiner to conduct error analysis in each of the three major areas of Conventions, Linguistics, and Content.

NORM SAMPLE. OWLS Written Expression was administered individually to a national sample of 1,373 subjects. The norm sample appropriately reflects characteristics of the population in age, gender, race, region, and socioeconomic status (determined by mother's education level).

RELIABILITY. Split-half, test-retest, and interrater reliability coefficients are provided. For all but 19-to-21-year old subjects, split-half reliability coefficients are .84 or higher. Test-retest reliability was studied with a median 9-week interval between test administrations using a group of 54 students between the ages of 8 and 11 and a group of 30 students ages 16-0 to 18-11. Coefficients were .88 and .87. Because of the subjective nature of much of the scoring, interrater reliability is critical. Interrater reliability was estimated using 15 subjects in each of the four age classes of students and the mean interrater reliability coefficient was .95.

VALIDITY. The author presents information about content, construct, criterion-related, and clinical validity. Content validity rests on the author's construction of a model of language and adherence in item generation to that model. No other information is provided.

The evidence for construct validity is presented as intercorrelations among the three OWLS scales. By age, the mean correlation coefficients of the Written Expression scale is .57 with Listening Comprehension and .66 with Oral Expression. One would expect a stronger relationship between Written Expression and Oral Expression than between Written Expression and Listening Comprehension.

Scores on the OWLS Written Expression were correlated with scores on the following achievement instruments in separate studies: Kaufman Test of Educational Achievement (KTEA), Peabody Individual Achievement Test—Revised (PIAT-R), and Woodcock Reading Mastery Test—Revised (WRMT-R). Most of the correlation coefficients exceed .80 for subtests of reading and spelling with OWLS Written Expression. Unfortunately, there are no criterion-related studies reported in the manual showing the relationship of scores on the OWLS Written

Expression and other achievement measures of written expression such as the Test of Written Language-3 (TOWL-3; T5:2731).

Separate groups of students with language impairments, mental retardation, hearing impairments, and learning disabilities were studied with significant results upholding the clinical validity premise that these groups do score systematically lower than peer groups on the OWLS Written Expression.

SUMMARY. OWLS Written Expression provides educational diagnosticians and researchers with a reliable and valid measure of written expression for a wide range of ages of students. Using the Written Expression scale in conjunction with Listening Comprehension and Oral Expression is an advantage over some other instruments because a Language Composite is available. Although the instrument is relatively easy to administer, scoring takes more time initially, but instructions are relatively clear given the subjective components of the instrument. Accompanying software aids in scoring and reporting.

OWLS Written Expression is a good assessment instrument. In the area of written language the instrument uses many frequently used means of measuring achievement and some formats that are less common. Common formats include writing sentences from dictation, combining sentences, and finishing stories. Less common formats include creating a cartoon character and writing a note to your mother. OWLS Written Expression does not require the subject to produce an extended writing sample like some other instruments such as the TOWL-3. Except for the lack of this feature used by some other written expression instruments, OWLS Written Expression appears to adequately measure important aspects of writing achievement.

Review of the Oral and Written Language Scales: Written Expression by KORESSA KUTSICK MALCOLM, School Psychologist, Augusta County School Board, Fishersville, VA:

It has been difficult to find a test of written language that taps into a broad array of writing skills, that measures the mechanics of writing as well as the creative process of written expression, that can be administered quickly and easily, and that carries good psychometric properties. The Written Expression Scale of the Oral and Written

Language Scales is a test that might address these assessment needs.

The Oral and Written Language Scales are composed of three separate scales: Listening Comprehension (55), Oral Expression (55), and Written Expression. The author advocates the administration of all three scales as part of a comprehensive assessment of language functioning; however, each scale may be administered independent of the other scales.

The Written Expression Scale of the OWLS was designed as a standardized test that measures an examinee's functional writing skills. Three major parts of the writing process are measured by this scale. These parts consist of: Conventions, measuring the applications of spelling, punctuation, and capitalization rules; Linguistics, measuring the use of language forms such as modifiers, phrases, verb forms, and complex sentences; and Content, measuring appropriate subject matter, coherence in writing, word choices, etc. Evaluation tasks of the Written Expression Scale require subjects to respond to a variety of open-ended writing tasks presented verbally by the examiner. Some tasks have accompanying pictures or printed materials. The writing tasks of this scale were designed to reflect typical writing assignments a student might encounter in a classroom setting. Writing activities include transcribing dictated sentences, writing notes or letters, retelling a story, completing a story, producing descriptive writing, and producing brief expository writing.

Administration of the Written Expression Scale takes 10 to 30 minutes depending on the age and skill levels of an examinee. Each examinee is presented a band of age-appropriate items. Items are arranged in ascending developmental order. This arrangement of items and levels allows for a good sampling of writing skills, while minimizing the effects of fatigue and frustration. Out-of-level testing is permitted to better assess the writing skills of lower functioning individuals or to tap into the upper limits of a bright student's writing skill range. The Written Expression Scale may be administered to examinees aged 5 to 21 years.

The Written Expression Scale may be given to individual or small groups of students. The ability to administer the scale to small groups of students may be of great value to special education teachers, school psychologists, and other professionals who must assess the writing skills of a large number of students each year. If group administration is used, examiners should limit the group size according to the age of the examinees. For example, three to five children would be the optimal group size for younger children as they might need more attention during the writing activities. As many as 10–15 students might comprise an assessment group of older students who are more independent in their writing habits.

Administration of the Written Expression Scale is straightforward. The manual is very clear in its presentation of the administration procedures of this test. The only materials needed for the administration process are a record booklet and an item card that contains the specific instructions for the test.

Scoring of the Written Expression Scale might prove to be somewhat of a challenge. Multiple scoring criteria are presented for each item. Practice will be necessary for examiners to master the specifics of the scoring rules. Scoring time can take as long as 17 minutes for the more advanced writing levels. The manual does provide good examples and explanations of scoring options for each item.

There are several positive features of the Written Expression Scale of the OWLS. Like the Listening Comprehension and Oral Expression Scales of this test, the Written Expression Scale is based on a strong theoretical foundation of language development and processes. All three scales were conormed, which allows for comparisons to be made between the different processes of language functioning. The range of obtainable standard scores for all three of the scales is another positive feature of the OWLS. Standard scores from 40 to 160 may be obtained. Few of the available writing tests on the market today provide this wide a range of standard scores. For example, on some assessments a score of 78 is the lowest standard score that can be obtained for some examinees. This level of score does not allow examiners to demonstrate point differences between ability and achievement that are often needed to document specific learning disabilities. With its lower range of standard scores, the Written Expression Scale of the OWLS may become the test of choice for many examiners charged with the task of defining significant weaknesses in a client's writing skills. A related positive feature of the Written Expression Scale of the OWLS is that it provides a Descriptive Analysis Sheet that allows examiners to chart items that examinees have passed or failed. Completion of the sheet provides a diagnostic view of particular writing strengths and weaknesses demonstrated by an examinee that can be translated into remedial activities.

No test is perfect and the Written Expression Scales does have a few weaknesses. The oral directions presented to examinees might be too complex. This may be especially true for those individuals who do have language processing difficulties. Even though readability estimates were presented for the directions read to the examinee, lower functioning individuals may have trouble understanding what is being asked of them.

The Written Expression Scale of the OWLS was standardized on 1,373 subjects ages 5 to 21 years. The standardization sample was representative of U.S. Census data for gender, geographic region, socioeconomic status (by mother's education level), and race/ethnicity.

The statistical properties of the test are good. Strong positive correlations were reported in the various reliability studies presented in the manual. Internal split-half correlations ranged from .77 to .94. The standard error of measurement of 5.5 points also gave support to the reliability of the scale. Test-retest studies with intervals from 18 to 165 days yielded correlations of .88 for younger subjects and .87 for older subjects. Interrater reliability correlations ranged from .91 to .98 depending on the level of items reviewed.

The author of the Written Expression Scale also provided good information on the validity of this scale. Content and construct validity support was offered through the descriptions of the development process of the scale. Construct validity evidence using interscale correlations ranged from .30 to .75 when the three scales of the OWLS were compared to each other. The Written Expression Scale tended to correlate higher with the Oral Expression Scale than with the Listening Comprehension Scale. The explanation for this was that both the Written Expression and Oral Expression Scales tapped into forms of language expression, whereas the Listening Comprehension Scale measured receptive language functioning. Comparisons of scores obtained by subjects on other language-based tests with results of the Written Expression Scale yielded similar results.

The Written Expression Scale tended to correlate more positively with tests of expressive language than it did with tests of receptive language.

Criterion-related validity was investigated by comparing scores from the Written Expression Scale with those obtained by subjects on various measures of achievement (the Peabody Individual Achievement Test—Revised, Kaufman Test of Educational Achievement, Woodcock-Reading Master Test—Revised). Strong positive correlations ranging from .63 —.88 were obtained. This is somewhat unusual for a test of written language, and may lend positive support for the inclusion of this scale in a battery of educational tests. Moderate to strong positive correlations (.41–.72) were also obtained between the Written Expression Scaled Score and scaled scores obtained on various measures of intellectual ability (such as the Wechsler Intelligence Scale for Children—Third Edition [WISC-III] and Kaufman Brief Intelligence Test). The Written Expression Scale tended to have stronger correlations with scales of verbal functioning than it did with scales of nonverbal abilities. Clinical studies conducted with the Written Expression Scale indicated that the test is able to discriminate between clients with language difficulties and those who do not demonstrate these problems.

With its assortment of writing tasks, ease of administration, and strong psychometric properties, the Written Expression Scale of the OWLS may become an instrument of choice when examiners must assess the written expression skills of school-aged individuals. The scale seems to meet many of the needs of a written language test, yet it is easy to administer and can be done so in a timely fashion.

[57]
Organizational Change-Readiness Scale.

Purpose: Constructed "to analyze the ability of an organization to manage change effectively and to plan improvement actions."
Population: Employees.
Publication Date: 1996.
Acronym: OCRS.
Scores: 5 scales: Structural Readiness, Technological Readiness, Climatic Readiness, Systemic Readiness, People Readiness.
Administration: Group.
Price Data, 1996: $6.50 per assessment inventory; $24.95 per facilitator's guide (24 pages).

Time: (20) minutes.
Comments: Redevelopment of Organizational Change-Readiness Survey.
Authors: John E. Jones and William L. Bearley.
Publisher: Human Resource Development Press.

Review of the Organizational Change-Readiness Scale by GARY J. DEAN, Associate Professor and Chairperson, Department of Adult and Community Education, Indiana University of Pennsylvania, Indiana, PA:

INTRODUCTION. The Organizational Change-Readiness Scale (OCRS) is a self-report measure through which members of an organization rate on a scale of 1 = *not at all,* 2 = *to a very little degree,* 3 = *to a little degree,* 4 = *to some degree,* 5 = *to a great degree,* and 6 = *to a very great degree,* 76 items regarding their organization's readiness for change. The items are grouped into five scales: Structural Readiness (21 items), Technological Readiness (6 items), Climatic Readiness (19 items), Systematic Readiness (13 items), and People Readiness (17 items). Each of these scales is measured in terms of both supports for change and barriers to change in a force-field analysis model. There are two booklets with the instrument: the inventory (which contains an interpretation guide) and a Facilitator's Guide.

DEVELOPMENT. The authors of the OCRS state that it is "a redevelopment of an instrument published earlier under the title *Organizational Change—Readiness Survey*" (facilitator's guide, p. 6), which was published in 1985 by Organization Design & Development. According to the authors, the model for the OCRS (the five scales of the instrument) is based on a thorough review of the literature on change readiness in organizations. The authors, stating that there is a scarcity of literature on the topic of change readiness in organizations, cite only two references, including what appears to be their primary source, an article by Pfeiffer and Jones (1978). Based on this review of literature and the previous Organizational Change-Readiness Survey, items were then developed for the OCRS to measure each of the five scales. The items were reviewed by "human resource development expert judges" (facilitator's guide, p. 6) and revised based on their comments. The resulting instrument was field tested prior to publishing the final version of the OCRS.

VALIDITY AND RELIABILITY. In the section of the Facilitator's Guide headed "Reliability and Validity," the authors discuss reliability but make no mention of specific attempts to establish validity beyond what is discussed in the section on the development of the OCRS. Because the authors provide only two references and no indication of the other literature they reviewed, it is difficult to determine the extent to which the five scales of the OCRS actually do reflect what the literature says.

Reliability was investigated using a small sample ($n = 88$), which was not further described. The following correlation coefficients were calculated for each scale using Cronbach's alpha: Structural Readiness = .79; Technological Readiness = .71; Climatic Readiness = .82; Systematic Readiness = .73; and People Readiness = .81. The authors correctly point out that the correlation coefficients for Technology and Systems are lower because of the limited number of items in these scales (6 and 13 respectively). In addition, the interscale correlations were calculated based on the same sample. These range from a low of .55 (Technology correlated with People) to a high of .80 (Comatic Correlated with People). The generally high interscale correlations indicate the interdependence of the scales, which the authors also acknowledge.

ADMINISTRATION AND SCORING. The inventory is contained in a booklet that includes an interpretation guide. The responses are recorded on NCR paper, the top page of which allows respondents to record their responses, and the bottom page of which allows for scoring. It took this reviewer less than 20 minutes to complete and score the inventory. The second page of the NCR answer sheet is divided so that the five scales appear as columns and are easily identifiable. Scoring is accomplished by recording the extreme positive and negative scores for each item. Items to which a respondent marked 1 (not at all) or 2 (to a very little degree) are recorded as an "X." Items to which a respondent marked 5 (to a great degree) or 6 (to a very great degree) are recorded as an "0." Items marked 3 (to a little degree) or 4 (to some degree) are not counted in computing the final scores for each scale. The effect of this system is that the scores are grouped into three categories: Scores of "1" and "2" are recorded as barriers (X), scores of "3" and "4" are disregarded, and scores of "5" and "6" are recorded as supports (0) for change readiness. These scores are recorded at the bottom of the second NCR page and again on an interpretation diagram.

INTERPRETATION. The total number of Xs for each scale indicates the extent to which there are barriers to change readiness, and the total number of 0s indicates the extent to which change readiness is supported in the organization. These scores are marked on a diagram based on Kurt Levin's model of force-field analysis. Supports can then be weighed against barriers to help determine what needs to be done to facilitate change readiness in the organization. The authors provide descriptions and examples for each of the scales to aid in interpretation. The inventory booklet also provides a section entitled, "Action Planning for Improving Change-Readiness," which respondents can use to help them become more specific about how to build on the supports as well as reduce the impact of the barrier that have been identified by the OCRS. In addition, the Facilitator's Guide describes three ways to use the OCRS and the Inventory provides 13 strategies to facilitate change in an organization.

The layout of the NCR answer sheet and the inventory booklet make them easy to use and understand. The facilitator's guide is also easy to use and has good material to help facilitators employ the OCRS effectively in their organizations.

SUMMARY. The OCRS is a well-designed instrument, which can be used effectively for the purposes described by the authors: as a tool to promote discussion and understanding of change readiness in an organization. The lack of specifics provided by the authors regarding the development and validity evidence of the instrument does promote some concern. The authors state that the instrument was designed as "a professional tool, not a research instrument" (Facilitator's Guide, p. 6). The applied nature of the instrument, however, does not excuse the authors from supplying more detailed information on the literature reviewed, the derivation of the conceptual basis for the instrument, and procedures used to develop items and field test the instrument. In short, scores from the instrument can be considered valid only to the extent particular users believe the five scales and the items used to measure those scales accurately reflect change-readiness issues in their organization.

REVIEWER'S REFERENCE

Pfeiffer, J. W., & Jones, J. E. (1978). OD readiness. In J. W. Pfeiffer and J. E. Jones, (Eds.), *The 1978 annual handbook for group facilitators* (pp. 219–228). San Diego, CA: University Associates.

Review of the Organizational Change-Readiness Scale by EUGENE P. SHEEHAN, Professor of Psychology, University of Northern Colorado, Greeley, CO:

The Organizational Change-Readiness Scale (OCRS) is a 76-item attitude survey designed to assess employees' perceptions of an organization's ability and readiness to change. The OCRS was developed from a literature review in which the authors identified the dimensions deemed critical to organizational change-readiness. This resulted in the questions being groups into five readiness scales: Structural 921 items), People (17 items), Systemic (13 items), Climatic (19 items), and Technological (6 items). Respondents indicate on a 6-point scale the degree to which their organization has a particular change-related characteristics (e.g., To what degree does this organization "stay on the lookout for new technology?" [facilitator's guide, p. 2]).

The instrument is professionally presented in a booklet (inventory), which also contains scoring directions, an Organizational Change-Readiness Profile, Force-Field Analysis of Change-Readiness, description of major change strategies, and an Action Plan for Improving Change-Readiness. Directions for responding to and scoring the inventory are clear and easily followed. Scoring is completed on an answer sheet that is separate from the inventory booklet. Respondents identify and graph supports and barriers to the change process in the Force-Field Analysis of Change-Readiness. This graph provides an indication of the organization's current standing with respect to organizational change-readiness. it also provides the impetus for discussion about how an organization might best initiate change. The outline of major organizational change strategies and Action Plan for Improving Change-Readiness are designed to augment and provide direction to this discussion. An accompanying facilitator's guide describes how the instrument can be used in several settings: training module, team-building session, and one-on-one consultation. Thus, it would seem that the most common use of the OCRS is to stimulate spirited and practical discussion regarding an organization's readiness for change and how to position an organization so as to increase its adaptability.

In both the inventory booklet and the facilitator's guide, the authors liken the concept of change readiness to reading readiness and go on to assert that once a child is ready to read almost any method of reading instruction will work. I would disagree with this assertion. Extensive research shows that learning to read is not a unidimensional task. Reading requires numerous intellectual processes and may depend on a variety of instructional strategies (Pressley & McCormick, 1995). Organizational change is a similarly complex process and the effectiveness of change strategies will vary across organizations and depend on the context in which change is implemented.

The OCRS facilitator's guide provides little psychometric data. The authors maintain the instrument is ideographic, designed for use in separate and idiosyncratic organizations, and thus any norms would be misleading. I would argue that the development of norms for any psychometric instrument is both useful and necessary. The authors wrote items they believed assess the five change-readiness dimensions. Human resource development experts reviewed these items, which the authors then rewrote. They also report testing different forms of the instrument with training and consulting groups prior to the development of the final version. However, the facilitator's guide provides no information regarding the criteria used to select or reject items. Similarly, it does not provide any details of the groups used to test early versions of the instrument.

Reliability estimates (Cronbach's alpha) on the change-readiness dimensions and intercorrelations between the dimensions are the only psychometric data provided. The reliability estimates very between .71 and .82. These estimates are based on responses from 88 cases, a very small sample. It would be useful to have other types of reliability, especially both short- and long-term reliability.

The intercorrelations among the five dimensions range from .55 to .80, suggesting, according to the authors, the existence of a general factor underlying organizational change-readiness. it would be useful to have data from a factor analysis to support this contention. We do not know that the instrument has the factor structure proposed. indeed, the authors propose that those who use the OCRS with large populations conduct their own factor analysis.

No validity evidence is provided. Data on the following two validity questions should be provided: How does this instrument fare when taken by employees from organizations with known differences in organizational change-readiness? Additionally, what are the correlations between this instrument and other organizational change instruments? Answers to these questions would provide some evidence regarding whether the OCRS is measuring change-readiness.

SUMMARY. Overall, the OCRS is an interesting instrument designed to assess organizational change-readiness. The graphic representation of the results, combined with the other literature presented to OCRS users in the inventory and facilitator's guide, should provoke an interesting discussion about the concept of organizational change-readiness and specifically the state of the users' organization with respect to change-readiness. The psychometric data, however, are sparse and in need of further development. This lack of data is a clear weakness of the OCRS.

REVIEWER'S REFERENCE

Pressley, M., & McCormick, C. (1995). *Advanced educational psychology for educators, researchers, and policymakers.* New York: Harper Collins.

[58]

Otis-Lennon School Ability Test®, Seventh Edition.

Purpose: "Designed to measure abstract thinking and reasoning ability."
Population: Grades K–12.
Publication Dates: 1977–1996.
Acronym: OLSAT®.
Scores, 3: Verbal, Nonverbal, Total.
Administration: Group.
Levels, 7: A, B, C, D, E, F, G.
Forms, 3: 1, 2, 3.
Price Data, 1999: $22.50 per examination kit including one test booklet and directions for administering (Form 3, Levels AG); $83.50 per 25 Type 1 machine-scorable test booklets including 1 directions for administering (Form 3, Levels AD); $60.50 per 25 test booklets (specify reusable or hand scorable, and level); $25.25 per 25 Type 1 machine-scorable answer documents; $25.25 per 25 hand-scorable answer documents; $65.25 per technical manual; $12.75 per separate directions for administering; $42.25 per side-by-side keys for hand-scorable test booklets; $22 per stencil keys for hand-scorable answer documents; $22 per

overlay keys for Type 1 machine-scorable answer documents; $5.25 per response keys (Form 3, specify level); $12.75 per 25 practice tests, including 1 directions for administering (Form 3, specify level); $6 per separate directions for administering practice tests; $65.25 per norms book; $5.75 per class records (Form 3, specify level).

Comments: Originally titled Otis-Lennon Mental Ability Test.

Authors: Arthur S. Otis and Roger T. Lennon.

Publisher: Harcourt Brace Educational Measurement—the educational testing division of The Psychological Corporation.

    a) LEVEL A.

Population: Grade K.

Time: (70) minutes over 2 sessions.

Comments: Orally administered.

    b) LEVEL B.

Population: Grade 1.

Time: Same as *a* above.

Comments: Orally administered.

    c) LEVEL C.

Population: Grade 2.

Time: Same as *a* above.

Comments: Partially self-administered.

    d) LEVEL D.

Population: Grade 3.

Time: (60) minutes.

Comments: Self-administered.

    e) LEVEL E.

Population: Grades 4–5.

Time: Same as *d* above.

Comments: Self-administered.

    f) LEVEL F.

Population: Grades 6–8.

Time: Same as *d* above.

Comments: Self-administered.

    g) LEVEL G.

Population: Grades 9–12.

Time: Same as *d* above.

Comments: Self-administered.

Cross References: See T5:1866 (45 references) and T4:1913 (8 references); for reviews by Anne Anastasi and Mark E. Swerdlik, see 11:274 (48 references); for reviews by Calvin O. Dyer and Thomas Oakland, see 9:913 (7 references); see also T3:1754 (64 references); 8:198 (35 references), and T2:424 (10 references); for a review by John E. Milholland and excerpted reviews by Arden Grotelueschen and Arthur E. Smith, see 7:370 (6 references).

Review of the Otis-Lennon School Ability Test, Seventh Edition by LIZANNE DeSTEFANO, Associate Professor of Educational Psychology, University of Illinois at Urbana-Champaign, Champaign, IL:

TEST BACKGROUND AND USES. The Seventh Edition of the Otis-Lennon School Ability Test (OLSAT-7) is the most recent in a series that began in 1918 with the Otis Group Intelligence Scale. The OLSAT is designed to measure abstract thinking and reasoning ability. The term "mental ability" has been changed from previous versions to "school ability" to reflect the purpose for which the current test is intended to serve: "To assess examinees' ability to cope with school learning tasks, to suggest their possible placement for school learning functions, and to evaluate their achievement in relation to the talents they bring to school learning situations" (Directions for Administration, p. 5). The use of "school ability" is also intended to discourage overgeneralization of the nature of the ability being measured (e.g., general intelligence). According to its publishers, the OLSAT is "based on the notion that to learn new things, students must be able to perceive accurately, to recognize and recall what has been perceived, to think logically, to understand relationships, to abstract from a set of particulars, and to apply generalizations to new and different contexts" (Directions for Administration, p. 5). Specific recommendations for appropriate uses and cautions against misuses of the OLSAT in educational settings, however, are not offered.

The Seventh Edition of the OLSAT contains items from the Fifth and Sixth Editions as well as new items. All items were reviewed and edited by editorial staff, measurement specialists, and psychologists for clarity, appropriateness of content, accuracy of correct answers, appropriateness of vocabulary, and absence of stereotyping or bias. Other than the changes made to item constituency, no discernible differences between the OLSAT Sixth and Seventh Editions were detected.

TEST STRUCTURE AND CONTENT. The OLSAT comprises seven levels (A through G) that are used for students in kindergarten to the 12th grade. Four separate levels are used for the early years (K through Grade 3) in order to provide a more precise measure of school ability during a developmental period recognized for steep gains in intellectual growth. One level, Level E, serves Grades 4 and 5; Level F serves Grades 6–8 and Level G Serves Grades 9–12. Levels A through G were normed using examinees whose age ranged from one year under and one year over designated school grades. Thus, out-of-level testing is possible within these limits.

Twenty-one different item types are organized into five clusters: Verbal Comprehension, Verbal Reasoning, Pictorial Reasoning, Figural Reasoning, and Quantitative Reasoning. Clusters I and II comprise the VERBAL component of the OLSAT and Clusters III-V form the NONVERBAL component. The classification of test items as verbal or nonverbal "hinges upon whether knowledge of language is requisite to answering the items" (Directions for Administering, p. 6). Verbal Comprehension includes Following Directions (Levels A–C), Antonyms (D–G), Sentence Completion (D–G), and Sentence Arrangement (D–G). Verbal Reasoning includes Aural Reasoning (A–C), Arithmetic Reasoning (A–G), Logical Selection (D–G), Word/Letter Matrix (D–G), Verbal Analogies (D–G), Verbal Classification (D–G), and Inference (E-G). Pictorial Reasoning includes Picture Classification (A–C), Picture Analogies (A–C), and Picture Series (K only). Figural Reasoning includes Figural Classification (A–D), Figural Analogies (A–G), Pattern Matrix (A–G), and Figural Series (A–G). Quantitative Reasoning is briefly samples (7 items) at Grade 3 (Level D), and used more extensively in Levels E through G. This cluster includes Number Series, Numeric Inference, and Number Matrix.

ITEM CHARACTERISTICS. All items on OLSAT tests use a multiple-choice format. Within each level, items are arranged according to certain criteria. For Levels A–C, items are arranged according to the kind of task performed by examinees (e.g., classifying or analogizing) and whether item stems are dictated by their teacher. This allows younger children, for whom test-taking may be an unfamiliar experience, to become more comfortable with these tasks. Within each of these three parts, items are spiraled by difficulty, with harder items "cushioned" by easier items so that children do not become discouraged once they have sensed that items are becoming increasingly more difficult to answer. At Levels E–G, items are arranged in a spiral omnibus format, wherein they are rotated throughout the test according to difficulty and item type. Level D (Grade 3) contains a section with figural and verbal items arranged according to increasing difficulty. In all other sections of Level D, items are arranged according to the spiral omnibus format of Levels E–G.

Equal numbers of verbal and nonverbal items are included in each level of the OLSAT. Levels A–C contain 30 items in both verbal and nonverbal components, whereas Level D contains 32 items and Levels E–G contain 36 items in each component.

CONSTRUCTION, DEVELOPMENT, AND STANDARDIZATION. OLSAT test development and norming efforts are extensive. The most recent national item tryout was conducted in 1994 with 10,000 students from schools across the country. School districts were selected according to a random sampling technique that resulted in samples of students that reflected the national school population in terms of SES, school district enrollment, and geographic region. Field-test items underwent a revision process that was intended to eliminate stereotypes and differential item functioning (DIF) with regard to gender and ethnic groups. Items that depicted differences in activities, emotions, occupations, or personality attributes with regard to gender, ethnic, or cultural group were identified by item editors, psychologists, and an advisor panel of minority educators and were subsequently removed from the OLSAT item pool. Following this review and elimination process, retained items were analyzed using the Mantel-Haenszel procedure to detect statistical differential item functioning (DIF) between gender and ethnic groups of students.

A stratified random sampling technique was invoked within each state to obtain standardization samples of examinees that were proportionate to total U.S. public and private school enrollment, and reflected percentages of students from different geographic, SES, and ethnic groups. The purpose of the standardization effort was to obtain normative and descriptive OLSAT data on students nationwide, to equate the levels of the Seventh Edition, to equate Sixth and Seventh Editions, and to document the statistical reliability and validity properties of scores from the test. Students participating in the OLSAT standardization samples were also administered the Ninth Edition of the Stanford Achievement Test Series (this is discussed in more detail in the section on Validity). Approximately 463,000 students participated in test standardization efforts in the Spring and Fall of 1995. The OLSAT Preliminary Technical Manual (PTM, released Spring, 1996) and Technical Manual (TM, 1997) provide information about standardization samples and statistical data relevant to test development including raw score means, standard deviations, and standard errors of measurement.

TEST SCORES. Total raw scores as well as those derived from Verbal and Nonverbal components of the OLSAT are converted to School Ability Indexes (SAIs), percentile ranks, stanines, and scaled scores SAIs (Mean = 100, Standard Deviation = 16). SAIs have been calculated for each 3-month age group (from 4 years, 6 months to 18 years, 2 months). SAIs have also been converted to stanines and percentile ranks—though not directly to scaled scores—within the same age groups. Although SAIs appear very similar to IQ scores, their exact meaning and significance are not clear. Scaled scores were developed by administering two adjacent OLSAT levels to student samples from Grades 1–4, 5, and 9. This allowed the scaled score system of the OLSAT to provide a single, continuous, uniform scale that allows comparison of performance of students across all levels of the tests, irrespective of the age or grade of the examinee. Uses of the scaled scores include comparing scores from different levels of the test, measuring changes in performance over time, and testing out of level. The OLSAT norming manual, the compendium that contains score information, is well organized, easy to read, and allows for quick conversions back and forth between raw scores, SAIs, stanines, and percentile ranks. It is not clear, however, how each type of score should be interpreted nor what the relative advantages and limitations of each are. Examples of students' score reports with explanations to the user would have been welcomed.

RELIABILITY. Estimates of internal consistency (Kuder-Richardson 20) for Total, Verbal, and Nonverbal components of the OLSAT are presented in the PTM. Within each level, separate estimates were calculated for 3-month age groups. The youngest age group used was 5 years, 2 months (Level A). The oldest was 19 years, 11 months (Level G). For total scores, estimates of reliability ranged from .78 (Level D, age 11 years, 0–2 months) to .97 (Level F, age 10 years, 0–2 months and Level G, age 13 years, 3–5 and 6–9 months). Estimates of reliability for the Verbal component ranged from .68 (Level A, 5 years 0–2 months and Level B, 8 years, 3–5 months) to .96 (Level G, 13 years, 6–9 months). Finally, KR-20

coefficients for the Nonverbal component ranged from .63 (Level D, 11 years, 0–2 months) to .95 (Level F, 10 years, 0–2 months and Level G, 13 years, 3–5 months). Low numbers of examinees in some of the age groups and extreme out-of-level testing groups may have contributed to lower-bound estimates of reliability. Measures of the stability of OLSAT scores over time, however, are not available.

VALIDITY. Separate sections of the Technical Manual address content, criterion-related, construct validity of the OLSAT. Correlational data are presented as the primary evidence of test validity with regard to these three issues. First, correlations between Sixth and Seventh Editions of the OLSAT are shown in order to demonstrate the relationship between the content of these two versions. Total score correlations for the Sixth and Seventh Editions range from .77 (Level F) to .87 (Level E). Ranges for Verbal and Nonverbal components range from .69 (Level A) to .83 (Level E) and .68 (Level F) to .83 (Level E), respectively. Correlations between the OLSAT and the Stanford Achievement Test (9th Edition) are presented to demonstrate the relationship between the OLSAT and academic achievement. Finally, the construct validity is evidenced by correlations between adjacent levels of the OLSAT. Correlations between Verbal components of Levels A and B, for example, would demonstrate the degree of consistency of the OLSAT in assessing the same skills across these levels. The level-to-level relationship is strongest for Total score, as would be expected for a scale comprising twice as many items as its two component scales. Correlations between Verbal components at adjacent levels range from .68 (Levels (C–D) to .82 (Levels B–C and E–F). Nonverbal component correlations range from .73 (Levels D–E) to .81 (Levels E–F). Correlations between Verbal and Nonverbal components at each testing level (and in each grade when one level is used to test multiple grade groups) are also presented. Correlations range from .67 (Level C) to .84 (Level E, Grade 5). The degree of these correlations indicates the extent to which each component (i.e., construct) contributes unique content to the test.

ADMINISTRATION, SCORING, AND REPORTING. Levels A–B are for use with Kindergartners and first graders, respectively. As such, these tests are dictated to examinees. Test items are organized into three sections and in a format that includes practice items. The first two sections are administered in one sitting; the third in a separate session, though it is not clear whether this should be scheduled on the same or a different day than the first two sections. Presumably, this decision is left to the discretion of the school/administrator. Level C (Grade 2) also has three sections, the last of which is dictated. Sections 1 and 2 are self-administered. Levels A–C each take approximately one hour to administer (37 minutes of actual testing time) and include examples of test items that students can try for practice. The "bubbles" that students use to indicate their responses are quite small, which may be a concern for youngsters who have underdeveloped fine motor skills. Levels D (two sections) and E–G (one section) are entirely self-administered in a one-hour session (40 minutes of actual testing time). Practice items precede each section in Levels D–G.

Manuals for administering all levels of the OLSAT include an introductory section that provides information on the background, structure, and content of the test, and general and specific directions for test administration. General directions include information about the scheduling of the test, the materials needed, and the use of machine-scorable answer booklets. Specific directions include step-by-step instructions on the distribution of materials and procedures and scripted directions to students.

Directions for administration are for the most part clear, straightforward, and concise. There are, however, some ambiguous references to supplemental testing materials (e.g., an achievement test battery) and confusing instructions on how to complete/coordinate student identification information on both kinds of test forms. Nevertheless, no specific training in test administration is required, although the publishers recommend that proctors take the test prior to actual administration. Directions to students are also easy to follow. For Levels A–C, place markers are available to students. These and the scripted instructions that are read aloud by the proctor reduce the likelihood that students will become distracted or get lost during testing.

Test items for all levels use a multiple-choice format. Students mark their responses in the test booklets for Levels A–D. All levels can either be machine scored or scored by hand. Separate answer forms are provided for Levels E–G and include two options: a combination answer-folder, OLSAT machine-scorable answer document, or OLSAT hand-scorable answer document. Based on the materials provided for review, it is not clear what the relative advantages and disadvantages of any of these scoring options are.

Practice tests are available for all levels of the OLSAT. According to its publishers, the Practice Tests, which include items and procedures that resemble those on the actual test, "help students understand what to expect …, thus reducing anxiety." The practice tests also offer students, particularly the younger ones, an opportunity to practice the mechanics of coding their answers and personal information on separate documents. The publishers recommend that practice tests are administered one week prior to actual test administration.

OLSAT scores are reported at student and classroom levels. Raw scores, SAIs, scaled scores, stanines, and age and grade percentiles are included in both reports. Narratives that include brief descriptions of the skills tested by each item cluster as well as students' performance relative to same age and grade cohorts are presented in the student reports.

SUMMARY OF CONCERNS. Despite the thorough treatment given to OLSAT development and relative ease with which it can be administered to large groups of students, the following limitations are noted as deserving special attention.

1. Perhaps the most serious weakness of the Seventh Edition of the OLSAT is the validity evidence presented in the Technical Manual. Moderate to high correlations between current and previous versions of a test are not sufficient evidence of content validity. Furthermore, readers of the Technical Manual must take OLSAT publishers on faith when they allude to an ongoing external review process that assesses the relationship between the skills measured by each item and the stated purpose of the test. A more detailed description of this process would have been welcome. Second, evidence of the construct validity of the OLSAT is also weakly presented. Again, correlations—this time between total and component scores at adjacent levels and between Verbal and Nonverbal components within each level of

the test—are insufficient. Results from confirmatory factor analyses that substantiate the differentiation of the verbal and nonverbal constructs of the OLSAT (and the degree to which each contributes to overall score variance) at all of its testing levels would also have been welcome. Third, correlations between the OLSAT and the Stanford Achievement Test scores represent an indirect measure of criterion-related validity in that a score on one measure can be used only to predict the score on another rather than the behavior of interest which, according to OLSAT publishers, is students' "ability to cope with school learning tasks." Direct evidence of this relationship as well as the implied relevance of the OLSAT to general success in school would improve the test's marketability among potential users. Another issue relevant to the validity of the OLSAT is whether total scores and those derived from its verbal and nonverbal components predict "school ability" equally well at all grade levels. That is, do OLSAT scores have greater relevance in the primary years of schooling when curriculum, it could be argued, is less differentiated than in the middle and upper levels when instructional content is more specialized? Furthermore, the use of the OLSAT for high school students would be a curious choice for at least two reasons. First, many high school students are nearing completion of their formal schooling. If this is true, then, what is the practical value of the OLSAT? Second, if college is an option for high schoolers, then use of the OLSAT seems less likely given the array of well-established measures of first-year college (e.g., ACT, SAT).

2. Despite extensive summaries of descriptive, correlational, and normative data, the interpretation of OLSAT scores is an ambiguous endeavor and thus increased the risk of misuse. The publishers should be more clear about what the OLSAT can and cannot do, particularly in the reports returned to teachers and other audiences; recommendations for OLSAT use should be accompanied by acknowledgment of its limitations.

3. The history of the OLSAT can be traced back to a period of testing that was dominated by hierarchical theories of intelligence that devolve from a general, omnibus single intelligence factor *g* into more specialized, though correlated, factors. In light of recent advances in cognitive theory, the theoretical foundations of the OLSAT should be questioned.

4. Satisfactory internal consistency estimates are presented, but no data relating to the stability of OLSAT scores over time are currently available.

SUMMARY. If the test users acknowledge the limitations of the test noted above and accept it as one of a variety of instruments that could be used for screening purposes (i.e., to identify students who may need extra help), then the technical characteristics of the OLSAT qualify its use for this limited role.

Review of the Otis-Lennon School Ability Test, Seventh Edition by BERT A. GOLDMAN, Professor of Education, Curriculum and Instruction, University of North Carolina at Greensboro, Greensboro, NC:

The Otis-Lennon School Ability Test, Seventh Edition (OLSAT-7) is the latest version of a series of ability tests begun by Arthur Otis with his Otis Group Intelligence Scale in 1918 and further enhanced by the work of Roger Lennon with the introduction into the series of the Otis-Lennon Mental Ability Test. This latest version employs "the same general conceptualization of the nature of ability" and "the same psychometric approaches" (Directions for Administration, p. 5) as its predecessors to measure thinking and reasoning abilities that are most relevant to school achievement. Given that the instrument is to be used in the school setting for the purposes of assessing school learning ability, suggesting school learning placement, and evaluating school achievement with respect to school learning potential, the label "school ability" is used rather than the label "mental ability." Also the term "school ability" is "intended to discourage overinterpretation of the nature of the ability being assessed" (Directions for Administration, p. 5).

Seven interrelated levels (A through G) of the test attempt to measure the ability range of students in Grades k through 12: Level A (Kindergarten), Level B (Grade 1), Level C (Grade 2), Level D (Grade 3), Level E (Grades 45), Level F (Grades 6–8), and Level G (Grades 9–12). Testing time per testing session takes from 27 minutes (Level C) to 50 minutes (each Level D–F) with Levels A, B, and C each requiring two testing sessions plus a 5-minute rest period within each session.

All levels contain both Verbal and Nonverbal items. The Verbal part consists of Verbal

Comprehension, which includes four subtests: Following Directions, Antonyms, Sentence Completion, and Sentence Arrangement; and Verbal Reasoning, which includes seven subtests: Aural Reasoning, Arithmetic Reasoning, Logical Selection, Word/Letter Matrix, Verbal Analogies, Verbal Classification, and Inference. The Nonverbal part consists of Pictorial Reasoning, which includes three subtests: Picture Classification, Picture Analogies, and Picture Series; Figural Reasoning, which includes four subtests: Figural Classification, Figural Analogies, Pattern Matrix, and Figural Series; and Quantitative Reasoning, which includes three subtests: Number Series, Numeric Inference, and Number Matrix. Although all levels contain Verbal and Nonverbal items, no level contains all subtests. For example, only Levels A, B, and C contain the Following Directions subtest.

Each test level has a separate brief practice test designed to familiarize students with that level's types of items to be administered in a session prior to the regular test session or sessions. Clearly written and easily followed directions are given in manuals for each test level.

Two types of answer sheet are available: machine-scorable by the test publisher and hand-scorable. A Preliminary Technical Manual and booklet containing National Spring Norms are provided. Demographic characteristics of the standardization samples are presented in the Preliminary Technical Manual and closely resemble those given for the total U.S. school enrollment. The demographics include: Geographic Region, SES Status, Urbanicity, Ethnicity, and Nonpublic Schools. Handicapping conditions are also included, but without comparable U.S. School Enrollment data.

Reliability data are given in the form of K-R 20 coefficients for Verbal, Nonverbal, and Total scores for each grade and for each age in years and months. Most of the coefficients appear to be in the .80s and .90s with a few in the .70s and one low of .68 for Level A, Verbal, 5 years 0–2 months. Although these coefficients are mostly good to excellent, they represent internal consistency rather than test-retest stability.

Given the one purpose of the OLSAT-7 is to assess school learning ability, it seems reasonable to expect that there be validity data showing the relationship between OLSAT scores and grades

in school. No such data are given in the Preliminary Technical Manual. Perhaps there will be a forthcoming technical manual containing this information. [Editor's Note: This information is provided on page 43 of the Technical Manual, which was provided in 1999 after this review was prepared.]

Data are presented containing correlations between the OLSAT-6 and OLSAT-7 for each grade levels (A–G) Total, Verbal, and Nonverbal scores. These correlations range from a low of .68 (Level F Nonverbal) to a high of .87 (Level E Total) with most in the upper .70s and mid to low .80s. Although all of these correlations appear to be statistically significant, if there are no major changes between the two test versions, one might expect the correlation to be much higher. This brings up the question of whether there are any major changes between OLSAT-6 and OLSAT-7. The Preliminary Technical Manual, Spring 1996, provides none.

Additional comparisons between the OLSAT-6 and OLSAT-7 are presented in the form of School Ability Index Scores (SAI) by age in years and months, which are one and two standard deviations above and below the mean. Generally, most of the mean SAI scores for OLSAT-6 and OLSAT-7 differ by one, two, or three points revealing similarity between the two instruments.

There appears to be consistency between each successive level and its preceding level as evidenced by correlations between them ranging from a low .68 to a high of .88 with most in the mid to upper .70s and low to mid .80s. Further consistency within the test appears in the correlations between Verbal and Nonverbal means for each grade level K–12. These correlations range from .65 to .84 with most in the low .80s.

Mean item difficulty levels for Total, Verbal, and Nonverbal items are presented for each grade K–12. The difficulty levels range from .49 to .63 and appear to be satisfactory. Median item discrimination indexes are presented for Grades K–12 and also appear to be satisfactory ranging from .48 to .61.

The OLSAT-7 National Spring Norms booklet enables raw scores to be converted to percentile ranks, stanines, or scaled scores. However, no information is given concerning the mean and standard deviation of these scaled scores. Also the Norms booklet enables raw scores to be converted to School Ability Indexes (SAI), which in turn may be converted to percentile ranks and stanines. There is no explanation of what the SAIs represent. They resemble IQs, but because this test is not presented as an intelligence test this reviewer wonders what they are and why they are introduced.

SUMMARY. The OLSAT-7 is designed to measure school ability for grades K through 12 by means of Verbal and Nonverbal items. It is a group test for which general conceptualization and psychometric approaches are those of its predecessors dating back to 1918. The demographic characteristics of the standardization samples closely resemble those of the total U.S. school enrollment. Estimates of reliability in the form of K-R 20 coefficients are mostly good to excellent. However, these data represent internal consistency rather than test-retest stability. Given that one purpose of the OLSAT-7 is to assess school learning ability, it is troubling that no validity data showing the relationship between OLSAT scores and school grades are provided.

Although the correlations between the OLSAT-6 and OLSAT-7 appear to be statistically significant, if there are no major changes between the two test versions (and we are not told whether there are), we should expect higher correlations between them. There appears to be consistency within the test as demonstrated by substantial correlations between successive levels and between Verbal and Nonverbal halves of the test. Item difficulty and item discrimination indexes appear to be satisfactory. Raw scores may be converted to School Ability Indexes, but there is no explanation of what these indexes are, although they resemble IQs. Until a more complete technical manual addressing the doubts raised by this review is prepared to replace the Preliminary Technical Manual, one should proceed with caution in using this instrument.

[59]
Parenting Satisfaction Scale™.

Purpose: Designed to assess "parents' attitudes toward parenting."
Population: Adults with dependent children.
Publication Date: 1994.
Acronym: PSS.
Scores, 3: Satisfaction with Spouse/Ex-Spouse Parenting Performance, Satisfaction with the Parent-Child Relationship, Satisfaction with Parenting Performance.

Administration: Individual.
Price Data, 1999: $96.50 per comprehensive kit including manual (47 pages) and 25 ReadyScore® answer documents; $31 per 25 ReadyScore® answer documents; $70.50 per manual.
Time: (30) minutes.
Authors: John Guidubaldi and Helen K. Cleminshaw.
Publisher: The Psychological Corporation.
Cross References: See T5:1888 (1 reference).

Review of the Parenting Satisfaction Scale by IRA STUART KATZ, *Clinical Psychologist, California Department of Corrections, Salinas Valley State Prison, Soledad, CA:*

OVERVIEW AND USES. The American family is under siege. Attacks on parents from the left and right are not uncommon. Biology thrusts individuals into social roles often unprepared, unschooled, and undifferentiated. The results of this lack of awareness, assessment, alignment, and attunement may lead to dysfunction and distress. Parenting role satisfaction appears to be related to behavioral outcomes. The Parenting Satisfaction Scale (PSS) is a refreshing step forward in closing the gap of awareness and promoting parenting skills and family healing.

The Parenting Satisfaction Scale (PSS) is a 45-item standardized assessment of parent's attitudes toward parenting with three discrete scales: Satisfaction with Spouse/Ex-Spouse Parenting Performance, Satisfaction with the Parent-Child Relationship, and Satisfaction with Parenting Performance.

A unique feature of the PSS is the recognition that more and more families are blended and fragmented. Parenting role behavior is not limited by court decrees. As an empathetic communication tool in assessing various issues in custodial disputes, such as parental support, the PSS offers practical hope to both clients and clinicians. Equally compelling about the PSS is the potential of increasing empathy among family members by having the spouse or child complete the scale as though he or she was the responding parent.

The PSS is a very client-friendly instrument. It is easy to administer and score. Each scale contains 15 items. The PSS can be completed in 20 minutes. The reading level eases administration. The ReadyScore Answer Document instructs parents to respond to each item by circling the dot for their response that appears in front of the item. This is easy on the parent and makes the process of responding easier. Clients have shared with me their satisfaction with the ease of reading and scoring of the PSS. More impressive to them was the clear focus of the items covered. These were issues that often came up in family therapy. That client endorsement reinforces the PSS as a good adjunct clinical tool.

John Guidubaldi and Helen Cleminshaw, who authored the PSS, provide an excellent 43-page manual that, like the PSS, is very reader- and clinician-friendly. A brief review of what the manual covers is in order.

TEST MATERIALS. The PSS is a 4-page self-score instrument. The ReadyScore Answer Document is very easy to understand and use. Parents (and/or respondents) are asked to provide responses that describe how she or he feel about the spouse's (or ex-spouse's) parenting, how the parent feels about his or her relationship with the child(ren), and how the parent feels about her or his own parenting. The parent may choose to strongly agree, agree, disagree, or strongly disagree with each statement. The administration and scoring are refreshingly straightforward. The overall feel of the PSS is more clinical than psychometric. This is based on the fact that "parenting satisfaction" per se is not expected to follow a normal distribution in the entire population.

NORMS AND STANDARDIZATION. Standardization of the PSS involved three steps: a pilot phase including item generalization, and the establishment of reliability, face validity, investigations of construct (initial factor analyses) and criterion-related validity evidence, a standardization phase involving administering the PSS to a large nationwide sample, a second factor analysis, calculating reliability, and further analyses of criterion validity, and the final phase was a 2-year follow-up study. The purpose of the final phase was to reassess reliability and establish validity over time. There are sample inherent limits in the norm and standardization process. The pilot sample was composed of 130 parents (78 mothers and 52 fathers). Of the participants, 122 were married, and 8 were single parents.

Ninety-one percent of the sample was White. This does not appear to promote psychometric generalization. Norms in this pilot sample may not be truly representative of the current increasingly diverse American family millennial mosaic.

There are alternative self-report inventories that may address this concern.

The Parent-Child Relationship Inventory (PCRI; 13:220) for example, authored by Anthony Gerard, was standardized with over 1,100 parents across the United States. An additional feature of the PCRI is that two validity scales alert the clinician to the possibility that a parent is responding inconsistently or portraying the parent-child relationship in an unrealistically positive light. The PCRI is also sensitive to the fact that "single dads" are becoming a more common factor in the parenting equation. The PSS could be strengthened in further revisions in these areas.

RELIABILITY. The PSS's internal consistency reliability indices, estimated using Cronbach's alpha, were very high with scores as follows: Satisfaction with Spouse/Ex-Spouse Parenting Performance, $r = .96$; Satisfaction with Parent-Child Relationship, $r = .86$; and Satisfaction with Parenting Performance, $r = .82$. A 2-year follow-up measuring internal reliability and test-retest reliability estimates indicated they were fair to good. Over a 2-year time period, satisfaction with the spouse's or ex-spouse's parenting style appears more stable than satisfaction with the parent-child relationship or than with one's own parenting style.

VALIDITY. Validity studies indicate good correlational factors of note. Specifically, correlations were shown between parenting satisfaction and children's social and academic performance, health ratings of family members, and between measures of family environment and the quality of the child's relationship with others. Worth noting here are two additional validity studies focusing on women, stress, and a Chinese Nationwide Child Adjustment Project. The women's project indicated parenting satisfaction highly correlates to satisfaction in spousal and employee roles as well as to life satisfaction in general. Stressors were shown to correlate negatively to parent satisfaction. The Chinese study resulted in expected correlations. The PSS was translated into Chinese and completed by 1,746 Chinese parents throughout the People's Republic of China. This is an exciting and needed step forward in bridging cultural and diversity gaps.

SUMMARY. The Parent Satisfaction Scale (PSS) is a clinically important tool that can help promote better understanding of the behavioral impact of various parenting roles. Its assessment of parent's attitudes toward parenting can be helpful to clients and clinicians. It can be strengthened by being more sensitive to various diversity issues including parental gender diversity. The PSS ease of reading and scoring are commendable and very client- and clinician-friendly. Future revisions should offer even more insights and clinical wisdom on the impact of parental roles attitude on behavior, communication, family relationships, therapy, and change. Drs. Guidubaldi and Cleminshaw have provided the gift of an excellent first step on a journey of needed clinical understanding for those focused on strengthening relationships and prosocial behaviors in families.

Review of the Parenting Satisfaction Scale by JANET V. SMITH, Assistant Professor of Psychology and Counseling, Pittsburg State University, Pittsburg, KS:

The Parenting Satisfaction Scale (PSS) is a 45-item self-report questionnaire designed to measure attitudes toward parenting and satisfaction with the parenting role. It can be used to assess satisfaction with parenting in general, or satisfaction with parenting of a specific child. The scale generates a total satisfaction score as well as scores on three separate subscales. Subscale 1 (Satisfaction with Spouse/Ex-Spouse Parenting Performance) provides information about satisfaction with a partner's role in parenting. Subscale 2 (Satisfaction with the Parent-Child Relationship) assesses level of satisfaction in the parent's relationship with their own child. Subscale 3 (Satisfaction with Parenting Performance) provides a measure of a parent's level of satisfaction with their own parenting role. The PSS was designed through a National Association of School Psychologists (NASP) project to predict child and family outcomes from levels of parenting satisfaction.

Test items were developed through relevant literature review as well as interviews with a nonclinical sample of adults to identify factors that were considered to be important to satisfaction and dissatisfaction with the parenting role. From this information, potential items were developed and these were reviewed by parents as well as experts in the field of child and family development. This process resulted in a pool of 211 items, which was then piloted on a sample of 130 parents to produce the final item selection for the test.

Test materials are very well designed, and the PSS is extremely simple and quick to both administer and score. The reading level of the test is upper elementary school. As the manual cautions, there is no check for social desirability, which could cause a problem given the high face validity of test items. The manual is comprehensive and easy to follow. Minimal qualifications are needed to administer and interpret the test. Although the manual suggests that the PSS may be completed in a parent's home, it would be desirable for the test to be taken in an office setting to ensure standardized administration conditions are met.

The normative sample appears adequate, other than fathers being significantly underrepresented in the sample. Of more concern is that the norms are already somewhat outdated, as the normative data were collected in 1981/1982. Tables are provided to obtain standard scores and percentile ranks. Standard scores are reported as nonnormalized T scores, which seems appropriate given that the distribution of raw scores on two of the subscales is somewhat skewed.

The test scores show adequate levels of reliability. Internal consistency was calculated using Cronbach's alpha and was found to be .96 for Satisfaction with Spouse/Ex-Spouse Parenting Performance scale, .86 for Satisfaction with Parent-Child Relationship scale, and .82 for Satisfaction with Parenting Performance scale. Test-retest reliability was investigated with 137 parents from the original normative sample, with a time interval of 2 years. Test-retest reliability coefficients were substantially lower than the internal consistency estimates: $r = .81$ for Satisfaction with Spouse/Ex-Spouse Parenting Performance, .59 for Satisfaction with Parent-Child Relationship, and .64 for Satisfaction with Parenting Performance. Although these coefficient values are rather low, this does not necessarily represent a problem with the test as it is quite reasonable to expect parenting satisfaction to change over time.

Factor analysis supports the existence of the three subscales on the PSS, although a small number of items do show rather low factor loadings. Alpha factor loadings for Factor 1 (Satisfaction with Spouse/Ex-Spouse Parenting Performance) vary from .61 to .84; for Factor 2 (Satisfaction with the Parent-Child Relationship) values range from .38 to .70; and for Factor 3

(Satisfaction with Parenting Performance) values range from .19 to .62.

Because no acceptable criterion for parenting satisfaction is available, evidence is provided for construct validity. In the pilot phase, the PSS was found to show significant correlations with other measures of satisfaction, although the scales used were measures of general life satisfaction and marital satisfaction rather than specific to the parenting role. The normative sample for the PSS was given a wide variety of instruments along with the PSS as part of the NASP project, and the three subscales of the PSS showed significant correlations with a large number of measures. Again, however, despite the vast amount of data collected, none of the measures were directly related to parenting satisfaction, but rather were predominantly in the areas of child's social competence, child's academic and intellectual achievement, family health, and family environment.

The authors describe several clinical applications of the test. For example, other family members may complete the PSS as though they were the responding parent, and this information could be used to increase communication and empathy. It should be noted, however, that these alternative applications may generate useful clinical hypotheses and qualitative impressions rather than psychometrically sound data, as no supporting data are provided in the manual.

SUMMARY. In summary, the test provides a much needed measure to assess levels of parenting satisfaction. The test provides a quick and easy measure of current levels of satisfaction, although it is not necessarily predictive of future levels. Psychometric properties are adequate for research purposes as well as for generating clinical hypotheses or facilitating the clinical/counseling process with families. However, additional evidence of validity would be helpful, rather than reliance on measures that have at best an indirect association with parenting satisfaction. Overall, the test fills a valuable role, as there previously has been no accepted measure of parenting satisfaction available.

[60]
PDI Employment Inventory and PDI Customer Service Inventory.

Purpose: Designed to identify job applicants most likely to display positive employee traits.
Population: Job applicants.

Publication Dates: 1985–1993.
Administration: Group.
Price Data: Available from publisher.
Time: (30) minutes.
Comments: Paper and pencil inventories of attitudes and self-descriptions; oral instructions; computer-scored.
Authors: George E. Paajanen, Timothy L. Hansen, and Richard A. McLellan.
Publisher: Personnel Decisions, Inc.
  a) PDI EMPLOYMENT INVENTORY.
  Purpose: Designed to identify job applicants who will be likely to be productive and to stay on the job at least 3 months.
  Publication Dates: 1985–1993.
  Acronym: PDI-EI.
  Scores, 2: Performance, Tenure.
  Foreign Language and Other Special Editions: Foreign and bilingual editions available include American Spanish/English, French-Canadian English, Mexican Spanish, British English, and Vietnamese/English.
  b) PDI CUSTOMER SERVICE INVENTORY.
  Purpose: Designed to identify job applicants most likely to exhibit helpful and positive behaviors in interacting with customers.
  Publication Dates: 1991–1993.
  Acronym: PDI-CSI.
  Score: Customer Service Knowledge and Skills (Total).
  Foreign Language Edition: Spanish-English edition available.

Review of the PDI Employment Inventory and PDI Customer Service Inventory by GORDON C. BRUNER II, Associate Professor, Marketing Department, Director, Office of Scale Research, Southern Illinois University, Carbondale, IL:

The PDI Employment Inventory (EI) was designed as a preemployment test to assist in the identification of applicants who are most likely to be productive and stay on the job for at least 3 months. The developers have positioned the instrument to be most appropriate for hourly workers who must be dependable but do not necessarily need high level skills. Likewise, the PDI Customer Service Inventory (CSI) was constructed in order to help identify applicants most likely to exhibit satisfactory behaviors related to interaction with customers of a business. The EI and the CSI can be administered separately or together, the latter being a 145-item form.

An impressive number of studies have been conducted to develop, purify, and gather validity evidence on the instruments. Evidence is provided to indicate that the tests meet the Federal Uniform Guidelines on Employee Selection Procedures as well as the Civil Rights Act of 1991.

The EI has four broad dimensions: Performance, Tenure, Infrequency, and Frankness, the last two being included as checks on careless and socially desirable responding, respectively. The authors described the items comprising the performance portion as representing 13 constructs but the instrument produces just one score to represent the set. Not surprisingly this leads to a low internal consistency (.74) as well as low one-month stability ($r = .62$). The reliability of the tenure portion of the EI was even lower (.64 [internal consistency], $r = .59$ [stability]). As for the CSI, it was developed to tap into some 16 personality dimensions that were thought to influence customer service behavior regardless of the work setting. The internal consistency estimate was .73 and the one-month stability value was .86. For both the EI and the CSI the authors argued that stability was the more important indicator of reliability. However, that position stands in opposition to what is now commonly accepted in psychometrics, that stability measures are confounded by various factors and should not be depended upon (e.g., Kelly & McGrath, 1988; Nunnally & Bernstein, 1994, p. 255). Further, if the score from an instrument is to be used for purposes such as hiring rather than just comparing groups then the internal consistency of the measure should be very high (i.e., greater than .90; Devellis, 1991, p. 86; Nunnally & Bernstein, 1994, p. 265).

Given this, it is this reviewer's position that due to the lack of unidimensionality and high reliability, the evidence of validity of scores from the instruments has not been established (e.g., Gerbing & Anderson, 1988). Only if we loosen that restriction are we impressed by the sheer quantity and variety of data presented in the manual in support of the validity of various uses in scores from the instrument.

Well over 100 correlation coefficients of the EI with other tests of personality and basic ability skills are presented in the manual as evidence of discriminant and convergent validity (pp. 31–35). Because the EI is multidimensional it is difficult to know how to interpret its correlation or lack thereof with the many other scales. On the positive side, it did have a moderate correlation with an employee reliability index; on the other hand, it had a much higher correlation with a test of reading comprehension. Obviously, it is premature for the authors to claim that the pattern of correlations shows a "sensible pattern" and is evidence of EI's validity (p. 31).

A variety of correlations are cited in support of the criterion validity of the EI and CSI. The figures are similar to what has been found in other recent studies of the effect of personality variables on customer service that indicate the portion of variance in service performance explained by personality ranges between 3% and 20% (e.g., Hurley, 1998). Although this suggests that some personality factors do appear to have a significant impact, especially in some settings, we must also be careful not to exaggerate personality's importance across work settings.

SUMMARY. In summary, the good news is that independent studies do appear to support the ability of the PDI (EI) to facilitate discrimination between employees based upon some sort of commitment factor (Collins & Schmidt, 1993; Woolley & Hakstian, 1992). The bad news is that the evidence of dimensionality, reliability, and validity of scores from the instruments are weak primarily because it is inappropriate for so many variables to be represented in the global scores composing PDI EI and CSI. Finally, managers should keep in mind that personality variables by themselves may not be the only or the best predictors of performance, and care must be taken not to overattribute causation to scores from any instruments that focus exclusively on such factors.

REVIEWER'S REFERENCES

Gerbing, D. W., & Anderson, J. C. (1988, May). An updated paradigm for scale development incorporating unidimensionality and its assessment. *Journal of Marketing Research, 25,* 186–192.

Kelly, J. R., & McGrath, J. E. (1988). *On time and method.* Beverly Hills, CA: Sage.

Devellis, R. F. (1991). *Scale development: Theory and applications.* Newbury Park, CA: Sage Publications, Inc.

Woolley, R. M., & Hakstian, A. R. (1992). An examination of the construct validity of personality-based and overt measures of integrity. *Educational and Psychological Measurement, 52,* 475–489.

Collins, J. M., & Schmidt, F. L. (1993). Personality, integrity, and white collar crime: A construct validity study. *Personnel Psychology, 46,* 295–311.

Nunnally, J. C., & Bernstein, I. H. (1994). *Psychometric theory* (3rd ed.). New York: McGraw-Hill.

Hurley, R. F. (1998). Customer service behavior in retail settings: A study of the effect of service provider personality. *Journal of the Academy of Marketing Science, 26*(Spring), 115–127.

Review of the PDI Employment Inventory and PDI Customer Service Inventory by ANNIE W. WARD, Emeritus Professor, University of South Florida, Daytona Beach, FL:

The PDI Employment Inventory (EI) and the PDI Customer Service Inventory (CSI) were developed by Personnel Decisions, Inc. to assist businesses and industries in making employment decisions. Both inventories deal with noncognitive aspects of employee behavior.

The inventories are quite short and they are available either in separate booklets or in a single booklet that combines both inventories. There are three types of items in both inventories: True-false; three-choice multiple-choice; and four-choice multiple-choice. The inventories are available in several language versions: American Spanish/English, British English, French-Canadian/English, Mexican Spanish, and Vietnamese/English. Three scores are reported on the combined inventories: Performance Score (EI), Tenure Score (EI), and Customer Service Score (CSI).

Although the test booklets themselves are not impressive, the manual is. It is well-written and contains much informative, useful information. Although it is directed primarily toward those who are responsible for hiring large groups of hourly employees, it also contains an impressive amount of technical information.

The manual starts with a brief discussion of personality tests in general and a longer discussion of counterproductive behavior and its relationship to satisfactory employee behavior. Then the authors describe the procedures used to develop the PDI inventories.

The authors are careful to recommend that users conduct their own studies and set their own cutoff scores based on local data. They also recommend that these inventories be used as only a part of hiring criteria, and that they be used in conjunction with other information. There is also a good discussion of "Adverse Impact and Fairness" and evidence to indicate that the PDI inventories are unbiased.

VALIDITY.

Development of the Employment Inventory (EI). In developing the EI, the authors followed procedures recommended in the literature. In order to define the construct, they started with a review of the literature, then they interviewed executives and managers of large companies and examined such materials as job descriptions, employee handbooks, training guides, and case files of counterproductive behavior.

From these materials they developed a set of 25 predictor constructs, mostly negative, separated into 10 major categories, which they used for item development. During the item development process they looked at a number of other instruments that seemed to be related to at least one of the constructs. A large number of items were written, but some of the constructs did not lend themselves to item writing, so the original 25 constructs were reduced to 13. Two of the original major headings were no longer there: "Excitement seeking" and "social influence." One subheading was apparently changed from "anomie" to "alienation." Careful study of the definition of the original constructs suggests that a different term for some of them might have been more informative. For example, the major heading "socialization," which has a positive connotation, is defined by the three headings of "delinquency," "fringe involvement," and "undeveloped values." Similarly, all of the subheadings under "Attitudes" are negative. It is clear that the items were directed at "nonproductiveness," which was the intent of the authors, but the terms used for some of them do not make this clear. The items were subjected to try-outs, concurrently with a sample of college students and with employees of a large retail chain.

Factor Analysis. Although the EI was not intended to be a factorially pure construct, a factor analysis was conducted with the data from the large department store. Of the 13 constructs that resulted from the original study and item writing, only five factors were identified and these factors accounted for only 15.7% of the total variance.

Predictive Studies. Scores on the EI were correlated with measures of job performance, with most of them being low positive (except when the hypothesized relationship is negative). Of the 167 relationships reported, 44% of the correlations were in the .20s and 27% were in the .30s. Eleven percent were higher than .40.

A comparison was also made of the percentage of satisfactory job performances of employees of one industry for those who "failed" and those who "passed" the EI, and for the situation with no use of the EI. There was a slight gain in the percentage of satisfactory employees with the use of the EI, ranging from 5–7% depending on where the cutting score was set.

Development of the Customer Service Inventory (CSI). The development of the CSI was based primarily on a study of the literature. Sixteen dimensions of personality that influence customer service were identified. Items were developed and administered to two groups of current employees and two groups of job applicants. Job analysis questionnaires were also administered to both job incumbents and supervisors. Four indicators of employee performance were developed and rank ordered. Only items that were related to job performance in more than one organization were selected for the final form of the inventory, which consists of 64 items.

Factor Analysis. Although the CSI was not intended to measure a factorially pure construct, a factor analysis was conducted. This analysis identified 10 factors that contributed 43.3% of the total variance of the inventory. The 5 largest factors contributed 28.2% of the total variance. It is easy to see the relationship between these factors and some of the original hypothesized constructs. However, a large percentage of the items did not load on any factor.

Predictive Studies. Scores on the CSI were correlated with four job ratings for eight employee groups. The correlations were mostly in the .20s.

A comparison was also made of the percentage of satisfactory job performances of employees of one industry for those who "failed" and those who "passed" the CSI, and for the situation with no use of the CSI. There was a slight gain in the percentage of satisfactory employees with the use of the EI, ranging from 3%–8%, depending on where the cutting score was set.

RELIABILITY. The internal reliability of the EI is reported as in the .60s and .70s, which the authors describe as acceptable, because the inventories were developed specifically to measure several different traits. The 4 week test-retest reliability estimate for the EI was only .60, which the authors attribute to the fact that it was obtained on a sample of university students, for which the scores have a restricted range.

For the CSI, the internal reliability was .73 and the one-month test-retest reliability was an impressive .86.

ADMINISTRATION AND SCORING. Both the EI and the SCI are essentially self-administering. There is a set of instructions to be read by the examiner while the examinee follows. A glossary of terms is provided in case the examinee needs help with a word.

There are 97 items on the EI, 64 on the CSI, and 145 on the combined instrument. Although there are no time limits, most examinees finish in less than 30 minutes. Both inventories use a set of "infrequent response" items to identify examinees who are not responding validly.

Both inventories may be scored quickly with the use of a computer disk. The disk keeps a record of each examinee and summarizes the records.

SUMMARY. In contrast with many other noncognitive instruments, the PDI inventories have much to commend them. The authors followed recommended procedures for identifying the constructs and writing items. They also collected empirical information, which they used to validate and select the items included in the inventories. Also, although the reliability information and the construct validation information came from the "convenient sample" of university students, the predictive validity data came from employees and supervisors in businesses and industry, as it should.

There are some problems, however. Unfortunately, neither the reliability nor the validity information is good enough to warrant uncritical use of these inventories as the sole, or even the primary, source of information to be used in making hiring decisions. This is true of most instruments of this nature. Whether use of the PDI inventories as part of the employment process will improve the percentage of satisfactory job performances depends very much on the local situation.

As is usual with noncognitive inventories, the statistical evidence for validity is not impressive. Scores on the inventories were correlated with scores on other personality and ability instruments and, in general, the significant correlations were in the hypothesized direction. Correlations were also run between scores on the inventories and supervisors' ratings, and again the correlations were in the right direction, but low. And some limited studies of satisfactory job performance demonstrated slight gains with the use of the inventories.

In addition to the relatively low statistical evidence, there are some problems with the face validity of the inventories. Although the concept of face validity is not highly regarded, it is still important in some situations. Testing for employment would seem to be one of those. With the low correlations between inventory scores and job performance ratings, it would be reassuring to find that the items look as if they would educe important information. This does not appear to be so for many of the items.

Examination of the items raises some question about just what is being measured by some of them. Furthermore, some of them require a great deal more self-insight than many of the targeted examinees are apt to have. And some items and/or options are so obviously negative that *aware* examinees would not choose them. It may be that these specific items are those that are included as a part of the "Infrequency scale," but they do not seem to be so.

CONCLUSION. As the authors correctly point out, no single instrument should be used as the sole basis for making decisions about hiring. Also, the PDI inventories deal only with attitude and ethics. Of even more importance for many jobs is the matter of the knowledge and skills needed to handle the job, which would have to be evaluated from some other data. The authors of the PDI inventories feel that with hourly (by which they apparently mean "low-level") employees, the attitude and ethics questions may be of equal importance. In situations in which this is true, these inventories may be useful adjuncts to the hiring information.

The information could make an important contribution to those decisions in certain situations. First, the situation would be one in which there was the need to hire large numbers of hourly employees. Second, a job analysis should be made to determine that the traits needed by the employees are essentially the same as those addressed on one or both of these inventories. And, finally, the employer would need to conduct an ongoing validation study to investigate whether scores on the inventory are really a help in identifying potential employee problems.

[61]

PEEK—Perceptions, Expectations, Emotions, and Knowledge About College.

Purpose: "Designed to assess prospective student's expectations about what college will be like."
Population: Prospective college students.
Publication Date: 1995.
Acronym: PEEK.
Scores, 3: Academic Expectations, Personal Expectations, Social Expectations.
Administration: Group.
Price Data, 1996: $1.75 per publisher scored form; $1.25 per software scored form (volume discounts available); $10 per software scoring kit (one-time purchase).
Time: (15–25) minutes.

Comments: Self-report questionnaire; can be machine scored by publisher, locally via software, or by hand in classroom settings.
Authors: Claire E. Weinstein, David R. Palmer, and Gary R. Hanson.
Publisher: H & H Publishing Company, Inc.

Review of the PEEK—Perceptions, Expectations, Emotions, and Knowledge About College by DAVID GILLESPIE, Social Science Faculty, Detroit College of Business, Warren, MI:

The PEEK—Perceptions, Expectations, Emotions, and Knowledge About College was designed to assess student expectations regarding college. Three domains of expectations are considered: Academic, Personal, and Social. Students compare their expectations to those of other individuals from the same institution who have also completed the questionnaire. This within-institution comparison was designed to provide more relevant comparisons. The authors believe that students who have unrealistic expectations are at-risk to encounter academic difficulties. Intervention and retention efforts could be targeted to these individuals who report unrealistic expectations.

The PEEK is a single-page, paper-and-pencil questionnaire consisting of 30 items. This questionnaire can be administered individually or in a group setting. Expectations for each area are assessed by 10 questions. Test respondents use a 4-point rating scale for their responses. The alternatives on this scale range from *Not at all likely* to *Extremely likely.*

The tests was constructed by polling over 3,000 college faculty and students over 4 years regarding expectations about college. The resulting information was used to develop a database of 300 items regarding differences in the personal, social, and academic environments of different colleges and schools. Test items were then selected from this pool.

The authors believe that a formal background in psychological test administration is not needed in order to administer, score, and interpret the results of this test. However, faculty or university staff using this test should have a thorough understanding of the information in the test manual, use of test results, and standard test administration. Test instructions are clearly written on the front of the questionnaire.

Although the PEEK can be hand scored, computer scoring and interpretation is also available. If computer scoring is desired, completed tests can be sent to the publishing company for scoring or software can be purchased for on-site scoring. The PEEK scoring software can generate three types of reports: PEEK Distribution Report, Peek Individual Report, and Peek Summary Report. The PEEK Distribution Report provides descriptive data for each of the 10 questions in each category, across all subjects who completed the form. The Individual Report provides the student who completed the questionnaire a comparison of his or her responses to those of peers, and the PEEK Summary Report provides summative information for all the students who completed the form.

The PEEK Individual Report uses z-scores to describe student responses. The patterns of these responses are compared to those of other students and faculty at the host institution. Although most students will be unfamiliar with the direct interpretation of z-scores, the manual and computer-generated reports provide good explanations of test interpretations.

The PEEK has a number of strengths. It can be quickly administered and scored. There is strong theoretical support for the effect cognitions have on behavior. The results of the PEEK can be used to increase student awareness of their own expectations and in student advising. These results can also assist the institution in better serving its students. Once discrepant cognitions are identified, a range of intervention options can be instituted. The PEEK and its scoring software are very reasonably priced. The PEEK is also easily hand scored.

Although the PEEK has its strengths, it also has a number of limitations. The manual is unclear as to how the final 30 test questions were selected. A review of the manual suggests the test developers made the final decisions based on their preferences and experiences. The use of z-scores as compared to the more commonly employed scaled scores could contribute to difficulty in score interpretation. As stated in the manual, the use of z-scores may lead to some counter-intuitive interpretations in extreme circumstances. Although z-scores are designed to indicate relative agreement/disagreement between the expectations of a particular student in relation to those of a larger group of students, certain circumstances could complicate score interpretation. If the majority of

students agree in their expectations with the institution, a low z-score may still indicate general agreement with institutional expectations. If a majority of students differ in their expectations from those of the institution, high z-scores may show little agreement with institutional expectations.

A related area of concern focuses on the comparison group used for score interpretation. The manual suggests that faculty, as well as students, complete the test. These respondents serve as the formal comparison group. However, this raises a number of issues. What relevance does a faculty member's perceptions have in relation to the expectations of the average undergraduate? It might be more effective to have upper-level students complete the PEEK based on their experiences. This information could serve as the comparison group for entry-level students. The authors of the PEEK also do not provide normative data to be used in test interpretation. This requires in-house comparisons. Although such comparisons can be useful, the issue of cohort effects can challenge the validity of test interpretation.

The scoring software also contains a default scoring system. This default scoring was created by the authors of the PEEK to reflect their experience with a number of institutions in the development of the instrument. The manual states that most institutions will find the default scoring is in close agreement with their own situations. However, there is no research cited to support this claim. The manual also states that the weights given to each of the 30 responses can be adjusted to reflect the expectations of the institution. However, an individual would need expertise in test construction and statistics before undertaking such a process. Additionally, when tests are hand scored, there is no procedure provided for aggregating the data across advisors for score comparisons and interpretation. There is no indication of how many students would be needed for a valid sample of the expectations of a general group of students. Perhaps most importantly, there are no psychometric data provided in the manual related to validity or reliability for score interpretation and use. This lack of information presents a formidable obstacle.

SUMMARY. The PEEK is a 30-item questionnaire used to assess entering college student's expectations related to college life in personal, academic, and social areas. It can easily be administered individually or in a group. Scoring can be facilitated by use of the computer-scoring package. Test results can be used by advisors or counselors to assist students in reformulating inaccurate expectations of college life. The weaknesses of the test include the lack of psychometric data, the use of z-scores to interpret test results, the lack of established comparison groups, and scanty information on test construction methods or institutional information related to its default scoring system.

Review of the PEEK—Perceptions, Expectations, Emotions, and Knowledge About College by DANIEL L. YAZAK, Assistant Professor and Chair, Department of Counseling and Human Services, Montana State University—Billings, Billings, MT:

Perceptions, Expectations, Emotions, and Knowledge (PEEK) About College is a 30-question self-report instrument designed to elicit responses that can be categorized according to Academic, Personal, and Social Expectations. Target users include prospective and current students, faculty, staff, and administrators in institutions of higher education. Results of the test can be used to provide an individual perspective or an individual score that can be compared with a peer group or another group using the PEEK. Uses of results include a basis for exploration of perceptions categorized into Academic, Personal, and Social experiences. The authors suggest that psychometric properties are established on a site-specific basis.

The PEEK was developed over a 7-year period. During that time, in excess of 3,000 individuals have contributed to the evolution of the 30-question item pool. No specific information is provided concerning psychometric properties of reliability and validity. National norms are not presented as PEEK is intended to provide information that can be compared on an institution-specific, time-limited basis. For example, perceptions, emotions, expectations, and knowledge data obtained from administering the PEEK can be used to identify differences within and between locally constituted groups. This idiosyncratic use of the test can be further developed by utilizing z-scores for additional comparisons. Software developed for the PC is available to provide percent responses of a local group, expanding comparison possibilities.

As no national norms have been developed for the PEEK, sources of error measure have not been reported. The self-report results are elicited from a Likert-type scale ranging from *not at all likely to be a part of my college experience* to *extremely likely to be a part of my college experience*. These results do not lend themselves to standard error of measure calculations. One test form is available for use. Due to the fact that local comparison situations are encouraged, interrater reliability calculations are not presented. Comparisons among groups by the test user is suggested; reliability estimates for different groups have not been made. Decisions concerning similarities and differences are possible using group data given the constraints of reliability evidence.

The PEEK relies on the self-report of individuals and/or groups at a specific location. Outside criteria have not been suggests to calculate correlations. As no distribution of scores for outside criteria has been presented, predictive accuracy is not appropriate in the case of the PEEK. The individual nature of self-report responses suggests use of the scores for comparison purposes without validity calculations.

Instructions for test administration are provided in the PEEK User's Manual. Group or individual administrations are appropriate for the test. Individuals familiar with standard test administration procedures will be able to administer the PEEK. Explanations for taking the test and potential uses of the PEEK are printed on one side of the test instrument. Test directions are made available in the PEEK User's Manual for use in group administration. An example question and response set is provided for test takers so that a uniform understanding among test takers is established. Likert-scale explanations are also provided so the test taker can consistently differentiate between the qualifying statements of the answer sequence.

Directions for test completion do not indicate a time limit. As the test seeks self-report information no reference materials or calculators are necessary. Standard testing requirements of a well-lit, well-ventilated room with minimal distractions are necessary. Test takers will require a writing surface and a number 2 pencil to complete the test.

A distribution report is available, which provides site score groups in three categories: Academic Expectations, Personal Expectations, and Social Expectations. Raw scores and percent responses are reported in addition to standard deviation, mean, median, and mode statistics for the category. Individual reports are available which convert raw scores to z-scores for the site and category. Summary reports provide a listing of individuals and z-scores by category. Interpretation of the individual z-score is provided in a narrative format along with a description of the category.

The PEEK is available in English written at a level appropriate for students who are able to read information concerning perceptions, expectations, emotions, and knowledge about academic, personal, and social experiences.

SUMMARY. Self-reported perspectives of Academic, Personal, and Social Expectations about College are elicited from a 30-question instrument. These reports provide individual and site-specific comparisons.

[62]

Personal Stress Assessment Inventory.

Purpose: A self-assessment instrument designed to identify those who would most likely benefit from participation in stress-management training.
Population: Adults.
Publication Dates: 1981–1993.
Acronym: PSAI.
Scores, 6: Predisposition, Resilience, Sources of Stress, Overall Stress Factor, Health Symptoms, Personal Reactions.
Administration: Group.
Price Data, 1998: $7.50 per inventory (volume discounts available).
Time: (20–30) minutes.
Comments: Self-administered; self-scored.
Author: Herbert S. Kindler.
Publisher: The Center for Management Effectiveness.

Review of the Personal Stress Assessment Inventory by E. SCOTT HUEBNER, Professor of Psychology, University of South Carolina, Columbia, SC:

The Personal Stress Assessment Inventory (PSAI) was designed "to reflect which respondents would most likely benefit from participation in stress-management training" (Kindler & Schorr, 1991, p. 4). This self-report inventory includes six scales: Predisposition, Resilience, Sources of Stress, Health Symptoms, Overall Stress, and a social desirability scale.

Scoring and interpretation procedures are described in a one-page attachment to the test protocol. Cut-points for elevated scores are provided. However, no data are offered to support their accuracy.

Overall, limited information is available regarding the technical properties of the PSAI. Item analysis information is absent. The standardization sample was small and described inadequately. No descriptive statistics for the sample are indicated.

Reliability information is limited to estimates of internal consistency (i.e., coefficient alpha), presumably for the five subscales (even though a total stress factor scores is calculated and interpreted). The alphas ranged from .51 (Predisposition scale) to .91 (unspecified scale); however, the authors state "the Predisposition scale was revised following this study and brought up to an adequate level of reliability" (p. 6). Nevertheless, further information regarding the manner in which the Predisposition scale (which was designed to measure Type A behavioral tendencies) was modified and the resulting reliability coefficient is not specified.

Validity information is also lacking. The authors state that intercorrelations among the scales were assessed, but fail to provide the correlation coefficients. Similarly, the authors state that the PSAI is unrelated to social desirability responding, but provide no data. On a positive note, the PSAI Predisposition, Resilience, and Sources of Stress scales cumulatively predicted the PSAI Health Symptoms score, and the various PSAI scales (except Predisposition) discriminated a group of employees enrolled in a stress management program from a group of employees "under more typical employee pressures" (p. 7). Nevertheless, considerable additional information is needed to support the content, criterion (including predictive), and construct validity of scores from the PSAI before it can be used confidently in individual decision making. For one example, factor analytic studies are crucial to the determination of the construct validity of the scale. For another example, evidence of convergent validity with respect to other more established measures of the same constructs (e.g., other Type A measures, stressful events measures), including reports from other raters (e.g., spouses, coworkers), would be helpful. Furthermore, the PSAI should be scrutinized to rule out the possibility of any racial or gender bias.

In sum, the PSAI should be considered to be in the preliminary stage of development. It awaits considerable further research support before it can be used for any purpose, even research purposes.

REVIEWER'S REFERENCE

Kindler, H. S., & Schorr, D. (1991). Stress management training programmes: Motivating participation using a self-diagnostic inventory. *Employee Counseling Today, 3*(1), 4–8.

Review of the Personal Stress Assessment Inventory by NORMAN D. SUNDBERG, Professor Emeritus, Department of Psychology, University of Oregon, Eugene, OR:

Appropriately the cover of the Personal Stress Assessment Inventory (PSAI) is a calming picture of flowers by the seaside. Inside, the 10 pages give instructions followed by 10 to 33 items and scoring instructions. The following examples illustrate the flavor of the item content and method of answering: (a) For the Predisposition scale respondents must choose along a line of numbers from 1 to 10 between *I often got annoyed when I waited in line* and *I rarely got annoyed when I waited in line.* (b) For Resilience on the next page, respondents must choose from 1 to 4 (*Frequently,* to *Not in the Last 30 Days*) on such items as *I seek places where I can find serenity.* (c) For Stress Sources on two pages, they write 1 to 10 (low to major impact) on personal items such as *A person close to me died,* and separately on work items *I was criticized by my boss.* (d) On an additional two pages they rate other sets of Stress Source items for whether each condition is within one's power to change or not. (e) For Personal Reactions, they write T or F by items measuring social desirability, such as *I like to gossip at times.* (f) Health Symptom items call for circling 1 to 4 on frequency for Physical Symptoms such as "Diarrhea" and Psychological Symptoms such as "Frightening dreams." The last two pages cover scoring and interpretation.

The content of PSAI items incorporates a variety of the ideas in the stress literature, particularly drawing on work on Type A and life change ideas. However, the changing nature of the method of answering the items could be confusing and the scoring is rather complex. The description says that the time required is 20 to 30 minutes. However, it seems likely that it would take longer, especially for people not used to taking tests, perhaps more than a half hour to answer and 15 minutes to score. The inventory could be improved by reducing it to only one or two different ways of answering the items and a simpler scoring system.

The purpose of the PSAI is to identify those who would benefit from stress-management training (Kindler & Schorr, 1991). As presented by Kindler and Schorr, the PSAI is used in the first session of a three-session group program and is self-administered and scored. They emphasize confidentiality of results and the voluntary nature of the training. Unless the inventory is a regular part of a training program, the respondents not only would need to take and score the instrument by themselves but also to self-identify and be motivated to seek training or counseling. There are no studies of whether tested employees actually seek help outside the training sessions.

The last page of the inventory tells respondents how to interpret their scores. The author, Herbert Kindler, does not present a table of norms or indicate how he chose the critical scores such as the following: On Resilience "scores above 50 suggest more caring attention can be given to gaining better emotional, physical, mental and spiritual balance," and on the Overall Stress Factor scores above 55 or below 15 deserve special attention. The current form of the PSAI evidently is revised; the instrument was originally copyrighted in 1981.

A survey of psychology publications revealed no reports on the psychometric properties of the PSAI other than the Kindler and Schorr article (1991), although Kindler has some articles on stress management training. The Kindler and Schorr study may serve as a manual but it is not so labeled. It is a report of the use of the PSAI with a sample of 82 white-collar middle managers and professionals from a variety of organizations and another sample of 20 employees who reported to the company medical department because of stress-related symptoms. All scales except Predisposition (.51) showed adequate internal consistency (.79 to .91), but no test-retest reliability is given. A table of intercorrelations among scales is not shown, but the authors report that social desirability (the Personal Reactions scale) did not affect other scales in a significant way. Except for the Predisposition scale, scales were significantly correlated with health symptoms, indicating some evidence of concurrent validity. Also a comparison of the two samples showed significantly more perceived stress with those employees who had reported for medical services with stress-related symptoms on all scales except Predisposition. The Predisposition scale, which is derived from Type A theory about proneness to heart trouble, did not work well in several instances; the authors argue that Type A theory is flawed and that irritability and hostility are symptoms that are easy to cover up. A regression analysis on health symptoms showed that Resilience and non-work sources of stress were particularly important in accounting for variance separate from other stress indicators. There is, therefore, some evidence of concurrent and construct validity, but no report on predictive validity. In the article the authors conclude that low resilience is an excellent "predictor" of excessive stress symptoms. Their recommendation for balance in life is mentioned but not theoretically explicated.

Several *Mental Measurements Yearbooks* contain reviews of self-report instruments for working adults. The closest to the PSAI seem to be the Meta-Motivation Inventory (9:698) published in 1979, the Stress Resiliency Profile (13:301) published in 1992, and the Work Temperament Inventory (13:368) published in 1993. None of these have been used in research efforts comparing them with the PSAI, and their purposes are somewhat different. The first one is the closest, because it is intended to help managers and others in leadership positions evaluate their own development in management and personal growth. It provides feedback on thinking styles relative to management theories. It would be useful to have some research comparing these and other such stress-related instruments. The Kindler and Schorr article makes no reference to the instruments just mentioned. They report that the PSAI is widely used in North America and the United Kingdom and has been translated into Japanese.

SUMMARY. What might one conclude about the PSAI? This self-report inventory offers an array of material about stress and its sources. It seems that it would be helpful for alerting employed people to possible problems in their own thinking and their work and non-work environments. It may be useful as a teaching tool in stress management programs. However, research on the inventory is very limited, and the format of the inventory is rather complex for self-administration

and scoring. The jury is out about whether the inventory would add anything to an employee assistance program beyond being a teaching tool alerting people to the nature of stress.

REVIEWER'S REFERENCE

Kindler, H. S., & Schorr, D. (1991). Stress-management training programmes: Motivating participation using a self-diagnostic inventory. *Employee Counseling Today, 3*(1), 4–8.

[63]

Police Selection Test.

Purpose: "Designed to measure abilities important for successful performance in training and on-the-job" as a police officer.
Population: Police officer applicants.
Publication Dates: 1989–1995.
Acronym: PST.
Scores: Total score only.
Administration: Group.
Price Data: Price information available from publisher for test material including Technical manual ('90, 17 pages), Administrator's Guide ('90, 8 pages), and Study Guide and sample questions ('90, 21 pages).
Time: (120) minutes.
Comments: Measures reading comprehension, quantitative problem solving, data interpretation, writing skills, and verbal problem solving.
Author: Psychological Services, Inc.
Publisher: Psychological Services, Inc.

Review of the Police Selection Test by JIM C. FORTUNE, Professor of Educational Research and Evaluation, Virginia Tech University, Blacksburg, VA:

PURPOSE. The Police Selection Test was designed to measure abilities important for successful performances in police training and on-the-job. The test is an entry-level test designed to select candidates for admission to the basic training program for police work.

DESCRIPTION. The test is a group-administered, multiple-choice test made up of 100 items organized in five sections. These sections include:

Section 1—reading comprehension—19 items measuring the ability to read, interpret, and apply information associated with police work.

Section 2—quantitative problem solving—20 items measuring the ability to work with number relationships, patterns, and organization principles.

Section 3—interpretation—23 items measuring the ability to read and use charts, tables, and maps and to follow written directions.

Section 4—writing skills—15 items measuring the ability to communicate with written language.

Section 5—verbal problem solving—23 items measuring the ability to use facts and make judgments from them.

RATIONALE. Criteria for any selection test for employment include: linkage of its content with the jobs for which the selection is being made and coverage of the relevant content, reliability, administrative ease, and production of results from which valid interpretations can be made. The linkage of content with the jobs for which the selection is being made is established through a quality job analysis. The coverage of the relevant content is assured through the table of specifications. Reliability must be adequate to make decisions on individuals and is shown through prestudy of the test performance. The manual for test administration gives evidence of administrative ease. The production of results from which valid interpretations can be made is evidenced through reported validity studies. These criteria form the basis for the review of the technical characteristics of this selection test.

TECHNICAL INFORMATION. The Technical Manual is concise, written with clarity, and easy to use. Perhaps its greatest fault is the omission of details needed to track the test development process.

The Technical Manual refers to but does not adequately describe the job analysis. The developers of the test report that three sources of information were used to determine job-relevant item types. It is assumed that determination of "item types" actually means test content. The sources were comprehensive job analysis, research literature, and police personnel. The job analysis was not described and a brief description of a meta-analysis is the information given on the literature search. Content selection appeared to be linked to training tests through current validity studies with training tests. Police personnel were asked to remember items that differentiated the most between superior and poor police performers. It appears that the linkage of content was made with the training for the job rather than with the job. It is unclear how the test developers assured the coverage of the relevant content. The Technical Manual does include a paragraph explaining that knowledge of the law, department

rules and regulations, and police procedures must be obtained on the job and are not appropriate for entry-level testing. Knowledge of human psychology and behavior should be part of the test as well as trainee personality and philosophical traits.

In the Technical Manual reliability in the form of coefficient alpha was reported for what was described as the total test scores, but it was actually a pooled estimate of the reliabilities of the subtest scores. This coefficient was .94, which is judged to be adequate to make decisions on individuals. The subtest reliabilities were not reported. The manual for test administration is brief and straightforward, serving as evidence of administrative ease. The production of results from which valid interpretations can be made is evidenced through reported validity studies linking test performance to training outcomes. The validation study linking the test to outcomes provided a product moment correlation of .53 corrected up for attenuation to .65. Note that this validity index is for success in the training program and not on the job.

EVALUATION. The test contains similar content to other police selection tests, but it is very important to note that the content is directed toward selection for training and not for the job. The test does not appear comprehensive enough to serve as a total criterion for selection, but it appears to be quite useful as part of a selection battery.

Review of the Police Selection Test by DENIZ S. ONES, Hellervik Professor of Industrial-Organizational Psychology, Department of Psychology, University of Minnesota, Minneapolis, MN:

As early as 1917, industrial-organizational psychologists looked for, created, or used ability tests in police personnel selection (e.g., Terman et al., 1917). This is with good reason: Police are entrusted with public safety and hiring incompetent police officers endangers public safety. The Police Selection Test (PST) was designed to test some of the abilities important to successful law enforcement and therefore, presumably, was developed to enable police departments to select the highest ability job applicants for the job.

DESCRIPTION. The purpose of the PST is to measure the ability of entry-level job candidates for police officer jobs. That is, the test is designed to predict "successful performance in training and on the job" (technical manual, p. 1) for police officers. It is intended for use with law enforcement job applicants. This ability test has a total of 100 items and is composed of five subsections with various numbers of items (see test development description below).

TEST DEVELOPMENT. Test development focused on abilities rather than job knowledge because it was important to be able to test job applicants at the entry level prior to acquiring specific job knowledge. It is expected that most of the job knowledge required to be a successful police officer would be acquired in training or later on the job. The domains to be tested by the PST were identified by drawing upon three sources: (a) job analytic information, (b) the research literature, and (c) job experts (police lieutenants). That is, development of the content of the PST was based on a detailed and comprehensive review of job analyses for police officer jobs coupled with a quantitative literature review on police selection using ability measures. In particular, test development heavily drew upon the findings of the Hirsch, Northrop, and Schmidt (1986) meta-analysis showing that across multiple studies and police departments, ability test showed sizable operational validities for predicting performance in training. In this meta-analysis, the operational validity of verbal ability tests for predicting training performance was .62. Police lieutenants were also involved in test development as job experts. They were asked to think of superior and unsuccessful police officers they knew and then to identify the characteristics that differentiated them. Characteristics that were consistently identified were included in the PST.

The subsections of the test are as follows: (a) reading comprehension, (b) quantitative problem solving (number series), (c) interpretation (ability to read charts, tables, maps, and instructions), (d) writing skills, and (e) verbal problem solving (verbal reasoning). Initially, 200 items were written and administered to 2,112 police officer job applicants (of the developmental sample providing demographic information on sex and race, the breakdown was as follows: 1,615 males, 487 females, 973 Whites, 876 Blacks, and 107 Hispanics). Items were written so that they did not contain any material that could be offensive to any ethnic group or sex. Two members of the test development team examined each item that was included on the experimental test.

Item analyses examined item difficulty, effectiveness of multiple-choice response option distracters, item-total and item-remainder correlations, and item bias. Items that were too difficult or too easy were eliminated. Poor distracters were identified by excluding those items with high distracter-total correlations. Also, distracters that were not being selected by many respondents were also identified as poor. Item-total correlations were examined to select those items yielding the highest item-total correlations. Item bias analyses used two different methods. First, items that were found to have differential probability of correct response for persons of the same ability level but different race were removed (Berk, 1982). Second, items that were disproportionately difficult for Hispanics and Blacks were removed (Angoff, 1982; Angoff & Ford, 1973).

The final measure includes 100 questions: 19 reading comprehension questions, 20 quantitative problem-solving questions, 23 interpretation questions, 15 writing skills questions, and 23 verbal problem-solving questions. All items are multiple choice. All but the verbal problem-solving questions use four response options (the last subscale uses three response options). Readability analyses of the test indicate that the mean reading ease index is at the 10th grade reading level.

RELIABILITY. The technical manual reports the reliability of the full test as .94 (reliability of the composite of five subsections included on the test). This reliability was computed on the developmental sample (n = 2,112).

CRITERION-RELATED VALIDITY. Given that for ability tests concurrent validities have been shown to approximate predictive validities (Barrett, Phillips, & Alexander, 1981), concurrent validity was investigated for the PST. For a sample of 105 police officers in training, overall scores on the PST were correlated with mean training test scores. In this validation study, the criterion was the mean of three job knowledge tests completed during training. Job relatedness of the criterion measures was established by expert judgments (by police officers). The observed correlation was .53. When this correlation was corrected for the downward biasing effects of unreliability in the criterion and direct range restriction, one obtains a more accurate estimate of the evaluation of the criterion-related validity of the test for performance in police training. This corrected correlation was .65. Thus, the PST is a valid predictor of acquiring the job knowledge necessary to be a good police officer. This level of criterion-related validity for training performance mirrors the previous literature on the validities of scores from ability tests for police work (Hirsch et al., 1986).

Another consideration relating to criterion-related validity is transportability of the validity. The technical manual makes a suggestion to ensure validity generalization to other law enforcement jobs: The test users should examine whether or not the job at hand is similar to the job for which the criterion-related validity was demonstrated. The cumulative literature from industrial psychology indicates that ability is the best predictor of job performance for entry level jobs and that validity generalizes across organizations, jobs, and situations (Schmidt, Ones, & Hunter, 1992). There is no reason to suspect that the validity of the PST will not be generalizable.

TEST FAIRNESS. The PST does reveal mean score differences between minorities and Whites (based on the information reported in the technical manual, I computed the mean Black-White difference to be .94 standard deviation units, favoring Whites). However, mean differences were also found on the criterion. The test publishers have examined the fairness of their test by computing subgroup validities for Blacks and Whites separately. Further, the regression lines for Blacks and Whites were compared. The results of these investigations revealed no differential validities for Blacks and Whites. Based on these data, the test was demonstrated to be fair to both Blacks and Whites in that training performance was not underestimated for Blacks.

NORMS. Mean and standard deviation information is available for the initial 2,112-participant developmental sample, as well as the 205-participant validation sample (broken out by racial group).

ADMINISTRATION AND USE. The subsections of the test are not separately timed but there is an overall 2-hour time limit to complete the 100 questions of the test. All the correct responses across all the sections of the test are summed to obtain an overall test score for each job applicant. The administrator's guide provides full text instructions to be read when administering the test. Scoring can be done by hand or by scanning machine. The scores on the PST can be used for ranking the job applicants, or a cutoff score can be established for hiring.

The ability items on the instrument are all job related, and therefore the test as a whole is likely to be perceived by applicants to be face valid. For example, the reading passage materials for the reading comprehension portion of the test were based on police introductory texts, police departmental notices, and manuals. This may enhance the usability of the measure for personnel selection. Further, because the test is not a measure of job knowledge and thus does not require any prior specialized training or knowledge, the test's usability for selecting entry level police work is enhanced.

MANUALS AND SUPPORTING DOCUMENTS. There are several manuals and supporting documents that accompany the PST. These are an informational brochure (7 pages), a study guide and sample questions (21 pages), an administrator's guide (8 pages), and a technical manual (17 pages). I found these materials to be extremely useful. Particularly the technical manual contained much of the psychometric information on the test.

SUMMARY. The PST is a good instrument. It is exemplary in making use of the past meta-analytic literature to guide test development. Further, the test's development and validation comply with the *Uniform Guidelines on Employee Selection Procedures* (U.S. Equal Employment Opportunity Commission, 1978) and the *Standards for Educational and Psychological Testing* of the American Psychological Association (AERA, APA, & NCME, 1985). The only psychometric data I found to be missing were on construct validity. Particularly, I would have liked to see some evidence of convergent and divergent validity. This should be reported in test manuals and can provide critically important information to potential users of the PST in designing *selection systems*. Also, both the test developers and users should continue to gather criterion-related validity for the criterion of job performance. These validity studies with the PST can contribute to future meta-analyses and can answer some important practical and scientific questions. Typically, ability tests have been shown to yield somewhat lower validities for job performance criteria than they do for training criteria (Hirsch et al., 1986). This has been attributed to both poor performance criteria (where raters have insufficient opportunity to observe) and the potential importance of noncognitive factors in police performance. To disentangle these two effects, it is essential that future validation studies with the PST attempt to develop good job performance criteria.

In 1917, Terman et al. wrote, "we know that 'general intelligence' can be measured with a fair degree of success, and we have reason to believe that this general intelligence, however we define it, is the most important single factor, apart from moral integrity, in determining fitness" (p. 18) for police positions. This statement still rings true over 80 years later. The PST appears to be a good measure of general cognitive ability and can be used as the cognitive ability component of police selection systems. As for "moral integrity," a class of tests referred to as integrity tests with fairly high demonstrated levels of criterion-related validity can be useful (Ones, Viswesvaran, & Schmidt, 1993).

REVIEWER'S REFERENCES

Terman, L. M., Otis, A. S., Dickson, V., Hubbard, J. K., Howard, L., Flanders, J. K., & Cassingham, C. C. (1917). A trial of mental and pedagogical tests in a civil service examination for policemen and firemen. *Journal of Applied Psychology, 1*(1), 17–29.
Angoff, W. H., & Ford, S. F. (1973). Item-race interaction on a test of scholastic aptitude. *Journal of Educational Measurement, 10*, 95–105.
U.S. Equal Employment Opportunity Commission, U.S. Civil Service Commission, U.S. Department of Labor, & U.S. Department of Justice. (1978). Uniform guidelines on employee selection procedures. *Federal Register, 43*, (166), 38295–38309.
Barrett, G. V., Phillips, J. S., & Alexander, R. A. (1981). Concurrent and predictive validity designs: A critical reanalysis. *Journal of Applied Psychology, 66*, 1–6.
Angoff, W. H. (1982). Use of difficulty and discrimination indices for detecting item bias. In R. A. Berk (Ed.), *Handbook of methods for detecting item bias* (pp. 96–116). Baltimore and London: The John Hopkins University Press.
Berk, R. A. (Ed.). (1982). *Handbook of methods for detecting item bias.* Baltimore, MD: The John Hopkins University Press.
American Educational Research Association, American Psychological Association, & National Council on Measurement in Education. (1985). *Standards for Educational and Psychological Testing.* Washington, DC: American Psychological Association, Inc.
Hirsch, H. R., Northrop, L. C., & Schmidt, F. L. (1986). Validity generalization results for law enforcement occupations. *Personnel Psychology, 39*, 399–420.
Schmidt, F. L., Ones, D. S., & Hunter, J. (1992). Personnel selection. *Annual Review of Psychology, 43*, 627–670.
Ones, D. S., Viswesvaran, C., & Schmidt, F. L. (1993). Comprehensive meta-analysis of integrity test validities: Findings and implications for personnel selection and theories of job performance. *Journal of Applied Psychology [Monograph], 78*, 679–703.

[64]
Posttraumatic Stress Diagnostic Scale.

Purpose: "Designed to aid in the diagnosis of posttraumatic stress disorder."
Population: Ages 17–65.
Publication Date: 1995.
Acronym: PDS.
Scores, 5: Symptom Severity Score, Number of Symptoms Endorsed, Symptom Severity Rating, Level of Impairment in Functioning, PTSD Diagnosis.

Administration: Group.
Price Data, 1997: $35 per hand scoring starter kit including manual (54 pages), 10 answer sheets, 10 scoring worksheets, and 1 scoring sheet; $117 per hand scoring reorder kit including 50 answer sheets, 50 scoring worksheets, and 1 scoring sheet; $17 per 25 MICROTEST Q answer sheets; $4.25 per MICROTEST Q profile report; $26 per manual; $35 per MICROTEST Q preview package including manual, answer sheets, and materials for 3 assessments.
Time: (10–15) minutes.
Author: Edna B. Foa.
Publisher: NCS (Minnetonka).
Cross References: See T5:2018 (1 reference).

Review of the Posttraumatic Stress Diagnostic Scale by STEPHEN N. AXFORD, Psychologist, Pueblo School District No. Sixty, Pueblo, CO, and University of Phoenix, Colorado Springs, CO:

With content aligned to DSM-IV criteria, the Posttraumatic Stress Diagnostic Scale (PDS) is a 49-item, paper-and-pencil or on-line, self-report clinical screening instrument designed to support assessment of the presence and severity of posttraumatic stress disorder (PTSD). As such, it is intended also to be used as a method for monitoring treatment progress. In fact, a computer-generated graphic Progress Report is available, utilizing NCS Assessments MICROTEST Q SYSTEM software, charting Symptom Severity and Number of Symptoms Endorsed. Although the PDS can be hand scored, a professional quality computer-generated interpretive report with tables, the Profile Report, is also available using the same software. The PDS requires approximately 10 to 15 minutes to administer and 5 minutes to score. Validated on clinical populations aged 18 to 65 years, the PDS is intended to be used with adults with at least eighth-grade reading level ability. As noted by the author, although clinical judgment may be used in deciding whether to administer the PDS to individuals falling outside the age range on which the PDS was normed, it should not be given to children because of the respective different DSM-IV criteria for diagnosing PTSD.

A well-written manual, cogently detailed, suitably addresses the conceptual and technical aspects of the PDS. As stated by the author and very evident in reviewing the test items, "the PDS was designed to correspond to DSM-IV diagnostic criteria for PTSD" (p. 3). Test items were revised following expert review. The PDS answer sheet, utilizing a combination of weighted or

Likert-type, dichotomous-choice (i.e., "yes/no"), and multiple-selection formats, is well organized and professional appearing, offering ample face validity.

Subjects were recruited for the normative sample (N = 248) from: Veterans Administration hospitals, anxiety and PTSD treatment clinics, women's shelters, emergency/trauma centers, fire stations, ambulance corps, and residential rehabilitation centers. A prerequisite for inclusion in the study was that the trauma-inducing event had to occur at least one month prior to administration of the PDS.

The author provides a detailed summary of the demographic characteristics for the PDS normative sample, specifically by: age, race, marital status, religion, employment status, occupation, education, and income. The author also furnishes a tabulation of types of traumatic events reported by the normative sample. As noted by the author, the distribution of traumas represented in the PDS normative sample "should not be considered indicative of the likelihood of a particular type of trauma producing PTSD or of the general population of individuals with PTSD" (p. 5). The author further states that the frequency distribution observed "is in part a reflection of the sites at which the data were collected" (p. 5). Indeed, a review of the norming sample demographics supports this disclaimer. For example, under the category of religion, only 20.2% of the participants are listed as Protestant, whereas 30.8% are listed as Catholic. This is an understandable sampling limitation given that the PDS focuses on such a very specific area of differential diagnosis, with PTSD having relatively limited representation in the general population. Nevertheless, future studies involving the PDS, particularly as this relates to norming, should attempt larger and more representative samples.

Although norm-referenced scores are not reported, the test results for the PDS include six components: PTSD Diagnosis (i.e., "yes/no"), Symptom Severity Score (ranging from 0 to 51, based on summation of weighted responses for items corresponding to the 17 DSM-IV PTSD Criteria B, C, and D), Number of Symptoms Endorsed, symptom onset and duration specifiers (Acute, Chronic, With Delayed Onset), Symptom Severity Rating (Mild, Moderate, Moderate to Severe, Severe), and Level of Impairment of Func-

tioning (No Impairment, Mild, Moderate, Severe). No validity index (e.g., measure of impression management) is provided. Future development and revision of the PDS should consider incorporation of such a component.

According to the author, "a diagnosis of PTSD is made if all six DSM-IV criteria … are met" (p. 5), specifically: exposure to a traumatic event, reexperiencing symptoms, avoidance symptoms, arousal symptoms, symptom duration of one month or more, and distress or impairment in functioning. Cut-points for the Symptom Severity Ratings "are based on the author's clinical judgment and experience … derived from a sample of 280 recent female assault victims and from a sample of 96 female assault victims with chronic PTSD" (p. 10). Future validation of the Symptom Severity Rating index should involve independent review of the cut-points by a group of experts. In addition, to the author's credit, users of the PDS are encouraged to interpret Symptom Severity Ratings data with caution, due to lack of validation research and because only female subjects were employed in establishing the cut-points. Of course, this could potentially affect generalizability of results. The author states that "at present, these cutoffs should be used only to roughly estimate the relative symptom severity manifested by a given individual compared to other trauma victims" (p. 10). However, even this practice would be questionable with regard to male subjects until further validation research is conducted on the Symptom Severity Rating index.

The manual for the PDS provides detailed discussion of the inventory's psychometric properties. Included is a summary of means and standard deviations for the Symptom Severity Score and Number of Symptoms Endorsed indexes, for subjects meeting (n = 128) and not meeting (n = 120) Structured Clinical Interview for DSM-III-R (SCID) PTSD criteria. Mean scores for subjects meeting SCID criteria for PTSD are significantly higher (p <.001) than for subjects not meeting SCID criteria. The study also compares PDS and SCID percent diagnostic agreement, yielding 79.4% agreement between the two measures, with a kappa of .59. PDS sensitivity (ability to correctly identify PTSD subjects) is reported to be 82.0% for the study. Specificity for the study (ability to correctly identify subjects not having PTSD) is reported to be 76.7%. These findings lend support that scores from the PDS are valid for screening for PTSD.

Convergent validity for the PDS was investigated by correlating (N = 230) the Symptom Severity Score with scales measuring constructs (depression, intrusion, avoidance, anxiety) associated with PTSD. This approach was taken because of the dearth of scales, particularly screening instruments, specifically designed to identify PTSD. Correlations between the PDS and the scales measuring related constructs are as follows: Beck Depression Inventory = .79, State-Trait Anxiety Inventory (State index) = .73, State-Trait Anxiety Inventory (Trait index) = .74, Impact of Event Scale (Intrusion index) = .80, Impact of Event Scale (Avoidance index) = .66. Although these data support the convergent validity of scores from the PDS, future research employing comprehensive scales that can be used in the differential diagnosis of PTSD (e.g., Personality Assessment Inventory [Morey, 1991; 12:290]) would further address, perhaps more directly, the issue.

Both internal consistency and test-retest stability were examined in investigating the reliability of scores from the PDS. A Cronbach alpha of .92 is reported for the 17 items used to calculate the Symptom Severity Score, indicating that this index has high internal consistency. Representing 110 retests with an average interval between administration of 16.1 days, a kappa of .74 is reported, with 87.3% diagnostic agreement between administrations. These data support the internal consistency and stability of scores from the PDS.

SUMMARY. The PDS represents a substantial achievement in the initial development of a conceptually and psychometrically sound PTSD screening instrument based on DSM-IV criteria. Besides providing professional quality interpretive reports, the PDS offers the innovative advantage of a convenient method for charting treatment progress. However, as the author notes, additional validation research is needed for more precise interpretation of the Symptom Severity Rating index (one of six PDS test results components provided). Nevertheless, the PDS meets its main objective of validly and reliably differentiating PTSD from non-PTSD subjects. In addition, both in the manual and computer-generated diagnostic report, to the author's credit, appropriate interpretation and use of PDS results are adequately addressed. Although the PDS would

benefit from additional validation research utilizing larger and perhaps demographically more representative samples, the PDS can appropriately be used as a clinical screening instrument for determining the presence of PTSD and charting changes in symptoms.

REVIEWER'S REFERENCE

Morey, L. C. (1991). Personality Assessment Inventory. Odessa, FL: Psychological Assessment Resources.

Review of the Posttraumatic Stress Diagnostic Scale by BETH DOLL, Associate Professor of School Psychology, University of Colorado at Denver, Denver, CO:

The author describes the Posttraumatic Stress Diagnostic Scale (PDS) as a 49-item, self-report scale to assist clinicians and researchers in diagnosing and judging the severity of Posttraumatic Stress Disorder as it is defined in the DSM-IV (*Diagnostic and Statistical Manual of Mental Disorders, Fourth Edition*; American Psychiatric Association, 1994). Despite this description, the PDS should be used principally as a research tool because evidence of its reliability and validity currently rests with a single, unreplicated study. As further evidence of the scale's technical adequacy emerges, the PDS could also prove to be a promising clinical tool.

The manual describes the use of the PDS in appropriately cautious terms. The author carefully advises that the scale not replace structured diagnostic interviews in making clinical decisions. The manual also notes that the scale should not be administered to persons under the age of 18, because the DSM-IV criteria are somewhat different for children and adolescents, and these differences are not represented in the PDS items. This latter caution may prove confusing to the scale's users because a prominent table in the manual maps the PDS against both adult and child criteria for the DSM-IV diagnosis of Posttraumatic Stress Disorder (PTSD). PDS items represent translations of the DSM-IV's technical language into common-use language suitable for adult clients: Items 1 through 21 serve to verify the respondent's experience of a traumatic event that involved actual or threatened death or injury to themselves or others and that left them feeling fearful and helpless (APA, 1994). Items 22 through 38 describe specific current symptoms of PTSD; respondents answer by indicating the presence and frequency of each symptom. Finally, Items 39 through 40 describe the duration of the symptoms and the degree to which these are interfering with the respondents' life.

Like all translations, the PDS language loses some of the richness of the original DSM-IV definition, and it is unclear how critical such omissions are. For example, the DSM-IV experience of "intense fear, helplessness or horror" (APA, 1994, p. 428) is translated into two items: "Did you feel helpless?" and "Did you feel terrified?" Is terror the same as intense fear? Are these the same as horror? The author reports that the item language was reviewed by other experts in the field in an attempt to evaluate the translations but stops short of describing how many experts reviewed the scale or the nature of their expertise. Consequently, the face validity of the scale's language is not entirely established.

Results of the PDS yield three judgments: (a) whether the six critical diagnostic criteria for PTSD have been met; (b) the Level of Impairment as judged by counting the number of life areas affected; and (c) the Symptom Severity Score created by summing severity ratings for the current symptoms list.

Although the manual refers to a "normative sample" underlying the PDS, the scale is not a norm-referenced measure. Instead, the PDS is criterion-referenced, with the objective of determining the degree to which PDS responses accurately reflect the "correct" DSM-IV diagnostic decision. Clinical labels are attached to the Level of Impairment and Symptom Severity Scores, but these labels do not appear to be derived from the performance of subjects in the scale's validity study.

Information assessing the reliability of the PDS and its adequacy as a criterion measure of the PTSD diagnosis is drawn wholly from a single 248-subject study reported in the manual. Unfortunately, the manual's description of the study omits critical information, whereas other details suggest that the study was not sufficiently representative to stand as a sole evidence of the technical adequacy of the scale. For example, subjects were drawn from agencies serving high-trauma populations in five East Coast states and two Midwestern cities. Figures presented in the PDS manual suggest that low- and upper-income subjects were somewhat overrepresented in the sample, and that Hispanic-American subjects and those of other minority groups were somewhat underrepresented. Subjects were included only if they had experienced a traumatic event meeting the DSM-IV criteria no less than one month before the study; consequently, the scale is most appropriately used to screen for PTSD among persons known to have experienced trauma.

Subjects were administered both the PDS and the Structured Clinical Interview for DSM-III-R (SCID; Williams et al., 1992), with the latter serving as the criterion measure against which the PDS was evaluated. The author never directly addresses the error introduced into the study by the SCID's origins in an earlier version of the DSM (the DSM-III-R; American Psychiatric Association, 1987). Moreover, the accuracy of such clinical interviews is highly dependent upon the skills of the interviewer, so it is a serious omission when the manual provides no information about the qualifications of the persons administering the SCID, the training those persons received, and interrater reliability of their diagnostic decisions.

These shortcomings aside, the results of the single validity study showed that diagnostic decisions made using the PDS agreed with those made using the SCID 79% of the time. Results suggest that the scale is both adequately sensitive (correctly identifying PTSD 82.0% of the time) and specific (correctly identifying non-PTSD 76.7% of the time). The robustness of these results would be more convincing if different examiners had administered the interview and the PDS, but the manual does not note whether this was the case.

Using the same study to assess scale reliability, the manual reports an impressive internal consistency alpha of .92 for the Symptom Severity Score. The more practical estimate of reliability is the percent agreement of diagnoses from two independent administrations of the PDS, separated by 10–22-day intervals. These diagnoses agreed 87.3% of the time, a relatively high degree of reliability. Again, these results would be most impressive if the two administrations were completed independently by different clinicians, but the manual fails to note whether this was the case.

SUMMARY. The PDS is a highly promising research tool developed to discriminate between those persons who, having experienced a significant traumatic event, do or do not meet the criteria for PTSD. Written to be parallel to the DSM-IV diagnostic criteria, a single validity study has shown the PDS to have high test-retest reliability across a 2-week interval and to show high agreement with a clinical interview designed around an earlier version of diagnostic criteria. The scale does not yet meet standards for general clinical use because it is based on a single, incompletely described and unreplicated validity study with a predominantly East Coast sample. The author acknowledges the scale's research status in recommending uses such as monitoring treatment outcomes or estimating prevalence of PTSD within specific populations.

REVIEWER'S REFERENCES

American Psychiatric Association. (1987). *Diagnostic and statistical manual of mental disorders* (3rd ed., rev.). Washington, DC: Author.

Williams, J. B. W., Gibbon, M., First, M. B., Spitzer, R. L., Davies, M., Borus, J., Howes, M. J., Kane, J., Pope, H. G., Rounsaville, B., & Wittchen, H. U. (1992). The structured clinical interview for DSM-III-R (SCID). *Archives of General Psychiatry, 49*, 630–636.

American Psychiatric Association. (1994). *Diagnostic and statistical manual of mental disorders* (4th ed.). Washington, DC: Author.

[65]

Psychosocial Pain Inventory [Revised].

Purpose: "Provides a standardized method of evaluating psychosocial factors important in maintaining and exacerbating chronic pain problems."
Population: Chronic pain patients.
Publication Dates: 1980–1985.
Acronym: PSPI.
Scores: Item scores only.
Administration: Individual.
Price Data: Price information available from publisher for complete kit including manual ('85, 38 pages) and 25 forms.
Time: Administration time not reported.
Authors: R. K. Heaton, R. A. W. Lehman, and C. J. Getto.
Publisher: Psychological Assessment Resources, Inc.
Cross References: See T4:2162 (1 reference).

Review of the Psychosocial Pain Inventory [Revised] by JULIE A. ALLISON, Associate Professor of Psychology, Pittsburg State University, Pittsburg, KS:

The Psychosocial Pain Inventory (PSPI) was developed to provide a standardized method of quantitatively evaluating psychosocial factors that may play a role in chronic pain. A basic assumption underlying the PSPI argues that both the genesis and the maintenance of chronic pain may be determined by a complexity of factors, including organic pathology, psychopathological factors, and psychosocial factors. Traditionally, chronic pain absent of organic pathology has often been considered psychopathological in nature. Because psychopathology may (or may not) play a role, and

the authors of the PSPI advocate obtaining Minnesota Multiphasic Personality Inventory (MMPI) results in juxtaposition with PSPI scores. In addition to a thorough physical/neurological evaluation, many psychosocial factors may contribute significantly to both the experience and the expressions of pain. These factors could be important to treatment programs for pain patients and may include, but are not limited to: (a) social reinforcement (both positive and negative) for behavioral expressions of pain; (b) financial compensation for pain; (c) emotional responses to environmental stress, which may be experienced as pain; (d) self-handicapping through pain; (e) using pain to obtain or validate the use of addictive drugs or alcohol; (f) social learning of pain behavior; (g) iatrogenic (induced inadvertently by physician or treatment) influences of present experiences with the health-care system; and (h) personality factors, which provide impetus for patient roles. The PSPI was designed specifically to measure these psychosocial categories.

The PSPI is an 8-page, 25-item structured interview for patients and their spouses. The interview begins with asking questions in an open-ended manner and any spontaneous responses are recorded following these responses, closed questions assessing frequencies for specific behaviors are given. Information from these latter questions are quantitatively coded. Even though a clear structure is provided by the PSPI, patients are encouraged to elaborate on problems not specifically covered in the interview, and clinicians are free to pursue issues that may seem important to a specific case. Upon completion of the structured interview, the patient is given a final total score based on the quantitative data obtained (instructions for scoring are clear and provided in the manual), which may range from 0 to 68. Higher scores indicate higher levels of psychosocial pain.

The content of PSPI items is quite extensive, and each is included with either a theoretical, clinical, or empirical rationale. They include duration of pain problem, disability income/litigation, life changes primary to pain problem, operations, time in hospital, number of primary physicians, relief obtained from previous treatments, pain-related stress, pain behavior at home, social reinforcement for pain behavior, pain-reducing behaviors, home/family-related responsibilities, work history, change in work status, plans if pain decreases, current medications, patient's past medical history, family history, history of physician usage, history of medication usage, alcohol abuse, pain contingent down time, and interview behavior.

RELIABILITY AND VALIDITY. Interrater reliability for the scoring of the PSPI was estimated as high ($r = .98$).

Data from validity studies on the PSPI do provide preliminary support for validity, but the research is not at a level that supports a general conclusion that scores from the measure are valid. All items on the scale have been found to correlate significantly with PSPI total scores. Significant correlations have been found between PSPI scores and several scores on the McGill Pain Questionnaire. And the authors report that research participants identified as improving 6 months posttreatment by their physician had originally scored significantly lower on the PSPI than those deemed to have not improved or even worsened. This support for the predictive validity of the PSPI is potentially weakened, however, by the confounding variable of treatment type, for which no results are reported. Furthermore, no additional studies replicating these results have been reported.

Normative data ($N = 169$) are provided from a sample of pain patients. These data may be helpful in identifying relative levels of psychosocial pain. The authors also suggest a cutoff level of 30 as a score that may predict poorer responses to treatments, particularly those that may put the patient at risk. However, the low N and the clinically derived cutoff level suggest that caution should be made in drawing any conclusions based on the PSPI score without corroborating information and/or data.

More research on the validity of scores from the PSPI is needed. Keeping this in mind, the PSPI does appear to be a potentially promising tool for identifying both the origins and the maintenance of pain and pain-related behaviors. In addition to identifying relative levels of both specific and general psychosocial pain, the PSPI may be used to aid in the identification of treatment for psychosocial components of pain, and to assist in the evaluation of treatment plans for pain patients. It is worth investigating.

Review of the Psychosocial Pain Inventory [Revised] by DENNIS C. HARPER, Professor of Pedi-atrics and Rehabilitation, College of Medicine, University of Iowa, Iowa City, IA:

PURPOSE. The Psychosocial Pain Inventory (PSPI) was designed to standardize the format of a clinical interview with adults who report chronic pain, and to provide a way to quantify data obtained in the interview. The authors described this process in the manual and in order to achieve these objectives they selected a structured interview format described by Fordyce (1976) as the basis for this interview. The authors describe a process without detail or verification of item development. Accordingly, the initial interview was subjected to pilot studies at the University of Colorado Pain Clinic. These deliberations reportedly resulted in a 31-item inventory; this inventory was employed in subsequent normative study validations. The information is vague as to its development.

NORMATIVE STUDY SAMPLE. The normative data on the PSPI were obtained from 169 consecutive chronic pain patients presenting at the University of Colorado Pain Clinic, date or type unspecified. Additional assessments were also completed on these patients, specifically the Minnesota Multiphasic Personality Inventory (MMPI) and the McGill Pain Questionnaire. The manual subsequently presents a series of MMPI profiles based on some group identification in relation to pain complaints. The authors present correlational data on the relationship between the Psychosocial Pain Inventory, general pain factors, the Minnesota Multiphasic Personality Inventory, and the McGill Pain Questionnaire. They conclude that the findings indicate that the Psychosocial Pain Inventory and the Minnesota Multiphasic Personality Inventory measure different variables in a population of patients with chronic pain. The authors also report correlational relationships between the McGill Pain Questionnaire and the Psychosocial Pain Inventory.

VALIDATION STUDIES. Two validation studies described in the manual attempt to identify relationships between specific responses on the Psychosocial Pain Inventory and specific patient indicators of pain and chronic disease. These authors indicate that the studies supported the conclusion that "it thus appeared that the total PSPI score could be used to predict outcome of treatment. Higher PSPI scores would predict increasing influence of psychosocial factors and poorer response to treatment plan" (p. 15). No other identifying information is provided.

GUIDELINES FOR ADMINISTRATION. The test authors have very specific guidelines for test administration and require that the questions be asked as written. Additional clinical suggestions for interviewing patients are offered as well. The manual then outlines the remaining 25 questions and the rationale and scoring for each. These are largely clinical interpretations.

SUMMARY. The Psychosocial Pain Inventory is a structured method of evaluating psychosocial factors common to chronic pain patients. The data presented by the authors in this manual are likely clinically useful; however, only limited, and insufficient, evidence of validity and reliability are presented. The PSPI seems useful as a structured interview based upon its face validity.

REVIEWER'S REFERENCE

Fordyce, W. R. (1976). *Behavioral methods for chronic pain and illness.* St. Louis: Mosby.

[66]
Quality of Life Inventory.

Purpose: Developed to provide a measure of a person's quality of life and their satisfaction with life.
Population: Ages 18 and over.
Publication Date: 1994.
Acronym: QOLI.
Scores: 17 scales: Health, Self-Esteem, Goals-and-Values, Money, Work, Play, Learning, Creativity, Helping, Love, Friends, Children, Relatives, Home, Neighborhood, Community, Overall Quality of Life.
Administration: Group or individual.
Price Data, 1999: $80 per starter kit for handscoring including manual (84 pages), 50 answer sheets, and 50 worksheets; $44 per preview package for computer scoring including manual, 10 answer sheets, materials needed for 10 assessments, and 10 profile reports; $63.50 per reorder kit for handscoring including 50 answer sheets and 50 worksheets; $17 per 25 computer answer sheets; $1.70 per profile report, $32.50 per manual.
Time: (5) minutes.
Comments: Useful for outcomes measurement as well as individual counseling.
Author: Michael B. Frisch.
Publisher: NCS (Minnetonka).

Review of the Quality of Life Inventory by LAURA L. B. BARNES, Associate Professor of Educational Research and Evaluation, School of Educational Studies, Oklahoma State University, Stillwater, OK:

The Quality of Life Inventory (QOLI) is theoretically grounded in a view of life satisfaction as a discrepancy between what a person has and what a person desires in valued areas of life. The model is linear and additive (i.e., overall satisfaction is the sum of satisfactions in particular areas of life deemed important). Satisfaction in highly valued areas is assumed to have greater influence on evaluations of overall life satisfaction than areas of equal satisfaction that are judged to be less important. The QOLI was developed as a measure of positive mental health to supplement measures of negative affect and psychiatric symptoms in both outcome assessment and treatment planning and to "focus the attention of health providers on a client's sources of fulfillment" (manual, p. 6). A chapter in the manual is devoted to general cognitively oriented treatment strategies for addressing the life areas assessed by the QOLI.

PRACTICAL EVALUATION. The QOLI can be administered via paper and pencil or online; scoring of the paper-pencil version can be accomplished by hand or by using available software. Only the hand-scoring version includes a form inviting respondents to identify problems that interfere with satisfaction in each of the 16 areas. The test materials are attractively packaged and easy to use. The meaning of the 16 areas is clearly defined for respondents. They are asked to rate both the importance of the area to their overall happiness and their level of satisfaction with that aspect of their life. The labels on the 6-point satisfaction scale may present a problem, however, because the scoring scheme assumes a higher level of satisfaction for a "somewhat satisfied" or a "a little satisfied" response than a "somewhat dissatisfied" or a "a little dissatisfied" response. For some respondents, to be only a little satisfied may seem more negative than to be only a little dissatisfied. The scale values suggest the intended interpretation because positive numbers are assigned to satisfied responses and negative numbers to dissatisfied responses. Nevertheless, I found the scale labels to be somewhat counterintuitive and distracting. Labeling only the end-points of the scale or using some other scale format would solve this problem.

Hand scoring is easily accomplished with step-by-step instructions on the worksheet. Total scale raw scores are converted to *T*-scores and percentiles, and finally to an overall classification (very low, low, average, high) by consulting the manual. A respondent's score profile across the 16 areas may also be plotted.

Interpretation of both the total satisfaction score and the life area profile is facilitated by a generally well-written section on test interpretation. According to the manual the overall QOLI classification scheme is based on both normative data from the standardization sample and on clinical data and suggests that the 20th percentile appears to distinguish between clinical and nonclinical samples. It would be helpful to have more specific information validating the classification cutoffs. Also lacking is a discussion of measurement error and confidence bands in the section on interpretation.

STANDARDIZATION. The nonclinical standardization sample matched the 1992 U.S. Census fairly closely with respect to race, but its match on other relevant characteristics cannot be determined from the manual. The sample consisted of 798 out of 1,924 individuals samples from 12 states across the U.S. The sampling procedure was not described but appears to have been a convenience sample (e.g., some respondents were paid). The description of the sample in the manual is inadequate for making judgments about its appropriateness.

RELIABILITY AND VALIDITY. The QOLI reports stability (2-week interval) and internal consistency reliabilities in the .70s. The samples were quite small ($n = 55$) and not described. Validity of scores of the QOLI was presented through moderate to large correlations with two other life satisfaction scales and a small correlation with the Marlowe-Crowne Social Desirability Scale. Significant results from a study of 13 clinically depressed patients treated with bibliotherapy were presented as evidenced for sensitivity to clinical treatment. An array of correlational data from a previous version of the QOLI showed moderate positive correlations with other measures of subjective well-being and moderate negative correlations with measures of psychopathology.

SUMMARY. The QOLI appears to be theoretically grounded and well integrated into a cognitive therapeutic modality. The discrepancy model upon which the instrument is based is not disguised in the instrument design. This may be a drawback psychometrically in that a person's awareness of discrepancy between what they value and what they have may influence their subsequent responses. On the other hand, this awareness of discrepancy may facilitate therapy. The QOLI has acceptable, but not outstanding, evidence of score reliability. The standard error of measurement must be taken into consideration in score interpretation and in assessing pre-post change. Validity data from the manual are scant but potentially promising. More information on the standardization sample and procedures needs to be made available—normative comparisons are tenuous at best without a clearer description of the make-up of the comparison group. The test itself appears to be solid and may be used with approrpriate caution for its stated purpose.

Review of the Quality of Life Inventory by RICHARD W. JOHNSON, Adjunct Professor of Counseling Psychology and Associate Director Emeritus of Counseling & Consultation Services, University Health Services, University of Wisconsin—Madison, Madison, WI:

The Quality of Life Inventory (QOLI) provides a broad measure of life satisfaction that complements measures of psychopathology used in clinical assessment. It evaluates one's quality of life in 16 different areas, such as Work, Love, and Health. Information of this nature is helpful in obtaining a fuller understanding of a client's issues and resources.

TEST DEVELOPMENT. The QOLI was developed by Michael Frisch based on a quality of life model that assumes four components underlie satisfaction with life in each of 16 areas. These four components (objective circumstances, attitudes toward one's circumstance, standards for evaluating one's situation, and relative importance attributed to an area of living) can be used both to explain an individual's scores and to suggest possible treatment approaches for improving scores.

The QOLI measures "weighted satisfaction" in each of the 16 life areas by the use of two questions for each area. Clients are asked first to rate their level of satisfaction (on a 6-point scale ranging from -3 to +3) for an area and then to indicate the relative importance (0, 1, or 2) that they place on that area. Satisfaction scores are multiplied by importance scores to obtain a total of 16 weighted satisfaction scores (ranging from -6 to +6), which are then added together to produce the QOLI Total score. The test questions, which are written at a 6th-grade reading level, are easy to understand and relevant to most therapy situations.

Most people can complete the QOLI in 5 or 6 minutes. Hand scoring of the instrument can be completed in 1 or 2 minutes. Because of its brevity, the inventory can be easily readministered to clients to help evaluate their progress in therapy.

Computer scoring is available as well as hand scoring. The hand-scoring version has the advantage of written comments supplied by the client that indicate the nature of problems or concerns in each of the 16 life areas. The computer version allows test scores from different administrations to be plotted in charts as a means of evaluating progress. All scores are reported as raw scores. Tables are provided for converting the Total score (but not the area scores) to T-scores or percentiles.

PSYCHOMETRIC CHARACTERISTICS. The QOLI has been standardized on a national sample that roughly matches the U.S. Census in regard to the distribution of racial and ethnic groups. The test results show no significant differences among the scores of Blacks, Whites, or Others; however, Hispanic respondents scored significantly higher (about one-third of a standard deviation) than both Blacks and Whites, indicating a higher quality of life for the Hispanic population. These results may be an artifact of the sampling process; additional research on this topic is needed. The author points out the value of collecting local norms for helping to determine treatment goals.

No significant sex or age differences were noted in the test scores. Test scores had low correlation ($r = .10$) with years of education. These data indicate that separate norms are not needed for different groups based on sex, age, or education.

The only test-retest reliability study reported in the manual for the current version of the QOLI yielded a relatively low correlation coefficient ($r = .73$ over a 2-week period). This result suggests a standard error of measurement of over one-half of a standard deviation unit. Two test-retest reliability studies reported in the appendix of the manual for an earlier version of the QOLI show higher correlations ($r = .91$ over 33 days and $r = .80$ over 18 days). This issue deserves further study.

Estimates of internal consistency for the Total score have been moderately high. Alpha

coefficients have ranged from .77 to .89 for studies conducted with the original and revised version of the QOLI. These results indicate that the Total score is a relatively homogeneous measure of quality of life.

Validation studies show both convergent and discriminant validity. QOLI Total scores of subjects in the normative sample were significantly correlated with two other measures of quality of life, the Satisfaction with Life Scale and the Quality of Life Index. Total scores for these same subjects were relatively independent of scores on a measure of social desirability. Similar studies conducted with the original version of the QOLI (which closely resembles the current version) also support the validity of scores from the instrument.

Additional validation studies are needed. What are the relationships among the 16 areas of living scores? What factors account for most of the variance in the QOLI scores? Do low QOLI scores predict clinical depression, sensitivity to pain, immune system vulnerability, or other health or psychological problems as suggested by the author? Information on each of these topics would help to clarify further the validity of the QOLI.

INTERPRETATION OF SCORES. Total scores are interpreted in terms of four levels, ranging from very low (10th percentile and below) to high (above 80th percentile). Scores at or below the 20th percentile indicate areas of concern that should be explored further in counseling. The manual is unusually helpful in listing possible causes for low scores in each of the 16 categories and in suggesting possible treatment strategies. Case studies indicate that the QOLI scores of clients are highly sensitive to changes in one's situation.

CONCLUSIONS. The QOLI inventory possesses the following advantages: It is brief, comprehensive in its scope, easy to administer and score, and closely related to a quality of life model that can be helpful both in explaining scores and in suggesting possible treatments. It is a new instrument that still needs research on a number of issues, including separate scale norms, test-retest reliability, construct (factorial) validity, predictive validity, and cross-cultural applications. Research and clinical experience thus far indicates that the instrument can provide valuable information in conceptualizing a case, in suggesting treatment approaches, and in measuring outcomes of interventions. It is the best instrument of which I am aware for evaluating a client's quality of life.

[67]
Recovery Attitude and Treatment Evaluator.

Purpose: Intended for use after diagnosis of alcohol or other drug dependency to determine the "patient's level of resistance to treatment and other important information" to be considered in treatment planning.
Population: Adults.
Publication Dates: 1987–1996.
Acronym: RAATE–CE; RAATE–QI.
Scores: 5 dimensions: Resistance to Treatment, Resistance to Continuing Care, Acuity of Biomedical Problems, Acuity of Psychiatric/Psychological Problems, Social/Family Environmental Status.
Administration: Individual.
Forms, 3: Clinical Evaluation, Initial Questionnaire, Automated RAATE–QI.
Price Data: Available from publisher.
Time: (30–45) minutes for Clinical Evaluation; [20–30] minutes for Initial Questionnaire or Automated RAATE–QI.
Comments: Automated RAATE–QI requires minimum 386 IBM compatible with Windows 3.1 or later, 8 MB RAM, mouse, printer, and color monitor.
Authors: David Mee-Lee, Norman G. Hoffmann, and Maurice B. Smith (manual).
Publisher: New Standards, Inc.

Review of the Recovery Attitude and Treatment Evaluator by PHILIP ASH, Director, Ash, Blackstone and Cates, Blacksburg, VA:

The Recovery Attitude and Treatment Evaluator (RAATE) instruments were developed in response to what was perceived as a need for more consistent and objective measures to plan treatment and to place into appropriate levels of care patients suffering from substance dependence and addiction problems. Clinical work with such patients, surveys of policies and criteria for patient care in several treatment facilities, and review of published reviews and research led to the identification of five dimensions on which to establish a clinically relevant and useful severity profile for the individual patient.

These dimensions as finally formulated include:

Dimension A. Resistance to Treatment: degree of resistance to treatment (including denial of addiction problems);

Dimension B. Resistance to Continuing Care: commitment to on-going recovery and degree of resistance to continuing care;

Dimension C. Acuity of Biomedical Problems: withdrawal problems, to determine the acuity and intensity of any needed physical treatment;

Dimension D. Acuity of Psychiatric Problems: whether independent of or secondary to addiction; and

Dimension E. Social/Family Environmental Status: degree to which the psychosocial environment is supportive of or detrimental to recovery (user's guide, p. 1-1).

An initial attempt to develop a 5-point rating scale for each of these dimensions, and a corresponding set of placement criteria, failed to be sufficient. This led to the development of two instruments, The Clinical Evaluation (RAATE-CE) (Smith, Hoffman, & Nederhoed, 1992) and the Questionnaire I (RAATE-QI) (Smith et al., 1992). The Questionnaire I (RAATE-QI) is in a pencil-and-paper-administered format; it is also available in a computer-compatible form, Automated RAATE-QI.

The RAATE-CE includes 35 Likert-type four-choice (from "Definitely Yes" to "Definitely NO," where the MOST FAVORABLE response, indicating lack of illness or a favorable condition, is scored "1") items in a structured clinical interview. It may be administered by a trained clinician or counselor in 20–30 minutes. The questions are divided among the five dimensions listed above (A = 6, B = 5, C = 6, D = 8, E = 10). A Guidelines table is provided to reduce each dimension to a 5-point LOW (1)/HIGH (5) Severity Profile score, which is further encoded to a Level of Care evaluation.

The RAATE-QI is a 94-item true-false self-report questionnaire that is answered by the patient, taking about 30–45 minutes to complete. The questions are divided among the five dimensions listed above. In the pencil-and-paper version, the five dimensions are scored by use of plastic templates. The raw scores are transferred to the QI Severity Profile, and converted to QI Severity Profile Scaled Scores, yielding a RAATE-QI Severity Profile. Finally, for each RAATE-QI dimension, the clinician circles the RAATE Severity Profile Scaled Scores under the appropriate ASAM (American Society of Addiction Medicine) Level of Care (Levels I–IV), where Level I is the most modest.

The RAATE manual presents a detailed introduction to the development and rationale of the RAATE, specific directions for administration and interpretation, and results of a reliability and validity study for the standardization sample ($N = 153$) drawn from recent enrollees of the Milwaukee County Mental Health Complex. Women comprised 43% of the sample, men 57%. The sample was largely composed of African-American drug abusers. The manual also includes an outline of desirable future studies and an extensive list of references.

RELIABILITIES. The RAATE-CE average interrater reliability estimates (across three clinicians) ranged from .59 to .77 ($N = 143$) and the internal consistency reliability values ranged from .65 to .87. The RAATE-QI internal consistency (KR-20) reliability ranged from .63 to .78, whereas test-retest reliabilities (over 24 hours) ranged from .73 to .87 (Allen & Megan, 1995, p. 476). Earlier, the manual (p. 5-5) reported test-retest (40 patients, 24 hours apart) reliability coefficients of .58 to .87 for the five dimensions. For the RAATE-CE, interrater reliabilities, by dimension, ranged from .58 to .70 (76 patients, 5 rater pairs) and from .51 to .87 (39 patients, one rater pair). Similar data were reported from the RAATE-CE by Smith et al. (1992, p. 361). The manual also contains extensive item analysis statistics.

As yet, very little evidence of criterion-related validity has been found by this reviewer, although a persuasive case may be made for the existence of content validity, as well as for arguing that the content and structure of the RAATE provides a basis for at least some components of construct validity. The manual itself suggests that "the inter-correlations of the five dimensions of the RAATE-CE demonstrated preliminary convergent and discriminant construct validity" (p. 5-4). Although the first two dimensions ("Resistance to treatment" and "Resistance to continuing care") were highly correlated, the other three dimensions appeared to be relatively independent, suggesting that the cited preliminary conclusion was justifiable.

SUMMARY. The RAATE-CE and RAATE-QI do seem to provide a way for trained clinicians to improve the accuracy and cost-effectiveness of treatment planning decisions for chemically dependent individuals. The instruments bring into focus issues in treatment decision-making that have not been extensively explored in available substance-abuse assessment devices. As the manual itself points out (pp. 6-1 to 6-3), extensive validity research is needed. Conduct of these studies should support the expectations set by the RAATE.

REVIEWER'S REFERENCES

Smith, M. B., Hoffmann, N. G., & Nederhoed, R. (1992). The development and reliability of the RAATE-CE. *Journal of Substance Abuse, 4*, 355–363.

Allen, P., & Megan, C. (Eds.). (1995). *Assessing alcohol problems: A guide for clinicians and researchers.* Washington, DC: National Institute on Alcohol Abuse and Alcoholism, NIAAA Treatment Handbook Series 4. Recovery Attitude and Treatment Evaluator (RAATE), pp. 474–477.

Review of the Recovery Attitude and Treatment Evaluator by TONY TONEATTO, Scientist, Clinical, Social and Research Department, Addiction Research Foundation, Toronto, Ontario, Canada:

The Recovery Attitude and Treatment Evaluator (RAATE) is the outcome of a program of clinical work conducted by David Mee-Lee (1988) who identified a small number of core variables critical to making clinical decisions about treatment placement, readiness for treatment, and treatment planning. Mee-Lee (1988) identified five key variables that form the basis of the five dimensions comprising the RAATE: (a) Resistance to Treatment (i.e., 6 items measuring awareness and acceptance of an addiction problem); (b) Resistance to Continuing Care, (i.e., 5 items measuring commitment to recovery); (c) Acuity of Biomedical Problems, (i.e., 6 items measuring health status); (d) Acuity of Psychiatric/Psychological Problems (i.e., 8 items assessing psychiatric status); and (e) Social/Family Environmental Status (i.e., 11 items assessing family support). There are presently two instruments that assess these dimensions, the 35-item RAATE-Clinical Evaluation (CE) to be administered in interview format, and the 94-item, true-false RAATE-Initial Questionnaire (QI), which is self-administered. The RAATE-CE items are rated on a 4-point scale. Both instruments require between 30 and 45 minutes to complete. The authors of the test manual state that neither instrument is designed to render psychiatric diagnoses nor to assess severity of addiction. Furthermore, the results of administering the two instruments are not intended to be compared directly because the content is not identical. Information describing the administration, scoring, interpretation, and psychometric properties of the two tests is provided in good detail in the 1992 test manual.

The interrater reliability of the RAATE-CE, based on 139 subjects, is suspect, due to the utilization of the Pearson product moment correlation coefficient, which "merely assesses the extent to which scores go together and not whether they are close to each other in absolute terms" (p. 58, Kazdin, 1982). Consequently, the coefficient may be quite high despite radically divergent scores by the raters. The appropriate statistic to assess interrater reliability would have been the intraclass correlation coefficient. It should be noted, however, that Smith, Hoffman, and Nederhoed (1992) reported a different reliability statistic (i.e., Fisher's r, p. 360) from the 1992 manual for these data. In any case, the correlations reported for the total scores averaged over the three interrater pairs ranged from .59 to .77, which can be judged to be fair to good. More recently, Najavits, Gastfriend, Nakayama et al. (1994) reported somewhat better interrater reliability coefficients, with a range of .66 to .92 for the five dimensions using a research version (RAATE-R) of the RAATE-CE in a sample of 116 cocaine-dependent outpatients. The internal consistency reliabilities reported in the 1992 test manual for each of the five dimensions are generally good (ranging between .79 and .86) with the exception of the dimension assessing availability of social support for which an unacceptable internal consistency estimate of .65 was reported. Najavits et al. (1997) reported internal consistency reliabilities for the five dimensions ranging from .45 to .71, which is generally considered poor.

Test-retest reliability on the RAATE-QI, based on two administrations of the test 8 to 10 hours apart (at least 24 hours may have been preferable), yielded generally excellent reliabilities, ranging between .73 to .87 with internal consistency (assessed with the KR-20 statistic) ranging between .63 and .77, which can be considered good. The relatively small number of items for most of the dimensions may have impacted on the estimates of reliability. A revised RAATE-QI, formed by deleting 17 items with low average item-scale correlations (< .25) and average test-retest correlations < .35, did not yield greatly improved internal consistency or test-retest reliabilities.

Construct validity for the two instruments was investigated by conducting interdimension correlations. The results show that for both instruments, Dimensions A and B, assessing Resistance to Treatment and Resistance to Continuing Care, tap into similar but not identical constructs (r = .76 and r = .73 between Dimensions A and B for RAATE-CE and RAATE-QI, respectively). Najavits et al. (1997) reported an r of .42 for RAATE-R between Dimensions A and B in cocaine abusers, considerably lower than would be desirable. The remaining three dimensions appear to be relatively independent constructs, with interdimension correlations ranging from -.06 to .45 for RAATE-CE and -.30 to .47 for RAATE-QI. Convergent-discriminant validity was further explored with the Multi-Trait Multi-Method approach, correlating the dimensions for both instruments. The result showed modest convergent validity, with coefficients ranging from .28 to .54, and good divergent validity with coefficients ranging from -.17 to .25. Najavits et al. (1997) found low correlations between the RAATE-R and the Circumstances, Motivation, Readiness, and Suitability Scales for Substance Abuse Treatment (CMRS; DeLeon, Melnick, Kressel et al., 1994) suggesting that the concurrent validity for scores from this instrument has yet to be established.

Further evidence for the construct validity of the measures (e.g., item-level factor analysis) and predictive validity have been planned but have yet to be reported. In addition, additional evidence for concurrent validity with other measures of readiness to change or psychiatric problems, for example, need to be conducted. There is some concern with the face validity of the RAATE-CE, particularly the Dimensions C and D measuring Acuity of Biomedical Problems and Acuity of Psychiatric/Psychological Problems. The questions comprising these dimensions require the patient to be able to assess what may often be very serious medical and psychiatric status, conditions best left to experts (i.e., physicians, psychiatrists). Many of the questions for Dimension D assess symptoms in a very superficial, general manner, and expect the patient to have insight into the relationship between symptoms and substance use, demanding interviewers be highly skilled in order to elicit valid responses. Thus, there is concern that considerable error can be introduced if the interview is administered by staff who are not highly skilled in medical or psychiatric diagnosis.

In summary, the RAATE-CE and RAATE-QI are intended to aid in the treatment planning and placement of treatment-seeking alcohol and drug abusers. However, the evidence for the reliability and validity for both instruments is, at present, too weak to conclude that this goal has been achieved. Representativeness of the sample and concerns about the size of the sample used in the psychometric analyses and the lack of extensive validity data (although the reliability data are generally good), indicate that further research is necessary before both instruments can achieve their goals.

REVIEWER'S REFERENCES

Kazdin, A. E. (1982). *Single-case research designs: Methods for clinical and applied settings.* New York: Oxford University Press.

Mee-Lee, D. (1988). An instrument for treatment progress and matching: The Recovery Attitude and Treatment Evaluator (RAATE). *Journal of Substance Abuse Treatment, 5,* 183–186.

Smith, M. B., Hoffmann, N. G., & Nederhoed, R. (1992). The development and reliability of the RAATE-CE. *Journal of Substance Abuse, 4,* 355–363.

DeLeon, G., Melnick, G., Kressel, D., & Jainchill, N. (1994). Circumstances, motivation, readiness, and suitability (The CMS Scales): Predicting retention in therapeutic community treatment. *American Journal of Drug and Alcohol Abuse, 20,* 495–515.

Najavits, L. M., Gastfriend, D. R., Nakayama, E. Y., Barber, J. P., Blaine, J., Frank, A., Muenz, L. R., & Thase, M. (1997). A measure of readiness for substance abuse treatment: Psychometric properties of the RAATE-R interview. *American Journal on Addictions, 6,* 74–82.

[68]
Rehabilitation Compliance Scale.

Purpose: Intended to provide a measurement of compliance to a rehabilitation program in the severely injured musculoskeletal patient.

Population: Severely injured patients ages 17–85 years.

Publication Date: 1994.

Administration: Group.

Price Data, 1998: $25 per sampler set including manual, test, and scoring sheets; $100 per one-year permission to reproduce up to 200 administrations of the test.

Time: Administration time not reported.

Author: Neil W. Rheiner.

Publisher: Mind Garden, Inc.

a) REHABILITATION COMPLIANCE SCALE.

Acronym: RCS.

Scores, 3: Appointment Compliance, Participation in Therapy, Progress in Therapy.

Forms, 2: A, B.

b) PATIENT EXPERIENCE QUESTIONNAIRE.

Acronym: IEQ.

Score: Total score only.

Review of the Rehabilitation Compliance Scale by MICHAEL P. GAMACHE, Clinical Assistant Professor of Psychology, Department of Neurology, University of South Florida, College of Medicine, Tampa, FL:

TEST COVERAGE AND USE. Musculoskeletal injuries are common and costly in terms of time loss from productive activities and the cost of rehabilitation. Despite advances in the ability to effect positive rehabilitation from these injuries, the cost effectiveness of rehabilitation efforts and the practical efficacy of such efforts is severely compromised by problems associated with noncompliance or failure to adhere to rehabilitation regimens. The Rehabilitation Compliance Scale (RSC) is a rating scale designed as a measure of compliance for the population of patients undergoing long-term rehabilitation from musculoskeletal injury in inpatient settings. The scale is completed by health care professionals (e.g., nurse, occupational therapist, physical therapist). It is most appropriate for use with severely injured, adult patients who are expected to remain hospitalized for at least a month or more and who do not suffer from injuries that would alter their cognitive status (i.e., head injury).

SIZE AND REPRESENTATIVENESS OF SAMPLE FOR VALIDATION AND NORMING. The test manual reports one validation study involving 50 patients undergoing long-term rehabilitation at a "Midwestern rehabilitation institution" (manual, p. 25). The patient sample was selected based on six criteria, including permission of attending physicians, willingness to participate, and the expectation that the severity of the patient's condition would require a minimum of 4 weeks of intensive inpatient rehabilitation. The author indicates that "40–50 percent" (p. 33) of the subjects selected were lost to the study because they did not remain available for the minimum 4-week observation period. It is not clear why they present a range of subject attrition rather than the specific percentage. There is no discussion of the percentage of patients excluded from the sample because of their unwillingness to participate in the study and how this may have affected the representativeness of the sample, particularly when the ultimate issue is compliance. The sample subjects were 60% male and 40% female and ranged in age from 17 to 85, with a mean age of 57 years. Despite characterizing the study sample as musculoskeletal injury patients, a review of the descriptive statistics regarding diagnosis, which were contained in a table in the manual, indicates that the primary diagnosis in more than one-third of the cases (38.0%) was neurological in nature and the modal diagnosis was cerebrovascular disease. In a discussion of subject selection problems the author states that subjects who were confused, aphasic, or who had head injury were excluded from the sample, which suggests that the criteria for determining the existence of confusion or other cognitive impairment were not particularly rigorous given the large number of neurological cases.

RELIABILITY. Reliability data for the RCS were derived from comparisons of the ratings of different disciplines (nurse vs. occupational therapist or physical therapist), different forms (Form A vs. Form B), and item analysis. The correlation between Form A and Form B was poor ($r = .167$), leading the author to conclude that Form B is measuring another construct than compliance and that further research is needed to determine the appropriate use of this form that they designed to be equivalent to Form A. The author also reports statistically significant differences between health care disciplines and their ratings of the same patients using the same form. They conclude that this finding is consistent with previous studies that have found differing perceptions of compliance between different disciplines. Despite acknowledging these differences, they offer a single mean score without differentiating between the professional disciplines of the raters. Internal consistency coefficients ranged from a low of .001 to a high of .916. Item correlation with total scores was only .167.

VALIDITY. The validity of the RCS was assessed by comparing RCS ratings with three external compliance measures: percentage of appointments kept, a rating of participation in therapy, and a rating by a multidisciplinary team of the patient's progress in therapy. The correlations were generally poor for the latter two. The only meaningful relationship was between the RCS and appointment keeping, which is the only one of the three criterion measures that is consistent with the usual definition of compliance. The correlation between Form A and the percentage of appointments kept was .737. Interestingly, in interpreting the study results, the author concludes that these criteria are "poor indicators of compliance" rather than concluding that the RCS is a poor predictor of compliance.

Content validity and item construction were based on the critical incident technique (Flanagan, 1954). The process entailed a survey of 330 health care professionals who provided representative descriptions of two examples of compliant behavior and two examples of noncompliant behavior each. A total of 2,201 critical incidents were generated for analysis and these were categorized and reduced to 28 types or categories of critical incidents for inclusion in a preliminary form of the rating scale, equally divided between examples of compliant and noncompliant behavior. They submitted this form to the original 330 health care professionals in order to obtain their opinion regarding the appropriateness of item content. Based on the feedback from these providers, the final form was revised to 24 items with a 5-point Likert rating for each item.

TEST ADMINISTRATION. The RCS is a 24-item Likert rating scale completed by a designated health care professional. For optimal analysis, the provider should have had direct contact with the patient to be rated for a minimum of at least 5 days before providing the rating. The patient should have been admitted to the rehabilitation program at least 2 weeks prior to rating, with at least 7 days of participation in a planned rehabilitation program, and an expected additional hospitalization of at least 4 weeks. The ratings are completed in pencil-and-paper format and a scoring key is included in the manual. The test would appear to take between 2 and 10 minutes to complete.

TEST REPORTING. There is no formal test reporting or interpretation offered. The author suggests that the mean score of 44 be used "as the point of demarcation between measurement of compliance and noncompliance" (p. 46). However, he rightfully cautions against the use of this score as a cutoff score suggesting instead that the greater the patient's score above 40, the less likely they are to comply with rehabilitation. This, in turn, might suggest that patients obtaining high ratings would be desirable candidates for some type of intervention aimed at improving compliance and reducing resistance to rehabilitation efforts. Factor analysis suggests that the test measures four aspects of compliance: self-destructive behavior, self-directing behavior, information seeking, and contradictory behavior.

TEST BIAS. There is insufficient normative data to determine test bias. The clinical validation sample was 60% male and had a mean age of 57. No other demographic data are offered.

SUMMARY. The ability to effectively and reliably predict compliance with rehabilitation regimens could be very important in tailoring rehabilitation techniques and resources to individual patients. Some research has demonstrated effective techniques for improving compliance and the ability to identify patients in advance who are likely to benefit from compliance interventions would be useful. The RCS is a rating scale for use with professionals involved in the rehabilitation process. It is derived from observations made by these professionals of critical incidents representative of compliance and noncompliance. It does not, however, have sufficient reliability or validity evidence at this time for use in practical decisions regarding treatment and patient compliance. The experimental or informal use of this instrument is all that can be recommended at this time. Such use might facilitate further interaction and discussion across disciplines with respect to the likely compliance or need for other interventions to facilitate rehabilitation.

REVIEWER'S REFERENCE

Flanagan, J. C. (1954). The critical incident technique. *Psychological Bulletin, 51,* 327–358.

Review of the Rehabilitation Compliance Scale by ROBERT A. LEARK, Associate Professor, Psychology Department, Pacific Christian College, Fullerton, CA:

INTRODUCTION. The Rehabilitation Compliance Scale (RCS) consists of two 24-item rating scales (Forms A & B). Items are rated using the following scale: *unable to determine, very much like, somewhat like, unlike,* and *very much unlike.* The rater circles the appropriate response on the one-page (front/back) response form.

The RCS is designed to measure "compliance to a rehabilitation program in the severely injured musculoskeletal patient" (manual, p. 5). The basis for the test is found in the author's logical statement:

> If one accepts the assumption that compliance to an effective rehabilitation regimen is desirable if the patient is to return to a maximal functional state, it follows that compliance to a rehabilitation program will lead to improved rehabilitation outcomes. Compliance, therefore, may lead to reduction in the length of major treatment regimes, the time in which the health team is involved in carrying out specific therapeutic programs, and the amount of medical facilities utilized at any one time by the injured. A marked improvement in rehabilitation outcomes offers the potential for dramatically reducing expenditures in the care of the injured. (Manual, p. 7).

VALIDITY AND RELIABILITY. The author utilized a critical incident technique to obtain items reported by health care professionals as significant in the outcome of severely injured patient rehabilitation. Initially, analysis of 2,201 behavioral indicators produced 246 specific behaviors with equal frequency by raters. This draft of items was distributed to health care professionals. At the end of the analysis and recommendations, the two 24-item parallel forms were created. These forms were then tested on a 50-patient sample undergoing a 24-month rehabilitation program. Each form has a mean score possible of 44. Thus, 44 was selected as the cut score for indications of compliance, scores above are seen as less indicative of compliance, scores below as more compliant. The overall predictive validity of scores from the RCS is limited. For example, correlations to Participation in Therapy (.178) and Progress in Therapy (.121) for the RCS Form A are disappointing.

Reliability of scores from the RCS was determined by calculating Cronbach alpha coefficients. RCS alpha coefficients are .806 for Form A and .854 for Form B. Factor analysis yielded four distinct factors (self-destructive behavior, self-directing behavior, information-seeking behavior, and contradictory behavior) for both forms. Individual item correlation between the two forms is weak (r = .167 for total scores).

COMMENTS. The RCS, Forms A and B, presents a novel attempt to measure rehabilitation outcome behaviors. Unfortunately, they fall far short of the mark. The author of the scales recommends continued research with Form A.

Clearly, continued research is needed for the RCS. However, a blanket disregard for the test is not warranted. The rehabilitation field is in need of outcome measures that can identify behaviors predictive of successful treatment. Rather than totally disregarding this instrument, the reader is encouraged to take up the author's call for further research. The author has gone to great lengths to begin the process for a successful outcome mesure for a highly specific patient population.

[69]

The Renfrew Bus Story.

Purpose: Designed as a "test of narrative recall."
Population: Ages 3.6–7.0.
Publication Date: 1994.

Scores, 4: Information, Sentence Length, Complexity, Independence.
Administration: Individual.
Price Data, 1997: $45 per complete kit including manual (56 pages), 15 record forms, and story booklet; $5 per 15 record forms.
Time: Administration time not reported.
Comments: American adaptation of original British version.
Authors: Judy Cowley and Cheryl Glasgow.
Publisher: Centreville School.

Review of The Renfrew Bus Story by SHERRY K. BAIN, Assistant Professor, Department of Psychology & Counselor Education, Nicholls State University, Thibodaux, LA:

RATIONALE FOR TEST. The Renfrew Bus Story (RBS) is an American adaptation of a British screening test of narrative recall for young children (Renfrew, 1977). The test involves measuring a child's ability to retell a story presented orally and with pictures by the examiner.

Cowley and Glasgow, the RBS authors, offer extensive justification for the use of a narrative testing format and cite several references to support their positions. In general, they claim that the narrative format of testing is more sensitive to language problems than traditional language tests involving short answers or brief, one-word responses. The narrative format requires that the child integrate and organize several skills, including visual and audio input, listening comprehension, memory, sentence formation, and narrative schema understanding. In addition, the task of narrative recall simulates natural occurrences in daily interactions as well as typical classroom demands.

ADMINISTRATION AND SCORING. To administer the RBS, the examiner reads a script to the child while sequentially exposing 12 pictures in a booklet. The child is then audio taped retelling the story, with the examiner supplying a prompt and a story-starting line. The child uses the same sequenced pictures to retell the story, which is transcribed from the audio tape, and scored by the examiner.

Scoring is based upon quantitative categories including (a) Information, described as content memory; (b) Sentence Length; (c) Complexity, described as sentences containing subordinate or relative clauses or attempts at using these clauses; and (d) Independence, measured by the absence of prompts from the examiner. Raw scores for Information and Sentence Length can be transformed into standard scores ($x = 100$, $sd = 15$) and percentiles according to tabled norms for 6-month age blocks. A qualitative assessment can also be completed using guidelines from the manual, and a style sheet may be filled out, indicating a child's positive and negative behaviors observed during testing.

Recommendations for training to administer the RBS could not be found in the manual. The complexity of recording and scoring young children's narratives indicates the need for several practice sessions on the examiner's part. The test is quick to administer, taking 15 or 20 minutes at the most, but results can be slow to transcribe and score initially. Instructions seem clear and fairly explicit although there are bound to be occasional problems with scoring children's language usage. Several examples of scored record forms are provided in the manual. Dialect variations are acceptable.

STANDARDIZATION, RELIABILITY, AND VALIDITY. Normative information for the RBS is provided in the manual; however, some gaps in information are apparent. The normative group included 418 children enrolled in public, private, and parochial schools across several states in the mid-Atlantic area (states not specified), Florida, and Illinois. Children were excluded if they did not speak English as a first language, or were hearing-impaired, language-delayed, learning-disabled, or suspected of having similar problems by their teachers. In addition, children not responding to the examiner's prompts to retell the story were excluded from analyses. Children's ages were distributed fairly evenly across the range for which the test was designed. Demographic information for gender, urban versus rural setting, and racial/ethnic groups are displayed in the manual along with raw score means for each demographic breakdown. The authors state that these results were investigated for bias and that none was found. For racial/ethnic makeup, the normative sample consisted of approximately 89% Caucasian, 8% Black, and 3% Hispanic or Other. The authors stated that a range of socioeconomic levels was represented but did not elaborate on this.

Evidence of test-retest and interrater reliability is presented in the RBS manual. Test-retest reliability estimates, based on a small sample ($n = 27$), produced an average coefficient of .70

(for a 4-week interval) across three subtests: Information, Sentence Length, and Complexity (range across subtests = .58 to .79). Interrater reliability estimates across three raters ranged from .22 to .92 across the same three subtests, with Complexity averaging .38. Low to moderate test-retest and interrater reliability coefficients are a strong indication that the RBS should remain a screening test, as the authors suggest, and not a formal assessment instrument.

The authors present evidence for validity of the RBS based on increasing means across subtests as ages increase. Concurrent validity evidence is based upon comparison of the British and American versions of the test, producing correlation coefficients of .98 for both Information and Sentence Length subtests. Further information about the number of subjects and their nationality was not provided for concurrent validity results. It is assumed the RBS authors were the experimenters.

Previous studies using the earlier British version of the RBS are cited by the test authors as providing discriminant validity for children with language delays. However, if studies cited originated in the United Kingdom, this could seriously affect generalizability of results to U.S. samples because of differences in diagnostic standards.

CONCLUSION. The RBS testing package is small, well organized, and attractively designed. It consists of an Examiner's Manual with administration instructions and normative tables, a *Story Booklet*, and a set of record forms. Instructions are clear and easy to follow. Administration is quick and straightforward. Scoring may require more time than does administration. Evidence of test-retest reliability and interrater reliability are provided with appropriate cautions. Construct and concurrent validity have been investigated for the RBS although more information should be gathered.

Some limitations of the RBS merit reviewing here. First, the test has a limited, geographically proscribed normative sample and specific information about the socioeconomic status of children in the sample is not supplied. Potential users are cautioned regarding the match between local populations and children represented in the normative data. In areas such as the Southeastern states, where racial makeup and socioeconomic conditions differ drastically from the RBS's normative sample, minority children and children from economically deprived backgrounds may find themselves overidentified and placed on a list for formal assessment. Locally collected norms for this screening test would provide an advantage in some geographic areas.

Secondly, children with identified language or learning problems or with suspected problems were intentionally excluded from the normative sample altogether, which may translate into poorer standard scores than these children might have received if such a group had been included. The normative sample should be extended to include these children. In addition, the need for updated research regarding discriminant validity based upon a sample of American children is evident. Additional concurrent validity based upon other language screeners would also be a welcome addition.

A third concern involves caution in scoring and interpreting the Complexity subtest, which exhibits the weakest reliability data and appears to have an inadequate floor at lower age levels. The test authors do advise caution in using this subtest. On the other hand, the Complexity subtest might prove useful in screening for characteristics of giftedness, an issue not discussed in manual, but perhaps worth investigating.

SUMMARY. The RBS is recommended by its authors as a language-screening instrument, a research instrument, or a tool within a battery of language tests. In general, these recommendations seem appropriate. The test could provide an inexpensive addition to screening packages for children suspected of having language problems if limitations of the normative sample are considered.

REVIEWER'S REFERENCE

Renfrew, C. E. (1977). *The bus story.* Oxford, England: 2a North Place, Old Headington.

Review of The Renfrew Bus Story by ROBERT R. HACCOUN, Professor and Chair, I-O Psychology, Université de Montréal, Montreal, Quebec, Canada:

The Renfrew Bus Story is the U.S.-based version of a British scale developed by C. Renfrew. The test is presumed to assess in young children (aged 3-6—6-11) the "ability to give a coherent description of a continuous series of events" (p. 1). Such ability is said to be useful in the analysis of the state of a child's progress towards the development of higher language skills. These skills are presumably required for academic achievement.

Performance on this task depends on a complex set of skills including the coordination of auditory and visual cues, attention, comprehension, and memory. The development of the test is based on an analysis of the dimensions that, on theoretical ground, appear to underlie language development and academic achievement. The test is supposed to indicate a need for further testing and it is not intended as a stand-alone diagnostic instrument that would lead to specific remedial interventions.

Examiners must read a story to the child who is prompted to retell it in his or her own words. The story itself is very short, recounting the experiences of a bus that runs away from its driver. Twelve pictures describing the key elements of the story are also presented and the child peruses the pictures as he or she is read the story and as it is retold to the examiner. The entire protocol is tape recorded and a content analysis is conducted by the test administrator who scores the verbal production along four dimensions: Information (level of story detail reproduced), Sentence Length (mean number of words for the five longest sentences), Complexity (use of sentences that contain subordinate and-or relative clauses), and Independence (level of prompting required). In addition, the examiner notes, on specific templates, information that may form the basis of a qualitative assessment. Specifically, the examiner may score the child's production for sequencing problems, off-topic remarks, organizational weaknesses, word difficulties, self-correction, and syntax. The examiner is also required to ask some questions that prompt the child to draw some logical inferences. Finally, the child's response style is also judged and recorded on a specific form.

The manual spends considerable time describing and exemplifying the scoring system. Appropriately, given the "open-ended" nature of the responses to be analyzed, scoring correctly is the essence of this measure. Very explicit directions and forms are provided to help the examiner in the scoring of a large number of possible verbal productions relevant to the information and the sentence length dimensions. Scoring for the Complexity and the Independence scores is explained with considerably less detail. Even though, based on the statistical information reported in the manual, these dimensions may prove more difficult to score reliably.

TEST PROPERTIES.

TEST STABILITY. The stability of the test results was assessed using a test-retest procedure with a 4-week delay with a sample of children aged 4 years 6 months to 6 years 11 months. Very young children (3.5 to 4.5 years) are not included in the sample. Data came from 27 children who were administered the test and their results were scored twice (by nondescribed raters).

The values of the pre-post correlations were .79 for Information, .73 for Sentence Length, and .58 for Complexity. The level of reliability estimate for scores from the Independence dimension is not reported. Except for the Complexity score, which is low (and the nonexistent information on Independence), the remaining coefficients are reasonable. However, the reliability estimates are based on a rather small sample and no information is provided as to the composition of the sample in terms of race, gender, or other parameters of importance. Moreover, the manual does not describe the raters nor the extent of their familiarity and training with the test. Of special significance is that the manual offers no information to define the reliability of protocols for the different age groups, which is important because scores are especially sensitive to age. The omission of data for the youngest people for whom the test is intended is also a glaring omission that requires correction.

INTERRATER AGREEMENT. Because the test involves the scoring of "open ended" response, the issue of interrater reliability is crucial. Here again, the authors conclude that the obtained label of interrater reliability is adequate. It is not clear how the procedure was carried out exactly though it appears that the mean rating obtained between the two authors was correlated with the results obtained by two (presumably independent) "special education teachers." These correlation coefficients, based on a sample of 25 children, ranged .70 to .90 for the Information scores; .79 and .81 for Sentence Length; and from .22 to .60 for the Complexity scores.

This methodology is suboptimal and interrater reliability level may be overestimated. First, any scoring variations between the authors would be washed out. Of course, it is possible that rather than the mean ratings obtained by the authors, each contributed an independent rating for some of the protocols. In this case, separate analyses for each author should have been reported. Second, the use of the correlation coefficient as opposed to the Kappa statistic as a basis for the estimation of agreement is not totally appropriate. Correlation coefficients are insensitive to any mean differences between raters, producing artificially high interrater agreement.

Despite the use of the problematic procedure, the reliability estimate of the Complexity scores is unacceptably low. Although the authors are prudent in advising test users to be especially diligent in scoring the test for complexity, it is doubtful that this prescription alone is sufficient. One can easily assume that the raters used in generating the results reported in the manual would have been very carefully monitored by the test authors. Therefore, the correlations obtained from their scores should be higher than those that would likely be found with raters in the field, where control over their training would most likely be less stringent. Consequently, and based on the reported data, it does not appear, at this point, that the Complexity scores are reliable enough to justify the use of this dimension to enable substantive decisions about children. The absence of technical information about the Independence score should trigger a great deal of caution in accepting the authors' claims about the usefulness of this dimension.

INDEPENDENCE OF THE DIMENSIONS. The manual does not report any information as to the intercorrelations between the dimensions. This is an important omission and a weakness that should be corrected. Until this is done, there is no basis for interpreting the dimensions separately.

VALIDITY. The validity of the use of scores from the scale requires further documentation. As a basis for validity the authors report a very high (r = .98+) concurrent correlation with the British version of the scale. However, no methodology is reported in the manual. The validity claim is further bolstered by the observation that the scores obtained by subjects increase "smoothly" with age. Once again, however, no statistical tests or, for that matter, description of the methodology used to support these claims, is presented. Given the paucity of the supporting documentation, validity claims would need considerable bolstering before one can agree with the authors that the test produces valid scores for identifying potential language difficulties.

TEST OR ITEM BIAS. The bus driver-mechanic in the story is a woman, which is a nice touch. The authors claim that the test appears to show no gender or race bias and present a table showing means (without variance information) for different groups. No further statistical information is available. Perusal of the table, however, shows that Black children (and to a lesser degree Hispanic children) appear to obtain lower scores. Therefore, and given the available evidence, the claim of no test bias—especially with regard to Blacks and Hispanics (populations of special importance in the United States)—is not entirely convincing.

NORMS AND INTERPRETATION. Norms are reported based on a sample of 418 children enrolled in school in the Mid-Atlantic states, Florida, and Illinois. The protocols for the normative samples were scored by the authors of the test. Here caution is required: (a) The reference sample excluded children for whom English was a second language or who did not respond to any prompts to tell the story as well as children who were previously identified as suffering from hearing loss, language delay, learning disabilities, or who were the object of unspecified "concerns" by the teacher; (b) the resulting sample is composed of 10 times more Caucasian than visible minorities though the gender balance is better; (c) the size of the normative sample for the various age groups is unknown; (d) given the low total sample sizes, the normative information for Blacks and Hispanics broken down by age group may be excessively thin.

The results are expressed as raw scores and a table in the manual translates these into standard scores and percentiles. The tables for the Information and Sentence Length dimensions are quite detailed and provided for children at 6-month intervals (3 years 6 months to 6 years 11 months). The norms tables are presented in a different format for the Complexity and the Independence scores leaving the impression that the two former scores are more important than the latter two. The reference chart for the Complexity dimension provides specific interpretations ("superior" to "concern") but the Independence chart only provides a global "average range" scores distribution. Separate norms are not given for gender, race, or other descriptions of the normative sample.

SUMMARY. The Renfrew Bus Story appears to be easy to administer and most young children might find it interesting. The scoring of the test, however, appears to be considerably more complex and difficult and errors are likely.

Although some of the reliability information is encouraging (though perhaps overestimated) the validity information is, at this point, much too scanty. Unless that information is seriously updated and strengthened, the test user who still chooses to use the test should follow the authors' advice and supplement it with additional testing. The claim of nonbias with respect to minority groups is not convincing. Of special significance, the test should not be used with those for whom English is a second language, who suffer previously diagnosed learning disabilities, or who have various sensory impairments as the norms sample specifically excludes these children. Leaving aside the omissions and technical ambiguities, the interpretation of results may prove somewhat taxing in practice.

Only the Complexity dimension (low scores flag "caution") is associated with explicit interpretation labels. This dimension is the very one that shows the weakest psychometric qualities.

The percentile information on the other dimensions may indicate a child's relative performance, but in the absence of validity information, it becomes difficult for the test interpreter to prepare any sort of convincing conclusion. We simply do not know if scoring at the 50th percentile on Information at age 6 is a valid precursor of difficulties in later school achievement.

It is not clear how one should interpret the profile of scores. The authors do provide one contingency (a two-by-two matrix, which relates Independence to Information), but this is very limited. Also, the linking of the qualitative and quantitative scoring systems is nowhere described.

Test users will find no help from the manual in defining the types of interpretations that may be reached given a particular pattern of scores. In the end, and after much complicated scoring, the evaluator is left pretty much on his or her own when it comes time to reach a conclusion about a child. They would then need to rely rather strongly on intuitive clinical sense. From a practical as well as a technical viewpoint, this considerably reduces the potential usefulness of this device.

[70]
Rey Complex Figure Test and Recognition Trial.

Purpose: Designed to "investigate visuospatial constructional ability and visual memory."

Population: Ages 18–89.
Publication Dates: 1995–1996.
Acronym: RCFT.
Scores, 9: Immediate Recall, Delayed Recall, Recognition Total Correct, Copy, Time to Copy, Recognition True Positives, Recognition False Positives, Recognition True Negatives, Recognition False Negatives.
Administration: Individual.
Price Data: Price information available from publisher for complete kit including manual ('95, 126 pages), 25 test booklets, stimulus card, and supplemental norms for children and adolescents ('96, 21 pages).
Time: (45) minutes, including a 30-minute delay interval.
Authors: John E. Meyers and Kelly R. Meyers.
Publisher: Psychological Assessment Resources, Inc.
Cross References: See T5:2227 (62 references).

Review of the Rey Complex Figure Test and Recognition Trial by D. ASHLEY COHEN, Clinical Neuropsychologist, CogniMetrix, San Jose, CA:

The Rey Complex Figure Test (RCFT) has appeared in various guises as a popular instrument in V.A. hospitals, academic neuropsychology training programs, rehabilitation facilities, and outpatient assessment offices. Its utility was apparent to many neuropsychologists (Kramer & Delis, 1998; Lynch, 1997) despite sometimes poorly reproduced and slightly varying versions of the stimulus figure, conflicting sets of administration and scoring instructions, differing times between the trials, and poor normative data, often requiring calculations and extrapolations. These factors almost completely precluded comparison of scores on ostensibly the same test, given in different facilities or regions, and contributed to unwanted variability in scores obtained from particular individuals. Data on older persons was virtually unavailable.

The present version of the RCFT addresses these shortcomings, and takes the concept from an error-variance-laden, rough approximation of an instrument with potential to a clean, well-constructed, modern neuropsychological test.

For those unfamiliar with the test in any of its extant forms, a line-drawing of a multipart geometric figure is shown, with the request to copy it exactly onto a separate paper. No mention is made of a memory task to come. Shortly following completion of the Copy trial, the subject is given a blank paper, and instructed to reproduce the same figure from memory. Thirty minutes after the Copy trial, the subject once again draws the figure. In the Meyers version (here reviewed), following the delayed recall, the subject is shown 24 smaller figures, half of which were part of the original stimulus, and is asked to mark the ones he or she has seen before.

The publisher lists the RCFT for use with individuals aged 6–89 years. A separate manual supplement is required to use the test with children and adolescents; this portion of the test is not discussed here as the publisher elected not to provide the children's manual for review. [Editor's Note: The publisher advises this was an oversight and provided the missing manual after the reviews were completed.]

IMPROVEMENTS AND UNIQUE FEATURES OF THE MEYERS AND MEYERS VERSION OF THE RCFT. The stimulus figure is provided with the test packet, and laminated to prevent deterioration. At many sites where the RCFT has been in use, it was customary to present the figure in "landscape" rather than "portrait" view. Examinees often gravitate to this orientation, as the figure is wider than it is tall. The manual states findings that the vertical presentation results in less inadvertent distortion of the figure by normal examinees.

The awkward practice of giving the examinee colored markers for doing the drawing, and having the examiner switch them at intervals, has been eliminated. As Meyers and Meyers observe, many neuropsychologically impaired individuals, or those with motor difficulties, are unduly distracted when drawing implements are exchanged. Examiners do not in practice switch colors reliably, and the process extends the administration time, which affects the time for copying, one of the important scores.

There were 601 subjects in the standardization sample in the 18–89-year age group, and 505 who were ages 6–17. All geographic regions of the U.S. and portions of Canada were included in the normative sample; both urban and rural areas were represented. A subset of the sample was selected to match year 2000 U.S. Census projections. The RCFT sample had slightly higher educational attainment than the U.S. population, although education was not found to be a factor in RCFT scores; neither was there an effect from gender. Age had by far the most significant influence on scores, and this version of the test provides normative data up to age 89 (the manual notes that relatively fewer of the oldest subjects are represented in the sample, however).

Because of the structure of the standardization sample, a given individual's score can be compared both to age-corrected scores, for purposes of diagnosis, and to the performance of the general adult population, when seeking to establish a level of performance in absolute terms.

Very precise scoring criteria, based on both placement of units of the figure, and accuracy in reproducing each unit, were developed empirically. The manual states experienced scorers do not need to use the detailed criteria for most protocols, and indeed they would be very time-consuming for everyday scoring. It is presumed, however, that the precise criteria were used in standardization, and the variability introduced hereby is unknown.

The Recognition Trial is an important addition to this test, enabling evaluation of the relative strengths of the processes of encoding, storage, and retrieval in a given subject. This trial is easy to administer, but recording and calculating the score is somewhat cumbersome. An additional feature of this trial is its potential utility in evaluating subjects suspected of questionable motivation; cutoff scores are suggested. Two types of errors are detailed, which are virtually never encountered in normals, extremely rarely seen in brain-injured patients, but are often found among malingerers.

Overall, strong reliability evidence was shown. Interrater reliability coefficients averaged .94. Test-retest reliability is a troublesome concept with this test, because once the examinee knows it is a memory test and has drawn the figure three times for the first administration, the situational demands change. Some of the obtained scores have a restricted range in normals, as well. Those portions of the test for which temporal stability is clinically meaningful yielded between .917 and 100% agreement in clinical rating or interpretation.

Good to excellent convergent and discriminant validities were found, using separate samples of both normal subjects and brain-injured patients. Construct validity was evaluated by comparing scores of the RCFT with the WAIS-R, and with related and unrelated neuropsychological tests, using both normal and brain-injured persons. As would be expected, the RCFT proved a strong measure of visuoconstructional ability and visuospatial memory.

Findings of a study were presented demonstrating the ability of the RCFT to discriminate among brain-injured patients, psychiatric patients, and healthy normal subjects. It was also found that the recognition trial provided incremental validity of 16.7%.

The authors present a "Profile Analysis" scheme similar, they state, to Roger Greene's (1991) codetype configuration analysis of the Minnesota Multiphasic Personality Inventory (MMPI). Five distinct patterns of scores were commonly found, and each pattern was associated with different recommendations for rehabilitation, as well as prognostic indicators for independence in activities of daily living.

GENERAL COMMENTS. In the manual, a brief historical summary of the RCFT is given, and research is cited on conditions and disorders with which the test has proven useful. Many helpful case illustrations, and detailed scoring examples, are provided. Overall, this version of the RCFT is easy to administer, and scoring, although still not simple, is much more likely to be accurate. Obtaining normative scores for a given protocol is efficient, and it is possible to compare the individual's score to both the general population, and to his or her appropriate age group, including elderly persons.

The newly developed Profile Analysis promises to increase clinical utility, and the Recognition Trial is a valuable addition to the test. It provides ability to locate where in the memory process the difficulty is occurring, and to measure the assistance, if any, obtained by provision of retrieval cues.

REVIEWER'S REFERENCES

Green, R. L. (1991). *The MMPI-2/MMPI: An interpretive manual.* New York: Allyn and Bacon.

Lynch, W. J. (1997). *Primary neuropsychological tests for use at the Brain Injury Rehabilitation Unit.* Palo Alto: Veterans' Affairs Medical Center.

Kramer, J. H., & Delis, D. C. (1998). Neuropsychological assessment of memory. In G. Goldstein, P. D. Nussbaum, & S. R. Beers (Eds.), *Neuropsychology* (pp. 333–356). New York: Plenum.

Review of the Rey Complex Figure Test and Recognition Trial by DEBORAH D. ROMAN, Assistant Professor and Director, Neuropsychology Lab, Departments of Physical Medicine and Rehabilitation and Neurosurgery, Director, Neuropsychology Lab, University of Minnesota, Minneapolis, MN:

The Rey Complex Figure Test (RCFT) has been around for over 50 years and has enjoyed popularity as a measure of constructional abilities

and nonverbal memory. This version of the test uses the traditional figure without modification. The administration procedure has been standardized and a recognition trial has been added. Consistent with previously established scoring criteria, 18 design elements are scored for a total possible score of 36, based on the accuracy and placement of the elements. The current system provides more detailed scoring criteria that should enhance interrater reliability. Additionally, the authors provide the largest normative sample ever published for this test, enabling more accurate age comparisons.

There are four parts to the test administration. First, subjects copy the design from a model. Then it is redrawn from memory after a 3-minute delay and again after a 30-minute delay. Finally, in the recognition trial, RCFT design elements are selected from arrays of options (12 target details, 12 foils).

The normative sample consisted of 601 subjects who had been screened for learning disability, substance abuse, psychiatric disorders, and depression. Subjects were pooled from various sources including college students (134), families and friends of rehabilitation patients (74), and community dwellers enlisted from a variety of sources (393). Subjects ranged in age from 18 to 89. A subset of this sample ($n = 394$) was selected to mirror the U.S. population in terms of age. The manual contains a breakdown of the various RCFT score means and standard deviations across 14 age groups.

Polynomial regression analyses were conducted to determine the effects of age, gender, and education on RCFT scores. There was a significant quadratic effect for age on Copy and Time to Copy scores. There was a significant linear effect for age on all of the other RCFT variables. Gender and years of education were not significantly related to RCFT scores. Demographically corrected normative scores are provided in Appendix C and enable conversion of raw scores to percentiles and T-scores for the Immediate Recall, Delayed Recall, and Recognition scores. All other scores were divided into five ranges (with >16th percentile as the top range and ≤1st percentile as the lowest range).

To estimate interrater reliability the senior author and two trained psychometrists independently scored the same 15 protocols. Interrater reliability coefficients (Pearson product-moment correlations) ranged from .93 to .99, suggesting very good reliability among well-trained scorers.

Temporal reliability (average retest interval was 184 days) was assessed using 12 subjects drawn from the normative sample. Immediate Recall, Delayed Recall, and Recognition Total Correct test-retest coefficients were .759, .888, and .874, respectively. There were no significant differences across the two testings for mean scores of the remaining variables (Copy, Time to Copy, Recognition, True Positives, Recognition False Positives, Recognition True Negatives, and Recognition False Negatives).

Convergent and discriminant validity were assessed using the 601 normative subjects. Immediate and Delayed Recalls were highly correlated (.881). Lower, but still significant, positive correlations were noted between Recall and Recognition scores. Copy scores also correlated significantly with Recall scores. Convergent and discriminant validity were also assessed in a heterogeneous group of 100 brain-injured patients. Again, Immediate and Delayed Recall scores were highly correlated (.961). Copy scores correlated significantly with Immediate and Delayed Recalls. Overall, the intratest correlations were similar for the normal and brain-injured groups. Given the very high correlations between Immediate and Delayed recalls, it may be possible to abbreviate the test by giving only the Immediate Recall and excluding the Delayed Recall.

Construct validity was assessed by correlating RCFT scores with the Wechsler Adult Intelligence Scale—Revised (WAIS-R) and various neuropsychological measures. Using the brain-injured sample ($n = 100$), RCFT measures generally correlated more strongly with the WAIS-R Performance subtests than the Verbal subtests, as expected. Copy scores correlated with the Benton Visual Retention Test (BVRT), Hooper Visual Organization Test, and Trail Making Test (Part B). Immediate and Delayed RCFT recall correlated with the BVRT and Rey Auditory Verbal Learning Test. Language measures such as the Benton Sentence Repetition and Controlled Oral Word Association Test were not significantly correlated with any RCFT measure.

Factor analysis of the RCFT yielded a five-factor solution, which accounted for 98.4% of the variance. These factors were labeled visuospatial

recall, visuospatial recognition, response bias, processing speed, and visuospatial constructional ability. The factor structure was very similar for the normal and brain-injured samples.

The RCFT was given to 30 brain-injured, 30 psychiatric, and 30 normal subjects. Analyses of variance revealed significant group differences for all RCFT variables. Post hoc analyses indicated that the brain-injured group scored significantly lower than the other two groups on the recall trials; the psychiatric group scored lower than the normal controls. For the other RCFT variables, the brain-injured group scored lower than the other groups and the psychiatric and normal groups did not differ from each other.

Discriminant function analysis was used to determine classification hit rates for the three groups. Using Copy and Time to Copy as the predictor variables, 58% of the subjects were correctly classified. Using Immediate Recall and Delayed Recall as the predictors, 61% were correctly classified. Finally, when using recall and recognition measures as predictors, 78% of the subjects were correctly classified. Overall, a larger number of psychiatric patients were misclassified. A substantial number of these patients were misclassified as brain injured. It may be that some of these patients had cerebral compromise. In any event, this test must be interpreted cautiously when used with psychiatric populations.

The clinical utility of the RCFT has been well established. It is a very useful measure of visuospatial processing abilities, constructional abilities, and nonverbal memory. The modifications made by these authors constitute significant improvements, which should enhance the usefulness of this measure. The more detailed scoring system should increase interrater reliability. The extended norms allow for better comparisons with age peers, including older adults. The addition of a recognition trial may prove especially useful in assessing neurobehavioral syndromes characterized by memory retrieval deficits (such as Parkinson's Disease and frontal lobe syndromes). In short, this is a valuable neuropsychological test.

The authors have demonstrated adequate test-retest and interrater reliability. The test scores also appear valid as a measure of brain dysfunction, as these scores have been shown to distinguish normals from brain-injured patients with a fairly high degree of accuracy. The extant literature suggests that the copy portion of the test is especially sensitive to parietal disease whereas recall scores are more sensitive to temporal disease. It remains to be seen whether the recognition trial developed by these authors is selectively sensitive to certain types of brain dysfunction, such as frontal lobe disease. Further studies with more homogeneous brain-injured populations are needed. It appears that many psychiatric patients score within the impaired range of this test, for reasons that are not yet clear. Again, studies with more homogeneous psychiatric populations are needed.

[71]
The Rivermead Behavioural Memory Test [Second Edition].

Purpose: "Developed to detect impairment of everyday memory functioning and to monitor change following treatment for memory difficulties."
Publication Dates: 1985–1991.
Acronym: RBMT.
Administration: Individual.
Price Data: Available from publisher.
Time: Administration time not reported.
Publisher: Thames Valley Test Company Ltd. [England].
a) THE RIVERMEAD BEHAVIORAL MEMORY TEST.
Population: Brain-damaged persons, ages 11 to elderly adult.
Publication Dates: 1985–1991.
Scores, 2: Screening Score, Standardized Profile Score.
Comments: For multiple administrations with the same subject, four parallel versions available.
Authors: Barbara Wilson (test, manual, supplementary manual 2), Janet Cockburn (test, manual, supplementary manuals 2 and 3), Alan Baddely (test, manual, supplementary manual 2), Robert Hiorns (supplementary manual 2), and Phillip T. Smith (supplementary manual 3).
b) THE RIVERMEAD BEHAVIOURAL MEMORY TEST FOR CHILDREN.
Population: Brain-damaged children, ages 5–10.
Publication Date: 1991.
Score: Standardized Profile Score.
Comments: Materials from adult version used for most subtests, but some additional materials needed.
Authors: Barbara A. Wilson (test and manual), Rebecca Ivani-Chalian (test and manual), Frances Aldrich (manual).
Cross References: See T5:2239 (35 references).

Review of the Rivermead Behavioural Memory Test [Second Edition] by ANTHONY M. PAOLO, Coordinator of Assessment and Evaluation, University of Kansas Medical Center, Kansas City, KS:

The Rivermead Behavioural Memory Test (RBMT) is not based upon any particular theoretical model of memory, rather it attempts to simulate the demands placed on memory by normal everyday life. It consists of 12 tasks that are analogues of everyday memory situations that may be problematic for persons with brain dysfunction. The tasks include remembering a person's first and last name, recalling a hidden belonging, remembering an appointment, face recognition, remembering a short story, picture recognition, remembering a new route, delivering a message, and answering typical orientation questions (i.e., date, place, etc.). The items for remembering a short story and new route have immediate and delayed recall components.

Interrrater reliability was excellent with 100% agreement between two raters for the scoring rules. Test-retest stability for the screening and profile scores was .78 and .85, respectively, for 118 patients tested twice. Performance on the second test administration was slightly better than the first. Although providing stability estimates is good practice, there is no information in the manual about which form(s) these coefficients were based on nor is there any information concerning the interval from test to retest. In addition, standard errors should be provided to allow users to be able to compute whether changes in RBMT scores reflect real change, rather than measurement error. The RBMT has four parallel forms that should reduce any meaningful practice effect that may occur with repeat testing. The correlations between Form A and Forms B and C are good and at least .80. The correlation between Forms A and D is lower (.67). Considering this lower coefficient, the interscale correlations among all of the parallel forms should be provided.

The RBMT demonstrates moderate correlations (.20 to .63) with other memory tests including the Warrington Recognition Memory Test, digit span, Paired Associate Learning Test, and Corsi Block Span. These relationships suggest that the RBMT does assess memory functions tapped by other measures of memory, but is not entirely redundant with them. More importantly, the RBMT correlates highest (greater than .70 in absolute value) with the therapist ratings of memory lapses for persons with central nervous dysfunction and with self-reported memory problems. The latter findings suggest that the RBMT is tapping other aspects of memory abilities, presumably memory functions required for everyday tasks. In addition to the above validity information, persons with brain damage or dysfunction tend to score lower than normal controls. When the brain-damaged subjects were grouped by etiology (i.e., right CVA, left CVA, head injury, etc.), the RBMT was not very successful in distinguishing among them. Thus, the RBMT seems to be sensitive to general memory disruption, but not necessarily specific to any particular etiology. It is also important to note that, in general, the memory tasks seem relatively easy, suggesting that the RBMT may not be sensitive to mild forms of memory impairment. As such, the RBMT should not be used as a screening device for detecting persons with early or mild memory problems.

The initial standardization samples consisted of 188 healthy persons between the ages of 16 and 69 (mean age = 41.17) with an average IQ of 106 (range 68 to 136) and a patient sample composed of 113 men and 63 women ranging in age from 14 to 69 years (mean = 44.40). No information concerning the gender, racial, or educational make-up of the healthy group is provided. Additional standardization samples have been collected on elderly and preteenage groups. The community-dwelling elderly sample consists of 44 men and 75 women ranging in age from 70 to 94 years (mean = 80.49; *SD* = 5.22) and have an average educational level of 9.51 years. The preteen sample consists of 43 girls and 42 boys ranging from 11 to 14 years of age.

For persons 16 to 69 years of age, percentile tables are provided in the manual, but because over 50% of the patient group scored below the 5th percentile relative to the normal subjects, these tables provide very little meaningful information. For this reason, the authors provide cutoff scores for severity of memory impairment based upon their clinical experience. In addition, separate cutoff scores are provided for persons with expressive language difficulty and persons with perceptual problems, as these difficulties significantly impact RBMT performance. These distinct cutoff scores are presented only for persons 16 to 69 years of age.

Very little information is provided for the preteenage standardization group. Only means and standard deviations for the total group and cutoff points for children with below average intellectual functioning are provided. For the elderly sample, tables are provided that allow for an individual's profile score to be compared with that expected for a normal person of similar age and estimated premorbid IQ. No such tables are provided for persons younger than 70 years of age.

SUMMARY. The RBMT represents one of only a few tests currently available for the assessment of everyday memory functions. The tasks appear relevant for everyday living situations and the validity information supports the claim that the RBMT measures meaningful everyday memory functions. The availability of four parallel forms is good, especially in situations where repeat testing will be necessary. Unfortunately, not knowing the test-retest interval and the lack of standard errors limits the usefulness of retest comparisons. Although the standardization samples cover a wide age range, different interpretive procedures are provided for the young and the elderly groups. A consistent method for interpreting scores across all age groups would improve the usability of the RBMT. Overall, if one needs to assess everyday memory functions in persons with known brain dysfunction, the RBMT is a good choice, but the manual could be improved by including some additional psychometric information.

Review of the Rivermead Behavioural Memory Test [Second Edition] by GORAN WESTERGREN, Chief Psychologist, Department of Clinical Psychology, State Hospital, Halmstad, Sweden, and INGELA WESTERGREN, Neuropsychologist, Licensed Psychologist, Department of Clinical Psychology, State Hospital, Halmstad, Sweden:

The Rivermead Behavioural Memory Test (RBMT) covers a broad spectrum of memory functions and in so doing permits the identification of many different memory dysfunctions. The RBMT's focus is built around everyday memory problems. The strength one can find in strict standardized tests for laboratory settings has been successfully combined in an excellent way with simple, practical behavior measurements for memory disturbances. Consequently, in the construction of the test the authors have tried to achieve what is called "ecological validity." The

RBMT assesses memory skills necessary for normal life. Thus it is not based on experimental data measuring the acquisition and retention or more or less abstract material that requires clinical judgment about practical consequences of the results. The type of reality-based functions the RBMT measures are things such as "if someone borrows something, then one must remember to get it back," "what must I remember when the bell rings," "orientation in time and space," "remember everyday information," "recognise people one has met," etc.

It is, then, a strength in the RBMT that, in comparison to more traditional tests such as the Wechsler Memory Scale (T5:2147) and the Recognition Memory Test (T5:2193), the user obtain a direct understanding of which types of everyday problems memory-impaired people are likely to face.

The test is constructed so that it can also be used on patients with severe brain damage and others with limited endurance. This is often difficult to carry out with normal memory tests and memory questionnaires. For some clinical groups, such as patients with expressive aphasia and specific perceptual problems, the relevant test sections are specified. In contrast to many other memory tests, the RBMT can also help therapists to find memory functions in patients that are possible to treat.

There are four parallel versions of the RBMT, therefore making it usable both in longitudinal studies and in situations involving change from before and after interventions. In addition to an adult version (16 to 69 years), there is a version for brain-damaged children in the age group 5–10 years.

The strength of the test is also its weakness. By being fast and easily administered it can be a little superficial and give a coarse picture of possible memory dysfunctions. Therefore, it functions best as a fast and practical screening test. In most cases of brain damage, however, it is usually quite satisfactory to obtain general assessment of the memory dysfunctions and for this the RBMT is quite sufficient. If the therapist requires more detailed information, supplemental tests that measure more specific memory functions will be needed. Examples of clinical questions where the RBMT can be supplemented with other memory tests are given in the manual.

The RBMT has validity evidence for a group of brain-damaged patients (113 men and 63 women, mean age 44.40). The sample contained 60 head-injury patients, 34 suffering from a left CVA, 42 a right CVA, 13 subarachnoid hemorrhage, and 27 others. The latter included cerebral tumors removed, carbon monoxide poisoning patients, multiple sclerosis, etc. The control group consisted of 118 subjects aged between 16 and 69 years (mean 41.17) with a mean IQ of 106 (range 68–136). A supplement of norms for the elderly (70–94 years) is also provided.

The interrater reliability was estimated by having 40 subjects scored separately but simultaneously by two raters. There was 100% agreement between the raters for scoring procedures. Test-retest reliability (administration interval not specified) was .78 for the screening score and .85 for the profile score.

The RMBT is based on empirical facts of everyday memory problems rather than on a clear theory concerning the memory's localization and function. Despite this, scores from the RBMT show high correlations with other standard memory tests. It also has a high face validity in observations made by therapists as well as subjective ratings by patients and their relatives.

SUMMARY. The RBMT is well constructed with clear and easily read questionnaires and manuals. It is also easy to learn to administer. The resistance against laboratory tests that sometimes occurs in many patient groups can be avoided in this test. The results are also easy to communicate to nonpsychologists, partly because of the test's practically founded, descriptive character. The RBMT is a well-structured, easily administered, and excellent screening test for memory dysfunctions.

[72]
Roberts Apperception Test for Children [with new Interpretive Handbook].

Purpose: Constructed to "assess children's perceptions of common interpersonal situations."
Population: Ages 6–15.
Publication Dates: 1982–1994.
Acronym: RATC.
Scores, 13: 8 Adaptive Profile Scales (Reliance on Others, Support—Other, Support—Child, Limit Setting, Problem Identification, Resolution 1, Resolution 2, Resolution 3), 5 Clinical Profile Scales (Anxiety, Aggression, Depression, Rejection, Unresolved Prob-

lems), 3 Indicators (Atypical Responses, Maladaptive Outcome, Refusal), and 3 Supplemental Measures (Ego Functioning, Aggression, Levels of Projection).
Administration: Individual.
Price Data, 1999: $120 per kit including manual ('82, 129 pages), 1 set of pictures (does not include test pictures for black children), and 25 record booklets; $17.50 per 25 record booklets; $59.50 per test pictures; $59.50 per test pictures for black children; $46.50 per manual; $59.50 per interpretive handbook ('94, 270 pages).
Time: (20–30) minutes.
Authors: Dorothea S. McArthur and Glen E. Roberts.
Publisher: Western Psychological Services.
Cross References: See T5:2242 (8 references) and T4:2285 (5 references); for a review by Jacob O. Sines, see 9:1054.

Review of Roberts Apperception Test for Children by MERITH COSDEN, Professor of Counseling/Clinical/School Psychology, Graduate School of Education, University of California, Santa Barbara, CA:

The Roberts Apperception Test for Children (RATC) is a projective test in which children are asked to tell stories about a series of pictures. As with other picture-story tests, the 16 cards are designed to "pull" for certain types of responses, but are also ambiguous enough to allow respondents to insert themselves into the stories. The examiner uses the structure and thematic content of the stories to make inferences about the psychological functioning of the child. Although the RATC shares the strengths and weaknesses of this approach with other similar assessment tools, such as the Children's Apperception Test (CAT; Bellak & Bellak, 1949; T5:466), and the Thematic Apperception Test (TAT; Murray, 1943; T5:2749), it also differs from these picture-story tests in some significant ways. Unlike the TAT, the RATC was designed specifically for children. By using line drawings of people in common interpersonal situations, the RATC appeals to a wider age range of children than the CAT, which uses pictures of anthropomorphized animals. Finally, the RATC is distinct from most picture-story tests in that it provides standardized procedures for administering and scoring the test, with interpretation of scores based on their comparison to a normative sample of well-adjusted children.

Although the RATC was first published in 1982, frequent updates of the Manual and the development of an Interpretive Handbook reflect efforts to increase the standardized use of this tool. Both texts state that use of the RATC in an informal manner (e.g., administration of a few cards with a subjective content analysis) is not desirable if the RATC is to be an effective assessment tool. The authors promote the administration of all 16 cards, in order, following standardized instructions for questioning children as they tell their stories. Detailed scoring procedures are described, with examples provided from well-adjusted, as well as clinical, samples of children. Methods for interpreting scores are detailed, along with case examples of test interpretations for both well-adjusted and maladjusted children.

Three types of scales are described in the manual: Adaptive Scales, Clinical Scales, and Clinical Indicators. Development of the eight Adaptive Scales was based on the thematic material presented in the stories of the standardization sample. Scores reflect the children's demonstration of problem-solving skills in their stories. For example, Reliance on Others is scored when the character in a story reaches out for help, and Resolution 1, 2, or 3 is scored as a function of whether the story problem is resolved unrealistically or constructively. The five Clinical Scales, including Anxiety and Depression, are scored based on feelings reflected in the stories. The cumulative number of coded responses in each area is used to infer the child's strength or pathology. The three Clinical indicators, Atypical Response, Maladaptive Outcome, and Refusal occurred rarely in the standardization sample, and are thought to reflect clinical problems.

Normative data are reported on 200 children in three school districts in California. The sampling procedures were designed to select "well adjusted" students on which to standardize the test. Teachers were asked to nominate three or four children from their classes who met the following criteria: good peer relationships, coping skills, academic performance, and the absence of any obvious psychological or behavioral difficulties. After this screening, stratified random sampling was conducted to assure equal numbers of boys and girls at each age level. The children ranged in age from 6–15, and were collapsed into four age groups (6–7, 8–9, 10–12, and 13–15) for the normative tables. Although the manual reports that the children represent a cross-section of socioeconomic groups, specific data on this, and the ethnic composition of the sample, are not reported. Further, the year in which the standardization sample was obtained is not provided. The lack of information about ethnicity, socioeconomic status, and cohort, allows one to question the generalizability of results based on comparison to this sample.

The validity of the scale, and its scores, for assessing adaptive behavior and psychopathology, is questionable. In one set of unpublished studies described in the manual, scores on the Adaptive and Clinical Scales for the standardization sample of well-adjusted children are compared to scores obtained from a sample of 200 children seeking services at a Child Guidance Center. The demographic characteristics of the children at the Child Guidance Center are not provided. Global differences are found between groups for scores on most of these scales; that is, the well-adjusted children tend to score higher on the Adaptive Scales and lower on the Clinical Scales than the other group of children. In a second series of studies, scores on the supplementary measures (ego functioning, aggression, and levels of projection) are used to distinguish children with different types of problems. Although the studies provide some support for these scores as indicators of specific types of problems, they were obtained through a nonstandardized administration of the RATC and they are not part of the clinical scoring protocol recommended in the manual.

Support for the relationship between specific Adaptive and Clinical Scales and external referents is missing. For example, there is no evidence that scores of Reliance on Others reflect patterns of behavior that, in fact, demonstrate reliance on others. Without studies to validate these scales, there is little support for the need for the elaborate scoring system presented in the manual.

SUMMARY. Although the RATC is presented as a standardized projective test with scoring protocols that address children's strengths as well as psychopathology, there is not sufficient data to support its use for this purpose. Even though the manual was last updated in 1995, none of the references are more recent than 1980. The authors' efforts to create a standardized projective test for children is laudable, but more evidence is needed to support the utility of this test, and its scoring system, for assessing children's strengths and needs.

REVIEWER'S REFERENCES
Murray, H. A. (1943). *Thematic Apperception Test manual.* Cambridge, MA: Harvard University Press.
Bellak, L., & Bellak, S. S. (1949). Children's Apperception Test. New York: CPS, Inc.

Review of Roberts Apperception Test for Children by NIELS G. WALLER, Professor of Psychology and Human Development, Vanderbilt University, Nashville, TN:

The psychological assessment of children is arguably one of the most important functions of the practicing psychologist. It is also one of the most difficult. Language limitations may restrict the usefulness of entire classes of tests, such as self-report measures. Assessment via direct interviews presents its own problems because of the unreliability of the young child's memory reconstructions (Loftus, 1993; Pendergrast, 1995). For these and other reasons, many psychologists have included thematic apperception tests (TAT) in their standard diagnostic battery for children. At least 23 such tests have been developed for children since Murray (1943) introduced his classic set of TAT stimulus cards. Currently, only 12 of these are used regularly (Kroon, Goudena, & Rispens, 1998).

Roberts Apperception Test for Children (RATC) is an objectively scored TAT measure that was designed specifically for the psychological assessment of children and adolescents. After reviewing the stimulus cards, the test manual, and the recently published (1994) Interpretive Handbook, I wondered why anyone uses the RATC to formulate diagnostic impressions or to make clinical decisions. When conducting research, individuals are free to use any psychometric device they wish (after all, it is a free country). When functioning as a practicing psychologist, however, we have an ethical responsibility to use tests with demonstrated validity. Although the RATC has been marketed for more than 15 years, it still has no established validity for its intended purposes.

Sines (1985) presented a scholarly review of the RATC in the *Ninth Mental Measurements Yearbook.* Because the RATC and the test manual have not been updated in the 13 years since that review, Sines's pronouncements concerning the utility of the RATC are still valid. In summary, Sines bemoaned that, "when we examine the relations of the several objectively scored RATC variables to external criteria we can only be disappointed" (Sines, 1985, p. 1290).

One of the weaknesses of the RATC manual is its heavy reliance on unpublished doctoral dissertations. The manual cites numerous dissertations that found the RATC useful in the diagnosis of childhood problems. While preparing this review, I naively assumed that many of these studies would have found their way into print during the last 15 years, and I was intent on reading some of them. Before trekking to the library, I logged onto the computer and conducted a literature search with the keywords "Roberts Apperception Test" and "RATC." I located 23 references. All but two of these references were unpublished doctoral dissertations. I decided to stay in the office. One can only wonder why so few studies that use the RATC end up in refereed journals.

One of the putative strengths of the RATC is that the test includes a set of objective scoring rules. The new Interpretive Handbook, which includes additional scoring guidelines, also advocates a more impressionistic approach to scoring. For example, the Handbook notes that "The RATC's standard administration and scoring procedures and age norms are not intended to replace or eliminate subjective interpretation of a child's stories" (Interpretive Handbook, p. 2).

The Handbook offers a wide sampling of RATC protocols from so-called well-adjusted children. These normative responses are provided to help clinicians identify possibly deviant stories to the 16 RATC stimulus cards. Unfortunately, because we are told virtually nothing about the individuals who gave these responses, it is impossible to evaluate their usefulness in calibrating our internal standards. At the very least, one would expect a summary of the demographic characteristics of this group of well-adjusted individuals. For example, questions that come immediately to mind include the following: What percentage of the children are girls? What percentage is from urban areas? Does the sample include kids from different ethnic and/or racial groups? Do any of these demographic variables relate to group differences? The Handbook is conspicuously silent on these issues.

SUMMARY. Recent meta-analyses (Spangler, 1992) and empirical studies (Cramer & Block, 1998) conclude that TAT stories can be reliably and validly scored. Because neither the authors nor the users of the RATC publish their findings in refereed journals, it is impossible to evaluate the validity of scores from this instrument for their intended purposes. The recently published Interpretive Handbook is a cornucopia of clinical impressions and poorly organized material. For these reasons, clinicians would be well advised to avoid the RATC. Our children deserve better.

REVIEWER'S REFERENCES

Murray, H. A. (1943). *Thematic Apperception Test.* Cambridge, MA: Harvard University Press.

Sines, J. O. (1985). [Review of the Roberts Apperception Test for Children.] In J. V. Mitchell, Jr. (Ed.), *The ninth mental measurements yearbook* (pp. 1290–1291). Lincoln, NE: Buros Institute of Mental Measurements.

Spangler, W. D. (1992). Validity of questionnaire and TAT measures of need for achievement: Two meta-analyses. *Psychological Bulletin, 112,* 140–154.

Loftus, E. F. (1993). The reality of repressed memories. *American Psychologist, 48,* 518–537.

Pendergrast, M. (1995). *Victims of memory: Incest accusations and shattered lives.* Hinesberg, VT: Upper Access.

Cramer, P., & Block, J. (1998). Preschool antecedents of defense mechanism use in young adults: A longitudinal study. *Journal of Personality & Social Psychology, 74,* 159–169.

Kroon, N., Goudena, P. P., & Rispens, J. (1998). Thematic apperception tests for child and adolescent assessment: A practitioner's consumer guide. *Journal of Psychoeducational Assessment, 16,* 99–117.

[73]
Roswell-Chall Auditory Blending Test.

Purpose: "Developed to evaluate a student's ability to blend sounds to form words when the sounds are presented orally."

Population: Grades 1–4 and "older students with reading difficulties."

Publication Dates: 1963–1997.

Scores: Total score only.

Administration: Individual.

Price Data, 1999: $9.80 (6+ packets) or $14.70 (1–5 packets) per packet of 24 test forms; $3.50 (6+ copies) or $5.25 (1–5 copies) per manual of instructions ('95, 5 pages).

Time: Administration time not reported.

Comments: Oral administration; useful for judging the ease with which students will learn phonics.

Authors: Florence G. Rosewell and Jeanne S. Chall.

Publisher: Educators Publishing Service, Inc.

Cross References: See T5:2253 (2 references), T4:2296 (1 reference), and T2:1674 (7 references); for reviews by Ira E. Aaron and B. H. Von Roekel of an earlier edition, see 6:830 (2 references).

Review of the Roswell-Chall Auditory Blending Test by JOYCE R. McLARTY, Principal Research Associate, Workforce Development Division, ACT, Inc., Iowa City, IA:

The Roswell-Chall Auditory Blending Test comprises three sets of 10 words of increasing complexity that the examiner reads to each examinee. In reading, the examiner is instructed to separate the sounds and the examinee is instructed to try to put the word back together. Although subtotals are calculated for each set of 10 words, no separate interpretation of either the sets or the subscores is provided, and the very high internal consistency of the test (.96 in one reported study) suggests that only the total score should be considered in interpreting examinee performance.

Results of this test are used to identify examinees who may experience difficulty in learning phonics. Ability to learn phonics is described as resulting from a combination of maturation and specific instruction in phonemic awareness, auditory blending, segmentations, rhyming, and the like. The instructions for the Roswell-Chall test tell the examiner to "Give the sounds at the rate of about 1/2 second for each sound. Avoid inserting extraneous sounds at the end of each of the separate consonants. The separation between the sounds should be almost imperceptible. Try to enunciate the consonant sounds clearly and elongate the vowel sounds, especially the short vowels" (p. 1). It appears likely that examiners' abilities to follow these directions will vary, and that this variation may impact the examinee's ability to correctly respond to the words. Therefore, the same examiner should administer the test to all of the examinees in a given group if the scores of individuals are to be compared.

To help examiners determine whether examinees are ready to learn phonics, tables are provided for determining whether blending skills are adequate or inadequate based on the grade level of the examinee. For example, a correct response to 14 of the 30 words is considered to represent adequate blending skills through Grade 2 and inadequate blending skills thereafter. The cutoff scores for this table were arrived at by inspection of the scores of 26 students tested annually in Grades 1 through 4 and 25 severely retarded readers tested in Grades 3 through 5. Although these longitudinal data are helpful in documenting the relationship between auditory blending and grade level, no information about student characteristics, other than their reading skills, is provided to help test users determine comparability to their own students. These students appear to have been assessed in the early 1960s, and it is likely that characteristics of both students and reading instruction have changed since then.

In addition, these sample sizes are too small to provide assurance of generalizable data. Without a larger and more current sample, and without more extensive information about the examinees on which the norms are based, those using the test would be well advised to consider the cutoff scores for the adequate/inadequate determination as guidelines rather than established facts. This is especially the case where the test is being used with students who have diverse cultural or language backgrounds.

A 1988 study (Yopp, 1988) referenced in the Roswell-Chall Manual of Instructions provides data for a larger and more current sample of examinees ($N = 104$). In this study, examinees were administered 10 tests of phonemic awareness and one test of the rate at which they learned to decode novel words. Factor analysis using oblique rotation identified two factors that correlated .77. These factors accounted for 59% and 10% of the variance, respectively, and were identified as simple and compound phonemic awareness. The Roswell-Chall test loaded .84 on the first factor, and .001 on the second, indicating that it is a strong measure of simple phonemic awareness. The Roswell-Chall test also correlated .63 with the test of the subsequent rate of learning to read novel words, which is reasonably good.

The Yopp-Singer Test of Phoneme Segmentation is provided with permission to reproduce in *The Reading Teacher*, Vol. 49, No. 1, September 1995. The reviewer also found a copy of the test available on the internet, so readers may want to check there as well. This 22-item test had a reliability of .67 and loaded .89 on the first factor in the study cited above. Although somewhat less reliable, and lacking guidelines for score interpretation, this test may be a good alternative where high stakes decisions are not being made.

This reviewer found a relevant research paper by P. B. Gough, K. C. Larson, and H. Yopp, titled *The Structure of Phonemic Awareness* on the internet, as well as additional information on language instruction for young children. Readers may wish to investigate these resources.

SUMMARY. The Roswell-Chall Auditory Blending Test appears to be a sound measure of phonemic awareness with very high reliability and a good correlation with ability to read novel words. The cutoff scores given for distinguishing adequate from inadequate blending, however, are outdated and based on insufficient sample sizes. Those using this test would be well advised to develop their own standards for when an examinee is adequately prepared to begin learning phonics.

REVIEWER'S REFERENCE

Yopp, H. K. (1988). The validity and reliability of phonemic awareness tests. *Reading Research Quarterly, 23,* 159–177.

Review of the Roswell-Chall Auditory Blending Test by JANET NORRIS, Professor of Communication Disorders, Louisiana State University, Baton Rouge, LA:

The Roswell-Chall Auditory Blending Test was designed to evaluate a student's ability to blend sounds presented orally to form words. A table for interpretation of raw scores is provided but no norms are available. Sound blending is measured using three tasks. Part I measures the ability to blend two sounds (b-e), Part II measures the ability to blend onset and rime (c-ake), and Part II measures the ability to blend CVC words (m-a-p). The test is intended to identify children who are at-risk for learning phonics and therefore learning to read. It is reported to be appropriate to children in Grades 1 through 4 and for older students with reading difficulties.

The entire test is composed of 30 items, and although no time requirements are given, it should be completed easily in less than 15 minutes. The instructions are simple and no pictures, blocks, or other materials are required, rendering the test easy to use and administer. Raw scores are directly compared to a grade level criterion score. The manual is five pages in length.

However, the simplicity of the test is reflective of its limitations. A brief description of test tasks and opinions on the significance of test results is provided. For example, the predictive power of Part III for phonics readiness is discussed and recommended instructional approaches for children who do or do not perform well on this skill are provided. However, despite over 25 years of research and dozens of studies on phonological awareness skills like sound blending, no research support is provided for these claims. Only five references are cited, most of them old. The instructional approaches recommended also are old and not consistent with the recommendations of the report from the Committee of the National Research Council (Preventing Reading Difficulties in Young Children, Snow, Burns, & Griffin, 1998).

The assessment is limited to three sound blending tasks, representing a very limited view of phonological awareness skills and an even narrower view of developmental reading skills. Other tasks, such as phoneme or syllable deletion, awareness of same or different beginning and ending phonemes, sound segmentation, and rhyme are examples of other tasks shown to be indicative of the ability to manipulate the sound structure of words and are predictive of reading ability (Brady & Shankweiler, 1991). Many other abilities, such as vocabulary, syntactic proficiency, story grammar, general knowledge, and visual skills have been shown to be equally important to reading proficiency (Weintraub, 1992–1996). The limitations of the Roswell-Chall tasks as a predictive measure of reading are reflected in the correlations obtained between the Auditory Blending Total Scores and six tests of reading achievement. Most of these were low to moderate, in the .4 to .5 range, with only one correlation (out of 24) above a .6. Thus, the predictive validity is not strong and the construct validity is limited to a task that may be related to one aspect of reading (i.e., phonics), although even this was stated but not supported by data in the manual.

The reliability, established using a split-half procedure, was good, ranging from .86 to .93 for Grades 1 through 4 (26 children). This finding was supported by a study conducted by Yopp (1988) who obtained a reliability coefficient of .96 for her 104 kindergarten subjects.

The Roswell-Chall does not provide norms, but only a chart designed to interpret the Total Score for each grade level as either "Inadequate Blending" or "Adequate Blending." Although information is limited, this table appears to be derived from the performance of 26 children who were tested in Grade 1 and followed up in succeeding grades through Grade 4. No information is available on these subjects, such as age, geographic location, reading ability, intellectual ability, gender, and so forth. Thus, the population is far too small and homogeneous to establish the validity of the cutoff scores for "adequate" or "inadequate" blending, so at best they serve as guidelines. There are currently other instruments on the market that test similar skills, such as the Test of Phonological Awareness (Torgesen & Bryant, 1994; T5:2708) and the Test of Awareness of Language Segments (Sawyer, 1987;

T5:2674) that are standardized on large representative samples of children and that do provide normative scores.

SUMMARY. In summary, the Roswell-Chall Auditory Blending Test measures a skill that is as popular in reading literature (i.e., phonemic awareness) as it was when the first edition was published in 1963. The 1997 version has not been updated in theory, research support, normative data, breadth of skills tested, or recommendations for intervention, so it is unclear why the instrument is being reissued with a new copyright date. Other instruments measuring similar skills may be better choices because of their stronger test construction and normative data.

REVIEWER'S REFERENCES

Sawyer, D. J. (1987). Test of Awareness of Language Segments. Austin, TX PRO-ED.
Yopp, H. K. (1988). The validity and reliability of phonemic awareness tests. *Reading Research Quarterly, 23*, 159–177.
Brady, S. A., & Shankweiler, D. P. (Eds.). (1991). *Phonological processes in literacy: A tribute to Isabelle Y. Liberman*. Hillsdale, NJ: Erlbaum Associates.
Weintraub, S. (Ed.). (1992–1996). *Annual summary of investigations relating to reading*. Newark, DE: International Reading Association.
Torgesen, J. K., & Bryant, B. R. (1994). Test of Phonological Awareness. Austin, TX: PRO-ED.
Snow, C. E., Burns, M. S., & Griffin, P. (1998). *Preventing reading difficulties in young children*. Washington, DC: National Research Council.

[74]
Sales Achievement Predictor.

Purpose: Constructed to assess "characteristics that are critical for success in sales."
Population: Adults.
Publication Date: 1995.
Acronym: Sales AP.
Scores, 21: Validity Scores (Inconsistent Responding, Self-Enhancing, Self-Critical), Special Scores (Sales Disposition, Initiative-Cold Calling, Sales Closing), Basic Domain Scores (Achievement, Motivation, Competitiveness, Goal Orientation, Planning, Initiative-General, Team Player, Managerial, Assertiveness, Personal Diplomacy, Extroversion, Cooperativeness, Relaxed Style, Patience, Self-Confidence).
Administration: Group.
Price Data, 1999: $175 per kit including manual (73 pages), 2 mail-in answer sheets, 2-use disk for on-site computer scoring, and 2 PC answer sheets; $45 per mail-in answer sheet; $50 per manual; $360 per 25-use computer disk (PC with Windows); $15 per 100 PC answer sheets; $39.50 per FAX service scoring.
Time: (20–25) minutes.
Comments: Microsoft Windows 3.1 or above required for computer scoring.
Authors: Jotham G. Friedland, Sander I. Marcus, and Harvey P. Mandel.
Publisher: Western Psychological Services.

Review of the Sales Achievement Predictor by GORDON C. BRUNER II, Associate Professor, Marketing Department, Director, Office of Scale Research, Southern Illinois University, Carbondale, IL:

The Sales Achievement Predictor, referred to as the Sales AP, was constructed in order to "assist in the selection, placement, and training of salespeople" (manual, p. 1). It is based upon a model that views achievement as being the product of many factors such as personality, work habits, and interpersonal style.

The instrument can be given as a paper-and-pencil test or taken on a PC. Several options for scoring the tests are offered. The manual seems to be clear in the instructions provided for administering the test as well as in interpreting the results. The authors indicated that multiple studies have shown little if any differences between groups based upon gender or ethnicity. Although fluency with English is needed, an assessment of readability level indicates the items are rather easy to read.

Estimates of internal consistency as well as one-year stability (test-retest) reliability were moderate to good for the 21 scales composing the instrument (ranging from .66 to .88 for internal consistency and .67 to .90 for test-retest).

However, the dimensionality of the various scales has not been established. This issue brings the reliability and validity into question if one accepts that dimensionality must be established first (Gerbing & Anderson, 1988). Putting that concern aside, the predictive validity might have been considered moderate to good had it not been based on disturbingly small samples (17 and 52). Further, the criterion in each case was a single item judgment made by sales managers about how salespeople met their expectations. The best that can be said is that about a quarter to a third of the variance of performance as determined by sales managers was predicted accurately by the Sales Disposition scale of the instrument.

Although convergent and discriminant validity were addressed in the manual, the evidence amounted to broad interpretation of correlation matrices. In fact, the naive reader would probably be overwhelmed by the quantity of data. Unfortunately, the manual fails to use theory to explain which correlations should be strong, which should not be strong, which should be positive, and which should be negative. Strong tests of relationships were not conducted (e.g., CFA, *SEM*). Even meager significance tests were missing from the correlation matrices that might assist in independently judging convergent and discriminant validity.

Maybe the most troublesome issue of the SalesAP has to do with its evidence related to content validity. The thoughtful reader wonders why we should expect these particular predictor variables to be associated with sales performance. The authors repeatedly assure the reader that their "combined clinical and business experience" (manual, p. 13) provided them with the insight to know which variables are important. Disturbingly lacking is any connection between the model with which the authors appear to be working and the considerable scholarly literature that has accumulated over the years in sales. What is one to think when in the 60+ pages of the manual no literature is cited from the very field for which an instrument is designed (personal sales) nor is the model tested (using the contemporary sense of model testing) in a sales context? For example, there is strong evidence that not only are there different types of sales occupations but sales people pass through different stages over time, each with its own distinct activities (Cron & Slocum, 1986; Wotruba, 1991). It seems reasonable, therefore, that test developers would want to find a relationship between variables that predict performance per sales activity rather than for selling in general.

SUMMARY. A review of the performance literature has led experts in the field to conclude that "no general physical characteristics, mental abilities, or personality traits appear to be consistently related to sales aptitude and performance in all companies and selling situations" (Churchill, Ford, & Walker, 1997, p. 388). Instead, it is recommended that the tasks involved in a sales job be identified and then tests of those skills and abilities be utilized in the selection process. Given this, the best that one can say about the SalesAP is that it may be appropriate in some sales situations and not in others depending upon the degree to which the constructs being measured by the instrument are related to the job of interest.

REVIEWER'S REFERENCES

Cron, W. L., & Slocum, J. W., Jr. (1986, May). The influence of career stages on sales person's job attitudes, work perceptions, and performance. *Journal of Marketing Research, 23*, 119–129.

Gerbing, D. W., & Anderson, J. C. (1988, May). An updated paradigm for scale development incorporating unidimensionality and its assessment. *Journal of Marketing Research, 25*, 186–192.

Wotruba, T. R. (1991). The Evolution of Personal Selling. *Journal of Personal Selling and Sales Management, 11*, 1–12.

Churchill, G. A., Jr., Ford, N. M., & Walker, O. C., Jr. (1997). Sales force management. Chicago: Richard D. Irwin, Inc.

Review of the Sales Achievement Predictor by BRENT W. ROBERTS, *Assistant Professor of Psychology, University of Tulsa, Tulsa, OK:*

The Sales Achievement Predictor (SalesAP) is designed to measure attributes associated with success in sales. The theory on which the SalesAP is based proposes that achievement at sales is determined by multiple factors, such as habits, interpersonal style, and personality, and thus the test takes a multidimensional approach to the assessment of sales success. A SalesAP test user receives scores on 15 Basic Domain scales, 3 Response Style scales, and an additional set of three scales meant specifically to predict success in sales. The SalesAP is a revised form of an unpublished test called the Motivation and Achievement Inventory (MAI). The MAI was originally developed to predict success in achievement-related settings. The primary difference between the SalesAP and the MAI is the addition of the three scales focusing on sales success. The SalesAP also includes interest scales that tap Holland's (1997) RIASEC (Realistic, Investigative, Artistic, Social, Enterprising, Conventional) model, but little or no information is provided on these scales in the manual.

The scales of the SalesAP are organized into six categories: (a) Sales Success, consisting of the Sales Disposition, Initiative-Cold Calling, and Sales Closing scales; (b) Motivation and Achievement, consisting of the Achievement, Motivation, Competitiveness, and Goal Orientation scales; (c) Work Strengths, consisting of the Planning, Initiative-General, Team Player, and Managerial scales; (d) Interpersonal Strengths, consisting of the Assertiveness, Personal Diplomacy, Extroversion, and Cooperativeness scales; and (e) Inner Resources, consisting of the Relaxed Style, Patience, and Self-Confidence scales. The sixth category, Response Style, is assessed via the inconsistent Responding, Self-Enhancing, and Self-Critical scales.

According to the manual the items for the SalesAP were written "based on the authors' years of professional experience in business and sales settings" (p. 23). The three Sales Success scales that warranted updating the MAI were developed from the existing item pool. It appears that the items for many scales were selected solely through a rational or logical approach. For example, the authors used their "combined clinical and business experience" (p. 13) to select items for the Cold Calling scale. For some scales, the authors claim to use criterion measures of sales success to help select scale items. Unfortunately, none of the item level evidence is presented supporting this empirical approach to scale development. In addition, the authors claim to use factor analytic techniques to define and refine scales, yet no factor analyses are reported.

The repeated claim that factor analysis was used to develop the SalesAP scales is ironic given the fact that the authors do not report a factor analysis of the SalesAP itself. Factor analysis can be a critical tool for understanding the construct validity of a test. Examination of the intercorrelations of the SalesAP scales would lead one to believe that there are fewer than 18 unique dimensions underlying the test. In fact, it would not be surprising to find that a factor analysis would not support the rational organization of scales into the five domains listed above. Of course, in the absence of a factor analysis all the reader can do is guess.

Convergent and discriminant validity were tested by correlating the SalesAP with the Sixteen Personality Factor Questionnaire (16PF; Cattell, 1986) and the Edwards Personal Preference Schedule (EPPS; Edwards, 1959). The magnitudes of the convergent validity coefficients were modest at best. The highest correlation across both tests was .66 and most convergent validity coefficients ranged from .20 to .45. The pattern of correlations supports the hypothesis that the SalesAP measures fewer than 18 constructs. Sixteen of the 18 SalesAP scales had substantive correlations with scales from the 16PF that measure extraversion (e.g., the Enthusiastic, Dominant, and Self-Doubting dimensions). A similar pattern of correlations was obtained on the EPPS.

The choice to use the 16PF and the EPPS to investigate the construct validity of the SalesAP is confusing. Several global personality measures that include "sales" subscales, such as the Hogan Personality Inventory (13:138) and the Jackson Personality Research Form (T4:2000) already exist. These instruments would have provided much

better tests of convergent and discriminant validity than the 16PF or EPPS.

The fact that the majority of the SalesAP scales tap the extraversion domain can be seen as both a blessing and weakness of the test. On the positive side, many studies have shown that the extraversion domain is the most critical for success in sales. On the negative side, it appears that the SalesAP is measuring far fewer than 18 independent dimensions. Take for example the Sales Success scales, the primary focus of the SalesAP test. Because the Sales Success scale items are drawn from the existing item pool on the MAI, these three scales tend to correlate quite highly with several of the remaining 15 scales. For example, the Cold Calling scale is a "content-based subscore" (p. 27) of the Initiative scale, and is thus correlated above .90 with the Initiative scale. Both the Sales Disposition and Sales Closing scales correlate above .70 with several Domain scales. Although scale overlap is often misunderstood and too often criticized (see for example, Gough 1996 for an alternative viewpoint), a correlation above .90 presses the acceptable level of independence. One must ask whether the user of the SalesAP is getting much more than a multiscale assessment of extraversion.

Establishing the criterion-related validity of an instrument is the most important standard for a scale developed to be used in the work place. Thus, for the SalesAP, the ability to predict success in sales is paramount. To the test's credit, a large majority of the SalesAP scales correlated highly with supervisor ratings of sales performance in both concurrent and predictive studies and across several types of salespeople. One quizzical finding was that the best predictor of sales performance was often not one of the three Sales Success scales. In fact, across 12 supervisor ratings (four studies), scales from the other domains of the SalesAP met or exceeded the level of prediction of the three Sales Success scales in at least eight cases. It appears that interested consumers could use many of the SalesAP scales to predict sales success.

The SalesAP scales exhibit acceptable if not excellent levels of reliability. The internal consistency scales estimates ranged from .66 to .88, with most estimates exceeding .80. One-year test-retest reliability estimates were just as impressive, ranging from a low of .67 to a high of .90 with most estimates averaging around .80.

The normative information provided is sufficient. The authors describe the norm sample in detail; they also provide scale scores for gender, race, and different occupational groups such as salespeople, managers, and job applicants. The authors also provide detailed scale descriptions and case studies related to selection and development of sales people. The manual also contains information on scoring services and a sample report.

The SalesAP has several strengths. First, it appears to do a respectable job of predicting ratings of sales performance. However, it should be noted that none of the validity studies have been reported in peer-reviewed journals, so the quality of these studies is still unclear. Second, the scales show good levels of reliability. Finally, the manual provides enough information for an informed consumer to judge the quality of the test in relation to other Sales performance predictors.

The primary weakness of the test is the false impression that it measures 18 distinct traits. Given the information in the test manual, the scales of the SalesAP fail to show adequate levels of construct validity. Furthermore, the addition of the three Sales performance scales adds little predictive utility over the original MAI scales. The lack of a factor analysis of the SalesAP scales is a second, related weakness of the test. Given the number of places that the authors invoke the use of factor analysis to develop specific scales, one would expect that an overall factor analysis of the SalesAP is feasible. A third flaw is the way the authors use the Response Style scales. Rather than using the scales to identify problematic protocols (e.g., people who may have lied), the authors argue that scale scores should be corrected for scores on the Response Style scales. To the contrary, numerous studies (e.g., Hough, 1998; Ones & Visweswaran, 1998) have shown that correcting for "response style" does little or nothing to the validity of personality scales.

SUMMARY. Overall, the SalesAP appears to be useful for predicting sales success. Before the test can be endorsed, additional evidence for the convergent and discriminant validity of the test needs to be provided. One must also question, as has been questioned before (Camara, 1995), the need for another personality-based predictor of sales success. There are numerous tests in existence to do just that, many of which are embedded in more comprehensive instruments that will provide more complete descriptions of people.

REVIEWER'S REFERENCES
Edwards, A. L. (1959). The Edwards Personal Preference Schedule. San Antonio, TX: The Psychological Corporation.
Cattell, R. B. (1986). The Sixteen Personality Factor Questionnaire. Champaign, IL: Institute for Personality and Ability Testing.
Camara, W. J. (1995). Review of the Sales Personality Questionnaire. In J. C. Conoley & J. C. Impara (Eds.), The twelfth mental measurements yearbook (pp. 886-887). Lincoln, NE: Buros Institute of Mental Measurements.
Gough, H. (1996). The CPI manual. Palo Alto, CA: Consulting Psychologists Press.
Holland, J. L. (1997). Making vocational choices: A theory of vocational personalities and work environments. Odessa, FL: Psychological Assessment Resources, Inc.
Hough, L. M. (1998). Effects of intentional distortion in personality measurement and evaluation of suggested palliatives. Human Performance, 11, 209-244.
Ones, D. S., & Visweswaran, C. (1998). The effects of social desirability and faking on personality and integrity assessment for personnel selection. Human Performance, 11, 245-270.

[75]
Scales for Predicting Successful Inclusion.

Purpose: Designed to identify students with disabilities for potential for success in general education classes.
Population: Ages 5–18.
Publication Date: 1997.
Acronym: SPSI.
Scores: 4 scales: Work Habits, Coping Skills, Peer Relationships, Emotional Maturity.
Administration: Group.
Price Data, 1999: $79 per complete kit including manual (47 pages) and 50 summary/response forms; $39 per 50 summary/response forms; $42 per manual.
Time: (5–10) minutes.
Comments: Ratings by teachers, parents, and/or assistants.
Authors: James E. Gilliam and Kathleen S. McConnell.
Publisher: PRO-ED.

Review of the Scales for Predicting Successful Inclusion by DAVID GILLESPIE, Social Science Faculty, Detroit College of Business, Warren, MI:

The Scales for Predicting Successful Inclusion (SPSI) is designed to identify those students with disabilities, ages 5 through 18, who could be successful in a regular education environment. The instrument can also be used to identify school adjustment problems children may demonstrate. Results can furthermore be employed to identify intervention targets, assess changes as a result of intervention, and identify students appropriate for referral.

The SPSI attempts to assess behavior in four domains. These areas include Work Habits, Coping Skills, Peer Relationships, and Emotional Maturity. Work Habits focuses on a student's ability to follow directions, obey rules, and listen to instructions. The Coping Skills scale assesses a student's ability to deal with the conflict and stress that might result from interacting with others. The Peer Relations scale assesses a student's social skills. The Emotional Maturity section focuses on a student's perceived emotional adjustment.

The instrument consists of 60 behavioral descriptions and is to be completed by teachers or those familiar with a student's behavior in the classroom. The rater compares the behavior of a target child with the behavior of normally developing students of the same age. A 9-point Likert scale is used to quantify rater perceptions. Individuals who are familiar with the target child and normative functioning in the school setting can complete the rating scale in approximately 5 to 10 minutes.

There is no specialized training needed to administer or score the SPSI. In order to properly interpret the test results one should be familiar with basic measurement concepts. Although the manual states that teacher assistants and parents can complete the scale, the scale was normed based on the perceptions of teachers. Certainly, further research appears appropriate to support the reliability and validity of these scores when the scale is completed by parents.

Scoring is achieved by converting raw scores to standard scores and percentile ranks by using tables located in the Appendix. The sum of the standard scores for each the subscales is then converted into a measure of overall functioning referred to as the Successful Inclusion Quotient (SIQ). The SIQ has a mean of 100 and a standard deviation of 15. These scores can be plotted on the front of the Summary/Response Form. Students with school adjustment problems will have low scores suggesting a low probability of successful inclusion, whereas high scores are more likely to be achieved by those individuals who have a greater likelihood of being successful in inclusive settings. The manual also contains guidelines for interpreting SPSI standard scores. The authors underscore the importance of not using this instrument as the only means of assessment. Clearly, educational placement decisions should be made on the basis of information gained from multiple informants, including the student in question.

The SPSI was normed on a sample of 1,715 school-age children in the United States. Of this group, 50% had some form of disability (educa-

tional and/or behavioral). One-half (approximately 429) of this group were identified as Learning Disabled, 12% (approximately 102) were identified as having speech impairments, and 9% (approximately 77) were identified as mentally retarded.

Students employed in the normative sample were identified by general and special education teachers and principals. The educators themselves were respondents to a recruitment mailing conducted by the test authors. The names of 5,000 educators were randomly selected. Approximately 100 teachers and principals agreed to collect data. In addition, 27 educators known to the authors took part in the standardization sampling.

Test items were developed after reviewing the literature and other rating scales. A pool of 20 items was developed for each scale. Special and general education teachers, university professors, and test construction experts reviewed these items.

Content validity was studied by examining the relationship between the various items and the scale or portion of the SPSI it represents. Item discrimination studies strongly supported internal consistency with median item-to-scale correlations ranging from .85 to .91. Construct validity was also supported in relation to group differentiation and item performance.

Concurrent and criterion-related validity studies examined the relationship between the SPSI and the Conners' Teacher Rating Scales, Adjustment Scales for Children and Adolescents, and the Comprehensive Scales of Student Abilities. Typically, significant negative correlations were found between the various subscales of the SPSI and the comparative behavior rating scales.

Overall reliability evidence was found to lie within acceptable limits. Internal consistency for the full scale and for the subtests, based on Cronbach's alpha, fell within the range of .80s and .90s. These findings suggest that the items within the scale are homogeneous.

Two test-retest studies were conducted in order to investigate the stability of the SPSI scores over time. The first study consisted of 18 subjects with disabilities. The teachers rated the subjects on the SPSI at 1-week intervals. Correlation coefficients ranged from .63 to .98. In the second study all the correlation coefficients were greater than .60 and significantly different from zero at $p<.05$. Although these results provide strong evidence of test-retest reliability, further research to support this stability over greater periods of time is warranted. Interrater reliability was also estimated (correlation coefficients ranged from $r = .84–.94$).

There are many aspects of this scale that reflect sound test development practices. However, the most significant limitation focuses on its use in relation to children who present the greatest challenge to education in the general classroom setting or full inclusion. Although the standardization sample reflected the general distribution of children with specific forms of disabilities found in the educational setting, the vast majority of the children who were evaluated as part of the normative sample fell into categories that are normally considered to reflect relatively mild impairments. By contrast, the term full inclusion is usually reserved for an approach to the educational placement of more severely impaired children, such as those with some level of cognitive impairment or mental retardation, autism, or severe emotional disturbance. The standardization sample only included about 77 students who were identified as mentally retarded and no children identified as autistically impaired. As such, further research employing this scale in relation to this more significantly impacted group of students is recommended.

SUMMARY. The SPSI is a 60-item scale designed to identify the probability of a child's successful inclusion in a regular education setting based on their behaviors in particular target areas. It is designed to be completed by teachers who are familiar with the child who has a handicapping condition, based on their knowledge of the child's behavior compared to the functioning of normally developing children. Although parents and paraprofessionals can also complete it, data were not gained based on their perceptions and interrater reliability across teacher and parent perceptions was not examined at the time of scale development. Test results can also be employed to identify intervention targets and to chart progress over time. The principal weakness of the scale focuses on the relative lack of more significantly impacted students, such as those with some level of mental retardation, in the normative sample. Although these individuals were included in the norm group in a manner equal to their proportion in the national population, it is this group of students who are normally considered the target of inclusionary education. Students who had been identified as LD or speech and language impaired made up the greatest proportion of the special education population employed in the normative sample. Yet these students are already largely educated in general education settings in most school districts.

Review of the Scales for Predicting Successful Inclusion by JOSEPH R. MANDUCHI, Clinical Associate, Susquehanna Institute, Harrisburg, PA:

The Scales for Predicting Successful Inclusion (SPSI) is identified by the authors as a Norm referenced instrument for identifying students with disabilities for successful inclusion into general education. It is a 60-item instrument that contains four scales for rater estimates of Work habits, Coping Skills, Peer Relationships, and Emotional Maturity.

Each scale consists of 15 questions that are all behaviorally based. Each question is prefixed with the statement, "Compared to average students of the same age, rate the student in terms of ..." (Protocol, p. 1), and then the item follows. Each item is scored on a 9-point Likert scale with ratings of Below, Average, and Above. Each rating is then subdivided into three numerical subratings that comprise the 9-point rating. Each scale then derives a "raw score," which is the sum for all ratings for the 15 questions of the scale. The raw scores are converted to a standard score between 1–20 (mean = 10, $SD = 3$) and subsequent percentile rankings. The sum of the scaled scores can be converted to a "Successful Inclusion Quotient" (SIQ), which is presented in customary fashion with a mean of 100 and a standard deviation of 15. Finally, the standard scores for the four SPSI scales can be converted to a probability rating for success in general education. The probability ratings are titled Extremely Probable, Highly Probable, Probable, Borderline, Unlikely, and Very Unlikely. The scores are easily interpreted by most professionals with only a casual knowledge of psychometrics and statistics.

Questions for each scale are presented in blocks of 15 questions. When rating questions about Coping Skills, for example, the rater answers all questions at one time. Therefore a mixing of the questions from the various scales is recommended.

The purpose of the test is to (a) identify specific problems in school adjustment, (b) identify strengths and weaknesses for intervention, (c) provide evidence of the need for referral to special education, (d) target goals for individualized education programs, (e) document progress, (f) provide evidence that students from special education are prepared for general education classes, and (g) to measure school adjustment skills and characteristics in research projects. Ostensibly this is all accomplished from the four scale scores, the Successful Inclusion Quotient, the Probability Ratings for Success, and the 60 rated questions. This seems ambitious.

The SPSI was normed on 1,715 school-aged children. The normative sample was collected by 100 experienced education professionals who taught students with disabilities as well as those without any known disability. The normative data did not yield differences based on age and as a result all students are scored and compared to the large norming sample. Conversion tables are provided for boys and girls both with and without known disabilities.

The test is a simple instrument with easy-to-understand questions and easy scoring procedures. It can be completed by most raters in less than 10 minutes. The test construction and administration practices may be somewhat biased because raters may have already made up their mind about the student's abilities. The SPSI seems more appropriate to be used by a rater who may have limited exposure to a student. Certainly exposure is required and therein may lie the source of rater bias. However, in the validity studies, there are high positive correlations for varying raters.

Reliability data are most impressive. Using Cronbach's alpha as an index for internal consistency, all values were above .95. The standard errors of measurement were low and ranged between .42 and .60. The data suggest that the SPSI is subject to little variability based on poor test construction. Correlation for stability over time (1-week interval) was high as well. Reliability evidence for the SPSI is strong.

The authors provide three sources of evidence for issues of validity. They provide data for content validity, criterion-related validity, and construct validity.

CONTENT VALIDITY. To assess content validity the authors calculated item to total correlations. For this procedure the scores for individual items are correlated with the scores obtained for the scale. The authors state that per Hammill, "item discrimination coefficients should be statistically significant at or beyond the .05 level and should reach or exceed .35 in magnitude" (p. 26). For the SPSI, the item to total coefficients were all at or above .8.

Every once in a while a test appears psychometrically too good. Based on these data, one is left with the notion that for each scale one and only one question needed to be asked. Given the simplistic nature of this test and the reliability and validity evidence, is this instrument of any more value than simply asking teachers, "Do you think this student is appropriate for inclusion in general education?"

CRITERION RELATED VALIDITY. The authors correlated data from the SPSI with the Conners' Teacher Rating Scales (CTRS), the Adjustment Scales for Children and Adolescents (ASCA), and the Comprehensive Scales of Student Abilities (CSSA). For the CTRS the correlations for the SPSI Scales to the CTRS scores that suggest behavioral difficulties were broadly significant. The correlations were generally not significant for the Work habits and the Coping Skills scales of the SPSI when compared to the scales of the ASCA. Under the scales of Peer Relationships, Emotional Maturity, and the Successful Inclusion Quotient consistent significant findings are present. Finally, for the CSSA, all but a few correlations were significant. When CSSA scales were correlated with the SIQ, every correlation was significant at the .01 level.

CONSTRUCT VALIDITY. Three hypotheses were used to study construct validity. They were:

1. The various scales of the SPSI should be positively related to each other.
2. Scale items should strongly relate to the scale total score.
3. Scores on the SPSI should discriminate persons who are successful (i.e., receiving passing grades) from subjects who are not successful (receiving failing grades). (p. 29)

For the interrelation of SPSI scales (Hypothesis 1), all correlations were significant at the .01 level. The item to total correlations (Hypothesis 2) were discussed earlier in this review but once again were all of high positive value. For group differentiation data (Hypothesis 3), a multivariate ANOVA was utilized. For all groups significant predictive relationships were found.

SUMMARY. Psychometrically, the developers of the SPSI present strong statistical data for their instrument. This reviewer is left with the belief that its simplicity lies outside psychometric scrutiny. This measure seems to be constructed in such a way as to permit considerable rater bias. A standardized measure is by its nature developed to provide objective measurements. I do not believe the SPSI provides that benefit. The SPSI does have value. It provides a source of documentation for teachers and other school personnel to base their recommendations for inclusion, but these recommendations are probably already crystallized prior to completing the SPSI ratings.

[76]
Scientific Orientation Test.

Purpose: "Designed to measure a range of affective outcomes for students of science or science-related subjects."
Population: Students in school years 5 to 12.
Publication Date: 1995.
Acronym: S.OR.T.
Scores, 4: Interest in Science, Scientific Attitude, Attitude to School Science, Total.
Administration: Group or individual.
Price Data, 1995: $120 per complete kit including manual (153 pages), 10 test booklets, and 10 response folios; $25 per 10 test booklets; $25 per 10 response folios; $75 per manual.
Time: (40) minutes.
Comments: Includes 5 subtests yielding 13 subscores; formerly titled A Test of Interests.
Author: G. Rex Meyer.
Publisher: GRM Educational Consultancy [Australia].

Review of the Scientific Orientation Test by BRUCE G. ROGERS, Professor of Educational Psychology, University of Northern Iowa, Cedar Falls, IA:

The Scientific Orientation Test (abbreviated in the manual as S.OR.T but, for ease of readability, abbreviated hereafter in this review as SORT) was designed to measure attitudes toward several science-related topics of students in grades 7 through 12. Because teachers and science educators frequently emphasize the value of positive orientations toward science as taught in the classrooms, there is a need for appropriate measuring instruments for assessing those attitudes. The SORT was constructed to address that need. For over 30 years, the SORT has been used in Austra-

lia, and more recently, has been used in several research projects in the United States. The author of the test is of the opinion that a wider use in the schools would be of benefit to both students and teachers. This review therefore addresses some of the factors that might be considered by potential users of the SORT and also presents constructive analysis of the instrument and its application.

Evaluation refers to our like or dislike of a thing. The centrality of evaluation is mirrored in the SORT by the emphasis on asking the students what they most like to do or not like to do. Psychologists also emphasize that attitudes are learned from experience, not inherited. Accordingly, the SORT was conceptualized to assess changes in attitude as a student is exposed to science activities in the school curriculum.

The construct of attitude is perceived by psychologists as a distinct, but complex, psychological entity. By constructing a total, unified score from a set of subscores, the SORT conforms to this view. It is an instrument, therefore, that reflects a professional approach to attitude measurement and therefore is worthy of careful consideration.

DEVELOPMENT. About 40 years ago, a research project at the University of London focused on the development of affective constructs in the areas of science education. Tests were assembled to measure these constructs, which were eventually developed, about 1965 in Australia, as the SORT. The development of each of the subtests began with a review of the literature to generate initial concepts and ideas, followed by consultation with psychologists, science educators, and teachers. After the items were submitted to various panels of experts, they were pilot-tested with groups of students and the resulting item analysis data were used for item modification. The final scales were administered to representative groups, in the Sydney, Australia area, and norm tables were developed. Although the details of the procedures are not as fully explicated in the manual as might be desired, sufficient explanation is given to lead the reader to believe that the standard professional procedures for attitude scale development were followed.

However, in the intervening three decades since the inception of the SORT, new developments have occurred in both science education and attitude measurement. Whereas achievement tests are typically revised every decade, there is no evidence in the SORT manual that any revision has occurred subsequently with this instrument. The test user today might expect that this attitude test would also have benefited if it had been revised during the subsequent years.

DESCRIPTION. Students are allowed 40 minutes to respond to a total of 170 items, presented in five subtests. Each item consists of a declarative sentence to be rated on a 5-point modified Likert-type scale. Three subtests measure scientific orientation, one subtest measures nonscientific interests, and a fifth subtest measures what the manual describes as "solving science problems by appeal to authority" (p. 23). These five areas can be further subdivided and combined to form a total of 18 scores. Instructions are given for creating several profiles to display the scores. The manual states that the function of the SORT is to "make available an easily administered battery of reliable and valid scales" (p. 13).

RELIABILITY. Evidence pertaining to the internal consistency of each of the subscales (called variables in the manuals) was obtained with the split-half method based on alternative items. These reliability indices had a median near .90, while the composite science orientation scales had reliabilities above that median. Test-retest reliability indices are also reported in the manual, with a median value for the 18 scales near .80. However, 16 of those values were based on a sample of 90 fifth grade students, tested across a 3-week interval, almost 40 years ago. Two of the values were based on a sample of 200 secondary students, over 30 years ago. Users of these tests could have more confidence in the reliability estimates if the data were available from larger samples and more recent administrations.

VALIDITY. As a check on "face" validity, the items were submitted to groups of teachers and other "criterion" groups (undefined in the manual), to obtain suggestions for rewording. Although this is a commendable procedure, it might be useful to also obtain comments from students when the test is revised in the future. Evidence for content validity was obtained by looking for agreement in judgments by judges. Although this is a desirable procedure, test users could have more confidence if there was an explanation of how phrases such as "high levels of

agreement between judges" and "conceptually homogeneous as perceived by judges" (p. 66) should be interpreted by the reader of the manual. Without such an explanation, the reader is actually left with only the opinion of the author of the test. This reviewer hopes that these matters will be addressed in a future revision.

The results of several studies of criterion-related validity are presented in the manual. Test scores of students were compared with essay scores on their opinion of science courses; with their indication of what type of courses they would like to take the next year in school; with self-ratings, peer ratings, and teacher ratings on their interest in science; and with other science interest tests. The validity of the test is certainly enhanced by these type of studies. However, all of the studies were over 10 years old at the time the manual was published and the majority of them were over 20 years old. Newer studies are to be encouraged, and this reviewer suggests that they be done with a revised edition of the test.

Evidence for construct validity was presented primarily as correlations with scores from intelligence tests, achievement tests, other science attitude and interest tests, and nonscience attitude scales. Factor analysis studies were also reported. These are certainly commendable, but the comments made above about the recency of the criterion-related studies apply in the same manner to the construct-related evidence.

NORMS. The manual shows percentile norms for one group in Australia. It also lists means and standard deviations for five groups. The test user will need to examine these norm data carefully to decide to what extent they are current, relevant, and representative. The norms for the SORT are not as current as the norms for many achievement batteries. The Australian norm data were 15 years old when the manual was published and the other norm data were over 20 years old. Because major curriculum changes have been made in science education during the past several decades, the test user would find the norms of more value if they were current within the most recent decade of their intended use. The relevancy of the norms may also be problematical. How relevant are Australian norms to the populations of the other countries? Unfortunately, this question is not addressed in the manual, even though the author encourages the use of the test by teachers in other countries. If the test is revised, perhaps arrangements will be made to collect data relevant to other countries where the test might be used. At that time, the issue of representativeness will need to be addressed. How confident can the test user be that the norm sample was representative of the intended population? Unfortunately, there was no description of how the Australian sample was selected. Three grade levels were reported from boys and girls, but the procedure for selecting geographical areas, schools, and students within grades is not described in the manual.

USABILITY. How convenient will teachers find this test to administer, score, and interpret in actual classroom use? The manual recommends that the test be administered by a "neutral" person. It explains that the teacher is not a "neutral" person, but it does not explain who is a "neutral" person. Is another teacher a "neutral" person? It would be very useful if such questions were addressed in the manual. The instructions for administering do not contain a set of sentences to be read verbatim, but rather consist of a set of 14 statements to the teachers, such as "Tell pupils that the book consists of lots of statements ... Write the following scale on the board ... Say the scale over twice" (p. 19). When this reviewer had the instructions read aloud by a teacher, it took over 5 minutes. The test user must consider how many students might lose interest during that time.

The manual recommends that students be allowed 40 minutes to respond to the 170 items in the test, but also states that most students finish within 35 minutes which implies that the students are responding to each item in about 12 seconds. Test users will need to decide if they wish to encourage such quick judgments about attitudes. The entire administration procedure might be perceived by some teachers as being excessively time-consuming and therefore they may consider eliminating some of the subtests. This should be considered when the test is revised.

The directions for scoring begin by adding the votes to obtain 13 totals on the pages within the booklet, transferring these totals to the cover, followed by 4 additions, 1 division, and 2 subtractions. Then, using the tables of norms, these scores are to be converted into standard scores and percentiles. The norm tables are arranged by grouping the raw scores into intervals encompass-

ing 8 points. For the other 7 points in any interval, the manual recommends interpolation. Over 200 words are devoted to describing the interpolation procedure, concluding with the sentence, "it is really simple and speedy" (p. 25). This reviewer does not consider interpolation in an 8-point interval to be either "simple" or "speedy." Furthermore, the manual explains that the relationship between raw scores and percentiles is nonlinear, yet linear interpolation is used within intervals as wide as 17 percentile points. For purposes of making comparisons, the manual recommends using standard scores, such a z-scores, but test users will also need to decide if they consider that computation to be "simple and speedy." In the opinion of this reviewer, the scoring procedures may be seen by many teachers as not being the best use of their time and thus they will be hesitant to use the instrument. The test user must again weigh the relative values of these activities.

When this test is revised, the authors might prioritize the type of decisions that teachers and pupils can make from the test and use that information to see if the test could be substantially reduced in length and time of administration. Because many schools now have, or plan to obtain, an optical scanner, it might be possible to arrange the items in a manner that the scanner could score the sheets. A computer program might be written to perform the score conversions, prepare profiles, and tabulate the results. This procedure is available for some other tests, and users might find it to be desirable for the SORT.

SUMMARY. The SORT is a set of attitude scales that were professionally constructed to assess interest in science. It reflects the state-of-the-art 30 to 40 years ago. Teachers will find the attitude constructs to be of value and students will find the items of interest as they respond. The results could, potentially, be of use to teachers in curriculum evaluation and to students in planning their courses of study. However, test users should be concerned that the test has not been revised in over 30 years, that there is a lack of supporting technical data, that the administration time is time-consuming, and that the scoring is labor intensive. The authors are urged to employ current technology and technical expertise to revise this instrument into one that teachers will find to be convenient to administer, score, and interpret.

Until that occurs, this reviewer would urge caution in the adoption of this instrument.

Review of the Scientific Orientation Test by HERBERT C. RUDMAN, Professor Emeritus of Measurement and Quantitative Methods, Michigan State University, East Lansing, MI:

The Scientific Orientation Test (S.OR.T.) was first developed in Australia in the 1960s under the title of *A Test of Interests.* It was revised again in 1975 and new norms were established in the 1980s. A third modification was published in 1995. This "commercial" version carries the misnomer of a "test" of scientific interests. A test usually signifies a correct or incorrect response. A test is a measure of the application of cognitive factors or the level of a skill, but interests as used in the *Scientific Orientation Test* are affective variables that can be measured but not tested. One might measure the frequency of interests or their depth, but a survey of interests is not the same as a test nor is it necessarily a predictor of future interests or future vocational skills (Ebel & Frisbie, 1986; Mehrens & Lehmann, 1991).

The S.OR.T. has been designed primarily for students in the middle school grades of 7 to 10. The author claims that it can be used "with care" in the primary school grades of 5 and 6 as well as the senior high school grades of 11 and 12. Unfortunately, he fails to identify just what "care" means. He also claims that with slight modifications in wording it can be sued in "nonformal and informal educational programs and other (non-specified) programs which are approximately equivalent to the school years specified" (manual, p. 1). Even though the title of the S.OR.T. deals with interests and attitudes towards science, the test booklet includes measures in two nonscientific areas, Literature and Fine Art. This adds some confusion to interpreting assessment results obtained. The manual states that each of the nonscientific areas are "sufficiently valid and reliable in its own right to stand on its own" (p. 1). It is not clear, however, why these two areas are part of the S.OR.T. battery. Ostensibly they offer a contrast to scientific interests but this reviewer cannot see what contributions they make to contrasts between nonscientific and science intereests. It is unclear to what end the S.OR.T. will be used.

COMPONENTS OF THE S.OR.T. BATTERY. The Scientific Orientation Test consists of a test manual, a test booklet, and a response folio. The test battery is an independently published product of the GRM Consultancy located in New South Wales, Australia. The English language used is idiosyncratic to Australia and introduces a few words connected with the test booklet that may puzzle the reader (e.g., "You will be asked to give 4 votes to the statement with which you agree very strongly, 3 to the next most sensible ones, 2 to the next, 1 to those with which you least agree, and 0 to the ones with which you do not agree at all. ... Be sure to give some kind of vote to each"). Most readers will come to see that "votes" are ratings on a nominal scale.

The test manual is confusing. The manuscript is filled with ambiguities related to the content level of the S.OR.T., to its description of the ages of students that are appropriate for the administration of the test, and to its claims of validity, reliability, and concepts that normally could illustrate the purposes for which the test is being used. The material presented for this review needs considerable editing.

The manual that accompanies the test and its scoring folio was meant to explain the S.OR.T.'s purpose, its content, how to administer the test booklet, and to serve as a technical manual, but unfortunately, it goes off on tangents and loses its focus. Instead of focusing on the test itself, the manual centers on the research of other investigators who have studied phenomena that are not necessarily related to the S.OR.T. test booklet.

Under the section entitled, "Uses of the Test" the author introduces the user of the S.OR.T. to what he describes as a rationale for the test. However, the "rationale" is more of a traditional review of the cognitive psychology literature that has been studied over the past 50 years than it is a rationale for the use of the Scientific Orientation Test. Although the author cannot be faulted for such a review, he is not addressing the rationale for the development and use of the test. Thirty-eight pages into the manual one finds still another section entitled "Using the Test Results," which is a far better discussion of test use. This latter description lists 17 topics ranging from "Grouping Pupils" to "Facilitating Basic Research."

NUMBER OF SUBTESTS. The Scientific Orientation Test booklet contains five "subtests" or components. These are identified as "School Holidays," "Finding Out About Things," "Learning Things," "Talking Together," and "Talking About Science At School." The students are asked to respond to statements under each of the components and rate each statement from 4 to 0. The format of these subtests is confusing. A major error in the construction of the test booklet is that too much is packed into what is designed to be a hand-scored booklet. Each page has a series of abbreviations along the top of the page that represent descriptors of what is being measured. For example, under "School Holidays," the student is asked to place a rating on a line that is under one of the abbreviations. This will then give the person assigned to scoring the responses an indication of what is ostensibly being measured. If the student offers a rating on a statement "Write the story" his rating will appear under the abbreviation "L," which stands for Literature. The student does not know what L stands for but they do see that there is a space in which to enter their response. Only the person who scores the "test" knows what it means.

TEST ADMINISTRATION. Instructions for administering the S.OR.T. seem to be relatively clear and detailed. The test booklet is obviously designed for hand scoring. The directions seem primitive in light of the availability of computer scoring in all but the most underdeveloped parts of the world. Most assuredly Australia is not an underdeveloped nation. What follows are excerpts from "Directions for Administering" the Scientific Orientation Test.

"It is not recommended that the test be administered by the class teacher as this may cause some pupils to answer in a manner which they assume is expected by the teacher." "Space pupils as widely as possible. Issue test booklets but tell the class not to open them or start work until told to do so." "Tell the pupils, though, not to spend too much time thinking about each vote. Read a statement and vote on it quickly. Vote on each statement in turn and do not leave any unanswered." "Stress that results will not be used for grading but to help teachers give better lessons." "It is not necessary to insist on completion unless the results are to be used for individual analysis" (manual, p. 19). (This last statement is quite a contradiction to earlier directions).

The last two pages of the test booklet are open-ended. The instructions on page 9 of the test booklet indicate to the test taker, "If you have time, use these two pages to write anything you would like to say about the science lessons in your school. You may write just a few lines or up to two pages according to the time you have left." The purpose served by these instructions is unclear to this reviewer.

The test manual is specific enough so that if a teacher, school administrator, or guidance counselor reads the supplied directions to those taking the test, the method for administering the test can be standardized. However, equally important is whether these directions have replicated the conditions under which the test was validated and normed. The Scientific Orientation Test appears to be a new test in name only. Its statistical descriptions utilize previous studies of its psychometric characteristics related to validity, reliability, and test construction. The research cited extends back more than 40 years. The various versions of this instrument were administered in four countries: England, Australia, Israel, and Bahrain.

DERIVATION OF AUSTRALIAN NORMS. S.OR.T. norms were gathered across three grade levels: 7th, 9th, and 11th. The norm sample consisted of 677 boys, and 640 girls for a total of 1,317 students. The students were not selected on a random base because classes remained intact. There appears to be no consideration given to randomizing a selection of schools from which the 50 classes could have been selected.

These norms were collected in mid year of 1980 in various areas of metropolitan Sydney. A remarkable jump in logic was made by the author when he observed that, "While the Australian norms were derived from only one city, evidence from international studies suggests that there are no significant differences between urban and rural groups or between geographic regions of a country" (p. 34). This singular observation is open for critical discussion. As one who has worked in schools abroad including the Middle East and Australia this reviewer finds this observation highly debatable.

A questionable practice in developing and using norms from which to draw conclusions is to be found on page 32 of the S.OR.T. manual. In discussing Australian norms for school years other than 7th, 9th, and 11th, the recommendation is made that grades 8, 10, and 12 use approximate norms by interpolation or extrapolation depending upon the level being approximated. The author does caution users to be careful in their generalizations.

DERIVATION OF BAHRAIN NORMS. Bahrain, we are told, is representative of the Arab States of Egypt, Iraq, Jordan, Kuwait, Libya, Oman, Qatar, Saudi Arabia, Sudan, Syria, and Yemen. The manual contains this generalization because the Arab states listed, ostensibly, have a common school structure, tend to follow the same or similar science curricula, and have a common culture and philosophy of education in relation to the teaching of science. Although all of the countries listed are Islamic in religion there are some considerable differences between Jordan, for example, and Saudi Arabia. The author draws generalizations from samples to populations too freely for this reviewer. Although it is likely that at some given point in time, sampling one Arab state or one city in a country might sound reasonable, generalizing from small samples to a population across decades, using data that ignore internal changes in a population over time, is a fundamental flaw in norm development.

TECHNICAL ASPECTS. The S.OR.T. manual describes the statistical analyses used to investigate the content, criterion-related, and construct validity of the test under review. Content validity is equated with "face" validity, which weakens the author's claims for content validity. A more substantive argument could have been made. From the beginning of the description of determining content validity, we can see what weakens the Scientific Orientation Test. In his desire to legitimize the bases of the "test" the author takes great pains to cite previous literature that is, at times, loosely linked to the content of the S.OR.T. booklet but does not deal directly with the S.OR.T. itself. As the manual states, "Content and 'face' validity are given credence ... [by] relying heavily on the cumulative findings of previous research, including in most cases published and validated relevant affective tests" (p. 66).

It would appear from the full description of how content validity was determined for the S.OR.T., that a Q-sort technique was used with teachers and other members of criterion groups to identify certain concepts that were related to each area of scientific interest. A high level of agreement was found using a 1929 scaling procedure by Thurstone and Chave.

The techniques described for obtaining evidence of criterion-related validity are a particularly strong and positive approach to establishing validity of the S.OR.T. Thirteen different studies are described. A positive element in the manual's discussion of criterion-related validity is the treatment of relationships between specific variables that make up the S.OR.T. and more generalized concepts of Science interests.

Construct validity evidence was obtained through statistical analyses of eight construct studies that used factor analysis, multiple regression, and discriminative analysis. As before, the discussion of construct validity leaned heavily upon studies of a variety of variables from differentiated studies not necessarily related or based upon the S.OR.T., and occurring at various periods in time. One would be hard-pressed to judge the excellence of the Scientific Orientation Test from the data reported in the test manual.

The manual reports reliability estimates by (a) split-half techniques using alternative items and (b) a Spearman Brown prophecy formula, (c) a test-retest estimate by a repeat testing 6-weeks later, and (d) Cronbach's alpha coefficient (an internal consistency measure).

The reliability estimates are reported by variables measured. The estimates are fragmented by year and by location. As an example, the split-half reliability estimate for "Science Orientation (variable 4.0)" is based on 200 randomly selected boys and girls in Forms 7, 9, and 11 in secondary schools in Sydney, Australia. This is contrasted with a test-retest at a 6-week interval. The estimates reported are given as split half (.968), and test-retest (.831). In the case of the example just cited, one cannot make much of a generalization about a scientific interest inventory under these conditions. Data are reported for different versions of the S.OR.T. (1959, 1965, 1985). This reviewer finds these data suspect because interests and attitudes are not always stable, and certainly they are not permanently fixed. Changing educational and social situations over time make disparate data of the kind described above not convincing.

The use of the reliability estimates is suspect, given the assumptions one would follow normally. It is essential to know the characteristics of the sample on which the reliability estimates were computed. The only characteristics identified in the descriptions given are gender, grade level, and location. Curriculums studied, science experiences in school, parental support, and the like are at least as important in the study of attitudes and interests, and in judging the reliability estimates computed. The use of coefficient alpha is most appropriate for personality measures, interest inventories, and other measures that are not scored for correct/incorrect responses. The use of Cronbach's coefficient alpha is mentioned in a review of a study conducted in Melbourne, Australia with 780 seventh graders. Unfortunately, this study had little to do with the development of the Scientific Orientation Test.

SUMMARY. The S.OR.T. is not representative of high-quality interest inventories usually reviewed in the *Mental Measurements Yearbook* series. The test manual reads more like a review of the literature in a doctoral dissertation than it does in (a) explaining how the interest inventory was developed, (b) the author's rationale for its use with students at various grade levels, (c) as a guide for administering the interest inventory, and (d) explaining other technical descriptions found in a test manual. The test manual as submitted for review only vaguely conforms to the *Standards for Educational and Psychological Testing* (AERA, APA, & NCME, 1985).

The overriding weakness of the S.OR.T. is that it overlooks the purposes that an interest inventory can serve. Scores derived from an administration of an inventory mean little if they are not interpreted correctly by a professional trained in the limitations of reported interests. Individual curiosities are rarely, if ever, stable. However, over time they can blossom into interests but even then they are not permanent. That being the case, the act of choosing vocations, or making advanced education choices based on interest inventory results is problematic.

This reviewer cannot recommend the Scientific Observation Test as it has been submitted. It needs severe editing and empirical use with a strong emphasis on currency of scientific concepts measured.

REVIEWER'S REFERENCES

American Educational Research Association, American Psychological Association, & National Council on Measurement in Education. (1985). *Standards for educational and psychological testing*. Washington, DC: American Psychological Association, Inc.

Ebel, R. L., & Frisbie, D. A. (1986). *Essentials of educational measurement* (4th ed.). Englewood Cliffs, NJ: Prentice-Hall.

Mehrens, W. A., & Lehmann, I. J. (1991). *Measurement and evaluation in education and psychology* (4th ed.). Fort Worth, TX: Holt, Rinehart and Winston, Inc.

[77]
Selby MillSmith Values Indices.

Purpose: "A measure of personal values associated with work and the working environment."
Population: Adults.
Publication Dates: 1985–1991.
Administration: Individual or group.
Editions, 2: Management Values Index, Supervisory Values Index.
Price Data: Available from publisher.
Comments: Test may be paper-and-pencil or computer administered.
Author: Adrian W. Savage.
Publisher: Selby MillSmith [England].

a) MANAGEMENT VALUES INDEX.
Purpose: "For selection, assessment and training and development at managerial and senior levels within an organisation."
Population: Managers.
Acronym: MVI.
Scores, 27: Core Scales [Achievement Values (Work Ethic, Responsibility, Risk Taking, Task Orientation, Leadership, Activity, Need for Status, Self Esteem), Expertise Values (Need for Mental Challenge, Innovation, Analysis, Attention to Detail), Consolidation Values (Need for Stability, Need for Structure, Career Development), Interpersonal Values (Sociability, Inclusion, Personal Warmth, Tactfulness, Tolerance)], [Second Order Indices (Executive Index, Stability Index, Conscientiousness Index, Expert Orientation Index, Team Orientation Index, Empathy Index, Motivational Distortion Index)].
Time: (30–45) minutes.

b) SUPERVISORY VALUES INDEX.
Purpose: "For selection, assessment and training and development at supervisory and 'A' level standard."
Scores, 26: Core Scales [Achievement Values (Work Ethic, Responsibility, Risk Taking, Task Orientation, Leadership, Activity, Need for Status, Self Esteem), Expertise Values (Need for Mental Challenge, Innovation, Analysis, Attention to Detail), Consolidation Values (Need for Stability, Need for Structure, Career Development), Interpersonal Values (Sociability, Inclusion, Personal Warmth, Tactfulness, Tolerance)], Second Order Indices (Initiative Index, Team Orientation Index, Stability Index, Enquiry Index, Conscientiousness Index, Motivational Distortion Index).
Time: (30–45) minutes.

Review of the Selby MillSmith Values Indices by PETER MILES BERGER, Area Manager— Mental After Care Association, London, England:

The Management Values Index (MVI) and Supervisory Values Index (SVI) are intended to measure fundamental work-related attitudes and beliefs. The manual indicates that these instruments can be used for selection, training, and/or development at managerial or senior level. Each instrument contains 252 questions, each answered on a scale of 0 to 4. The instruments take approximately one-half hour to complete. Questionnaires have to be scored by computer, and the publisher supplies several PC-based scoring packages.

The instruments are available for interactive use on PCs. The interactive version was quite user friendly and appealing. The questions were stimulating and engaging, encouraging self-examination that seemed like a helpful, if unintended, outcome.

Of three available report formats I clearly preferred the briefer narrative report as it was most clear and incisive. The longer report differs from the briefer only in stating elaborate definitions for each scale. This information is particularly superfluous for scales falling in the average range.

Validity studies, reliability studies, and normative data were developed for the MVI using groups including managers, final year students, trainee airline pilots, and police inspectors. Of 1,158 norm group subjects, 319 are unclassified.

For the SVI, airline cabin crew, police superintendents, engineers, members of the fire brigade, and supervisors were used. Of 919 norm group subjects 337 are unclassified. These norm groups hardly represent the broad spectrum of different professions and trades. The norms offer a point of reference, rather than an authoritatively representative view; therefore, interpretation based on these norms should be cautious in the extreme. Workers will differ from these norms according to characteristics of each job.

The manual emphasizes the construct validity of scores from these instruments. No studies of predictive validity are presented, nor studies of performance against criteria. As a result, findings should be considered theoretical, rather than grounded in real life performance or behavior. This shortcoming undermines the author's proposal for use in selection or recruitment.

The manual details a conscientious effort to clearly define constructs articulating a wide range of work-related values. As a result, the user has little doubt about what is being measured. This documentation offers rationale for the face validity of the instruments.

The manual presents a number of studies testing concurrent validity by comparing results with The Myers-Briggs Type Indicator, the FIRO-B, The Jackson Personality Inventory, and the California Psychological Inventory. A number of strikingly significant correlations support construct validity. Findings offer evidence that the other instruments measure some factors in common with the MVI and SVI.

Reliability is examined solely through the alpha method. These coefficients are very acceptable, within the limits of the method. No impression of stability can be gained through the documentation. It would be interesting to know how stable work-related values are, and which values represent state or trait factors. Test-retest studies would reflect on the confidence that could be placed in findings.

The author makes a point of foregoing factor analytic methods for developing subscales. Subscales are devised by commonsense grouping. The result of eschewing a more rigorous factor-analytic approach is that boundaries between subscales seem fuzzy with single factors potentially contributing to several identified scales. The documentation surprisingly does not present a breakdown of which items are included in which scales. This vital information would allow users to better understand and evaluate the instruments.

More global "Second Order Scales" are produced by amalgamating several basic scales. Examples of these scales include "Executive Index," "Team Orientation Index," and others. These scales amplify the difficulties of intuitive rather than technical scale development. Scales contributing to the Second Order Scales can cancel each other out, so that these amalgamated scores can become nearly useless.

The impression of using and interpreting my personal results was that the scores mostly agreed with my self-perceptions. The report described me accurately in many respects. I felt that some of the narrative comments might be interpreted negatively by employers, to my disadvantage in selection.

I must raise several points of caution. The developers propose that the instrument be used for selection for employment. Use of these tests for selection does not seem appropriate, especially within an equal opportunities selection framework. No predictive validity is offered to indicate correlation between scale results and success in jobs. The tester-selector is asked to make an inductive leap from constructs to predicting job performance, and there appears to be no evidence to justify this proposed use. It may be tempting to recruiting employers to propose the desired profile for candidates, and select (or reject) candidates who meet (or do not meet) the hypothetical profile. This approach to using these test findings is speculative and creates fundamental unfairness in selection. My view is that these instruments should not be used for selection in recruitment or promotion.

Another important factor with these instruments is that they are comparatively expensive. The publishers require a license fee of approximately 500 pounds (700 USD) per year plus fees for each administration of 11 or 14 pounds (17 to 22 USD), with some discounts available. Thus, the instruments seem to be targeted for corporate use in organizations that can justify this level of expenditure for this type of information.

SUMMARY. Overall, these instruments were interesting to use. Results encouraged me to think more about values and my personal beliefs and conduct. Test consumers need to consider if these instruments justify their cost, or if perhaps other less costly instruments can be found to analyse an individual's values. After all, values are rather abstract constructs lending themselves to many different schemata, and there can be little argument about the relative merits of such schemata, as they are more in the eye of the beholder than grounded in any true life reality.

Frankly, I am troubled by the suggestion that these tests could be used in employee selection. Their use for that purpose, in absence of relevant predictive validity studies, seems indefensible. With an appreciation of these tests' limitations, organizations that can comfortably bear the cost may find these instruments useful in stimulating employees' self-examination, to facilitate team building and effective supervision, and for assisting employees to plan their future development and training needs.

Review of the Selby MillSmith Values Indices by GERALD R. SCHNECK, Professor of Rehabilitation Counseling, Mankato State University, Mankato, MN:

The Selby MillSmith Values Indices was developed by the authors in the United Kingdom for applied use in the "selection, assessment, training, development and employment or career counselling" of predominantly adults within employment settings. There are two versions of the Selby MillSmith Values Indices, those being the Management Values Index (MVI) and the Supervisory Values Index (SVI). The MVI "demands a level of knowledge of English broadly compatible with the ability to read a serious daily newspaper," whereas the SVI "uses simpler English, broadly compatible with a popular tabloid newspaper" (manual, p. 1). The MVI is designed to be used with "management," "graduates and first year student" populations, whereas the SVI is intended for "people who may broadly be described as being of Supervisory level, or alternatively for school leavers of A-level standard" (manual, p. 1). The manual and user guide for the Selby MillSmith Values Indices provides a thoughtful discussion of the importance of values in the hierarchy of psychological constructs, particularly as they relate to beliefs and attitudes and to applications within the field of Human Resource Management.

Preliminary items for inclusion in the Values Indices instruments were developed through the guidance of the hypothetical framework of values and then administered to a sample of respondents. Items were excluded if they were ambiguous or unclear, with the remainder being weighted onto scales based on item-to-scale correlation. The scales were then checked on a cross-validated sample and split-half reliability coefficients were estimated using coefficient alpha. The authors state that this process resulted in the currently used scales owing their inclusion to: "(a) relevance to real-life; (b) evidence from the literature that those scales represent stable and widely recognised values; and (c) having had their relevance established statistically" (manual, p. 3). A combination of both "global" values and job-specific attitudes and preferences were ultimately included by the authors, to provide balance and relevance to the work situation, rather than to other life activities. The Values Indices scales have two formats: (a) item for response is placed into a context; and (b) presentation as single, context-free words. Responses made to items on the questionnaire are grouped and scored against 21 Core scales, which represent the basic value-structure of the subject, as measured by the instrument. In addition, Second Order scales are derived from combinations of scores on the Core scales. The MVI has six of these scales, whereas the SVI has five. Core and Second Order scales are as listed in the descriptive entry for this instrument.

Although both the MVI and SVI questionnaires are administered in a paper-pencil format, the scoring of the Values Indices is complex, requiring a licensed computer-scoring program (IBM PC or truly compatible machine only). Raw scores for each subject are converted to standardized score, specifically the STENS system (standard TENS). The manual provides a short explanation of each point in the STENS scale (ranging from 1 at the lowest to 10 at the highest) and appropriate manner of interpreting these scores, including various cautions regarding overinterpretation.

Comments within the manual addressed important issues surrounding instrument usage, such as: (a) strongly encouraging appropriate training of persons involved in administering, interpreting, and utilizing the instruments; and (b) providing one-on-one feedback to the subject, rather than only offering a written or diagrammatic summary that they might misunderstand. Manual appendices included extension reliability and other correlation data pertaining to the development of the Values Indices, normative data for Core and Second Order scales for total sample, and subsamples classified by primary occupational assignment (i.e., managers, first year students, trainee airline pilots and police inspectors for the MVI; airline cabin crew, police superintendents, engineers, supervisors, and fire brigade members for the SVI). Additional validation data were also provided in the Appendices, which included the principal correlations found between the Core scales of the Values Indices and each of the following tests: The Myers-Briggs Type Indicator; FIRO-B; Jackson Personality Inventory; and the California Psychology Inventory. Next, Core scales, which comprise the various Second Order scales or indices for the MVI and the SVI, were listed along with their related factor weightings. Finally, the weightings of each component scale of the MVI and SVI were listed along with their respective weightings, as they related to the Motivational Distortion Index for the Indices.

The review package provided by the test publisher also included sample computer-generated reports for both the MVI and SVI. The questionnaires and separate answer sheets for the MVI and SVI included the administration instructions for the test taker, which were not provided nor expanded upon anywhere within the manual and user guide that was provided for the administrator. Computer-generated reports provided both a Score Chart (list of the 20 Core scales with raw and sten scores, as well as a graphic representation of the scores) and a Full Narrative interpretation for each of the Core scales and summary paragraphs for each of the Second Order index scales. Either of these two choices in report formats can be requested from the test-scoring program. No mention was made of whether the test user or administrator must key in actual item responses, raw or sten scores from the hand-corrected copy of each test, or if the questionnaire could be scanned into the program, thus saving time and effort. Review of narrative sample reports showed that the developers utilized gender references of he/his and she/her in an alternating format, leaving some discomfort on this reviewer's part with the manner in which the report spoke to an individual's specific results. Many other instruments that utilize computer scoring to generate a narrative report are able to incorporate the individual's name into the report to enhance personalization of results. Also, narrative discussion of individual results as compared to normative data emphasized "comparison to other UK (United Kingdom) supervisors" or "managers." This raises the point of the norm groups being taken from a rather limited range of supervisory and managerial occupations within the United Kingdom (although geographic or other demographic information was not provided to aid the reviewer in determining the actual representativeness of the norm groups, such as if they were taken from individuals only residing within England and/or the British Isles, or if the norm group(s) were also representative of other member countries).

The MVI and SCI may lend themselves to computer administration.

Selby MillSmith and other organizations have launched websites on the Internet that are designed to assist job seekers and employers in identifying qualified personnel for positions that are available within a particular organization.

The Selby MillSmith *Inter-Work* (http://www.selbymillsmith.com/1ststep.htm) and Career Direct (http://www.careersdirect.com) websites are unique, in that they include an assessment capability for determining whether or not an individual is best suited for a particular type of occupation and work situation. Given the global nature of the Internet and the rapid acceleration of the number of websites that address employment listing and screening, the use of the MVI and SVI show tremendous potential to aid both employers and job seekers throughout the world, if the instrumentation that is used and its normative data facilitate application to other countries, participants, languages, and a wider array of occupational opportunities. This reviewer feels that although the Selby MillSmith Values Indices appears to provide important information about a relatively wide variety of values that appear to be appropriate to supervisory and managerial personnel, it does not fully explain the full range of this work behavior construct as evidenced by cross-validation data provided for the Myers-Briggs Type Indicator, FIRO-B, Jackson Personality Inventory, or the California Personality Inventory. Likewise, use of the results of instruments such as the MVI and SVI necessitate integration with other subject-linked information and measures of knowledge, skills, and abilities that are also relevant to successful career choices and human resource management activities. Current normative data do not provide any basis for the application of the MVI and SVI to populations located outside of the United Kingdom, other than by indirect and partial encouragement provided by the validation data included in the manual. Availability of alternative language format(s) are not addressed and it is therefore assumed that none are currently available.

SUMMARY. Although the manual and sample reports for the Selby MillSmith Values Indices (MVI and SVI) present a rather impressive package at first glance, this reviewer is of the opinion that other alternatives are currently available that would better address the issues raised. The publisher, Selby MillSmith, has indicated that the instruments and manual for the MVI and SVI are currently under revision, but these materials were not fully available at the time of this review. The aforementioned instruments reported in the validation studies for the MVI and SVI, in fact, would each be stronger choices for use in a package for employment assessment for persons not living in the United Kingdom. However, all of these and comparable instruments within this area of psychological tests and measures, need to be enhanced through better content analysis, particularly with the increasing demands for essential task representativeness and accuracy being placed on human resource operations with the implementation of the Americans With Disabilities Act and other efforts to overcome discriminatory practices in employment settings.

[78]
Silver Drawing Test of Cognition and Emotion [Third Edition Revised].

Purpose: Designed as a nonverbal measure of ability in three areas of cognition: sequential concepts, spatial concepts, and association and formation of concepts; and to screen for depression.

Population: Ages 5 and over.

Publication Dates: 1983–1998.

Acronym: SDT.

Scores, 5: Predictive Drawing, Drawing from Observation, Drawing from Imagination, Self-Image, Projection.

Administration: Individual or group.

Price Data, 1998: $10 per set of 10 test booklets, layout sheet, and scoring forms; $32 per manual ('96, 147 pages); $15 per manual entitled "Updating the Silver Drawing Test and Draw A Story Manuals" ('98, 32 pages).

Foreign Language Edition: Brazilian translation and standardization available.

Time: (12–15) minutes.

Comments: Revision of Silver Drawing Test of Cognitive Skills and Adjustment.

Author: Rawley Silver.

Publisher: Ablin Press Distributors.

Cross References: See T4:2462 (1 reference); for reviews of an earlier edition by Kevin D. Crehan and Annie W. Ward, see 11:362; for reviews of the original edition by Clinton I. Chase and David J. Mealor, see 10:333.

Review of the Silver Drawing Test of Cognition and Emotion [Third Edition Revised] by TERRY OVERTON, President, Learning and Behavioral Therapies, Inc., Farmville, VA:

DESCRIPTION AND PURPOSE. The Silver Drawing Test of Cognition and Emotion was designed to assess cognitive development and to screen for possible emotional problems in children and youth. The original concept of the test was to assess the cognitive and emotional problems in children with hearing impairments who were non-verbal. The test author states that hearing children use language concepts to label perceptions, organize experiences, and attempt to make sense of and control their worlds. The basic foundation of the theoretical base of this instrument is conceptualized in the writings of Piaget, Bruner, Arnheim, Torrance, and Sinclair-de-Zwart. The Silver Drawing Test focuses on assessing the child's spatial, conceptual, and sequential ability through structured and semistructured drawing tasks. The tasks include Predictive Drawing, Drawing from Observation, and Drawing from Imagination. Predictive Drawing measures sequential ability by asking the child to predict a sequence, to predict "horizontality," and to predict "verticality." This task presents stimuli for which the child is asked to draw what would happen under specific conditions, such as the liquid in a glass decreasing as it is consumed through a straw. Drawing from Observation is designed to measure concepts of space and spatial relationships between objects. Objects are placed within the environment in a standardized format and the child is required to draw the objects. Drawing from Imagination assesses the ability of the child to select content, combine content (visual stimuli), and represent ideas and feelings, or creativity. Drawing from Imagination is the task that the author states screens for emotional disturbance in children. This task presents visual stimuli: 15 pictures of people and objects, from which the child is asked to select 2 and is then asked to imagine something happening between the 2 pictures. The child is to then draw what they have imagined. Next, the child is requested to write a title or story for the drawing. Drawing from Imagination includes two sets of stimulus pictures, Form A and Form B.

ADMINISTRATION AND SCORING. According to the manual, the test can be administered without any prior training by a variety of professionals who work with children. The test is untimed but the author states administration usually takes from 12 to 15 minutes. The test may be administered in a group setting. Directions for arranging the stimuli are provided; however, the instructions for the examinee are not presented as standardized instructions but rather as a casual suggestion of what the examiner might say. The instructional format allows for the presentation of

the test to nonhearing children and includes using pantomime or manual language as needed. Scoring takes 3 to 6 minutes according to the manual; however, the novice examiner would most likely be unable to complete the scoring within this time limit. The guidelines for scoring are provided as are examples of 1-to-5-point responses for Predictive Drawing. The predictive task is scored on predicting a sequence, predicting "horizontality," and predicting "verticality." Scoring criteria for Drawing by Observation are provided for horizontal or left-right relationships, vertical relationships, and front-back relationships or depth. The Drawing from Imagination subtest includes scoring for ability to select the content; ability to combine, or the form of the drawing; and the ability to represent, or creativity in form, content, title, or story. The Drawing from Imagination subtest scoring includes a projection scale for assessing the emotional content of responses on the dimensions of negative themes, moderately negative themes, neutral themes, moderately positive themes, and strongly positive themes. A self-image scale is also provided for the Drawing from Imagination subtest and includes criteria for scoring the drawing on morbid fantasy, ambiguous or ambivalent fantasy, pleasant fantasy, and wish-fulfilling fantasy.

TECHNICAL INFORMATION. The Silver Drawing Test provides no specific test construction information such as how the items were designed and selected on the basis of field trials or expert judges. The normative data are based on a sample of 624 children and adults. No substantial descriptive information is provided about the sample. The sample sizes by grade or age range from 16 tenth graders to 127 third graders. The adult group included 77 persons and there was no information provided in the table regarding the ages of the adults. The manual includes results from a variety of reliability and validity studies. Five interrater reliability studies were conducted. These studies compared scores from raters who were trained in the scoring methods and those from persons with no training. Various professions were represented across the studies. The largest number of tests scored in any of the interrater studies was 36. The interrater reliability coefficients ranged from .45 to .99 for the reliability of raters across tasks or subtests. One interrater reliability study is described that compared results from raters across the emotional content scale (n = .94) and the self-image scale (r = .74). This study compared results from five judges. Reliability studies include estimates of internal consistency reliability for the subtests and test-retest research. Two test-retest studies are included with sample sizes of 12 students with learning disabilities and 10 third grade students (interval of approximately 1 month for both of the studies). These reliability coefficients ranged between .08 and .84.

The validity studies include research on discriminant validity of clinical samples, criterion-related validity studies, and evidence of construct validity through developmental changes. The conclusions from the validity studies are mixed and most of the research described involved studies using small sample sizes. The data are presented in an inconsistent format in the validity chapter. The manual includes a chapter of validity studies conducted from 1990–1995 ranging from gender comparison studies to studies on constructs such as aggression and attitude to comparison studies of scores from "deaf" and hearing children.

EVALUATION. The theoretical foundation of this instrument is intriguing and the author provides an interesting rationale. The author provides some evidence that this instrument may have the capability to measure the constructs that are purported to be measured. The test construction, standardization, and normative process lack a solid research base. The reliability and validity studies are based on very small samples and the author does not provide consistent information about the sample selection or the variables considered in selecting the samples (such as ages, socioeconomic status, geographic representation). The manual does not present the reliability and validity research studies in a consistent format and this results in extremely difficult interpretation for test consumers. The test instrument itself provides two sets of stimulus pictures for the Drawing from Imagination task; however, the author does not address the purpose of the two forms nor does the consumer know if these are equivalent forms. The scoring is fairly subjective and the examiner is not provided with diagnostic or interpretive information.

SUMMARY. In summary, the ideas proposed by the author are quite interesting and the concept of assessing nonverbal children, verbal children, and children in clinical populations in these areas is an excellent concept. This test may be able to assess the cognitive development of children on the dimensions proposed in the Predictive Drawing subtest in a manner not assessed by other instruments. The cognitive development areas assessed appear to have some validity as evidenced by the results of the validity studies included on developmental changes in samples. This aspect of the instrument deserves additional research. The test lacks the scientific rigor expected of an instrument designed to be used in the manner the author states.

Review of the Silver Drawing Test of Cognition and Emotion [Third Edition Revised] by JANET V. SMITH, Assistant Professor of Psychology and Counseling, Pittsburg State University, Pittsburg, KS:

The Silver Drawing Test of Cognition and Emotion (SDT) is a revised version of the Silver Drawing Test of Cognitive and Creative Skills (1990), previously known in the original version as the Silver Drawing Test of Cognitive Skills and Adjustment (1983). Despite the name change, the third edition is essentially the same as the previous version of the test, with some improvements that attempt to address past criticisms of the test. According to the manual, the major changes from the earlier edition are: (a) addition of a second set of stimulus drawings; (b) addition of a new Self-Image scale; (c) two new chapters in the manual, one summarizing recent studies conducted on the SDT and one tying assessment to intervention techniques; (d) improvement of scoring guidelines; and (e) improvement of theoretical background and statistical analyses.

The SDT is designed for use with hearing-and/or language-impaired individuals, and is based on the premise that art can provide an effective medium for assessment of individuals with language deficiencies. The test can be used for examinees aged 5 years to adult, and provides measures of both cognitive and emotional functioning. The cognitive component is based on Piaget's concepts related to sequencing ability, space, and class inclusion. The emotional component is based on the assumptions of projective assessment. Previous versions of the test have been criticized for lack of adequate theory base. The third edition reports that the theoretical background has been expanded. However, certain aspects of the theoretical rationale for the test continue to be lacking and some references are rather dated.

There are three subtests to the SDT. Predictive Drawing involves asking subjects to draw predicted changes in appearance of objects and is designed to assess "ability to predict and represent horizontality, verticality, and sequential order" (manual, p. 10). Drawing from Observation involves presenting subjects with an array of simple objects and asking them to draw what they see. This subtest is designed to assess spatial relationships. Finally, Drawing from Imagination requires individuals to draw a picture of what they imagine happening between two subjects selected from a set of 15 stimulus drawings. This subtest is intended to assess functional grouping and relationships, as well as creativity. The Drawing from Imagination subtest is also the basis for the emotional component of the SDT, with the assumption that responses to this subtest will reveal attitudes toward self and others as well as facilitate early identification of depression. In addition, an individual's score for the new Self-Image scale is obtained from responses to this third subtest. Very little is said in the manual about the new scale but "it is theorized that the SDT Self-Image Scale can be useful in screening children and adults for depression or masked depression" (p. 20).

Administration of the test takes approximately 15 minutes, with an additional 3 to 6 minutes for scoring. Responses are scored on a 0- to 5-point scale. For the most part, scoring guidelines appear adequate, although it seems that there would still be room for subjectivity in scoring the emotional component of the test. Tables are provided to convert raw scores into T scores and percentile ranks. Normative data continue to be inadequate, with small, nonrepresentative samples. Data are pooled for males and females, which presents a problem given reported gender differences in subject responses. It is also troubling that the mean cognitive scores for some older age groups is lower than the mean for younger subjects, given the assumption that cognitive abilities should increase with age. No normative data are provided for the new Self-Image Scale.

Evidence for reliability of scores from the test is presented in the form of interscorer reliability as well as test-retest reliability. Although the manual for the third edition reports that "scoring guidelines have been tightened" (p. 1), there are no new data presented either in terms of interrater reliability or test-retest reliability. Previous criticisms of small, inadequate samples continue to be applicable. Reliability of scores from the SDT remains questionable.

Reviews of previous editions of the SDT also criticized the test for lack of adequate evidence of validity. The third edition of the SDT includes a new chapter entitled "1990–1996 Studies Showing Validity." The chapter reports findings from 11 different studies. However, 6 of the studies address gender and/or age differences in responses to the SDT, one study simply involves case examples, and another study involves comparing the stimulus drawings of the SDT with Silver's Draw a Story instrument in terms of likelihood to elicit negative responses. Unfortunately, the results of these studies contribute little to the establishment of validity of the scores from the SDT.

Of more importance in the new chapter are three studies that compare SDT scores of children with various disabilities to SDT scores of those without disabilities. However, these studies still fall short of establishing validity of scores from the test. It was predicted that scores from language- and/or hearing-impaired individuals should be equivalent to those from nonimpaired children in terms of spatial skills, but weaker in terms of verbal and sequencing skills. Overall, deaf children were found to have equivalent scores to nonimpaired children on most spatial tasks, except for lower scores on the Drawing from Observation subtest. No significant differences were found between the groups in terms of sequencing ability. In an expansion of this study, both of these groups of subjects scored higher on some spatial relationship tasks than did a group of learning-disabled students. In a third study, a small group of learning-disabled, dyslexic, and normal children in grades 3, 4, and 5 were administered both the California Achievement Test (CAT) and the SDT. The group of normal children had the highest mean scores on both the CAT and the SDT, followed by the learning-disabled group, with dyslexic students having the lowest mean scores on both instruments.

The last major change in the third edition of the SDT is a new chapter describing several art intervention techniques to remedy deficits identified by the SDT. The techniques appear to be potentially useful for art therapists in particular, but it is difficult to assess the effectiveness of these interventions as no evidence of validity is provided in the chapter, other than an illustrative case example.

SUMMARY. The underlying concept of using art to assess individuals with language difficulties is very appealing. The author appears to have responded to several criticisms of previous editions of the test. However, despite attempts to remedy serious deficits, psychometric properties of the test remain very weak. Overall, this reviewer concurs with reviews of previous editions of the SDT, concluding that this test should only be used for experimental purposes at this time, and cannot be recommended over other existing measures of cognitive and emotional abilities for hearing- and/ or language-impaired individuals.

[79]
SIPOAS: Styles in Perception of Affect Scale.

Purpose: "Measures the preferred style in the awareness of, and response to, the minute changes in bodily feelings that lead to emotions and responses."
Population: Age 18 to adult.
Publication Date: 1995.
Acronym: SIPOAS.
Scores: 3 styles: BB (Based on Body), EE (Emphasis on Evaluation), LL (Looking to Logic).
Administration: Individual or group.
Price Data, 1996: $20 per 25 copies of questionnaire; $22.50 per complete research report (203 pages).
Time: [20–30] minutes.
Author: Michael Bernet.
Publisher: Institute for Somat Awareness.

Review of the SIPOAS: Styles in Perception of Affect Scale by BRIAN F. BOLTON, University Professor, Rehabilitation Research and Training Center, University of Arkansas, Fayetteville, AR:

The Styles in Perception of Affect Scale (SIPOAS) is a self-report inventory designed to measure the construct known in the humanistic psychology literature as "Being in touch with one's feelings." Specifically, the SIPOAS purports to quantify three styles of perceiving one's emotions. Based on Body (BB) refers to integrated awareness of bodily feelings, Emphasis on Evaluation (EE) involves interpretation of feelings through introspection, and Looking to Logic (LL) assesses the use of reasoning to understand feelings.

Consistent with the author's theoretical and professional orientation, and supported by some

research on the SIPOAS, a higher score on the BB scale is considered to be indicative of better mental health. The BB scale indicates whether respondents are sufficiently in touch with their feelings. Conversely, higher scores on the EE and LL scales reveal how the awareness of feelings is blocked. Participation in body and spiritual approaches to therapy is hypothesized to enhance the client's ability to attend to bodily feelings.

The author states that the SIPOAS is suitable for use in clinical, counseling, and human resource settings. Specific diagnostic applications suggested in psychology and medicine include depression, eating disorders, substance abuse, post-traumatic stress disorder, and career and family counseling. The author also offers training programs and workshops in the use of the SIPOAS.

The SIPOAS consists of 31 items that require respondents to choose among three alternatives. All 31 items are phrased in the first person, such as "When I feel frightened," followed by three alternatives, each representing one of the perceptual styles. An innovative forced-choice format gives respondents three options: Select one alternative and reject the other two (3, 0, 0); order the three alternatives from most to least preferable (2, 1, 0); or rate the three alternatives as equally preferable (1, 1, 1). This is accomplished by allocating 3 points to the alternatives in the patterns listed above.

Total scores are calculated for the three perceptual styles by summing the choice scores (3, 2, 1, 0) for the 31 alternatives that represent each style. The scoring process is facilitated by use of a tally sheet that incorporates the scoring key. The result is that respondents receive three raw scores that indicate *relative* preferences for the three perceptual styles. It is important to emphasize that the forced-choice response format guarantees that higher scores on one or two styles will necessarily be accompanied by lower scores on the other style(s).

There are no norms for the SIPOAS. The reason for this omission is that the instrument has not been administered to any broadly representative sample of respondents. Instead, members of a variety of organizations and populations were recruited for research purposes. For example, the three largest segments of the research sample were volunteers from the Association for Humanistic Psychology, the National Association of School

Psychologists, and North American Mensa (the high IQ society). The majority of the approximately 1,000 research participants were college-educated professionals. Another indication of the nonrepresentativeness of the research sample is that one-half reported personal experience in some form of psychotherapy.

The SIPOAS is a revision of an earlier instrument called the Perception of Affect (POA) Profile. Development of the POA Profile began with 22 items taken from existing self-consciousness and self-awareness inventories and an equal number of items generated by graduate students. Several cycles of item analyses resulted in a 39-item version of the POA Profile that measured three perceptual styles named Propriocentric, Xenocentric/Vigilant, and Repressor. An interim version of the SIPOAS was created through further item revision and reconceptualization of the three styles. Continued refinement of the items produced the current version of the SIPOAS.

This sequence of progressive item revision and refinement, guided by the author's theoretical orientation and based on statistical analyses of the items, generated three homogenous scales that measure the SIPOAS perceptual styles. The average corrected item-scale correlations are: Based on Body (.45), Emphasis on Evaluation (.39), and Looking to Logic (.42). The internal consistency reliability coefficients for the three scales are .86, .81, and .84, respectively. Finally, the interscale correlations (-.51, -.62, and -.34) are artifacts of the forced-choice response format and do not provide any evidence about the "distinctiveness" of the three styles.

To clarify the trait validity of the three perceptual styles, the author conducted a comprehensive investigation of the relationship between the SIPOAS and selected scales from the NEO Personality Inventory and the Sixteen Personality Factor Questionnaire, the Toronto Alexithymia Scale, and several scales devised to measure body awareness, personal values, and experience in various forms of therapy. The correlational patterns generated detailed descriptions of the three styles. For example, individuals who score higher on Based on Body tend to be adaptable, mature, trusting, self-assured, and insightful. In contrast, high scorers on Emphasis on Evaluation are more likely to be apprehensive, angry, guilty, self-doubting, and suspicious. And respondents who score

higher on Looking to Logic are typically impersonal, nondisclosing, unemotional, intellectually focused, and self-reliant. Correlations with gender, age, and affiliation were consistent with these characterizations.

There is no manual for the SIPOAS. The author's dissertation is offered as a substitute for a test manual. Because the 200-page dissertation contains much irrelevant, redundant, and speculative material, it is a major task for the reader to locate the necessary data about the SIPOAS. The test author is always responsible for providing essential information for the user of the instrument in a standard manual.

SUMMARY. The SIPOAS purports to measure three styles of perceiving emotions that have a variety of diagnostic applications in psychology and medicine. The self-report inventory is the product of a series of developmental analyses guided by a theoretical framework with origins in the human potential movement. The research evidence is generally supportive of the validity of the three perceptual styles. However, the SIPOAS should not be used for client assessment at this time because of the absence of appropriate norms and the lack of a published manual. When these deficiencies are addressed, the SIPOAS may be useful to practitioners who share the author's professional therapeutic orientation.

Review of the SIPOAS: Styles in Perception of Affect Scale by S. ALVIN LEUNG, Associate Professor, Department of Educational Psychology, The Chinese University of Hong Kong, Shatin, N. T., Hong Kong:

The Styles in Perception of Affect Scale (SIPOAS) was designed to measure the degree that a person is in touch with his/her feelings and emotions. The SIPOAS was developed and researched by the author through a doctoral dissertation project (Bernet, 1995). Currently, no test manual is available. The unpublished dissertation presents technical information about the construction of the instrument. A two-page brief description of the instrument and the meaning of the scores is also available for test users.

According to Bernet (1995), the SIPOAS is based on an earlier instrument called the "Perception of Affect" Profile developed by the same author. The SIPOAS has 31 items. For each item stem (e.g., "When I come up against a difficulty I find a solution by") there are three options from which to choose, and a test taker is given 3 points to allocate to the options, depending on the degree that each option describes the preference of the test taker. In other words, the test taker could give either 0, 1, 2, or 3 points to each of the three options as long as the cumulative total equals 3. This method of responding to the SIPOAS is somewhat complex and unusual, and test takers have to read the instructions very carefully to understand what is required. A "tally sheet" is available for test users to compute a total score for each of the three scales: Based on Body (BB), Looking to/for Logic (LL), and Emphasis on Evaluation (EE). According to the author, these scales represent three different personality styles related to "being in touch with one's feelings" (p. 49).

According to the two-page test description, persons with high BB scores (45 to 60) are in touch with their own emotions. They are emotionally healthy, insightful, and free of excessive worries and guilt. They are likely to have healthy personalities and good interpersonal relationships. A score of 25 or below in the BB scale is considered low and education in emotional awareness through therapy is recommended. Individuals with high EE scores (35 or higher) are out of touch with their own feelings and emotions. They are tense, easily discouraged, and overly sensitive to the opinions of others. Consequently their social and interpersonal skills are impaired. The author also suggested that high EE scores are associated with a lack of confidence in daily decision making. Individuals with high LL scores (40 or above) are logical, impersonal, and distant, and they rely on intellectualization and rationalization. They have little regard for emotions, and consequently they do not have adequate awareness of their emotional life. The author suggested that the BB scale should be used as an indicator of "being in touch with one's feelings" (p. 3), and the EE and LL scales indicate whether the blockage to awareness is due to an overreliance on logic, or having low confidence in one's inner processes.

Data on the SIPOAS (N = 997) were collected from participants through 10 different sources, including members of professional organizations (e.g., International Primal Society, National Association of School Psychologists) and a number of special settings (e.g., on display in practitioner's waiting room, computer bulletin board, and multicultural middle-class neighborhood). It was not clear how many copies of the instruments were sent out or the response rate. The sampling process was not systematic and the resultant normative sample was not representative of the general population. Several established instruments, including the NEO PI-R, Cattell's 16-PF (Fifth Edition), and the Toronto Alexithymia Scale, were administered to some of the participants in order to generate information related to the criterion validity of the SIPOAS. A number of so called "ad hoc measures," including a "Body-awareness scale," an "Emphasis on Intellect" scale, a "Personal Values and Attributes scale," and a "Practitioner's Checklist" were also administered to all or some of the participants. However, it was not clear which sample source completed these additional instruments.

Information on the reliability and validity for scores from the SIPOAS was summarized by the author (Bernet, 1995). The author suggested that the internal consistency of the scales was "well within accepted guidelines" (p. 68), but the alpha coefficients were not reported. The author instead reported split-half reliability coefficients for the BB, EE, and LL scales, which were .86, .81, and .84, respectively. It is not clear how the items were divided into halves to perform this analysis. Test-retest reliability coefficients for the scales were not available. In terms of validity, the author claimed that the correlation between the SIPOAS and the other criterion measures (e.g., 16-PF) supported the validity of scores from the instrument. The results of the correlation analyses were used to generate interpretative ideas for the three SIPOAS scales. Similarly, the relationship between the SIPOAS scales and some of the criterion measures suggested that "being in touch with one's feelings" was related to mental health, therapy preference, and experience. In addition, factor analyses were computed on the scales. The results were only briefly reported, and it was not clear how the results were used to aid in the construction of scales and in the interpretation of scores.

The SIPOAS suffers from a number of limitations. First, the intercorrelations among the three scales are high. The correlation coefficients between the BB scale and the EE and LL scales were -.52 and -.62, indicating substantial overlapping between the scales. Such findings pose a challenge to the claim that these scales represent divergent personality styles. Second, with only limited normative information, it is risky to make decisions about what constitutes high and low scores. The cutoffs suggested by the author appeared to be quite arbitrary and were not based on sufficient research data. Third, the author developed a number of "ad hoc" scales and inventories (e.g., the Practitioner's Checklist) to serve as criterion variables for the SIPOAS. However, the validity of these scales and checklist have not been demonstrated. Finally, the author made a number of claims regarding the use of the SIPOAS in psychodiagnosis, different forms of psychotherapy, and medicine (Bernet, 1995, pp. 120–125). These claims, however, have not been substantiated through research.

SUMMARY. The SIPOAS appears to be an instrument that is at the beginning stage of development. Efforts should concentrate on refining the inventory and on accumulating research data to substantiate reliability and validity of the scores. At present, there are not enough research data on the reliability and validity to justify using the results in any psychotherapeutic or clinical settings. It is premature at this point to market and sell the instrument to professional and nonprofessional users, which the author is apparently doing. The author promised in his two-page SIPOAS description that related books and materials are forthcoming, and that in-house training programs and seminars are available to train users on the use of this instrument and on heightening emotional awareness. The author should only consider marketing the instrument for professional use when sufficient data on reliability and validity are available, and when a comprehensive manual about the instrument is ready for test users to use as reference.

REVIEWER'S REFERENCE

Bernet, M. (1995). *Styles in the perception of affect and its relation to mental health.* Unpublished doctoral dissertation, The City University of New York.

[80]
Slosson Full-Range Intelligence Test.

Purpose: Constructed as a "quick estimate of general cognitive ability."
Population: Ages 5–21.
Publication Dates: 1988–1994.
Acronym: S-FRIT.
Scores, 8: General Cognition (Full-Range Intelligence Quotient, Rapid Cognitive Index, Best *g* Index), Cognitive Subdomains (Verbal Index, Abstract Index, Quantitative Index, Memory Index, Performance Index).
Administration: Individual.

Forms, 2: Item Profiles/Score Summaries Form, Brief Score Form.
Price Data, 1996: $115 per complete kit including examiner's manual ('94, 80 pages), normative/technical manual ('94, 93 pages), picture book, 50 motor response forms, 50 brief score forms, and 50 item profiles/score summaries: $20 per 50 forms (specify Motor response, brief score, or item profiles/score summaries); $26 per examiner's manual; $24 per normative/technical manual; $22 per picture book.
Time: (20–35) minutes.
Authors: Bob Algozzine, Ronald C. Eaves, Lester Mann, H. Robert Vance, and Steven W. Slosson (Brief Score Form).
Publisher: Slosson Educational Publications, Inc.

Review of the Slosson Full-Range Intelligence Test by GERALD S. HANNA, Professor of Education, Kansas State University, Manhattan, KS:

PURPOSE. Screening is a major suggested use of the Slosson Full-Range Intelligence Test (S-FRIT). Although there are circumstances in which one might reasonably use a quick, individually administered screening test, in this regard, I see only limited utility. If screening is sought for the general population, I would consider the convenience and economy of group instruments. If screening is used only for students who have been referred for suspected problems, I would wonder if the referral process itself had not served the screening function, thereby justifying more comprehensive assessment than a short screening test can offer.

In addition, the examiner's manual indicates that the S-FRIT is a quick, easily scored cognitive instrument intended to supplement the use of more extensive cognitive assessment instruments such as the Wechsler Intelligence Scale for Children, Third Edition (WISC-III), the Kaufman Assessment Battery for Children (K-ABC), and the Kaufman Adolescent and Adult Intelligence Test (KAIT) in assessing cognitive progress. In pursuit of this, the S-FRIT assesses cognition in ways similar to the Stanford-Binet Intelligence Scale, Fourth Edition (SB-IV). Several subscores are provided to help make tentative diagnoses of cognitive abilities, strengths, and weaknesses. By way of explanation of their purpose, the technical manual (p. 1) indicates:

Though the … S-FRIT is a screening instrument, … [it can be used for] tentative diagnosis of intellectual strengths and weaknesses. It must be understood that … implementation must be considered as tentative, awaiting further confirmation by other diagnostic and remedial procedures. Many students will receive the S-FRIT for screening and it will be determined that they will not proceed through further diagnostic evaluation. The techniques outlined in this Manual can be applied to these students to help them educationally.

The authors are to be commended for discouraging use of subscores on a short screening test for full-blown diagnosis. However, one is puzzled as to which students are to be helped educationally from the *tentative* diagnosis. Those for whom no further diagnostic evaluation is obtained? If so, both the method of confirmation and the need for diagnosis are obscure. Or those for whom the screening use of the S-FRIT leads to full diagnostic evaluation with more sophisticated procedures? If so, the tentative findings would seem to be of limited utility. Or those for whom one wishes to complement more sophisticated Wechsler or Kaufman tests with SB-IV type items? If so, the SB-IV itself might be more attractive than a short screening instrument.

TESTING MATERIALS AND ADMINISTRATION. Test materials are clear and well designed. Administration seems relatively easy and adequately standardized. Excellent use is made of color in aiding administration and scoring. Generally clear scoring criteria are very conveniently placed with the items in the manual.

Verbal items comprised about 36% of the test and were used as much for young children as for the older examinees. Item types included body parts, simple commands, verbal analogies, general information, verbal absurdities, explanation of sayings and proverbs, and vocabulary.

Performance items constitute 48% of the test and include, among others, counting, drawing shapes, picture completion, number and letter series, abstract figures, block counting (from printed materials), and a variety of quantitative items. Manipulatives are restricted to a few common objects (e.g., pencils and coins) and to drawings; this seems sensible for a screening instrument in that it keeps cost down, simplifies administration, and enhances mobility of testing materials.

Quite a few memory items require exact repetition of words, phrases, or sentences. Rote memory is also assessed with pictures, and digits forward and backward. The emphasis on memory—16% of the items—seemed a bit heavy.

Basals and ceilings are each established by eight-in-a-row criteria. It is interesting that the same basals and ceilings are used for all of the subscores, even though eight consecutive items may contain as few as one or even zero items of a particular subpart. This would not seem justified, unless the subparts are intrinsically highly correlated. Otherwise, the use of common basals and ceilings would tend to artificially inflate correlations among the part scores.

I fret that examiners are provided no place to record examinees' responses; rather, they record only the score—1 or 0—for each item. Although most items could easily be scored during testing, there would surely be some for which one could profitably return at one's leisure to reconsider the scoring. Moreover, the absence of answers makes it difficult for scoring accuracy to be investigated, monitored, or improved.

SCORES. A variety of derived scores are provided. The General Cognitive Index is based on the conventional and sensible standard scores with $M = 100$ and $SD = 16$. Unfortunately, this index is labeled an IQ. This and the use of the word "intelligence" in the test's name do not help users to steer clear of the many misconceptions that attend these dated terms.

The four major cognitive subdomains have standard scores with $M = 50$ and $SD = 8$. The use of a standard deviation large enough to avoid introducing substantial grouping error, such as that found in Wechsler scales, is commendable.

THEORY, DEVELOPMENT, AND STANDARDIZATION. Item development is described only as being based on current cognitive assessment practices and theory. Theoretical foundations and rationale are not described.

In developing the test, 600 items were tried out on an unknown number of undescribed examinees and culled down to 355. These items were normed and then culled further to 252. Therefore, the norms appear to have been gathered under conditions of item order and item context that differ from those of the final version. This, of course, compromises their utility.

Overall, the description of sampling procedures for the norming sampling is meager. Field examiners were apparently instructed on how to sample and then were left to it. It seems possible that the adequacy of sampling among the examiners may have varied considerably.

A laudable feature of the technical manual is provision of comparative tables showing the sample of 1,509 in comparison with 1980 census data on a number of demographic characteristics.

RELIABILITY. In individually administered tests, there are four major sources of measurement error that are present in practice. Ideal reliability research would shed light on all of these sources of error.

Occasion Sampling Error. This was investigated with a test-retest study involving 14 children. Because the manual failed to report descriptive statistical data for this sample, the results are not interpretable.

Content Sampling Error. Reliability of the S-FRIT was investigated mainly by use of KR-20. However, a number of issues prevent the KR-20 data from being interpretable. First, the sample is not described; it may well have been the entire norming sample, but this is not made clear.

Second, if there is any sound rationale for the various subscores, then there would be more homogeneity of content within subscores than across subscores. Therefore, KR-20 would not be appropriate for the total score. Yet it is reported.

Third, internal consistency methods of estimating reliability, such as KR-20, are not appropriate for instruments having basal and ceiling levels because the double truncation inflates the results to an unknown extent.

Examiner Error. No data are presented on this topic.

Scoring Error. No data are presented on scoring error. In justice, it should be noted that, although unfortunate, the absence of these latter two kinds of reliability data is common among individually administered tests.

VALIDITY. The treatment of validity in the technical manual is disappointing. The terminology is, at best, of a pre-1985 vintage and it is not used in conventional ways. Empirical findings are reported rather meagerly, often without summary descriptive data. No data are provided that shed light on the statistical independence, or discriminant validity, of the several subscores.

Under the heading "Content Validity" is a description of S-FRIT content. Some data concerning the SB-IV are reviewed, but none reported for the S-FRIT.

A section on "Construct Validity" also provides description of kinds of test content, but no construct-related validity evidence for scores from the test. This, of course, is the place where data demonstrating the discriminant validity of the subscales would be expected.

Under "Concurrent Criterion Validity" are summaries of several studies. One group reports relationship of S-FRIT scores with those of other aptitude tests. In general the studies report impressive concurrent validity coefficients; however, the samples are very small and the accompanying data are reported rather haphazardly. For example, means and standard deviations of the samples are not reported in several studies. However, *SD*s are reported in a study in which the limited variability was used to explain the small correlation coefficient. Correction for restriction of range was used in another study for which *SD*s were not reported.

Another group of concurrent validity studies concerned special populations. Here too, the findings seem reasonable, yet the reporting omits essential important detail.

A methodological issue common to the above studies is the need for the examination of the S-FRIT and the other tests to be independent. That is, different examiners should administer the tests and they should not know each other's results until they are finished. As is typically the case in test manuals, no information was provided as to whether this condition was met.

Yet another group of validity studies reports correlation of S-FRIT scores with scores of achievement tests. Although the correlational findings seem adequate, they must be disregarded because descriptive data (*M*s and *SD*s) are not reported for the samples.

Missing, as mentioned above, is systematically presented information about the correlations among the several S-FRIT subscores. Without data suggesting some degree of statistical independence of the subscores, users cannot use them with confidence that they are not unduly redundant. Indirect data on this topic can be gleaned from three sources. First, Table 8 in the technical manual provides, for a sample lacking summary statistics, the intercorrelations among four basic S-FRIT subscores as well as the correlation between WISC-R Verbal and Performance IQs. The correlation between the two Wechsler scores was .71, that between pairs of the (much shorter, thus presumably less reliable) S-FRIT scores ranged from .77 to .90. Thus, there appears to be great redundancy among the S-FRIT subscores.

Second, in comparing the KR-20s for the subscores with that of the total score, one could not expect the KR-20 of the total to be as high as it is compared with those of the parts if the parts were not quite highly intercorrelated.

Third, a comparison in the norms tables of deviant status on the subscores and total scores reveals that it is not very much more unusual for people to be consistently deviant than to be occasionally deviant; this suggests that the subparts are highly correlated. Consequently, on the basis of the indirect data available, I believe the parts of the S-FRIT lack sufficient independence to warrant their use.

SUMMARY. The S-FRIT is a short, individually administered instrument offered for use in screening and in making tentative diagnoses. In those situations in which one wished an individually administered test for screening purposes, the S-FRIT seems quite serviceable. However, the absence of sound reliability information about the instrument precludes its being recommended for this purpose. Deficits including insufficient reliability information and the probability of poor discriminant validity among the subscales leave me unable to recommend the test for any diagnostic purposes, tentative or otherwise.

Review of the Slosson Full-Range Intelligence Test by GERALD TINDAL, Professor of Behavioral Research and Teaching, University of Oregon, Eugene, OR:

The Slosson Full-Range Intelligence Test (S-FRIT) is designed to screen students on intelligence and provide a tentative diagnosis of intellectual strengths and weaknesses. In reviewing the technical manual, the following perspectives and issues emerge.

ADMINISTRATION. The materials provided by the authors include the following: (a) an examiner's manual, (b) a picture book and a Motor Response Form (to be used with a subset of the problems listed in the examiner's manual), (c) Item Profile/Score Summaries Form, (d) a Brief Score Form, and (e) a technical manual, including a Slosson Classification Chart.

In the examiner's manual, directions are provided to obtain optimal performance from students. Examiners are provided explicit strategies for establishing rapport, annotating performance, establishing basal and ceiling levels (even when more than one is obtained), computing chronological age, establishing and maintaining an appropriate testing environment, managing students who are reticent or recalcitrant, and reminding examiners of the importance of standard administration procedures (including prompts on items that should be timed, the use of scratch paper and pencil, and breaks in testing). The materials for administration are coordinated so that the examiner is provided verbatim directions on how to present each item and is cued when to present a figure in the Picture Book or to use the Motor Response Form.

When administering the test, the examiner records individual item responses as either correct or incorrect directly on either an Item Profiles/Score Summaries Form or a Brief Score Form.

The Item Profiles/Score Summaries Form is composed of four major sections:

1 and 2. A cover sheet with basic summary performance information listed above demographic data.

3. Two pages of performance levels on the 252 items (with age levels listed at intervals of the cumulative list) for four subdomains and the Best *g* Index (B*g*I). Each of the items is color coded so that the examiner knows in which subdomain or B*g*I (some of which are precoded) to add the score. For each subdomain, the total number of items coded is cumulatively listed at the bottom of each column.

4. The last page consists of three sections: (a) recording of scores (for general cognition and the cognitive subdomains), (b) comparison of subdomain scores, and (c) score profiles. A supplementary mode of interpretation is provided with the two scores from the Abstract and the Quantitative Indices added together to form the Performance Index.

The Brief Score Form is color coded so that three major test results can be recorded: Verbal Index (VI), Performance Index (PI), and Memory Index (MI), with these three indices added to form the Full-Range Index (FRIQ)

The S-FRIT takes about 20–35 minutes to administer, though the Brief Form can be used with fewer items and the scores copied from the Profiles/Score Summaries Form. The test is relatively efficient in great part because a basal is used for the administrator to find the level in which the student answers eight successive items correctly and then proceeds until the examinee hits a ceiling in which eight items are successively failed. This approach, like other traditional intelligence tests, keeps the test oriented to those items most appropriate for the student.

SCORING AND INTERPRETATION. Three S-FRIT Scores are available from administration of this test: (a) the Full-Range (FRIQ), (b) Rapid Cognitive Index (RCI), and (c) Best g Index (BgI). These scores are based on the following items:

The Full-Range Intelligence Quotient (FRIQ) is based on the total test performance (all 252 items). The S-FRIT's General Cognitive Index (CGI) is composed of four subdomains, each with subtest scores: Verbal Index (VI) with 36% of the total items, Abstract Index (AI) with 25% of the total items, Quantitative Index (AI) with 23% of the total items, and Memory Index (MI) with 16% of the total items.

The Rapid Cognitive Index (RCI) provides a quick estimate of general cognitive ability based on approximately half the items in the full S-FRIT (134 of the 252). No subdomain analysis is available when administering the RCI.

There are two supplementary interpretations for the Best g Index (BgI) and Abstract/Quantitative Performance Index (PI). The BgI is based on those items that, regardless of the specific domains to which the items belong, correlate highest with the S-FRIT total score (with 181 items serving as the base for this index).

The directions include clear descriptions for obtaining any of these three indices as well as the subdomain scores and supplementary summaries. The examiner records the basal (including all items passed before it) and adds all items answered correctly until the ceiling. In cases of two basals, the examiner is directed to take the earlier one; in cases of two ceilings, the higher one is taken. The examiner is clearly directed which items fit into which domains and summary scores through the use of color-coded and "stippled" recording boxes on the response form.

When interpreting performance through the use of derived scores, the examiner is directed to a technical manual that includes a norms table providing standard scores. This table is clearly organized with the raw scores listed inside the table text and the standard score on the left side. Each page of the norms contains a 3-month interval of age and three major cognitive indices on the left side and the four subdomains on the right side. The normative tables provide well-scaled conversions from ages 5 years to 21 years, 11 months. A mean of 100 and a standard deviation of 16 are used for the CGI scores and a mean of 50 and a standard deviation of 8 are used for all subdomain scores. Separate tables also are provided for obtaining confidence intervals, standard errors of measurement, and statistically significant score differences between S-FRIT subtests at both the 85% and 95% levels of confidence. Finally, for the S-FRIT, a table is provided for obtaining standard score conversions to several other tests (Wechsler, General Aptitude Test Battery, and College Entrance Examination Board) and other metrics (z, T, normal curve equivalent scores, stanines, and percentile rank).

TECHNICAL ADEQUACY INFORMATION. The normative sample is composed of 1,509 children from 37 states, ages 5–21. This sample is generally consistent with the 1980 census data with several exceptions, all of which are detailed in the manual. For example, gender, ethnicity, parent education, region, and community size are included in the comparison between the population participating in the normative sample and base rate of individuals in the U.S. For the most part, some deviations exist between them; furthermore, the test user should be cautioned that the normative sample was tested 10 years ago and comparisons made to census data from 20 years ago.

The technical manual provides clearly displayed data on reliability and validity information for the S-FRIT, though most of the studies are somewhat dated (conducted a decade ago). Both internal consistency and test reliability data are presented.

Construct validity is presented by reference to two types of intelligence (g): Crystallized and Fluid, with quantitative reasoning and recall information also considered. The authors assert that g, global ability, is the "composite of abilities, especially verbal abilities, that enables an individual to learn and recall information, communicate with others, recognize likeness and differences, reason quantitatively, and to apply these abilities in solving unique problems and dealing effectively with the environment" (examiner's manual, p. 8). Crystallized intelligence is a product of native ability, culture, and life experiences. "Fluid intelligence is defined as a relation perceiving capacity which represents one's potential intelligence, independent of socialization and education" (p. 9). Quantitative reasoning is the ability to make numerical comparisons. Recall information is the ability to remember what has been learned.

The authors assert that the test measures both general intelligence and specific subdomains. In the technical manual, the items are crosswalked for each subdomain. As they note, however, the Verbal Index (VI) dominates with 90 of the 252 items coded in this area. In each of these descriptions, the authors provide labels for the types of problems and reference confirmatory factor analyses conducted over 15 years ago.

A series of concurrent criterion-validity studies has been summarized in which other measures of intelligence were administered concurrently with the S-FRIT. Most conclusions resulted from studies conducted by the second author in the late 1980s. Generally, the correlations have been high-moderate to high, and when not as high as expected, the authors described very plausible explanations (such as age restrictions leading to reduced variance, etc.).

TEST SUMMARY AND RECOMMENDA-TIONS. The authors present a test of intelligence that provides school psychologists and others interested in measuring ability with a quick screener. The manuals and materials are clearly organized with details explicitly listing how to administer the test and interpret performance. The test is loosely based on a theory of intelligence that incorporates both inherited and learned components of performance, though no attempt is made to fit the items into the constructs of crystallized or fluid intelligence. Rather, the items follow this orientation and only vaguely range from those that may be answered indirectly by inference (generalization or induction-deduction) or directly from experience (learning in and out of school). For example, several items require the examinee to visually reassemble a picture displayed in parts. Is this a component of crystallized or fluid intelligence; or is it a component of quantitative or recall information? In other items, the examinee is directed to repeat sentences or numbers, which clearly are part of recall information. In summary, the construct validity of the test is not substantive with

depth; rather, it provides an organizing logic with thin data supporting it and fails to connect the items with summary constructs. The primary validity data comprise concurrent measures administered with the S-FRIT. Although the data consistently reveal reasonable correlations, an emphasis on decision making is lacking.

Several different summaries are presented, though some of them are questionable. For example, although the authors address the limitations of age equivalent scores, they assert that the scores are not inherently misleading but simply need to be used in the proper manner. And difference scores are presented among the various subdomains; yet they fail to mention that the reliability of difference scores is less than the reliability of the actual subdomain scores.

[81]

Social Competence and Behavior Evaluation, Preschool Edition.

Purpose: "Designed to assess patterns of social competence, affective expression, and adjustment difficulties."

Population: Children aged 30 months to 76 months.

Publication Date: 1995.

Acronym: SCBE.

Scores: 8 Basic scales (Depressive-Joyful, Anxious-Secure, Angry-Tolerant, Isolated-Integrated, Aggressive-Calm, Egotistical-Prosocial, Oppositional-Cooperative, Dependent-Autonomous); 4 Summary scales (Social Competence, Internalizing Problems, Externalizing Problems, General Adaptation).

Administration: Group.

Price Data, 1999: $75 per complete kit including 25 AutoScore™ forms and manual (67 pages); $33.50 per 25 AutoScore™ forms; $45 per manual.

Time: (15) minutes.

Comments: Ratings by teachers or other child care professionals.

Authors: Peter J. LaFreniere and Jean E. Dumas.

Publisher: Western Psychological Services.

Review of the Social Competence and Behavior Evaluation, Preschool Edition by RONALD A. MADLE, School Psychologist, Shikellamy School District, Sunbury, PA and Adjunct Associate Professor of School Psychology, Pennsylvania State University, University Park, PA:

TEST PURPOSE AND DESIGN. The Social Competence and Behavior Evaluation (Preschool Edition; SCBE)—previously known as the Preschool Socio-Affective Profile—is designed to "assess patterns of social competence, affective expression, and adjustment difficulties" (manual, p. 1). The authors indicate its function is to describe behavioral tendencies for the purposes of socialization and education rather than to classify children within diagnostic categories. The scale was formulated from a "developmental/adaptational perspective … which emphasized the functional significance of affect in regulating social exchange" (p. 33). As such as it appears that the SCBE is more appropriately thought of as a personality instrument or measure of temperament than a typical behavior rating scale.

The SCBE provides eight basic scales and four summary scales. Each basic scale includes five items describing successful adjustment and five describing adjustment difficulties. Three basic scales describe the child's manner of emotional expression (Depressive-Joyful, Anxious-Secure, Angry-Tolerant), three describe social interactions with peers (Isolated-Integrated, Aggressive-Calm, Egotistical-Prosocial), and two describe teacher-child relations (Oppositional-Cooperative, Dependent-Autonomous). The four summary scales were developed based on statistical analyses and include Social Competence (40 items), Internalizing Problems (20 items), Externalizing Problems (20 items), and General Adaptation (all 80 items).

ADMINISTRATION, SCORING, AND INTERPRETATION. The SCBE is easy and straightforward to use. It comes as an AutoScore™ form that combines administration, scoring, and display of the score profile.

Completion of the 80 items should take a caregiver approximately 15 minutes, although considerable exposure to the child is needed before completing the ratings. Although many items are observable, numerous ones will require considerable interpretation and value judgments by the rater (e.g., using terms such as "takes pleasure," "enjoys," or "delights in playing"). All items are scored on a 6-point scale ranging from *Almost NEVER occurs* to *Almost ALWAYS occurs*. A number of items are "reversed" to minimize response sets by the rater.

Scoring takes about 10 minutes. Procedures for calculating raw scores for each scale are clearly specified in both the manual and on the scoring form. Raw scores are then converted to normalized *T*-scores by plotting them on the SCBE Profile. Although numerical *T*-scores are clearly noted on the Profile, actual percentiles are difficult

to obtain and there is no table in the manual. Because the *T*-scores are normalized, percentiles could be obtained from standard tables; it would be useful to have this information in the manual. Completed scales are considered scorable if as many as seven items are left blank by substituting median values printed on the scoring form. This practice seems questionable because almost 10% of the items could have been left blank.

The manual presents extensive information on the interpretation of each scale, as well as nine detailed case studies describing the use of the scale in applied situations.

STANDARDIZATION. Early development of the SCBE was completed in Quebec with French-Canadian children and the manual details this work. The published scale was designed to make the measure available to the U.S. clinician and educator. The U.S. standardization sample consisted of 1,263 children between the ages of 30 and 78 months. They were selected from six sites in Indiana and Colorado. All respondents were preschool teachers and were overwhelmingly (95%) female. Only a small percentage (8.3%) of the sample was below age 4. Although the gender distribution of the children was good compared to 1991 U.S. Census data, the norm group oversamples low SES parents, although statistical simulation studies indicated this made no difference. The manual also states that the percentage of black children was "slightly above" the census distribution. The tabular breakdown, however, suggests considerable overrepresentation (20.6% versus 15%). Only separate norms for males and females are presented.

RELIABILITY. Estimates of interrater agreement and internal consistency are reported for each of the eight basic scales. The manual fails, however, to report reliability information on any of the four composites.

Interrater agreement was assessed only with the Indiana sample. Interrater agreement estimates were in the range of .72 to .89, similar to earlier Canadian results.

Internal consistency (coefficient alpha = .80 to .89) was reported across the Indiana and Colorado samples combined. No U.S. test-retest information is presented, although the Canadian information indicated estimates of 2-week test-retest reliability (.74–.87) and 6-month (.59–.70) stability for the eight subscales.

VALIDITY. Both construct and criterion validity research is reported. It is stated that content validity evidence is available in the manual, but it is not clear to what information this refers. Construct validity was examined primarily through independent factor analyses of the Colorado and Indiana samples. A relatively consistent factor structure, consisting of Internalizing Problems, Externalizing Problems, and Social Competence was obtained in each sample, as well as in the earlier Canadian research.

Convergent and discriminant validity were examined through correlation of the SCBE with the Achenbach Child Behavior Checklist (CBCL) for 177 of the French-Canadian children. Only the Internalizing and Externalizing dimensions were considered. Although convergent validity appears to be adequate for the scales, discriminant validity evidence was less convincing. For example, Internalizing Problems correlated equally well with the CBCL Internalizing and Externalizing scores.

Criterion validity was assessed in a study of 126 children in Montreal using peer sociometrics and direct observation criterion measures. The study primarily validated the social competence and anxious-withdrawn aspects of the scale. A subsequent chapter in the manual presents three additional studies that expand on the validity of scores from the scale. Each uses the "SCBE Typological Approach" (socially competent, anxious-withdrawn, angry-aggressive, or average). Although this system is described in the research in the manual, it is not a formal component of the published scale.

SUMMARY. The SCBE presents a promising approach to assessing preschool social and emotional characteristics. Its development, however, is incomplete and flawed and it cannot be recommended for use as other than a supplemental scale. The norm sample's quality is more typical of that seen in scales developed 10 or more years ago. Also, most development research stresses the basic scales and less information is available on more global composites or the typological approach used in some of the research. Other better developed measures such as the Achenbach Child Behavior Checklist (13:55) or the Behavior Assessment System for Children (13:34) are more rigorously developed and remain the instruments of choice.

Review of the Social Competence and Behavior Evaluation, Preschool Edition by G. MICHAEL POTEAT, Associate Professor of Psychology, East Carolina University, Greenville, NC:

The Social Competence and Behavior Evaluation, Preschool Edition (SCBE) is a rating scale designed to measure the social competence and affective, expressive, and adjustment difficulties in children from 30 to 78 months of age. The SCBE is a standardized and commercially published version of an earlier instrument—the Preschool Socio-Affective Profile (PSP)—designed to be completed by the student's teacher. Each item is a behavioral descriptor (e.g., Active, ready to play), which is rated as *Never* (1), *Sometimes* (2 or 3), *Often* (4 or 5), or *Always* (6). The SCBE is described as providing (a) a standardized description of behavior, (b) a measure of social competence, (c) a differential assessment of emotional and behavioral problems, (d) data that are reliable and consistent, and (e) a method for evaluating changes that are functions of growth or treatment.

The 80 items are divided into eight basic scales (10 items each) and four summary scales. Three of the basic scales describe the child's typical or "characteristic" manner of emotional expression and are labeled using negative and positive poles: Depressive-Joyful, Anxious-Secure, and Angry-Tolerant. Three other basic scales are designed to describe social interactions with peers: Isolated-Integrated, Aggressive-Calm, and Egotistical-Prosocial. The last two scales are measures of teacher-child interactions: Oppositional-Cooperative and Dependent-Autonomous. Four summary scales are described as being developed on the basis of extensive statistical analysis and are labeled: Social Competence (based on 40 items), Internalizing Problems (20 items), and Externalizing Problems (20 items). The last summary scale is labeled General Adaptation and is based on all 80 items.

Scoring the SCBE is done by opening the score form, which employs carbon paper and then summing items following the printed directions. The raw scores are next transferred to the profile sheet, which has *T*-scores and percentile ranks. One side of the profile sheet has *T*-scores based on norms for boys and the other side has norms for girls. The instructions are clear and math checks are included to help reduce the number of scoring errors. Teachers should have no problem in obtaining the raw scores and transferring the raw scores to the profile sheet. The manual also contains a completed example of a form and profile sheet but the instructions on the form are satisfactory. All scales are constructed so that high *T*-scores are positive and low *T*-scores are indicative of problems. The *T*-scores are based on raw scores that have been transformed and normalized. *T*-scores of 63 or higher are indicative of good adjustment and *T*-scores of 37 or lower are interpreted as indicative of adjustment problems.

The technical and psychometric properties of the SCBE are overall very good. The initial version of the SCBE was published in French and preliminary data and psychometric properties are reported based on a sample of 979 French-Canadian preschool children. Based on the results obtained with the French version, the instrument was translated into English and standardized on a sample of 1,263 U.S. children at six sites in two states. The sample includes 631 girls and 632 boys from Colorado and Indiana who were enrolled in preschool classes. Modal age was 5 years (41.7%). Children aged 4 years (27.5%) and 6 years (22.5%) were also well represented but only 8.3% of the children were in the 3-year-old group. Age was significantly positively correlated with social competence and negatively correlated with behavioral problems, but the norms did not indicate any practically significant age differences. The magnitude of the correlation between age and the SCBE scales ranges from .09 to .32 with most of the correlation coefficients clustering around .20.

Comparison of the demographic characteristics of the normative sample to those of the U.S. show that children with less education and from Black families were overrepresented. Children from Hispanic families and children from families with some college or a college degree were underrepresented. The authors report the SES effects were relatively small and none of the correlations between SES and the SCBE were statistically significant. Significant differences were found between boys and girls using multiple *t*-tests with probability levels adjusted using Bonferroni's correction. Boys were found to have significantly more negative ratings than girls for Externalizing Problems and the four associated basic scales. Boys also had significantly less positive ratings on Social Competence and General Adaptation.

The reliability and internal consistency estimates for the SCBE are good. Interrater reliability estimates for the ratings of the 824 students in the Indiana sample were between .72 and .89. The internal consistency (using Cronbach's alpha) indices for the eight standard scales ranged from .80 to .89 in both the Indiana and Colorado samples.

Numerous data are presented to support the validity of the SCBE. Construct validity is evidenced in the factor structure of the SCBE, which demonstrates that the theoretical structure of the instrument (as a measure of social competence, externalizing problems, and internalizing problems) is supported by the data obtained in both the Indiana and the Colorado sample. Other evidence for the construct validity of the SCBE was obtained in a convergent and discriminant analysis comparing the SCBE with the Child Behavior Checklist (CBCL; Edelbrock & Achenbach, 1984). The pattern of correlations between the scales of the SCBE and CBCL is supportive of the construct validity of the SCBE (e.g., the Anxiety scale of the CBCL had a high correlation with Internalizing Problems and a low correlation with Externalizing Problems on the SCBE).

Criterion-related validity was evaluated by comparing the SCBE with measures of peer sociometrics and direct observations of behavior. Based on a random sample of 126 children enrolled in preschool in the Montreal area, four groups were identified as socially competent (S-C), anxious-withdrawn (A-W), angry-aggressive (A-A), and average (AV). Analysis of variance demonstrated significant differences between the groups with the A-W children spending more time in noninteraction than the other groups, and the A-A group receiving significantly more peer rejection (negative peer nominations). The data are presented in some detail and were the basis for a publication (LaFreniere, Dumas, Capuano, & Dubeau, 1992). Additional information is presented on three other developmental and clinical studies using the SCBE, which are also indicative of the instrument's validity and utility.

In summary, the SCBE is a well-developed instrument with reasonably good psychometric properties. The test manual is well done with a great deal of technical information and details from a number of case studies. The manual contains information related to both research and clinical applications. Caution is advised in using the norms with 3-year-old children, and the limitations of the normative sample (the lack of geographical variation and the underrepresentation of children from higher SES families) should be noted. The SCBE is recommended for use as an aid in the identification of preschool children who have problems in the area of social competence and in research on children's social development. As the authors of the SCBE point out, the instrument should not be used as the sole basis for clinical identification but should be viewed as providing a basis for hypotheses about the behavior of individual children, which requires other collaboration.

REVIEWER'S REFERENCES

Edelbrock, C. S., & Achenbach, T. M. (1984). The teacher version of the child behavior profile: I. Boys aged 6–11. *Journal of Consulting and Clinical Child Psychology, 52*, 207–217.
LaFreniere, P. J., Dumas, J. R., Capuano, F., & Dubeau, D. (1992). The development of and validation of the preschool socioaffective profile. *Psychological Assessment: Journal of Consulting and Clinical Psychology, 4*(4), 442–450.

[82]
STAR Reading™.

Purpose: A computer-adaptive reading test and database designed "to quickly and accurately place students in books at the appropriate reading level."
Population: Grades 1–12.
Publication Date: 1997–1998.
Scores: Total score only.
Administration: Individual.
Price Data, 1998: $1,499 per school license for up to 200 students, including administrator's manual (173 pages), 5 teacher's guides, norms/technical manual (94 pages), 1-year Expert Support Plan, and pre-test instruction kit; $399 per single-computer license, including administrator's manual, Quick Install card, 1-year Expert Support Plan, and pretest instruction kit.
Time: [10] minutes.
Comments: Provides grade equivalents, percentile scores, and instructional reading level; available for both Macintosh and IBM/Windows computers; can be repeated through school year to track growth at no extra cost.
Author: Advantage Learning Systems, Inc.
Publisher: Advantage Learning Systems, Inc.

Review of the STAR Reading by THERESA VOLPE-JOHNSTONE, Clinical and School Psychologist, Pleasanton, CA:

The STAR Reading is a computerized system developed to serve two purposes: (a) provide quick and accurate estimates of instructional reading levels (IRL), and (b) provide an estimate of students' reading levels compared to national norms. In doing so, this test purports to diagnose reading ability and help assess reading progress in 13 minutes or less with little administration effort. The test is dynamically scored using Item Response Theory through Adaptive Branching where the program weighs each answer provided by the student and presents the next question at an appropriate difficulty level. It is used primarily in the school setting and can yield valuable information at the teacher level in identifying children who need remediation/enrichment, at the principal level in obtaining class grade or year-to-year comparison, and at the district level for comparing data across schools, grades, or special student populations. The program may be installed on a Macintosh 68020 or an IBM-compatible 80386 with other provisions, such as space availability and installed memory. STAR Reading can be installed as a stand-alone program or placed on the network server (reviewer recommended) with a student capacity of 200 before necessitating the purchase of expansion codes in units of 50.

A sample size of 13,846 was used for pilot testing for content development and approximated the national school population well. Participation rates by grade were appropriate but ranged from 1,504 for Grade 8 to 573 for Grade 12. Item difficulty values provided an adequate basis for validating and norming the STAR Reading with sufficient variations in test scores. Normative data were subsequently based on a large sample (approximately 42,000), which was representative of the national population and balanced for demographics, SES, geographic region, and school type. In the development it is important to note that minority students typically scored lower than white grade peers with differences on the order of one-half to one standard deviation. This test should not be used with nonnative English speakers until English proficiency has been established. Special care was taken to minimize the influence of cultural factors including evaluating items for offensiveness. The normative data (percentile ranks and grade equivalents) are based on the unit-interval frequency distributions of the scaled scores of the students' first test. The data were weighted by demographic region and then by the type/size and SES of the school system. However, the tabled values indicated very minimal differences between weighted and unweighted scores.

In estimating reliability, measuring the internal-consistency of the STAR Reading was deemed inappropriate because it is a computer-adaptive test with many test forms. The authors chose test-retest estimation with alternative forms that were incorrectly stated as resulting in coefficients of stability and equivalence. This coefficient would be produced if there were relatively long periods of time separating administration. In this instance, "the median date of administration for the first test was April 25, 1996; the median date for the second test was April 30, 1996" (manual, p. 30), which suggests a coefficient of equivalence was obtained. This method was done to insure that no measurable growth in reading ability occurred between the two tests. Content-sampling would be a source of error, but given the method of content development, all individuals would be affected uniformly. Reliability estimates ranged from .85 to .95 for scaled scores, and from .79 to .91 for instructional reading levels (IRLs). Although there was consideration of practice effects, (a) the nature of adaptive branching would not allow for it, and (b) the retest scores were slightly lower than were the results of the first test, suggesting that practice was not an influencing factor. The standard errors of measurement (*SEM*) for the IRLs were impressive, with no more than a 1.1 grade level fluctuation due to chance across the grade span.

For the STAR Reading, it was sufficient to demonstrate content validity for the assessment of reading ability. The instrument appears to have strong content validity at least up to Grade 8. It was developed using 1995 updated vocabulary lists that were based on the Educational Development Laboratory's *A Revised Core Vocabulary* (1969), which the authors report is widely used in creating educational instruments. The STAR Reading correlated highly with at least three different, and common, reading tests spanning Grades 1 through 8. However, the coefficients were based on the STAR Reading versus older data by at least one year. There were too few comparisons with insufficient sample sizes to be considered as having established validity for Grades 9 through 12. The authors welcome additional data for validation purposes and continued supporting evidence is needed. The STAR Reading is prescriptive rather than predictive. It purports to measure growth based on external program implementation.

The STAR Reading makes use of instructional reading levels as a construct but validation was not conducted. It was simply defined as the "highest reading level at which the student can answer 80% or more of the items correctly" (manual, p. 45). Therefore, the STAR Reading does provide quick estimates of the IRLS but their accuracy may be questionable.

Administrating the STAR Reading to replicate conditions used to demonstrate validity is a simple task. Directions come with easy-to-use transparencies for pretest instructions that can be taught to a class or one student at a time and can be administered up to five times per year. The STAR Reading comes with administrator, teacher, and pretest instruction guides that are all well-written, user-friendly manuals with excellent indices. This includes installing the program, setting up program preferences, working with lists of students, testing the students, and working with the various reports. The computer monitors the student progress item-by-item and guides the student toward completion without allowing frustration levels to be reached.

Results are reported through one, or all, of the program's 10 types of standard or customized reports for evaluating student test performance. Scores are delineated via the criterion-referenced Instructional Reading Level (IRL), and the norm-referenced Grade Equivalent (GE), Percentile Rank (PR), and Normal Curve Equivalent (NCE) scores.

Instructional Reading Levels indicate the reading level at which students can recognize words and understand instructional material with some assistance. The GE indicates the normal grade placement of students for whom a particular score is typical. Grade equivalents are not linear and therefore this is not an equal-interval scale. Caution should be taken in averaging GE scores across grades particularly when using the Summary Report. Percentile ranks show how an individual student's performance compares to same-grade peers. Normal Curve Equivalents act similarly to PRs but are based on an equal interval scale. The norm-referenced scores are based on the grade placement of the student at the time of the test. Therefore, it is crucial to use the correct grade placement values in order for the results to be accurate.

Two additional scores may be obtained: the Zone of Proximal Development (ZPD) and Diagnostic Codes, both derived from GEs. The ZPD defines the reading range from which students should be selecting books to achieve optimal reading growth without experiencing frustration. The Diagnostic Code ranges from 01 to 09 (the higher the GE, the higher the diagnostic code) and represents behavioral characteristics of readers at particular stages of development. These codes were not statistically validated. Scaled scores are available only on the Test Record Report, which generates results of every test taken during a specified time period for the student selected. Scaled scores range from 50 to 1,350 and are based on a Bayesian statistical model. Although scaled scores allow comparability among tests and were used to obtain PRs and NCEs, these scores were not clearly explained and are not easily interpreted.

Several assets were built into the STAR Reading. Each time the student takes a test, the program automatically begins just below the last tested reading level. The number of items presented reduces each time the student tests. Therefore, the STAR Reading does assess reading progress in 13 minutes or less. Teachers can group or sort students in characteristic ways. The program can be used in conjunction with, and may have been developed for, the Accelerated Reader™ to help match the right books for an individual's reading level. Program safeguards prevent unauthorized access to test content by program encryption, password protection, access levels, keydisk requirement, and test monitoring. The norming sample was of more than adequate size, and was sufficiently representative to establish appropriate norms and to provide evidence of students' reading ability from Grades 1 through 8.

SUMMARY. It seems that the STAR Reading was specifically developed to work well with Accelerated Reader. This is a shortcoming. If this program were not part of the curriculum, another type of organized reading program would need to be in place for this test to be useful. The results of the tests are based on grade placement and the ensuing reports are boilerplate—based on standard score and sequencing paradigms for the field of reading education that may not fit the profile of a student. Insufficient validity evidence is presented for 9th through 12th grades or for IRLs. This test has great potential but continued validation studies to support conclusions regarding the use of the STAR Reading for its entire intended purpose is needed.

Review of the STAR Reading by SANDRA WARD, Associate Professor of Education, The College of William and Mary, Williamsburg, VA:

The STAR Reading is an individually administered, computerized test of reading for Grades 1–12. The publishers state two main purposes of the STAR Reading: (a) to provide instructional reading levels, and (b) to compare reading levels to national norms. The test is not intended for use in promotion/placement decisions. The average completion time for the test is 7–8 minutes with an average of 30 items per administration. The computer input necessary for test completion is limited to four numeric keys, so necessary computer skills are minimized for examinees.

The items of the STAR Reading represent a vocabulary-in-context format that is similar to a cloze technique. Each item consists of a sentence with a missing word. The examinee must select the correct response for the missing word from three or four choices, within a 60- or 45-second time limit, depending on grade level. The correct response fits both the semantics and syntax of the sentence. Although the item format was chosen because success depends on comprehension of reading material, there is some concern regarding the artificial nature of the task. The presentation of only one sentence may not provide sufficient context for the reader. It appears that this instrument represents a measure of vocabulary development as well as reading comprehension.

In addition to careful writing, reviewing, and editing of items, an extensive item validation study included 13,846 students who were tested on a pool of 1,330 items. Although this sample matched national percentages for socioeconomic status and school type and enrollment, it was not representative for geographic region. The editing process included review of all items for possible gender and/or ethnic group bias; however, no statistical procedures were implemented. Final item selection was based on analyses of increased performance across grade levels, discrimination ability, reduced variability in item difficulty, and average response latency. The final selection resulted in a large item pool from which test items are selected. Consequently, the repetition of items in multiple administrations is minimized. A major advantage of the STAR Reading computer administration is the adaptive testing component. The program administers items of varying difficulty based on the students' responses, until a sufficient amount of data is gathered to obtain a reliable scaled score and indication of instructional level.

The STAR Reading was normed on 42,000 students from 171 schools. Sample sizes ranged from 326 in Grade 12 to 5,977 in Grade 5. The size of this sample is sufficient at every grade level. The variables controlled for in the standardization included geographic region, school system type, school system size, and socioeconomic status. The whole sample closely matched national characteristics on these variables; however, the representativeness at each grade level is not reported. Although school system location and instructional expenditures were not controlled for, the data on these variables closely matched national averages. With respect to ethnicity, only Hispanic students were underrepresented. The publishers noted that minority groups showed an average score between 1/2 to 1 standard deviation below the mean, which is consistent with other standardized tests of ability and achievement. The normative data for the test consist of percentile ranks and grade equivalents. Although scaled scores are discussed, the mean and standard deviation are not provided.

Average test-retest reliabilities are adequate for screening purposes and ranged from .79 to .91 with an average of 5 days between administrations. The publishers correctly acknowledge that the computer-adaptive testing restricts the methods for determining internal consistency reliability. However, the publishers do not adequately explain how they determined item functioning in relation to item response theory. Although *SEM* estimates are provided, these are difficult to interpret because the standard score scale is not explained.

Data are provided to support concurrent and construct validity of test scores. Scores from the STAR Reading correlate sufficiently (.60 or higher) with scores from widely used standardized tests of reading ability across grade levels. Support for content validity is demonstrated through the purposeful approach in developing the instrument. Furthermore, STAR Reading scores increase with grade level, as would be expected for reading ability. It should be noted that the content validity is for a single item type that is highly dependent on vocabulary knowledge as well as reading comprehension. No evidence is presented for predictive validity; however, the publishers openly state that this test should not be used for placement or promotion decisions.

A proprietary Bayesian statistical model was used to convert scores to a common scale. Because the parameters and methodology of this model are not disclosed, it cannot be fully evaluated. Although scaled scores were reported to range from 50 to 1,350, no mean or standard deviation was reported. The norm-referenced score emphasized for interpretation is the grade equivalent. The publishers do an excellent job explaining the interpretation and pitfalls of grade equivalents. It is possible to convert scores to percentile ranks and normal curve equivalents. The instructional reading level is computed based on the level at which the examinee earned 80% proficiency. The program produces a Zone of Proximal Development score that is the readability level range from which students should select books to achieve optimally without frustration.

The Test Administrator's Manual and the Teacher's Guide are written in a straightforward and step-by-step manner. They assume minimal computer expertise and are very user-friendly. These manuals include information on program installation and a tutorial. Additionally, basic set-up, testing, and reporting procedures are outlined. Directions are brief with many examples, and they provide useful practical information. A number of different reports are available from the STAR Reading, depending on the type of information the examiner desires. These reports include Test Activity Report, Growth Report, Summary Report, Test Record Report, and Diagnostic Report.

SUMMARY. The STAR Reading is a computerized measure of reading ability that produces grade equivalents and instructional reading levels. Directions for administration and scoring are straightforward and user-friendly. Although the standardization sample is adequate, the discussion of standard scores is confusing because the scale is never provided. The publishers provide excellent guidelines for the interpretation of grade equivalents. Specific information is provided to support the test's stability reliability and validity. A major concern regarding the use of the STAR Reading in establishing reading levels is its reliance on a single item type that represents an artificial reading task and depends heavily on vocabulary development. Consequently, this measure should be used as a screening device. Supplementary data on reading ability should be collected to support conclusions regarding reading level. The STAR Reading should not be used for the diagnosis of reading disabilities nor used for placement decisions.

[83]
START—Strategic Assessment of Readiness for Training.

Purpose: Designed to diagnose adult's learning strengths and weaknesses.
Population: Adults.
Publication Date: 1994.
Acronym: START.
Scores, 8: Anxiety, Attitude, Motivation, Concentration, Identifying Important Information, Knowledge Acquisition Strategies, Monitoring Learning, Time Management.
Administration: Group.
Price Data, 1996: $19.95 per user's manual (21 pages); $9.95 per assessment and learner's guide (volume discounts available).
Time: (15) minutes.
Comments: Self-administered; self-scored.
Authors: Claire E. Weinstein and David R. Palmer.
Publisher: H & H Publishing Company, Inc.

Review of START—Strategic Assessment of Readiness for Training by PHILLIP L. ACKERMAN, Professor of Psychology, Georgia Institute of Technology, Atlanta, GA:

The START is described by the authors as a "powerful assessment tool designed to diagnose adults' learning strengths and weaknesses and to provide prescriptive information and guidelines for both trainers and learners" (user's manual, p. 2). The authors state that the START is an outgrowth of the LASSI (Learning and Study Strategies Inventory), and was developed for human resource development specialists and trainers to assess adults in the workplace, to design remediation treatments, and to "modify and adapt instruction" (p. 14) in the workplace. They advise that the START "has excellent psychometric properties and is based on a model of strategic learning" (p. 2). The manual indicates that START is not designed for selection for employment "or as the sole criteria [*sic*] for participation in training opportunities" (p. 2). START is recommended for providing diagnostic feedback to employees/trainees, and as an aid to match training methods to trainee characteristics. There are no references in the manual to any research with the instrument or to the model that underlies the instrument.

RELIABILITY/VALIDITY. The only quantitative "reliability" data provided are actually measures of internal consistency (coefficient alpha), and these range from .65 to .87, but only two scales exceeded an alpha of .80, suggesting that most of the subscales are relatively heterogeneous. No aggregation of scale scores is recommended in the manual. No data are provided that indicate whether the START is capable of assessing the kinds of remediation-based changes that are mentioned as a purpose of the measure. Content validity was established by one survey of experts about a list of scales, and then a follow-up review by "more than 40 experts" of "more than 200 items" (p. 14). No criterion-related validity data are presented, either predictive or concurrent. No correlations between the scales of the START are presented with any other instruments. Minimal data are presented about the standardization sample, only a description of the sample as "226 persons enrolled in training programs at several different corporations" (p. 15). The only construct validity data presented are wholly inadequate for evaluation of the validity of the START. They consist of the intercorrelations of the eight scales, and a "factor analysis" that was a "principal components" analysis (obviously a confusion of the two different methods of analysis). Regardless, eight factors were extracted from the eight-variable correlation matrix, a fact that the authors regard as showing: "It is clear from this table that each scale loads on one and only one dimension" (p. 15). Such an analysis is completely uninformative, because it clearly violates a central tenet of factor analysis (that is, to represent a matrix of correlations by means of a smaller number of latent hypothetical factors). When eight factors are derived from eight variables, the result is a foregone conclusion, and not a property of the constructs. My own calculation of a factor analysis of the eight variables showed clearly that the largest number of defensible underlying factors was four (three by Kaiser's rule, and four by the Humphreys-Montanelli parallel analysis), and clearly demonstrated a lack of independence of the eight scales. Therefore, in the absence of any additional evidence, the only validation data presented in the manual suggest that the START should not be used to assess eight different constructs.

NORMS. Reported norms are inadequate to make judgments about which persons may appropriately take this test, such as education or experience background characteristics. No data describe gender or race ethnic group differences in scores. One of the more distressing aspects of the START is that discrepancies exist between the means and standard deviations shown for the norming sample (where scale means range from 22.04 to 29.18, and standard deviations range from 3.93 to 5.81), and the self-scoring graph for respondents to interpret their scores (which show "high scores" to be any scale score higher than 29, and "low scores" to be any score lower than 21). Thus, any respondent who obtains a mean score on the Attitude scale is told that they are "high" on this scale, and any respondent with a z-score of -.22 (corresponding to 41% of the norming sample) is told that they are "low" on "Time Management."

ADMINISTRATION/INTERPRETATION. Administration of the START is straightforward. The respondent is told that the measure is to be used to "provide you with valuable information about yourself" (p. 1); that the START "provides a list of suggestions for improving your skills" (p. 1); and that it "can be used by your trainers to help adapt their instruction" (p. 1). The START is self-scoring; the respondent tallies and then graphs the scale scores on another page (although the key for each scale is presented so participants can see the scheme while completing the form).

After completing the summation of scale scores, the rest of the test booklet is devoted to directions for interpreting the scale scores. There are separate recommendations for only low scores on each scale. Low Anxiety (where a low score indicates high anxiety) respondents are told that "You may want to think about why you are in the training program" (p. 14) or "you may want to use stress management techniques like muscle relaxation or mediation before each training session" (p. 14). Low Motivation respondents are told to "consider some of the actions suggested in the discussion of low Attitude Scale scores" (p. 15). Respondents who are low on Concentration are told to "get a good night's sleep before training sessions" (p. 16). Such recommendations are given without any documentation in the manual suggesting differential effectiveness with persons of different attributes, or whether the recommendations often take the form of Barnum statements, those that are clearly true, regardless of scale scores. (For example, imagine telling any trainee

that he/she need *not* get a good night's sleep before training, regardless of score.)

The recommendations to the trainer are no better than those to the respondent. Trainers with a group of persons showing high levels of anxiety are told to "Check the level of difficulty of the course materials for the target population" (p. 9); for a group that is low in Attitude, trainers are told to "Try to create a supportive and friendly environment so that the trainees enjoy being there" (p. 10); and for those low on Identifying Important Information, trainers are told to "Make sure the instructional pace is not too fast for your participants" (p. 11).

SUMMARY. As a diagnostic instrument for trainees, a structured remediation plan for respondents, and a mechanism for trainers to tailor instruction for their trainees, this instrument has not demonstrated any of the characteristics that are concordant with standard guidelines. Both construct and criterion-related validity data are lacking, and the data that exist fail to support the assertions of the independence of the eight scales. The interpretations of scale scores are flawed by placing average or nearly average responses into high-score or low-score categories, without any diagnostic validation data to support such categorizations. The recommendations for both respondents and trainers are either not demonstrated to be supported by data of differential treatment effects, or are so general as to be self-evident or tautological.

Review of the START—Strategic Assessment of Readiness for Training by PATRICIA A. BACH-ELOR, Professor of Psychology, California State University at Long Beach, Long Beach, CA:

The Strategic Assessment of Readiness for Training (START) is designed as a self-administered and self-scored assessment of an adult's learning strengths and weaknesses. START is composed of eight scales that serve as a prescriptive and diagnostic measure that establishes a baseline, identifies areas of weaknesses and strengths, and thereby enables trainers to tailor instruction to create an effective and efficient learning environment. The transfer and extension of newly acquired ideas, knowledge, and skills beyond a specific learning or training experience may also be enhanced by the identification and targeting of a participant's responsiveness to a learning program. The eight scales, which assess key aspects of an adult's ability to benefit from training/education, are: *Anxiety* (degree of tension associated with performance in a learning environment), *Attitude* (level of commitment to training or value placed upon training), *Motivation* (acceptance of responsibility for active participation in training environment), *Concentration* (ability to focus and maintain attention on learning tasks or presentation of material), *Identifying Important Information* (ability to select and transfer important information), *Knowledge Acquisition Strategies* (ability to learn new information and skills), *Monitoring Learning* (degree to which learning is monitored/reviewed during learning program), and *Time Management* (ability to create and adhere to an effective schedule).

START is a self-administered, self-scored 56-item instrument. Most participants can complete the instrument in 15 minutes, although there is no time limit. The scores for each scale are derived by summing the responses to the seven items comprising each of the eight scales. This calculation is facilitated by a "scoring page" provided in the test manual. Also included is a graph grid with preprinted lines indicating the range of high scores (top 25%), middle scores (next 25%), and low scores (bottom 50%). These ranges of performance were not further detailed or justified. However, experts who were consulted agreed upon these designations (user's manual, p. 8). The plot of scale scores results in a visual presentation of the participant's responses and serves as a reference during the interpretative phase of the assessment. Low or even middle scorers on any of the scales are referred to the corresponding "Suggestion" section. Each of the "Suggestion" sections interprets the scale, describes behaviors/attitudes that may lead to low scores, and offers strategies to improve performance. Learners, trainers, and/or program developers may design and modify instructional and learning environments to enhance learning readiness based on this knowledge. The language is upbeat, positively stated, and clearly articulated. The 10 to 16 suggestions per scale are appropriate and specific to producing an effective learning environment. The suggestions can be modified and tailored to a variety of learning situations and learners.

DEVELOPMENT. Thirty learning, adult education, and human resource development specialists generated the concept of nine scales in the initial version of the START. Psychometricians and learning specialists prepared 200 items, which were critically reviewed by 40 experts (half new to the START). These items were revised, pilot tested, and reanalyzed to produce 126 items, which were pilot tested and revised to 90 items. Thirty experts (two-thirds were among the earlier experts) reviewed and field tested this version of the START on trainees and participants in professional organizations, continuing education settings, manufacturing plants, and technical services. The current version of the START (56 items) is the result of these trials.

RELIABILITY. Evidence of the internal consistency reliability of the START was assessed by computing coefficient alpha indices for each scale. These coefficients were: *Anxiety* .87, *Attitude* .71, *Motivation* .65, *Concentration* .83, *Identifying Important Information* .75, *Knowledge Acquisition* .78, *Monitoring* .78, and *Time Management* .76. These seven-item scales can be considered to possess evidence of modest internal consistency reliability.

VALIDITY. The START manual does not contain a "Validity" section. However, content validity evidence can be inferred by the description of a series of reviews by experts in the fields of human learning, adult education, and resource development. The reported consensus of approximately 50 experts can be taken as sufficient evidence of the existence of content validity of the START scales. No attempt was made to address the construct validity of the START scales. The *Standards for Educational and Psychological Testing* (AERA, APA, & NCME, 1985) require such an investigation. In an otherwise carefully prepared manual, the assessment of such a critical psychometric quality was an obvious and glaring omission. Without an inquiry into the accuracy of the START scales, the usefulness of the instrument in practical applications is dubious.

NORMATIVE GROUPS. Unfortunately, no demographic or other information is provided about the adults who participated in the standardization sample. Without such information about the normative sample of the START, test users would be unable to evaluate if the test is appropriate for a specific application or to interpret performance with any confidence.

SUMMARY. The START consists of eight scales that assess an adult's learning strengths and weaknesses. It is a self-administered and self-scored prescriptive and diagnostic measure that may facilitate learners and trainers to modify an educational setting to enhance learning readiness. The user's manual of the START is a clearly articulated instructional guide that will benefit a variety of practitioners in the educational arena. The suggestions are relevant and appropriate for the stated target audience. Internal consistency estimates of the START scales reveal modest reliability; however, evidence is lacking regarding construct validity. The appropriateness of the use and interpretation of the START is questionable until such an assessment is presented to test users. The standardization sample needs to be described in detail. Additionally, normative and interpretative data are required before meaningful comparisons can be made. Test users cannot interpret scores or justify conclusions reached without such information.

REVIEWER'S REFERENCE

American Educational Research Association, American Psychological Association, & National Council on Measurement in Education. (1985). *Standards for educational and psychological testing.* Washington, DC: American Psychological Association, Inc.

[84]
State-Trait Anger Expression Inventory.

Purpose: Designed to measure "the experience and expression of anger."
Population: Ages 13 and up.
Publication Dates: 1979–1996.
Acronym: STAXI.
Scores, 8: State Anger, Trait Anger (Angry Temperament, Angry Reaction), Anger-in, Anger-out, Anger Control, Anger Expression.
Administration: Group or individual.
Editions, 2: Hand-scored, machine-scored.
Price Data, 1996: $74 per kit including manual ('96, 46 pages), 50 item booklets, and 50 rating sheets; $27 per manual; $29 per 50 item booklets; $29 per 50 rating sheets.
Time: (10–12) minutes.
Comments: Test forms are entitled Self-Rating Questionnaire; Self-rating; Form G recommended for large scale research.
Author: Charles D. Spielberger.
Publisher: Psychological Assessment Resources, Inc.
Cross References: See T5:2496 (6 references); for reviews by David J. Pittenger and Alan J. Raphael of the Revised Research Edition, see 13:296 (52 references); see also T4:2562 (12 references); for reviews by Bruce H. Biskin and Paul Retzlaff of the STAXI-Research Edition, see 11:379 (8 references).
[Editor's Note: These reviews are based on test materials received prior to 1999. The publisher advised in August 1999 that this test has been revised. The STAXI-2 will be reviewed in a future *MMY.*]

Review of the State-Trait Anger Expression Inventory by ROBERT J. DRUMMOND, Professor, Division of Educational Services and Research, University of North Florida, Jacksonville, FL:

The State-Trait Anger Expression Inventory (STAXI) is a 44-item inventory developed for two major purposes: first, to help assess components of anger that could be used in the assessment of normal and abnormal behavior, and second, to investigate the role of various components of anger to the development of medical conditions. Spielberger's construct of anger has two major components, state anger and trait anger. The STAXI consists of six scales and two subscales. The inventory has three parts: How I feel right now (10 items), How I generally feel (10 items), and When angry or furious (24 items). A 4-point Likert scale is utilized—*not at all* to *very much so* and *almost never* to *almost always.*

State Anger assesses the intensity of angry feelings the client has at a particular moment of time. Trait Anger, on the other hand, reflects the disposition of the individual to experience anger and is made up of two subscales, Angry Temperament and Angry Reaction. Anger-in measures how often the individual's anger is turned inside or suppressed. Anger-out taps anger directed toward other individuals and objects in the environment. Anger Control asks for the frequency the individual tries to control the expression of anger. Anger Expression measures the degree to which anger is expressed regardless of the direction of expression.

The STAXI can be administered to individuals age 13 through adulthood and is at the fifth grade reading level. The author presents norms for adolescents, college students, adults, and special populations. The average respondent takes from 10 to 12 minutes to complete the test. Scoring can be completed in 4 minutes or less. There are two versions of the STAXI, a handscorable version and a machine-scored version.

The STAXI has gone through elaborate validation proceedings and the manual presents considerable information of how the scale was developed, the conceptual issues, and the results of factor analysis. The STAXI has been compared to the Eysenck Personality Inventory and the State-Trait Personality Inventory. The STAXI has also been compared with physical correlates such as blood pressure. Alpha coefficients provide evidence of the reliability of the anger scales.

The red print on the test booklet and answer sheet make them harder to read. The layout of the test, however, is good. Overall, the manual is more of a scholarly treatise on the technical aspects of the test. Notably missing are several case studies to illustrate the use and interpretation of the test. The manual could present data to the clinician that would facilitate the interpretation and proper use of the test.

Although the author comments on age and gender differences, I would like to see ethnic and cultural group comparisons. Some evidence of the test-retest reliability would be helpful. It would also be useful to see comparisons with other scales from the Minnesota Multiphasic Personality Inventory (MMPI) so we could have more information on whether response set, faking, and social desirability affect the scores.

SUMMARY. The STAXI appears to be a well-developed measure of state and trait anger. The test is widely used as a research tool and can be a valuable clinical tool if the manual becomes more user friendly.

Review of the State-Trait Anger Expression Inventory by STEPHEN E. TROTTER, Associate Professor, Department of Educational & Counseling Psychology, University of the Pacific, Stockton, CA:

The recent revision of the State-Trait Anger Expression Scale (STAXI; 1996) represents a significant shift from its earlier stated use. Previously, the STAXI stated use was primarily as a research tool. Clinicians were instructed to be cautious in its use with clinical populations. The new version attempts to widen the potential pool of users by aiming more at the practitioner rather than the researcher. In addition, previous versions were consistent in suggesting that training in psychometrics was required. This seems somewhat softened in the new version, as training is required to interpret but not administer the instrument. This is in keeping with many checklists and self-report inventories on the market.

The instrument purports to measure the experience and expression of anger. It further divides these factors into state and trait anger. It also addresses patterns of overtly or covertly expressing anger. Finally, it attempts to measure the dimensions of control and frequency of anger expression.

The test comprises 44 items with responses rated from 1–4 along a consistent direction of *almost never* to *almost always*. It is helpful that Spielberger varied the polarity of the questions to make it less likely for respondents to autocorrelate their ratings. A fairly large number of items (9) need to be omitted before overall validity is compromised. However, on some scales the omission of one item will render it invalid. The items have a high degree of face validity, with the questions divided into three sections: How I feel right now, How I generally feel, When angry or furious. The majority of the questions are five words or less and reading level is referenced as the fifth grade. This should be well within the range of the majority of subjects 13 years of age and above for which the instrument is designed.

The STAXI is composed of two forms, HS (hand scored) and Form G (OCR Scored). The OCR format is returned to the publisher for scoring and is returned with percentiles and *t*-scores for each individual.

The manual is clearly written and provides guidelines for interpreting high scores. It is relatively brief, approximately 50 pages including references. It is divided into well-written sections addressing administration and interpretation, conceptual issues and scale development, validity studies, and current research. It is helpful that Spielberger provides the examiner information regarding the skewness of the distribution of scores that prevents it from discriminating between individuals with low scores. In addition, a thorough description of the normative sample is provided. The sample is composed of responses from more than 9,000 individuals. Separate norms are provided as a function of gender and further delineated by adolescent, college, or adult. The scores are transformed into *T* scores and percentiles.

The shortcomings of the STAXI appear to be centered on the norming sample. Issues of ethnicity and race raised in Pittenger's (1998) *MMY* review are very briefly addressed in the revision. Spielberger reports that approximately 18% of the high school norming population were Black (African-American). This suggests an overrepresentation based on the current census. In contrast the data for Hispanics are not reported, but rather referenced as a smaller proportion. The reader is left unaware of the representation, if any, for Asians and Native-Americans.

Ethnicity and racial data are not provided for the remaining norms. This greatly limits their usage across ethnic and racial groups.

However, the largest threat to generalizability appears to be the use of approximately 2,000 individuals from the National Defense University. The reader is left uninformed as to differences in mean scores for these individuals in relationship to other adults in the norming population. This may be particularly problematic for adult male scores because 1,890 of the National Defense University pool were males. Therefore, the adult male normative group is largely composed of these individuals. Without reported comparative data this greatly limits the use with other males who are not members of this group. This flaw is continued in the college student normative group with 640 (600 males, 40 females) students selected from the United States Military Academy. The relatively low number of West Point females suggests that representation in the female normative group is less than 5%. In contrast West Point males represent approximately 45% of the college male group. Spielberger addresses this factor when he reports a 7-point higher score on S-Anger for Military Academy males when contrasted with urban undergraduate college males. He credits this with providing the impetus for reporting scores by gender. However, he notes that the scores are almost identical independent of gender for college students. Therefore, an alternative hypothesis might be that gender is not as large a factor as reported but rather that anger management and/or response style is reflected in career choice. This is also evident in differences between reported alpha coefficient estimates of internal consistency reliability as a function of college or Navy recruit membership.

The manual does an excellent job reporting factor loadings for the scales that support the construct of Anger-in and Anger-out as distinct styles. The manual is very thorough and provides an excellent and concise review of the literature associated with the STAXI and Anger Expression. It concludes with "Validity Studies and Current Research," which provides comparison data with the Minnesota Multiphasic Personality Inventory (MMPI), Eysenck Personality Questionnaire, and Buss-Durkee Hostility Inventory. The bulk of the research cited in the manual is dated and carries over from earlier editions. How-

ever, Anger-in scores were reported to correlate with blood pressure levels—finding that suggests a meaningful, real-world application for the STAXI in the treatment of elevated blood pressure levels.

SUMMARY. In closing the STAXI has much to offer the well-informed clinician. The reviewer's concerns center around the makeup of the normative group. Specifically, there appears to be an overrepresentation of military and allied individuals in both the college and adult normative group. In addition, the lack of data for Hispanic representation and the apparent absence of Native-Americans from the sample provide problematic. Moreover, the lack of a validity scale and the obvious intent of the items negate its use with populations that might be motivated to fake bad or good.

REVIEWER'S REFERENCE

Pittinger, D. J. (1998). [Review of the State-Trait Anger Expression Inventory, Revised Research Edition]. In J. C. Impara & B. S. Plake (Eds.), *The thirteenth mental measurements yearbook* (pp. 948–949). Lincoln, NE: Buros Institute of Mental Measurements.

[85]
Symptom Scale—77.

Purpose: "Designed to reflect specific symptom changes ... capable of modification by psychotherapy or neuropharmacology."

Population: Adolescents and adults.

Publication Dates: 1992–1995.

Acronym: SS—77.

Scores: 10 scales: Somatic Complaints, Depression, Alcohol and Other Drug Abuse, Anxiety, Obsessive—Compulsive Symptoms, Panic Disorder Without and With Agoraphobia, Traumatic Stress, Minimization of Symptoms, Magnification of Symptoms, Guardedness Index.

Administration: Individual or group.

Price Data: Not available.

Time: (15–20) minutes.

Comments: Computer administration requires IBM-compatible with at least 4 MB RAM and 1.4 MB disk drive and mouse and Windows 3.1.

Author: Judith L. Johnson and William McCown.

Publisher: DocuTrac, Inc. [No reply from publisher; status unknown].

Review of the Symptom Scale—77 by HERBERT BISCHOFF, Licensed Psychologist, Psychology Resources, Anchorage, AK:

With the advent of managed care there has been a growing need for the quantification of clinical constructs that are typically viewed as being "qualitative" in nature. The Symptom

Scale—77 (SS-77) attempts to do this by providing a 77-item questionnaire to be completed by an individual currently receiving some form of psychotherapy. The survey's intention is three-fold: (a) to provide the therapist/clinician with an indication of current symptoms, (b) to demonstrate to third party payers progressive easement of symptoms thereby qualifying the need for current and possible further interventions, and (c) to provide a tracking device for a therapist/clinician to gain an overall estimate of the efficacy of specific techniques with certain populations. The first two goals are accomplished by relying on the client's self-reported measure of expressed symptom severity by taking the SS-77 at various times for an individual. The third goal is accomplished by compiling information from many respondents.

The SS-77 comes in a disk format and can be administered on-line or by a clinician. The format is user friendly and has options useful in printing reports and graphs. The scoring package provides the ability to access different reports for different administrations for comparison and then, as is recommended by the test author, a clinician/ therapist can compile test results for all of their clientele to provide an overall indication of a particular practitioner's or agency's ability to successfully mitigate presenting symptoms. This can be done by selecting time frames and then asking the program to produce a summation of levels of symptoms.

However, if complications arise or there is a need to query the free help desk, the number provided in the test manual was no longer in service and no alternate was provided. Although the software is user friendly, the question is raised whether or not it is worth the risk with the inherent possibility of malfunction. Should this occur there are no immediate resources available to provide assistance.

A shortcoming of the SS-77, as with many self-report measures, is the 77-item survey's ability to accurately represent current self-reported symptoms. This is especially problematic when considering potential inherent limitations to insightfulness with certain clinical populations (e.g., delusional schizophrenics). However, the information may be helpful for a client who typically suffers from extreme variations of symptomatology by having them take the survey at various points during treatment providing valuable insight for them and their therapist/clinician. The symptom survey

results may assist in the development of more proactive techniques and monitor the course of symptomatology (e.g., how levels of anxiety may be provoked/lessened by introducing various stimuli into the environment). Regardless of the intention of administering the SS-77, it still requires a fairly high level of insight, self-awareness, and intelligence.

Although the testing manual is written in an understandable format and the author has apparently taken into consideration the limitations of the manual, there is limited discussion regarding normative data. The author recommends individual clinicians compile their own normative data for their particular populations of interest and geographic area, with no way of comparing this information to other normative samples. Providing information to third party payers, demonstrating the need for continued interventions, or quantifying progress would have qualitative limitations.

Reliability is reported at acceptable levels using internal consistency indices. The author points out test-retest reliability is an inappropriate measure for this test, given the desired variance of levels of symptomatology from test to test. Test-retest reliability studies were conducted with individuals who were not currently in treatment and not excessively stressed. There was a high level of test-retest consistency found over a one-week interval suggesting the test's ability to detect real symptom change.

SUMMARY. In summation, the SS-77 is a 77-item survey intended to measure change in levels of symptoms chosen specifically because they are considered representative of "mainstream" symptomatology and considered treatable through typical psychotherapeutic or neuropharmacological techniques. The manual is well written, adequately covering evidence of score reliability. Problems with the SS-77 including lack of normative data and an assumption of insight needed to accurately self-report symptom severity. Also, there is a problem with the help desk number that was no longer in service with no available alternate.

Review of the Symptom Scale—77 by TONY TONEATTO, Scientist, Clinical, Social and Research Department, Addiction Research Foundation, Toronto, Ontario, Canada:

The Symptom Scale-77 (SS-77) is a 77-item test intended to screen for nonpsychotic psychiatric symptoms in psychiatric and medical patients. The SS-77 can be used to establish the need for treatment or indicate the need for a diagnostic assessment. The scale can also be used as a measure of baseline functioning to evaluate the effects of psychosocial and psychopharmacological interventions. One of the unique features of the SS-77 is the inclusion of symptoms that are potentially modifiable by treatment (psychological or medical). The authors of the SS-77 stress that the scale cannot be used to make psychiatric diagnoses, as a psychological test, or to supplant clinical judgment. The scale excludes symptoms that were either rare (e.g., hysterical paresis) or so common that they would routinely be observed by a clinician or self-reported by a patient (e.g., phobia). Instead, symptoms that are more subtle, difficult to self-report, or difficult to ascertain in a clinical interview by a clinician were selected. Norms for nonpatients and outpatients provide the user with direction on establishing the need for, and evaluate the result of, treatment. The manual author advises, however, that the regular user of the SS-77 should develop their own norms due to regional, ethnic, and cultural differences in symptom presentations.

The ease and rapidity with which the SS-77 can be administered make it useful for clinicians and researchers as prepurchased score sheets, computerized scoring, or mail-in services are not required.

The SS-77 consists of seven clusters of symptoms that correspond to commonly diagnosed psychiatric disorders: Somatic Complaints (8 items), Depression (10 items), Alcohol/Drug Abuse (8 items), Anxiety (10 items), Obsessive-Compulsive Symptoms (9 items), Panic Disorder without Agoraphobia (9 items) or with Agoraphobia (2 additional items), and Traumatic Stress (9 items). Three validity scales have also been included: Minimization of Symptoms (8 items), Magnification of Symptoms (6 items), and a Guardedness Index (2 items). The domain of the disorders they have defined does not include social phobia, a very common disorder, as well as hypomanic symptoms, which may frequently occur in mood disordered patients but are difficult to assess directly. An examination of the content of the clinical symptom scales reveals considerable symptom overlap. For example, the Somatic Complaints scale includes "feeling sick to my stomach" vs. "stomach problems"; the Alcohol/Drug Abuse scale includes "problems from alcohol or taking drugs" vs. "arguments with family or friends about my alcohol or drug use" and "feeling guilty about using drugs or drinking" vs. "feeling ashamed about using drugs or drinking"; the Anxiety Scale includes "feeling restless" vs. "feeling nervous" vs. "feeling anxious" vs. "feeling keyed up or edgy." In each of these examples, the symptoms are either very similar or potentially difficult for the patient to distinguish or discriminate. The discussion of the Guardedness Index, consisting of only two items, is accompanied by several recommendations on the interpretation of the scores; this appears to be premature given that no evidence on the reliability or validity of this subscale is provided.

A serious limitation of the SS-77 is the decision to use a Likert scale with ratings ranging from *not at all bothered* to *constantly bothered*. The choice of the label "bothered" is problematic as many symptoms may be clinically significant even if the patient is not "bothered" by them (e.g., "thoughts of hurting or killing myself," "fear of going outside alone," "fear of going crazy"). Because patients may not always understand, recognize, or have insight into the significance of symptoms, it would have been more appropriate to assess the presence or frequency of such symptoms and then to explore how bothersome or significant they were later. Furthermore, the effects of treatment cannot be unambiguously evaluated because symptoms that are less "bothersome" may not have necessarily diminished or disappeared.

The SS-77 manual reports good internal consistency reliability data for the nine subscales across several populations (e.g., normal college, geriatric, chronic pain) with about half of Cronbach alpha coefficients above .80. Test-retest reliability is judged to be an inappropriate reliability measure for the SS-77 as the symptoms may fluctuate rapidly. However, good test-retest reliability statistics for college students/adult nonstudents are reported (although they do not indicate the interval period between tests). Such data would have been useful to have for other populations as well, using brief intervals between administrations (e.g., 24 hours) in order to assess reliability of symptom report but not long enough to reflect treatment effects. One week test-retest data were presented for four subscales (i.e., Somatic Complaints, Depression, Alcohol Abuse, Anxiety) that are identical to a previous version of the SS-77 were administered to nonpatients. Results showed poor to fair reliability (coefficients ranging from .60 to .77). Split-half reliability is estimated to be generally very good (generally above .80); unfortunately, however, the manual reports data combining clinical and nonclinical populations, making interpretation difficult.

The data for the validity of SS-77 scores are generally poor. Allusion to studies assessing criterion validity are made but no data are reported. Limited data for the concurrent validity of the Anxiety subscale are presented and almost none for the remaining subscales. Validity data for the validity subscales are again alluded to, but very little reported. It is noteworthy that no mention is made in the SS-77 manual of the Symptom Checklist-90 (Derogatis, 1983; T4:2674), a 90-item instrument with similar purposes and structure to the SS-77, especially measuring treatment-related clinical change. The Symptom Checklist-90 has considerably more sound psychometric data supporting its use. A briefer version of the instrument is also available; the 58-item Brief Symptom Inventory has also been shown to be a suitable instrument (Royse & Drude, 1984; T4:324). Future studies of the SS-77 should include concurrent validity evidence for these instruments. Furthermore, brief screening instruments for alcohol abuse, such as the Alcohol Use Disorders Identification Test (AUDIT; Saunders, Aasland, Babor, de la Fuente, & Grant, 1993; see 2) have received considerable support and may be more effective as screening measures than the SS-77 Alcohol/Drug subscale.

At the present time, the SS-77 suffers from serious weaknesses (e.g., questionable content validity, limited validity data). Therefore, caution should be exercised when interpreting the scores from this measure. The existence of alternative, better established instruments should be used until the weaknesses noted above have been rectified.

REVIEWER'S REFERENCES

Derogatis, L. R. (1983). *SCL-90-R: Administration, scoring and procedures manual-II for the revised version and other instruments of the psychopathology rating scale series.* Baltimore, MD: Clinical Psychometrics Research.

Royse, D., & Drude, K. (1984). Screening drug abuse clients with the Brief Symptom Inventory. *The International Journal of the Addictions, 19,* 849–857.

Saunders, J. B., Aasland, O. G., Babor, T. F., de la Fuente, J. R., & Grant, M. (1993). Development of the Alcohol Use Disorders Identification Test (AUDIT): WHO collaborative project on early detection of persons with harmful alcohol consumption-II. *Addiction, 88,* 791–804.

[86]
Target Mathematics Tests.

Purpose: Designed "to provide achievement tests which reflect the content of the National Curriculum in Mathematics" in Great Britain.
Population: Levels 2–5, 2–6.
Publication Date: 1993.
Scores: Total score only.
Administration: Group.
Forms, 2: Test 4, Test 5.
Price Data, 1999: £8.50 per 20 test booklets (specify test); £7.99 per manual; £8.99 per specimen set.
Time: [30] minutes.
Author: D. Young.
Publisher: Hodder & Stoughton Educational [England].

Review of the Target Mathematics Tests by KEVIN D. CREHAN, Associate Professor of Educational Psychology, University of Nevada, Las Vegas, NV:

The Target Mathematics Tests are designed as norm-referenced measures of Britain's National Curriculum in Mathematics that was adopted in 1991. The two tests, Test 4 and Test 5, are targeted at the ends of Key Stage 1 and Key Stage 2 and are recommended for administration at the end of Years 4 and 5, respectively. The intent of the tests is to provide teachers with help in monitoring student progression through Key Stage 2 of the mathematics curriculum in order to identify individual and class weaknesses in a timely fashion.

Target Test 4 has 55 items presented on four pages. Most of the items are supply type but a few provide options from which the student may select. The first 30 items consist of a display of information (e.g., coins, clock face, diagrams, graphs) with the basis for answering supplied orally by the teacher. The oral presentation of the first 30 items is designed to discount the effect of reading difficulties in the assessment of mathematics achievement. The remaining 25 items are presented on the test booklet and the student is allowed 20 minutes to respond. Target Test 5 contains 50 items, all of which are presented on the four-page test booklet. Again, most of the items are supply type, but several items present options from which the student selects. Administration time is 30 minutes.

TECHNICAL CONSIDERATIONS. Test items, at least in part, were taken from the former

Y Mathematics Series. There is no indication of other sources of test content. The manual states that the "validity is based on substantive rather than associative considerations" (p. 5). However, no indication of the basis for the substantive judgments is provided. That is, there is no mention of formal content validation procedures. No direct evidence of reliability is presented; however, the manual provides standard errors for the two tests obtained from reliability estimates derived from test-retest administrations within 10 days for sample sizes of 95 for Test 4 and 115 for Test 5. Based on the standard errors provided, the correlations of scores from the test-retest administrations would have been in the .96 range over the 10-day period.

SCORE INTERPRETATION. Age level norm tables, with 2-month intervals, are provided for each test. Test 4 age intervals go from 8 years-4 months to 10 years-3 months and the Test 5 intervals are from 9 years-4 months to 11 years-3 months. The norm data are based on samples from 18 schools of 359 males and 348 females for Year 4 and 370 males and 387 females for Year 5. The tables allow easy conversion of raw scores to age level "quotients" that appear to be normalized standard scores with a mean of 100 and standard deviation of 15 for each age interval. Standard errors for individual score interpretation are about 3 points or one-fifth of a standard deviation.

The manual suggests interpretation of results can be both norm-referenced, using the accompanying tables, and criterion-references, using raw scores. That is, a student's performance can be compared to his or her age peers or against the national curriculum standards. Additional suggested uses of the tests and test results may derive from teacher observations during scoring; that is, the teacher may informally identify points for further examination. The teacher is also directed to give special attention to differences in performance between orally presented and non-orally presented items as a check for the potential effect of poor reading ability.

OBSERVATIONS AND RECOMMENDATIONS. The Target Mathematics Tests should give the British teacher results that are useful as an aid to instructional decisions; however, the measures could easily be improved in both presentation and the provision of additional supporting interpretive information. There is some concern with the format, presentation, and arrangement of the individual items. For example, in some cases the student provides his or her answer as the solution to a problem and in other cases a separate answer space is provided. This inconsistency may cause difficulty in responding and scoring. Additionally, a few items could benefit from editing. For example, hand position in the clock face problems is ambiguous and caused this reviewer some pause in interpretation. Also, the ordering of items should be examined to place easier items of a type before more difficult items measuring similar content (e.g., the item asking the perimeter of a regular shape should be placed before the item asking the area of an irregular shape).

Given the effort needed to administer and hand score these tests, more in the way of suggested uses of results might be expected. For example, given the variety of content and the apparent broad range of item difficulties, subarea means and/or item difficulty data might be used to aid the teacher in diagnosing individual and class strengths and weaknesses both in a norm-referenced interpretation and for comparison to the national curriculum standards.

Finally, the choice to construct the norm tables using only normalized standard scores is questioned. Because the proposed prime user of these scores is the classroom teacher, norm tables presenting percentile rank conversion of raw scores may provide greater interpretive power.

SUMMARY. The Target Mathematics Tests have the potential for usefulness to the teacher in both norm-referenced and criterion-referenced interpretations. The usefulness of the tests could be expanded by the addition of item difficulty data and norm tables presenting percentile ranks.

Review of the Target Mathematics Tests by *GERALD E. DeMAURO, Coordinator of Assessment, New York State Education Department, Albany, NY:*

TEST COVERAGE AND USE. The Target Mathematics Tests 4 and 5 are designed to measure achievement of the National Curriculum of Great Britain in mathematics between the end of Key Stage 1 and Key Stage 2, Years 4 and 5. This is equivalent to American grades 4 and 5.

APPROPRIATE SAMPLES FOR TEST VALIDATION AND NORMING. The tests' normative samples were drawn from 18 schools.

The Year 4 sample was composed of 707 children (359 boys and 348 girls) with an average age of 9 years and 2.5 months. The Year 5 sample was composed of 757 children (370 boys and 387 girls), with an average age of 10 years and 2.5 months.

Quotients referenced to these samples are provided for Tests 4 and 5 based on a mean of 100 and standard deviation of 15. Test 4 has 54 possible scores and provides quotients for children in each of 12 two-month intervals ranging from 8-4 to 10-3, yielding 648 possible quotients. Test 5 has 49 possible scores and provides quotients in each of 12 two-month intervals, ranging from 9-4 to 11-3, yielding 588 possible quotient cells. The sizes of the normative samples suggest that these cells reflect considerable interpolations rather than observed performance throughout the ranges for all ages.

The author quite rightly states that raw scores are more helpful for the criterion-referenced interpretation of results. However, evidence of formal standard setting studies that reference performance to levels of competence is not presented.

CRITERION RELATED VALIDITY. The criterion of interest is achievement of the National Curriculum in mathematics. Formal validity data are not presented. Rather, the author states that the tests were designed in stages, beginning with *Y Mathematics Series* items and finalizing the item pool on the basis of the standardization trials. Scores of about 25 on Test 4 and 23 on Test 5 are held to be equivalent to Level 2 on the National Curriculum and the transitions between Levels 3 and 4, respectively.

CONTENT VALIDITY. Items on the two tests are proportionally distributed over four mathematics content areas and four and five ability levels, respectively. There do not appear to be sufficient items to provide reliable subscores related to these divisions.

The author states, "Since the tests are based on the content of the National Curriculum, the validity of the tests is based on substantive rather than associative consideration" (p. 5). Although these substantive considerations are vital to content validity, it would help readers evaluate their strength to present documentation of the expert judgments that support the substantive relationships between the curricular domain and the con-figuration of the tests. Analyses of 50 students at four ability levels in each year are said to confirm the appropriate item ability and discriminatory characteristics.

CONSTRUCT VALIDITY. Evidence is presented of attempts to purify the construct. Items are presented orally for 30 of the 55 items on Test 4 to avoid reading confounds. Cautions are raised that there may be common abilities that underlie both mathematics problem solving and reading comprehension.

TEST ADMINISTRATION. Test administration is completely specified, taking about 18 minutes for the orally administered section and 20 minutes for the read section of Test 4. Test 5, entirely read, takes 30 minutes to administer.

TEST REPORTING. As mentioned above, reporting may be in quotients or raw scores. Although there are recommended levels of performance, there is no indication of how these were determined. Interpretations seem to depend on achieving the average of the normative sample, and extreme performances are judged with reference to the performance of the normative sample rather than with reference to the probabilities that students possess certain knowledge or skills.

TEST AND ITEM BIAS. No information is reported on differential item functioning or differential test validity.

SUMMARY. The Target Mathematics Tests are referenced to specific portions of the National Curriculum of Great Britain in mathematics. They are undoubtedly reliable and useful for this purpose. The user would be aided with greater detail concerning the derivation of test specifications from the curriculum.

[87]
Teacher Observation Scales for Identifying Children with Special Abilities.

Purpose: Designed as an assessment instrument for identifying gifted children, tailored to be culturally appropriate for use in New Zealand.

Population: Junior and middle primary school.

Publication Date: 1996.

Scores, 5: Learning Characteristics, Social Leadership Characteristics, Creative Thinking Characteristics, Self-Determination Characteristics, Motivational Characteristics.

Administration: Individual.

Price Data, 1996: NZ$12.50 per 20 observation scales; $12.50 per teacher's handbook (9 pages).

Time: Administration time not reported.
Authors: Don McAlpine and Neil Reid.
Publisher: New Zealand Council for Educational Research [New Zealand].

Review of the Teacher Observation Scales for Identifying Children with Special Abilities by IRA STUART KATZ, Clinical Psychologist, California Department of Corrections, Salinas Valley State Prison, Soledad, CA:

TEACHERS NEED TOOLS. Funds are not unlimited to assess and address the special needs of gifted children. School boards, parents, and the general public can be very critical about where and how education dollars are best spent for the greatest return on investment. The Teacher Observation Scales for Identifying Children with Special Abilities is designed as an instrument to identify gifted children tailored for use in New Zealand. Various methods have been utilized to assess giftedness ranging from scales for parents, teachers, peers, and students.

Teacher judgment continues to play a pivotal role in accurate assessment. Renzulli and Hartman (1971) addressed this need with a rating scale. The Scale for Rating Behavioural Characteristics of Superior Students (SRBCSS) has been widely used in the United States and elsewhere. The SRBCSS has not been effective for the needs of students and teachers in New Zealand. Three issues—composite scale statements, scale statement ambiguity, and lack of cultural relevance—were all not well addressed by the SRBCSS. Ultimately, with much empirical research effort, five scales emerged: Learning Characteristics, Social Leadership Characteristics, Creative Thinking Characteristics, Self-Determination Characteristics, and Motivational Characteristics. The Teacher Observation is a valuable assessment tool with some clear advantages and disadvantages.

SCALES. Advantages include the ease of use, clear language, focus of behavioral characteristics, scoring, and recognition of the unique traits incumbent with the gifted, or children with special abilities (CWSA). Despite some cultural nuances, the instrument appears to be culture-friendly and could be used beyond New Zealand with some minor modifications. A clinical and empirical advantage is its recognition of the psychological aspects of giftedness or special abilities. Ellen Winner (1996) in her wonderful contribution to the field, *Gifted Children: Myths and Realities,*

provides insight on this unique population that is covered in the Teacher Observation Scales.

The authors of the scale, McAlpine and Reid, have given teachers a gift in identifying and working with children with special abilities. Combining the empirical research and clinical wisdom of Winner's work should be an adjunct for any teacher before using this scale or any other for this population. The Teacher Observation Scales Teacher's Handbook is a valuable tool that should be read and understood before any assessment. The handbook makes some valuable suggestions on utilization concerning timing and reliability of observations that should be followed scrupulously to increase empirical accuracy and effectiveness. Some of the suggestions are valuable for any teacher utilizing any tool.

Specifically, these suggestions include evidence to be familiar with the children (don't use the scales too soon in the school year), provide a wide range of learning experiences that encompass the behaviors measured in the scales, assess a small group of children (e.g., 4 or 5) concurrently over a brief period, record observations soon after events have highlighted a particular behavior, avoid the "halo" effect of allowing one or two "good" behaviors to affect ratings on other unrelated behaviors, and reassess from time to time because children change their behaviors as the result of new experiences.

Technical factors (validity and reliability) are well supported in the preliminary empirical data. Most striking here is the similarity with the SRBCSS validity research of a decade ago. Reliability evidence was less well grounded. The authors indicate accurately that intrarater reliability in the circumstances in which scales will be used makes little sense as a teacher's ratings will change based on the range of afforded observations. Hence, change, that is a *lack* of stability, is to be expected.

The authors close the handbook with some suggested curriculum models for the education of the CWSA and the integration of the Teacher Observation Scales.

SUMMARY. The Teacher Observation Scales for Identifying Children with Special Abilities is an assessment instrument with a future despite some preliminary limitations. It would be helpful to accelerate the process of closing the cultural diversity gap and put more emphasis of teacher development in future handbooks. Assessing the psychological aspects of giftedness should receive more treatment in future revisions of both the instrument and handbook. It can be hoped that the Educational Research and Development Center and New Zealand Council for Educational Research could combine the synergy of its counterparts and colleagues worldwide to better serve the needs of students, peers, teachers, and parents in our ever more culturally diverse and pluralistic world. The Teacher Observation Scales for Identifying Children with Special Abilities is on the vanguard of that needed change.

REVIEWER'S REFERENCES
Renzulli, J. S., & Hartman, R. K. (1971). Scales for rating behavioural characteristics of superior students. *Exceptional Children, 3,* 243–148.
Winner, E. (1996). *Gifted children: Myths and realities.* New York: Basic Books.

Review of the Teacher Observation Scales For Identifying Children With Special Abilities by KENNETH A. KIEWRA, Professor of Educational Psychology, University of Nebraska–Lincoln, Lincoln, NE:

This review focuses on the Teacher Observation Scales in terms of (a) purpose, (b) composition and development, (c) use (administration, scoring, and interpretation), and (d) technical information (validity and reliability).

PURPOSE. The Teacher Observation Scales are for screening and selecting talented students for inclusion in enriched or accelerated school programs. Although the scales are intended to offer a broader means for identifying talented students than conventional means such as intelligence testing, they are best used in conjunction with other identification methods.

COMPOSITION AND DEVELOPMENT. There are five Teacher Observation Scales: Learning Characteristics (13 items), Social Leadership Characteristics (12 items), Creative Thinking Characteristics (11 items), Self-Determination Characteristics (9 items), and Motivational Characteristics (8 items).

The scales were reportedly derived from the literature on gifted and talented, and then modified and confirmed through statistical techniques. The scales are not tied explicitly to any theoretical model of talent or intelligence such as Gardner's (1997) or Sternberg's (Sternberg & Kagan, 1986), and the literature base from which the scales were purportedly drawn is unspecified. Therefore there

is reason to question the scales' conceptual basis. As such, the five scales seem arbitrary.

USE. The scales appear, on the surface, simple to administer. Teachers or school personnel simply mark a checklist showing the degree (*seldom, occasionally, often,* or *almost always*) to which a particular student demonstrates each of the 53 characteristics. At a deeper level, it might be difficult for a teacher to make certain student judgments such as: "easily grasps underlying principles," "jumps stages in learning," "takes the initiative in social situations," "synthesises ideas from group members to formulate a plan of action," "enjoys speculation and thinking about the future," and "relates well to older children and adults and often prefers their company" (scoring booklet, pp. 2–5). Teachers obviously must first know their students well in varying situations before using the Teacher Observation Scales.

Another problem in administering the Teacher Observation Scales is the ambiguity associated with scale points ranging from "seldom" to "almost always." No operational definition is provided for these scale points and users might be hard pressed deciding whether a student engages in certain scale behaviors "occasionally" or "often."

Use of the Teacher Observation Scales is appropriate for students at all levels but is recommended for students at middle, primary, intermediate, and junior secondary levels. The Teacher Observation Scales are not to be used with all students. They are best used to select or confirm those few students being considered for gifted or accelerated programs.

The developers also recommend administering the Teacher Observation Scales to students who are "puzzling," "unknown," or "new to the school" (manual, p. 3). This recommendation though is at odds with the developers' recommendation to know the children well before administering the scales.

Scoring is done separately for each special ability scale. Scale scores are never combined to provide a general special ability score. Scoring is simple. For each scale, sum the responses marked "often" and multiply the sum by 3; sum the responses marked "almost always" and multiply the sum by 4. Then, add those two products to derive the total scale score.

Interpretation of scale scores is unclear. There are no national norms or predetermined cutoff scores for selection. Teachers are directed to "interpret scale scores in light of their particular circumstances and experience teaching children with special abilities" (manual, p. 4). Obviously, this directive offers little guidance. Consequently, test developers do offer tentative estimates of what they consider the upper ranges for selection.

Another concern in interpreting scores is that the scales are tipped in favor of quantity over quality. Because points are not earned for "occasionally" demonstrating a behavior, a student could conceivably write a single best selling novel and earn no points for the item "creates original stories."

TECHNICAL INFORMATION. The Teacher Observation Scales are problematic in some aspects of validity and reliability. In terms of validity, content validity has already been questioned. The scales are not tied to any existing model of talent or intelligence. Moreover, the scales do not reflect important aspects of talent such as hard work, time on task, and background knowledge. The Creative Thinking Scale, in particular, lacks validity. Creativity is an incremental process marked by small and predictable steps toward a solution (Weisberg, 1993) rather than the stereotypical characteristics found in the Creative Thinking Scale such as: "generates unusual insights" and "seeks unusual rather than conventional relationships" (scoring booklet, p. 4).

The Teacher Observation Scales also lack predictive and criterion validity. The predictive power is unknown because students selected into gifted programs through use of the Teacher Observation Scales have not been evaluated later in terms of actual success in their gifted programs or their talent areas. Similarly, criterion validity is lacking because there are only minimal data linking scale performance with performance on other established and related measures. For three of the five scales, there have been no attempts to establish criterion validity.

Regarding reliability, each of the five scales is internally consistent. This means that items within a scale generally measure the same attribute.

The test developers report consistently strong indices of interrater reliability. That is, pairs of teachers independently rate students similarly on the scales. Unfortunately, the numbers of teacher raters and students rated are unreported. The test developers themselves cast some doubt on the objective value of the Teacher Observation Scales.

They state: "Over time, as teachers working together in schools moderate on another's interpretations of scale ratings ..., it is anticipated that the degree of agreement will increase still further" (manual, p. 7).

SUMMARY. Although the Teacher Observation Scales are a convenient means for identifying exceptional students, they were not developed along any established or defensible theoretical model of intelligence or expertise. Once developed, there is not clear evidence that they measure what they purport to measure. Finally, their fundamental value is questionable given that teachers, in most cases, must first know a student well and recognize that student as exceptional before using the Teacher Observation Scales. Given the Teacher Observation Scales' subjective nature, it is possible teachers using the scales will find just what they intended to find.

REVIEWER'S REFERENCES
Sternberg, R. J., & Kagan, J. (1986). *Intelligence applied: Understanding and increasing your intellectual skills.* San Diego, CA: Harcourt Brace Jovanovich.
Weisberg, R. W. (1993). *Creativity: Beyond the myth of genius.* New York: W. H. Freeman.
Gardner, H. (1997). *Extraordinary minds: Portraits of exceptional individuals and an examination of our extraordinariness.* New York: Basic Books.

[88]

TerraNova.

Purpose: Constructed as a "comprehensive modular assessment series" of student achievement.

Population: Grades K–12.

Publication Date: 1997.

Administration: Group.

Levels, 12: 10, 11, 12, 13, 14, 15, 16, 17, 18, 19, 20, 21/22.

Price Data, 1997: $12.50 per practice activities (specify battery and level); $2.70 per directions for practice activities (specify battery and level); $25 per teacher's guide; $11.25 per additional test directions for teachers (specify battery and level); norms book available from publisher.

Foreign Language Edition: Available in English and in Spanish editions.

Time: Administration time varies by test and level.

Comments: Instruments may be administered alone or in any combination; revision of the Comprehensive Tests of Basic Skills, Fourth Edition (T5:665).

Author: CTB/McGraw-Hill.

Publisher: CTB/McGraw-Hill.

a) CTBS COMPLETE BATTERY AND COMPLETE BATTERY PLUS.

Population: Grades K–12.

Scores, 10: Complete Battery (Reading, Language Arts, Mathematics, Science, Social Studies),

Complete Battery Plus (Word Analysis, Vocabulary, Language Mechanics, Spelling, Mathematics Computation).

Price Data: $115.50 per 30 Complete Battery consumable test booklets (specify level); $122 per 30 Complete Battery Plus consumable test booklets; $86 per 30 Complete Battery reusable test booklets (specify level); $92.50 per 30 Complete Battery Plus reusable test booklets (specify level); $30.75 per 50 reflective answer sheets (specify battery and level); $770 per 1,250 continuous foreign answer sheets (specify battery and level); $3.53 per student basic service scoring for Complete Battery; $3.80 per student basic service scoring for Complete Battery Plus.

b) CTBS BASIC BATTERY AND BASIC BATTERY PLUS.

Population: Grades K–12.

Scores, 8: Basic Battery (Reading, Language Arts, Mathematics), Basic Battery Plus (Word Analysis, Vocabulary, Language Mechanics, Spelling, Mathematics Computation).

Price Data: $108.15 per 30 Basic Battery consumable test booklets (specify level); $114.65 per 30 Basic Battery Plus consumable test booklets (specify level); $83.75 per 30 Basic Battery reusable test booklets (specify level); $90.25 per 30 Basic Battery Plus reusable test booklets (specify level); $30.75 per 50 reflective answer sheets (specify battery and level); $770 per 1,250 continuous form answer sheets (specify battery and level); $3.53 per student for Basic Battery basic service scoring; $3.80 per student for Basic Battery Plus basic service scoring.

c) CTBS SURVEY AND SURVEY PLUS.

Purpose: Designed as a norm-referenced measure of academic achievement.

Population: Grades 2–12.

Scores, 10: Survey (Reading, Language Arts, Mathematics, Science, Social Studies); Survey Plus (Word Analysis, Vocabulary, Language Mechanics, Spelling, Mathematics Computation).

Price Data: $103 per 30 Survey consumable test booklets (specify level); $109.50 per 30 Survey Plus consumable test booklets (specify level); $81.25 per 30 Survey reusable test booklets (specify level); $87.75 per 30 Survey Plus reusable test booklets (specify level); $30.75 per 50 reflective answer sheets (specify battery and level); $770 per 1,250 continuous form answer sheets (specify level); $3.37 per student for Survey basic service scoring; $3.64 per student for Survey Plus basic service scoring.

d) MULTIPLE ASSESSMENTS.

Purpose: Intended to assess academic achievement using "a combination of the selected-response items of the Survey edition and a section of constructed-response items that allow students to produce their own short and extended responses."

Population: Grades 1–12.

Scores, 5: Reading, Language Arts, Mathematics, Science, Social Studies.

Price Data: $125 per 30 consumable test booklets (specify level); $9.80 per student for basic service scoring.

e) SUPERA.

Purpose: Constructed as a "TerraNova Spanish edition."

Price Data: $13 per 30 practice activities (specify battery and level); $2.60 per directions for practice activities (specify battery and level); $24.25 per 30 locator tests (specify test and level); $21.50 per 50 locator answer sheets; $16.50 per SUPERA technical bulletin; $11.25 per SUPERA additional test directions for teachers (specify battery and level); $8.50 per locator manual.

1) *SUPERA Survey.*

Population: Grades 1–10.

Scores, 3: Reading, Language Arts, Mathematics.

Price Data: $103 per 30 consumable test booklets (specify level); $81.25 per 30 reusable test booklets (specify level); $30.75 per 50 answer sheets; $1,540 per 2,500 continuous feed answer sheets; $23.05 per 25 ScorEZE answer sheets; $2.83 per student for basic service scoring.

2) *SUPERA Multiple Assessments.*

Population: Grades 1–10.

Scores, 3: Reading, Language Arts, Mathematics.

Price Data: $87.50 per 30 consumable image-scorable test booklets (specify level); $6.35 per student for basic service scoring.

3) *SUPERA Plus.*

Population: Grades 1–10.

Scores, 5: Word Analysis, Language Mechanics, Vocabulary, Math Computation, Spelling.

Price Data: $30 per 30 test booklets (specify level); $30.75 per 50 answer sheets (specify regular or survey); $11.25 per manual (specify level).

Comments: Intended for use with either SUPERA Multiple Assessments or SUPERA Survey.

f) PERFORMANCE ASSESSMENTS.

Purpose: Constructed to "meet the needs of educators who wish to use context-based tasks or open-ended assessments."

Scores, 4: Communication Arts, Mathematics, Science, Social Studies.

Comments: Available only through contract with publisher; additional scores can be provided for broad competencies such as communication or problem solving.

Cross References: For information on the Comprehensive Tests of Basic Skills, see T5:665 (95 references); see also T4:623 (23 references); for reviews by Kenneth D. Hopkins and M. David Miller of the CTBS, see 11:81 (70 references); for reviews by Robert L. Linn and Lorrie A. Shepard of an earlier form, see 9:258 (29 references); see also T3:551 (59 references); for reviews by Warren G. Findley and Anthony J. Nitko of an earlier edition, see 8:12 (13 references); see also T2:11 (1 reference); for reviews by J. Stanley Ahmann and Frederick G. Brown and excerpted reviews by Brooke B. Collison and Peter A. Taylor (rejoinder by Verna White) of Forms Q and R, see 7:9. For reviews of subtests of earlier editions, see 8:721 (1 review), 8:825 (1 review), 7:685 (1 review), 7:514 (2 reviews), and 7:778 (1 review).

Review of the TerraNova by JUDITH A. MONSAAS, Associate Professor of Education, North Georgia College and State University, Dahlonega, GA:

DESCRIPTION. The TerraNova comprises the revised versions of the Comprehensive Tests of Basic Skills with several optional packages including the CTBS Survey assessing Reading/Language Arts, Mathematics, Science, and Social Studies; the CTBS Complete Battery covering the same subjects but with more items per subject for more precise norms (according to the publisher) and for criterion-referenced test scores interpretations; and the CTBS Basic Battery, which only includes the Reading/Language Arts and Mathematics subtests. Each of these three Batteries has a Plus Version that includes supplemental tests in Word Analysis (Grades 1–3 only), Vocabulary, Language Mechanics, Spelling, and Mathematical Computation. The final set of assessments in the basic four subjects, called Multiple Assessments, includes a combination of the selected-response items from the Survey edition and constructed-response items, which allow students to produce their own responses. TerraNova Levels 10–22 cover Grades K–12. Additional testing materials, including performance assessments (reviewed in the *Thirteenth Mental Measurements Yearbook*), SUPERA, the Spanish edition, customized tests, and the CTB Writing Assessment (13:88) are available to supplement the TerraNova or as stand alone tests, but are not included in this review.

PURPOSE AND USES. The TerraNova, like other achievement test batteries, is designed to assess individual student learning in the basic subjects. When used in conjunction with other information, it can be used to assess individual and group status and change over time as well as provide information about the effectiveness of educational programs. The test results can be used to make comparisons with school, district, and national norm groups. Standardized achievement tests can provide important information for teachers about the knowledge and skills of their students and can be used for planning instruction based on analysis of individual student or class performance on educational objectives. The addition of performance standards to the TerraNova Batteries is helpful for schools and systems moving toward a standards-based curriculum framework. CTB/McGraw-Hill suggests that the TerraNova and other standardized achievement tests can assist in decision making in the following areas: evaluation of student progress, needs assessment, instructional program planning, curriculum analysis, program evaluation, class grouping, and administrative planning and direction. Given the multitude of assessment batteries and supplemental assessments, this claim appears to be quite supportable.

MANUALS AND OTHER ANCILLARY MATERIALS. Several manuals for test users and reviewers were provided with the TerraNova. The two most useful documents for test users are the Teacher's Guide and a separate guide for interpreting test scores and using test results. These are both well written and user friendly. The guide for interpreting test scores provides definitions and descriptions of the different score reporting methods and has a helpful section on appropriate uses of test data. This guide is relatively short and could be read or skimmed by conscientious test users to help them correctly use and interpret their students' test scores. The Teacher's Guide is a much more comprehensive description of the test content and purposes, the various score reporting profiles, and suggestions for communicating test scores to parents. In fact, there is a particularly useful question and answer section for parents embedded in the middle of the manual under the "Using Test Results" section that might be missed by someone not reading the lengthy manual carefully. The detailed description of the test development process, the content, the thinking skills framework, as well as comparisons with the CTBS/4 for previous users of the CTB tests are very useful for schools and districts attempting to determine the validity of the content for their particular curriculum and test use.

The tests are very engaging and user friendly, as well. The directions are clear and easy to follow and the tests are attractively packaged. According to the manuals, the tests were designed to look more like instructional materials than traditional achievement tests. To a certain extent, the test publishers were successful. Several test questions are linked to themes, which provide some continuity from item to item for students, making the test more closely resemble typical classroom material. Also, the constructed-response questions in the Multiple Assessments tests resemble instructional materials. Nonetheless, although these tests are attractive and more engaging than most achievement tests I have inspected, I doubt that students will forget that they are taking a test.

STANDARDIZATION AND NORMS. Norming of the TerraNova was completed in 1996 providing a relatively current set of national norms. The standardization sample was large and generally representative. Schools participating in the standardization completed a demographic survey and the results of the survey were compared to national demographic data. The norm group tended to have somewhat fewer minorities than the general population, but had more students on free and reduced-price lunch and more students from single-parent families. The final norms were, of course, weighted to reflect the national proportions. Thirty-four percent of the norm group were current users of the CAT/5 or CTBS/4, indicating that there was not an overrepresentation of CTB customers. The publishers did not specify how many schools and systems from the original sample declined to participate in the norming of the TerraNova. This information would have been helpful in evaluating the quality of the standardization sample.

A full complement of norms are available including local and national percentile ranks, normal curve equivalents, stanines, and grade equivalents. Developmental scale scores ranging from 0 to 999 span all the grade levels tested. This scoring method is especially useful for evaluating student change over time, but is not readily understandable to lay people (e.g., parents); the scores typically must be changed to derived scores such as

percentiles to be useful to parents. The manuals clearly explain the benefits and limitations of each of these normative score reporting methods so that users can know when to use which method and why the various methods are used. A section on "Avoiding Misinterpretation" when using grade equivalents clearly explains the limited use of these scores and is clear on ways the scores should not be used. This disclaimer may not satisfy hard-core opponents of grade equivalents, but if teachers carefully read this section of the Teacher's Guide, they would be very circumspect in their use and interpretation of these scores.

CRITERION-REFERENCED INTERPRETATIONS. Two criterion-referenced reporting systems are provided for the TerraNova: an objectives mastery report and a performance level/standards report. The objectives mastery reports are similar to the criterion-referenced reports provided for most standardized test batteries in that students' levels of performance on subsets of objectives are provided. This is somewhat controversial, though common, because the number of items associated with each objective is sometimes too small for valid inferences regarding student performance on that objective. Also, items are typically not selected to determine mastery of the objectives, but to discriminate among students. The publishers provide an Objectives Performance Index (OPI), which is an estimate of the number of items that a student could be expected to answer correctly if there had been 100 such items for that objective. A Bayesian procedure, used to estimate the OPI, takes into account overall test performance as well as actual performance on a given objective, which serves to improve the reliability of the scores on the objectives. This procedure is an improvement on the "number correct" method considering the small number of items per objective. The score reports show student (class or district) performance on the objective using this 100-point index. The number of items used to assess the specific objectives is not provided on the score report, thus a user does not know if this index is based on the minimum of four items or considerably more. The number of items per objective would lead to more "truth in testing" and to more cautious interpretation of objectives with fewer items. Although it is possible that a test user may question how an OPI for a four-item objective is not divisible by four, it is also possible that a user might assume that an OPI of say, 79, was based on considerably more items than four. A somewhat questionable interpretation is the classification of OPI into mastery levels. An OPI of 75 and above is defined as Mastery, 50–74 as Partial Mastery, and 49 and below as Non-Mastery. These Mastery designations seem arbitrary. No standard-setting has been performed to indicate what experts (curriculum specialists, teachers) might consider mastery. If the average OPI is similar to the mean p-value the average child appears to be defined as having partial mastery of the grade level material because the average p-value per subtest ranges from about .50 to .70.

In addition to performance on the objectives, performance levels have been set that describe what a student can do in terms of the content across the grade spans: Grades 1–2 (primary), Grades 3–5 (elementary), Grades 6–8 (middle) and Grades 9–12 (high). Student performance is reported in terms of five Performance levels: Level 1 (Starting out or Step 1); Level 2 (Progressing); Level 3 (Nearing Proficiency); Level 4 (Proficient); and Level 5 (Advanced). Standard setting committees made up of curriculum experts and accomplished teachers set standards that included the setting of cut scores and development of performance level descriptors for each level of each subject. CTB used an IRT-based Bookmark Standard Setting procedure (Lewis, Mitzel, & Green, 1996) to set the cut scores for the TerraNova. For the Multiple Assessments, both the selected-response and constructed-response items are located on the same scale for developing performance standards. The procedure for setting the cut scores and performance descriptors is well-described and defensible. I wish that the procedure for defining Mastery levels using the OPI were as defensible, especially because that is the information schools are most likely to use in planning and evaluating instruction.

RELIABILITY. Reliability coefficients for the subtests and composite scores on the TerraNova were consistently high. KR-20 was used to estimate the reliability of the Survey Plus and the Complete Battery Plus and coefficient alpha was used to estimate the reliability of the Multiple Assessments. Reliability coefficients were computed separately for the fall and spring standardization samples. The reliability coefficients were consistently in the .80s and .90s. The only subtest

demonstrating consistently lower coefficients was Spelling. Spelling also had consistently lower p-values indicating that it was more difficult. Slightly lower coefficients were also found at the lower grade levels (Grades 1 and 2) and for the fall standardization sample. Because the differences were slight and most testing is conducted in the spring, this coefficient discrepancy should not be of concern. It should be noted that the reliability coefficients for the Multiple Assessments were as consistently high as those of the other batteries. Finally, interrater reliability studies were conducted on the constructed response items At selected grade levels (3, 6, and 8). The mean score points awarded by two raters were very close and the correlations were very high indicating high rater agreement. The technical manual reports that monitoring techniques are in place to ensure that interrater agreement and accuracy remain high.

VALIDITY. The process used to develop the test and ensure content validity was very thorough and clearly explained both in the Teacher's Manual and the Technical manual. Texts, basals, and numerous other publications, as well as standards developed by the states and the professional associations, were used in the development of the series. Frequent and thorough tryouts, reviews, and revisions were completed by a wide variety of classroom teachers and experts in the subject fields. Other data obtained included usability studies and sensitivity/bias reviews to ensure that the test materials were clear and appropriate and did not reflect possible bias in language, subject matter, or group membership. The *Dimensions of Thinking* (Marzano, et al., 1988) was used as a framework to ensure that the test reflected a full range of thinking skills. Tables for each test level show that the subtests assess a range of thinking skills. Not surprisingly, the Multiple Assessment battery has a greater number of items reflecting higher level thinking skills. Another feature that enhances the content validity of these tests is the thematic integration of subsets of items on the tests. This integration makes the tests more similar to materials to which students are exposed in the classroom and in their everyday lives.

Criterion-related validity studies were being planned at the time the various manuals were published. The publishers plan to correlate the TerraNova with the National Assessment of Educational Progress (NAEP), the Third International Mathematics and Science Study (TIMSS), and the SAT and ACT. Based on similar studies relating the California Achievement Tests with the SAT and ACT, the publishers expect strong relationships. These data are necessary to determine whether scores on this new test are related to other independent measures of achievement.

To support the construct validity of this test, the publishers cited the careful test development process to support the content validity and comprehensiveness of the test. A series of construct validity statements describe the skills, concepts, and processes measured in each of the subject areas. Detailed information on the subskills and objectives supports the content validity and further supports the construct validity of these tests. Convergent and discriminant validity evidence was supported by the correlations among the TerraNova subtests and total scores, and the subareas and total scores on the Test of Cognitive Skills, Second Edition. The pattern of correlations provides construct support for the TerraNova. Item review and item analysis were performed to support construct relevance and minimize construct irrelevance.

SUMMARY. The TerraNova is an innovative, well-developed set of achievement test batteries. The materials are all well constructed, attractive, and user friendly. The norming and score reporting methods are well developed. The performance standards development is state-of-the-art. My only serious reservation is with the mastery classifications for the criterion-referenced interpretations—the "cut scores" are arbitrarily defined. Although the Objectives Performance Index is technically sound and does increase the reliability of the criterion-referenced interpretations, these interpretations can still be misleading without reporting the number of items associated with each objective. Further, using technically sophisticated scaling methods and then using arbitrary, and possibly misleading, definitions of mastery, seems to be indefensible. Although I would caution teachers and schools to use the criterion-referenced scores carefully and devise their own mastery levels, in all other respects, this test is extremely well constructed. The content and construct validity evidence support the test and its appropriate uses in schools. The reliability evidence is strong as well. Planned criterion-related validity studies will likely provide additional validity support for these tests. As with all achieve-

ment tests, it is necessary that the users determine the extent to which the content of the TerraNova matches the curriculum in their schools.

REVIEWER'S REFERENCES

Marzano, R. J., Brandt, R. S., Hughes, C. S., Jones, B. F., Presseisen, B. Z., Rankin, S. C., & Suhor, C. (1988). *Dimensions of thinking: A framework for curriculum and instruction.* Alexandria, VA: The Association for Supervision and Curriculum Development.
Lewis, D. M., Mitzel, H. C., & Green, D. R. (1996, June). Standard setting: A bookmark approach. In D. R. Green (Chair), *IRT-based standard setting procedures utilizing behavioral anchoring.* Symposium conducted at the meeting of the Council of Chief State School Officers, National Conference on Large Scale Assessment, Phoenix, AZ.

Review of the TerraNova by ANTHONY J. NITKO, Professor, Department of Educational Psychology, University of Arizona, Tucson, AZ:

The TerraNova is the fifth revision of the Comprehensive Tests of Basic Skills (CTBS5). This edition's revisions to the established CTBS series are rather substantial. To understand this edition, it is first necessary to note that TerraNova is a general name for several overlapping, but distinct products, each tailored to specific purposes that potential users may have. Some understanding of the scope and purposes(s) of each of these products, in relation to individual assessment needs, is necessary to select the product that is appropriate.

ORGANIZATION OF THE TERRANOVA. The main products are the Survey Battery, Complete Battery, and Basic Battery. Each of these may be purchased with additional supplemental subtests. The word "Plus" is added to the preceding product titles when the supplemental tests are included.

The Survey Battery is a multiple-choice test. It has the fewest items per subtest. As a consequence of using a shorter test, the publisher correctly states that individual students' scores are somewhat less reliable. Thus, the publisher provides only norm-referenced information for individual students. However, curriculum-referenced information is provided at the class, school, and district levels. The Survey Battery includes subtests and scores for Reading/Language Arts, Mathematics, Science, and Social Studies. The Survey Battery Plus, contains additional subtests of Language Mechanics/Word Analysis, Vocabulary, Spelling, and Mathematics Computation. When the Survey Battery Plus product is used, composite scores are provided in reading, language, and mathematics that include the appropriate supplemental subtests.

The Complete Battery is a multiple-choice test also. To create the Complete Battery, the publisher used the items from the Survey Battery along with additional items. The consequences of lengthening the subtests are having more reliable individual student subtest scores and being able to report on each student's mastery of the objectives assessed within each subtest. These latter scores can be used to identify each student's strengths and needs within each curricular area assessed. The Complete Battery Plus includes the same supplemental subtests as were provided with the Survey Battery Plus. The composite scores the publisher reports include these supplements.

The Basic Battery is a multiple-choice test with sufficient reliability for individual student scores but only assesses reading and mathematics. It contains the same Reading/Language Arts and Mathematics subtests as the Complete Battery. The Basic Battery Plus includes the same set of supplemental subtests and also yields composite scores.

The Multiple Assessments Battery contains both multiple-choice and constructed-response items. It has the same subtests and multiple-choice items as the Survey Battery. At the end of each subtest, the publisher added short-response and extended-response items.

CHANGES AND NEW FEATURES. A distinguishing new feature of all the above-described TerraNova products is the way test items are organized within subtests. Items within each subtest are organized according to contextual themes, thus countering to some degree the often-heard criticism that standardized tests assess strictly decontextualized knowledge and skills. For example, a set of several mathematics items may be presented in the context of a neighborhood theme.

Within each subtest there are several themes. The themes are grade-appropriate so as to encourage students to engage and interact with the tests' materials. The publisher's studies of the impact of thematic graphical material concluded that there was no statistical difference in students' performance using illustrated and non-illustrated items. However, "below level" students liked the way the pages were designed, believed the illustrations helped them, and said when illustrations were present they knew more about the passages to be read.

VALIDITY AND USABILITY. The approach used to design and organize the TerraNova was thorough and careful. As is typical for better-developed standardized tests, the developers began with a thorough analysis of curriculum guides from around the country, of statements of national and state goals and standards, and of textbook series. Efforts were made to align the test content with the NAEP (National Assessment of Educational Progress) and NCTM (National Council of Teachers of Mathematics) frameworks. Teachers, curriculum experts, and other educators reviewed the test specifications and test materials for appropriateness, fairness, and accuracy. At the high school levels, attention was paid to school-to-career skills by requiring test items to assess students' abilities to apply knowledge to real-life situations.

In addition, the publisher conducted several usability studies to support the new test design and content, and the design of the reports available to a school district. Among the studies the publisher conducted were: impact of the graphical page design (referred to previously), readability of the background colors, clarity and usability of the directions to teachers, how students navigate their way through the test material, preferences students have for a specific test design, and verification of whether students responded to items using the processes that item developers intended them to use. Some of these studies were conducted in "cognitive lab" settings where under the watchful eyes of researchers and video cameras, individual students used their fingers to navigate test pages; talked aloud as they worked through the items; and expressed their concerns, confusions, and preferences. The results of these studies were used to improve test items, teachers' directions, and page designs.

There are important differences in the way earlier editions of the CTBS and TerraNova assess reading, language arts, mathematics, science, and social studies in the "non-Plus" subtests. The organization of the items into thematic context groups was discussed above. Beyond that, the subtests attempt to reflect recent developments in how each curriculum area teaches and integrates its unique base of knowledge, skills, and ability. For example, items from reading comprehension, language expression, vocabulary, and reference skills are intermixed within themes. Reading items tend to focus on comprehending the central message of the passage, and are sequenced systematically from lower level comprehension through extension, interpretation, and inference. Vocabulary items usually assess understanding the meaning of selected words in the context of the theme and passage reading. Items assessing language expression are similarly linked to the same passage or its thematic context. Passages are often extracted from published works and are presented in their original format. Unlike previous editions, the TerraNova reading passages tend to be realistically long.

To illustrate, consider one Reading/Language Arts section at Level 19 (Grade 9), Basic Battery. The thematic section begins with an approximately 520-word biographical sketch of an author, including the author's photograph. This is followed by four items: one reading comprehension and three about a related timeline printed on the page. Timeline items refer to events stemming from the author's biography. These are followed by an extended extract from one of the author's books (approximately 1,100 words). The extract is preceded by a paragraph introducing the material and setting the context. The extract is followed by six items assessing various aspects of comprehension and interpretation. Next, are two items assessing comprehension across both the extract and the biographical sketch. The next five items assess a student's language expression and usage, all within the theme of the author and the author's work. The material for applying language expression is a report written by a fictitious student about the author's book.

Mathematics, Science, and Social Studies subtests are comparably organized around applied themes with integrated skill assessment. In this manner, the publisher hopes to mirror the way language and reading are taught in schools.

You should note that the Plus subtests do not have the same organization and orientation as do the main batteries. They follow a more traditional presentation, using multiple-choice items to assess skills in isolation and without engaging themes.

A criticism of the CTBS4 was that no evidence was presented concerning the speededness of the test (Hopkins, 1992). In this edition, this shortcoming is corrected. The data presented show that typically fewer than 4% of the students fail to respond to the last multiple-choice item on the Survey Plus and the Complete Battery Plus. Data are not provided for the Multiple Assessments Battery in which constructed-response items are found. Experience in some large scale assessment programs indicates that students may respond less frequently to constructed-response items, not because the tests are speeded, but because students do not understand the question, think they cannot write a response that is worthy of full marks, or think the question requires too much writing. It would be useful for the publisher to explore these issues with the TerraNova. The item difficulty data for the constructed-response items show that there may be a tendency for them to be slightly more difficult than multiple-choice items, which is to be expected because students responding to multiple-choice items may answer correctly using partial knowledge and receive full credit. Whether this is a signal that there is not enough time to complete all constructed-response items cannot be ascertained from the data.

Throughout all the manuals and teacher's guides, the publisher addresses evidence of validity. Much of the evidence is provided in the technical publications. However, the bulk of the validity *argument* is presented in the Teacher's Guide to the TerraNova. Details are provided on the development procedures, the thinking skills frameworks, the rationales for the curriculum approaches taken, the proper interpretations and limitations of the scores, and the items' contents. A five-page appendix is devoted to an argument for the content validity of scores from the test. The publisher has provided one of the most complete discussions of validity currently available for standardized achievement batteries.

NORMS AND SCALES. The publisher provides fall, winter, and spring norms. Fall standardization included 71,366 students (Grades 1–12), and spring standardization included 100,650 students (K–12). Winter norms are generally interpolated, but over 8,000 students in Kindergarten and Grade 1 were sampled. The sample appears to be reasonably representative of the nation's students and not overrepresentative of former CTBS users. However, test users are urged to test in the spring or fall because empirical norms are available for late April and October, respectively.

The now-standard set of norm-referenced scores is provided: percentile ranks, normal curve equivalents, grade-equivalents, and stanines. The standard score scale, spanning all grades in a range of 0 to 999, is the main interpretive educational development growth scale. It is derived from an IRT item scaling in which multiple-choice and constructed-response items were scaled simultaneously using CTB/McGraw-Hill's proprietary software, PARDUX. This software uses marginal maximum likelihood implemented via the EM algorithm.

The norm-referenced scores and the IRT scoring (called "pattern scoring") are very well described in two excellent publications: the Teacher's Guide and *Beyond the Numbers*. Both publications should be read before using the test results. School principals, in particular, should not attempt to use the TerraNova unless they have studied both publications.

As with earlier editions of the CTBS, Anticipated Achievement Scores are provided when the Test of Cognitive Skills (TCS) is administered along with a TerraNova battery. These multiple-regression-based scores are a useful adjunct to other battery scores. They estimate what students of similar age, grade, and TCS score do on the average on each TerraNova subtest. However, the anticipated score should not be used as a goal or an "expectation." One should not expect a student to be "average" for his or her age and grade. It is inappropriate, also, based on these scores, to describe a student as an "overachiever" or "underachiever." One can say the student is above (or below) the average for his (her) age and grade.

CRITERION-REFERENCED INFORMATION. If the Complete or Basic Batteries are used, then each student can receive a score on each of the objectives the test measures. This score is called an Objective Performance Index (OPI). Each objective on which a score is reported is measured by at least four items. The score is an estimate of the percent of items for an objective that a student can answer correctly. The automated score report interprets the estimated percentage in this way: nonmastery (0–49%), partial mastery (50–74%), and mastery (75–100%). The hope is that teachers will use these scores to identify specific subject-matter objectives on which a student needs more instruction.

Objective-based information for the entire class (average OPI) is available for all three batteries. Average OPIs may help teachers plan instruction either for the current group or for next year's class.

Students' test results can also be reported as performance levels. Scores range from 1 to 5. The respective verbal labels are: Starting Out (or Step 1), Progressing, Nearing Proficiency, Proficient, and Advanced. This type of reporting mimics the way that the National Assessment of Educational Progress and several states report performance.

Performance levels were set using the Bookmark Standard Setting Procedure (Lewis, Mitzel, & Green, 1996). The standard errors for the cutscores resulting from this procedure seem reasonably small. Teachers and administrators are provided verbal description for each subject (reading, language arts, mathematics, science, and social studies) of the skills, knowledge, and concepts of which students at each performance level are supposed to be able to have reasonable mastery. These skills are described in the Performance Levels Handbook.

SUMMARY. The TerraNova is a technically well-built achievement test. It is one of the better batteries of its type. The new features of embedding items in thematic contexts, using more real-world item formats, and incorporating constructed-response items with the multiple-choice subtests seem to be educationally sound. The three versions (Survey, Complete, Basic), with their "Pluses," and the Multiple Assessment Battery have something to offer everyone, albeit as a confusing array on first blush. Teachers' materials are exceptionally well done and informative. The score reports that are available are also well done, having been, themselves, field tested. If the TerraNova's content and approach are a close fit to a school district's curriculum framework, it should be seriously considered for adoption. If this close match is not there, look elsewhere.

REVIEWER'S REFERENCES

Hopkins, K. D. (1992). [Review of the Comprehensive Tests of Basic Skills, Fourth Edition]. In J. J. Kramer & J. C. Conoley (Eds.), *The eleventh mental measurements yearbook* (pp. 215–217). Lincoln, NE: The Buros Institute of Mental Measurements.

Lewis, D. M., Mitzel, H. C., & Green, D. R. (1996, June). Standard setting: A bookmark approach. In D. R. Green (Chair), *IRT-based standard-setting procedures utilizing behavioral anchoring.* Symposium conducted at the meeting of the Council of Chief State School Officers National Conference on Large Scale Assessment, Phoenix, AZ.

[89]

Test of Children's Language: Assessing Aspects of Spoken Language, Reading, and Writing.

Purpose: "Designed to measure important aspects of spoken language, reading, and writing."

Population: Ages 5-0 to 8-11.

Publication Date: 1996.

Acronym: TOCL.

Scores, 11: 7 Component Scores (Spoken Language, Knowledge of Print, Word Recognition, Reading Comprehension, Writing Skills, Writing From Memory, Original Writing); 4 Combined Scores (Spoken Language Quotient; Reading Quotient, Writing Quotient; Total Language Quotient).

Administration: Individual.

Price Data, 1999: $139 per complete kit including manual (62 pages), "A Visit with Mr. Turtle" storybook, story picture sheet, 25 student workbooks, and 25 profile/examiner record forms in storage box; $39 per 25 student workbooks; $44 per 25 profile/examiner record forms; $44 per manual; $5 per storybook picture sheet; $12 per "A Visit with Mr. Turtle" storybook.

Time: (30–40) minutes.

Authors: Edna Barenbaum and Phyllis Newcomer.

Publisher: PRO-ED.

Review of the Test of Children's Language: Assessing Aspects of Spoken Language, Reading, and Writing by STEVE GRAHAM, Professor of Special Education, University of Maryland, College Park, MD:

The Test of Children's Language (TOCL) was developed to assess selected aspects of young children's spoken language, reading, and writing. According to the authors, the test is unusual in that it bridges the gap between traditional, standardized assessment and nontraditional, performance-based assessment, measuring the language skills of children between the ages of 5-0 and 8-11 using authentic and real-life tasks. The assessment of students' spoken language and reading skills is primarily conducted within the context of a storybook entitled *A Visit With Mr. Turtle*. The storybook is read to the child, with the examiner asking questions either before or after reading the material on a specific page. The only exception involves the last three printed pages of text that are read by the child if she or he is capable of doing so. Writing skills are assessed by asking the child to rewrite the story from memory, using the pictures from the storybook to facilitate recall, and by asking them to write letters, words, and a story about animal friends.

Although the use of the storybook provides an interesting and reasonably method for collecting a variety of information, it is unlikely that teachers will view this task as authentic or real-life. The story is constantly interrupted and parts of each page repeated as the examiner asks the student to carry out specific tasks, such as identifying the letters a specific sound makes, putting words together to form a sentence, and determining what a particular sentence means.

The TOCL can be administered in approximately 30 to 40 minutes, and the authors indicate that the test can be given in several sessions if the examiner decides that this is advisable. Administering the test across multiple sessions is likely to inflate estimates of the child's relative standing, however, especially on the task where the child is asked to rewrite the information in the storybook from memory. When the child is not administered this task immediately after the story is read, the examiner is directed to reread the storybook to the child. Rereading the story without the constant interruptions involved in the initial administration of the storybook tasks is likely to make the process of recalling information easier.

The authors are to be commended for indicating the type of children for which the TOCL is most appropriate, detailing the necessary qualifications for administering the test, and noting specific cautions that should be observed in interpreting the obtained scores. The TOCL is easy to administer and score, although examiners may experience some frustration when trying to determine the part of a word the child is pointing to when completing some of the items on the storybook task. The authors do, however, provide an alternative form of assessment for these items.

According to the authors, the TOCL can be used to determine students' relative standing in terms of their language and literacy skills, pinpoint individual strengths and weaknesses in these skills, identify children at-risk for failure in reading and writing, and document students' progress. Unfortunately, the developers of the TOCL do not present a strong or convincing case for each of these claims. For example, alternate forms of the test are not available and the instrument samples a relatively small range of behaviors in each of the domains tested, undermining the authors' contention that the test can be used to monitor student progress. Similarly, the only evidence to support the claim that the test is helpful in identifying children at-risk for failure in literacy were two small studies conducted by the authors. In the first study, TOCL scores of 43 kindergarten children identified by teachers as at-risk were lower than the scores of kindergarten students in the normative sample. In the second study, TOCL scores of 41 second grade students were related to final report card ratings in major subject areas. Additional research employing stronger outcome measures is needed before this instrument should be used as a device for identifying children at-risk for developing reading and writing difficulties.

Items for the TOCL were developed in response to a number of different theoretical positions concerning language and literacy development. Although the authors asked eight experts to classify items according to the content measured, they used a criterion of agreement barely better than chance to assign an item to a specific domain. There is also some question about the subclassifications given to some items. For instance, the authors indicated that some of the items on the test measure phonological awareness (an oral language skill). Instead, the items appear to assess the child's ability to produce an appropriate sound for an identified letter in a written word.

The initial pilot study for the TOCL involved a small number of participants—75 kindergarten through second grade children. Data form the pilot were used to make minor revisions in the instrument and it was then standardized on a relatively small sample of 908 children. The normative sample was reasonably representative of the population of children residing in the United States at the time of the 1990 census.

Overall, the reliability estimates for scores from the instrument appear adequate. Measures of internal consistency computed on the standardization sample were, in almost all instances, above .80 and often above .90. Although test-retest (with a 14–21 day interval) reliability coefficients were computed from a sample of only 45 children, they ranged from .82 to .98. The only exception involved the Reading Comprehension subtest for which the test-retest reliability coefficient was .77. It is important to note, however, that test-retest reliability coefficients were not available at different ages, and the authors failed to provide any information in intra- or interrater reliability.

It is possible that the TOCL is too easy for older children. There was very little difference in the test performance of 7- and 8-year-old children in the normative sample and the item analysis conducted by the authors on the test indicated that items measuring spoken language and reading were fairly easy for students at these ages. In contrast, results of the item analysis indicated that

the criteria used to score two of the writing subtests, Writing From Memory (i.e., retelling the storybook) and Original Writing (writing a story about animal friends), are overly difficult for younger children—those who are 5 and 6 years of age.

Finally, the authors conducted several studies establishing that scores on the TOCL were related to other measures of early reading, language, and intelligence. They further provided evidence that students who typically have language-related problems scored lower on the TOCL than children in the normative sample. Unfortunately, these studies involved small numbers of children, and require replication before the authors of the TOCL can make a strong or convincing case regarding the validity for scores from the instrument. At this point, the TOCL appears to be best suited as a screening device for identifying young children who may benefit from additional testing in spoken language, reading, or writing.

Review of the Test of Children's Language: Assessing Aspects of Spoken Language, Reading, and Writing by RICHARD M. WOLF, Professor of Psychology and Education, Teachers College, Columbia University, New York, NY:

The Test of Children's Language (TOCL) is an individually administered test that measures proficiency in three areas of children's language: spoken language, reading, and writing. It is intended for use with children from age 5-0 to 8-11. It yields a number of scores in each area. A single score is obtained in the area of Spoken language, three scores in the area of reading (Knowledge of Print, Word Recognition, and Reading Comprehension), and three scores in writing (Writing Skills, Writing From Memory, and Original Writing). A total score can also be obtained. Administration time is estimated to be between 30 to 40 minutes and can be given in one or two testing periods. Much of the test material is based on a short book that is given to the student to read and answer questions. In addition, the student is asked to do some writing.

The testing situation is somewhat similar to a clinical interview. Detailed directions are provided to the examiner and a sheet for recording the student's answers is used. The recording sheet also contains the directions. An answer sheet is furnished the student. The testing situation attempts to combine elements of a conventional testing situation along with a whole language approach. The testing situation clearly depends heavily on the ability of the examiner to develop rapport with the student and to maintain a relaxed flow to the testing situation. Although no special training seems to be required, as the manual states, it seems that some experience in administering the test is needed in order to become proficient. Classroom teachers should be able to administer and score the test after a period of study and practice. Whether a classroom teacher would have the time to individually administer the test to some or all members of his or her class is open to question.

Raw scores are obtained for each subtest, which can then be converted to standard scores. These standard scores can then be aggregated into subscores for the three areas of language and, finally, into a total score. The total score can be expressed either as a quotient (really a standard score with a mean of 100 and a standard deviation of 15), an age equivalent, a percentile rank, or a stanine. It is also possible to obtain a total score based on from three to all seven subtests although this is questionable because it is not specified which three subtests are included in the derived total score.

Although the TOCL is intended for use with students from ages 5-0 to 8-11, the use of the test with 5-year-olds and 8-year-olds is questionable. Five-year-olds have usually had little formal instruction in reading, so testing at this age level is dubious. At the 8-year-old level, the tests show a distinct ceiling effect. For example, for 7-year-olds, the average percent correct for the test items ranges from .29 for Writing From Memory to .93 for Word Recognition with an average item difficulty of .71. At age 8, the average percent correct for the items ranges from .34 to .96 with an average item difficulty of .74. One would expect to see a much greater difference in the average item difficulties from age 7 to 8.

The TOCL was standardized on a sample of 908 students drawn from 15 states from around the country. The demographic characteristics of the standardization group fairly closely match characteristics of the U.S. population, based on the 1990 Census data. However, the number of students tested at each grade level varies from 136 at age 5 to 317 at age 7. Item analyses were carried out for each subtest at each age level. Median item difficulties increase substantially for each subtest at each age level except from age 7 to 8. Median discrimination indices appear to be acceptable. However, individual item difficulties and discrimination indices are not provided. The authors attempt to show that the tests do not exhibit any gender or racial bias by presenting correlations between delta values for gender and racial (white/nonwhite groups). However, this merely shows that the items are of the same order of difficulty for the groups being studied. It says nothing about the actual item difficulties. One gender group could systematically score .50 higher than the other gender group on every item, for example, and the correlation would be +1.0.

Reliabilities of the subtests were estimated both by internal consistency and by test-retest. Internal consistency reliability estimates are generally above .80 with a number of tests yielding values above .90. A few subtests have internal consistency reliability values at some age levels between .73 and .77. Test-retest reliabilities (time interval ranged from 14 to 21 days) ranged from .77 for Reading Comprehension to .98 for Word Recognition. Most are .90 or higher. Clearly, the reliability scores from the tests is satisfactory. Validity information is provided in the form of correlations with other tests of reading and language ability. The correlations range from .56 (Writing From Memory vs. Reid, Hresko, & Hamill's Test of Early Reading Ability—2nd ed.) to .83 (Knowledge of Print vs. the same test). Total scores on the TOCL correlate .84 and .88 with other tests of reading ability and language ability. Evidence of construct validity inheres in increasing means with age except for the fact that the means for 8-year-olds are only slightly higher than the means for 7-year-olds. Total scores on the TOCL correlate .86 with Wechsler Intelligence Scale for Children—Revised (WISC-R) total scores, but the analysis is based on only 33 second grade students. All subtests of the TOCL correlate significantly with WISC-R scores except for Writing From Memory and Original Writing.

In summary, the TOCL is an individually administered test based on a whole language concept and yields scores in spoken language, reading, and writing. Although intended for students from ages 5-0 to 8-11, it is probably best used with 6- and 7-year-olds. Testing time per student is from 30 to 40 minutes. The test items appear to have been carefully constructed and there is much testing of language in context. Reliability and validity information is generally acceptable. Whether teachers or other school personnel would want to administer such a labor intensive test is a question that can only be answered by prospective users.

[90]
Test of Language Development—Intermediate, Third Edition.

Purpose: To determine strengths and weaknesses in language skills.
Population: Ages 8-0 to 12-11.
Publication Dates: 1977–1997.
Acronym: TOLD-I:3
Scores, 12: General Intelligence/Aptitude Quotient, Spoken Language Quotient (SLQ), Listening Quotient (LiQ), Speaking Quotient (SpA), Semantics Quotient (SeQ), Syntax Quotient (SyQ), Sentence Combining (SC), Picture Vocabulary (PV), Word Ordering (WO), Generals (GL), Grammatic Comprehension (GC), Malapropism (MP).
Administration: Individual.
Price Data, 1999: $154 per complete kit.
Time: (30–60) minutes.
Comments: Primary edition also available.
Authors: Donald D. Hammill and Phyllis L. Newcomer.
Publisher: PRO-ED.
Cross References: See T5:2694 (27 references) and T4:2767 (7 references); for reviews by Rebecca McCauley and Kenneth G. Shipley of the TOLD-I:2, see 11:436 (5 references). For a review by Doris V. Allen of an earlier version of the entire Test of Language Development, see 9:1261 (5 references).

Review of the Test of Language Development— Intermediate, Third Edition by DAVID P. HURFORD, Director of the Center for the Assessment and Remediation of Reading Difficulties and Associate Professor of Psychology and Counseling, Pittsburg State University, Pittsburg, KS:

The Test of Language Development—Intermediate, Third Edition (TOLD-I:3) is to be used to measure the language skills of children between the ages of 8-0 and 12-11. The TOLD-I was originally developed to bridge the age gap between the Test of Language Development—Primary (TOLD-P), intended to examine the language development of children between the ages of 4-0 and 8-11 years, and the Test of Adolescent Language (TOAL), intended to examine the language development of children between the ages of 12-0 and 18-5 years. The age range for the

TOLD-I:3 overlaps the age ranges for the TOLD-P and the TOAL. The revisions that resulted in the TOLD-I:3 occurred as a function of previous reviews. The TOLD-I:3 includes a new subtest, Picture Vocabulary, that replaced the Vocabulary subtest. The other subtests remain the same.

The TOLD-I:3 assesses overall spoken language, semantics, syntax, listening, and speaking. The test evaluates these skills with six subtests that produce five composite scores expressed as quotients. Although the TOLD-I:3 produces subtest scores, the authors recommend using the composite quotients. The description of each subtest in the order of their intended presentation is as follows. Sentence Combining measures the ability to combine two or more sentences into one complex or compound sentence while retaining all of the relevant information from the shorter sentences (e.g., I am big. I am tall. = I am big and tall.). Picture Vocabulary assesses the individual's ability to comprehend the meaning of two word phrases by pointing to a picture depicting the phrase. Word Ordering measures the ability to combine randomly presented words into meaningful sentences (e.g., big-am-I = I am big or Am I big?). Generals measures the ability to identify the similarities among three words (e.g., Monday, Tuesday, Wednesday). Grammatic Comprehension requires the individual to identify the word that has been used in an ungrammatical way (e.g., Me play ball). Malapropisms measures the ability to realize that a similar sounding word has been incorrectly substituted for another (.e.g., We should brush our feet every morning). All age groups begin with the first item on each subtest and proceed until ceiling. Each item is scored as 1 for correct and 0 for incorrect. Raw scores are simply the number of correct items per subtest that can be transformed into age equivalent scores, percentile ranks, and standard scores.

There are five composite scores, which are represented as quotients: spoken language (Spoken Language Quotient, SLQ), semantics (Semantics Quotient, SeQ), syntax (Syntax Quotient, SyQ), Listening (Listening Quotient, LiQ), and speaking (Speaking Quotient, SpQ). All six subtests are involved in the Spoken Language Quotient, which is the test's best indicator of a child's language ability. The Semantics Quotient is composed of the Picture Vocabulary, Generals, and Malapropisms subtests. The Syntax Quotient is composed of the Sentence Combining, Word Ordering, and Grammatic Comprehension subtests. The Listening Quotient is composed of the Picture Vocabulary, Grammatic Comprehension, and Malapropisms subtests. Finally, the Speaking Quotient is composed of the Sentence Combining, Word Ordering, and Generals subtests. The composite scores reflect the theoretical two-dimensional model that guided the design and construction of the test. The first dimension of the model includes the linguistic systems of reception (listening) and expression (speaking) and the second dimension of the model includes the linguistic features of syntax (the structure of the language) and semantics (the meaning associated with the language). The composite scores represent the various combinations of the two levels of the dimensions of the model: listening, speaking, semantics, and syntax. The Spoken Language Quotient reflects both dimensions and provides an overall evaluation of language ability. The composite quotients have a mean of 100 and standard deviations of 15 and easily converted from subtest standard score totals into quotients with the use of a table.

The TOLD-I:3 was normed with 779 children from 23 states. The norming sample closely approximated the U.S. Bureau of the Census information with regard to geographic area, gender, race, residence (urban vs. rural), ethnicity, family income, parents' educational attainment, age, and disability status (i.e., no disability, learning disability, speech-language disorder, mental retardation, other). The TOLD-I:3 provides standard scores with means of 10 and standard deviations of 3, age equivalents, and percentile ranks for the subtests, and, as mentioned above, quotients that have means of 100 and standard deviations of 15.

Reliability was examined with internal consistency and test-retest correlation coefficients. Cronbach's coefficient alphas for 8-, 9-, 10-, 11-, and 12-year-old participants ranged from .80 to .97 for the subtests (Mdn = .88). The coefficient alphas for the composites were considerably larger ranging from .92 to .96 (Mdn = .94). Coefficient alphas were generated for the subgroups within gender, ethnicity, and disability status which resulted in coefficients ranging from .70 to .97 for the subtests and .90 to .97 for the composites. Test-retest reliability coefficients ranged between .83 to .93 for the subtests and .94 and .96 for the

composites. The test-retest study involved only 55 participants with the time between administrations of only one week. Interrater reliability was examined with the assistance of two staff personnel from PRO-ED's research department who scored 50 protocols chosen at random. Interrater reliability ranged from .94 to .97 on the subtests and .96 to .97 for the composites.

Validity was examined using content, criterion-related, and construct validity. The items for the subtests were created with the two-dimensional model described above as a guide. As a result, the items should reflect adequately the content they were purported to tap. To assess how closely the items represented the particular domains of interest, 71 individuals who had applied or theoretical experience in language were asked to rate the formats of the six subtests according to how closely they matched the two-dimensional model. The raters generally rated the subtests in a manner that was consistent with the model used to create the subtests. Criterion-related validity was assessed by correlating the subtest and composite scores on the TOLD-I:3 and the TOAL-3. The coefficients ranged from .58 to .86 for the subtests and .74 and .88 for the composites. The correlation coefficient between the Spoken Language Quotients for the TOLD-I:3 and the TOAL-3 was quite large (.85). No other tests were used to establish criterion-related validity.

Construct validity was evaluated by several approaches. If the TOLD-I:3 properly assessed language ability, subtest scores should increase with age as language skills develop. Positive correlation coefficients were reported for age and subtest scores that ranged between .32 to .47 on the various subtests. If scores from the TOLD-I:3 had construct validity, one would expect that disability groups (i.e., speech and language disabilities, learning disabilities, mental retardation, and attention-deficit/hyperactivity deficits) could be differentiated from nondisabled children. Although no results of statistical analyses were reported, the groups with disabilities had smaller standard score and composite means than the nondisabled group. Subtest correlation coefficients ranged from .38 to .63 indicating that the subtests are measuring a similar construct, language ability. The TOLD-I:3 composite scores were correlated with the Comprehensive Scales of Student Abilities (CSSA) test in a study examining 24 students. The correlation matrix included the five composites of the TOLD-I:3 and the five values (Verbal Thinking, Speech, Reading, Writing, and Mathematics) from the CSSA. Of the 25 coefficients, 17 were significant indicating that the TOLD-I:3 was related to school achievement. The subtest scores from the normative sample were also subjected to principal component analysis. The results indicated that all six subtests strongly loaded on a single factor. This factor accounted for 88% of the variance with loadings ranging from .59 to .79. It would have been interesting to see if the bidimensional model would have been supported by rotating the principal components solution. Rotating the principal components solution would allow one to determine if the resulting factors support the model used to build the TOLD-I:3.

To guard against test bias, the normative sample was diverse and representative of the U.S. population as reflected in the U.S. Bureau of Census information, which reduces the likelihood that a test will be biased. In addition, test bias was not indicated by the consistency of reliability and validity coefficients for the various ethnic and disability groups. Item response theory and Delta scores analyses were applied to the subgroups in the normative sample. Each approach suggested that bias was not present in the TOLD-I:3. Researchers have indicated that timed tests might underestimate the ability of certain groups. The authors point out that none of the subtests are timed, as such, and that the test should not be biased in this regard.

The Record Booklet has sections for identifying information (e.g., name, gender, age, etc.), recording the scores (e.g., raw scores, standard scores, age equivalents, percentile ranks, and quotients), and score profiles (graphical display of the standard scores and quotients). The subtests along with their brief instructions are contained within the Record Booklet. There is a Comments section after the first subtest that should be used to record the disposition of the examinee, the environment of the examination, and other pertinent information. The examiner should realize that the Comments section refers to the entire test and not just the first subtest.

The TOLD-I:3 examiner's manual is well written, quite thorough, and informative. There are two points that need to be mentioned and

further clarified. It is stated on page 5 that "No subtests were developed to measure the phonology feature. This is because children older than 6 or 7 usually have already incorporated successfully most phonological abilities into their language." Although this may be true for nondisabled children, it is most likely the case that individuals who will be assessed with this instrument will be suspected for language deficiencies. It has long been determined that children with language deficiencies are also likely to have phonological processing deficiencies as well. Assessing phonology would be a welcome addition to this test, particularly because one of its intended uses is to identify children who are experiencing learning and other language-related disabilities. On pages 29 and 30 a case sample is presented. The Spoken Language Quotient and an IQ score (Comprehensive Test of Nonverbal Intelligence) for this fictitious individual is 77 and 90, respectively. On page 30, the authors state "Comparison of Steve's SLQ (77) with his IQ (90) … suggest that his poor language might be accounted for by low mental ability." Although Steve's SLQ is quite low (77, more than 1 standard deviation below the mean), his IQ is well within what most psychometricians would consider low average to average ability. Referring to an IQ score of 90 as low mental ability is not justified and certainly does not explain the relatively low Spoken Language Quotient.

SUMMARY. The TOLD-I:3 is a carefully constructed test of language ability to be used with children between 8-0 and 12-11 years of age. The theoretical framework that guided its creation is appropriate and item construction closely matched the framework. Reliability and validity seem to be well established, although in some cases the sample sizes of the studies were quite small. The TOLD-I:3 provides information concerning listening, speaking, semantics, and syntax abilities as well as an overall measurement of spoken language ability. This information is useful for the diagnosis of weaknesses and the planning of interventions.

Review of the Test of Language Development—Intermediate, Third Edition by PAT MIRENDA, Associate Professor, University of British Columbia, Vancouver, British Columbia, Canada:

The Test of Language Development—Intermediate, Third Edition (TOLD-I:3) is a 1997 revision of one of the most widespread measures of language skills of children between the ages of 8-0 and 12-11 who speak English and are not deaf or hard-of-hearing. Like its predecessor, the TOLD-I:3 requires approximately 1 hour to administer, and is meant to be used by examiners who have some formal training in assessment, including (ideally) supervised practice. The test manual is easy to read and well organized, and provides appropriate instructions to examiners with regard to test administration, scoring, and interpretation. It also contains an excellent, albeit brief, chapter that provides information about the usefulness and limitations of standardized tests in general, as well as resources related to language instruction and remediation.

The TOLD-I:3 measures both receptive (i.e., listening) and expressive (i.e., speaking) English language skills in each of two areas: semantics (the meaning of language) and syntax (the structure of language). With regard to semantics, the test includes subtests that measure the child's knowledge of picture vocabulary items, ability to identify malapropisms in spoken sentences, and ability to explain the similarities between three words spoken by the examiner. With regard to syntax, the test includes subtests related to the child's ability to recognize incorrect grammar in spoken sentences, to form one sentence from two or more spoken by the examiner, and to reorder a series of spoken words to form a complete sentence. Composite scores can also be calculated in each of five areas: semantics, syntax, listening, speaking, and spoken language overall.

The revision was undertaken to address some of the limitations of the previous version. In terms of the test items themselves, a new subtest, Picture Vocabulary, replaces Vocabulary from the previous edition; and children's names used in the test items were revised to reflect the current demographic makeup of U.S. schools. In addition, the rationale for the test has been updated to reflect current theories and research regarding oral communication.

The TOLD-I:3 was normed in 1996 on a sample of 779 persons in 23 states representing all regions of the U.S. Norming was done by 37 experienced examiners who were selected at random from a database of professionals who purchased the TOLD-I:2 within the previous 2 years. Characteristics of the normative sample were keyed to the 1990 U.S. Census data and are representative of the current U.S. population as well with regard to gender, race, ethnicity, family income, disabling conditions, and several other factors. Extensive demographic data for the sample are provided in the test manual. Normative data (percentiles and standard scores) are provided for each of the six subtests and five composite areas in an Appendix. Age equivalents are also provided, along with an appropriate note in the manual advising examiners to exercise caution when using such equivalents.

Content sampling error (i.e., internal consistency reliability) was evaluated using Cronbach's alpha as applied to five age intervals from the entire normative sample. All of the coefficients for the subtests exceeded .84, and all for the composites exceeded .90, indicating high degrees of internal reliability. In addition, alpha values for 11 selected demographic subgroups (including those related to gender, race, and various disabilities) within the normative sample are also reported. All but one exceeded .81, indicating that the TOLD-I:3 is about equally reliable for all subgroups investigated and contains little or no bias relative to those groups.

Test-retest reliability was measured with 55 fourth- fifth-, and sixth-grade students who attended regular classes in Texas, with a time lapse of one week between the two test administrations. Test-retest coefficients for all subtests were .83 or above, indicating that the test contains little or no time sampling error. Interscorer reliability was measured by having two individuals independently score a set of 50 completed protocols that were randomly selected from the normative sample. The correlation coefficients were all .94 or above, indicating a high degree of scorer reliability for the test. Overall, scores from the TOLD-I:3 are highly reliable and show little evidence of significant test error when used as intended.

Content validity was established on the basis of the extant research and theoretical literature in the areas contained in the TOLD-I:3 and in other tests that measure the same constructs. In addition, 71 professionals who were "known to have a practical or theoretical interest in spoken language" (p. 59) read descriptions of the formats of the six subtests and rated them on two 9-point scales. On one scale, a low score indicated that the rater thought the test format was more a measure of semantics than syntax. On the other scale, a low score indicated that the test was seen as more a measure of listening than speaking. In general, the mean ratings provide support that the subtests were perceived by the experts to measure what they were intended to measure.

Quantitative evidence for content validity was measured using the point-biserial correlation technique to determine item discrimination. On the basis of the results, items that did not satisfy the item discrimination and item difficulty criteria were eliminated from the final version of the test. In the end, an item analysis was undertaken with the entire normative sample; the results indicated an acceptable degree of content validity. In addition, the Item Response Theory (IRT) approach was used to compare item performance between five demographic groups on the sample, including males/females, African Americans/non-African Americans, and learning-disabled/non-learning-disabled students. Only a few of the items (2.5–6.0%) were found to be potentially biased with regard to the groups studied. The Delta scores approach was applied to nine groups and the resulting correlation coefficients were generally .90 or above, with the exception of three scores of .82, .84, and .88. Together, these measures indicate that the test items contain little or no bias with regard to the groups investigated.

Criterion-related validity (i.e., predictive validity) was examined by correlating relevant TOLD-I:3 subtest scores with those from the Test of Adolescent and Adult Language—Third Edition (TOAL-3) (Hammill, Brown, Larsen, & Wiederholt, 1994). Both tests were administered to a group of 26 nondisabled fifth and sixth graders from Texas. Pearson product-moment coefficients were .58 or above for the selected subtests, indicating at least moderate correlations. In addition, five TOAL-3 composite score were correlated with 11 TOLD-I:3 variables, and the results indicated an overall correlation of .85. From these data, it appears that the TOLD-I:3 measures similar spoken language constructs to the TOAL-3.

Construct validity was measured in several ways, including calculations of (a) correlations between age and performance of the students in the normative sample on the subtests, (b) standard score means for 392 children with identified disabilities from the normative sample, (c) intercorrelations for the subtests for the entire normative sample, and (d) correlations between the TOLD-I:3 composite scores and school achievement scores as measured by the Comprehensive Scales of Student Abilities (CSSA) for a sample of 24 elementary-age students in Texas. Across all four of these measures, construct validity evidence was found to be well within the acceptable range. In addition, factor and item analyses provided additional evidence for a moderate to high degree of construct validity.

SUMMARY. The TOLD-I:3 is significantly improved from the previous versions, especially with regard to psychometric evidence that scores from the test are valid and reliable when used with a wide variety of demographic subgroups are well as with the general population. Examiners who read the manual thoroughly will be impressed with both its breadth and its depth, and with the extent to which it attempts to place the test in an appropriate theoretical and practical context.

REVIEWER'S REFERENCE

Hammill, D. D., Brown, V. L., Larsen, S. C., & Wiederholt, J. L. (1994). Test of Adolescent and Adult Language (3rd ed.). Austin, TX: PRO-ED.

[91]
Test of Language Development—Primary, Third Edition.

Purpose: To determine children's specific strengths and weaknesses in language skills.

Population: Ages 4-0 to 8-11.

Publication Dates: 1977–1997.

Acronym: TOLD-P:3.

Scores, 15: Subtests (Picture Vocabulary, Relational Vocabulary, Oral Vocabulary, Grammatic Understanding, Sentence Imitation, Grammatic Completion, Word Discrimination [Optional], Phonemic Analysis [Optional], Word Articulation [Optional]); Composites (Listening, Organizing, Speaking, Semantics, Syntax, Spoken Language).

Administration: Individual.

Parts, 2: Subtests, Composites.

Price Data, 1999: $218 per complete kit.

Time: (60) minutes.

Comments: Intermediate edition also available; orally administered; examiners need formal training in assessment; PRO-SCORE Computer Scoring System available for Macintosh, Windows, and DOS (1998).

Authors: Phyllis L. Newcomer and Donald D. Hammill.

Publisher: PRO-ED.

Cross References: See T5:2695 (72 references) and T4:2768 (21 references); for reviews by Linda Crocker and Carol E. Westby of a previous edition, see 11:437 (20 references).

Review of the Test of Language Development—Primary, Third Edition by RONALD A. MADLE, School Psychologist, Shikellamy School District, Sunbury, PA and Adjunct Associate Professor of School Psychology, Pennsylvania State University, University Park, PA:

TEST PURPOSE AND DESIGN. The purpose of the Test of Language Development—Primary, Third Edition (TOLD-P:3) is to provide reliable and valid scores for identifying English-speaking children who show significant delays in language proficiency. It also is intended to determine specific strengths and weaknesses in language development.

The TOLD-P:3 measures children's expressive and receptive competencies in major linguistic areas. The manual thoroughly discusses the constructs upon which the instrument is based. Specifically, it details the use of a two-dimensional conceptual model with linguistic features (Semantics, Syntax, and Phonology) on one dimension, and linguistic systems (Listening, Organizing, and Speaking) on the other. Although not all aspects of spoken language are assessed, the authors explicitly acknowledge this and suggest that some areas, such as pragmatics, are more appropriately assessed through informal methods rather than norm-referenced testing.

The most significant change in the TOLD-P:3 is the addition of integrating-mediating language to the systems measured. Two new subtests, Relational Vocabulary and Phonemic Analysis, were added to the existing Sentence Imitation task to accomplish this. The TOLD-P:3 also moves all phonological subtests from the core battery and now treats them as supplemental measures. This results in a clearer differentiation between the "language" and "speech" systems assessed by the test.

ADMINISTRATION AND SCORING. All materials are well constructed and durable. In keeping with trends in recently developed or revised tests, the pictures are now presented in full color rather than as black-and-white line drawings.

The time to administer the TOLD-P:3 core battery is estimated as 30 to 60 minutes. The supplemental phonology subtests take an additional 30 minutes. The administration and scoring procedures are presented clearly in the manual and should be followed easily by examiners with adequate preparation in individual assessment techniques. A complete discussion of issues such as testing of limits, interpretation, and local norms is included in the manual. Basal and ceiling procedures are followed easily with each subtest beginning at the first item and continuing until five consecutive items are failed.

Subtest raw scores are converted to standard scores (mean = 10; SD = 3) and percentiles. Although test users are advised not to employ them, age equivalents are also included, apparently as a concession to agencies that require them. In addition to the overall Spoken Language Quotient, five composites (mean = 100; SD = 15) are available. Two measure linguistic features (Semantics and Syntax) and three assess linguistic systems (Listening, Organizing, and Speaking). No composites are utilized for the phonological subtests.

STANDARDIZATION. The TOLD-P:3 was standardized on 1,000 children between the ages of 4 and 8, with all data collected in the spring of 1996. A significant criticism of the TOLD-P:2 was addressed with this renorming as the normative data previously had been aggregated across all earlier versions, resulting in some data being collected as early as 1976. The number of children at each age varies from 107 (age 4) to 258 (ages 7 and 8). Because standard score conversion tables use 6-month intervals, however, it is not clear how many children were used for each table. Information presented in the manual indicates the normative sample closely approximated the 1990 U.S. Census data on most demographic variables utilized, including geographic region, gender, race, rural versus urban status, ethnicity, educational attainment of parents, and disability status. Generally, the TOLD-P:3 standardization sample is quite appropriate. There was, however, a slight overrepresentation of lower income families.

RELIABILITY. The authors present reliability information covering each of the three primary sources of error variance: content sampling (internal consistency), time sampling (test-retest reliability), and scorer differences (interrater reliability). The internal consistency data for the TOLD-P:3 are comparable to those of major intelligence tests, typically the best developed of all measures. The internal consistency of the subtests is uniformly in the .80 to low .90 range, whereas composite data are in the low .90 range. The overall Spoken Language Composite internal consistency is .95 or higher across all ages. Data for each scale also are presented by gender, racial status, and disability with no meaningful variation being present across these variables. Although the associated standard errors of measurement are presented in the manual, there is no systematic method to note these on the record form. This is disappointing because most contemporary tests encourage consideration of this information by having spaces to record confidence intervals on the test booklet.

The test-retest reliability estimates for the TOLD-P:3 over a 4-month interval are somewhat lower, but quite acceptable, ranging from .81 to .92. Interrater reliability is reported to be uniformly high (.99) across all scales.

VALIDITY. Several validity studies are provided in the manual. Content validity was investigated qualitatively, through item reviews, as well as quantitatively by using classical item analysis and differential item functioning analysis. Generally, the results support a high degree of content validity, although there is limited item difficulty at ages 4 and 5. This is also evident by examining the subtest and composite floors at these ages. They do not meet Bracken's (1987) suggested criterion of at least two standard deviations below the mean until age 5 1/2. In fact, the minimum Spoken Language Quotient at age 4 is 85, only one standard deviation below the mean. This substantially compromises the authors' stated purpose of identifying children who show significant delays in language proficiency at these ages.

Criterion-related validity was examined by correlating scores from the TOLD-P:3 with those from the Bankson Language Test—Second Edition for 30 primary age students. Uniformly high correlations were found supporting convergent validity. There was limited support, however, for discriminant validity as scores from all subtests and composites correlated similarly with both the semantic and morphological/syntactic scales on the Bankson. More thorough validation studies would have been desirable, although the manual also contains a summary of research on the previous edition that has continuing relevance for the current version.

Construct validity was investigated through documentation of age differentiation, group differentiation, subtest interrelationships, factor analysis, and item validity. The factor analysis revealed all six core subtests loaded on a single factor rather

than validating the theoretical structure of the test. This may, however, be due to "construct underrepresentation," a problem currently being dealt with in the area of intellectual assessment (cf. McGrew, 1997).

Several studies are also detailed documenting the absence of test bias for various dimensions such as gender and racial groups, responding to prior criticisms that the TOLD-P:2 included insufficient information about cultural fairness.

SUMMARY. The TOLD-P:3 represents a significant revision that has taken feedback from earlier test reviewers quite seriously. The manual summarized prior criticisms of the TOLD-P:2 and details how each has been addressed systematically in the current revision. Although a few shortcomings are present, the TOLD-P:3 remains one of the best developed and psychometrically sound measures of children's language available today. Special care should be taken, however, when using it with children below the age of 5 1/2 due to its limited floors. At these ages an alternative measure (e.g., Test of Early Language Development; T5:2680) would be a better choice.

REVIEWER'S REFERENCES

Bracken, B. A. (1987). Limitations of preschool instruments and standards for minimal levels of technical adequacy. *Journal of Psychoeducational Assessment, 4,* 313–326.

McGrew, K. S. (1997). Analysis of the major intelligence batteries according to a proposed comprehensive Gf-Gc framework. In D. P. Flanagan, J. L. Genshaft, & P. L. Harrison (Eds.), *Contemporary intellectual assessment: Theories, tests, and issues* (pp. 151–179). New York: Guilford.

Review of the Test of Language Development— Primary, Third Edition by GABRIELLE STUTMAN, Private Practice, Westchester and Manhattan, NY:

The Test of Language Development—Primary, Third Edition (TOLD-P:3) is represented as the only comprehensive test of oral language abilities that uses a purely linguistic orientation. Its subtests were specifically designed to assess children's receptive and expressive spoken English language competence in the areas of semantics, syntax, and phonology. This third edition of a test originally published in 1977 is substantially improved from previous versions. Major improvements include two new subtests (Phonemic Analysis and Relational Vocabulary), a new composite score, "Organizing" (used to represent mediating processes between reception and expression), and new norms.

PURPOSE AND USE. The TOLD-P:3 is a standardized diagnostic tool that was developed to assess spoken English language. It is used to identify students who need special help, to document their strengths and weaknesses, monitor progress, and measure language for research studies.

The TOLD-P:3 uses a two-dimensional linguistic model that incorporates both linguistic components and linguistic systems of the English language. Three major component features of language are assessed: phonology (the 36 phonemic sounds of the English language), syntax (the morphological structure of English), and semantics (the relation between the spoken and the thought). The three organizing systems addressed are receptive systems (listening), integrating and mediating systems (organizing), and expressive systems (speaking). As each of these organizing systems are assessed via their related semantic, syntactic, and phonological subtests, a three-by-three matrix of linguistic ability is created. The three phonological subtests are supplemental and need not be administered. This two-dimensional organization of test components is very useful in pinpointing the source of linguistic strengths and weaknesses and structuring appropriate intervention.

The authors are clear and thorough in their rationale for and description of each of the subtests. The TOLD-P:3 appears appropriate for its intended population, practitioners, and uses.

ADMINISTRATION AND SCORING. The TOLD-P:3 is designed to be individually administered by a professional with graduate training in test characteristics and administration. The chapter devoted to test administration and scoring includes a section of instructions regarding motivation, the testing situation, etc., to guide the quality of administration. Testing materials have been updated and improved: The pictures are drawn in color and more contemporary names are used in the text. Some additional changes in the testing materials, however, would facilitate their use. The Picture Book would be easier to use if it was structured like an easel to be free standing. Tabs at the different sections would facilitate movement to the next subtest. Also the Record Booklet would be less awkward to use if the "correct response" column were adjacent to the "score" column, rather than at a maximum distance.

Although the instructions are precise, some practice and training should precede the use of this test, and those who are not specifically qualified to administer complex psychological tests should take extra precautions. Many of the subtests will be familiar to the experienced examiner. Scoring is objective for all subtests.

TOLD-P:3 raw subtest scores can be converted into percentiles, age equivalents, and standard scores (with a mean of 10 and a standard deviation of 3) for the subtests. One may compare the standard scores on the various subtests with each other and draw conclusions as to relative strengths and weaknesses of specific linguistic functions. To the authors' credit, strong warnings are issued against the use of age or grade equivalents, which are given only because of legal and administrative necessity. The composite scores are based on several subtests and are given in Quotients with a mean of 100 and a standard deviation of 15 in order to conform with the conventions of IQ testing. These Quotients indicate a child's ability relative to higher order categories. The Spoken Language Quotient (SLQ), calculated using all essential subtests, provides the most comprehensive measure of overall language ability. Comparisons among Quotients may also be made and are considered to be more reliable than comparisons among subtests, as they are based on more data. A sample case is also given to aid the formulation of interpretation and intervention. Because the scoring process is complex and time-consuming, an optional computer scoring/report program should be made available.

RELIABILITY AND VALIDITY. Sample selection procedures, demographic characteristics, reliability, and validity measures are fully documented. The authors have also given clear definitions and explanations of each type of reliability, validity, source of error variance, and the procedures used to gather the evidence.

Reliability was measured in terms of errors of content sampling (internal consistency coefficients), time sampling (4-month time lapse), and scorer differences. All content and time sampling coefficients were in the range of .80 to .90 except for the Word Discrimination subtest. Its time sampling coefficient was only .77, largely as a result of increased variance on the second testing. Scores of different scorers were correlated .99. The magnitude of these coefficients of reliability suggest that the TOLD-P:3 evidences a consistently high degree of reliability across all three types of test error. What the test lacks is a table of coefficients to partial out practice effects when retesting to assess intervention effectiveness.

Three types of validity—content, criterion-related, and construct validity—were investigated. The logical basis for content validity is given in the context of each subtest's derivation from longstanding approaches to the assessment of specific language abilities. Subtests that were changed in this new edition were extensively field tested. In addition, all new and revised subtests were subjected to a classical Item Analysis in which an item inclusion criteria of .3 or greater was used for point-biserial coefficients. Item difficulty analysis, although generally indicating sufficient dispersion, shows compression across the upper age categories for the phonemic subtests (Word Discrimination, Phonemic Analysis, and Word Articulation). Specifically, after about age 7 there is a ceiling effect such that only large age delays will be revealed. Although the authors state that these skills are mastered by that age, more difficult items (e.g., the use of nonsense syllables instead of meaningful words in the Word Discrimination subtest) might have revealed important developmental differences. Relational Vocabulary shows a floor effect for 4- and 5-year-olds.

Item and test bias were dealt with at length. Item bias was measured using the Item Response Theory (IRT) approach with the entire normative sample and a 3.5% level of potential bias was accepted. Test bias was carefully controlled through the use of a demographically representative sample with regard to gender, race, social class, and disability groups in the normative sample.

Criterion-related validity was assessed by correlating TOLD-P:3 scores with the Bankson Language Test—Second Edition (Bankson, 1990). All relevant correlations were significant beyond the .05 level. Strong and convincing evidence is presented for the construct validity through factor, correlational, and logical analysis. Problems with the phonemic scales are dealt with by assigning these tests a supplemental role and advising that they be interpreted strictly in terms of their individual contents.

NORMATIVE INFORMATION. The normative sample, comprising 1,000 children in 28 states, was tested in 1996. The characteristics of the sample with regard to geographic region, gender, race, residence, ethnicity, family income, educational attainment of parents, and disabling condition are representative of the Statistical Abstract of the United States (U.S. Bureau of the Census, 1990) for the school-aged population. Despite small sample size, the representation of population segments within each different age group, is preserved. However, the authors properly caution that, whenever possible, local norms should be developed and used.

SUMMARY. The TOLD-P:3 is substantially improved from earlier editions. As an evaluative and diagnostic tool it serves its stated purpose. It is also helpful in targeting general goals for remediation. Strengths of this test include objectivity of scoring, the three-by-three-matrix organization of test components useful in pinpointing the source of linguistic difficulties and structuring appropriate intervention, its strong historical and logical foundation, relative freedom from bias, acceptable subtest reliability (except for the Word Discrimination subtest), and generally good evidence of validity. Its weaknesses include unnecessarily awkward test materials, no option for computer scoring [Editor's Note: PRO-SCORE System for Macintosh, Windows, and DOS available 1998] , low ceilings on the phonemic measures, a high floor on the Relational Vocabulary subtest, and the lack of a table of test-retest coefficients that would enable the administrator to partial out practice effects when using the instrument to measure intervention effectiveness.

REVIEWER'S REFERENCES
Bankson, N. W. (1990). Bankson Language Test (2nd ed.). Austin, TX: PRO-ED.
U.S. Bureau of the Census. (1990). *Statistical abstract of the United States.* Washington, DC: Author.

[92]

Test of Nonverbal Intelligence, Third Edition.

Purpose: "Developed to assess aptitude, intelligence, abstract reasoning, and problem solving in a completely language-free format."

Population: Ages 6-0 through 89-11.

Publication Dates: 1982–1997.

Acronym: TONI-3.

Scores: Total score only.

Administration: Individual.

Price Data, 1999: $229 per complete kit including manual ('97, 160 pages), picture book, and 50 each Form A and Form B answer booklets and record forms; $39 per 50 answer booklet and record forms (specify Form A or B); $96 per picture book; $59 per manual.

Time: (15–20) minutes.

Authors: Linda Brown, Rita J. Sherbenou, and Susan K. Johnson.
Publisher: PRO-ED.
Cross References: See T5:2704 (47 references) and T4:2775 (10 references); for reviews by Kevin K. Murphy and T. Steuart Watson of the Second Edition, see 11:439 (9 references); for reviews by Philip M. Clark and Samuel T. Mayo of the original edition, see 9:1266.

Review of the Test of Nonverbal Intelligence, Third Edition by JEFFREY A. ATLAS, Associate Clinical Professor (Psychiatry), Bronx Children's Psychiatric Center, Albert Einstein College of Medicine, Bronx, NY:

Tests of nonverbal intelligence are a critical part of mental health and educational workers' assessment tools in considering differential diagnostics, treatment and placement recommendations, and grade placement. Although tests such as the Peabody Picture Vocabulary Test (T5:1903), Goodenough-Harris Draw-A-Person Test (T5:1097), and Raven Progressive Matrices (T5:2163), from which the Test of Nonverbal Intelligence (TONI) draws, have aided in nonverbal assessment, each suffers from various weaknesses ranging from oblique reliance upon verbal skills to outdated or constricted norms. It is unusual for a test to feature well-constructed norms while also making such minimal demands on the examinee such that nearly all populations except the blind may be evaluated for intelligence, viewed as the capacity to reason abstractly. The TONI-3 provides such a measure, which may be applied to the gifted, dyslexic, attention-deficit/hyperactive, learning-disabled, emotionally disturbed, and non-English-speaking groups (all having norms within the average range), while distinguishing such groups from mentally retarded individuals. In this manner, each group's particular handicapping conditions need not confound estimates of intelligence, which optimally could tailor educational and psychotherapeutic programming so as to maximize each person's potential in acting upon the world. Labels (or epithets) such as deaf-dumb, anachronistic yet still occasionally encountered, are reduced as we develop more sensitive means, such as the TONI-3, of recognizing and developing the potential of exceptional groups.

A limitation of the TONI-3, however, is the two-fold problem that special placement decisions do continue to be based primarily on Intellectual Quotient (IQ) scores derived from groundbreaking instruments, such as the Wechsler scales, and that the TONI-3 manual overstates the value of its concurrent validity. Correlations ranging from .53 to .63 between the TONI-3 and Wechsler Intelligence Scale for Children, Third Edition (WISC-III; the primary assessment instrument for the exceptional population served) are at best moderate (accounting for a little over one-third of the variability in scores) and based upon a small sample (of 34 students). Although this limitation is not insignificant, the TONI-3 is probably the best instrument we have in making some sort of comparison to the standard Wechsler scale when it cannot be validly administered due to sensory limitations of the subject. The authors of the TONI-3 are to be commended in presenting the instrument as a work-in-progress, to be revised with the accrual of data, despite validity and reliability estimates that already place it ahead of most "tests" on the market.

The TONI-3 is attractively packaged, with sturdy test plates featuring successively more difficult abstract design entries requiring indication by the subject of the logical complimentary or penultimate design. The manual is a model of historical background information, review of research, reflective consideration of limitations, and care of presentation, and is written in a manner accessible to psychometrically trained students and practitioners.

SUMMARY. The TONI-3 is best seen as a replacement intelligence test for individuals who do not speak English or who suffer sensory deficits. It correlates only moderately with the WISC-III and its pantomimic administration procedure, although as favorably "nonverbal" an administration procedure as one is likely to find, may render test administration to gifted or nonhandicapped students unnecessarily awkward. For those testing situations requiring minimal (mainstream) cultural interference or minimal dependence upon full sensory capacities of examinees, the TONI-3 is to be highly recommended.

Review of the Test of Nonverbal Intelligence, Third Edition by GERALD E. DEMAURO, Coordinator of Assessment, New York State Education Department, Albany, NY:

TEST COVERAGE AND USE. The third edition of the Test of Nonverbal Intelligence

(TONI-3) is described as "a language-free measure of cognitive ability" (cover). It is preceded by the TONI and TONI-2 and is designed to assess aptitude of people from 5-0 to 85-11 years of age whose cognitive, linguistic, or motor skills would interfere with optimal performance on traditional intelligence measures. The authors believe the design and development of the test and its focus on problem solving makes its use particularly valid for a wide range of population groups. Specifically, Jensen's (1980) seven criteria for reducing the impact of language and culture served to guide the development of the two 45-item forms of the instrument.

SAMPLES FOR TEST VALIDATION AND NORMING. The TONI-3 was administered in 1995 to 2,060 individuals and again in 1996 to another 1,391 individuals, for a total of 3,451 examinees chosen to represent the United States population geographically, and by gender, community type, ethnicity and races, disabling condition, and socioeconomic status. The test provides deviation quotients for 23 age groups, demarcated by half years from 6-0 to 10-11, by whole years from 11-0 to 16-11, from 17-0 to 54-11, by 5-year intervals from 55-0 to 79-11 and from 80-0 to 89-11. The 46 raw scores yield 980 conversions to quotients (age intervals by raw scores). Within whole year intervals, the samples range from 54 (80-0 to 89-11) to 1,373 (17-0 to 59-11). The quotients are converted to percentile ranks with varying stability depending upon the size of the samples at the different score points and age groups.

Many validity studies are cited in the 1997 examiner's manual. Specific studies range in sample sizes from 16 (Brown, Sherbenou, & Johnsen, 1982) to item analysis based on the entire normative sample.

The normative data show a rise in mean raw scores over the age intervals up to the 17-0 to 54-11 interval. At 55-0 to 59-11, the means start dropping. Examinees in the 6-0 to 6-5 interval averaged only seven correct items of the 45, whereas examinees in the 17-0 to 54-11 interval averaged 31 correct items.

RELIABILITY. Coefficients alpha and standard errors of measurement (*SEM*s) were calculated for 20 age intervals, delineated by whole years until age 19 and by decades thereafter. The average coefficient for both forms was .93, and the

ranges were .89 to .97. *SEM*s ranged from 3 to 5. Coefficients alpha were: .96 on both forms for males; .95 on both forms for females, Hispanic examinees, and for deaf examinees; .94 on both forms for African Americans and for learning-disabled examinees; and .92 on both forms for gifted examinees.

Alternate form correlations within the 20 age intervals ranged from .74 to .95, and test-retest correlations with a one-week separation ranged from .89 to .94 for both forms for 13-year-olds, 15-year-olds, and 19–40-years-olds. Rescoring of test protocols from the normative sample by staff members of PRO-ED's research department yielded .99 correlations for each form of the test, providing strong evidence of interrater reliability for trained scorers. The reliability studies support test-based decisions about individuals.

CRITERION-RELATED VALIDITY. Several small studies suggest that the convergence of TONI-3 scores with these other intelligence measures increases as their verbal demands decrease. For example, correlations for 19 students on Forms A and B were .57 and .51, respectively with the WAIS-R (Wechsler Adult Intelligence Scale—Revised) Verbal Scale but .75 and .76 with WAIS-R Performance Scales.

These discriminant and convergent properties are less evident for younger examinees. Correlations for 34 seven- to 17-year-olds with the WISC-R (Wechsler Intelligence Scale for Children—Revised) Performance Scale were .56 and .58 for Forms A and B, respectively, whereas those with the WISC-R Verbal Scale were .59 and .53, respectively.

Median correlations of studies of the two earlier versions of the test demonstrate the same relationships, .52 with measure of general aptitude, .45 with measures of verbal aptitude, and .60 with measures of nonverbal aptitude. These correlations appear to be attenuated.

Taken in isolation, these studies contribute to the criterion-related evidence. Taken together, they elaborate the construct in terms of the test's discriminant and convergent properties. Purely from the perspective of criterion-related evidence, information about the types of decisions made about people of different ages and at different scoring ranges and empirical support for those decisions from other sources would be valuable to users.

CONTENT VALIDITY. The authors (Brown, Sherbenou, & Johnson) base their arguments for content validity on rationales for format and items, classical item analysis, and differential item functioning (DIF) analysis. The argument for content validity rests heavily on the fidelity of the test items to the domain. Therefore, evidence that the items are not biased supports the argument when success in the domain is equally likely for equally skilled examinees. The domain focuses on problem solving, and the format is abstract drawing, in light of logistical ease of administration and Jensen's (1980) criteria for language-free tests.

Originally, 307 items were reviewed by experts in psychology, testing, and nonverbal assessment. The 183 surviving items were field-tested, subjected to classical item analysis, and reduced to two parallel 50-item forms (TONI, in 1982). In 1990, the TONI-2 revision, 23 more difficult items were passed through the same screens, and 5 survivors were added to each form. These two forms were reduced to 45 items each on the basis of item analysis and bias analyses of the TONI-3 normative study.

Item analyses used criteria of point-biserial correlations of .33 or higher and p values ranging from .02 to .86 with a mean of .50. Forms were pre-equated on the bases of item p-values for the common normative sample.

DIF analyses employed IRT item characteristic curves and delta item difficulty correlations. Neither identified DIF problems in the surviving item pool related to gender, race, gifted status, or learning disabilities. The IRT approach utilizes hypothetical ability points, whereas the delta approach, without analysis of distance from the regression line of individual items, estimates whole test fairness.

CONSTRUCT VALIDITY. The authors base their construct validity argument on six types of evidence. First, the observed relationship of age to TONI-3 scores follows patterns observed on other intelligence measures. Second, they summarize studies relating TONI-3 scores to school achievement. Third, studies of the normative sample revealed that gifted examinees score highest, examinees with nonintellectual disabilities score lower than gifted examinees, and mentally retarded examinees score lowest. African-American examinees scored about a third of a standard deviation below the total sample, raising the question of culture-bound test content.

Fourth, a study by Vance, Hankins, and Reynolds (1988) is cited that indicates that the TONI-2 is as strong a predictor of the WISC-R Full Scale IQ as is the Quick Test (Ammons & Ammons, 1962). Fifth, exploratory factor analytic studies indicate a single strong factor (59% and 60% of the variance for the two forms, respectively after Promax rotation, and two weaker factors). Sixth, the median item point biserials by age group (medians of .49 for Form A and .50 for Form B) are presented as evidence of fidelity to the construct.

TEST ADMINISTRATION. The test administration procedures are clear and reasonable. They approximate those involved in the normative administration. Questions are nonverbal, and administrations may be curtailed when a ceiling is reached. Because items are arranged by difficulty, a criterion of three incorrect responses among five contiguous questions determines the ceiling. However, there is a provision for administering all 45 items. Three concerns arise under such conditions: (a) The ceiling criterion needs to be studied to assure that answers beyond ceiling are in fact guesses; (b) by not uniformly applying the ceiling criterion, some examinees may be credited with guessing whereas others are not; and (b) if the above concerns are without base, misfitting examinees may still be able to answer more difficult questions after failing earlier questions.

TEST REPORTING. TONI-3 information is summarized on the Answer and Record Form. The information provides quotient, reliability, and raw and percentile rank scores. Provisions are made for other information, some of which involves subjective interpretations of the examiner.

CONCLUSION. The TONI-3 offers much evidence to support its use. It would also be useful to examine differential validity for examinees of different degrees of verbal skills.

REVIEWER'S REFERENCES

Ammons, R. B., & Ammons, C. H. (1962). The Quick Test: Provisional manual. *Psychological Reports, 11,* 11–161.

Jenson, A. R. (1980). *Bias in mental testing.* New York: Free Press.

Brown, L., Sherbenou, R. J., & Johnsen, S. K. (1982). Test of Nonverbal Intelligence manual. Austin, TX: PRO-ED.

Vance, B., Hankins, N., & Reynolds, F. (1988). Prediction of Wechsler Intelligence Scale for Children—Revised Full Scale IQ from the Quick Test of Intelligence and the Test of Nonverbal Intelligence for a sample of referred children and youth. *Journal of Clinical Psychology, 44,* 793–794.

Tests of Achievement and Proficiency, Forms K, L, and M.

Purpose: Designed to "provide a comprehensive and objective measure of students' progress in a high school curriculum."

Population: Grades 9–12.

Publication Dates: 1978–1996.

Acronym: TAP.

Forms, 3: K, L, M; 2 batteries: Complete and Survey.

Administration: Group.

Levels, 4: 15, 16, 17, 18.

Price Data, 1999: $17 per 25 practice test booklets including 1 directions for administration; $3 per practice test directions for administration; $7 per Preparing for Testing with the Tests of Achievement and Proficiency; $98 per 25 Form K or L Complete Battery reusable test booklets including 1 directions for administration; $12.50 per Forms K and L Complete Battery directions for administration; $98 per 25 Form K or L Survey Battery reusable test booklets including 1 directions for administration; $12.50 per Forms K and L Survey Battery directions for administration; $98 per 25 Form M Complete Battery reusable test booklets including 1 directions for administration; $12.50 per Form M Complete Battery directions for administration; $98 per 25 Form M Survey Battery reusable test booklets including 1 directions for administration; $12.50 per Form M Survey Battery directions for administration; $52 per 50 Forms K and 1 Listening Assessment answer documents including 1 directions for administration and score interpretation; $10 per Forms K and L Listening Assessment directions for administration and score interpretation; $44 per 50 Form M Listening Assessment answer documents including 1 directions of administration and score interpretation; $9.50 per Form M Listening Assessment directions for administration and score interpretation; $99 per Form K Complete Battery Braille Edition test, Braille administration notes, and supplement to the directions for administration; $118 per Form K Survey Battery Braille Edition test, Braille administration notes, and supplement to the direction for administration; $60 per Form K Complete Battery large-print edition including test booklet and general instructions for testing visually impaired students; $42 per Form K Survey Battery large-print edition including test booklet and general instructions for testing visually impaired students; $38 per 50 Forms K and L Complete Battery answer documents; $35 per 50 Forms K and L Survey Battery answer documents; $38 per 50 Form M Complete Battery answer documents; $35 per 50 Form M Survey Battery answer documents; $1,260 per 1,500 Forms K and L Complete Battery continuous-form answer documents; $1,260 per 1,500 Forms K and L Survey Battery continuous-form answer documents; $31 per 25 Form M Survey Battery easy-score answer documents including 1 class record folder; $25 per scoring key; $50 per Forms K and L Complete Battery scoring masks; $50 per Form M Complete Battery scoring masks; $44 per Complete Battery norms and score conversions booklet; $44 per Survey Battery norms and score conversions booklet; $47 per special norms booklets (large city, Catholic, high socioeconomic, international, or low socioeconomic); $120 per Forms K and L keyscore norm look-up software including program disk (3.5-inch) and user's guide; $6 per 5 class record folders (specify form); $9.50 per 25 student profile charts (specify form); $10 per 25 profile charts for averages; $16 per interpretive guide (Form M, '96, 140 pages; Forms K and L, '93, 149 pages) for teachers and counselors; $26 per interpretive guide for school administrators; $15 per 25 report to students and parents; $15 per 25 reporte para estudiantes y padres; $26 per content classifications with item norms booklets; $25 per Technical Summary 1.

Special Editions: Braille and large-print editions available.

Authors: Dale P. Scannell, Oscar M. Haugh, Brenda H. Loyd, and C. Frederick Risinger.

Publisher: Riverside Publishing.

a) COMPLETE BATTERY.

Scores, 15: Vocabulary, Reading Comprehension, Written Expression, Math Concepts and Problem Solving, Math Computation [optional], Social Studies, Science, Information Processing, Reading Total, Math Total, Core Total, Composite, plus Advance Skills Scores for reading, language, and mathematics.

Time: (255) minutes; (275) minutes with optional test.

b) SURVEY BATTERY.

Scores, 10: Reading (Vocabulary, Comprehension, Total), Written Expression, Math Concepts and Problem Solving, Math Computation [optional], Total, plus Advanced Skills Scores for reading, language, and mathematics.

Time: (90) minutes; (100) minutes with optional test.

Cross References: See T5:2735 (1 reference), T4:2810 (1 reference), and 11:445 (4 references); for a review by Elaine Clark of Forms G and H, see 10:375 (2 references); for reviews by John M. Keene, Jr. and James L. Wardrop of an earlier form, see 9:1282.

Review of the Tests of Achievement and Proficiency, Forms K, L, and M by SUSAN M. BROOKHART, Associate Professor, School of Education, Duquesne University, Pittsburgh, PA:

The Tests of Achievement and Proficiency (TAP) are part of the Riverside Integrated Assessment Program that also includes the Iowa Tests of Basic Skills (ITBS; T5:1318), the Iowa Tests of Educational Development (ITED; T5: 1319), and the Cognitive Abilities Test (CogAT; T5:560). The ITBS measures basic skills for students in Grades K through 8, the ITED measures skills important for continued learning in adult life for students in Grades 9 through 12; the TAP measures skills commonly emphasized in the secondary school curriculum for students in Grades 9 through 12; and the CogAT measures cognitive abilities for students in Grades K through 12. The ITBS, ITED, and TAP were standardized and scaled in the same series of studies. Therefore, school districts that use the ITBS may use either the TAP or ITED for their secondary school students, depending on what kind of information they desire. A useful feature of this continuity is the availability of developmental standard scores (SS) on the same scale for all grades.

TESTS AND MATERIALS. Four levels (15 through 18) of Forms K, L, and M are available, for Grades 9 through 12, respectively. Two versions, a Complete Battery and a Survey Battery, are available. The Complete Battery takes more than twice as long to administer as the Survey Battery; the major difference is the inclusion of subtests in Science, Social Studies, and Information Processing (see the test description above for complete lists of the scores associated with each battery). The Complete Battery also composes a Life Skills score based on a subset of the more practically oriented items, such as those dealing with extracting information from a newspaper or using mathematical reasoning in everyday life.

The booklets for the TAP student test batteries are well designed. The print is large, illustrations are clear, and two-color printing helps present the content well. There is plenty of white space, the pages are not cluttered, and page turns are in logical places. Practice tests for students follow the same format. Booklets for parents include sample test items.

Supporting materials for school personnel are also well designed. The manuals have been redesigned for Form K, L, and M in a manner that parallels the recent redesign of the ITBS manuals. Previous versions included both technical and administrative material in a daunting *Manual for School Administrators.* The present version includes

two very helpful manuals, the *Interpretive Guide for School Administrators,* and the *Interpretive Guide for Teachers and Counselors.* These guides contain materials that would be useful for the kinds of tasks administrators, teachers, and counselors actually perform. One of the best features of these manuals is the inclusion in each of an extensive set of samples, explanations, and potential uses for each kind of score report. This reviewer recommends that schools and districts that use the TAP buy multiple copies of these interpretive guides and make them widely available to professional staff members, so as to maximize their use.

The technical data have been removed to a series of manuals, Technical Summary I, Technical Summary I Supplement, and Norms and Score Conversions with Technical Information for the various forms of the TAP. These technical manuals are well indexed and clear. A *Research Handbook,* in preparation, will complete the available technical information; its table of contents indicates that it will contain valuable information about TAP development, norming and scaling, reliability, and validity.

Both the Complete and Survey Batteries include a questionnaire asking students about future plans, current study habits, library use, and the like. In the sample tests provided to this reviewer, all forms of both batteries included this questionnaire only in Levels 17 and 18, for Grades 11 and 12. The manuals and accompanying materials implied that the questionnaires would be available at all levels, and indeed "Questionnaire" was listed on the contents pages of the tests at Levels 15 and 16. The sample reports in the Interpretive Guides for both School Administrators and Teachers and Counselors include example questionnaire data from ninth graders taking Form 15. So the omission of the questionnaire in the test materials is curious.

Supplemental assessments in Listening and Writing are available, and the table of contents of the *Research Handbook* in preparation also refers to a Constructed Response Supplement for the TAP. These supplemental tests and their technical documentation were not provided for review. Therefore, this reviewer is not able to comment beyond noting that, assuming appropriate validity and reliability evidence, such supplements might provide useful information for some of the individual and group purposes of the TAP.

NORMS. The TAP Forms K and L were published in 1993, and TAP Form M was published in 1996. Norming data were obtained in 1992 and 1995 from well-described, nationally representative samples of schools. In the 1995 studies, Form M was equated to Form K, and 1995 norms were calculated for all three forms. Users may use either the 1992 or 1995 norms. Mathematics norms are calculated for students taking the tests both with and without calculators. Separate norms are available for fall, midyear, and spring administrations and for specific populations: Catholic/Private, Large City, International, High Socio-Economic Status, and Low Socio-Economic Status Schools. This reviewer encourages users to take advantage of this information, especially for purposes such as reviewing the effectiveness of school curriculum. This will require a little extra work on the part of school administrators, counselors, and teachers, because the individual and class score reports are printed with national percentile ranks.

The TAP yields a variety of scores and score reports. Norm-referenced and criterion-referenced scores are available. Reports can be prepared with various units of analysis in mind: for individuals, classes, and buildings. School norms are available for building level analyses. The *Interpretive Guide for School Administrators* includes a helpful section on Selecting Score Reports, suggesting which reports would be best for different purposes and different roles (e.g., teacher, principal). This reviewer recommends that users pay more attention to norm-referenced scores and interpretations than to criterion-referenced ones. Most of the design and statistical analysis for the TAP has been aimed at creating a state-of-the-art norm-referenced test, so that is what it should do best. Besides, the "criteria" for the criterion-referencing are general categories of items (e.g., "real numbers") and the subsets of items are relatively short. However, any of the scores or reports the TAP yields can be useful to educators if the information is matched to an intended purpose or decision, especially if used in combinations with additional appropriate sources of information.

VALIDITY. The publisher claims that TAP content has been selected to assess progress toward widely accepted secondary school curriculum goals. Content validity is carefully documented. For each form, items are classified according to content. Content categories include both simple knowledge and more complex cognitive activities such as making inferences or interpretations from written material. This reviewer spot-checked a sample of the items and agrees that they indeed tap the intended content and cognition categories. In addition to such logical and content review, a panel of experts reviewed the items for the appearance of bias.

The test manuals carefully and wisely point out, in several places, that the ultimate content validity review must rest with the school or district that uses that test. The information is available for school or district committees to review the item content for its coordination with valued local curriculum goals. Test users should exercise this responsibility before selecting the TAP. This reviewer agrees that content validity is of utmost importance for a test like the TAP.

Purposes for using TAP scores are listed as studying individual student and class strengths and weaknesses, studying student progress through the high school curriculum, planning instruction, selecting areas for remedial and enrichment activities, and revising courses of study and instructional activities (*Technical Summary I*, p. 32). These purposes, rephrased but essentially the same in meaning, are restated in the *Interpretive Guide for Teachers and Counselors* (p. 7) and in the *Interpretive Guide for School Administrators* (pp. 6–7). In these guides, three inappropriate purposes for using TAP scores are also listed (p. 7); "to judge the secondary school curriculum," "to encourage or discourage students from seeking formal education beyond high school," and "to steer students into certain career choices." It is not clear to this reviewer what the effective difference would be between "reviewing the overall effectiveness of the curriculum" or "revise courses of study and instructional activities," listed as appropriate purposes, and "to judge the secondary school curriculum" listed as an inappropriate purpose. In any case, some validity studies specifically targeted to the list of uses would strengthen the case for using the TAP for its intended purposes.

The publisher did provide some statistical evidence of construct validity in the *Manual for School Administrators* for Forms G and H, received by this reviewer with the publisher's note that this material will soon be updated and included in the new *Research Handbook* for Forms K, L, and M. This evidence included intercorrelations among standard scores for the TAP and correlations between TAP scores and CogAt scores, both of which featured expected patterns. For example, the correlation between CogAT Verbal scores and TAP Reading Comprehension scores is .78 or .79, compared with .69 or .70 with the TAP Mathematics score, whereas the opposite pattern obtains for the CogAT Quantitative score. As the reader can see, all of these correlations are high enough to suggest that a general academic achievement construct may underlie them. For a sample of four high schools, correlations of TAP scores with course grades, grade-point averages, and ACT and SAT scores are given. Correlations with grades are moderate as expected, higher for the relationships with other tests (ACT and SAT).

RELIABILITY. Reliability evidence is well reported in the TAP materials. All in all, the nature and quality of the reliability evidence presented is a strength of the TAP.

KR-20s and standard errors of measurement are reported for each form, level, and subscale. The KR-20 values are mostly between .85 and .95, with a few values above or below that range. The Mathematics Advanced Skills scale has consistently low KR-20 values, with many forms falling below .80. This may be explained by the difficulty of the test, where 10% to 20% of examinees, depending on the level and time of year, score below chance on this subtests; this is the only subtest reporting a consistent floor effect of this nature across forms and levels.

Several other kinds of statistical evidence for reliability are reported. Equivalent forms reliability estimates are given, based on data from a sample of examinees who took both the Complete and Survey Batteries. These values range from .52 to .97, with most falling in the .60 to .90 range for subtests and above .90 for the Math and Reading composites and total scores. Score-level standard errors of measurement are reported for standard scores. The reliabilities of differences among TAP scores are reported in the *Manual for School Administrators* for Forms G and H, in the material that the publisher claims will be updated soon for Forms K, L, and M.

SUMMARY. The TAP is a reliable indicator of basic academic skills commonly emphasized in the secondary school curriculum. It was normed and scaled on a nationally representative sample and provides information that, on the basis of the evidence presented in a wide array of manuals, is appropriate for the purposes of interpreting both individual and curricular strengths and weaknesses. The tests themselves are well designed; well-intentioned students should have no trouble understanding what is called for and doing their best.

In the opinion of this reviewer, the publisher has accomplished its intention with the redesigned manuals and companion materials. For Forms G and H, technical material was mixed with material for administrators in one manual. For Forms K, L, and M, separating the two has allowed for the presentation of more comprehensive technical material on the one hand and more useful, appropriately written material for administrators, teachers, and school counselors on the other. This reviewer encourages users of the TAP to take full advantage of all available material to reap for their schools and districts the maximum benefits of the information the TAP can provide because the scores themselves are only as good as the purposes they help users accomplish.

Review of the Tests of Achievement and Proficiency, Forms K, L, and M by DARRELL L. SABERS, Professor of Educational Psychology, University of Arizona, Tucson, AZ:

The Tests of Achievement and Proficiency (TAP), Forms K, L, and M, replace the earlier versions G and H. Forms K and L were published in 1993; Form M in 1996. These three forms make up the latest edition of TAP, which is part of the integrated assessment system of The Riverside Publishing Company that also includes the Iowa Tests of Basic Skills (ITBS; T5:1318), the Iowa Tests of Educational Development (ITED; T5: 1319) and the Cognitive Abilities Test (CogAT; T5:560). Also available as part of this system are listening assessments, Iowa writing assessments, and performance assessments. Excluding the CogAT, the three achievement tests are also referred to as the Iowa Tests, although some documents referring to the integrated assessment system (also called Riverside 2000 assessment series) do not include information about the CogAT. A thorough review of the TAP requires examining material pertaining to the other aspects of the series; however, this review is intended to focus only on the TAP.

Forms K, L, and M of the TAP are published in two booklet formats: a Complete Battery and a Survey Battery. The Survey Battery consists of short tests (30 minutes each) in Reading, Written Expression, Math Concepts and Problem Solving, and Math Computation (optional). The Survey Battery is not comparable to the "basic battery" of previous forms; rather, the basic battery has been replaced by a scoring option (called the Core Battery), which consists of full-length Complete Battery tests in Reading, Language, and mathematics. The Core Battery is ignored in the rest of this review; the comments will apply to both the Complete and Survey Battery.

The TAP are multiple-choice tests intended to assess basic academic skills relevant to the curriculum for Grades 9–12. The authors make it clear that their definition of basic skills includes thinking skills necessary for academic success; thus the tests do not include an abundance of factual questions. The best evidence of the level of thinking required to answer the items can be obtained by the reader who "takes" the test personally. The potential user is encouraged to examine the content of the items in any achievement test prior to selection; such examination provides better information than viewing the classification of item content. The exercise of taking the TAP should be an enjoyable one for the potential user, because the selections in the tests constitute interesting reading and the items are of very high quality. Item content information is contained in the booklet "Content Classifications with Item Norms" that describes the content and process intended to be measured by each item. Also in that booklet are p-values for each item for fall, midyear, and spring for the Complete and Survey Batteries. The *Interpretive Guide for Teachers and Counselors* provides an overview of the domain of the test and classifies the content and process of each item. One or more of these different ways to describe the relevance of the items should provide a user-friendly examination of the content. How well the collection of items in the tests represents a school's curriculum must be judged by local personnel.

Forms K, L, and M of the TAP continue the tradition of the TAP forms reviewed previously, and all of the praises and most of the cautions mentioned in those reviews (9:1282 & 10:375) apply to the new forms as well. Strengths include sound procedures for test development and standardization, well-written test materials that emphasize application of knowledge and skills

rather than specific content, and clear presentation of information to the potential user. Although adequate technical data are available for the subtest and total scores, there are no adequate data to support the scores derived from items selected across subtests or for "criterion-referenced" scores. Any element deemed to be a shortcoming of the TAP is likely to be a shortcoming in any competing test battery.

One tradition the current forms continue is the multilevel nature of the TAP. Items from each level can be found in an adjacent level within a form, although separate booklets are provided for each grade. The advantage of the overlap is evident in the added amount of information available from students in adjacent grades who have taken the same items. The Survey Battery contains items found in the Complete Battery; this overlap should create no problem as there is not likely to be any user who would use both batteries for students at the same level.

The norms for the series were made more current by an advantageous combination of standardization sample data and information from users. Typically user norms are suspect, because users may differ systematically from schools in general. However, in the case of the TAP, norms that were originally obtained from a large, well-documented, carefully chosen national sample were adjusted based on the amount of change found in user norms. The assumption was made that the users do not differ substantially from the original sample in how much their students grow each year. If the tests were really used to modify and improve instruction, this assumption might be very questionable. Reviewers may disagree on the extent to which the above assumption is justified, but there should be agreement that the combination process is better than employing user norms (and it is unreasonable to expect a national standardization every few years). Potential users who worry about meeting psychometric assumptions will likely approve the traditional statistical techniques used in the development of the TAP.

The norms for the TAP are exemplary in that there are norms for many different populations and for school averages. The interpretation guides give a good explanation of the need for school norms and of the difference between building and system norms. Given the current misuse of pupil norms for reporting school standings that is prevalent in the press, this explanation might be helpful to school personnel presenting scores to the public.

Something new to the TAP is the way grade equivalents (GEs) are reported. The ITBS and TAP now use the decimal between the year and month; in this respect they report GEs like everyone else does. This improvement is relatively unimportant for the TAP because GEs are not useful at the high school level; perhaps it is another sign that there are becoming fewer differences among the major test batteries.

There is an abundance of validity information for the series, although it may not be easy to locate. Because TAP information is relevant to other tests, that information might be found in places where the potential TAP user would not look. In making most relevant information available to different user groups, the author teams have created many separate documents. How advantageous this proliferation of documents becomes will depend on the user; it is likely that what makes the TAP difficult to review comprehensively might also make it much easier for school personnel to use because each individual will read only those documents of interest. Because content is the most important category of validity evidence for an achievement test, examining the Content Classifications With Item Norms and taking the test will provide sufficient validity information to the user. After selecting the test, the user would be well advised to read the *Interpretive Guide for Teachers and Counselors,* which includes a good section on common misunderstandings about scores.

The *Interpretive Guide for Teachers and Counselors* suggests that a class average should be interpreted as the score for a typical student; this appears to misrepresent the meaning of the average (mean). Would a counselor use this wording with a student or parent who is familiar with the correct interpretation? The example on page 55 suggests that the typical student in the class would have the same pattern of scores as the class average, but there may be no student in the class who would have a pattern similar to that shown by the average scores. No evidence supporting this interpretation is found in the material reviewed. Granted this is a minor point, but misinterpretation of test scores is identified as a concern of the TAP authors.

The interpretive guides present clear descriptions of the many scores available for the TAP. There are clear directions for score conversions that should enhance users' understanding of the relationships among scores; these directions and score descriptions are found in enough documents to be easily accessible to individuals who read only the particular document intended for their use.

The massive amount of technical information includes data on longitudinal growth, floor and ceiling effects, and score level standard errors of measurement. The growth data provide a comparison of norm groups for the years 1985, 1988, and 1992 but do not relate to the stability of the TAP. Reliability data are extensive, with standard errors presented as raw scores or as standard scores, and internal consistency data provided for fall and spring testing. Higher order thinking items are expected to produce slightly lower reliability estimates than factual items, but there is ample evidence that the scores produced by the TAP continue to be highly reliable. Naturally, the Complete Battery is more reliable than the Survey Battery because each test is longer, and total scores are more reliable for the same reason.

SUMMARY. It is clear that the TAP are among the best of the high school testing batteries. A major complaint about all of the batteries is that the goal of improving instruction is not likely to be met because their content is not the content of high school courses—perhaps that is why no validity data are provided to support the major intended use of the batteries: To improve instruction. Supporters of the batteries can point to the items in the batteries and contend that the proficiencies measured by the tests are desirable outcomes of schooling. The TAP will not satisfy those who want the content to be organized like high school courses, but may satisfy those who want academic proficiencies measured. No high school test battery is likely to be better, but one might be found that is different enough in content to satisfy potential users. The Riverside 2000 series contains one such competitor, the ITED— different, but not necessarily better. The TAP are an excellent choice for those schools looking for a norm-referenced achievement test battery.

[94]
Toddler and Infant Motor Evaluation.

Purpose: Designed to be used for "diagnostic, comprehensive assessment of children who are suspected to have motor delays or deviations, the development of appropriate remediation programs, and treatment efficacy research."

Population: Ages 4 months to 3.5 years.

Publication Date: 1994.

Acronym: TIME: Version 1.0.

Scores: 5 Primary Subtests: Mobility, Stability, Motor Organization, Social-Emotional, Functional Performance; 3 Clinical Subtests: Quality Rating, Component Analysis Rating, Atypical Positions.

Administration: Individual.

Price Data, 1999: $395 per complete kit including manual (324 pages), 10 record forms, timer, rattle, 2 balls, squeak toy, toy car, 3 containers, toy telephone, 2 shoelaces, 6 blocks, and nylon tote bag; $35 per 10 record forms; $125 per manual.

Time: (15–40) minutes.

Comments: Diagnostic assessment tool designed to be used by licensed/highly trained physical and occupational therapists, or appropriately trained adaptive physical educators, special education teachers, or others with expertise in the motor domain; administered utilizing a partnership between parent(s) or caretaker(s) and a trained examiner.

Authors: Lucy J. Miller and Gale H. Roid.

Publisher: Therapy Skill Builders—A Division of The Psychological Corporation.

Review of the Toddler and Infant Motor Evaluation by LARRY M. BOLEN, Professor and School Psychology Trainer, East Carolina University, Greenville, NC:

The Toddler and Infant Motor Evaluation (T.I.M.E.) is purported to be a comprehensive assessment of motor ability for children 4 months to 3.5 years of age. The intent was to develop an instrument useful in the diagnostic assessment, treatment planning, and treatment efficacy research of very young children. The test is administered by observing a parent or caregiver interacting/playing with the child. Prompting by the examiner to elicit specific motor abilities allows for the measurement of movement in five positions: supine, prone, sit, quadruped, and stand positions.

The T.I.M.E. manual, for the most part, could serve as a model for test developers to emulate. Detailed explanations for all aspects of test development, item content, standardization, and psychometric properties are presented. The authors identify in the Preface the one major concern potential test users may have: "While waiting for sufficient funding to complete a large-scale national standardization ... [the] ... issue became whether to publish The T.I.M.E.™ or

await large-scale funding" (p. xv). The decision was made to use volunteer testers and decrease standardization from a target number of 100 boys and 100 girls in each age group to a minimum of 30 boys and 30 girls. Therefore, in that sense, the T.I.M.E. may be viewed as an experimental test even though there was extensive attention to construct and content development between 1986 and 1993.

The test is not intended for the novice user. Extensive familiarity with motor development and assessment expertise is required. The test is expected to be used by occupational and physical therapists and other professionals with specific skill in motor assessment. Two competency levels are involved: Administration of the five primary scales is straightforward and should be adequately accomplished by professionals with, at least, moderate training. The three clinical scales, however, require advanced training and comprehensive training and knowledge are required.

Item development began in 1986 at the Developmental Disabilities Research Symposium in Boston. A panel of 12 pediatric occupational therapists reviewed the related literature and existing motor assessments for infants and toddlers. A table of specifications for the measurement of motor development in infants and toddlers was developed encompassing four subdomains: neurological foundations, stability, mobility, and motor organization. The relative importance of each was rated in each of the age groups from birth through 3.5 years. The initial item pool was field tested by the same 12 clinicians ($n = 100$ children, 10 in each age group). Data analyses were completed and changes in procedure and items incorporated.

Two additional pilot testings were completed in 1988. The final try-out edition occurred in 1989 with 25 pediatric occupational and physical therapists, all with 10 or more years of experience, testing an average of 15 to 16 children each (total $n = 390$). There were 257 children included without motor delays and 133 with motor delays distributed across 10 age groups. Gender was evenly distributed (52% female) with 89% White, 6% Black, and 4% Hispanic. Geographically, 41% of the sample was from the East, 21% West, 15% South, 14% Central, and 8% Canadian.

The final edition of the T.I.M.E. was developed by having a methodical review by a panel of seven national subject matter experts who refined the table of specifications and construct definitions during a 3-day symposium. Additionally, the validity of each item was discussed and changes made to improve interrater reliability.

The final standardization was begun in 1992. The sample (n = 731) was divided into 10 age groups: four groups of 3 months each in the 0–12-month age span, three groups of 4 months each in the 13–24-month age span, and three groups of 6 months each in the 25–42-month age span. A team of 75 volunteer testers evaluated a randomly selected sample, stratified by race/ethnicity, gender, socioeconomic status, and age, based on the 1990 U.S. Census Bureau demographic statistics. The sample consisted of two groups of children: those with motor delays and those without motor delays. Children classified as "at-risk," however, were not included. These included children whose birth weight was below 1000 grams or who were premature by less than 32 weeks as well as those who were environmentally "at-risk" (extreme poverty, parental substance abuse, etc.). The samples were taken from 10 states: California, Oklahoma, Kansas, Colorado, Texas, Ohio, New York, New Jersey, and Pennsylvania.

Raw score conversions to age-based standard scores are provided for the five primary scales, with a mean of 10 and a SD of 3. Corresponding percentile ranks and a standard score for corrected age are also provided. Cutoff score points of -1.5 SDs are suggested for classification accuracy. That is, using scaled scores of 5 or 6 or lower to denote motor impairment decreases false positive significantly compared to using a 1.0 SD cutoff.

Item stability (n = 33) was examined for retest-retest and internal (alpha) consistency, and for interrater reliability (n = 34). Test-retest was completed by the participating examiner testing the same child within a period of 1 to 3 weeks. Test-retest coefficients were computed across age groups and across group inclusion (i.e., 91% of the children included were without motor delays whereas 9% included in the test-retest sample had motor delays). Thus, the reliabilities reported for each of the subdomains may be spuriously high (all coefficients ranged from .965 to .998) due to the dichotomous nature of the sample. Internal consistency estimates were calculated using Cronbach's alpha. Generally, these reliability estimates were computed on a sample of children without motor delays except for Stability and Atypical Total where the sample was a mix of children

with and without delays. Within each test subdomain, alpha values ranged from .79 to .93 for the 0–6-month age group; .88 to .97 for the 7–12-month age group; .79 to .96 for the 13–24-month age group; and .72 to .96 for the 25–42-month age group. Interrater reliability was examined by having a second examiner unobtrusively observe and independently score a child during the same test session. Several pairs of examiner-observers participated. Consistency between the pairs resulted in correlations of .90 or higher.

Validity indices were assessed in four ways: content validity; construct validity denoted by differentiating age/developmental trends and factor analysis; discriminant validation; and classification accuracy. The authors' utilization of expert subject matter specialists to develop specification tables, to develop items, and the various item validity reviews suggests excellent content validity for the five primary subdomains.

Construct validity was investigated by examining the age trend of increasing performance or mastery across items as a function of increase in age for each of the subdomains. This pattern is identifiable, on the standardization sample of 731 children without motor delays, for the Mobility subdomain until the 19–21-month age group. Here, only 2 points separate this group from the 22–24-month age group performance. Similarly, only 1 point separated the 25–28-month age group from the 29–32-month age group; and the 37–42-month age group actually scored lower than the 33–36-month age group. Additional construct validity was studied using factor analysis and unidimensionality was concluded. Limited data are presented, however, and the authors' conclusion that the various methods of factoring support their construct claim requires additional documentation.

Discriminant validity studies were reported on a sample of 153 children with motor delays (20 more than the 133 previously indicated as comprising this sample) compared to the 731 children without motor delay. Significant differences were obtained for all subdomain comparisons, levels of motor organization, and clinical scales except for Atypical age, Reactivity, and Social/Emotional age. However, none of the comparisons report sample sizes, post-hoc follow-up tests of the four levels of age, or alpha error rate adjustments.

Classification analysis was completed for the Mobility, Stability, and Atypical Positions subtests total score. Data suggest a high degree of accuracy for identifying children correctly as with or without motor delay. False positives were highest for Mobility (11.8%) scores if one standard deviation was used as the cutoff point. The rate decreases to 6.2% when the recommended -1.5 *SD* cutoff point is used.

The test equipment is remarkably limited in scope and size. Toy cars, a small and large ball, toy telephone, rattle, a squeaky toy, blocks, a timer, and containers make up the majority of items furnished in the test kit. The examiner supplies items such as masking tape, cereal pieces, pencils, and a blanket (if the test surface is cold). The record form is simultaneously complex and extremely comprehensive. One glance, and it becomes apparent the degree of training and knowledge necessary to adequately administer and prompt while observing the child's motor behavior, score, and interpret the various test subdomains. The manual does include detailed, but easy to follow, testing procedures and guidelines, pictorials of motor actions, and a glossary of terms and definitions. Moreover, an appendix provides description of positions for the Mobility, Component Analysis, and Atypical Positions subtests clarifying testing for supine, side, prone, quadruped, bear, squat, sit, support, transition stand, kneel, and run/walk positions.

In sum, the T.I.M.E. has evidence of good face validity. National standardization should be a primary goal for the test authors. The knowledgeable professional should be able to use the test effectively. Considerably more research is needed at the infant level to determine the T.I.M.E.'s usefulness and sensitivity in differentiating motor delays versus normal fluctuation in development sequence. Moreover, the utility of the test for treatment planning, and treatment efficacy has yet to be determined. The authors indicate continued ongoing research in a variety of movement areas. As an experimental instrument, the test has promise.

Review of the Toddler and Infant Motor Evaluation by WILLIAM R. MERZ, SR., FPPR, Professor-School Psychology Training Program, California State University, Sacramento, CA:

The Toddler and Infant Motor Evaluation (T.I.M.E.) is a new diagnostic assessment that evaluates motor proficiencies and difficulties of children from 4 months to 3.5 years. It uses parent-elicited responses from children allowing qualified professionals to obtain accurate quantitative and qualitative observations of children's motor skills. This standardized instrument includes eight subtests for observing a child's motor development; these subtests are divided into two types: (a) Primary Subtests that include: Mobility—the ability to move one's body in space; Stability—the dynamic and discrete balance of muscles; Motor Organization—the ability to perform unique motor skills requiring visual and spatial skills, balance and complex sequential motor abilities, also called praxis and sequencing; Social/Emotional Abilities—ratings of behaviors observed during the test session (i.e., state, activity level, emotionality, reactivity, temperament, interaction level, and attention span); Functional Performance—adaptive skills such as feeding, dressing, toileting, grooming, self-management and mastery, relationships and interactions, and functioning in the community; and (b) Clinical Subtests that include: Quality Rating—detailed descriptions in tone, reflex integration, balance, balance between flexion and extension; Component Analysis—completed separately for each of seven positions and for transitions between positions; and Atypical Positions—atypical movement patterns.

The authors categorize the scales into three groups: Screening Instruments, Comprehensive Assessments, and Diagnostic Assessments. They are administered through a partnership between a parent or caregiver and a trained examiner. The examiner must be familiar with motor development, with assessing motor development, and have formal training in administering the T.I.M.E. Usually occupational or physical therapists administer this test but, according to the authors, appropriately trained educators, medical professionals, and mental health professionals may use it, too.

The authors demonstrate through their review of research on motor performance that there is a need for a diagnostic motor assessment that measures quality of movement in young children, is sensitive to small changes in motor performance, and has documented evidence of reliability and validity. Assessing the quality of movement is the focus of this instrument. The authors developed a taxonomy to define quality of movement and identified a set of measurable constructs to assess it. In the process, quality of movement was defined in objective, measurable terms based on constructs defined by experts.

Different levels of performance are determined by briefly observing the child or asking the parent for input. The authors identify a general order of subtest administration. The observations on which scoring is based include free-play as well as structured subtests. There are screening and assessment subtests. Observations can be quite confusing if an assessor is not familiar with the development of movement and the subtle observations of that development. For the five primary subtests, raw scores are converted to scaled scores that range from 1 to 19. Scaled scores can be converted to percentile ranks. There are clinical scores for out-of-age-range, atypical mobility patterns, and Motor Organization subtest growth. There are rules for obtaining total raw scores, the most complicated of which is for the Mobility subtest.

The Motor Organization subtest lends itself to traditional item analysis methodology including p-values, item-total correlations, item intercorrelations, discrimination indices, and correlation of items with age in months, along with Rasch item analysis. The Social/Emotional Abilities subtest consists of 20 Likert-type items that were examined for statistically significant age trends across five age groups. Other internal psychometric properties such as item-total correlations and factor structure are examined, as well. Performance on tasks making up the Functional Performance subtest and the Atypical Positions subtest was examined with analysis of variance for differences between delayed and not delayed groups as well as for difference among age categories.

The T.I.M.E. was developed carefully from 1986 through its release in 1994. A grant from the American Occupational Therapy Foundation funded the Pilot I study. On the basis of findings of Pilot I, a revised test was administered by 18 pediatric occupational and physical therapists in Colorado. In this Pilot II study approximately 150 children were assessed; some of the children experienced delays and deviations and some did not. In 1989 a try-out edition was used to accumulate item data on 390 children. Twenty-five pediatric occupational and physical therapists participated in training in standardized test administration and scoring and in methods of random,

stratified sampling before assessing children. Results of this try-out yielded a new taxonomy as well as tried items that were incorporated into the T.I.M.E. Pilot III study.

Norming was completed during 1992 and 1993. A team of 75 trained and closely supervised testers was recruited. A sample of children was randomly selected and stratified by race/ethnicity, gender, parents' education, and age based on 1990 U.S. Census statistics. Children without delays and deviations as well as children with delays and deviations were included. The sample included 875 children between the ages of 3 and 42 months.

Interrater, internal consistency, and test-retest reliabilities were computed. Coefficient alpha for internal consistency reliabilities ranged from .72 to .97. Test-retest (1- to 3-week interval) reliabilities ranged from .965 to .998 and interrater reliabilities ranged from .897 to .996.

Investigations supporting validity include content-related evidence, construct-related evidence, and criterion-related evidence. The three studies that included expert panels give evidence that the content applies to the construct being assessed. Age trends and factor analysis give evidence that the T.I.M.E. functions as one would hypothesize it should. Means increase with age, and factor analysis yields evidence of unidimensionality for the Motor Organization subtest. Factor analysis of the Social/Emotional subtest shows that items load onto three factors as one would expect, and this finding held across three different factoring methods. Criterion-related evidence of validity includes discriminant validity studies that show the T.I.M.E. discriminated between groups of children with motor delays and those without motor delays. Classification accuracy studies yield excellent rates of accurate identification.

SUMMARY. The information gathered is important for early intervention with young children under IDEA (federal Special Education law and regulation) and Section 504 (Vocational Rehabilitation provisions applied to those with disabilities). The data generated evaluate a child's level of function, help develop appropriate interventions, and can evaluate the efficacy of those interventions. The instrument is not easy to administer unless the examiner is very familiar with motor function and development and has been trained to administer the T.I.M.E. Collaborating with parents as partners in evaluating a child's function requires the examiner to have excellent people skills. It is essential that the examiner elicit the desired behaviors by directing the parent's work with the child, observe astutely, and be very familiar with the test. The examiner must record observations accurately in order to interpret the data collected and translate the data into appropriate remedial activities or efficacious accommodations. The disadvantage here is that these are skills beyond the experiences of most educators and mental health professionals. Also, physicians may not have the time to administer, record, and interpret the information much less to develop appropriate intervention strategies.

Devising this instrument is an important step toward objective assessment of motor development. It is one of the few norm-referenced tests that targets younger children. With "child find" provisions of IDEA, having such an instrument becomes even more important. The T.I.M.E. provides objective, standardized, norm-referenced assessment of young children's motor development. The device is built on a sound developmental base and has had input from specialists and practitioners in the area of children's motor and movement development.

[95]
Transition Planning Inventory.

Purpose: To identify and plan for the comprehensive transition needs of students.

Population: High school and middle school students with disabilities who need future planning.

Publication Date: 1997.

Acronym: TPI.

Scores: Ratings in 9 areas: Employment, Further Education/Training, Daily Living, Leisure Activities, Community Participation, Health, Self-Determination, Communication, Interpersonal Relationships.

Administration: Individual or group.

Forms, 4: Student, Home, School, Profile and Further Assessment Recommendations.

Price Data, 1999: $126 per complete kit; $35 per Administration and Resource Guide (232 pages), $24 per 25 Profile and Further Assessment Recommendations Forms; $24 per 25 School Forms; $24 per 25 Home Forms; $24 per 25 Student Forms; $24 per 25 Spanish Home Forms.

Foreign Language Edition: Spanish version of Home Form available.

Time: Administration time not reported.

Authors: Gary M. Clark and James R. Patton.

Publisher: PRO-ED.

Review of the Transition Planning Inventory by ROBERT K. GABLE, Professor of Educational Psychology, and Associate Director, Bureau of Educational Research and Service, University of Connecticut, Storrs, CT:

The Transition Planning Inventory (TPI) addresses the area of transition of adolescents from school to adult living. Although it can be used for any student, it is most appropriate for students needing special and/or related services. Consistent with the Individuals with Disabilities Education Act of 1990 (IDEA), the TPI addresses four critical transition planning areas (i.e., instruction, community experience, employment, and post-school goals).

The TPI contains 46 transition-planning statements reflecting the nine planning areas listed earlier in the descriptive entry. Each area is assessed by three or more items regarding knowledge, skills, or behaviors associated with successful adjustment in the respective area.

Ratings and written comments are obtained from the student, the student's parents or guardians, and one or more school professionals using one of four forms. While maintaining parallel item content across the forms, appropriate modifications in the item wording are included on the Student, Home, and School forms based upon the respondent groups. Ratings are obtained using a 6-point Likert scale with end-point anchors of *Strongly Disagree* (0) and *Strongly Agree* (5); *Not Appropriate* (NA) and *Don't Know* (DK) options are also provided. The scale appears appropriate for this type of survey; the completion instructions are clearly presented. Overall, the layout of the survey foldout is well done.

The Profile and Further Assessment Recommendations Form includes sections for recording the results of other assessment, student preferences and interests, and likely postschool setting(s). In addition, a profile section is included for recording the ratings obtained from the School, Home, and Student forms.

ADMINISTRATION. Well-written, specific directions are provided for administering the Student and Home forms using three options as deemed appropriate: independent self-administration, guided self-administration, or oral administration. A suggested self-administration time of 15–20 minutes, and oral administration time of 20–30 minutes seem appropriate. Teachers or school personnel can complete the School form in 15–20 minutes. Completion of the entire Profile and Further Assessment Recommendations form would most likely take at least one hour.

VALIDITY. Comprehensive and appropriate evidence is offered in support of content validity. A literature review on follow-up studies, adult adjustment of persons with disabilities, and transition needs was conducted; references are provided. Expert judges (direct service personnel in schools, individuals in higher education or special education) reviewed the items in relation to transition planning needs. Limited correlational evidence is presented to support the concurrent validity aspect of criterion-related validity. Based on the proposed nine dimensions assessed by the TPI, it is surprising that the authors have not reported any confirmatory factor analytic evidence of construct validity. Given the alpha reliabilities to be discussed in the next section of this review, it appears the TPI Teacher, Parent, and Student data could fit the proposed model. Without such empirical support for construct validity called for in the *Standards for Educational and Psychological Testing* (AERA, APA, & NCME, 1985), the meaningfulness of the TPI score interpretations could be in question. The authors should report the results of these analyses on existing and future data sets. We do note that the DK and NA response options mentioned earlier will reduce the numbers of complete sets of data desired for these analyses.

RELIABILITY. Impressive alpha internal consistency and stability reliabilities are reported. Average alpha reliabilities across 329 school-based personnel, 227 parents, and 288 students (grade level not identified) ranged from .70 to .94 for the nine planning areas. The students rated had been identified as having a learning disability or mental retardation. Stability reliabilities based on a small sample of 36 students averaged from .70 to .98 across the three survey forms; the time interval between testing was not identified.

SCORING AND SCORE INTERPRETATION. A comprehensive, well-done section is included regarding interpretation and use of results in transition planning. As noted by the authors, "The comprehensive gathering of information about a student's transition needs does not ensure that these needs will be addressed" (manual, p. 26). The TPI manual provides valuable infor-

mation for "moving from assessment to planning" (p. 28). Included are sections regarding interpreting transition needs data using TPI forms provided, further needs assessment instrument references, individualized transition planning goals, and turning plans into action. Three well-done case studies illustrating completed TPI surveys and forms are presented. Users will find these materials quite useful.

SUMMARY. The TPI is a well-developed and comprehensive set of materials for needs assessment and transition planning for high school students with disabilities. In addition to the assessment materials, the TPI manual is an excellent transition planning resource with over 140 appendix pages devoted to such topics as: planning notes, additional interpretive case studies, resources for professionals and parents, transition goals, and developing a transition portfolio. Overall, the TPI represents a well-designed and delivered set of materials. Future development efforts should be focused on providing empirical evidence of construct validity to support meaningful score interpretations.

REVIEWER'S REFERENCE

American Educational Research Association, American Psychological Association, & National Council on Measurement in Education. (1985). *Standards for educational and psychological testing*. Washington, DC: American Psychological Association, Inc.

Review of the Transition Planning Inventory by ROSEMARY E. SUTTON, Professor of Education, and THERESA A. QUIGNEY, Assistant Professor, Cleveland State University, Cleveland, OH:

The Individual Educational Plans (IEPs) of all students with disabilities aged 14 and older must address educational needs and/or services to assist the transition from school to post-school activities (Individuals with Disabilities Education Act, 1997). The Transition Planning Inventory (TPI) was designed to help the IEP team develop an individual transition plan by assessing students' strengths, weaknesses, preferences, and interests.

The focus of the inventory is 46 transition planning statements categorized into nine areas: Employment, Further Education/Training, Daily Living, Leisure Activities, Community Participation, Health, Self-Determination, Communication, and Interpersonal Relationships. These statements indicate the current level of competence of the student and occur on each of three forms: Student, Home, and School. For example, the item on the Student form is "I know how to get a job," whereas on the School form the equivalent item is "Knows how to get a job."

The format of the three forms is consistent: a 6-point Likert scale for the 46 transition planning statements; a brief checklist on likely post-school settings; and an area for open-ended comments. In addition, there is a section on the Student form entitled "Student Preferences and Interests" with items such as "Where do you plan to live after high school?" (p. 5) and "What type of friendships do you plan on having?" (p. 6). The TPI also includes a "Profile and Further Assessment Recommendations Form," which allows the test administrator to summarize and display the data from the three previously described forms, and to identify planning strategies.

ADMINISTRATION. The Student, School, and Home forms are designed to be completed independently. However, the manual contains extensive instructions for guided self-administration and oral administration for the Home and Student forms. These instructions, according to the authors, are not intended to be prescriptive, but should be considered as a guide to enhance understanding and elicit appropriate responses. Ensuring that students and parents understand the items is more important than standardized instructions as the TPI is not norm-referenced.

The detailed instructions for nonindependent administration are a strength of the TPI. They allow test administrators to use the instrument with a broad range of students with disabilities. However, the need for such detailed instructions is particularly great because the directions and the wording of the items are often complex and vague. For example, "I know how to use a variety of services and resources successfully" (p. 2), and "I have the work habits and attitudes for keeping a job and being promoted—with or without special help" (p. 1). Field testing of the instrument raised this and other issues. The authors state that, "Self-administration of the TPI for students and parents should be offered selectively" (manual, p. 15). In addition, they discuss other concerns and provide recommendations to address these.

RELIABILITY AND VALIDITY. The authors provide two types of reliability data. An internal consistency index, Cronbach's alpha, was calculated for the three forms (school personnel, parents, and students) and ranged from .70 to .95, with the majority of indices over .80. These data

are based on three groups, Learning Disabled (LD), Mentally Retarded (MR), and "Total." Unfortunately the authors do not state who comprises the total group. Nor do they provide the sample size or demographic information about the three groups. The second type of reliability evidence provided by the authors, test-retest, was based on 36 students in Kansas. The indices ranged from .70 to .98. The authors do not state what interval occurred between the test and retest.

The omission of descriptive information about the sample and test-retest interval is puzzling because detailed reliability index tables are provided. It is also surprising that only two disability groups, LD and MR, were included in the reliability studies because the manual states that this instrument is designed for all students with disabilities.

The authors provide both content and concurrent validity evidence. Two aspects of content validity are examined. First, the authors provide a rationale for the format of the TPI by critiquing other related instruments. Second, they describe the process of developing and narrowing the item pool through a review of the literature and expert judgments. Concurrent validity evidence was derived from 48 students who had previously been administered the Weschler Intelligence Scale for Children—Third Edition (WISC-III) (Weschler, 1991) and the Vineland Adaptive Behavior Scales (Harrison, 1985). The actual correlations between the TPI and these two measures are not provided. The authors argue that many of the correlations are not statistically significant because the sample size is small and yet they conclude that, "The limited data available suggest that the TPI is valid with regard to concurrent validity" (p. 76). We disagree for two reasons. First, the WISC-III is an inappropriate criterion as it is not directly related to transition planning assessment. The authors should compare scores on the TPI with other currently available transition skills assessments. Second, the statistical data on concurrent validity are inadequate. The authors admit that more validity data are needed but it is disappointing that they did not provide these in this edition of the TPI.

SUMMARY. The TPI has a number of strengths. It systematically addresses critical transition areas required by the Individual With Disabilities Education Act (1990) by including data from nine domains and input from three raters: student, parent, school personnel. It provides a framework to assist the IEP team link the assessment data to IEP goals and activities. The manual contains a wealth of supplemental materials including case studies, suggested transition goal statements, and additional forms. Although the goal to develop an inventory for all students with disabilities is laudable, it created some problems related to format, item wording, and administration. The authors do provide two types of reliability evidence but the sample size and composition are limited. The validity information is weak. The concept of the TPI is very good and the need for such a planning inventory is great. We hope that the authors continue to refine this instrument and collect more reliability and validity data.

REVIEWERS' REFERENCES

Harrison, P. (1985). *Vineland Adaptive Behavior Scales: Classroom Edition manual.* Circle Pines, MN: American Guidance Service.
Weschler, D. (1991). Weschler Intelligence Scale for Children—Third Edition. San Antonio: Psychological Corporation.
Individuals with Disabilities Education Act of 1990. P.L. 101–476, 101ˢᵗ Congress, 20 U.S.C. §1401 *et seq.*
Individuals with Disabilities Education Act Amendments of 1997, P.L. 105–17, 105ᵗʰ Congress.

[96]
Vulpe Assessment Battery—Revised.

Purpose: Designed as "a comprehensive, process-oriented, criterion-referenced assessment that emphasizes children's functional abilities."
Population: Children functioning between full term birth to six years of age.
Publication Date: 1994.
Acronym: VAB-R.
Scores: 8 scales: Basic Senses and Functions, Gross Motor, Fine Motor, Language, Cognitive Processes and Specific Concepts, Adaptive Behaviors, Activities of Daily Living, Environmental Assessment.
Administration: Individual or group.
Price Data, 1994: $65 per complete kit including manual ('94, 480 pages) and 50 record sheets; $12 per 50 record sheets.
Time: Administration time not reported.
Comments: Ratings by person familiar with the child.
Author: Shirley German Vulpe.
Publisher: Slosson Educational Publications, Inc.

Review of the Vulpe Assessment Battery—Revised by THERESA GRAHAM, Assistant Professor of Educational Psychology, University of Nebraska-Lincoln, Lincoln, NE:

The Vulpe Assessment Battery—Revised (VAB-R) is a comprehensive developmental assessment battery for children with special needs from birth through 6 years of age. As a criterion-referenced test, it is intended to provide an overview of children's strengths and weaknesses for enhancing programming and intervention. The VAB-R purports that it can be used with children with a variety of developmental disabilities. The VAB-R includes three sections: Assessment of Basic Senses and Functions of the central nervous system, Assessment of Six Domains of Developmental Behaviors (Gross Motor, Fine Motor, Language, Cognitive Processes, Adaptive Behaviors, and Activities of Daily Living), and Assessment of the Environment. The six domains include 60 skill sequences. The individual activities (over 1,300 activities) were developed through examination of relevant literature. The activities are organized according to domain, skill sequence, and age. For each activity, a description of the equipment needed and directions are provided. In addition, the supporting references and cross referencing to other skills are noted. The VAB-R can be individually tailored to the specific needs of the child. It can be administered in multiple settings and different materials can be used to elicit the same developmental skill.

The scoring system consists of the Vulpe Performance Analysis Scale (VPAS), Task/Activity Analysis, and Information Processing Analysis. The VPAS uses a 7-point scale for evaluating a child's performance in terms of type of assistance (if any) needed by the child to perform the task. This continuum system provides the examiner with a much better picture of the child's abilities than a dichotomous "yes"/"no" assessment of performance. Task/Activity Analysis considers aspects of the child's abilities that may inhibit the child's performance of a particular activity. Information Processing Analysis requires the examiner to consider the activities in terms of input, integration, and output.

Although there are many strengths to the VAB-R (e.g., the focus on intervention, appreciation of the family, and a dynamic approach to assessment; flexibility in administration; the variety of activities provided; the literature-based activities; cross-referencing of activities; etc.), there are a number of weaknesses. Flexibility in administration and variety of activities may make administration difficult for examiners with less skilled backgrounds. Making appropriate modifications within a testing situation may be a difficult task for individuals who have not had extensive training.

Scoring of the VAB-R may be difficult for both experienced and inexperienced examiners. First, although the VPAS is unique in its evaluation approach, it may be problematic in that it may be an inappropriate technique for certain activities. For example, how does an examiner provide physical assistance for verbal tasks? Also, the VPAS may be influenced by the examiner. Given the focus on flexibility and adaptation, an examiner may be more likely to provide assistance when it may not be needed. The Information Processing Analysis might be difficult given the paucity of the description of what the examiner is supposed to do. In addition, it is not clear how it differs from the Task/Activity Analysis and what additional information it provides.

In terms of reliability, three studies were described. Although the studies indicated interrater agreement rates between 87%–95%, there may be weaknesses in the studies that may limit their usefulness. For example, none of the studies provided much, if any, information regarding the children used in the studies (e.g., age, developmental abilities) or information about the raters and their training (although in the present version a training packet for examiners to use is provided). In addition, none of the samples were very large, which may limit the generalizability of the findings across evaluators and children. Finally, little information was provided regarding on what the percent agreements were based. Given the types of interpretations that hinge on the VPAS scoring, one-point disagreements may be very meaningful.

Bias, content validity, curriculum validity, and concurrent validity were each discussed. The author claimed that there is no unsystematic error bias citing that the VAB-R has been used by various disciplines and in a variety of settings and countries. The reliability of scores was also cited as evidence of lack of bias. However, the concerns raised earlier concerning the studies used to assess reliability still apply. The author stated that the inherent flexibility of the VAB-R reduces possible bias that may occur with children with atypical development. However, in both cases of bias, no studies were reported.

Content validity was considered by examining various sources, including relevant psychological and educational literature, and professionals, and child development experts, to assess validity of the placement of items in each domain and the placement of items at various age levels. Curriculum validity was examined by comparing the six domains and the 60 skill sequences to typical early child curricula. The VAB-R was seen as similar to the developmental tasks attended to in preschools and to the developmental sequences used in treatment activities.

Only one study was reported to examine concurrent validity. This study examined the concurrent validity of the gross motor items from the Vulpe Second Edition and the Peabody Developmental Scales. No other items were examined. In addition, very little information was given regarding the sample used. For example, was the test better suited for children with physical disabilities? Thus, it is difficult to assess the concurrent validity of the test for other domains included in the VAB-R or for particular populations.

SUMMARY. The goal of the VAB-R is "to enable appropriate early intervention in the child's life as soon as possible, to support families in the difficult task of raising a special child and to help children learn to the maximum of their endowed abilities" (p. xiii, VAB-R manual). Although the information regarding validity and reliability is weak and the preparation for and administration of the VAB-R may be somewhat burdensome, the VAB-R meets its goal of providing a comprehensive view of a child with special needs. The flexibility in administration is well suited to tap the "best" performance of these children, and the information gained will provide caregivers with a better sense of the child's strengths and weaknesses in order to create appropriate environments to best meet the child's needs.

Review of the Vulpe Assessment Battery—Revised by DIANE J. SAWYER, Murfree Professor of Dyslexic Studies, Middle Tennessee State University, Murfreesboro, TN:

DESCRIPTION. The Vulpe Assessment Battery—Revised is the third edition of this test. Originally published in 1969, it is intended for use with individuals who evidence atypical development related to medical or social conditions that affect developmental potential. It may be used with individuals functioning between full-term birth to 6 years of age regardless of one's chronological age. The authors indicate that the test is appropriate for all children regardless of disabling condition, sex, or cultural background (manual, p. 1). They also indicate that it may be used by any responsible person who knows the child well or who was trained in child development. Further, the authors indicate that the battery may be administered to individuals or to groups of children and that it may be used in multiple settings where the child spends time. For example, it may be used at home, in a hospital, or in a school setting.

The Vulpe Assessment Battery—Revised is made up of six subscales: Gross Motor skills, Fine Motor skills, Language, Cognitive Processes and Specific Concepts, Adaptive Behaviors, and Activities of Daily Living. Each scale is composed of observable activities. These activities are arranged according to developmental expectations from 0–1 month through age 6 years. Each activity may be interpreted into a scale-score devised by the authors. This score is intended to quantify observations of behaviors observed or elicited. The 7-point scale ranges from 1, indicating that the child shows no interest in the activity, to 7, indicating that the child can demonstrate the ability to successfully transfer performance of a task to unfamiliar situations (such as a test situation) as well as to other tasks demanding equal skills in different forms and contexts (manual, p. 28). Two other assessments are also included in this battery: the Basic Senses and Functions Assessment and the Assessment of the Environment. The former addresses issues with visual acuity, auditory acuity, the sense of smell and touch, as well as various aspects of growth and fine motor development. Assessment of the Environment offers questions to raise and discuss with the caretakers responsible for the child being assessed. Questions address the adequacy of the environment, the degree of stimulation available within the environment, the degree of psychological support available in the environment, and the degrees to which the environment adapts to the needs of the child. These last two assessments yield comments and interpretations that are not subsequently quantified. All of the developmental assessment scales are arranged hierarchically by the age at which an activity is expected to be developmentally appropriate. For each age (e.g., 0–1 month) activities to be elicited or observed are described, the equipment and directions for eliciting or observing the behavior are listed, and the 7-point scale used to transform the behavior observed into a quantitative index is provided. Space for comments is also provided on the record sheet. A total of 1,014 items appeared in the six main assessment scales. Entry into the assessment is determined by the examiner based upon personal observation and/or discussions with one or more of the caregivers.

Another component of these scales is the Special Scales section. There are Special Scales presented for gross motor, fine motor, functional tests, and analysis of posture and mobility. These special scales include items drawn from the primary developmental scales that specifically address particular subsets of behavior specific to each scale. This reviewer could find no discussion of these special scales that would assist in understanding when they should be used and how these special scales relate to the primary scales in the battery.

An interesting feature of the assessment battery is the assessment references. The authors have indexed each activity in the battery to professional references that support the importance of that activity in scaling an individual's development. References include assessment tools, professional journal articles, text references, and instructional guides, as well as government documents.

The battery includes three appendices. The first details a study of interrater reliability for applying the 7-point Performance Analysis Scale. The second offers illustrations of how to scale behavior, including a sample developmental report for a young child (22 months) and one for an older individual (23 years). Illustrations are also provided for home-based programs for various individuals, individualized education plans, an individual program progress plan, and daily and weekly classroom schedules. Appendix 3 details the application of the performance analysis scale as it is applied to some of the assessment items. Authors state that this scale may be used to teach a task or to enhance performance on a task by attending to a sequence of steps for gaining a child's attention or to manipulating the task, or the environment, to improve task performance (manual, p. 16). In this way, the authors indicate that the assessment is directly linked to subsequent instruction as well as to subsequent evaluation of progress.

RELIABILITY. Estimates of reliability are based upon two elements. The first is the number of items in the battery. Authors cite references that indicate that the greater the number of items used to make an assessment of a child's functioning in a particular area, the more likely it is that the assessment will reflect the actual ability of the child (manual, p. 67). Secondly, the authors indicate that three studies of interrater reliability have been conducted. They report interrater agreement ranging from 87%–95% and interrater reliability coefficients reported for two studies range from .74–.94. These studies involved five and eight children, respectively, with various developmental handicaps. No scores are reported for interrater reliability in studies of group administration. Neither does the manual clearly indicate how a group administration might be managed. Further, in two studies for which details are provided, only professionally prepared individuals were involved in administering the battery. However, the authors state that anyone who is familiar with the child may reasonably administer this battery. It is not clear how a parent or daycare provider would be supported in evaluating the outcome of the assessment even if the tasks could be adequately presented and recorded.

VALIDITY. The authors offer little evidence of validity. They claim content validity and reference a report that evaluated face validity of the second edition. The authors also claim concurrent validity, based upon a study conducted on the second edition comparing the gross motor scales with the Peabody Developmental Scales gross motor scales. No other evidence of test validity is provided. The authors do claim, however, that extensive field testing has removed any unclear measurement descriptions (manual, p. 69) and thereby has essentially eliminated the source of unsystematic error, which might be associated with poorly described measures. They further indicate that the potential impact of a child's handicapping condition or of differing cultural experiences on the assessment of the child's development is addressed directly in the administration of this battery. Examiners are required to modify directions to the child, performance expectations, testing materials, as well as sources of information to assure that the child's full scope of abilities may be observed and recorded.

SUMMARY. The Vulpe Assessment Battery—Revised is a comprehensive but cumbersome tool developed for the assessment of development among individuals with medical or sociocultural limitations that might impede development. No evidence is provided to document that this tool effectively distinguishes between individuals who experience typical development and those who evidence atypical development in any one or combination of domains assessed by this battery. The primary utility of this battery would appear to be in identifying the particular state or stage of development an individual has achieved when that individual has already been identified as evidencing delays in development. This battery might then identify entry points for intervention within specific domains.

The authors provide little direction for interpreting the battery results into a plan of intervention. One page (p. 31) offers suggestions for things to consider in designing a program. These include such global recommendations as, "what is the basal age at which the child accomplishes tasks without assistance within any given skill area?" "Is there a particular type of assistance that helps the child perform most often?" The authors also refer users of the battery to Appendix 2 for sample report formats prepared by the authors. These samples support the impression that highly trained professionals should administer, interpret, and develop intervention plans based upon the Vulpe Assessment Battery. It is not likely that parents or other caregivers could effectively administer, interpret, and build intervention plans of the sort provided, without a great deal of guidance and support. A statement by the authors seems to underscore this reality. "Admittedly, the flexibility and choices inherent in the VAB-R are a challenge and can be considered very complex for persons with limited experience and knowledge" (p. 36).

In the hand of skilled professionals, it may be that the Vulpe Assessment Battery—Revised can accomplish the purpose for which it was developed.

[97]
Wechsler Adult Intelligence Scale—Third Edition.

Purpose: Designed to assess the intellectual ability of adults.

Population: Ages 16–89.

Publication Dates: 1939–1997.

Acronym: WAIS-III.

Scores, 22: Verbal (Vocabulary, Similarities, Arithmetic, Digit Span, Information, Comprehension, Letter-Number Sequencing, Total), Performance (Picture

Completion, Digit Symbol-Coding, Block Design, Matrix Reasoning, Picture Arrangement, Symbol Search, Object Assembly, Mazes, Total), Verbal Comprehension Index, Perceptual Organization Index, Working Memory Index, Processing Speed Index, Total.

Administration: Individual.

Price Data, 1999: $682.50 per complete set in attaché case; $625 per complete set in box; $35 per 25 response books; $134 per 100 response books; $68.50 per 25 response forms; $263.50 per 100 response forms; $73.50 per administration and scoring manual ('97, 217 pages); $42 per technical manual ('97, 370 pages).

Time: (60–90) minutes.

Author: David Wechsler.

Publisher: The Psychological Corporation.

Cross References: See T5:2860 (1422 references) and T4:2937 (1131 references); for reviews by Alan S. Kaufman and Joseph D. Matarazzo of the revised edition, see 9:1348 (291 references), T3:2598 (576 references), 8:230 (351 references), and T2:529 (178 references); for reviews by Alvin G. Burstein and Howard B. Lyman of the original edition, see 7:429 (538 references); see also 6:538 (180 references); for reviews by Nancy Bayley and Wilson H. Guertin, see 5:414 (42 references).

Review of the Wechsler Adult Intelligence Scale—Third Edition by ALLEN K. HESS, Distinguished Research Professor and Department Head, Department of Psychology, Auburn University at Montgomery, Montgomery, AL:

When planning concerts during his later years Frank Sinatra lamented that if he sang his classic ballads, the audience would complain that he had done nothing new in years. If he sang new songs, the audience would complain that they were disappointed because they came to hear their old favorites. Such a dilemma confronts those who revise a classic test such as the Wechsler Adult Intelligence Scale. Let us examine some of the constancies and changes in the WAIS-III.

During the last three decades, the Cohen (1952a, 1952b, 1957a, 1957b) factor scores became a major alternative to the traditional Wechsler dichotomy of Verbal (VIQ) and Performance (PIQ) intelligence quotients and are finally incorporated into the structure of the new WAIS. The WAIS-III is composed of a core of 9 subtests: Picture Completion (PC), Vocabulary (V), Digit Symbol—Coding (CD), Similarities (S), Block Design (BD), Arithmetic (A), Matrix Reasoning (MR), Digit Span (DS), and Information (I). The examiner who wishes to determine the traditional VIQ,

PIQ, and Full Scale intelligence quotient (FSIQ) can administer the Picture Arrangement (PA) and Comprehension (C) subtests in addition to the core 9 and determine these quotients on the basis of the 11 subtests. If the examiner wants to determine the new index scores [Verbal Orientation Index (VOI), Perceptual Organization Index (POI), Working Memory Index (WMI), and Processing Speed Index (PSI)] based on the Cohen factors, the Symbol Search (SS) and Letter-Number Sequencing (LN) subtests are given in addition to the 9 core subtests. To determine both the traditional and factor quotients, the examiner needs to administer 13 subtests. The Object Assembly (OA) is now optional unless one needs to substitute it for a "spoiled" performance subtest. The OA is still the best measure of perceptual-organization (technical manual, p. 105) and worth administering. The administration manual claims that the whole battery takes about 80 minutes to administer, though this examiner finds his colleagues and students take longer when carefully administering the WAIS-III.

The WAIS-III technical manual documents how the mental processes that underlie the subtest scores, the index scores, and the intelligence quotients articulate with the language, theory, and research of information processing models. The WAIS-III technical manual is a model of how a test manual should be composed. It reviews the theoretical rationale and the extensive procedures and data upon which the WAIS-III is constructed and has but one typographical error (p. 174, a PSI should read POI). It would help the reader if future printings of the 350-page manual included a subject index.

A number of changes mark the WAIS-III. In addition to the inclusion of the index scores, the SS, LN, and MR subtests are new subtests. The SS subtest measures processing speed by using 60 items that include a pair of symbols and a set of five symbols to the right of the pair. The examinee is to mark whether or not either of the target pair of symbols appears in the search set. This subtest can replace a "spoiled" CD administration in calculating the VIQ. The LN subtest measures working memory and attention by having the examinee listen to a set of numbers and letters, then recomposing them so the examinee repeats back the numbers in ascending order and then the letters in alphabetical order. The LN can substitute for a "spoiled" administration of the DS in determining the PIQ. The MR measures nonverbal untimed abstract reasoning by having the examinee point to the one of five responses that would complete the incomplete stimulus target. The OA was dropped from the required sets of subtests because the developers determined the MR has a higher split-half reliability, the MR is easier and quicker to administer, the MR is a better measure of nonverbal, fluid reasoning, and the MR draws less on the ability to respond quickly so perceptual-organization is not confounded with processing speed. However, the manual identified OA as still the best indicator of perceptual-organization.

The WAIS-III is paired with the revised and embellished Wechsler Memory Scale-III (WMS-III; T5:2863). The two tests share subtest LN, which was standardized on the WMS-III sample of 1,250, not the WAIS-III sample of 2,450. More central, the conceptual link regarding memory processes is well-stated in the technical manual that the two tests share. Though the manual presents the WAIS-III data then the WMS-III data in each of the chapters' sections, one can easily parse the sections in order to learn either the WAIS-III or the WMS-III with little interference by material about the other test. However, the pairing will encourage professors to teach both instruments to graduate students. Given the necessity to examine memory for geriatric, forensic, and neuropsychiatric purposes, this is a positive development.

The WAIS-III retained some 68% of the WAIS-R items in their original or slightly modified form but revamped the others based on datedness, clinical utility, content relevance, and psychometric considerations. Artwork was updated. The timed nature of some subtests was de-emphasized so processing speed would not confound other attributes measured by the subtests. Because performance speed is important, there are still timed aspects of the WAIS-III, and the clinician should note the examinee's functioning under time pressure. Those familiar with the Stanford-Binet (T5:2485) will find the WAIS-III uses the reverse sequence procedure in determining the basal level for the subtests; that is, if a certain number of items are missed in the beginning of a subtest, the examiner administers the easier items until a success criterion (basal level) is reached,

then testing proceeds forward (through the harder items) until a ceiling level is ascertained.

The WAIS-III extends the intelligence quotient band from 45 to 155 points. The new standardization sample carefully matches 1995 census data with respect to gender, socioeconomic status, race and ethnicity, educational attainment, and geographical residence. It is stratified for 13 age bands, extending the WAIS-III's applicability to people from 16 to 89 years of age.

RELIABILITIES. Evidence suggests that the subtests are reliable. Test-retest reliabilities, based on 2- to 12-week spans (mean = 34.6 days), range from the .70s (OA, DS, LN, PA, MR, C, and BD) to the .80s (SS, PC, S, CD, and A) to the .90s (V and I). The VIQ, PIQ, and FSIQ have stability coefficients in the low .90s and the indexes range from the .80s to the .90s, again demonstrating excellent stability. The manual notes a gain of about a half subscale point for the subtests, of about 3 points for the intelligence quotients, and of about 5 points for the indexes due to the practice effect upon retesting. The technical manual claims the simple and objective scoring criteria lead to high interscorer agreement as shown by .95 (V), .92 (S), and .91 (C) coefficients. Whether this agreement is achieved by examiners in general remains to be determined. There is one error on the scoring template for Coding that the examiner must correct: Item 14 is rotated 90 degrees so the examiner scoring Coding must change the "]" to "U" in order not to penalize the examinee.

VALIDITY. The technical manual claims the three foci of the WAIS-III are to help assess psychoeducational disability, neuropsychiatric and organic dysfunction, and giftedness. In keeping with the intended purposes of the WAIS-III, studies are presented that show how groups of people with neurological disorders (Alzheimer's, Huntington's, and Parkinson's diseases; temporal lobe epilepsy; traumatic brain injury; and Korsakoff's syndrome) are portrayed on the WAIS-III. Then a study is presented on how a schizophrenic group functions on the WAIS-III. Finally, people with psychoeducational and developmental disorders (mental retardation, attention-deficit/hyperactivity, learning disorders, and deaf and hearing impaired) are depicted on the WAIS-III. The descriptions of the disorders are of the highest caliber. The data support the differences expected in people with their respective disorders, lending credence to the validity of the WAIS-III. However, there is no mention as to whether the WAIS-III data were accessible to those making the diagnostic determinations. If they were, then criterion contamination may have occurred. Assuming the absence of criterion contamination, the technical manual presents an impressive array of studies supporting the construct validity of the WAIS-III.

The WAIS-III was examined for content coverage and relevance. It covers well the traditional views of intellectual functioning. However, the newer focus on emotional intelligence, or what used to be called social intelligence on tests such as the Vineland, is not directly assessed. Of course, the competent clinician has plenty of opportunities to observe the examinee over the varied WAIS-III materials and in the social exchange that occurs over the course of the testing in order to estimate emotional intelligence.

The factorial analyses presented are elegant and support the four factor or index model. The conceptual validity of the WAIS-III includes its articulation with the WISC-III. The WAIS-III VIQ (.88), PIQ (.78), FSIQ (.88), and index scores correlate well with their WISC-III counterparts. Also, the WAIS-III correlates .88 with the Stanford-Binet-IV. Compelling evidence on the concordance of WAIS-III scores with measures of cognitive ability, attention, memory, language, fine motor speed and dexterity, spatial processing, and executive functioning provide convergent and construct validity evidence. Research needs to be done to see the degree to which the subtests and indexes are saturated with fluid or crystallized intelligence. Little in the way of discriminant validity is presented, but given the scope of the construct "intelligence," its inclusion of so many attributes, and its relationship to so many outcome variables, conceiving attributes that diverge from intelligence presents a challenge. Still discriminant validity needs to be ascertained.

FUTURE CONCERNS. A number of research questions are posed by the WAIS-III. Interscorer reliability of clinicians not trained by the WAIS-III team need to be determined. The test-retest reliabilities and practice effects over different interims are unknown. Even though there is a bounty of outcome research (i.e., future educational and economic success) concerning measures of intelligence, studies specific to the WAIS-III, and especially the new index scores, need to be conducted. Disciminant validity needs to be determined. The technical manual provides group differences data that support convergent validity but do not provide validation for using the WAIS-III for classification purposes. If the WAIS-III will be used for classification then studies concerning its classification efficiency, or hits and misses, must be conducted. Determination of test reliability and validity should be made independent of the Wechsler research team in order to provide ecological validity of the WAIS-III.

Despite the administration manual admonishing against using short forms of the WAIS-III for specialized purposes, it seems inevitable in this era of "cost containment" that the full and careful examination of the individual may be sacrificed. Also, the length of the WAIS-III may impel some to abbreviate the WAIS-III. Any such short cuts vitiate the validity of using the standardization tables, especially with respect to the intelligence quotients and the index scores. Using short forms may constitute poor practice unless compelling reasons force their use and norms are developed for any derived summary or "estimated" subtest, index, or intelligence quotient scores.

SUMMARY. There is no way to overstate the importance of the role of intelligence in the history of psychology, in the success of individuals in society, and in the assessment of people. William James and his contemporaries saw psychology through a prism of affective, cognitive, and conative domains.

The study of individual differences is marked by Galton's landmark 1893 work, which was followed by Binet's development of a measure to assess the ability of Parisian children to succeed in school. During World War I, Wechsler worked with Spearman and Pearson (Matarazzo, 1979). Subsequently Wechsler was awarded a fellowship allowing him to study in Paris with Lapique and Pieron and to meet Simon and Janet. Thus was Wechsler steeped in the best of the British psychometric tradition as well as the French experimental and clinical methods; both influences heavily mark the initial and all subsequent Wechsler scales. About 30 years after the development of the Binet-Simon scales, David Wechsler was faced with trying to assess the strengths and weaknesses of patients at New York's Bellevue Hospital, leading him to develop the Wechsler-Bellevue scales.

Both aspects of cognition, the general laws of learning and information processing and the differences in the individual's capacities, are central in the person's ability to adapt and adjust to the world—in a Darwinian sense, to survive and master life's tasks. In the century preceding Darwin, John Locke expressed the view that the learning process and the individual's capacities and limitations must be brought into harmony:

He, therefore, that is about children should well study their natures and aptitudes, and see, by often trials, what turn they easily take; and what becomes them; observe what their native stock is, how it may be improved, and what it is fit for; He should consider, what they want; whether they be capable of having it wrought into them by industry, and incorporated there by practice; and whether it be worthwhile to endeavor it. For in many cases, all that we can do, or should aim at, is to make the best of what nature has given; to prevent the vices and faults to which such a constitution is most inclined, and give it all the advantages it is capable of. Everyone's natural genius should be carried as far as it could, but to attempt the putting another upon him, will be but labor in vain; and what is so plaister'd on, will at best fit but unto-wardly, and have always hanging to it the ungracefulness of constraint and affectation. (Traxler, Jacobs, Selover, & Townsend, 1953, p. 1)

In their pursuits to assess children and adults, both Binet and Wechsler proved to be sensitive clinicians in composing their tests to be vehicles by which the tester interacted with the testee. The rich array of tasks allowed the clinician to develop a sense of the person both globally and with specific regard to strengths and deficits, both intellectually and with respect to how the capacities and inabilities fit in the totality of the person.

The WAIS-III retains the best features of the classic WAIS-R, and it incorporates the Cohen factor scores and an information processing orientation in its linkage to the WMS-III. The WAIS-III accomplishes what Frank Sinatra aimed for in his artistic performance—the blending of the beloved classics with the best of contemporary developments. Similarly, the psychometric excellence of the WAIS-III blended with the continuing emphasis on the rich clinical material that makes a psychological examination a portrait of a person

would delight David Wechsler. John Locke, too, would be encouraged in that we might be approaching a nexus between optimally matching the needs and abilities of the people we test with learning regimens and employment that make capital of each person's "natural genius."

REVIEWER'S REFERENCES

Cohen, J. (1952a). A factor-analytically based rational for the Wechsler-Bellevue. *Journal of Consulting Psychology, 16,* 272–277.

Cohen, J. (1952b). Factors underlying Wechsler-Bellevue performance of three neuropsychiatric groups. *Journal of Abnormal and Social Psychology, 47,* 359–365.

Traxler, A. E., Jacobs, R., Selover, M., & Townsend, A. (1953). *Introduction to testing and the use of test results in public schools.* New York: Harper & Brothers.

Cohen, J. (1957a). The factorial structure of the WAIS between early adulthood and old age. *Journal of Consulting Psychology, 21,* 283–290.

Cohen, J. (1957b). A factor-analytically based rationale for the Wechsler Adult Intelligence Scale. *Journal of Consulting Psychology, 21,* 451–457.

Matarazzo, J. D. (1972). *Wechsler's measurement and appraisal of adult intelligence* (5th ed.). Baltimore, MD: Williams & Wilkins.

Review of the Wechsler Adult Intelligence Scale—Third Edition by BRUCE G. ROGERS, Professor of Educational Psychology, University of Northern Iowa, Cedar Falls, IA:

The Wechsler Adult Intelligence Scale formally began in 1939 as the Wechsler-Bellevue Intelligence Scale. At that time, it set a precedent by incorporating both verbal and performance scores into a composite intelligence score. Although new, it reflected David Wechsler's experience of administering intelligence tests during World War I to those who had failed the group tests as he observed how these individuals performed on a variety of tasks that were individually administered. Through his practical experiences and his studies under James Cattell, Edward L. Thorndike, Charles Spearman, and others, he came to envision intelligence both as a unitary concept (the *g* factor of Spearman) and as a composite of distinct abilities (as espoused by Thorndike) and he merged those two concepts into a theory that many psychologists and educators have found acceptable. Wechsler's definition of intelligence, now over 50 years old, is still regarded as an eloquent description because it emphasizes the ability to act with a purpose in mind, to think in a logical manner, and to interact with the current environment. Or, as some would say, to use common sense!

This third revision of the scale, completed after Wechsler's death, reflects this strong theoretical tradition and builds on it by attempting to incorporate the latest theoretical concepts and emerging technical procedures such as confirmatory factor analysis and item response theory. The developers of the WAIS-III sought to retain the original structure while updating the norms, extending the age range (ages 16 through 89), and modifying the items both from theoretical and aesthetic perspectives. The WAIS-R has been the most used individually administered test of intelligence for adults and this revision will likely continue that acceptance by professionals.

DESCRIPTIONS. The WAIS-III consists of 14 subtests that yield two sets of summary scores. First, there are the traditional Verbal, Performance, and Full Scale scores. Second, there are four index scales, based on more refined domains of cognitive functioning, which are labeled Verbal Comprehension, Perceptual Organization, Working Memory, and Processing Speed. The first set is likely to be of most frequent use in educational settings, and the second set is more likely to be interpreted in clinical settings. However, all administrators of the test will find both sets of scores to be of complementary use.

Although the overlap between the items on the WAIS-R and WAIS-III is considerable, many revisions have been made for this edition. The artwork shows both more color and reflection of diversity in gender and minorities. The wording of the items has also been addressed to reflect the gradual evolution of language patterns in adult society. New items were added to both the floors and ceilings (i.e., easy and hard items) to obtain more accurate measures at those extremes. The Object Assembly tests was made optional and replaced by a new Matrix Reasoning test that places more emphasis on fluid reasoning and abstract mental operations. Details of the subtest revisions have been described in the manual, so that users of the WAIS-R can make comparisons between it and the WAIS-III.

Overall, the revisions are positive improvements. However, this reviewer feels that some of the artwork may potentially contribute to irrelevant variance in the scores. Attention to detail may be interpreted in different ways. For example, suppose that an item showed a picture of a venetian blind with one slat missing. Gestalt theory suggests that our mind will see a pattern and fill in the empty space. Is that to be counted toward intelligence or against it? It appears to be the latter in this scale. In the real world, sometimes it is important to focus upon overall patterns and ignore details whereas at other times minor

details are very important. The administrator will need to keep the examinee focused upon the concept being tested in order to insure that the resulting scores can be properly interpreted. In one example of a picture of a pair of shoes, this reviewer found differences other than the keyed response. The administrator may be faced with the problem of how to score a response in such a situation. The authors may want to consider examining the artwork very carefully with the intent of reducing the possibility of ambiguities.

PURPOSES AND USES. The term "intelligence" has accrued many meanings in our society, as seen in any dictionary. The authors of this test have attempted to reflect the views given by Wechsler, thus emphasizing a multitude of verbal and nonverbal skills. Accordingly, the test is appropriate for the purpose of educational planning and placement with older adolescents and adults of any age. Although group-administered tests are most commonly used for this purpose, decisions of special education placement sometimes necessitate an individually administered test for persons of low cognitive ability. Similarly, at the other extremity, superior cognitive ability is one of the components of "giftedness" and thus evaluations of it typically include an assessment of intelligence. Toward this type of application, the test ceiling has been raised to 155 to improve the reliability of the scores for high achieving adolescents and adults. Another purpose of the test is the diagnosis of the extent to which neurological and psychiatric disorders may affect mental functioning. When used in the context of interviews and other psychological measures, this instrument can add an important dimension to this diagnosis. In addition to its applied uses in these contexts, it can also be appropriately used in research studies of the relationships among hypothetical constructs.

It is important to emphasize that because of the test's complexities, examiners should have received professional training and experience in its use. Although the test publisher attempts to insure that the test is made available only to qualified applicants, the successful implementation of that policy is dependent upon the ethical and professional behavior of the potential users. For those with professional experience in the use of the WAIS-R, the transition to the WAIS-III will be straightforward because the differences are clearly described in the manuals.

VALIDITY. Traditionally, the degree to which any test measures what it purports to measure is emphasized throughout the professional literature as the most important aspect of a test. In recent years, this aspect has been explicated with an emphasis upon the defensibility of the interpretations of the test scores. The appropriateness of the interpretations of the WAIS-III scores is evaluated with both empirical and theoretical rationales. Thus, in one sense, validity can be viewed as a very subjective procedure, but its objectivity increases as professionals in the field communicate, confer, and concur on the interpretation of the evidence that is presented.

EVIDENCE SUPPORTING CONTENT VALIDITY. The content of this intelligence test should focus on cognitive functions that are considered important for persons aged 16–89 years. To ensure this, the authors state that they conducted literature reviews to identify problems with the WAIS-R. Several consultants, including school psychologists and clinical psychologists, examined the items for content coverage, potential biases, and theoretical relevance. An advisory panel of appropriate experts was formed to review and critique all of the procedures of test development. Even though these are most desirable procedures, the reader must accept the word of the authors of the technical manual as to what was actually done. In the appendix, the names of the reviewers and consultants are listed. Although there were undoubtedly differences of opinion within this group, most readers are likely to assume that each of the reviewers and consultants agreed that the test was constructed in a professional manner or else they would have declined to have their name associated with it.

EVIDENCE FOR CRITERION-RELATED VALIDITY. This evidence consists of the correlations of the test with other measures. Although there is not a specific criterion, there are measures that purportedly tap intellectual ability and it is this set of correlations that is presented in the technical manual as evidence. When the subtests of the WAIS-III were correlated with the corresponding subtests of the WAIS-R, the median value was about .80; when correlated with the corresponding subtests of the Wechsler Intelligence Scale for Children—Third Edition (WISC-III), the median value was about .75. When compared with the Stanford-Binet, the correlation

of the composite scores was .88. When compared with an academic achievement test, all of the subtests on the achievement test were predicted best by the verbal intelligence score. There appears to be considerable evidence that the test scores will predict appropriate criterion measures with reasonable accuracy.

EVIDENCE FOR CONSTRUCT VALIDITY. Both exploratory and confirmatory factor analyses yielded results that can be interpreted as consistent with the hypothesized four-factor hierarchical model corresponding to the four Index scores that combine to form the g-factor. Factor analysis within age bands was reasonably consistent, although the 75 through 89 year age band results appeared not as consistent as those of the other age bands. Some have asked if the factorial composition has been fully resolved, and the answer is no. A more fruitful question may be to ask if the four-factor hierarchical model is useful in interpreting the results, and the answer to that question is yes. The four-factor approach also appears to be fruitful in suggesting avenues for further research. The traditional two-factor hierarchical model appears to be the one for which the data most often will be first interpreted, followed by further examination of the four-factor model. The evidence for convergent and divergent construct validity shows reasonable support for the two-factor hierarchical model, although the results could be interpreted as showing that the full scale score is more heavily loaded with the verbal component than with the perceptual component. The technical manual does not evaluate the convergent and divergent construct validity for the four-factor model, but that may be a fruitful avenue for further research. Also contributing to the evidence supporting construct validity are correlations with other measures that are theoretically related to intelligence, such as the Standard Progressive Matrices, the Wechsler Memory Scale, and the Boston Naming Test. These correlations lend support for the full-scale score, and for the two-factor model to a lesser degree.

EVIDENCE FOR CLINICAL VALIDITY. Data from clinical groups with various mental disorders such as Alzheimer's Disease, Parkinson's Disease, and Mental Retardation were analyzed. As was expected, the scores of persons with these types of disorders were, on the average, lower than those in the standardization sample, thus suggesting that the WAIS-III may be found to be a useful tool when used in conjunction with other clinically appropriate procedures. Studies in this area are very problematical, because of the challenge of obtaining a reasonably randomly drawn representative sample of the special groups. However, the authors were aware of these limitations, and their interpretations are presented with the necessary precautions. Those who expect a definitive connection between intelligence measures and mental disorders are likely to be disappointed with the WAIS-III, but those who employ it in conjunction with other measures are more likely to find it to be a useful supplement.

EVIDENCE FOR BIAS REDUCTION. According to the technical manual, considerable attention was directed toward the detection of item bias, including formal reviews by appropriate experts and item analysis based on both the traditional Mantel-Haenszel bias analysis and item response theory (IRT). The use of these contemporary methodologies is exemplary and would be further enhanced if examples of some of the statistical results were presented in the manual for perusal by the interested reader.

RELIABILITY. To assess the internal consistency of scores from the WAIS-III, each subtest was analyzed with the split-half estimation procedure. The reader with a strong technical background will likely understand why this procedure was used in preference to the widely used Kuder-Richardson Formula 20, but an explanation of it would be appropriate in the technical manual, as that manual will be consulted by many persons who may not fully understand how adapting the test to the ability level of the respondent affects this decision. Subtest reliability estimates are quite high, with the median about .85. The Verbal, Performance, and Full Scale have values above .90, as do three of the Index scores. Furthermore, the values are consistent across all of the age groups, 16 through 89. Stability coefficients were also obtained, most with a time span of approximately one month, and showed results similar to those found with the internal consistency indices.

Estimates of the standard error of measurement are also provided for each subscale by age group. These values are used to create tables in the administration manual wherein the scaled scores are converted to confidence intervals. For the middle of the Full Scale, the standard error is about two points. At the extremes, a confidence interval is not symmetric around the estimated score, reflecting the regression toward the mean. The authors are to be commended for the improvement in clarity of interpretation that derives from this procedure. Users would be wise to always report the results in terms of these confidence intervals and treat the single score as a step in the procedure of generating the confidence interval. This emphasis on the interpretation of scores in the context of the estimated error is again reflected in the tables that show observed differences between the Intelligence scores and the Index scores, to address the question "Is the observed difference larger than what would be expected by the chance error in the scores?" The tables show the minimum value for the difference to be statistically significant at the .05 and .15 level. Even though this is a commendable procedure, it might be useful, in the future, to consider reporting them at the .05 and .10 level, corresponding to the levels reported for the confidence intervals. As an alternative, this information could also be reported as confidence intervals. Again, it is important to avoid interpreting a difference score until some probability estimate can be made concerning the error involved.

NORMS AND SCORES. The sampling plan for the standardization sample was carefully constructed to attain a representative sample of adults stratified on age, sex, race/ethnicity, education level, and geographic region using the then current census data (corrected for 1995). Marketing research firms were employed to recruit participants, who were paid a fee for their participation. Although the actual sampling procedure was not strictly mathematically random, the results do indicate that the national sample was reasonably close to approximating the census data on the stratified variables.

A variety of scores is offered by the WAIS-III, for use in different settings. The subtest raw scores are converted to standardized scale scores, which are then summed and adjusted by age group to form the Verbal, Performance, and Full Scale scores. In a similar manner, the Index scores were formed. A commendable improvement in the third edition of this test is the transformation of the scores based on age-appropriate norms. Without this transformation, older adults are likely to show a decline in mental functioning when compared to a younger group. When interpreting the scores from the WAIS-III, the new appropriate norm reference group is the particular age group rather than the previously used reference group aged 20–34, or adults combined from all age groups. As for the proper interpretations of the names of the 14 subtests, the three intelligence scores and the four index scores, very good explanations are given in the two manuals. These explanations are written at a level at which it is assumed that the reader has had appropriate professional training and for that audience, the explanations are a good review of what was learned in that training.

Tables are given to convert Intelligence scores and Index scores to confidence intervals and percentile ranks. This conversion of the intelligence scores to confidence intervals is a most desirable procedure; however, no conversion was done for the percentile ranks. To help the administrator do that using the data in the tables, directions would be helpful. Although the procedure is straightforward, it is, nevertheless, a tedious task because it involves the construction of a nonsymmetric interval in many cases. Because it is "traditional knowledge" that intelligence scores have a mean of 100, most of the adult population knows whether or not a given intelligence score is above or below the mean. However, an understanding of the standard deviation on the normal curve is not "traditional knowledge," so most of the adult population will find it a challenge to give further interpretation to a given intelligence score. Therefore, the reporting of percentile ranks is a commendable feature for this test, because those test scores can be readily explained to almost all adults.

The labeling of the normalized intelligence scores as "IQ" scores appears to this reviewer to give a misleading connotation. The acronym "IQ" was derived from Intelligence Quotient, namely, the quotient of the "mental age" and the chronological age. The authors of the manuals carefully explain why the concept of mental age is not used with this test and why deviation scores are to be preferred to quotient scores. But then the term "deviation IQ" is used, which appears to be self-contradictory because there is not a quotient of two scores. Authors of other tests have adopted terminology that avoids the word "quotient" and this reviewer would be pleased if the term IQ would not be used in the technical literature or in the popular literature.

MANUALS AND MATERIALS. The supporting material for the test is divided into two manuals, one for administration and scoring, and the other for technical materials. The administration manual is spiral bound for ease of frequent use. Both manuals are printed in readable format that does not detract from the content being presented. The test materials, including pictures and puzzle-type pieces, appear to be of high professional quality that will endure repeated use. Because the test is certainly not inexpensive, administrators can reasonably expect it to remain in good condition for use with many subjects.

SUMMARY. The WAIS-III is the oldest and most frequently used intelligence scale for individual administration to adults. It is composed of a set of 14 subtests that have been improved with extensive research while maintaining the historical continuity. Reviewers of the two previous editions have made criticisms and suggestions that have been addressed by the authors, and the changes appear to result in improvements for those practitioners and researchers who use the test. The scores from the test are reliable enough to be used in all of the designated age ranges and the validity evidence gives confidence that the test scores measure those intellectual constructs that it purports to measure. Psychologists in educational institutions will find it to be a useful tool for assessing those persons who are not adequately evaluated with group intelligence tests. Clinicians and clinical researchers will probably continue to employ the test as their primary instrument for assessing adult intelligence. The manuals are written in a clear, readable manner for those with proper training. Although there are areas in which the manuals could be improved, they provide more information than the manuals of most other tests. The WAIS-III gives promise of continuing the evolutionary trend toward improved measurement. Those who are looking for a revision with major changes, such as a multiplicity of factors, will not find it here, although the verbal and performance scores have been supplemented with more refined index scores. Those users who are looking for an improved interpretation of a parsimonious approach toward intelligence testing will find considerable in the WAIS-III.

[98]
Wisconsin Card Sorting Test, Revised and Expanded.

Purpose: "Developed … as a measure of abstract reasoning among normal adult populations" and "has increasingly been employed as a clinical neuropsychological instrument."

Population: Ages 6.5–89.

Publication Dates: 1981–1993.

Acronym: WCST.

Scores, 11: Number of Trials Administered, Total Number Correct, Total Number of Errors, Perseverative Responses, Perseverative Errors, Nonperseverative Errors, Conceptual Level Responses, Number of Categories Completed, Trials to Complete First Category, Failure to Maintain Set, Learning to Learn.

Administration: Individual.

Price Data: Price information available from publisher for complete kit including manual ('93, 234 pages), 2 decks of cards, and 25 record booklets; price information also available from publisher for computer version.

Time: (20–30) minutes.

Comments: Additional materials necessary for testing include a pen or pencil and a clipboard.

Authors: Robert K. Heaton, Gordon J. Chelune, Jack L. Talley, Gary G. Kay, and Glenn Curtiss.

Publisher: Psychological Assessment Resources, Inc.

Cross References: See T5:2892 (309 references) and T4:2967 (96 references); for reviews by Byron Egeland and Robert P. Markley of an earlier edition, see 9:1372 (11 references).

Review of the Wisconsin Card Sorting Test, Revised and Expanded by ELAINE CLARK, Professor of Educational Psychology, University of Utah, Salt Lake City, UT:

The Wisconsin Card Sorting Test (WCST) was originally published in 1981 and was intended as a measure of abstract reasoning and ability to shift cognitive strategies when faced with changing stimuli. In as much as the WCST requires strategic planning, organized searching, and the use of environmental feedback to shift strategies to solve problems, it has been considered to be a measure of "executive function." The WCST is one of the most widely used tests in neuropsychology and is likely to be used more since some useful revisions in 1993. For one, age and education corrections were provided for the normative sample of adults 20 years and older. Secondly, normative data have been expanded to include individuals from the age of 6.5 through 89. Finally, the authors developed a computer-administered version of the test. The primary focus of this review, however, is on the manually administered version of the WCST.

ADMINISTRATION AND SCORING. The WCST still consists of four stimulus cards and two sets of 64 response cards that depict four forms (circle, crosses, triangles, and stars), four colors (red, yellow, blue, and green), and four numbers (one, two, three, and four). Adequate performance on the test requires that the examinee determine the correct sorting principle and maintain that set across changing stimulus conditions. Failure to maintain the set or perseveration on an older, and ineffective, principle is taken into consideration in the scoring. The procedures for administering the test are standardized, and the same instructions are considered adequate for children and adults. The authors, however, suggest that examiners introduce the test as a "game" to young children.

Four stimulus cards are placed in front of the examinee in a specific order from left to right. Examinees are then given the first deck of 64 cards and asked to match each of the cards with one of the four stimulus cards that they think it matches. Feedback is provided by the examiner as to whether the examinee's response is correct or incorrect. Although instructions can be repeated, no other information is given that might help examinees figure out the correct matching principle. After 10 consecutive correct matches to color, the sorting principle shifts to number. The test is then repeated in the same order (color, form, and number) using the remaining response cards. The examiner records the examinee's response on a record booklet. The record booklet is clearly printed, and, for the most part, self-explanatory. The responses that examinees give, however, need to be considered on three dimensions (i.e., correct and incorrect, ambiguous and unambiguous, and perseverative and nonperseverative). These dimensions are described thoroughly in the manual. The test is not timed and examinees can pace themselves as they wish.

According to the manual, the test can be administered by "any trained person with a background in psychological testing" (p. 3). Clinical interpretation of the test, however, is said to require "professional training and expertise in clinical psychology and/or neuropsychology … and a clear understanding of brain-behavior relationships and the medical and psychological factors that affect them" (p. 4). Potential test users are warned, and rightfully so, that the procedures used to administer, record, and score the test need to be carefully studied and mastered before using the WCST clinically. Although Heaton and his colleagues have provided about as comprehensive an instructional manual as possible, some of the scoring is difficult. This is especially true of the rules for scoring perseverative response and error scores. Fortunately, the authors have provided in the manual sample protocols to illustrate difficult scoring situations (e.g., discriminating ambiguous from unambiguous errors in order to score perseverations). Although with practice scoring can be mastered, it is time-consuming. For novice examiners the time it takes to score the test is likely to be estimated in hours, not minutes. To give the test, however, even the novice can be finished in 20 or 30 minutes (excluding the amount of time needed to reorder the response cards for each administration). The computer version of the WCST provides an immediate solution to the scoring problem. It is unclear, however, how comparable the computer-generated scores are to those obtained through the manual administration. As with any computer-administered test there are potential drawbacks. For one, examinees who need this type of test are often uncomfortable with unfamiliar tasks, in particular, computers. Experience with computer testing has also shown that some examinees get confused during the test. For example, some examinees have difficulty keeping track of what they are matching to, that is, mistakenly matching to the bottom row of response cards instead of the top row of stimulus cards. Examinees with reduced vision may also find the computer version more difficult to see. Of course, this often depends on the size and quality of the monitor displaying the stimuli.

NORMATIVE DATA. The revised WCST was normed on a group of 899 "normal" subjects between the ages 6 years, 6 months and 89 years, 11 months. The 899 subjects were drawn from six distinct samples. For example, one group of 150 subjects was described as being in the original WCST manual and normative study published in 1991 by Heaton and his colleagues, whereas another was a group of 124 commercial airline pilots participating in a study of computerized neuropsy-

chological testing. Given a lack of information on the consistency of administration and scoring procedures, it is unclear how reliable and valid these normative data are. It is also unclear how representative these data are for examinees living in various geographic regions, and of various socioeconomic and racial/ethnic backgrounds. According to the manual, the majority of subjects in the norming groups were selected from the southeastern and southwestern/Rocky Mountain regions of the United States. Data pertaining to race were reported in only one sample, a group of 379 children from an urban setting in the southeast. No race data were provided for the remaining subjects, and no socioeconomic data were included for any subjects. Gender data were provided, and for the most part, evenly distributed. Age and education data were also provided; however, the mean age of the child and adolescent samples was not given.

The mean age of the 384 adult subjects (i.e., 20 years and older) was noted to be 49.89 with a standard deviation (*SD*) of 17.94. The data were compared to the 1995 census data and showed an underrepresentation of younger adults, and an overrepresentation of older adults. This, however, does not mean that all groups of older adults are adequately represented in the norming sample. In fact, only four subjects comprise the 85 years and older group. The mean adult education level given was 14.95 (*SD* of 2.97). Comparing this with the 1987 U.S. Census data (the most recent education data available at the time) showed that the WCST sample education mean was 3 years higher. Although it would have been preferred to equate on education, the analyses of the normative data showed that the demographic variable with the greatest relationship to WCST performance was age. According to regression analyses, performance on the WCST steadily increases from 6.5 through about 19 years of age. Performance remains stable from the 20s through the 50s, after which time it begins to decline. The data indicate that individuals with higher levels of education perform better on the WCST.

RELIABILITY AND VALIDITY. Reliability data reported in the manual pertain to interscorer and intrascorer agreement for the child/adolescent and adult samples, and generalizability coefficients and standard error of measurement values for the child and adolescent data only. The interscorer and intrascorer reliability studies reported in the manual were conducted with 30 adult psychiatric inpatients. The first study used experienced clinicians and showed a range of interscorer reliability between .88 and .93 and a range of intrascorer coefficients between .91 to .96. Coefficients found for novice examiners were also adequate (i.e., coefficients ranged from .75 to .97 for both inter- and intrascorer data). Similar data were obtained for a sample of children and adolescents. With the exception of the Learning to Learn score, interscorer coefficients ranged from .90 to 1.00 (the Learning to Learn coefficient was .66). Intrascorer coefficients for the same set of data ranged from .83 to 1.00.

Generalizability coefficients intended to assess fidelity of measurement (i.e., how well the instrument measures a subject's true score) were calculated for the child and adolescent data only. Generalizability coefficients for 46 subjects ranged from .39 to .72, and averaged .57 (a coefficient of .60 or higher is considered to be indicative of "very good" scale reliability). Standard errors of measurement (*SEM*) were also calculated for the child and adolescent "reliability sample." These data are provided in the manual for each of the WCST standard scores (i.e., scores with a mean of 100 and *SD* of 15). Because the sample was "normal", further data are needed to determine what the *SEM*s would be for a clinical group of children and adolescents, as well as for a clinical and normal group of adults.

A number of validity studies, in particular, correlational and discriminant function analyses, were described in the manual. The data from these studies support the use of the WCST for a variety of neurological and psychological problems, and with a variety of populations. Studies of adults with closed head injuries, demyelinating diseases, seizure disorders, and schizophrenia, and children with traumatic brain injuries (TBI), seizures, learning disabilities (LD), and attention deficit hyperactivity disorders (ADHD) indicate that the WCST may be useful in assessing "executive functions" in these groups. Although some correlational data have shown that the WCST is sensitive to frontal lesions, data provided in the manual and in the research literature suggest that the WCST is also sensitive to dysfunction in other areas of the brain.

TEST SCORE INTERPRETATION. Raw scores from 9 of the 13 WCST variables can be converted to *T* scores, standard scores (mean of 100 and *SD* of 15), and percentile ranks. The other remaining WCST variables (i.e., the Number of Categories Completed, Trials to Complete the First Category, Failure to Maintain set, and Learning to Learn) can only be converted to percentile ranks. Appendix D of the manual provides data that have been demographically corrected for age and education. Demographic corrections are provided for each decade of life from 6 years, 6 months through 89 years, 11 months (with the exception of only a half decade being represented for children between ages 6 years, 6 months and 7 years). Categories of educational attainment, however, begin at age 20. These categories include 8 years of education or less, 9 to 11, 12, 13–15, 16 to 17 years of education, and greater than or equal to 18 years of education. These data allow examiners to compare an examinee's score with those of individuals who are similar in age and from similar educational backgrounds.

Examiners may also compare an adult examinee's score with the general adult population. These data represent the U.S. Census age-matched adult sample. Base rate data are also provided for examiners who wish to assess the likelihood that an examinee's score is more similar to a clinical (i.e., neurologically impaired) population than a normal (non-neurologically impaired) one. The "normal" sample was represented by data from the normative group, whereas the clinical sample consisted of subjects who had frontal, frontal plus (i.e., focal lesions involving frontal and nonfrontal areas), diffuse damage, and nonfrontal brain lesions. Base rate data for the diagnostic categories, TBI, seizure disorder, ADHD, and LD, are also provided in Appendix E for comparative purposes.

SUMMARY. The WCST has essentially remained unchanged since its publication in 1981. The test's normative data, however, have been expanded to include children as young as 6 years, 6 months and adults as old as 89. Although the small number of adults in the 85 and older category makes it difficult to interpret test scores for this age group, the authors should be commended for their recognition of the need to include these individuals in normative studies of this type. The authors also demonstrate a recognition for the need of base rate information to compare an individual score and draw conclusions about impairment. These data are conveniently provided in the manual so that comparisons can be made between an examinee's WCST scores and those of "nonimpaired" or normal individuals with those of individuals with known neurologic impairments and psychological/behavioral problems (e.g., ADHD).

It is not surprising to find that Heaton and his colleagues have also included demographically corrected normative data to compare an examinee's test scores. These scores were intended to allow comparisons of an examinee's score to that of individuals of similar age and educational background. These norms, however, were obtained by combining test scores of control subjects involved in six different studies. Little information was found in the manual about the subjects or procedures used to collect the data. Demographic information important in interpreting test scores (e.g., racial/ethnic and socioeconomic background) is missing. Knowing so little about the normative sample makes it somewhat difficult for test users to interpret any differences they find between their examinees and the normative group. Although it is recognized that conducting large normative studies is extremely expensive, equating procedures such as those used by educational test publishers need to be considered. "Equating" the normative data of the WCST with those of similar tests (e.g., tests of reasoning) may provide more convincing support for the test norms.

The WCST has enjoyed a long history of use in neuropsychological research and clinical practice. The 1993 revisions of the test are likely to insure that it retains its place. Although investigations with the WCST indicate that it does not have sufficient specificity to warrant its use as a frontal lobe sign (i.e., it is also sensitive to nonfrontal lesions), it has been shown to be particularly sensitive to frontal lesions and useful as a measure of "executive function." Whether the number and/or complexity of hypotheses needed to solve the sorting problem of color, form, and number is sufficient for higher functioning individuals, however, needs to be further evaluated. As a measure of executive function, the WCST provides information that many other executive function measures do not, even those that are considered more conceptually complex. Rather than generating a total or cutoff score to determine success or failure on the tasks, the WCST

yields scores that help one to understand how well a person conceptualizes the problem of the card sort (i.e., how efficiently they learn) and how flexibly they shift strategies to solve the problem. These features are likely to insure that the WCST continues to be one of the most frequently used tests for "executive" skill.

Review of the Wisconsin Card Sorting Test, Revised and Expanded by DEBORAH D. ROMAN, Assistant Professor and Director, Neuropsychology Lab, Departments of Physical Medicine and Rehabilitation and Neurosurgery, University of Minnesota, Minneapolis, MN:

The manual for the Wisconsin Card Sorting Test (WCST) provides extended norms and some new research findings for this popular test. The scoring system is unchanged relative to the system proposed by Heaton (1981), though scoring criteria are described in greater detail and illustrated with numerous examples.

The normative sample is composed of 899 normal subjects including 453 children and adolescents. Subjects ranged in age from 6.5 to 89 years. To correct for irregularities in the distribution of scores, continuous norming was used to derive norms for a census-matched sample of the entire normative group. Regression analysis showed a significant quadratic effect for age on all WCST variables. Scores improved with age between ages 6.5 and 19 and then tended to be stable throughout most of adulthood. Performance declines after age 60. Gender was not significantly related to performance.

The WCST yields a number of scores measuring different aspects of problem solving including the efficiency with which hypotheses are generated and tested and the extent to which defective strategies are abandoned and revised. The advantage of these various scores is that it enables the examiner to determine more specifically the nature of executive deficits. The disadvantage is that it makes for a complex scoring system. The test is time-consuming to score and would take practice to master. Studies are cited indicating acceptable levels for inter- and intrascorer reliability estimates.

Reliability was further evaluated through a study design based on Cronbach's generalizability theory (Cronbach, Glaser, Nanda, & Rajaratnam, 1972). Subjects were 46 children and adolescents tested twice over the span of a month. Based on a single test administration, generalizability coefficients ranged from .39 to .72, with a mean of .57 and median of .60. Previous authors had suggested that coefficients of .60 or better are considered good. Using this criteria, most of the WCST scores showed good reliability evidence. Scores for the Percent Perseverative Responses and Percent Perseverative Errors had lower reliability estimates. Standard errors of measurement are provided for most WCST scores, but only for this subsample.

There seems to be ample evidence that the WCST scores are valid measures of executive abilities and provide a sensitive measure of brain dysfunction. Defective WCST performance has been observed in organic disorders characterized by executive dysfunction, such as schizophrenia and Parkinson's disease. Poor WCST performance has also been reported in children with Attention Deficit Disorder.

Accordingly, the WCST has come to be regarded as a frontal lobe test and has been used as such in the context of neuropsychological evaluations. But given the complexities of the task, it is unclear whether it is selectively sensitive to frontal lobe disease. In this regard the literature is mixed. In one of the earliest neuropsychological studies, Milner (1963) reported significantly lower card sort performance in epilepsy patients with focal frontal lobe disease. Since then, some studies have confirmed these results (Heaton, 1981) and others have refuted them (Anderson, Damasio, Jones, & Tranel, 1991; Grafman, Jones, & Salazar, 1990). The authors caution against using the WCST in isolation to diagnose frontal lobe dysfunction.

In reaching decisions about focal brain disease, the WCST should be used in conjunction with other neuropsychological measures and clinical observations. Because the ecological validity of scores from the test has not been established, it is not possible to predict the kinds of problems low scorers are apt to have in the real world. Further studies are needed to determine the effects of practice on test performance, as neuropsychological measures are commonly given repeatedly in assessing conditions that may be progressive or reversible.

The WCST is one of only a small handful of executive tests. Of these it is one of the best normed and most extensively researched measures. It can be used with both children and adults. These factors, combined with good reliability and acceptable validity, make it one of the best executive measures available. Despite its imperfect specificity as a frontal lobe test, it has a well-deserved place in the neuropsychological battery.

REVIEWER'S REFERENCES
Milner, B. (1963). Effects of different brain lesions on card sorting. *Archives of Neurology, 9,* 90–100.
Cronbach, L. J., Gleser, G. C., Nanda, H., & Rajaratnam, N. (1972). *The dependability of behavioral measurements.* New York: Wiley.
Heaton, R. K. (1981). *A manual for the Wisconsin Card Sorting Test.* Odessa, FL: Psychological Assessment Resources.
Grafman, J., Jones, B., & Salazar, A. (1990). Wisconsin Card Sorting Test performance based on location and size of neuroanatomical lesion in Vietnam veterans with penetrating head injury. *Perceptual and Motor Skills, 71,* 1120–1122.
Anderson, S. W., Damasio, H., Jones, R. D., & Tranel, D. (1991). Wisconsin Card Sorting Test performance as a measure of frontal lobe damage. *Journal of Clinical and Experimental Neuropsychology, 13,* 909–922.

[99]
Work Readiness Profile.

Purpose: "Developed as a tool for the initial descriptive assessment of individuals with disabilities."
Population: Older adolescents and adults with disabilities.
Publication Date: 1995.
Scores, 14: Physical effectiveness (Health, Travel, Movement, Fine Motor Skills, Gross Motor Skills and Strength, Total Average), Personal effectiveness (Social and Interpersonal, Work Adjustment, Communication Effectiveness, Abilities and Skills, Literacy and Numeracy, Total Average), Hearing, Vision.
Administration: Group.
Price Data, 1995: $75 per set including manual (64 pages), 10 answer books, 10 group record forms, and 10 individual record forms; $15 per 10 answer books; $6 per 10 group record forms; $6 per 10 individual record forms; $45 per manual.
Time: (10–15) minutes.
Comments: Self-administered or ratings by informant.
Author: Helga A. H. Rowe.
Publisher: Australian Council for Educational Research Ltd. [Australia].

Review of the Work Readiness Profile by JEAN POWELL KIRNAN, Associate Professor of Psychology, The College of New Jersey, Ewing, NJ:
[The reviewer wishes to acknowledge the contributions of Monica Chlupsa. Her careful research and thoughtful insights contributed greatly to this review.]

The Work Readiness Profile is designed as a quick measure of the work effectiveness of differentially abled adolescents and adults who are entering or reentering the workforce. The instrument provides measures of physical, personal, and sensory effectiveness with a focus on the client's abilities and level of support needed to function properly in a work environment. The focus on abilities and strengths, rather than disabilities and weaknesses, is refreshing and fits in well with the spirit of the Americans with Disabilities Act of 1990.

There are three methods of administration: (a) self-administration, (b) completion by an informant who knows the client very well, or (c) ratings obtained by the test administrator during an interview(s) with the client or informant(s). The form of administration suggested for use varies depending upon the client's ability level, although self-report is preferred.

With the exception of the recommendation to administer this test in a quiet environment, free of interruptions, there were no special instructions given regarding the setting. Test materials include a well-written test manual, a 17-page answer booklet that contains both the test statements and an answer column to mark responses, an Individual Record Form, and a Group Record Form. The Work Readiness Profile has no set time limit, but is estimated to require about 10 to 15 minutes.

The instrument consists of 12 separate sections each measuring a different factor. Arithmetic averages of specific factors are calculated to derive the summary scores of Physical Effectiveness (Health, Travel, Movement, Fine Motor Skills, and Gross Motor Skills), and Personal Effectiveness (Social and Interpersonal, Work Adjustment, Communication Effectiveness, Abilities and Skills, and Literacy and Numeracy). There are separate factor scores for Hearing and Vision and an overall Summary Score that is the average of all 12 factors.

Each section contains statements that the rater is required to answer as true (applicable to the client's present condition), not true (nonapplicable to the client's present condition), or 0 (the rater does not know). Although the "0" option can only be used in the informant or interview mode of administration, the instructions for informant administration fail to mention its use. Additionally, it is unclear how a "0" response is scored.

Score ranges vary from section to section, but the higher the score, the more capable the individual is in that area. For example, scores for Vision can range from 4 to 6, whereas scores for Communication can range from 1 to 8. This variation in score range leads to differential weightings of the factors when one derives the summary scores for Personal Effectiveness, Physical Effectiveness, and overall Summary. This may be intentional on the part of the test author, yet no documentation was provided to explain or justify this.

The differential starting and ending points for the various factors may be confusing to the respondent. For six of the factors, one is to begin at the highest rating; whereas for the other six one begins responding at Level 5. These are marked in the answer book with an arrow and instructions. After responding to the statements at the starting point, the respondent either proceeds down the page to statements representing a lower rating of the factor, up the page to statements representing a higher rating of the factor, or considers him/herself finished and moves on to the next factor. The decision of how to proceed depends on whether this particular factor begins at the highest level or Level 5, and if the respondent answers "true" to all statements at a rating level. It seems unwise to burden the respondent with the responsibility of deciding when a factor is complete. Such knowledge might also influence their responses.

Another troublesome aspect of the scoring is the possible occurrence of what the author terms "patchy performance," defined as when one cannot assign a rating for a client because they do not answer "true" for all the statements at any one level. Fortunately, the author suggests that this is rare for if it were to occur with any frequency, it would suggest that the statements are not grouped properly and/or that the linear ordering of the ratings does not reflect a corresponding increase in the factor.

Factor scores are transcribed onto the Individual Record Form and then graphed to determine the aspect(s) of the work environment that will require support. Factors with a score of 6 or greater are interpreted as strengths and those rated 4 or less are indicative of work areas that will require some level of intervention and/or support. Suggestions for the level and type of support needed can be derived from this form, interpretive guidelines in the manual, and case studies.

The development of the Work Readiness Profile should be better documented in the test manual. Although various groups of subject matter experts and service providers were consulted in the initial stages of test development, it is unclear how critical decisions were made in the final stage. Further documentation of how items were selected/deleted, why factors vary in score range, and how the ratings were assigned to each item is needed.

These gaps in information about the development of the instrument are also reflected in the description of the normative sample, which is lacking. It is specifically stated in the test manual that the client is compared with people in the general population; indeed, a score of 6 is considered "average" on all factors. Yet, a specific normative group is never defined.

The test manual presents evidence of validity through a series of factor analytic studies with four distinct samples varying in terms of presence of disability, type of disability, and employment status. The 12 variables loaded similarly in the studies producing four factors of Work Readiness, Health and Physical Effectiveness, Hearing, and Vision. These findings provide initial support for the construct validity of the Work Readiness Profile.

An adequate demonstration of construct validity, however, calls for an accumulation of evidence through a variety of techniques. The authors are encouraged to continue research along these lines. For example, a comparison of mean scores on the factors between a known disabled population and a nondisabled population would be useful. Similarly, pre/post measures of work readiness with the intervention of a training program should show an increase in scores. Although these are not stand-alone validation techniques, such studies would add to the "accumulation of evidence" that constitutes construct validity.

The author specifically cites the purpose of the Work Readiness Profile as one of describing and not predicting performance. However, it seems reasonable to expect that clients scoring low on the Work Readiness Profile would take longer to learn a job, have difficulty reaching acceptable production levels, and express less satisfaction in the workplace relative to high scorers or low scorers receiving adequate support. Again, evidence of this type would support the test's validity.

Very good reliability measures were obtained for scores on the Work Readiness Profile utilizing two techniques: test-retest and interrater reliability. Test-retest reliability coefficients ranging from .74 to 1.00 were obtained for the 12 factors utiliz-

ing the total sample with no obvious major disabilities tested over an 11-day interval. An additional measure of "agreement rate" was calculated for this data and is a percentage determined from number of observations agreed upon. The agreement rate for the 12 factors ranged from 71% to 100%. In both analyses the majority of the factors showed agreement or correlation above 80% or .80, respectively. It would be interesting to demonstrate test-retest reliability in a sample of disabled subjects.

Interrater reliability is critical for this instrument as it may be completed by an informant rather than by the clients themselves. Although the sample size was very small, excellent interrater reliability for total sample was demonstrated with correlations ranging from .89 to 1.00 and agreement ratings ranging from 69% to 100%.

A few minor editorial details should be addressed. These include modification of wording to better fit a U.S. population, consistency in the use of italics in the behavioral statements, and correction of inconsistencies between the Individual Record Form and the answer booklet. Also, the administration should be completely standardized by eliminating the optional section in the verbal instructions and enforcing a precise order of the questions in the interview mode of administration.

To summarize, the Work Readiness Profile represents a good "first attempt" at the measure of work effectiveness in a differentially abled population. The manual and record forms are clearly written and easy to understand with a much-needed emphasis on what the individual can do rather than on what they are lacking. Noted discrepancies and editorial errors should be corrected. Similarly, more detail on the development and normative sample need to be provided. Future research should aim at providing additional evidence of validity. To the credit of the author, she points out that the instrument is in the early stages of development. This reviewer looks forward to continued research and revision of the Work Readiness Profile.

Review of the Work Readiness Profile by S. ALVIN LEUNG, Associate Professor, Department of Educational Psychology, The Chinese University of Hong Kong, Shatin, N.T., Hong Kong:

The Work Readiness Profile was developed to assess individuals with disabilities on their readiness to engage in work or employment. According to Rowe, the author, this instrument was designed to provide descriptive information on how a person functions within his/her environment, and to highlight personal strengths rather than deficiencies. The objective was to describe current characteristics and behavior, instead of predicting long-term future behavior. The Work Readiness Profile was intended for adolescents and adults with a range of disabilities, including people with intellectual, physical, and multiple disabilities.

The manual of the Work Readiness Profile briefly described how the instrument was developed. The process appeared to be systematic. Initially, a number of factors related to the work performance of disabled individuals were identified through literature search and consultation with professionals. A set of items related to each factor was then written. A "multidiscipline panel" of experts and service providers then reviewed these items. It was not clear, however, who these experts were in terms of training, education, and actual experiences. The number of factors and items were eventually reduced after several trials of the instrument. The nature and procedures of the trials were not clearly described in the manual. The process resulted in a Work Readiness Profile that has 12 factors or scales, which were: Health (H), Hearing (D), Vision (V), Travel (T), Movement (M), Fine Motor Skills (MF), Gross Motor Skills and Strength (MS), Social and Interpersonal Skills (SI), Work Adjustment (WA), Communication Effectiveness (C), Abilities and Skills (AS), and Literacy and Numeracy (LN).

An important feature of the Work Readiness Profile is that respondents are asked to rate themselves or a target person by comparing with people in the general population. The belief is that the identification of handicaps could help organizations determine what supports are needed for disabled workers and job applicants so as to facilitate their work adjustment. A criterion-referenced approach was used in the design of items and factors. Items in each factor were arranged to reflect progressive levels of behavior competence. The higher the level, the higher the degree of competence a person has achieved in relation to the required skill area. Of the 12 factors, 6 factors (the MS, SI, WA, C, AS, and LN scales) have eight competency levels (1–8). The V factor has three competency levels (4–6),

the D factor has four competency levels (3–6), the H factor has five competency levels (2–6), and the T, MF, and M factors each have six competency levels (1–6). Three of the 12 factors (the H, D, and V scales) have a single item at each competency level, and other factors have multiple items at each competency level. The varying structures of the factors could be confusing for test-takers and users.

Items are written using behavior terms, and respondents are asked to indicate whether each item is "true" or "not true" in describing themselves or a target person. A respondent's score on each factor is the highest level in which a "true" response is given to all the items at that level. For five factors, respondents are asked to start at the highest level, and if the answer is "true," the highest level would be their score. For other factors, respondents are asked to start at Level 5, and they move up or down depending on whether or not their answers to all items at that level are in the "true" direction. For all the factors, a score of 6 or above reflects competencies of individuals without disabilities. The 12 factors are arranged into three clusters, which are Physical Effectiveness, Personal Effectiveness, and Sensory Effectiveness. An average score for each cluster, as well as an average score for all the 12 factors, is also computed. Overall, the method of scoring is somewhat complex because the number of competency levels for each factor is not the same. The instructions for test administration are somewhat complex, particularly for individuals who might have some intellectual disabilities. Also, these instructions are printed in the manual, and they are not printed on the text booklet. Printing the instructions on the text booklet is important, especially for individuals with disabilities.

The Work Readiness Profile could be completed in about 10–15 minutes. A person could rate himself/herself directly. A service provider could rate a client through an interview or through information provided by an informant. Test scores are arranged and summarized using a profile form. An organization could also aggregate and summarize test scores for a group of individuals and plot their average scores using a group profile form. Both the individual and group profile forms are well designed, which should facilitate the process of test interpretation.

Information regarding reliability and validity is summarized in the manual. The average test-retest (11 days) reliability coefficient for the 12 factors is .89, and the range of the coefficients is between .74 and 1.0. The average test-retest agreement rate for the 12 factors is 90%, and the range is between 71% and 100%. The average interrater reliability coefficient for the 12 factors is .95, and the range of coefficients is between .89 and 1.0. The average interrater agreement rate for the 12 factors is 85%, with a range between 69% and 100%. The levels of test-retest reliability and interrater reliability appear to be adequate.

The manual of the Work Readiness Profile reported five studies that were done to investigate the validity of scores from the instrument. The five studies were actually five factor analyses of the 12 scores using different samples. The author claimed that the findings supported the existence of a Work Readiness factor as well as a Physical Effectiveness factor across different samples. The factor analysis procedure suffered from two major limitations. First, the five studies used overlapping samples of participants with and without disabilities. For example, the 229 intellectually disabled participants whose responses were used in the first factor analysis were also included in the second study focusing on people with disabilities. Also, the fifth factor analysis consisted of participants examined in Study 1, 2, and 4. One could argue that similar structures were found across studies because overlapping samples were used. Separate factor analyses on independent samples should be performed if the author would like to show that the factor structure across samples was similar. Second, the sample size used in Study 3 was too small ($N = 57$). A bigger sample should be used to ensure that the resultant factor structure is valid and stable.

More research work should be done to examine the validity of the Work Readiness Profile. A more vigorous approach to factor analysis is only one way to examine the validity of scores from the instrument. If the goal intention of the instrument were to help disabled individuals to identify strengths that could be used in an occupational setting, some form of predictive validation would be necessary. Rowe insisted that the purpose of the Work Readiness Profile is to describe and not to predict. However, if the scores of this test cannot accurately predict work-related competencies at least in the short term, the test scores would not be useful to test takers or organizations that are using the data. Moreover, the test scores were expected to "predict" the degree of support a disabled worker might need in a work setting. Consequently, I believe that evidence on the predictive and concurrent validity of scores from the instrument is important and necessary.

The Work Readiness Profile suffers from three other limitations. First, a group form is available and group data could be computed. However, there is no information on how to use the group data, and on the validity of using group data. Second, the manual suggested that informants could be used as sources of information about a disabled person. Test interpretation based on informants without actually meeting a target client is quite risky. Finally, the utility of the aggregated scores (Physical Effectiveness and Personal Effectiveness) and the total score should be more clearly explained in the manual. The validity of these aggregated scores should be examined through research work.

SUMMARY. Overall, the Work Readiness Profile is a carefully designed instrument that could provide useful information for practitioners and employers about the status of disabled individuals in relation to their work competencies and potential. The manual is concisely written and well designed to help test users understand the construction and use of the test. At this point, the amount of research evidence to support the validity of scores from the instrument is inadequate. Consequently, practitioners are advised to use the instrument and interpret the test scores with caution.

[100]
Working—Assessing Skills, Habits, and Style.

Purpose: "Designed to assess personal habits, skills, and styles that are associated with a positive work ethic."

Population: High school and college students and potential employees.

Publication Date: 1996.

Scores: 9 competencies: Taking Responsibility, Working in Teams, Persisting, Having A Sense of Quality, Life-Long Learning, Adapting to Change, Problem Solving, Information Processing, Systems Thinking.

Administration: Group.

Price Data, 1996: $4 each for 1–49 instruments, $3.50 each for 50–499; $3 each for 500–1999; $2.50 each for 2000–4999; $2 each for 5000+; technical and applications manuals available upon request (price information available from publisher); user's manual free with each order.

Time: (30–35) minutes.

Comments: Inventory for self-rating; can be self-administered and self-scored.

Authors: Curtis Miles (test and user's manual) and Phyllis Grummon (test, user's manual, and technical manual), and Karen M. Maduschke (technical manual).

Publisher: H & H Publishing Co., Inc.

Review of Working—Assessing Skills, Habits, and Style by WAYNE CAMARA, Executive Director of Research & Development, The College Board, New York, NY:

Working is a self-assessment designed to address nine broad-based competencies associated with high-performance workplaces and based on findings of the Secretary's Commission on Achieving Necessary Skills (SCANS) (1992, Department of Labor). The workplace skills framework proposed by SCANS and others goes beyond the basic skills in reading, writing, and mathematics. Thinking skills and competencies in understanding systems, technology, resource allocation, teamwork, and acquisition/analysis of information are viewed as essential for jobs in an increasingly competitive, technologically sophisticated, global economy (Linn, p. 1996).

This self-assessment is designed for use as a counseling or career/job planning tool for students planning to enter the workforce, or adults first entering or re-entering the workforce. It is described as a "launching pad for discussion, instruction, application, planning … the basis of seminars, counseling sessions, classes, orientations" (manual, p. 4). It provides information to the test taker, which may also be of use to teachers, trainers, and others when used as part of a group exercise in a counseling or learning situation.

Working includes a user's manual that briefly describes the directions for administration, scoring, and the development of the instrument. The publisher also provides a modest technical document that provides an overview of results from field testing and a description of the scales, a test booklet, and an optional applications manual describing possible uses for the instrument. Working is part of a series of products marketed by H&H Publishing Company labeled "the mindful workforce portfolio" designed for transitioning from school to entry level work.

Working's nine competencies provide a framework of broad applied learning competencies that are not targeted to specific jobs or groups of occupations. The competencies are not skilled based in the traditional sense of job analyses and personnel selection, but rather broader enabling skills and productive work behavior. Working's competencies appear to tap aspects of three of the five SCANS competencies (interpersonal skills, information, and systems, but not resources and technology) and two of three foundation skills (thinking skills and personal qualities, but not basic skills). Together these nine competencies include broad thinking and reasoning skills, as well as positive work behaviors and productive predispositions that together are believed to be transferable across high performance workplaces. The nine competencies include:

1. Solving Problems—interest and skill in using systematic problem solving methods with complex problems.

2. Information Processing—managing one's learning and using multiple strategies when learning.

3. Thinking in Terms of Systems—understanding the relationship among parts in a system and effects of actions within a system.

4. Adapting to Change—comfort with frequent or major changes in one's environment.

5. Having a Sense of Quality—understanding of how exceeding expectations can help one succeed (e.g., "more than expected" vs. "just enough").

6. Interest in Life Long Learning—interest in engaging in learning across a variety of settings.

7. Working in Teams—degree to which one is comfortable working in teams and using skills associated with effective teamwork.

8. Persistence—willingness to expend time and effort to ensure that what is started is completed.

9. Taking Responsibility—Desire to take personal responsibility for task completion. (Technical manual, pp. 2–7)

The nine scales were developed through a content validation process that began with a review of the surveys of workplace skills and a review by a panel of experts. No empirical evidence is provided (e.g., correlations of items across scales) to support the reporting of nine separate subscores and it is likely that subscores across several of these scales are highly related.

The scales and items are more appropriately considered a self-reporting of interests, attitudes, or self-perceptions about competencies rather than a cognitive measure of these competencies. This is a critical distinction for potential users to understand. As a self-report instrument, Working resembles personality, attitude, or career interest inventories rather than objective skill assessments. Items on the test further reinforce this distinction: I like working in teams (Working in Teams Scale); I follow through on things no matter what it takes (Persisting Scale); When learning something, I think carefully about the very best way to tackle it (Information Processing Scale); I know how to get things done in a system or an organization (Thinking in Terms of a System Scale).

Working provides a measure of individuals' perceived and self-reported interests and understanding of these competencies, not objective competency profiles. This distinction is made quite clear in all material on the test. The authors are very cautious in describing what the test does and how it can be appropriately used, yet potential users must understand this distinction. Working is not designed for individual decision making such as with hiring, job placement, or performance appraisals.

A field test with a longer 85-item draft instrument was conducted with students at 13 community colleges and 4-year institutions across geographic regions, resulting in a final sample of 640 students completing the items. About two-thirds of these students were freshmen, 17% were sophomores, 3% were high school seniors, and the remaining 4% were upper-class college students. Over half of the participants in the field test were 18–19 years of age, with an additional 30% between the ages 20—29. Seventy percent of students worked at least part-time and about half of those had worked for 5 years or more. English teachers were recruited at each site to administer the test.

The final instrument is composed of 50 items that are answered using a 5-point scale. Individuals read each statement and circle one of five statements that best described (or fits) them: (e) Almost always like me, (d) Quite a bit like me, (c) Moderately like me, (b) Occasionally like me, and (a) Almost never like me. The 50 items are each scored for only one of the nine competencies, resulting in nine separate scale scores. Each scale has only four to six items, a relatively small number of items to produce a reliable subscore. Coefficient alphas for the longer field test instrument ranged from .52 to .75 across the nine scales. The median coefficient alpha was .59, however, final reliability for the shorter final instrument is not reported. Coefficients in the .5 range have marginal reliability and the reliability of the final 50-item test will likely be lower. This level of reliability may be adequate for initiating discussions of career exploration and interest but insufficient for many other uses.

The instructions note, "remember that this is not a 'test'—there are no right answers. Merely *your* answers based on *your* personality" (test booklet, p. 2). Administration time is estimated at 10–20 minutes. The instructions are simple and clear. The items are printed on pressure-sensitive pages so responses are recorded on the scoring sheet used to compute each subscore. The scoring sheet assigns values of 1–5 to each response and also indicates which items correspond to each of the nine scales. Scale scores are computed by copying the circled value for each item into a box placed under the appropriate column corresponding to the scales. The test taker then adds the total points achieved on those items in each scale. Scores for 16 reverse-coded items are inverted on the score sheet so that more positive responses always result in more points. Score scales range form 6–30 points for the six-item scales and 4–20 points for the four-item scales. The final step in scoring is to convert the scale score for the nine competencies to a percentile score on profile charts. Two additional pressure-sensitive pages are provided for this task and the test taker is instructed to remove these pages from the booklet prior to testing (this is presumably required so that marks will not go through all four pages). Two profile charts are provided—one for the test taker and one for the administrator. Again, all directions for scoring the instrument are quite clear and examples are very helpful. Most secondary students and young adults should be able to complete this instrument independently.

Working is a norm-referenced instrument where scale scores and percentiles are based on responses from up to 566 students completing each scale in the field test and also providing criterion data. However, the manual does not provide adequate explanations of how criterion data were determined and criteria were used to generate these scores.

Working is described as a "diagnostic and prescriptive instrument" (user's manual, p. 1). This description is questionable because more than a profile among subtest scores is required to provide diagnostic value. The only materials discussing interpretation simply note that higher scores are better. There is no prescriptive information, rather all test takers are told "you can improve yourself in any or all of the nine areas. Build on your strengths; improve those areas where you already score well. Find ways to improve on any scores that are lower than you would like" (test booklet, p. 9).

There is limited evidence of validity for the instrument at this time. Students completing the field test were asked for two types of data that served as criteria for the validity study and were also used to determine the scale and percentile scores: (a) self-reported GPA and (b) years of work experience. There are problems with these criteria. First, years of work experience is related to age and is not a convincing indicator of high skills in the workplace. Second, difficulties in using grades as a criteria are summarized in Camara (1998), but are more problematic with an instrument such as Working where there is no evidence that success in traditional college courses is a sufficiently credible and valid predictor for work place skills such as adapting to change, working in teams, and life-long learning, which may not be factored into college grades. About 560 students provided criterion data. Results illustrate 14 of 18 correlations were statistically significant ($p<.01$) but that 5 of 9 scales have correlations of .20 or higher with work experience (Taking Responsibility, Persisting, A Sense of Quality, Life-Long Learning, and Adapting to Change) and 3 of 9 scales have a moderate correlation with GPA (Taking Responsibility, Persisting, and A sense of Quality). Working in Teams was not significantly related to work experience or GPA. The authors attempted to collect additional criterion data from teachers and work supervisors. English teachers returned completed assessments of Working for 98 students. Student and teacher perceptions correlated between .11 and .33 across the scales, yet English teachers may interact with students for less than 45 hours in a typical college course and it is questionable the extent that they could pro-

vide objective and valid evaluations of students on several of these competencies. The authors emphasize that although no single line of validation evidence may be overly convincing, together, data from teacher and students ratings provide a lien of convergent validity for the instrument.

SUMMARY. Working is a self-assessment designed to measure nine competency areas that are associated with high-performance workplaces. In general, there is insufficient evidence in the literature linking the skills and competencies prescribed by SCANS and other state and national efforts to high performance workplaces or job success and satisfaction. Despite this void in the research, some employers and policymakers continue to define such broad-based competencies as essential for future workplaces. Even though there is insufficient empirical basis supporting these skill frameworks, Working does attempt to meet a need for educators and employers who believe in the common foundation of generic and broad-based competencies. It appears to be the first assessment designed to address SCANS-like competencies and may be useful for providing students and entry-level workers with a profile of their self-perceived competencies and interests. The instrument is easy to administer, score, and interpret. The authors are quite open in emphasizing the instrument's use for initiating discussions, career explorations and guidance, and not for any high stakes purposes. The reliability and independence of the separate scales are often questionable, and additional items may be needed in nine separate scales are to be reported. Additional validation evidence is also required as are more appropriate criteria for validation studies. Ultimately, employer ratings may be the only defensible criteria in measuring competencies associated with high-performance workplaces. College GPA, teacher ratings, and years of experience do not provide the type of qualitative evidence or have a conceptual link to the types of competencies instruments such as Working attempt to measure.

REVIEWER'S REFERENCES

Secretary's Commission on Achieving Necessary Skills. (1992). *Learning a living: A blueprint for high performance: A SCANS report for America 2000.* Washington, DC: U.S. Department of Labor.

Linn, R. L. (1996). Work readiness assessment: Questions of validity. In L. B. Resnick & J. G. Wirt (Eds.), *Linking school and work* (pp. 249–266). San Francisco: Jossey-Bass Publishers.

Camara, W. (1998). *High school grading policies.* Research Notes (RN-04) New York, NY: College Board.

Review of Working—Assessing Skills, Habits, and Style by JOYCE MEIKAMP, Associate Professor of Special Education, Marshall University Graduate College, South Charleston, WV:

NATURE AND USES. Working—Assessing Skills, habits, and Style (Working) is a self-administered and scored inventory for either individuals or groups. It was designed to be used for both diagnostic and prescriptive purposes, purportedly tapping workplace skills beyond academic competencies and technical skills. Its intent was to be a simple, inexpensive way to measure competencies that may be necessary for productive and rewarding employment into the 21st Century in the United States.

Reportedly employers describe successful employees as individuals who can do more than perform specific job tasks. They have skills that are essential and transferable across workplace settings. Based on the Secretary's Commission on Achieving Necessary Skills (SCANS) Report released by the United States Department of Labor, Working taps nine transferable workplace skills. In addition to working in teams, orientation to learning, problem solving and decision making abilities, and the ability to adapt to change, these skills include persisting and taking personal responsibility for task completion. Working also addresses focusing on work quality and understanding how an individual's work fits into the overall goals of the organization.

The nine scales that comprise Working assess each of nine constructs via 50 statements. Subjects are asked to record their responses, using a 5-point Likert scale, directly beside each of the statements in the Working inventory booklet. A unique feature of the booklet is that it has pressure sensitive pages corresponding to the scoring page for ease in scoring. Raw scores generated from the nine scales are each converted to percentile ranks.

According to the authors, Working is a diagnostic tool that can be used to identify relative strengths and weaknesses. Results are to be used to develop individual plans for intervention or as a counseling tool.

DEVELOPMENT AND STANDARDIZATION. Based upon review of the literature and national and state level surveys, skill areas most critical to employers were identified. As a result, a matrix of 24 potential competencies was given to a panel of experts for review. From this review, 24 competencies were collapsed into the nine Working scale areas and then the items were developed. No mention was made in the technical manual as to how these competencies were "collapsed." Apparently only review rather than statistical procedures was utilized.

Items were pilot tested and reviewed by psychometricians. Items correlating with social desirability were eliminated. The technical manual only alludes to this correlation and does not specify the exact statistical procedures performed nor results.

Standardization procedures for Working are cause for concern. For example, no mention is made of the total number of students initially administered Working. The authors make note that a number of student participants did not take the assignment seriously and completed it in a haphazard manner. As such, 640 student responses were usable.

Moreover, the sample was not randomly stratified for age, gender, race, geographic region, work experience, or community setting. Although Working's target population is supposed to include high school students, none were used in standardization. Participants were from 13 institutions, consisting of community, technical, and 4-year colleges. These institutions were recruited via the Internet and personal contact. In fact, of the 13 institutions participating, nine were community colleges.

RELIABILITY AND VALIDITY. Alpha coefficients for each of the scales ranged from .52 to .75. However, no other measures of reliability were reported.

Relative to content validity, rater judgments were used. However, in the technical manual no mention was made about their relevant training, experience, or qualifications.

Convergent validity relating teachers' perceptions of strengths and weaknesses of students and the students' performances on Working was investigated for 98 of the students' self-assessments. Pearson r correlations ranged from .11 to .33. Adapting to Change was not significantly correlated with the teachers' perceptions. Working scale correlations were also reported for work experience and grade-point average. Work experience did not correlate significantly with Working in Teams. In addition, grade-point average correlated significantly with six of the nine scales.

The authors cited these patterns of correlations as supportive of convergent and divergent validity.

INTERPRETATION HAZARDS. Although the rationale supporting Working seems to have merit, given the limited research cited in the technical manual, results must be interpreted with caution. Until additional research is conducted relative to construct and criterion validity, Working results can be interpreted within the constraints of relative strengths and weaknesses for only the nine scales. Due to the very limited research to date, one cannot make assumptions as to how Working results may generalize to future workplace success.

SUMMARY. Working is a self-administered and scored inventory to assess relative strengths and weaknesses on nine scales related to workplace competencies other than academic/technical skills. Although the premise supporting Working may be worthwhile, due to technical limitations results should be interpreted with caution.

[101]
Young Adult Behavior Checklist and Young Adult Self-Report.

Purpose: "Designed to provide standardized descriptions of behavior, feelings, thoughts, and competencies."

Publication Date: 1997.

Scores, 11: Anxious/Depressed, Withdrawn, Somatic Complaints, Thought Problems, Attention Problems, Intrusive, Aggressive Behavior, Delinquent Behavior, Internalizing, Externalizing, Total.

Administration: Group.

Price Data, 1997: $10 per 25 test booklets (specify instrument); $10 per 25 profiles for hand scoring (specify instrument); $25 per manual (217 pages); $7 per template for hand scoring (specify instrument); $220 for computer program scoring.

Authors Thomas M. Achenbach.

Publisher: Child Behavior Checklist.

a) YOUNG ADULT BEHAVIOR CHECKLIST.
Population: Young Adults.
Acronym: YABCL.
Time: (10–15) minutes.
Comments: Ratings by parents.

b) YOUNG ADULT SELF-REPORT.
Population: Ages 18–30.
Acronym: YASR.
Time: (15–20) minutes.

Review of the Young Adult Behavior Checklist and Young Adult Self-Report by PATTI L.

HARRISON, Professor of School Psychology and Assistant Dean of the Graduate School, The University of Alabama, Tuscaloosa, AL:

The Young Adult Self-Report (YASR) and Young Adult Behavior Checklist (YABCL) are designed to provide an assessment of the problem behaviors and competencies of adults aged 18–30 years. The YASR is self-administered by young adults, and the YABCL is completed by parents and other adults who know the young adult, although users are cautioned that norms are based on parent reports only. The YASR and YABCL represent an upward extension of instruments developed by the same author, including the Child Behavior Checklist/4–18 (CBCL; Achenbach, 1991a; T5:451), Teacher's Report Form (TRF; Achenbach, 1991b; T5:451), Youth Self-Report (YSR; Achenbach, 1991c; T5:451), and Semistructured Clinical Interview for Children and Adolescents (McConaughy & Achenbach, 1994). The YASR, YABCL, and other instruments use an empirical paradigm based on statistical procedures for deriving taxonomic groupings of specific problem behaviors and evidence that the problem behaviors distinguish among people with and without mental problems.

CONTENT AND SCORING. The Problem Scales are the major components of the YASR and YABCL. Most of the 116 YASR problem behavior items have counterparts in the 113 YABCL problem behavior items. Each problem behavior item of the YASR and YABCL is scored by the respondent on a 3-point scale of 0, 1, or 2 to indicate if the behavior is *not true, somewhat or sometimes true,* or *very true or often true* for the young adult over the past 6 months.

The problem behavior items form three global scales (Total problems, Internalizing, and Externalizing) and eight syndromes scales. The Anxious/Depressed and Withdrawn syndrome scales comprise the Internalizing global scale, and the Intrusive, Aggressive Behavior, and Delinquent Behavior syndrome scales comprise the Externalizing global scale. Somatic Complaints, Thought Problems, and Attention Problems are not categorized on the Internalizing or Externalizing global scales, but are included in the Total problems scale. Each syndrome scale has 7–17 items. In addition, 35 items on the YASR and 25 items on the YABCL are not included on a syndrome scale or the Internalizing or Externalizing global scales, but are included on the Total Problems scale.

The YASR, but not the YABCL, includes brief Adaptive Functioning and Substance Use scales. Five scales of Adaptive Functioning (Friends, Education, Job, Family, Spouse) include 3–7 items each; a mean Adaptive Functioning Score also is provided. The three Substance Use scales (Tobacco, Alcohol, and Drugs) have one item each, and a mean Substance use score is provided. A criticism of the CBCL (Doll, 1998; Furlong, 1998) was the incomplete measurement of the strengths and competence of children and adolescents. The young adult extensions also place very little emphasis on adaptive functioning.

The raw scores for the three global scales and eight syndrome scales are converted to normalized T scores, based on the scores of normative samples for each gender. The T scores were normalized to result in comparable percentile ranks across the eight syndrome scales. Because large percentages of the normative sample obtained scores of 0 and 1 on the syndrome scales, a minimum T score of 50 (raw scores at the 50th percentile or lower) was set for the syndrome scales. The T scores for most syndromes have a maximum of 100. The normative sample exhibited more variability in the raw scores for the three global Problem Scales, and T scores for the global scales range from 20–100. The T scores for the Adaptive Functioning and Substance Use Scales of the YASR were developed in a similar manner. Higher T scores on the problem Scale and Substance Use Scales indicate poorer functioning, and higher T scores on the Adaptive Functioning Scales indicate better functioning.

Profiles allow professionals to graph the scores from the YASR and YABCL and identify the percentile rank and a "normal," "borderline," and "clinical" category for each score. For the eight problem syndromes, T scores below 67 (percentile ranks below 95) are classified in the normal range. T scores between 67 and 70 (percentile ranks 95–98) fall in the borderline range, and T scores greater than 70 (percentile ranks greater than 98) form the clinical range. For the Total Problems, Internalizing, and Externalizing Scales, T scores of 60 (82nd percentile) and 63 (90th percentile) were selected to demarcate the normal, borderline, and clinical categories. Similar profiling systems are used with the Adaptive Function-

ing and Substance Use Scales of the YASR. The author indicates that the selection of T-scores to demarcate the categories was based on discrimination of scores for referred and nonreferred samples, but recommends that other cutoffs be tested for their effectiveness. The author cautions professionals to use the scores and the normal, borderline, and clinical categories as estimates, an important caution given that a difference of only 2–3 raw score points differentiates the clinical and normal categories for some syndromes.

Scoring and profiling the YASR and YABCL can be accomplished by hand or with a computer-scoring program. Because the hand scoring is tedious and prone to clerical errors, professionals are encouraged to use the computer-scoring program. A similar recommendation was made for the CBCL (Doll, 1998; Furlong, 1998).

TECHNICAL DATA. The YASR and YABCL have a wealth of supporting data from numerous pilot, normative, reliability, and validity studies, and comprehensive descriptions of these studies fill most of the manual. Similarly, the empirical base of the CBCL has been identified as its major strength (Doll, 1998; Furlong, 1998). Development of the YASR and YABCL began with a generation of large pools of items, and items were deleted and modified during testing of five successive pilot editions with young adults and their parents. The eight syndromes were derived using principal components analysis by gender with data from large samples of clinically referred and nonreferred young adults. The Internalizing-Externalizing groups were formed using principal factor analyses with the same samples.

T scores for the YASR and YABCL are based on normative samples of nonreferred young adults. The 575 females and 484 males for the YASR and 553 females and 521 males for the YABCL were selected from a national representative sample. Although the manual does not include national percentages with which to compare the sample demographics, the normative samples appear to be fairly comparable to the U.S. population. The sample appears to be somewhat underrepresented in the lower SES group, with only 18% of the sample falling in the lower SES.

Large, matched samples of nonreferred and referred young adults were used in reliability studies. Test-retest reliability studies with a one-week interval yielded generally acceptable correlations for the YASR (mean r = .84, Total Problems r = .89, Mean Adaptive scale r = .82) and YABCL (mean r = .87, Total Problems r = .93), although some syndromes had correlations in the .60s and .70s. Long-term stability studies resulted in a mean correlation of .58 for the YASR, over an average of 39 months, and a mean correlation of .60 for the YABCL, over an average of 44 months. Internal consistency analyses yielded alphas primarily in the .70s and .80s for the syndrome scales, .88–.95 for Internalizing and Externalizing, and .96–.97 for the Total Problems scales. Alpha coefficients are not reported for the Adaptive Functioning scales of the YASR; the Adaptive Functioning scales have fewer items than the Problems scales, which not only affects the computation of alpha coefficients but also suggests that the Adaptive Functioning scales should have limited use only. The reliability data suggest that the Total Problems scale provides the most reliable measure and that individual syndrome scales and Adaptive Functioning scales should be interpreted cautiously.

The author emphasizes the importance of cross-informant ratings and provides data in the manual to support the cross-information approach. Reliability studies found an average correlation of .60 between mothers and mothers on the YABCL and .42 between informants on the YASR and YABCL. The author also provides a method for using a cross-informant approach in the interpretation of scores for an individual. The computer-scoring program provides cross-informant Q correlations between item, syndrome, and global scores, if the YASR and YABCL are administered to several informants, and compares the Q correlations to typical correlations of a reference sample.

A variety of validity studies for the YASR and YABCL report differences between referred and nonreferred samples. The author supports content validity with the finding that, with one exception, all items were scored significantly higher for referred than nonreferred individuals; however, most items had small effect sizes. Several studies investigated criterion-related validity. All problem syndromes and global scores were significantly different for referred and nonreferred samples, although multiple regression analyses suggested referral status generally accounted for small amounts of variance in scores. Other analyses found that proportions of referred subjects

significantly exceeded nonreferred subjects who scored in the clinical range. These analyses suggested that the largest proportion of subjects would be correctly classified on the YASR according to a combination of the Total Problems, Mean Adaptive Functioning, and Mean Substance Use scores (67% accuracy) and the Total Problems score of the CBCL (71% accuracy). This accuracy in classification was not improved substantially as a result of a series of discriminant analyses of items and individual syndromes. Another analysis reported that Total Problems T-scores in the clinical range had a 74%–82% probability of being from referred samples.

Construct validity studies investigated the relationship between the YASR and YABCL and other measures of psychopathology. Studies found significant longitudinal relationships between the CBCL and YSR and later YABCL and YASR scores for American and Dutch samples. Other studies found significant relationships between YASR syndrome scores and some DSM diagnostic constructs for American and Dutch samples. Dutch studies indicated that the YASR discriminated between referred and nonreferred samples as well as or better than other adult measures of psychopathology. A Turkish study found significant correlations between the YASR and Minnesota Multiphasic Personality Inventory—2 (MMPI-2). Although there are only a few construct validity studies presented in the manual and limited support for using the YASR and YABCL in identifying psychopathology, it is anticipated that many additional construct validity studies will be conducted by the author and other researchers, as has been done with the CBCL.

APPLICATIONS. Although the manual for the YASR and YABCL provides a detailed analysis of technical data, a major disappointment is that the manual is not directed to the clinical user. The limited information about scoring, interpretation, and use of the instrument by practitioners has been a weakness also cited for the children and youth versions (Doll, 1998; Furlong, 1998). Most of the limited information for everyday, clinical use is in an appendix on hand scoring and a chapter with answers to common questions or is embedded in technical chapters. For example, a brief description of the hand-scored and computer-scored profiles and a sample profile are in the same chapter as the description of the principal components analysis for deriving syndromes and data about the normative sample. A sample printout and description of cross-informant comparison for a person are in the chapter on reliability. A clinician will not find a chapter with detailed, comprehensive, sequential presentation of sample case studies and recommendations for interpretation.

Although the author describes practical uses in a brief chapter, the chapter is limited to a general, vague, and unsupported discussion of the use of the instrument in managed care, fee-for-service, and forensic contexts. The author suggests several uses of the instruments, including using individual items to select targets for treatment and using the instruments for pretreatment and outcome assessment, that were not investigated or supported by validity studies summarized in the manual. Similarly, the chapter includes a table relating YASR and YABCL syndromes to DSM-IV disorders; although a validity study did investigate the relationship between syndromes and DSM classification, the table is not consistent with the results of the validity study reported in the manual. Fortunately, the author does include a chapter outlining needed research studies to support these practical applications of the instruments.

SUMMARY. The strength and weakness of the YASR and YABCL are similar to those for the children and adolescent versions: The comprehensive empirical foundation is far stronger than translation of research into clinical use. The development and research for the YASR and YABCL can serve as a model for comprehensive test development procedures and reliability and validity investigations for new instruments. The technical data support that scores from the instruments have adequate reliability and validity to distinguish between referred and nonreferred samples, although studies suggest that users should rely on the Total Problems score and have limited interpretation of the individual problem syndrome and Adaptive Functioning scores. The manual includes only a few investigations of construct validity, but the author provides guidelines for future research to support different uses of the instruments.

The clinician will be disappointed by the lack of information in the manual to guide the everyday use of the instrument with clients experiencing problems and with the general, vague, and unsupported suggestions for the practical settings in which the instrument may be used. The clinician will appreciate the research data that comprise most of the manual, but also would have appreciated chapters dedicated to case studies and guidelines for interpretation of scores. It is strongly recommended that the author develop future manuals with far greater emphasis on the needs of practitioners in clinical settings.

REVIEWER'S REFERENCES

Achenbach, T. M. (1991a). *Manual for the Child Behavior Checklist/4–18 and 1991 Profile.* Burlington, VT: University of Vermont Department of Psychiatry.
Achenbach, T. M. (1991b). *Manual for the Teacher's Report Form and 1991 Profile.* Burlington, VT: University of Vermont Department of Psychiatry.
Achenbach, T. M. (1991c). *Manual for the Youth Self-Report and 1991 Profile.* Burlington, VT: University of Vermont Department of Psychiatry.
McConaughy, S. H., & Achenbach, T. M. (1994). *Manual for the Semistructured Clinical Interview for Children and Adolescents.* Burlington, VT: University of Vermont Department of Psychiatry.
Doll, B. (1998). [Review of the Child Behavior Checklist.] In J. C. Impara & B. S. Plake (Eds.), *The thirteenth mental measurements yearbook* (pp. 217–220). Lincoln, NE: Buros Institute of Mental Measurements.
Furlong, M. J. (1998). [Review of the Child Behavior Checklist.] In J. C. Impara & B. S. Plake (Eds.), *The thirteenth mental measurements yearbook* (pp. 220–224). Lincoln, NE: Buros Institute of Mental Measurements.

Review of the Young Adult Behavior Checklist and Young Adult Self-Report by JONATHAN SANDOVAL, Professor and Acting Director, Division of Education, University of California, Davis, Davis, CA:

This paired set of self-reports and other-reports of problems experienced by young adults is an extension of the author's earlier work with children and adolescents. These initially developed measures—The Child Behavior Checklist (T5:451), the Teacher's Report Form (T5:451), and the Youth Self-Report (T5:451)—have been widely adopted for use in schools, clinics, and research studies. It seems reasonable to extend them to an older population of young adults. In so doing, the author breaks new ground in developing instruments explicitly for this age group, which includes many students in college.

The manual for the test is really a short text on the research and theory that have been done to develop the concepts of internalizing and externalizing symptoms of behavior. The manual is dense with information. An unusual amount of detail about the test development efforts may be found in the manual, and the reader in a hurry may be overwhelmed or frustrated, although others will appreciate the thoroughness of this approach. The author has used the statistical techniques of principal component analysis, analysis of variance, regression analysis, and discriminant analysis to construct and validate the measures. We should look forward to the application of other modern techniques such as structural equation modeling to examine the latent traits that may underlie these scales.

The intent of the Young Adult Self-Report (YASR) and the Young Adult Behavior Checklist (YABCL) is to identify behavioral and emotional problems of young adults and discriminate between those individuals who are considered relatively normal and those who are considered maladaptively deviant. The items on the two scales overlap in content to a large extent. The measures yield normalized T scores and percentiles by gender in relationship to a representative U.S. norm group. The reports and ratings produce eight scales, two composites (internalizing and externalizing), and a Total Problems score. In addition, the YASR contains items related to adaptive functioning with friends, family, education, job, and spouse. These items combine into an adaptive scale. Some of these adaptive scales may not be relevant to a particular individual, such as the spouse scale for someone unmarried, and need not be administered. The YASR also has items related to alcohol, drug, and tobacco use, which combine into a substance use scale. The YABCL does not include these or other items thought to be unreliably observed by parents or other adults who know the subject well. In addition, the manual contains information about the prevalence rate of each item, inasmuch as they are discrete problems such as "Self-conscious," "Nausea," and "Brags" that may need to be followed up. The percent reporting each problem is listed by gender and by referral status. Absent from the measures is a social desirability scale or a lie scale. We have little information about the extent to which informants may be minimizing problems or faking problems. Although useful, such scales would add to the length of the measures. The author recommends that extreme scores be considered carefully in light of other information about the informant.

The reporting forms for the scales are simple and laid out in a straightforward manner. There is limited space available for the respondent to elaborate or to list additional concerns. The problems listed, on their face, seem to be appropriate to this age group. The items, however, are general in nature and subject to interpretation. A strength of the scales is the inclusion of items related to Attention Deficit Hyperactivity Disorder, Oppositional Defiant Disorder, and Conduct Disorder, items often missing from scales designed for older adults.

The norms for the scales were obtained from the same subjects used in norming previous measures developed by the author. There was some attrition in the sample over time, and one can speculate that this factor may have biased the norms as being conservative, in that more unstable individuals may have been lost over time.

The norm sample consisted of over 1,200 individuals across the country, from different ethnicities and different socioeconomic statuses, who did not report receiving mental health or substance abuse treatment, who did not report being suicidal or having experienced a traumatic event, or who had not been incarcerated during the previous year. Those who did *report* receiving clinical services were retained in the "referred" sample along with others who had been obtained from clinical settings. This referred sample, used extensively in the validation of the scale, is not described in any detail, although further description of what kind of services they sought would have been informative. The lack of information about this clinical sample is a serious omission. Undoubtedly they are a heterogeneous group. The norm sample is also referred to as the "nonreferred sample" (manual, pp. 41, 86). They are somewhat representative of the nation but underrepresent the western region of the country and the Latino population, to some degree. More seriously, they underrepresent the lower socioeconomic status group, a population from which a larger number of problems may come.

Test-retest stability over one week is good, ranging from .72 for Thought Problems to .89 for Total Problems and Anxious/Depressed on the YASR. Values for the special Substance Use scale reached .92. Many of the coefficients are in the low .90s for the YABCL with the glaring exceptions of Somatic Complaints and Thought Problems (.43 and .64, respectively), which reflects the difficulty in observing these phenomena by others. Longer term stability coefficients over 3 years are lower, but the same patterns are present. The correlations of scores average around .60 over this relatively long interval.

Internal consistency reliability measures are also quite good, with the Cronbach alpha statistic for the main scores of Internalizing and Externalizing on both measures averaging around .90 and the Total Problems score equaling .96. Here too, the reliabilities for Thought Problems are lowest, ranging from .56 to .77. The user should be most concerned about the reliability of this score.

Interrater reliability on the YABCL is fairly good. The manual reports an average correlation of .60 between the ratings of mothers and fathers. The correlations across the YABCL and YASR are in the .4 range, which is not unusual for the agreement between a self-report and another's report. The lowest correlation, not unexpectedly, is on the scale Thought Disorders. An interesting feature of the computer scoring program for the scales is the side-by-side listing of ratings of each item by different informants as well as the Q correlations between the self-report and up to five informants on the YABCL.

The validity evidence for the two scales is based on the history of the utility of the items in the author's and other's previous work, the ability of the items to discriminate between the referred and nonreferred individuals in the large sample used for test development and norming, and correlations with previous status and other measures. The evidence presented is persuasive that the measures can discriminate between referred and nonreferred populations, and that there is consistency between younger adjustment status and older in both U.S. and Dutch populations. Little evidence is available on the extent to which these measures correlate with other conventional measures of problem behaviors in adults, although the manual reports encouraging findings in U.S., Dutch, and Turkish samples. It will be important for more studies to be done on the concurrent validity of the scale, although it is likely to do as

good a job as any in predicting future difficulties with the law or future mental health needs.

It would also be useful to have support for the validity of the scale by the performance of carefully diagnosed groups of young adults with aggressive behavior, depression, emotional disturbance, somatic complaints, etc. This kind of validation will be necessary for clinical applications of the scales.

Many of the criticisms that have been leveled at Achenbach's other measures have applicability to the YABCL and the YASR (Drotar, Stein, & Perrin, 1995). The measures may have limited sensitivity in detecting less serious and subtle problems and changes in problem behavior below the threshold for disturbance. The assessment of adaptive functioning and substance use may be limited in scope, and there may be problems in interpreting data on clients who are culturally, ethnically, or economically diverse. Nevertheless, because of the focus on the young adult population, these measures deserve serious consideration for use in screening and research.

SUMMARY. In summary, the YASR and YABCL are a well-designed and potentially useful set of measures for the assessment and identification of young adults with emotional disturbances and behavioral disorders. By combining information from two sources and comparing them, it is possible to have a richer picture of an individual's functioning than just from one measure alone. Those familiar and comfortable with the author's previous work will welcome the availability of these new measures.

REVIEWER'S REFERENCE

Drotar, D., Stein, R. E. K., & Perrin, E. C. (1995). Methodological issues in using the Child Behavior Checklist and its related instruments in clinical child psychology research. *Journal of Clinical Child Psychology, 24,* 184–192.

CONTRIBUTING TEST REVIEWERS

PHILLIP L. ACKERMAN, Professor of Psychology, Georgia Institute of Technology, Atlanta GA

JULIE A. ALLISON, Associate Professor of Psychology, Pittsburg State University, Pittsburg, KS

PAUL A. ARBISI, Minneapolis VA Medical Center, Assistant Professor Department of Psychiatry and Assistant Clinical Professor Department of Psychology, University of Minnesota, Minneapolis, MN

PHILIP ASH, Director, Ash, Blackstone and Cates, Blacksburg, VA

JEFFREY A. ATLAS, Associate Clinical Professor (Psychiatry), Bronx Children's Psychiatric Center, Albert Einstein College of Medicine, Bronx, NY

STEPHEN N. AXFORD, Psychologist, Pueblo School District No. Sixty, Pueblo, CO, and University of Phoenix, Colorado Springs, CO

GLEN P. AYLWARD, Professor of Pediatrics, Psychiatry and Behavioral and Social Sciences, Southern Illinois University School of Medicine, Springfield, IL

PATRICIA A. BACHELOR, Professor of Psychology, California State University at Long Beach, Long Beach, CA

SHERRY K. BAIN, Assistant Professor, Department of Psychology & Counselor Education, Nicholls State University, Thibodaux, LA

LAURA L. B. BARNES, Associate Professor of Educational Research and Evaluation, School of Educational Studies, Oklahoma State University, Stillwater, OK

JAMES K. BENISH, School Psychologist, Helena Public Schools, Adjunct Professor of Special Education, Carroll College, Helena, MT

PETER MILES BERGER, Area Manager—Mental After Care Association, London, England

HERBERT BISCHOFF, Licensed Psychologist, Psychology Resources, Anchorage, AK

LARRY M. BOLEN, Professor and School Psychology Trainer, East Carolina University, Greenville, NC

NANCY B. BOLOGNA, Clinical Assistant Professor of Psychiatry, Louisiana State University Medical Center, Program Director, Touro Senior Day Center, New Orleans, LA

BRIAN F. BOLTON, University Professor, Rehabilitation Research and Training Center, University of Arkansas, Fayetteville, AR

JEFFERY P. BRADEN, Professor, School Psychology Program, Department of Educational Psychology, University of Wisconsin-Madison, Madison, WI

SUSAN M. BROOKHART, Associate Professor, School of Education, Duquesne University, Pittsburgh, PA

ROBERT BROWN, Carl A. Happold Distinguished Professor of Educational Psychology Emeritus, University of Nebraska—Lincoln, and Senior Associate, Aspen Professional Development Associates, Lincoln, NE

GORDON C. BRUNER II, Associate Professor, Marketing Department, Director, Office of Scale Research, Southern Illinois University, Carbondale, IL

WAYNE CAMARA, Executive Director of Research & Development, The College Board, New York, NY

KAREN T. CAREY, Professor of Psychology, California State University, Fresno, CA

JANET F. CARLSON, Professor of Counseling and Psychological Services, Associate Dean School of Education, Oswego State University, Oswego, NY

DALE CARPENTER, Professor of Special Education, Western Carolina University, Cullowhee, NC

MARY MATHAI CHITTOORAN, UC Foundation Assistant Professor of School Psychology, The University of Tennessee at Chattanooga, Chattanooga, TN

JOSEPH C. CIECHALSKI, Professor of Counselor and Adult Education, East Carolina University, Greenville, NC

ELAINE CLARK, Professor of Educational Psychology, University of Utah, Salt Lake City, UT

D. ASHLEY COHEN, Clinical Neuropsychologist, CogniMetrix, San Jose, CA

LIBBY G. COHEN, Professor of Special Education, University of Southern Maine, Gorham, ME

MERITH COSDEN, Professor of Counseling/Clinical/School Psychology, Graduate School of Education, University of California, Santa Barbara, CA

ANDREW A. COX, Professor of Counseling and Psychology, Troy State University, Phenix City, AL

KEVIN D. CREHAN, Associate Professor of Educational Psychology, University of Nevada, Las Vegas, NV

THOMAS J. CULLEN, JR., Clinical Psychologist, Cullen Psychological Services, P.C., Fairless Hills, PA

JACK A. CUMMINGS, Professor and Chair, Department of Counseling and Educational Psychology, Indiana University, Bloomington, IN

STEPHEN F. DAVIS, Professor of Psychology, Emporia State University, Emporia, KS

GARY J. DEAN, Associate Professor and Chairperson, Department of Adult and Community Education, Indiana University of Pennsylvania, Indiana, PA

GERALD E. DeMAURO, Coordinator of Assessment, New York State Education Department, Albany, NY

LIZANNE DeSTEFANO, Associate Professor of Educational Psychology, University of Illinois at Urbana-Champaign, Champaign, IL

BETH DOLL, Associate Professor of School Psychology, University of Colorado at Denver, Denver, CO

E. THOMAS DOWD, Professor of Psychology, Kent State University, Kent, OH

ROBERT J. DRUMMOND, Professor, Division of Educational Services and Research, University of North Florida, Jacksonville, FL

RICHARD F. FARMER, Associate Professor of Psychology, Idaho State University, Pocatello, ID

ROBERT FITZPATRICK, Consulting Psychologist, Cranberry Township, PA

JOHN W. FLEENOR, Director of Knowledge Management, Center for Creative Leadership, Greensboro, NC

JIM C. FORTUNE, Professor of Educational Research and Evaluation, Virginia Tech University, Blacksburg, VA

MICHAEL FURLONG, Professor, Counseling, Clinical, School Psychology Program, University of California, Santa Barbara, Graduate School of Education, Santa Barbara, CA

ROBERT K. GABLE, Professor of Educational Psychology, and Associate Director, Bureau of Educational Research and Service, University of Connecticut, Storrs, CT

MICHAEL P. GAMACHE, Clinical Assistant Professor of Psychology, Department of Neurology, University of South Florida, College of Medicine, Tampa, FL

DAVID GILLESPIE, Social Science Faculty, Detroit College of Business, Warren, MI

BERT A. GOLDMAN, Professor of Education, Curriculum and Instruction, University of North Carolina at Greensboro, Greensboro, NC

STEVE GRAHAM, Professor of Special Education, University of Maryland, College Park, MD

THERESA GRAHAM, Assistant Professor of Educational Psychology, University of Nebraska—Lincoln, Lincoln, NE

ROBERT M. GUION, Distinguished University Professor Emeritus, Bowling Green State University, Bowling Green, OH

ROBERT R. HACCOUN, Professor and Chair, I-O Psychology, Université de Montréal, Montreal, Quebec, Canada

GERALD S. HANNA, Professor of Education, Kansas State University, Manhattan, KS

DENNIS C. HARPER, Professor of Pediatrics and Rehabilitation, College of Medicine, University of Iowa, Iowa City, IA

PATTI L. HARRISON, Professor of School Psychology and Assistant Dean of the Graduate School, The University of Alabama, Tuscaloosa, AL

SANDRA D. HAYNES, Assistant Professor, Department of Human Services, The Metropolitan State College of Denver, Denver, CO

ALLEN K. HESS, Distinguished Research Professor and Department Head, Department of Psychology, Auburn university at Montgomery, Montgomery, AL

THOMAS P. HOGAN, Professor of Psychology and Director of Assessment and Institutional Research, University of Scranton, Scranton, PA

E. SCOTT HUEBNER, Professor of Psychology, University of South Carolina, Columbia, SC

DAVID P. HURFORD, Director of the Center for the Assessment and Remediation of Reading Difficulties and Associate Professor of Psychology and Counseling, Pittsburg State University, Pittsburg, KS

CARLOS INCHAURRALDE, Professor of Linguistics and Psychologist, University of Zaragoza, Zaragoza, Spain

CARL ISENHART, Coordinator, Addictive Disorders Section, VA Medical Center, Minneapolis, MN

JILL ANN JENKINS, Psychologist, Mary Sheridan Child Development Centre, London, United Kingdom

RICHARD W. JOHNSON, Adjunct Professor of Counseling Psychology and Associate Director Emeritus of Counseling & Consultation Services, University Health Services, University of Wisconsin-Madison, Madison, WI

IRA STUART KATZ, Clinical Psychologist, California Department of Corrections, Salinas Valley State Prison, Soledad, CA

ALAN S. KAUFMAN, Clinical Professor of Psychology, Yale University School of Medicine, New Haven, CT

NADEEN L. KAUFMAN, Lecturer, Clinical Faculty, Yale University School of Medicine, New Haven, CT

MICHAEL G. KAVAN, Associate Dean for Student Affairs and Associate Professor of Family Practice, Creighton University School of Medicine, Omaha, NE

CAROL E. KESSLER, Assistant Professor of Education, Chestnut Hill College, Philadelphia, PA, and Adjunct Professor of Special Education, West Chester University, West Chester, PA

KENNETH A. KIEWRA, Professor of Educational Psychology, University of Nebraska—Lincoln, Lincoln, NE

JEAN POWELL KIRNAN, Associate Professor of Psychology, The College of New Jersey, Ewing, NJ

HOWARD M. KNOFF, Professor of School Psychology, University of South Florida, Tampa, FL

JOSEPH G. LAW, JR., Associate Professor of Behavioral Science and Educational Technology, University of South Alabama, Mobile, AL

ROBERT A. LEARK, Associate Professor, Psychology Department, Pacific Christian College, Fullerton, CA

STEVEN B. LEDER, Professor of Surgery, Yale University School of Medicine, New Haven, CT

FREDERICK T. L. LEONG, Associate Professor of Psychology, The Ohio State University at Columbus, Columbus, OH

ALVIN LEUNG, Associate Professor, Department of Educational Psychology, The Chinese University of Hong Kong, Shatin, N. T., Hong Kong

MARY A. LEWIS, Director, Human Resources, Chlor-Alkali and Derivatives, PPG Industries, Inc., Pittsburgh, PA

STEVEN J. LINDNER, Executive Director, Industrial/Organizational Psychologist, The WorkPlace Group, Inc., Morristown, NJ

HOWARD A. LLOYD, Neuropsychologist, Hawaii State Hospital, Kaneohe, HI

CHARLES J. LONG, Professor of Psychology, The University of Memphis, Memphis, TN

KAREN MACKLER, School Psychologist, Lawrence Public Schools, Lawrence, NY

RONALD A. MADLE, School Psychologist, Shikellamy School District, Sunbury, PA, and Adjunct Associate Professor of School Psychology, Pennsylvania State University, University Park, PA

KORESSA KUTSICK MALCOLM, School Psychologist, Augusta County School Board, Fisherville, VA

JOSEPH R. MANDUCHI, Clinical Associate, Susquehanna Institute, Harrisburg, PA

GARY L. MARCO, Consultant, Chapin, SC

WILLIAM E. MARTIN, JR., Professor of Educational Psychology, Northern Arizona University, Flagstaff, AZ

JOYCE R. McLARTY, Principal Research Associate, Workforce Development Division, ACT, Inc., Iowa City, IA

JOYCE MEIKAMP, Associate Professor of Special Education, Marshall University Graduate College, South Charleston, WV

WILLIAM R. MERZ, SR., Professor—School Psychology Training Program, California State University, Sacramento, CA

DANIEL C. MILLER, Associate Professor of Psychology, Texas Woman's University, Denton, TX

PAT MIRENDA, Associate Professor, University of British Columbia, Vancouver, British Columbia, Canada

JUDITH A. MONSAAS, Associate Professor of Education, North Georgia College and State University, Dahlonega, GA

KEVIN L. MORELAND, Psychologist, Private Practice, Ft. Walton Beach, FL

SCOTT A. NAPOLITANO, Adjunct Assistant Professor, Department of Educational Psychology, University of Nebraska—Lincoln, Lincoln, NE, and Pediatric Neuropsychologist, Lincoln Pediatric Group, Lincoln, NE

ANTHONY J. NITKO, Professor, Department of Educational Psychology, University of Arizona, Tucson, AZ

JANET NORRIS, Professor of Communication Disorders, Louisiana State University, Baton Rouge, LA

DENIZ S. ONES, Hellervik Professor of Industrial-Organizational Psychology, Department of Psychology, University of Minnesota, Minneapolis, MN

TERRY OVERTON, President, Learning and Behavioral Therapies, Inc., Farmville, VA

ABBOT PACKARD, Instructor, Educational Psychology and Foundations, University of Northern Iowa, Cedar Falls, IA

ANTHONY M. PAOLO, Coordinator of Assessment and Evaluation, University of Kansas Medical Center, Kansas City, KS

ILA PARASNIS, Associate Professor, Department of Applied Language and Cognition Research, National Technical Institute for the Deaf, Rochester Institute of Technology, Rochester, NY

RENEE PAVELSKI, Doctoral Candidate, Counseling, Clinical, School Psychology Program, University of California, Santa Barbara, Graduate School of Education, Santa Barbara, CA

G. MICHAEL POTEAT, Associate Professor of Psychology, East Carolina University, Greenville, NC

THERESA A. QUIGNEY, Assistant Professor, Cleveland State University, Cleveland, OH

BIKKAR S. RANDHAWA, Professor of Educational Psychology, University of Saskatchewan, Saskatoon, Canada

ALAN J. RAPHAEL, President, International Assessment Systems, Inc., Miami, FL

JAMES C. REED, Chief Psychologist, St. Luke's Hospital, New Bedford, MA

ROBERT C. REINEHR, Professor of Psychology, Southwestern University, Georgetown, TX

PAUL RETZLAFF, Professor, Psychology Department, University of Northern Colorado, Greeley, CO

ROGER A. RICHARDS, Consultant, Office of Certification and Credentialing, Massachusetts Department of Education, Malden, MA, and Adjunct Professor of Communication, Bunker Hill Community College, Boston, MA

MICHELE L. RIES, Research Assistant, Psychology Department, The University of Memphis, Memphis, TN

BRENT W. ROBERTS, Assistant Professor of Psychology, University of Tulsa, Tulsa, OK

BRUCE G. ROGERS, Professor of Educational Psychology, University of Northern Iowa, Cedar Falls, IA

CYNTHIA A. ROHRBECK, Associate Professor of Psychology, The George Washington University, Washington, DC

DEBORAH D. ROMAN, Assistant Professor and Director, Neuropsychology Lab, Departments of Physical Medicine and Rehabilitation and Neurosurgery, University of Minnesota, Minneapolis, MN

HERBERT C. RUDMAN, Professor Emeritus of Measurement and Quantitative Methods, Michigan State Univesity, East Lansing, MI

MICHAEL LEE RUSSELL, Commander, 47th Combat Support Hospital, Fort Lewis, WA

DARRELL L. SABERS, Professor of Educational Psychology, University of Arizona, Tucson, AZ

VINCENT J. SAMAR, Associate Professor, Department of Applied Language and Cognition Research, National Technical Institute for the Deaf, Rochester Institute of Technology, Rochester, NY

JONATHAN SANDOVAL, Professor and Acting Director, Division of Education, University of California, Davis, Davis, CA

DIANE J. SAWYER, Murfree Professor of Dyslexic Studies, Middle Tennessee State University, Murfreesboro, TN

GERALD R. SCHNECK, Professor of Rehabilitation Counseling, Mankato State University, Mankato, MN

EUGENE P. SHEEHAN, Professor of Psychology, University of Northern Colorado, Greeley, CO

EVERETT V. SMITH JR., Assistant Professor of Educational Psychology, University of Illinois, Chicago, IL

JANET V. SMITH, Assistant Professor of Psychology and Counseling, Pittsburg State University, Pittsburg, KS

JANET E. SPECTOR, Assistant Professor of Education and Human Development, University of Maine, Orono, ME

GARY J. STAINBACK, Senior Psychologist I, Developmental Evaluation Clinic, East Carolina University School of Medicine, Department of Pediatrics, Greenville, NC

MARGOT B. STEIN, Clinical Assistant Professor of Psychiatry, UNC School of Medicine, Director of Training, Center for the Study of Development and Learning, University of North Carolina at Chapel Hill, Chapel Hill, NC

STEPHANIE STEIN, Professor of Psychology, Central Washington University, Ellensburg, WA

TERRY A. STINNETT, Associate Professor, School Psychology Programs, Oklahoma State University, Stillwater, OK

DONALD LEE STOVALL, Assistant Professor of Counseling & School Psychology, University of Wisconsin—River Falls, River Falls, WI

GABRIELLE STUTMAN, Private Practice, Westchester and Manhattan, NY

NORMAN D. SUNDBERG, Professor Emeritus, Department of Psychology, University of Oregon, Eugene, OR

ROSEMARY E. SUTTON, Professor of Education, Cleveland State University, Cleveland, OH

DONALD THOMPSON, Dean and Professor of Counseling and Psychology, Troy State University Montgomery, Montgomery, AL

GERALD TINDAL, Professor, Behavioral Research and Teaching, University of Oregon, Eugene, OR

TONY TONEATTO, Scientist, Clinical, Social and Research Department, Addiction Research Foundation, Toronto, Ontario, Canada

MICHAEL S. TREVISAN, Assistant Professor, Department of Educational Leadership and Counseling Psychology, Washington State University, Pullman, WA

STEPHEN E. TROTTER, Associate Professor, Department of Educational & Counseling Psychology, University of the Pacific, Stockton, CA

SUSANA URBINA, Professor of Psychology, University of North Florida, Jacksonville, FL

JOHN J. VACCA, Certified School Psychologist, Assistant Professor of Special Education, Advisor, Graduate Program in Early Intervention, Loyola College, Baltimore, MD

WILFRED G. VAN GORP, Associate Professor of Psychology in Psychiatry, Director, Neuropsychology, New York Hospital—Cornell Medical Center Mental Health System, New York, NY

THERESA VOLPE-JOHNSTONE, Clinical and School Psychologist, Pleasanton, CA

WILLIAM J. WALDRON, Administrator, Employee Testing & Assessment, TECO Energy, Inc., Tampa, FL

NIELS G. WALLER, Professor of Psychology and Human Development, Vanderbilt University, Nashville, TN

ANNIE W. WARD, Emeritus Professor, University of South Florida, Daytona Beach, FL

SANDRA WARD, Associate Professor of Education, The College of William and Mary, Williamsburg, VA

BETSY WATERMAN, Associate Professor, Counseling and Psychological Services Department, State University of New York at Oswego, Oswego, NY

GORAN WESTERGREN, Chief Psychologist, Department of Clinical Psychology, State Hospital, Halmstad, Sweden

INGELA WESTERGREN, Neuropsychologist and Licensed Psychologist, Department of Clinical Psychology, State Hospital, Halmstad, Sweden

KEITH F. WIDAMAN, Professor of Psychology, University of California at Davis, Davis, CA

WILLIAM K. WILKINSON, Consulting Psychologist, Boleybeg, Barna, Co. Galway, Ireland

CARRIE L. WINTEROWD, Assistant Professor of Counseling Psychology, College of Education, Oklahoma State University, Stillwater, OK

RICHARD M. WOLF, Professor of Psychology and Education, Teachers College, Columbia University, New York, NY

DANIEL L. YAZAK, Assistant Professor and Chair, Department of Counseling and Human Services, Montana State University—Billings, Billings, MT

JAMES YSSELDYKE, Birkmaier Professor of Educational Leadership, University of Minnesota, Minneapolis, MN

INDEX OF TITLES

INDEX OF ACRONYMS

This Index of Acronyms refers the reader to the appropriate test in The Supplement to the Thirteenth Mental Measurements Yearbook. *In some cases tests are better known by their acronyms than by their full titles, and this index can be of substantial help to the person who knows the former but not the latter. Acronyms are only listed if the author or publisher has made substantial use of the acronym in referring to the test, or if the test is widely known by the acronym. A few acronyms are also registered trademarks (e.g., SAT); where this is known to us, only the test with the registered trademark is referenced. There is some danger in the overuse of acronyms, but this index, like all other indexes in this work, is provided to make the task of identifying a test as easy as possible. All numbers refer to test numbers, not page numbers.*

CLASSIFIED SUBJECT INDEX

The Classified Subject Index classifies all tests included in The Mental Measurements Yearbook *into 18 major categories: Achievement, Behavior Assessment, Developmental, Education, English and Language, Fine Arts, Foreign Language, Intelligence and General Aptitude, Mathematics, Miscellaneous, Neuropsychological, Personality, Reading, Science, Sensory-Motor, Social Studies, Speech and Hearing, and Vocations. This Classified Subject Index for the tests reviewed in* The Supplement to the Thirteenth Mental Measurements Yearbook *includes tests in 15 of the 18 available categories. (The categories of Fine Arts, Foreign Languages, and Social Studies have no representative tests in this volume but will be represented in the* 14th MMY*.) Each category appears in alphabetical order and tests are ordered alphabetically within each category. Each test entry includes test title, population for which the test is intended, and the test entry number in* The Supplement to the Thirteenth Mental Measurements Yearbook*. All numbers refer to test entry numbers, not to page numbers. Brief suggestions for the use of this index are presented in the introduction. The classifications have been used in the previous editions of the* MMY *and* TIP*. Revised definitions of the categories are effective with this* Supplement *and the upcoming* Fourteenth Mental Measurements Yearbook *and are provided at the beginning of this index.*

Achievement

Tests that measure acquired knowledge across school subject content areas. Included here are test batteries that measure multiple content areas and individual subject areas not having separate classification categories. (Note: Some batteries include both achievement and aptitude subtests. Such batteries may be classified under the categories of either Achievement or Intelligence and Aptitude depending upon the principal content area.)

See also Fine Arts, Intelligence and General Aptitude, Mathematics, Reading, Science, and Social Studies.

Behavior Assessment

Tests that measure general or specific behavior within educational, vocational, community, or home settings. Included here are checklists, rating scales, and surveys that measure observer's interpretations of behavior in relation to adaptive or social skills, functional skills, and appropriateness or dysfunction within settings/situations.

Developmental

Tests that are designed to assess skills or emerging skills (such as number concepts, conservation, memory, fine motor, gross motor, communication, letter recognition, social competence) of young children (0-7 years) or tests which are designed to assess such skills in severely or profoundly disabled school-aged individuals. Included here are early screeners, developmental surveys/profiles, kindergarten or school readiness tests, early learning profiles, infant development scales, tests of play behavior, social acceptance/social skills; and preschool psychoeducational batteries. Content specific screeners, such as those assessing readiness, are classified by content area (e.g., Reading).

See also Neuropsychological and Sensory-Motor.

Education

General education-related tests, including measures of instructional/school environment, effective schools/ teaching, study skills and strategies, learning styles and strategies, school attitudes, educational programs/ curriculae, interest inventories, and educational leadership.

Specific content area tests (i.e., science, mathematics, social studies, etc.) are listed by their content area.

English and Language

Tests that measure skills in using or understanding the English language in spoken or written form. Included here are tests of language proficiency, applied literacy, language comprehension/development/proficiency, English skills/proficiency, communication skills, listening comprehension, linguistics, and receptive/expressive vocabulary. (Tests designed to measure the mechanics of speaking or communicating are classified under the category Speech and Hearing.)

Fine Arts

Tests that measure knowledge, skills, abilities, attitudes, and interests within the various areas of fine and performing arts. Included here are tests of aptitude, achievement, creativity/talent/giftedness specific to the Fine Arts area, and tests of aesthetic judgment.

Foreign Languages

Tests that measure competencies and readiness in reading, comprehending, and speaking a language other than English.

Intelligence and General Aptitude

Tests that measure general acquired knowledge, aptitudes, or cognitive ability and those that assess specific aspects of these general categories. Included here are tests of critical thinking skills, nonverbal/verbal reasoning, cognitive abilities/processing, learning potential/aptitude/efficiency, logical reasoning, abstract thinking, creative thinking/creativity; entrance exams and academic admissions tests.

Mathematics

Tests that measure competencies and attitudes in any of the various areas of mathematics (e.g., algebra, geometry, calculus) and those related to general mathematics achievement/proficiency. (Note: Included here are tests that assess personality or affective variables related to mathematics.)

Miscellaneous

Tests that cannot be sorted into any of the current MMY categories as listed and defined above. Included here are tests of handwriting, ethics and morality, religion, driving and safety, health and physical education, environment (e.g., classroom environment, family environment), custody decisions, substance abuse, and addictions. (See also Personality.)

Neuropsychological

Tests that measure neurological functioning or brain-behavior relationships either generally or in relation to specific areas of functioning. Included here are neuropsychological test batteries, questionnaires, and screening tests. Also included are tests that measure memory impairment, various disorders or decline associated with dementia, brain/head injury, visual attention, digit recognition, finger tapping, laterality, aphasia, and behavior (associated with organic brain dysfunction or brain injury).

See also Developmental, Intelligence and General Aptitude, Sensory-Motor, and Speech and Hearing.

Personality

Tests that measure individuals' ways of thinking, behaving, and functioning within family and society. Included here are projective and apperception tests, needs inventories, anxiety/depression scales; tests assessing substance use/abuse (or propensity for abuse), risk taking behavior, general mental health, emotional intelligence, self-image/-concept/-esteem, empathy, suicidal ideation, schizophrenia, depression/hopelessness, abuse, coping skills/stress, eating disorders, grief, decision-making, racial attitudes; general motivation, attributions, perceptions; adjustment, parenting styles, and marital issues/satisfaction.

For content-specific tests, see subject area categories (e.g., math efficacy instruments are located in Mathematics). Some areas, such as substance abuse, are cross-referenced with the Personality category.

Reading

Tests that measure competencies and attitudes within the broadly defined area of reading. Included here are reading inventories, tests of reading achievement and aptitude, reading readiness/early reading ability, reading comprehension, reading decoding, and oral reading. (Note: Included here are tests that assess personality or affective variables related to reading.)

Science

Tests that measure competencies and attitudes within any of the various areas of science (e.g., biology, chemistry, physics), and those related to general science achievement/proficiency. (Note: Included here are tests that assess personality or affective variables related to science.)

Sensory-Motor

Tests that are general or specific measures of any or all of the five senses and those that assess fine or gross motor skills. Included here are tests of manual dexterity, perceptual skills, visual-motor skills, perceptual-motor skills, movement and posture, laterality preference, sensory integration, motor development, color blindness/discrimination, visual perception/organization, and visual acuity. (Note: See also the categories Neuropsychological and Speech and Hearing.)

Social Studies

Tests that measure competencies and attitudes within the broadly defined area of social studies. Included here are tests related to economics, sociology, history, geography, and political science, and those related to general social studies achievement/proficiency. (Note: Also included here are tests that assess personality or affective variables related to social studies.)

Speech and Hearing

Tests that measure the mechanics of speaking or hearing the spoken word. Included here are tests of articulation, voice fluency, stuttering, speech sound perception/discrimination, auditory discrimination/comprehension, audiometry, deafness, and hearing loss/impairment. (Note: See Developmental, English and Language, Neuropsychological, and Sensory-Motor.)

Vocations

Tests that measure employee skills, behaviors, attitudes, values, and perceptions relative to jobs, employment, and the work place or organizational environment. Included here are tests of management skill/style/competence, leader behavior, careers (development, exploration, attitudes); job- or work-related selection/admission/entrance tests; tests of work adjustment, team or group processes/communication/effectiveness, employability, vocational/occupational interests, employee aptitudes/competencies, and organizational climate.

See also Intelligence and General Aptitude, and Personality and also specific content area categories (e.g., Mathematics, Reading).

ACHIEVEMENT

BEHAVIOR ASSESSMENT

DEVELOPMENTAL

EDUCATION

ENGLISH AND LANGUAGE

INTELLIGENCE AND GENERAL APTITUDE

MATHEMATICS

MISCELLANEOUS

NEUROPSYCHOLOGICAL

PERSONALITY

READING

SCIENCE

SENSORY-MOTOR

SPEECH AND HEARING

VOCATIONS

PUBLISHERS DIRECTORY
AND INDEX

This directory and index gives the names and test entry numbers of all publishers represented in The Supplement to the Thirteenth Mental Measurements Yearbook. *Current addresses are listed for all publishers for which this is known. Those publishers for which a current address is not available are listed as "Address Unknown." As a new feature beginning in* Tests in Print V, *this directory and index also provides telephone and FAX numbers and email and Web addresses for those publishers who responded to our request for this information. Please note that all test numbers refer to test entry numbers, not page numbers. Publishers are an important source of information about catalogs, specimen sets, price changes, test revisions, and many other matters.*

Ablin Press Distributors
700 John Ringling Blvd., #1603
Sarasota, FL 34236-1504
Telephone: 941-361-7521
FAX: 941-361-7521
Tests: 78

Academic Therapy Publications
20 Commercial Boulevard
Novato, CA 94949-6191
Telephone: 800-422-7249
FAX: 415-883-3720
E-mail: atp@aol.com
Web URL: www.atpub.com
Tests: 48

Advantage Learning Systems, Inc.
P.O. Box 8036
Wisconsin Rapids, WI 54495-8036
Telephone: 800-338-4204
FAX: 715-424-4242
E-mail: answers@advlearn.com
Web URL: www.advlearn.com
Tests: 82

American Guidance Service, Inc.
4201 Woodland Road
Circle Pines,MN 55014-1796
Telephone: 800-328-2560
FAX: 612-786-5603
E-mail: agsmail@agsnet
Web URL: www.agsnet.com
Tests: 50, 55, 56

Assessment Systems Corporation
2233 University Avenue, Suite 200
St. Paul, MN 55114-1629
Telephone: 651-647-9220
FAX: 651-647-0412
E-mail: info@assess.com
Web URL: www.assess.com
Tests: 47

Assessment Systems International, Inc.
15350 W. National Avenue, Suite 205
New Berlin, WI 53151-5158
Tests: 41

Australian Council for Educational Research Ltd.
19 Prospect Hill Road
Private Bag 55
Camberwell, Victoria 3124
Australia
Tests: 43, 99

Behavior Science Systems, Inc.
P.O. Box 580274
Minneapolis, MN 55458
Telephone: 612-929-6220
FAX: 612-920-4925
Tests: 11, 33

Nancy E. Betz, Ph.D.
2758 Kensington Place, West
Columbus, OH 43202
Tests: 9

Brunner/Mazel, Inc.
1900 Frost Road, Suite 101
Bristol, PA 19007-1598
Tests: 3

The CATI Corporation
10 East Costilla
Colorado Springs, CO 80903
Tests: 22

The Center for Management Effectiveness
P.O. Box 1202
Pacific Palisades, CA 90272
Telephone: 310-459-6052
FAX: 310-459-9307
E-mail: kindlerCME@aol.com
Tests: 62

Centreville School
6201 Kennett Pike
Wilmington, DE 19807
Telephone: 302-571-0230
FAX: 302-571-0270
E-mail: language@del.net
Tests: 69

Child Behavior Checklist
University Medical Education Associates
1 South Prospect Street, Room 6434
Burlington, VT 05401-3456
Telephone: 802-656-8313
FAX: 802-656-2602
E-mail: checklist@uvm.edu
Web URL: checklist.uvm.edu
Tests: 10, 101

CTB/McGraw-Hill
20 Ryan Ranch Road
Monterey, CA 93940-5703
Tests: 88

Development Associates, Inc.
1730 North Lynn Street
Arlington, VA 22209-2023
Telephone: 703-276-0677
FAX: 703-276-0432
E-mail: tstephenson@devassoc1.com
Web URL: www.devassoc1.com
Tests: 1

Diagnostic Counseling Services, Inc.
P.O. Box 6178
Kokomo, IN 46904-6178
Tests: 51

DocuTrac, Inc.
[Address Unknown]
Tests: 85

Educators Publishing Service, Inc.
31 Smith Place
Cambridge, MA 02138-1089
Telephone: 800-225-5750
FAX: 617-547-0412
E-mail: cps@epsbooks.com
Web URL: www.epsbooks.com
Tests: 73

Golden Educational Center
857 Lake Blvd.
Redding, CA 96003
Tests: 35

GRM Educational Consultancy
P.O. Box 154
Beecroft, New South Wales 2119
Australia
Telephone: 61-2-9484-1598
FAX: 61-2-9875-3638
Tests: 76

H & H Publishing Co., Inc.
1231 Kapp Drive
Clearwater, FL 33765
Telephone: 800-366-4079
FAX: 727-442-2195
E-mail: hhservice@hhpublishing.com
Web URL: www.hhpublishing.com
Tests: 61, 83, 100

Harcourt Brace Educational Measurement
555 Academic Court
San Antonio, TX 78204-2498
Telephone: 800-211-8378
FAX: 800-232-1223
E-mail: CUSTOMER_SERVICE2@HBTPC.COM
Web URL: WWW.HBEM.COM
Tests: 58

High/Scope Educational Research Foundation
600 North River Street
Ypsilanti, MI 48198-2898
Telephone: 734-485-2000
FAX: 734-485-0704
E-mail: info@highscope.org
Web URL: www.highscope.org
Tests: 30

Hodder & Stoughton Educational
Hodder Headline PLC
338 Euston Road
London NW1 3BH
England
Telephone: 0171 873 6000
FAX: 0171 873 6024
E-mail: chas.knight@hodder.co.uk
Tests: 29, 43, 86

Human Resource Development Press
22 Amherst Road
Amherst, MA 01002-9709
Telephone: 800-822-2801
FAX: 413-253-3490
E-mail: marketing@hrdpress.com
Web URL: www.hrdpress.com
Tests: 45, 57

Imaginart International, Inc.
307 Arizona Street
Bisbee, AZ 85603
Telephone: 520-432-5741
FAX: 520-432-5134
E-mail: IMAGINART@AOL.COM
Tests: 6

The Institute for Matching Person & Technology, Inc.
486 Lake Road
Webster, NY 14580
Telephone: 716-671-3461
FAX: 716-671-3461
E-mail: impt97@aol.com
Web URL: members.aol.com/IMPT97/Mpt.html
Tests: 42

Institute for Somat Awareness
Michael Bernet, Ph.D.
1270 North Avenue, Suite 1-P
New Rochelle, NY 10804
Telephone: 914-633-1789
FAX: 914-633-3152
E-mail: mBernet@aol.com
Tests: 79

Jossey-Bass/Pfeiffer
350 Sansome, 5th Floor
San Francisco, CA 94104
Tests: 19

Mind Garden, Inc.
1690 Woodside Road, Suite #202
Redwood City, CA 94061
Telephone: 650-261-3500
FAX: 650-261-3505
E-mail: info@mindgarden.com
Tests: 16, 44, 68

Multi-Health Systems, Inc.
908 Niagara Falls Blvd.
North Tonawanda, NY 14120-2060
Telephone: 416-424-1700
FAX: 416-424-1736
E-mail: CUSTOMERSERVICE@MHS.COM
Web URL: www.mhs.com
Tests: 4, 15, 20, 23, 25, 31, 37, 39

Multiple Intelligences Research and Consulting, Inc.
1316 South Lincoln Street
Kent, OH 44240
Telephone: 330-673-8024
FAX: 330-673-8810
E-mail: sbranton@kent.edu
Web URL: WWW.ANGELFIRE.COM/OH/
    THEMIDAS
Tests: 46

National Clearinghouse of Rehabilitation Training
    Materials
5202 N. Richmond Hill Drive
Oklahoma State University
Stillwater, OK 74078-4080
Tests: 54

NCS [Minnetonka]
Sales Department
5605 Green Circle Drive
Minnetonka, MN 55343
Tests: 8, 28, 64, 66

New Standards, Inc.
8441 Wayzata Blvd., Suite 105
Minneapolis, MN 55426-1349
Telephone: 800-755-6299
FAX: 612-797-9993
E-mail: tjk@newstandards.com
Tests: 67

New Zealand Council for Educational Research
Education House West
178-182 Willis Street
Box 3237
Wellington 6000
New Zealand
Tests: 87

Norland Software
P.O. Box 84499
Los Angeles, CA 90073-0499
Telephone: 310-202-1832
FAX: 310-202-9431
E-mail: emiller@ucla.edu
Web URL: www.calcaprt.com
Tests: 7

Personnel Decisions, Inc.
2000 Plaza VII Tower
45 South Seventh Street
Minneapolis, MN 55402-1608
Tests: 60

PRO-ED
8700 Shoal Creek Blvd.
Austin, TX 78757-6897
Telephone: 800-897-3202
FAX: 512-451-8542
E-mail: proedrd2@aol.com
Web URL: WWW.PROEDINC.COM
Tests: 75, 89, 90, 91, 92, 95

Psychological Assessment Resources, Inc.
P.O. Box 998
Odessa, FL 33556-9908
Telephone: 800-331-8378
FAX: 800-727-9329
Web URL: www.parinc.com
Tests: 17, 36, 65, 70, 84, 98

The Psychological Corporation
555 Academic Court
San Antonio, TX 78204-2498
Telephone: 800-211-8378
FAX: 800-232-1223
E-mail: customer_service@HBTPC.com
Web URL: www.HBEM.com
Tests: 5, 13, 18, 26, 27, 32, 34, 49, 53, 59, 97

Psychological Services, Inc.
100 West Broadway, Suite #1100
Glendale, CA 91210
Telephone: 818-244-0033
FAX: 818-247-7223
Web URL: www.psionline.com
Tests: 63

Riverside Publishing
425 Spring Lake Drive
Itasca, IL 60143-2079
Telephone: 800-323-9540
FAX: 630-467-7192
Web URL: WWW.RIVERPUB.COM
Tests: 24, 93

Selby MillSmith, Ltd.
30 Circus Mews
Bath BA1 2PW
United Kingdom
Telephone: +44 1225-446655
FAX: +44 1225-446643
E-mail: Info@Selby MillSmith.com
Web URL: www.Selby MillSmith.com
Tests: 77

Slosson Educational Publications, Inc.
P.O. Box 280
East Aurora, NY 14052-0280
Tests: 80, 96

Stoelting Co.
Oakwood Center
620 Wheat Lane
Wood Dale, IL 60191
Telephone: 630-860-9700
FAX: 630-860-9775
E-mail: psychtests@stoeltingco.com
Web URL: www.stoeltingco.com/tests
Tests: 40

Thames Valley Test Company, Ltd.
7-9 The Green
Flempton, Bury St. Edmunds
Suffolk IP28 6EL
England
Telephone: +44 1284 728608
FAX: +44 1284 728166
E-mail: TVTC@MSN.COM
Tests: 71

Therapy Skill Builders-A Division of The Psychological Corporation
555 Academic Court
San Antonio, TX 78204-2498
Telephone: 800-211-8378
FAX: 800-232-1223
Web URL: www.hbtpc.com
Tests: 14, 21, 94

Western Psychological Services
12031 Wilshire Blvd.
Los Angeles, CA 90025-1251
Telephone: 310-478-2061
FAX: 310-478-7838
Tests: 12, 38, 52, 72, 74, 81

World Health Organization
[Address Unknown]
Switzerland
Tests: 2

INDEX OF NAMES

This analytical index indicates whether a citation refers to authorship of a test, a test review, or a reference for a specific test. Numbers refer to test entries, not to pages. The abbreviations and numbers following the names may be interpreted as follows: "test, 73" indicates authorship of test 73; "rev, 86" indicates authorship of a review of test 86; "ref, 45(30)" indicates authorship of reference number 30 in the "Test References" section for test 45.

SCORE INDEX

This Score Index lists all the scores, in alphabetical order, for all the tests included in The Supplement to the Thirteenth Mental Measurements Yearbook. *Because test scores can be regarded as operational definitions of the variable measured, sometimes the scores provide better leads to what a test actually measures than the test title or other available information. The Score Index is very detailed, and the reader should keep in mind that a given variable (or concept) of interest may be defined in several different ways. Thus the reader should look up these several possible alternative definitions before drawing final conclusions about whether tests measuring a particular variable of interest can be located in this volume. If the kind of score sought is located in a particular test or tests, the reader should then read the test descriptive information carefully to determine whether the test(s) in which the score is found is (are) consistent with reader purpose. Used wisely, the Score Index can be another useful resource in locating the right score in the right test. As usual, all numbers in the index are test numbers, not page numbers.*